Springer Japan KK

Fujio Yamaguchi

Computer-Aided Geometric Design

A Totally Four-Dimensional Approach

With 401 Figures

Springer

Fujio Yamaguchi
Department of Mechanical Engineering
School of Science and Engineering
Waseda University
3-4-1 Ohkubo, Shinjuku-ku, Tokyo 169-8555, Japan

Front-cover image designed by Atsushi Umemura

ISBN 978-4-431-68007-9

Library of Congress Cataloging-in-Publication Data

Yamaguchi, Fujio, 1935-
[Yojigen riron ni yoru zukei. English]
Computer-aided geometric design : a totally four-dimensional approach / Fujio Yamaguchi.
p. cm.
Includes bibliographical references and index.
ISBN 978-4-431-68007-9 **ISBN 978-4-431-67881-6 (eBook)**
DOI 10.1007/978-4-431-67881-6
1. Geometrical drawing--Data processing. 2. Engineering design--Data process ing. 3. Computer graphics. I. Title

QA464 .Y8213 2002
620'.00425'0285--dc21

2002030248

This translation is based on the Japanese original.
F. Yamaguchi; Yojigen Riron ni yoru Zukei·Keijou Shori Kougaku
published by Nikkan Kogyo Shinbunsha
1996 © Fujio Yamaguchi

Printed on acid-free paper

Originally published by Springer-Verlag Tokyo Berlin Heidelberg New York in 2002
Softcover reprint of the hardcover 1st edition 2002

SPIN: 10877483

This is a photograph of a maze garden (Somerleyton, Norwich, England), typical of the type found in the gardens of English castles or manor houses. The author intentionally placed a bird overlooking the garden.

For those on the ground, the view is limited by the garden hedges making navigation through the maze. A maze garden presents a very difficult two-dimensional problem for us. For a bird having three-dimensional information, or, additional height information, however, it would be a very simple task.

The "bird approach" to navigation of the maze and the four-dimensional approach which the author is going to propound in this book, have something in common: an n-space problem is often solved more easily in $(n+1)$-space than in n-space.

Dedicated to Ivan E. Sutherland,

from whom the author learned many invaluable lessons

Preface

This is a long research paper arranged in the style of a book, in which the author proposes a paradigm shift in computer-aided geometric design, from that of conventional "Euclidean Processing" to "Totally Four-dimensional Processing" or "Four-dimensional Processing."

Today, computer graphics (CG), computer-aided design (CAD) and computer-aided manufacturing (CAM) are employed in a wide array of creative activities. The area of study known as computer-aided geometric design provides the basis of such technologies. Indeed, CG/CAD/CAM are used in today's society to such an extent that modern economic activities would cease to function without them. When we recall that only three decades ago, these technologies were thought to belong to the realm of fantasy, we realize what great changes have taken place since then. In those days, a fortune spent on computer equipment and software yielded very crude results by today's standards, whereas today a desktop computer purchased with one's pocket money can execute incomparably faster and accomplish far more difficult tasks. This change was brought about by developments in computer-aided geometric design as well as by technological advances in computers.

Yet when a CAD system, for instance, is examined carefully, we notice that some important but unresolved basic issues remain. Namely, that the system has many elements that are inaccurate or non-robust, and that the system itself has become too complex. These problems have a direct bearing on a system's reliability. Reliability is critical in practical systems; an unreliable system may malfunction at any time during the course of a daily routine, which would make it extremely difficult to observe work schedules.

The author argues strongly that as long as Euclidean Processing provides the basis for computer-aided geometric design, there will always be a limit to the level of reliability in a system. In other words, Euclidean Processing seems to contain within it elements that inevitably lead to a system's inaccuracy, non-robustness and complexity.

Over the author's course of study, he has come to realize the major cause of such inherent problems of Euclidean Processing: namely, that *a division operation is the root cause of all evil.*

An n-space problem accompanies with it a corresponding $(n + 1)$-space problem. In today's Euclidean Processing, n-space problems are processed in n-space, which is why a division operation becomes necessary. In geometric terms, a division operation can be considered as a projection from a space that is of the next-higher-dimension. Therefore, if processing is entirely carried out in $(n+1)$-space, i.e., without projection, it becomes possible to avoid the various problems that accompany a division operation. When this idea is carried to its logical conclusion, we arrive at a paradigm, namely, "Totally Four-dimensional Processing," which is the subject of this book.

This book can be considered as a systematic collection of research results obtained by the author and his students during the fifteen years since the author joined the Department of Mechanical Engineering at Waseda University.

Research over the years has only strengthened the author's conviction of the necessity of the paradigm shift he proposes. While there is much opportunity for future research to take place in the application of Four-dimensional Processing, particularly with respect to curves and surfaces, the author believes that the developments thus far are of a level sufficient for practical applications. The author would like to invite comments and criticisms from all readers, and in particular from those who practice CG/CAD/CAM in the workplace on a daily level.

The book is made up of four parts.

In Part I, various problems existing in the conventional processing method, i.e., Euclidean Processing, are pointed out and the causes of the problems are investigated. We conclude that performing a division operation is *the root cause of all evil.* We then try to incubate a new geometric processing paradigm where we can do away with division operations.

In Part II, Four-dimensional Processing is presented as a solution. A collection of techniques on Four-dimensional Processing is discussed in detail, and constitutes the central part of the book.

In Part III, the characteristics of the proposed Four-dimensional Processing are shown experimentally on various items and compared to those of Euclidean Processing.

Part IV gives an evaluation of Four-dimensional Processing conclusively: the simpler method, i.e., Four-dimensional Processing, is superior to the more complex Euclidean Processing in terms of exactness, robustness, generality, unifiability, duality and transformation invariance. This conclusion may sound like a paradox, and reasons for its existence are discussed.

Lastly, the author discusses the role of a division operation in computer-aided geometric design.

Chapters 1-6 constitute Part I.

Chapter 1 demonstrates various problems of non-exactness, non-robustness and non-compactness which exist in conventional processing. It points out that performing division operations is the root cause of these problems.

In order to construct a geometric processing method and do away with division operations, we must study relevant mathematics. Chapters 2, 3 and 4 discuss such topics as homogeneous coordinates, classical projective space and two-sided space, respectively.

Chapter 5 discusses some of the conventional approaches using homogeneous coordinates from a critical point of view, and concludes that they are insufficient for our purpose.

In considering and evaluating a processing paradigm of computer-aided geometric design, it is important to examine the types of transformations involved because we desire that all the data, geometry definitions, theories and algorithms are not influenced by these transformations, or are, in other words, invariant under these transformations.

Chapter 6 reviews the transformations used in computer-aided geometric design. It points out that we very often come across projective transformations and thus require projective invariance.

Chapters 7-24 constitute Part II.

Chapter 7 presents Four-dimensional Processing as a solution to the problems pointed out in Chapter 1. It discusses the concept and theoretical background of the processing paradigm.

Chapters 8-11 deal with homogeneous geometric definitions:

Chapters 8 and 9 present introductory and detailed discussions on homogeneous geometric definitions, respectively. Geometric elements are defined using homogeneous coordinates or coeffcients, as elements in classical projective or two-sided space.

Chapters 10 and 11 deal with homogeneous curves and surfaces, respectively. These chapters list some problems that accompany rational polynomial curves or surfaces, and then show, by contrast to Euclidean processing, how the problems can be resolved in Four-dimensional Processing.

Chapters 12-16 deal with four-dimensional geometric computations:

Chapter 12 presents basic homogeneous intersection formulas.

Chapter 13 discusses the Euclidean 4×4 determinant method and the homogeneous 4×4 determinant method. These 4×4 determinant methods require reference points to be specified.

The 4×4 determinant methods discussed in Chapter 13 are generalized to the homogeneous determinant method in Chapter 14, which does not require reference points. This chapter presents a detailed discussion on projectively invariant interference conditions between homogeneous simplices. These are expressed concisely using Plücker coordinates or Plücker coefficients.

Chapter 15 discusses the homogeneous geometric Newton method and compares it with the conventional Euclidean method. While the latter often shows non-robust characteristics when applied to rational polynomial curves or surfaces, the former method shows superior robustness. Furthermore, if homogenization is extended to the parameters defining rational curves or surfaces, the method also exhibits much better characteristics on the local uniqueness of intersection points with respect to initial values. Applications of the homogeneous method to complex root determinations are also mentioned.

Chapter 16 discusses long integer representation and adaptive error-free sign detections of scalar products and determinants made up of long integer components. An application of the floating-point unit (FPU) to the adaptive error-free sign detection is also mentioned.

Chapter 17 explains the basic elements of topology, and Chapter 18 discusses critically three types of data structure needed to describe shape topology. In order of increasing complexity, they are winged edge, half edge and quarter edge data structures. Totally Four-dimensional Processing employs the quarter edge data structure, which allows for duality. Chapters 17 and 18, which pertain to topology, are included to explain total duality in geometric computations.

Chapter 19 deals with Euclidean quantities and affine concepts in the four-dimensional environment.

The subsequent three chapters then deal with the applications of Four-dimensional Processing:

Chapter 20 presents a completely robust set operation algorithm between polyhedra. This algorithm relies on the property that Four-dimensional Processing does not require a division operation and thus enables exact computation. It uses long integers, but limits the increase in data length to a certain extent. This chapter also presents a fundamental technique for dealing with set operations on curved objects.

Chapter 21 shows a simple application of Four-dimensional Processing to surface generation by polyhedron subdivision. This shows an example of how generality is increased by a simple homogenization.

Chapter 22 deals with the reconstruction of three-dimensional points from a pair of projected images on two spherical surfaces. This chapter also shows another example of how the application of Four-dimensional Processing simplifies processing and increases generality.

Chapter 23 reviews the four-dimensional techniques of viewing pipe-line processing.

Chapter 24 presents a guideline of which projective space should be used in a given application; classical projective or two-sided space.

Part III includes only one chapter, Chapter 25, which shows various experimental tests to evaluate Four-dimensional Processing in comparison to the Euclidean method.

Chapters 26-28 constitute Part IV.

Chapter 26 presents a comprehensive comparison of Euclidean Processing and Four-dimensional Processing in terms of exactness, robustness, compactness, generality, unifiability, duality and transformation invariance, and concludes that Four-dimensional Processing is superior to the Euclidean method on almost all terms.

The conclusions of Chapter 26 may sound too favorable toward Four-dimensional Processing and Chapter 27 discusses the reasons for such a paradoxical situation.

Chapter 28 gives various algebraic and geometric interpretations of Four-dimensional Processing.

Appendices include: the fundamentals of Euclidean processing, various geometries, the plane determinant method, analytical geometry in associated vector space and others.

Five years ago the author published a book in Japanese entitled *Geometric Processing Based on Four-dimensional Theories* from Nikkan Kogyou Shinbunsha. The present book is an extended version of this earlier one. The author would like to thank Nikkan Kogyou Shinbunsha for permitting the use of some parts from the predecessor in this book.

In acknowledging the help of others, first, the author expresses his thanks to all students who studied with him during their acquisition of bachelor's, master's or doctoral degrees.

Second, he would like to express his thanks to Professors A.A. Ball, A. Bowyer, B. Bruderlin, E. Cohen, A.R. Forrest, C.M. Hoffmann, A.E. Middleditch, N.M. Patrikalakis, R.R. Patterson, H. Pottmann, M.J.D. Powell, R.F. Riesenfeld, and H.P. Seidel for helpful discussions; particularly to Dr. M.A. Sabin for his support, advice and discussions given to the author while he was in Cambridge for six months.

Third, the author would like to thank Professor J. Stolfi for the extensive quotations (in Chapter 4) from his book.

Fourth, he largely owes the English translation to Mr. R. Takeguchi.

Finally, the author would like to thank his wife Yukiko for her constant encouragement and support during the many, many days that have led to this finished product.

Fujio Yamaguchi
Hino, Tokyo, April 2002

Notation used in this book

The notation system used in this book and described below has the following common guidelines:

a. Points and vectors in two- and three-dimensional Euclidean space or its associated vector space are represented by lower case letters, while those in classical projective space, two-sided space or its associated vector space are represented by uppercase letters.

b. Vectors and matrices are represented by letters in italic bold type.

c. The coordinates or coefficients of points, lines and planes are enclosed by parentheses ( ), within which the components are separated from each other by commas. Vectors are enclosed by brackets [ ], and the vector components are separated from each other by a space.

d. The homogeneous coordinates or coefficients of points, lines and planes, as well as Plücker coordinates or coefficients, are overlined. These vector representations are overlined as well. The overline represents the equivalence class.

1. **Space symbols**

   Spaces are represented by uppercase letters in bold type. For example,

   $\mathbf{E}^3$....three-dimensional Euclidean space,
   $\mathbf{P}^3$....three-dimensional classical projective space,
   $\mathbf{T}^3$....three-dimensional two-sided space,
   $\mathbf{R}^4$....four-dimensional vector space.

2. **Points in Euclidean space**

   Points in $\mathbf{E}^2$ or $\mathbf{E}^3$ are represented by lowercase letters; their coordinates are enclosed in parentheses ( ) and separated by commas. For instance,

   $$q = (x, y), \quad q = (x, y, z).$$

3. **Vectors in the associated vector space with Euclidean space**

   Vectors in the associated vector space, $\mathbf{R}^2$ or $\mathbf{R}^3$, with Euclidean space, are represented by lowercase letters in italic bold type, and the vector components are enclosed in brackets [ ] and separated by a space. For instance,

   $$\boldsymbol{v} = [x \ y], \quad \boldsymbol{v} = [x \ y \ z].$$

4. **Vectors in the associated vector space with projective spaces**

   Vectors in the associated vector space $\mathbf{R}^3$ or $\mathbf{R}^4$ with classical projective space or two-sided space are represented by bold italic uppercase letters or bold Greek letters. That is, homogeneous coordinate vectors corresponding to points in classical projective or two-sided space are represented by bold uppercase letters as in

$$\boldsymbol{Q} = [w\ X\ Y],\ \ \boldsymbol{Q} = [w\ X\ Y\ Z]$$

and homogeneous coefficient vectors corresponding to lines in $\mathbf{P}^2$, $\mathbf{T}^2$ and planes in $\mathbf{P}^3$, $\mathbf{T}^3$ are represented by Greek letters in bold type as in

$$\boldsymbol{\gamma} = \begin{bmatrix} a \\ b \\ c \end{bmatrix},\ \ \boldsymbol{\gamma} = \begin{bmatrix} a \\ b \\ c \\ d \end{bmatrix}.$$

5. **Points in classical projective space or two-sided space**

Points in $\mathbf{P}^2$, $\mathbf{P}^3$ or $\mathbf{T}^2$, $\mathbf{T}^3$ are represented either by uppercase letters, as in Q, or, when defined using vectors, by overlined, uppercase letters in bold type (vectors), as in $\overline{\boldsymbol{Q}}$, with their elements separated by commas. For instance,

$$Q = \overline{(w, X, Y)}, \qquad Q = \overline{(w, X, Y, Z)};$$
$$\overline{\boldsymbol{Q}} = \overline{[w\ X\ Y]} = \overline{(w, X, Y)},\ \ \overline{\boldsymbol{Q}} = \overline{[w\ X\ Y\ Z]} = \overline{(w, X, Y, Z)}.$$

Plücker coordinates are also overlined (see guideline 9).

6. **Lines and planes in projective space or two-sided space**

Lines in $\mathbf{P}^2$, $\mathbf{T}^2$ and planes in $\mathbf{P}^3$, $\mathbf{T}^3$ are represented by Greek letters, either in plain type, as in γ, or in overlined, bold type (vector). Each component is shown as a column. For instance,

$$\gamma = \overline{\begin{pmatrix} a \\ b \\ c \end{pmatrix}} = \overline{(a, b, c)^T},\ \ \gamma = \overline{\begin{pmatrix} a \\ b \\ c \\ d \end{pmatrix}} = \overline{(a, b, c, d)^T},$$

$$\overline{\boldsymbol{\gamma}} = \overline{\begin{bmatrix} a \\ b \\ c \end{bmatrix}} = \overline{[a\ b\ c]^T},\ \ \overline{\boldsymbol{\gamma}} = \overline{\begin{bmatrix} a \\ b \\ c \\ d \end{bmatrix}} = \overline{[a\ b\ c\ d]^T}.$$

As in homogeneous coefficients, Plücker coefficients are also overlined (see guideline 9).

7. **Transformations**

Projective transformation matrices are represented by uppercase letters in italic bold type. Transposed, inverse and adjoint matrices are expressed by adding the superscripts ^{T}, $^{-1}$ and ^{a}, respectively, as in $\boldsymbol{M}^T$, $\boldsymbol{M}^{-1}$ and $\boldsymbol{M}^a$.

The equivalence class of projective transformations is represented by an attached overline, as in $\overline{\boldsymbol{M}}$.

8. **Simplex and flat**

A simplex is represented by a lowercase letter, and expressed by vertices which are separated by semicolons and enclosed by parentheses. For instance,

$$s = (V_a; V_0; V_1), \quad e = (E_0; \; ..... \; ; E_\nu).$$

Flats determined by simplices are denoted by uppercase letters. For instance,

$$A = (V_0; V_1).$$

9. **Plücker coordinates and Plücker coefficients in space geometry**

Plücker coordinates and coefficients, which are generalized forms of homogeneous coordinates and homogeneous coefficients, respectively, are represented with an attached overline on their components. For instance, a line expressed in Plücker coordinates would be written as:

$$L_{01} = \overline{(P_{01}, Q_{01}, R_{01}, S_{01}, T_{01}, U_{01})}.$$

Flats expressed by Plücker coordinates and Plücker coefficients, and their components are represented as follows:

· Flats expressed by Plücker coordinates are denoted by regular uppercase letters, and their components are also represented by uppercase letters.
· Flats expressed by Plücker coefficients are denoted by lowercase Greek letters, while their components are represented by lowercase letters. However, T_{0123} is an exception.

Plücker coordinates

Point: $V_0 = \overline{(w_0, X_0, Y_0, Z_0)}$
Line: $L_{01} = \overline{(P_{01}, Q_{01}, R_{01}, S_{01}, T_{01}, U_{01})}$
Plane: $F_{012} = \overline{(A_{012}, B_{012}, C_{012}, D_{012})^T}$
Universe: $U_{0123} = \overline{(S_{0123})}$

Plücker coefficients

Plane: $\gamma_0 = \overline{(a_0, b_0, c_0, d_0)^T}$
Line: $\lambda_{01} = \overline{(p_{01}, q_{01}, r_{01}, s_{01}, t_{01}, u_{01})}$
Point: $\pi_{012} = \overline{(w_{012}, x_{012}, y_{012}, z_{012})}$
Vacuum: $\tau_{0123} = \overline{(T_{0123})}$

· Plücker coordinates or Plücker coefficients given in bold type indicate that they are vectors defined by Plücker coordinates. For instance,

$$\boldsymbol{L}_{01} = [P_{01}\ Q_{01}\ R_{01}\ S_{01}\ T_{01}\ U_{01}], \quad \boldsymbol{F}_{012} = [A_{012}\ B_{012}\ C_{012}\ D_{012}]^T.$$

· f_{012} represents one of the Plücker coordinates for plane, F_{012}; and p_{012} represents one of the Plücker coefficients for point, π_{012}. In other words,

$$f_{012} \in \{A_{012}, B_{012}, C_{012}, D_{012}\}, \; p_{012} \in \{w_{012}, x_{012}, y_{012}, z_{012}\}.$$

· l_{01} represents one of the Plücker coordinates for line, L_{01}; and m_{01} represents one of the Plücker coefficients for line, λ_{01}. In other words,

$$l_{01} \in \{P_{01}, Q_{01}, R_{01}, S_{01}, T_{01}, U_{01}\}, \; m_{01} \in \{p_{01}, q_{01}, r_{01}, s_{01}, t_{01}, u_{01}\}.$$

As for Plücker coordinates and coefficients in plane geometry, see Appendix C.1.

10. **Logic symbols**

"A or B" and "A and B" are expressed using the logic symbols $\vee$ and $\wedge$, respectively, as follows:

$$A \vee B, \quad A \wedge B.$$

11. **Operational symbols for join and meet**

The *join* of flats A and B and *meet* of flats A and B are expressed by the operational symbols $\cup$ and $\cap$, respectively, as follows:

$$A \cup B, \quad A \cap B.$$

12. **Flats in join and meet operations**

A flat expressed by a point set is represented by an overlined matrix in which each row comprises the homogeneous coordinates of point. For instance, a line defined by V_0 and V_1 is expressed as:

$$V_0 \cup V_1 = \overline{\begin{pmatrix} w_0 & X_0 & Y_0 & Z_0 \\ w_1 & X_1 & Y_1 & Z_1 \end{pmatrix}}.$$

A flat expressed by a plane set is represented by an overlined matrix in which each column comprises the homogeneous coefficients of plane. Thus, a line defined by γ_0 and γ_1 is expressed as:

$$\gamma_0 \cap \gamma_1 = \overline{\begin{pmatrix} a_0 & a_1 \\ b_0 & b_1 \\ c_0 & c_1 \\ d_0 & d_1 \end{pmatrix}}.$$

In other words, multiple rows of homogeneous coordinates or multiple columns of homogeneous coefficients, when overlined, implicitly contain a *join* or a *meet* operation, respectively.

13. **Fundamental vectors**

The following homogeneous fundamental vectors are used:

$$\boldsymbol{I} = [1\;0\;0\;0], \; \boldsymbol{J} = [0\;1\;0\;0], \; \boldsymbol{K} = [0\;0\;1\;0], \; \boldsymbol{L} = [0\;0\;0\;1]$$

and

$$\vec{\boldsymbol{I}} = \begin{bmatrix} 1 \\ 0 \\ 0 \\ 0 \end{bmatrix}, \quad \vec{\boldsymbol{J}} = \begin{bmatrix} 0 \\ 1 \\ 0 \\ 0 \end{bmatrix}, \quad \vec{\boldsymbol{K}} = \begin{bmatrix} 0 \\ 0 \\ 1 \\ 0 \end{bmatrix}, \quad \vec{\boldsymbol{L}} = \begin{bmatrix} 0 \\ 0 \\ 0 \\ 1 \end{bmatrix}.$$

The fundamental vectors in three-dimensional Euclidean space are defined similarly, that is,

$$\boldsymbol{i} = [1\ 0\ 0], \ \boldsymbol{j} = [0\ 1\ 0], \ \boldsymbol{k} = [0\ 0\ 1]$$

and

$$\vec{\boldsymbol{i}} = \begin{bmatrix} 1 \\ 0 \\ 0 \end{bmatrix}, \quad \vec{\boldsymbol{j}} = \begin{bmatrix} 0 \\ 1 \\ 0 \end{bmatrix}, \quad \vec{\boldsymbol{k}} = \begin{bmatrix} 0 \\ 0 \\ 1 \end{bmatrix}.$$

14. **Graphical representation in two-sided space**

Graphical representation of the straight model in two-sided space follows the pattern of Stolfi [53]. Points and lines (line segments) in the front range are represented by solid dots and solid lines respectively. Points and lines in the back range are represented by open dots and dashed lines, respectively.

15. **Differentiation**

Differentiation with respect to an ordinary parameter t is shown by a dot symbol. For instance, the first derivative function vector of a simple curve is written as $\dot{\boldsymbol{P}}(t)$ (as for "simple curve," see Section 9.5).

16. **Scalar triple product**

The scalar triple product of vectors $\boldsymbol{p}$, $\boldsymbol{q}$ and $\boldsymbol{r}$ is denoted by:

$$[\boldsymbol{p}, \boldsymbol{q}, \boldsymbol{r}].$$

Contents

List of Figures

List of Tables

Part I

Problem Definitions

Chapter 1

Problems of Euclidean Approach

It is of vital importance that a computer-aided geometric design system is sufficiently reliable. We will examine the conventional geometric processing approach in terms of exactness, robustness and compactness which have a direct bearing on the system's reliability.

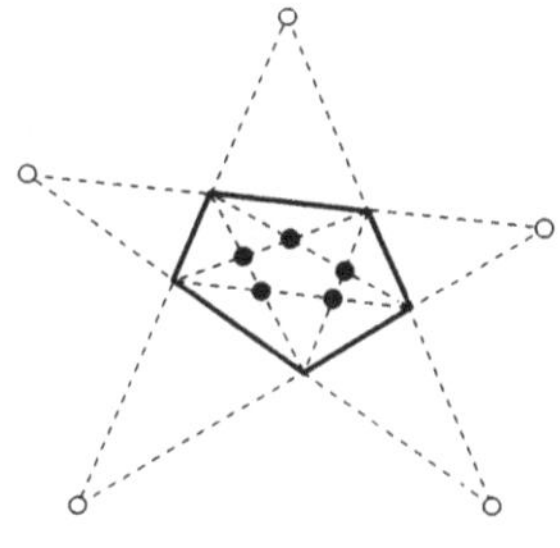

Figure 1.1: Going-in and going-out operations of a pentagon.

1.1 Non-Exactness

We consider the pentagon problem [24]. Given a pentagon in the plane (Fig. 1.1), we draw the five diagonals; their intersections define a contained, smaller pentagon. This operation is called *going-in*. Similarly, we call the operation *going-out*, when we define a larger pentagon by extending the five sides of the original pentagon. Let us iterate the going-in operation n times and then iterate the going-out n times. The coordinates of the vertices of the final pentagon should be equal to those of original ones. In practice, however, they differ by a large error, even for small values of n.

The intersection computations in this case can be written as follows:

$$a_0 + b_0 x + c_0 y = 0,$$
$$a_1 + b_1 x + c_1 y = 0,$$

$$\Delta = \begin{vmatrix} b_0 & c_0 \\ b_1 & c_1 \end{vmatrix}, \ \Delta_x = \begin{vmatrix} -a_0 & c_0 \\ -a_1 & c_1 \end{vmatrix}, \ \Delta_y = \begin{vmatrix} b_0 & -a_0 \\ b_1 & -a_1 \end{vmatrix}, \tag{1.1}$$

$$x = \frac{\Delta_x}{\Delta}, \ y = \frac{\Delta_y}{\Delta}. \tag{1.2}$$

Even if Δ, Δ_x and Δ_y are assumed to be represented exactly, exact coordinates (x, y) can not be expected because of the division operations in eq.(1.2). There the (x, y) is derived, which includes some error, and is input to the next process. Therefore the error is accumulated by the repetition of the process. It would be almost impossible to expect to restore the exact coordinates of the vertices of the original pentagon.

The example above deals with plane geometry. As an example of space geometry, let us consider defining exactly a face of a polyhedron in terms of vertex coordinates, where the coefficients of the plane equations of the faces of the polyhedron are expressed in rational numbers. The coordinates of a vertex, (x, y, z), are then obtained by the following set of equations:

$$\begin{aligned} a_0 + b_0 x + c_0 y + d_0 z &= 0, \\ a_1 + b_1 x + c_1 y + d_1 z &= 0, \\ a_2 + b_2 x + c_2 y + d_2 z &= 0, \end{aligned} \tag{1.3}$$

where $(a_0, b_0, c_0, d_0)^T$, $(a_1, b_1, c_1, d_1)^T$ and $(a_2, b_2, c_2, d_2)^T$ are the homogeneous coefficients of three faces comprising the vertex.

When this is solved, and letting

$$\Delta = \begin{vmatrix} b_0 & c_0 & d_0 \\ b_1 & c_1 & d_1 \\ b_2 & c_2 & d_2 \end{vmatrix}, \ \Delta_x = \begin{vmatrix} -a_0 & c_0 & d_0 \\ -a_1 & c_1 & d_1 \\ -a_2 & c_2 & d_2 \end{vmatrix},$$

$$\Delta_y = \begin{vmatrix} b_0 & -a_0 & d_0 \\ b_1 & -a_1 & d_1 \\ b_2 & -a_2 & d_2 \end{vmatrix}, \Delta_z = \begin{vmatrix} b_0 & c_0 & -a_0 \\ b_1 & c_1 & -a_1 \\ b_2 & c_2 & -a_2 \end{vmatrix}, \tag{1.4}$$

we obtain

$$x = \frac{\Delta_x}{\Delta}, \ y = \frac{\Delta_y}{\Delta}, \ z = \frac{\Delta_z}{\Delta}. \tag{1.5}$$

In general, it is not possible to exactly express the Euclidean coordinates, (x, y, z), obtained after division operations in terms of finite-length computer words. This means that polygonal faces can not be exactly represented, in general, using Euclidean coordinates.

The vertices thus derived do not lie on the plane of the face in the exact sense. Thus the vertex data has the contradiction that a point to be on a plane does not, in reality, satisfy the condition. This could cause some serious troubles in set operations of solid modeling.

1.2 Non-Robustness

One of the most important issues in geometric modeling today might be the problems of non-robustness that appear in set operations of solid modeling. This non-robustness originates from some errors of geometry definitions and computations. Therefore this would belong to the problem of previous section.

The simplest and commonest type of non-robustness occurs when a number is divided by zero or some extremely small number. This non-robustness might occur, for example, in computing a "distant" intersection point of two almost parallel lines.

Another type of non-robustness may occur when we compute an intersection between a rational polynomial curve or surface with some geometric element by using the geometric Newton-Raphson method [36],[64] (see Chapter 15).

Let us consider, for example, the problem of determining a point of intersection between a planar rational polynomial curve and a line segment. The rational polynomial curve is expressed by the following equation:

$$\boldsymbol{p}(t) = [x(t)\ y(t)] = [\frac{X(t)}{w(t)}\ \frac{Y(t)}{w(t)}]. \tag{1.6}$$

Here, the parameter increment δt is as follows:

$$\delta t = -\frac{\begin{vmatrix} 1 & \frac{X(t)}{w(t)} & \frac{Y(t)}{w(t)} \\ 1 & x_A & y_A \\ 1 & x_B & y_B \end{vmatrix}}{\begin{vmatrix} 0 & \frac{X'(t)w(t)-X(t)w'(t)}{w(t)^2} & \frac{Y'(t)w(t)-Y(t)w'(t)}{w(t)^2} \\ 1 & x_A & y_A \\ 1 & x_B & y_B \end{vmatrix}} \tag{1.7}$$

$$\equiv -\frac{f(t)}{f'(t)}. \tag{1.8}$$

As an example, consider the intersection between the following rational Bézier curve and line segment [36](Fig. 1.2).

Data for the rational Bézier curve

$$\boldsymbol{p}(t) = \frac{\sum B_{j,3}(t) w_j \boldsymbol{q}_j}{\sum B_{j,3}(t) w_j}, \quad (0 \leq t \leq 1), \tag{1.9}$$

where

$$B_{j,3}(t) = \binom{3}{j}(1-t)^{3-j}t^j.$$

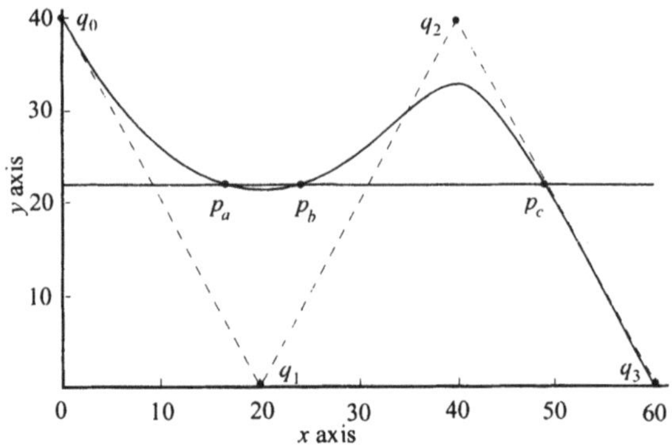

Figure 1.2: Computing intersection points for a rational Bézier curve and a line segment.

The data for the control points are

$$\begin{aligned} &\boldsymbol{q}_0 = [0 \;\; 40], \quad \boldsymbol{q}_1 = [20 \;\; 0], \quad \boldsymbol{q}_2 = [40 \;\; 40], \quad \boldsymbol{q}_3 = [60 \;\; 0], \\ &w_0 = 1, \qquad\quad w_1 = 3, \qquad\quad w_2 = 9, \qquad\quad w_3 = 1. \end{aligned}$$

Data for the line segment

$$\begin{aligned} \boldsymbol{v}(u) = (1-u)\boldsymbol{v}_a + u\boldsymbol{v}_b, \quad 0 \le u \le 1, \\ \boldsymbol{v}_a = [0 \;\; 22], \qquad \boldsymbol{v}_b = [100 \;\; 22]. \end{aligned} \tag{1.10}$$

Experimental results show that if the initial value falls within the following ranges:

$$\begin{aligned} -0.231 \le t \le -0.230, \quad -0.227 \le t \le 0.160, \quad 0.164 \le t \le 0.507, \\ 0.511 \le t \le 0.654, \qquad 0.884 \le t \le 1.039, \end{aligned}$$

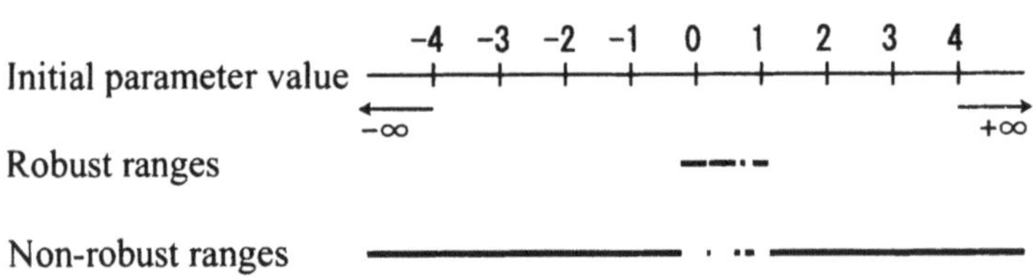

Figure 1.3: Ranges of parameter initial values for robust and non-robust processing.

then the parameter converges to a finite value and a solution is obtained, anyway. Conversely, if the initial value falls outside of these ranges, however, the parameter value will diverge and finally halt the algorithm (Fig. 1.3). Note the extensiveness of the range of parameter initial values for which non-robustness phenomenon occurs.

From eq.(1.8), we see that the geometric Newton-Raphson method amounts to solving for the roots of the algebraic equation $f(t)=0$. A plot of $f(t)$ in this example is shown in Fig. 1.4. We see that $f(t)$ has a complex plot with asymptotes in both axis directions, indicating that the parameter value may diverge under the repetitive processing of geometric Newton-Raphson method. (It is shown in Chapter 15 that this uncertainty is inherent in the processing of the geometric Newton-Raphson method when applied to rational curves and surfaces.)

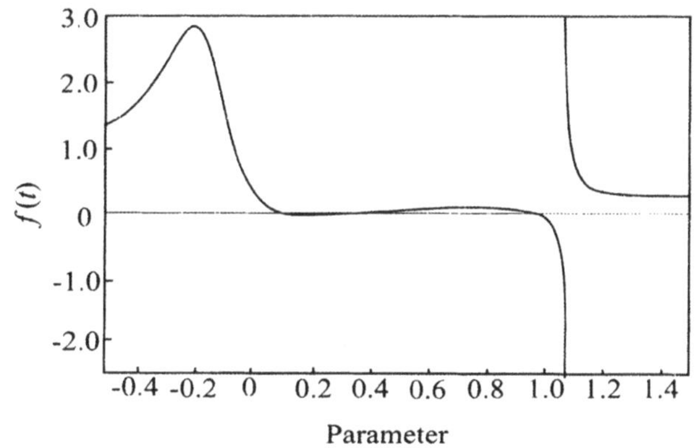

Figure 1.4: An equivalent function for the geometric Newton-Raphson method.

Choosing an initial value for which the parameter falls within the narrow robust ranges is not an easy matter, since there is no way of determining this range beforehand. This non-robustness phenomenon is a characteristic feature that accompanies the processing of rational polynomial curves and surfaces, and does not occur for ordinary polynomial curves (see Chapter 10). The non-robustness issue poses a particularly serious problem because the use of rational polynomial curves and surfaces has become widespread in recent years. Normally all w values are restricted to positive values in the processing of rational polynomial curves and surfaces, but this condition does not prevent the non-robustness phenomenon from occurring, seen from the many examples in Chapter 15 and Section 25.2.1, along with the present example.

1.3 Non-Compactness

Generally speaking, geometric elements in a CAGD system are considered to be subjected to projective transformations . Therefore we want geometric theories and algorithms to be projectively invariant. For details, see Chapter 6.

Imagine the case where we are to write a software package to test an intersection between two line segments, or between a line segment and a triangle.

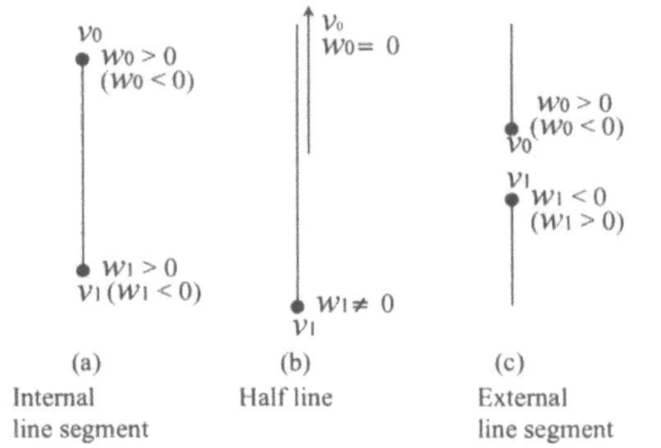

Figure 1.5: Three possible shapes of a line segment after a general projective transformation.

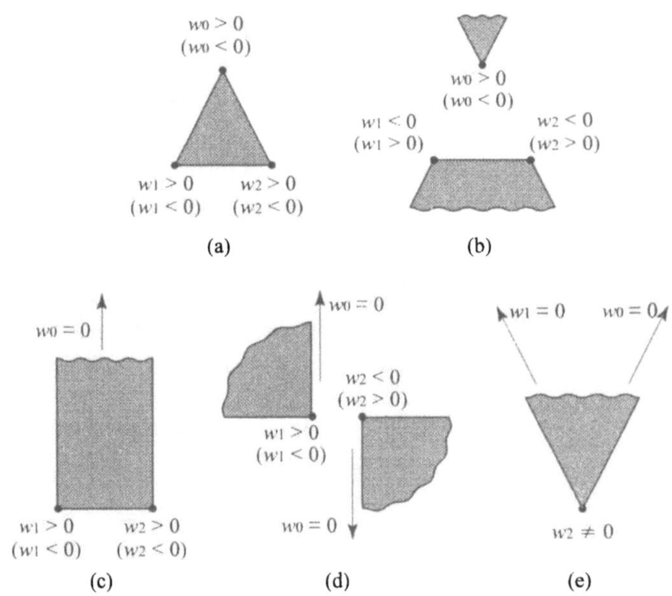

Figure 1.6: Five possible shapes of a triangle after a general projective transformation.

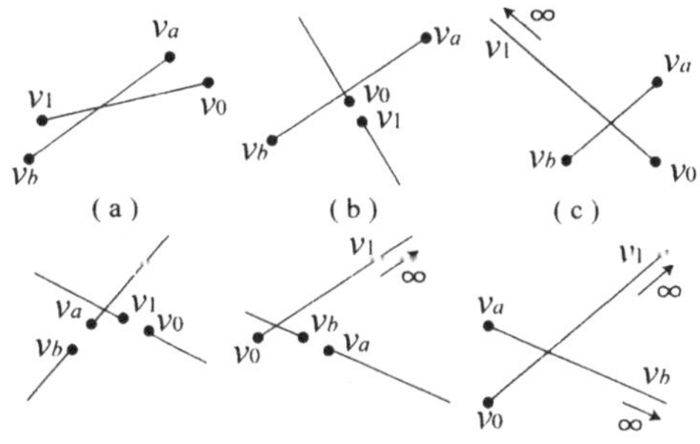

Figure 1.7: Six cases of line segment intersections.

Since a line segment could be transformed into three shapes (Fig. 1.5), and a triangle into five shapes (Fig. 1.6), by a general projective transformation, we have to make $3 \times 2 = 6$ (Fig. 1.7) or $3 \times 5 = 15$ separate routines respectively to cover all the possible cases.

In actual processing, the three types of line segments must each be treated with separate mathematical expressions. For instance, if we denote two endpoint vectors by $\boldsymbol{v}_0$ and $\boldsymbol{v}_1$, we can write as follows:

$$\text{Internal line segment} : \boldsymbol{v} = (1-t)\boldsymbol{v}_0 + t\boldsymbol{v}_1, \quad (0 \le t \le 1), \tag{1.11}$$

$$\text{Half line} : \boldsymbol{v} = \boldsymbol{v}_0 + \boldsymbol{\alpha} t, \quad (t \ge 0), \tag{1.12}$$

$$\text{External line segment} : \boldsymbol{v} = \boldsymbol{v}_0 + \boldsymbol{\alpha} t, \ \boldsymbol{v} = \boldsymbol{v}_1 - \boldsymbol{\alpha} t, \quad (t \ge 0). \tag{1.13}$$

In the package, the program, first of all, has to test among all the possible cases which the present case is and pass the control to a corresponding routine. This is not an easy task again. Thus, a seemingly simple problem becomes highly complex by the time a complete program is written.

1.4 Problems of Rational Curves and Surfaces

Because of the high representational capabilities, rational polynomial curves and surfaces are becoming standard descriptions in computer aided geometric design systems.

In dealing with a rational polynomial curve or surface, however, we come across various difficulties.

First, a rational polynomial curve does not allow us to generate an exact point on the curve corresponding to a parameter value because it forces to perform division operations in computing the rational expression itself. Therefore in reality an exact point can not generally be obtained, for example, from a quadratic rational polynomial curve although it is an exact expression of conics.

Second, as mentioned in Section 1.2, the geometric Newton-Raphson method sometimes fails when it is applied to a rational polynomial curve while it does not when applied to an ordinary one.

Third, formulas and algorithms tend to be more complex than those for an ordinary polynomial curve. The projective transformation of the curve is this complex and is not linear with respect to the position vector $\boldsymbol{p}(t)$:

$$\boldsymbol{p}^*(t) = \frac{\boldsymbol{p}(t)\begin{bmatrix} a & b & c \\ d & e & f \\ g & h & i \end{bmatrix} + [t_x\ t_y\ t_z]}{px + qy + rz + s}. \tag{1.14}$$

There are many other formulas and algorithms for rational polynomial curves which take much more complex forms than those for ordinary ones.

Fourth, there is a strict sign restriction on weights w_i, i.e., the signs of w_i must not be mixed in the processing of a rational polynomial curve because various inconveniences, such as non-convex hull property, zero denominator of tangent vectors and so on, may arise if the restriction is not observed. This restriction drastically reduces the high representational capability of rational polynomial curves and surfaces.

Suppose $\boldsymbol{q}_0$, $\boldsymbol{q}_1$ and $\boldsymbol{q}_2$ define an ellipse (Fig. 1.8). The negation of the weight of $\boldsymbol{q}_1$ generates its complementary segment. This is a simple way of generating a whole curve. This curve segment is, however, not allowed for processing because the signs of the weights of the control vertices are mixed.

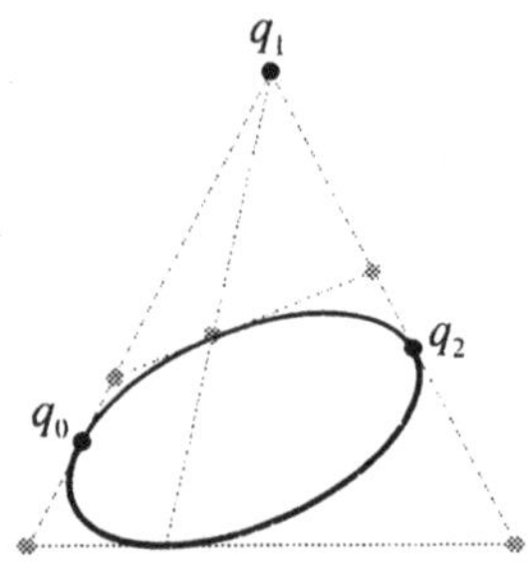

Figure 1.8: Complementary segment.

1.5 Root Cause of All Evil

We have so far pointed out various types of problems inherent in the conventional processing. Let us consider the cause of each problem in the order presented above.

As for the example of non-exactness, it is evident that the cause of non-exactness in the pentagon problem lies in performing the division operations to generate Euclidean coordinates.

In the case of the non-robustness problem of the Newton-Raphson method applied to rational curves and surfaces, it is also self-evident that the cause of the non-robustness lies in the divisional expression of the rational curves and surfaces because this type of non-robustness does not arise when it is applied to ordinary polynomial curves and surfaces.

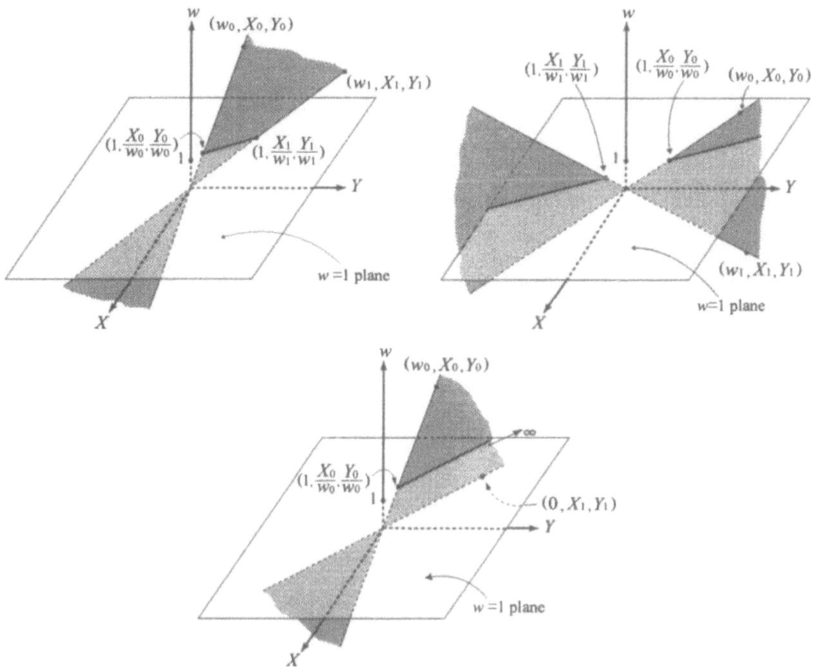

Figure 1.9: Three types of line segments.

As for the example of non-compactness, the cause may be a little difficult to find out. Let us consider this way; the three types of line segments are the cuts of wedge-shaped planes with the apexes at the origin of three-space O-wXY (Fig. 1.9). Then we understand that the three types of line segments are the results of division operations, and that division operations could cause to increase the number of shape types of a geometric element.

In Section 1.4, we listed up various problems inherent in the processing of rational curves and surfaces. Because these do not appear in the ordinary curves and surfaces, it is evident that the divisional forms of rational curves and surfaces are the causes of these problems.

Considering the discussion above, it does not seem to be difficult for us to conclude that these problems are caused by division operations. Thus we say that *"the division operation is the root cause of all evil."* (This will be borne out by various test results shown in Chapter 25) This observation invites us to consider the data set immediately before division operations, that is, the denominator w and the numerators X, Y, Z as coordinates of a point in place of the coordinates $(x, y, z) = (X/w, Y/w, Z/w)$. While the post-division data set is called *ordinary coordinates* or *Euclidean coordinates*, the pre-division data set (w, X, Y, Z) is called *homogeneous coordinates.*

It is now the time to study homogeneous coordinates.

Chapter 2

Homogeneous Coordinates

2.1 History

Homogeneous coordinates were used when proving theorems in projective geometry. An n-dimensional problem has corresponding to it an $(n+1)$-dimensional problem, and in most cases the $(n+1)$-dimensional problem is more easily solved than the n-dimensional one. Thus, by projecting the result of the $(n+1)$-dimensional case, one can obtain the result for the n-dimensional case [40]. With homogeneous coordinates, points at infinity can be treated in the same manner as points at finite distances.

In the early years of computer graphics (around the 1960s), it was L. G. Roberts and S. A. Coons of MIT who first introduced the methods that employ homogeneous coordinates into the field. Although Roberts' original purpose in using homogeneous coordinates was to obtain perspective drawings, he and Coons extended and generalized the method, developing a system where matrices based on homogeneous coordinates are used to projectively transform points, lines, planes, conical curves and conical surfaces [50],[11].

Furthermore, Roberts, Coons and A. R. Forrest showed the relation between rational curves and surfaces, and their homogeneous coordinate representations, and developed methods for their matrix representations [50],[10],[19].

Thus, in this regard, methods using homogeneous coordinates provided a basis in the development of systems of "transformations" and "curves and surfaces" within the field of computer aided geometric design. By treating two-dimensional problems as problems in three-dimensional space using homogeneous coordinates, and three-dimensional problems as those in four-dimensional space, the use of homogeneous coordinates can bring about considerable simplification, unification and generalization.

Other attempts to perform three-dimensional geometric computations in four-dimensional space, particularly with respect to clipping, were presented by I. E. Sutherland and G. W. Hodgman in 1974 [54], and by J. F. Blinn and M. E. Newell in 1978 [4]. In 1985, the author presented a method whereby various geometric interference problems can be uniformly processed by computing 4×4 determinants constructed from homogeneous coordinates, and proposed a processor based on this method [57].

It was R. F. Riesenfeld [49] and Blinn [4] who pointed out that, although a space composed of points expressed in homogeneous coordinates has local properties similar to Euclidean space, its topological structure on a macroscopic scale differs greatly and instead is that of projective space.

As the relation between algebra and geometry was established by the introduction of cartesian coordinates into Euclidean geometry, so too were homogeneous coordinates introduced originally into projective geometry to enable its algebraic treatment.

Projective space has properties that uniquely differ from those of Euclidean space. That is, 1) projective space is non-orientable, i.e., it is not possible to define "clockwise" or "counter-clockwise" in a consistent manner throughout the entire space; 2) a plane in projective space has only one side, and so two points cannot be separated from each other by placing a plane in between. Perhaps it is such peculiar properties of projective space that has given rise to the impression of it being an unwieldy, difficult subject and the major reason that it has not seen wider processing applications in computer aided geometric design, although it is routinely used in transformations as a readily accepted fact.

In conventional homogeneous coordinates, multiplication by an arbitrary non-zero scalar yields the same result, and so no distinction is made as to the sign. It is therefore sometimes called *unsigned homogeneous coordinates.* In his 1991 book ,"Oriented Projective Geometry," however, Jorge Stolfi proposes using *signed homogeneous coordinates* for geometric computations [53]. He points out that in space represented by signed homogeneous coordinates (which he calls *oriented projective space* or *two-sided space*), it is possible to treat oriented lines (or planes), signed angles, line segments and convex sets, which could not be treated with classical projective space, while still retaining the useful properties for geometric computations existing in classical projective space [1)].

Subsequently, the present author has proposed a new paradigm for geometric computation which is based on "Totally homogeneous processing," where various geometric computations in three-dimensional Euclidean space are consistently and uniformly processed in four-space [59],[60],[61].

2.2 Definitions and Properties

We have seen in the previous chapter that division operations give rise to various difficulties in geometric computations. Homogeneous coordinates are thus interesting in carrying out geometric computations without divisions.

---

1) Since two-sided space is also a kind of projective space, when it is necessary in this book to distinguish it from space represented by unsigned homogeneous coordinates, the term "classical projective space" is used to refer to the latter.

We first examine three-dimensional homogeneous coordinates, which should provide the reader with an understanding of the geometric meanings. We begin by presenting the definition of three-dimensional homogeneous coordinates from two-dimensional Euclidean coordinates.

Definition 2.1 (Three-dimensional homogeneous coordinates) *The (unsigned) three-dimensional homogeneous coordinates of a point* (x, y) *in* $\mathbf{E}^2$ *are given by* $\overline{(w, X, Y)} = \overline{(w, wx, wy)}$, *where* w *is an arbitrary non-zero scalar.*

The homogeneous coordinates $\overline{(0, a, b)}$ *represent a point at infinity (or ideal point) in the direction of vector* $[a\ b]$ *in* $\mathbf{E}^2$.

$\overline{(0, 0, 0)}$ *is not defined in homogeneous coordinates.* (x, y) *is called ordinary or non-homogeneous coordinates* [2].

When the following relations exist between two sets of homogeneous coordinates, $\overline{(w, X, Y)}$ and $\overline{(w', X', Y')}$:

$$w = kw', X = kX', Y = kY', \quad k \neq 0, \tag{2.1}$$

these two correspond to identical ordinary coordinates. That is, multiplication of homogeneous coordinates by an arbitrary non-zero scalar will not change the corresponding ordinary coordinates. The two sets of homogeneous coordinates are said to be "in an *equivalence relation*" if these two satisfy eq.(2.1). This is expressed by the following equation:

$$\overline{(w, X, Y)} = \overline{(w', X', Y')}. \tag{2.2}$$

All the sets of homogeneous coordinates in an equivalent relation with a given set of homogeneous coordinates is called an *equivalence class*, which is represented with an overline. When an equivalence class is referred to as a point, the set consisting of all such points forms the projective plane $\mathbf{P}^2$ (see Chapter 3).

The following statements can be made concerning homogeneous coordinates.

1. For any given ordinary coordinates in $\mathbf{E}^2$, an infinite number of corresponding homogeneous coordinate representations exist. Conversely, for given homogeneous coordinates $\overline{(w, X, Y)}$, where $w \neq 0$, the corresponding ordinary coordinates (x, y) are uniquely determined by $(x, y) = (\frac{X}{w}, \frac{Y}{w})$.

2. In homogeneous coordinates, directions are equivalent to points. That is, the direction of vector $[a\ b]$ on a Euclidean plane is expressed as $\overline{(0, a, b)}$ in homogeneous coordinates. This also expresses a point at infinity in the direction $[a\ b]$ [44].

3. Since $\overline{(0, a, b)}$ and $\overline{(0, -a, -b)}$ represent the same point, a point at infinity in the direction $[a\ b]$ and one in the opposite direction are considered to be identical.

---

[2] The meaning of an overline will soon be explained.

4. When w of homogeneous coordinates $\overline{(w, X, Y)}$ is varied with X and Y fixed, the corresponding Euclidean coordinate values are magnified or reduced. In this sense, w is called a *scale* or *weight.*

5. In vector space wXY, the projective plane $\mathbf{P}^2$ is represented by a set of lines going through the origin.

   Every line going through the origin except for those on the $w=0$ plane has a one-to-one correspondence to a point on the $w=1$ plane, which can be considered to be the Euclidean plane.

   Lines on the $w=0$ plane, on the other hand, have no corresponding points on the Euclidean plane.

   Thus the projective plane is the sum of Euclidean-coordinate points (x, y) and points at infinity of all directions on the Euclidean plane, in terms of point set.

6. In homogeneous coordinate representations, points at finite distances and those at infinity are treated as algebraically equivalent.

   Furthermore, when, say, the equation, $a+bx+cy=0$, of a line in the Euclidean plane is expressed in homogeneous coordinates, it becomes $aw+bX+cY=0$, where the constant term has disappeared and all terms are of the first degree.

   In the case of the Euclidean line equation, $[b \;\; c]$ represents the normal vector to the line, while a is a quantity proportional to the normal distance from the origin to the line. In homogeneous representation, on the other hand, $[a \;\; b \;\; c]$ expresses a normal vector of a plane in wXY space, with a, b and c playing equal roles [3] (see Appendix C.2).

7. Homogeneous coordinate representations are not unique. Therefore, vector addition does not hold in homogeneous coordinates.

   If, for instance, we assume that addition is satisfied, then

   $$\overline{(1,2,3)} + \overline{(3,2,1)} \to \overline{(4,4,4)}.$$

   Yet, if $\overline{(2,4,6)}$, which represents the same point as $\overline{(1,2,3)}$, is used, we have

   $$\overline{(2,4,6)} + \overline{(3,2,1)} \to \overline{(5,6,7)}.$$

   These two results do not represent the same point. That is, homogeneous coordinates do not possess the structure of a vector space [44].

[3] According to the Oxford English Dictionary, the word "homogeneous" has the following definitions [5].

(a) Of the same kind so as to be commensurable.

(b) Of the same degree or dimension: consisting of terms of the same dimension.

8. An element in $\mathbf{R}^3$ taken from an equivalence class is called a "*representative element*" (or simply "*representative*"). For example, [2 4 6] is a representative element of $\overline{(1, 2, 3)}$.

9. A "standardized" representation of homogeneous coordinates is often used. By standardization, the following operation is meant:

   for a point at a finite distance: $\overline{(1, x, y)}$, (x and y are two-dimensional Euclidean coordinates.),

   for a point at infinity: $\overline{(0, a, b)}$, ($[a\ b]$ is a direction vector on the two-dimensional Euclidean plane.).

10. The homogeneous coefficients of lines can be defined in a symmetric manner, that is, dualistically, to homogeneous coordinates of points.

Similar statements can be made concerning four-dimensional homogeneous coordinates and points in $\mathbf{P}^3$, as well as three-dimensional homogeneous cordinates and points in $\mathbf{P}^2$.

The definition of four-dimensional homogeneous coordinates follow:

Definition 2.2 (Four-dimensional homogeneous coordinates)
The four-dimensional homogeneous coordinates of a point (x, y, z) *in* $\mathbf{E}^3$ *are given by* $\overline{(w, X, Y, Z)} = \overline{(w, wx, wy, wz)}$, *where* w *is an arbitrary non-zero scalar.*

The homogeneous coordinates $\overline{(0, a, b, c)}$ *represent a point at infinity (or an ideal point) in the direction of vector* $[a\ b\ c]$ *in* $\mathbf{E}^3$.

$\overline{(0, 0, 0, 0)}$ *is not defined in homogeneous coordinates.* (x, y, z) *is called ordinary or non-homogeneous coordinates.*

2.3 Signed Homogeneous Coordinates

While the discussion on homogeneous coordinates in the previous section concerned conventional homogeneous coordinates, a different kind of homogeneous coordinate system has been proposed in recent years, as stated in Section 2.1 [53]. The former is known as "unsigned homogeneous coordinates," and the latter "signed homogeneous coordinates." The only difference in the definitions of these two is that the former makes no sign distinctions, while the latter does.

Definition 2.3 (Signed three-dimensional homogeneous coordinates)
The signed three-dimensional homogeneous coordinates of a point (x, y) *in* $\mathbf{E}^2$ *are given by* $\overline{(w, X, Y)} = \overline{(w, wx, wy)}$, *where* w *is an arbitrary positive or negative scalar, depending on whether the point is in front or back ranges, respectively* [4].

The homogeneous coordinates $\overline{(0, a, b)}$ *represent a point at infinity (or ideal point) in the direction of vector* $[a\ b]$ *in* $\mathbf{E}^2$.

[4] As for front and back ranges, see Section 4.2.

$\overline{(0,0,0)}$ *is not defined in homogeneous coordinates.* (x, y) *is called ordinary or non-homogeneous coordinates.*

Below, we describe only how signed homogeneous coordinates differ from unsigned ones.

1. The equivalence relation for three-dimensional signed homogeneous coordinates is expressed as follows:

$$w = kw', X = kX', Y = kY', \quad k > 0. \tag{2.3}$$

   For example, $\overline{(2,6,4)}$ and $\overline{(-2,-6,-4)}$ both represent the same Euclidean coordinates $(3,2)$, but they are distinguished as belonging to different *ranges* [5]. Points with positive w belong to the front range, while those with negative w to the back range.

   Thus, the points at infinity, $\overline{(0,a,b)}$ and $\overline{(0,-a,-b)}$, are considered to represent different points.

2. When an equivalence class in signed three-dimensional homogeneous coordinates is referred to as a point, the set of these points form a *two-sided plane* $\mathbf{T}^2$.

   In the vector space $\mathbf{R}^3$, the two-sided plane is represented by the set of half-lines originating from the origin of the space and having the same sign of w (see Section 4.5.3).

2.4 Normalizations

Repetitive computations using homogeneous coordinates have a tendency to make coordinate and coefficient data very long since division operations are not usually performed. Therefore it is strongly recommended to "normalize" coordinate and coefficient data often to prevent the computations from getting excessively inefficient, from causing excessive deterioration of data accuracy in some cases, or from getting into overflow situation (see Sections 16.5, 25.1.1 and 25.1.2). The normalizations are done among homogeneous coordinates or coefficients, or more generally, among Plücker coordinates or coefficients, or even between the denominator and numerator of a rational number. In some cases the normalizations are performed among the components of a homogeneous transformation matrix.

2.4.1 Integer Homogeneous Components

When coordinates or coefficients are expressed in integer format, the normalization means to delete the greatest common divisor from each integer homogeneous component. This helps to prevent the computations from getting excessively inefficient while keeping the exactness of data (see Table 25.10).

[5] As for ranges, see Section 4.2.

In the following we shall explain how to compute the greatest common divisor of four-dimensional integer components, making use of the properties of the greatest common divisor:

We suppose u and v are integers.

1. When u and v are both 2's multiples,

$$gcd(u, v) = 2 \cdot gcd(u/2, v/2).$$

2. When u is 2's multiple and v not,

$$gcd(u, v) = gcd(u/2, v).$$

3. When $u > v$,

$$gcd(u, v) = gcd(u - v, v).$$

By using the properties above, we have the following algorithm for determining the greatest common divisor of four-dimensional integer coordinates (w, X, Y, Z).

a. Consider only non-zero elements in w, X, Y and Z.

b. Shift each element right by one bit until some element is not 2's multiple. Denote the number of the bit-shift by k.

c. If any element is 2's multiple, shift it right until it is not.

d. Determine the smallest element. Subtract it from the other elements.

e. Delete a zero element after the subtraction above, if any, from consideration.

f. When there is only one non-zero element left, the non-zero number$\times 2^k$ is the greatest common divisor that we seek.

2.4.2 Floating-point Homogeneous Components

There are two types of normalizations about floating-point format homogeneous components. One is for keeping the truncation error as little as possible, and the other for preventing the overflow of the data.

1. **Mantissa normalization**

   In order to prevent the chances of data overflow from mantissa as few as possible and thus keep the deterioration of data accuracy as small as possible, we normalize the mantissa data of homogeneous coordinates (coefficients) such that we look upon them as integers, apply the integer homogeneous component normalization technique mentioned in the previous section and return them with $1 \leq$ mantissas of w, X, Y and Z (a, b, c and d) < 2 (IEEE standard case)(supposing any of the mantissas is not zero). This normalization does not affect the data accuracy at all.

Although this method is computationally expensive, we can expect more accurate processing because the data length of each coordinate tends to be shorter by this technique (see Section 25.1.1).

2. **Exponent normalization**

   In order to prevent data overflow, we subtract from each exponent of the coordinates (coefficients), that of w-coordinate (a-coefficient). This is equivalent to dividing each component by $2^{\text{exponent of } w}$ ($2^{\text{exponent of } a}$). This helps to prevent the data from overflowing while keeping the accuracy of data. After the normalization, w (a) becomes the value of its mantissa, that is, $1 \leq w < 2$ ($1 \leq a < 2$).

The best normalization routine would be realized by uniting the two types into one.

Next, we study, in the subsequent two chapters, the properties of the two types of projective spaces that homogeneous coordinates represent, that is, classical projective space and two-sided space.

Chapter 3

Classical Projective Space

3.1 Definition by Vector Space

As stated in the previous chapter, conventional unsigned homogeneous coordinates represent a space called (*classical*) *projective space.*

Alternatively, projective space can be defined by the use of vector space. In the following we will give this definition.

Definition 3.1 (Classical projective space)
In $(\nu+1)$-dimensional numerical vector space on real field, define a vector space ${}^*\mathbf{R}^{\nu+1}$:

$$ {}^*\mathbf{R}^{\nu+1} = \mathbf{R}^{\nu+1} - \{\mathbf{0}\} $$

and an equivalence relation $\sim$ between two vectors $\boldsymbol{P}$ and $\boldsymbol{Q}$ in the space such that

$$ \boldsymbol{P} \sim \boldsymbol{Q} \Leftrightarrow \exists \lambda \in \mathbf{R}^1, \lambda \neq 0 : \boldsymbol{Q} = \lambda \boldsymbol{P}. \tag{3.1} $$

Denote the set of all of the equivalence classes derived by classifying ${}^*\mathbf{R}^{\nu+1}$ by the equivalence relation $\sim$, such that

$$ \overline{\mathbf{R}}^{\nu+1} = {}^*\mathbf{R}^{\nu+1}/\sim . \tag{3.2} $$

We refer to $\overline{\mathbf{R}}^{\nu+1}$ as ν-dimensional projective space and denote it by $\mathbf{P}^{\nu}$ [29]. The equivalence class which includes $\boldsymbol{Q} \in {}^*\mathbf{R}^{\nu+1}$ is a point in projective space and is denoted by $\overline{\boldsymbol{Q}}$ in the present book. We shall call $\mathbf{R}^{\nu+1}$ associated vector space [1] *of $\mathbf{P}^{\nu}$.*

[1] The relation by which a vector space is associated with projective space is similar to that by which a vector space is associated with Euclidean space (see Appendix A.1). Just as it is necessary to clearly distinguish between a point in Euclidean space and a vector in vector space (see Appendix A.2), so is it necessary to make a clear distinction between a point in projective space and a vector defined by its homogeneous coordinates. Geometric shapes defined in projective space is processed by making use of the associated vector space, similarly to the manner in which the processing in Euclidean space is carried out by means of a vector space.

As we know, a point Q in projective space, for example in $\mathbf{P}^3$, is defined by homogeneous coordinates, like $Q = \overline{(w, X, Y, Z)}$. From the definition above, the point can also be defined by specifying a vector $\boldsymbol{Q} = [w\ X\ Y\ Z]$ like $\overline{\boldsymbol{Q}} = \overline{[w\ X\ Y\ Z]}$. That is, $Q = \overline{(w, X, Y, Z)} = \overline{\boldsymbol{Q}} = \overline{[w\ X\ Y\ Z]}$.

Geometrically speaking, a point in $\mathbf{P}^\nu$ is represented as a line through the origin in $\mathbf{R}^{\nu+1}$ and every point on the line except the origin constitutes an equivalence class. Therefore $\mathbf{P}^\nu$ can be said to be represented as the set of all lines through the origin in $\mathbf{R}^{\nu+1}$ and this set is called *vector space model* of classical projective space. The set of all lines through a point is called a *bundle.*

3.2 Models of Projective Space

We discuss below one- and two-dimensional projective spaces, that is, projective line $\mathbf{P}^1$ and projective plane $\mathbf{P}^2$, using four models, following Stolfi [53].

1. **The straight model**

   The straight model of projective line $\mathbf{P}^1$ is the real line $\mathbf{R}^1$ to which is added points at infinity, $+\infty$ and $-\infty$, which are taken to be the same point (Fig. 3.1).

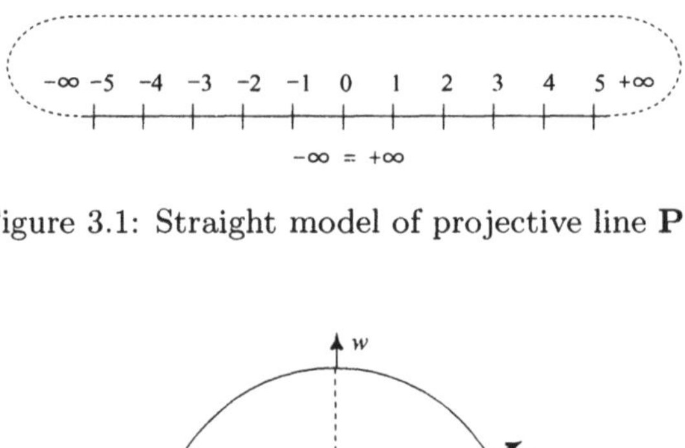

Figure 3.1: Straight model of projective line $\mathbf{P}^1$.

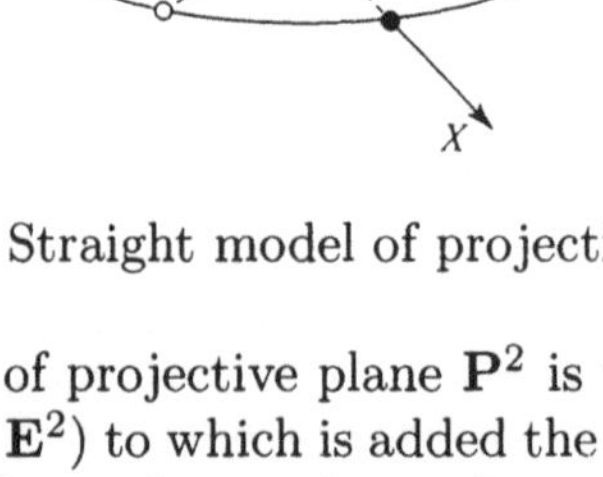

Figure 3.2: Straight model of projective plane $\mathbf{P}^2$.

   The straight model of projective plane $\mathbf{P}^2$ is the real plane $\mathbf{R}^2$ (same as the Euclidean plane $\mathbf{E}^2$) to which is added the line at infinity Ω_2 [2)], where a single point at infinity $\boldsymbol{d}\infty$ corresponds to a direction pair $\{\boldsymbol{d}, -\boldsymbol{d}\}$ ($\boldsymbol{d}$ is a unit vector representing a direction.). Thus, $\boldsymbol{d}\infty = (-\boldsymbol{d})\infty$ lies on

2) We shall denote the line at infinity of $\mathbf{P}^2$ or the plane at infinity of $\mathbf{P}^3$ by Ω_2 or Ω_3 respectively in this chapter.

the line at infinity Ω_2 (Fig. 3.2). Furthermore, all lines parallel to the direction of $\boldsymbol{d}$ passes this point at infinity $\boldsymbol{d}\infty$.

2. **The analytical model**

   The analytical model of projective line $\mathbf{P}^1$ is simply represented by two dimensional homogeneous coordinates (w, X).

   In the analytical model, a point on $\mathbf{P}^2$ is represented by homogeneous coordinates (w, X, Y), and a line by homogeneous coefficients $(a, b, c)^T$.

3. **The spherical model**

   The spherical model of projective line $\mathbf{P}^1$ is a circle for which antipodal points are identified (Fig. 3.3).

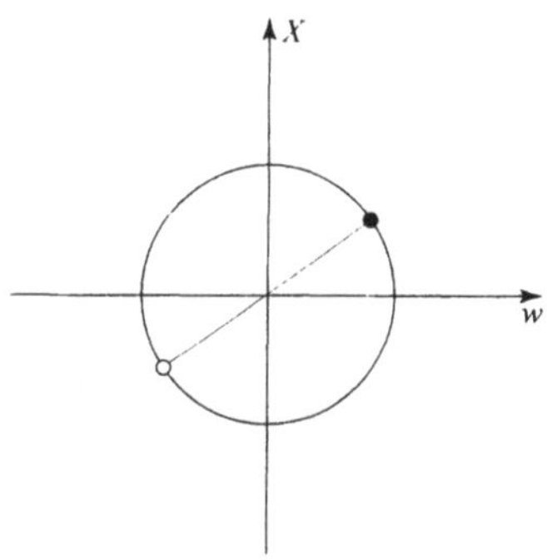

Figure 3.3: Spherical model of $\mathbf{P}^1$ embedded in vector space wX.

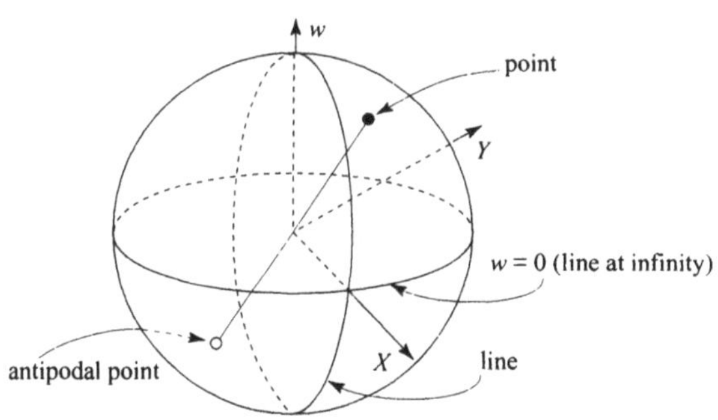

Figure 3.4: Spherical model of $\mathbf{P}^2$ embedded in vector space wXY.

The spherical model of projective plane $\mathbf{P}^2$ is a spherical surface for which a point and its antipodal are considered to be identical (Fig. 3.4). A line in $\mathbf{P}^2$ is represented by a great circle on the spherical model. A point and its antipodal on this great circle are also considered as identical.

The spherical model clearly demonstrates that all points, including those at infinity, are treated on equal terms, and that all lines including that at infinity (the great circle, which is the intersecting line of the sphere's surface and $w=0$ plane) are treated on an equal basis.

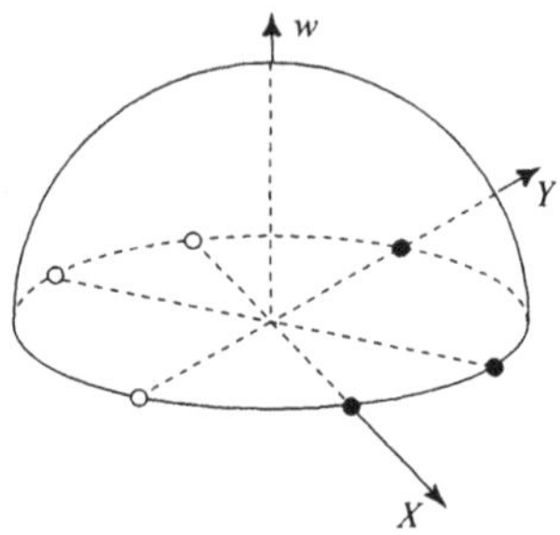

Figure 3.5: Half spherical model of $\mathbf{P}^2$ embedded in vector space wXY.

Because antipodal points are considered to be the same point in this model, the upper half sphere is all we need (Fig. 3.5). In this case, only those points on the great circle of $w=0$ forming a semicircle are included. It is known that the closed surface obtained by connecting antipodal points on the circle cannot be realized in Euclidean space (see Section 3.4, where we try to realize a model of perfect projective plane).

4. **The vector space model**

   A point $\overline{(w, X)}$ in $\mathbf{P}^1$ can be represented in vector space $\mathbf{R}^2$ by a line going through the origin and point (w, X) (Fig. 3.6).

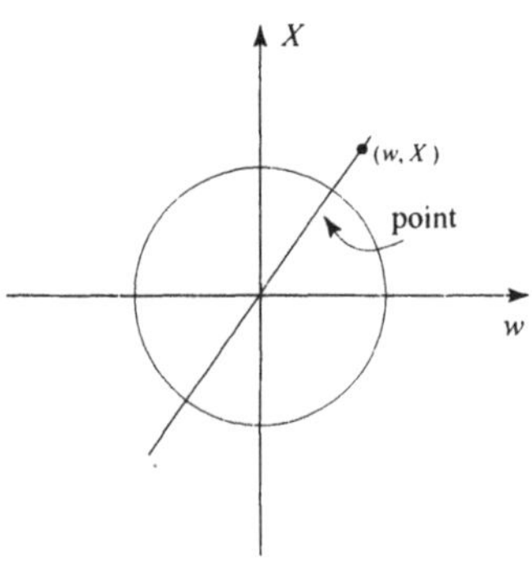

Figure 3.6: Vector space model of point in $\mathbf{R}^2$.

A point $\overline{(w, X, Y)}$ in $\mathbf{P}^2$ can be represented in vector space $\mathbf{R}^3$ by a line going through the origin and point (w, X, Y), and a line $\overline{(a, b, c)^T}$ in $\mathbf{P}^2$ by a plane containing the origin and normal to vector $[a\ b\ c]$. In other

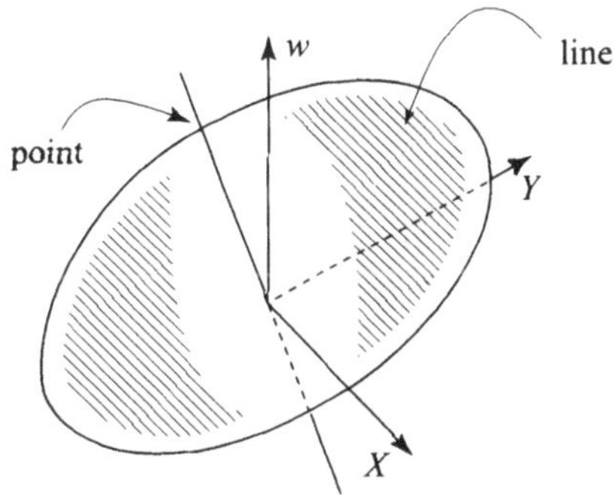

Figure 3.7: Vector space models of a point and line.

words, points and lines in $\mathbf{P}^2$ correspond to one- and two-dimensional linear subspaces, respectively, in three-dimensional vector space. The vector space models of a point and line are shown in Fig. 3.7.

In general, a geometric shape in $\mathbf{P}^\nu$ is represented by a linear subspace of dimension higher by one than that of corresponding Euclidean shape, in vector space $\mathbf{R}^{\nu+1}$.

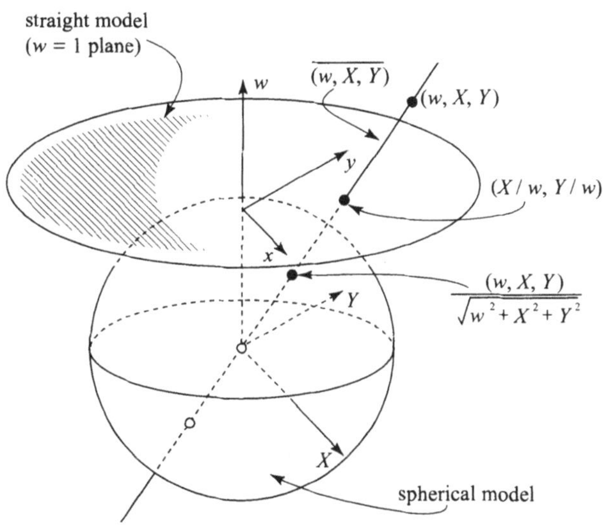

Figure 3.8: Relations among the four models.

3.3 Relations among Models

The relation between the analytical and straight models is expressed by that between homogeneous coordinates $\overline{(w, X, Y)}$ and ordinary coordinates (x, y).

That is, if $w \neq 0$, then $(x,y)=(\frac{X}{w},\frac{Y}{w})$, but if $w=0$, then $\overline{(0,X,Y)}$ represents a point at infinity in the direction of vector $[X\ Y]$ in Euclidean space.

Meanwhile, a point (w,X,Y) in $\mathbf{R}^3$ is transformed to a point in the spherical model by the following expression:

$$\frac{(w,X,Y)}{\sqrt{w^2+X^2+Y^2}}. \tag{3.3}$$

The relations among the four models are illustrated in Fig. 3.8. Geometrically, the relations are illustrated by the intersections that the unit sphere and $w=1$ plane have with a central projection from a point in $\mathbf{R}^3$ into the origin. The great circle for $w=0$ in the spherical model is projected in the straight model to the line at infinity. Furthermore, each point and line are projected to a point and a line respectively, and the incidence relationships between geometric elements are preserved in the projection.

3.4 Topological Properties

We begin with projective line, which is a closed space formed by adding a point at infinity to the Euclidean line. It is topologically equivalent to a circle (Fig. 3.9).

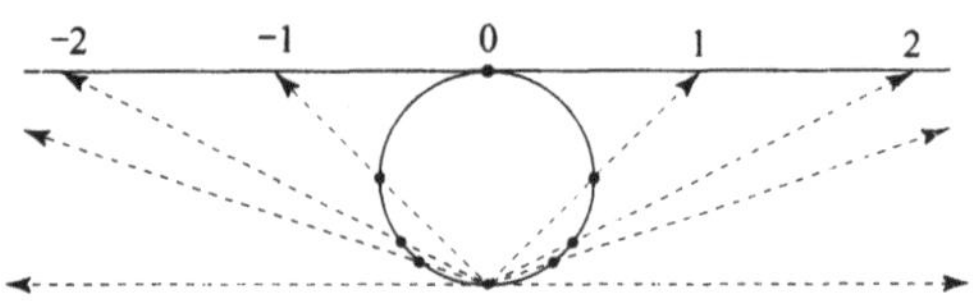

Figure 3.9: Spherical model showing topology of projective line.

We next examine the Möbius band so as to gain some insight into the topology of projective plane. A Möbius band is a closed surface obtained by twisting one end of a band by half turn and connecting it to the remaining end (Fig. 3.10).

The Möbius band has the interesting property of possessing only a one-sided edge and a one-sided surface.

We shall try to realize a model of perfect projective plane by making use of the property of the Möbius band.

Take now a disk whose circumference is equal in length to the edge of the Möbius band, and connect the edges of the two so that the points, p and q, of the disk meet the corresponding points on the band [49]. This operation cannot be done in Euclidean space, and so must be "visualized" in the reader's imagination. This disk is just like any other normal disk except that, when the width of the Möbius band is zero, diametrically opposite (i.e., antipodal) points become identical. Although the surface has local properties similar to a Euclidean plane, it clearly differs from a macroscopic standpoint.

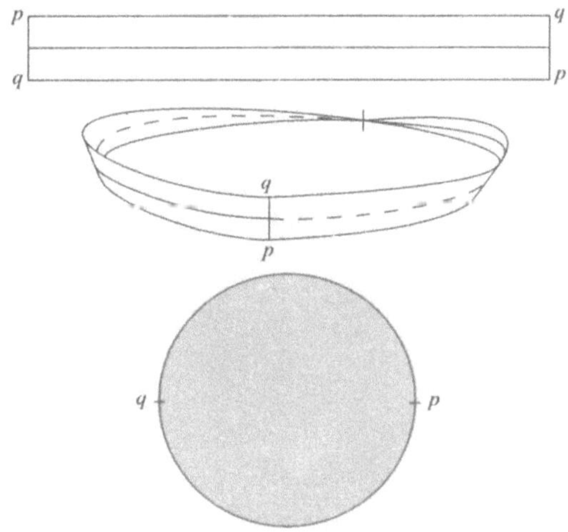

Figure 3.10: Making a Möbius band.

This closed surface represents a model of projective plane $\mathbf{P}^2$. The disk's interior represents the Euclidean plane. This model explains why projective plane is non-orientable [3)] as is the Möbius band.

We examine further topological properties of projective plane $\mathbf{P}^2$ [49]. Consider first a line on the two-dimensional Euclidean plane as follows:

$$\boldsymbol{v} = (1-t)\boldsymbol{v}_0 + t\boldsymbol{v}_1, \qquad -\infty \le t \le +\infty, \tag{3.4}$$

where $\boldsymbol{v}=[x\ y]$, $\boldsymbol{v}_0=[-1\ -1]$ and $\boldsymbol{v}_1=[1\ 1]$.

Eq.(3.4) represents a line going through points v_0 and v_1, and separates the Euclidean plane into two half spaces.

We now examine whether a projective line separates projective plane, as a Euclidean line does in the Euclidean plane. We have seen before that three-dimensional homogeneous coordinates represent projective plane. To examine the properties of projective plane, therefore, we consider the following two equations expressed in homogeneous coordinate vectors (Fig. 3.11):

$$\overline{\boldsymbol{P}} = \overline{(1-t)\boldsymbol{P}_0 + t\boldsymbol{P}_1}, \qquad t \ge 1 \text{ or } t \le 0, \tag{3.5}$$

$$\overline{\boldsymbol{P}} = \overline{(1-t)\boldsymbol{P}_0 + t\boldsymbol{P}_1}, \qquad 0 \le t \le 1, \tag{3.6}$$

where $\overline{\boldsymbol{P}}=\overline{[w\ X\ Y]}$, $\boldsymbol{P}_0=[1\ -1\ 1]$ and $\boldsymbol{P}_1=[-1\ -1\ 1]$.

Eq.(3.5) represents a line segment connecting points P_0 and P_1. Originating at P_0 at $t=0$, it passes the origin at $t=\pm\infty$, and ends at P_1 at $t=1$ (solid bold line in Fig. 3.11). Meanwhile, eq.(3.6) represents a line segment that begins at

---

3) **Definition 3.2 (Surface orientability)**
A surface is orientable when, after triangulating the surface, the orientation of all triangles can be set such that the directions at a common side for two adjacent triangles are opposite to one another.

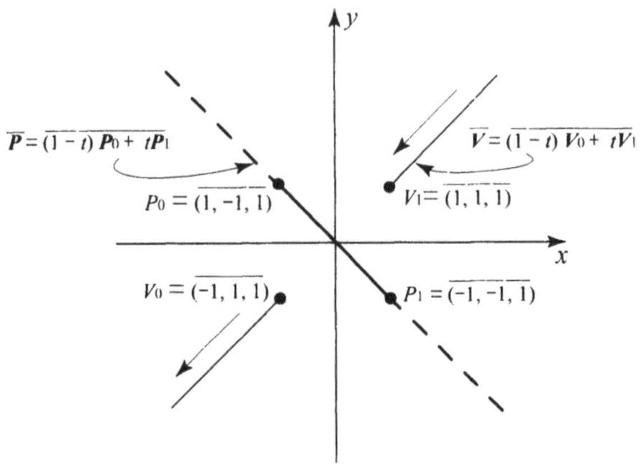

Figure 3.11: Separation of projective plane.

P_0 at $t=0$, passes a point at infinity $\overline{(0,-1,1)}$ at $t=\frac{1}{2}$, and ends at P_1 at $t=1$ (dashed bold line in Fig. 3.11). So

$$\overline{\boldsymbol{P}} = \overline{(1-t)\boldsymbol{P}_0 + t\boldsymbol{P}_1}, \qquad -\infty \le t \le +\infty \tag{3.7}$$

is a closed line going through points P_0 and P_1, and therefore represents a projective line.

Consider now the next equation which has the same form as eq.(3.7):

$$\overline{\boldsymbol{V}} = \overline{(1-t)\boldsymbol{V}_0 + t\boldsymbol{V}_1}, \qquad -\infty \le t \le +\infty, \tag{3.8}$$

where $\overline{\boldsymbol{V}} = \overline{[w\ X\ Y]}$, $\boldsymbol{V}_0 = [-1\ 1\ 1]$ and $\boldsymbol{V}_1 = [1\ 1\ 1]$. Eq.(3.8) represents a closed line that intersects with line (3.7) at the origin.

As we saw, projective plane is formed by adding a line at infinity to the Euclidean plane. The two lines, (3.7) and (3.8), intersect only at the origin on the Euclidean plane. Meanwhile, they do not intersect with each other at the line at infinity, with which they meet at points of infinity, $\overline{(0,-1,1)}$ and $\overline{(0,1,1)}$, respectively. Thus, the two lines intersect only at the origin on projective plane. Because it is possible to start out at V_0, pass a point at infinity, and reach V_1 without intersecting with line (3.7), the line of (3.7) does not separate points V_0 and V_1. This is a property of projective plane that differs greatly from that of the Euclidean plane. To separate projective plane (or space) into two distinct regions, it is necessary to specify two lines (or hyperplanes) (see Section 7.2).

3.5 Cross Ratios

Consider a coordinatized line t in Euclidean space; if a, x, y and b are four points on this line, the ratio of ratios, denoted by $(x:y|a:b)$ and defined as follows, is called a *cross ratio* or *anharmonic ratio* (Fig. 3.12):

$$(x:y|a:b) = \frac{x-a}{b-x}\Big/\frac{y-a}{b-y}. \tag{3.9}$$

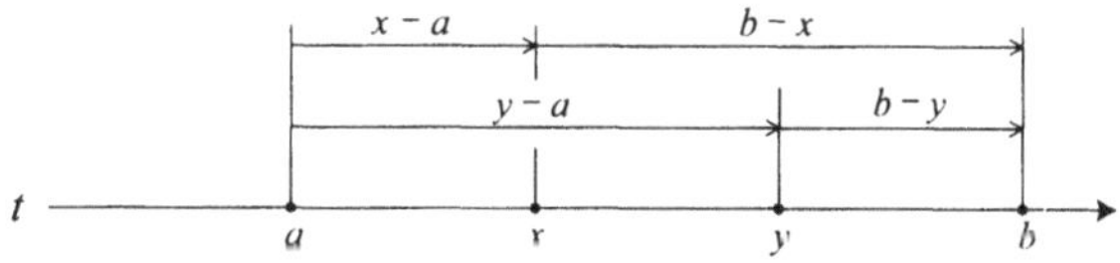

Figure 3.12: Cross ratio

If the cross ratio is to have real number values including $\pm\infty$, eq.(3.9) can be defined as long as three of the four points are distinct. The four points can be assigned any real numbers including $\pm\infty$. Fig. 3.13 shows cross ratios with point y fixed somewhere between a and b, and x varied from $-\infty$ to $+\infty$. Fig. 3.14 shows the same cross ratio plotted.

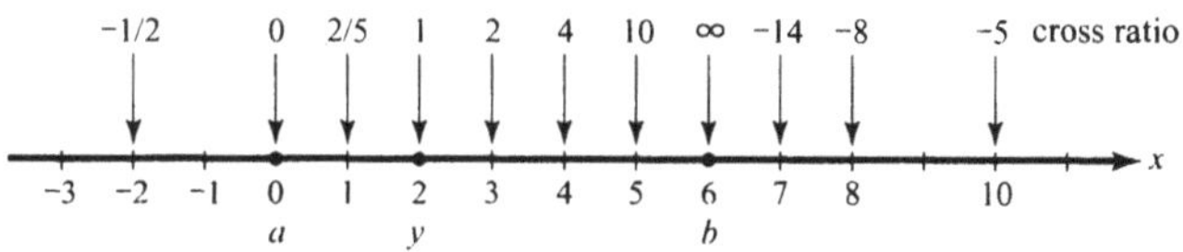

Figure 3.13: Cross ratio as a function of x.

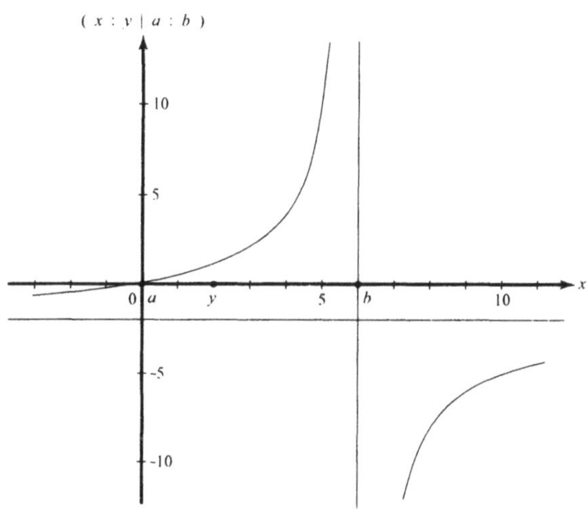

Figure 3.14: Plot of cross ratio.

Now if we take an arbitrary point o outside of line t, and draw radial lines from o through the four points, a, x, y and b, then denote by a^*, x^*, y^* and b^* the points at which those radial lines intersect with some arbitrary line, t^*, that does not contain o (Fig. 3.15), then the following relation holds:

$$(x : y|a : b) = (x^* : y^*|a^* : b^*). \tag{3.10}$$

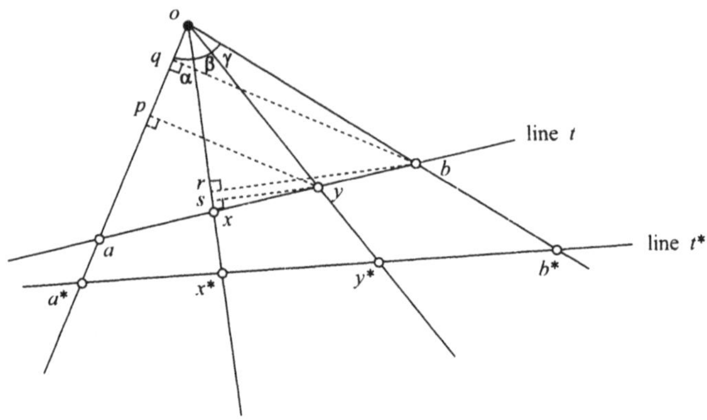

Figure 3.15: Cross ratio is preserved through projection.

It is easy to prove this with simple geometry using angles, α, β and γ, between the radial lines, and some length relations. In fact, cross ratios stay invariant through projective transformations, and eq.(3.10) expresses the most fundamental relation in projective geometry. For this reason, it is not entirely consistent to employ angles, lengths, or any other quantities that vary with projection when proving a proposition concerning projective invariance. For the projective proof that cross ratios are invariant under projective transformations, refer to Stolfi [53].

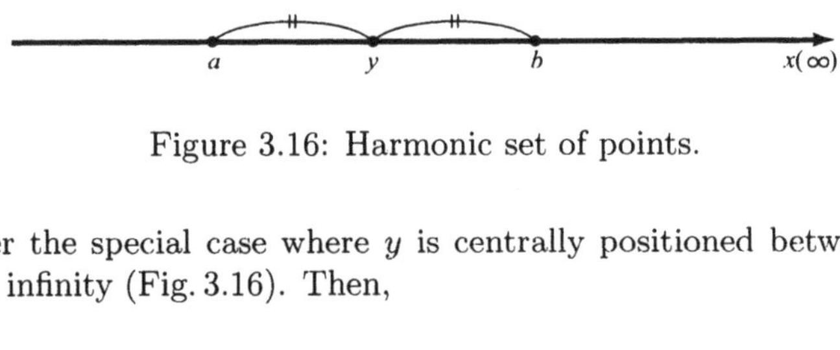

Figure 3.16: Harmonic set of points.

Consider the special case where y is centrally positioned between a and b and x is at infinity (Fig. 3.16). Then,

$$\begin{aligned}(x : y|a : b) &= \frac{\infty - a}{b - \infty} \Big/ \frac{y - a}{b - y} \\ &= \frac{\infty - a}{b - \infty} \cdot \frac{b - y}{y - a} \\ &= -\frac{b - y}{y - a} = -1. \end{aligned} \tag{3.11}$$

When a set of points having the conditions shown in Fig. 3.16 is projectively transformed to obtain a new set of points, the new set also has a cross ratio of -1. A set of points with a cross ratio of -1 is called a *harmonic set of points.*

In projective space, a cross ratio is defined using homogeneous coordinates as follows: when four points in $\mathbf{P}^1$ are given in homogeneous coordinates by

$V_a = \overline{(w_a, X_a)}$, $V_x = \overline{(w_x, X_x)}$, $V_y = \overline{(w_y, X_y)}$ and $V_b = \overline{(w_b, X_b)}$, then

$$
\begin{aligned}
(V_x : V_y | V_a : V_b) &= \frac{(\frac{X_x}{w_x} - \frac{X_a}{w_a})/(\frac{X_b}{w_b} - \frac{X_x}{w_x})}{(\frac{X_y}{w_y} - \frac{X_a}{w_a})/(\frac{X_b}{w_b} - \frac{X_y}{w_y})} \\
&= \frac{\frac{w_a X_x - X_a w_x}{w_x w_a} \cdot \frac{w_y X_b - X_y w_b}{w_b w_y}}{\frac{w_x X_b - X_x w_b}{w_x w_b} \cdot \frac{w_a X_y - X_a w_y}{w_a w_y}} \\
&= \frac{\begin{vmatrix} w_a & X_a \\ w_x & X_x \end{vmatrix} \cdot \begin{vmatrix} w_y & X_y \\ w_b & X_b \end{vmatrix}}{\begin{vmatrix} w_x & X_x \\ w_b & X_b \end{vmatrix} \cdot \begin{vmatrix} w_a & X_a \\ w_y & X_y \end{vmatrix}}.
\end{aligned}
\tag{3.12}
$$

Since a cross ratio can be expressed in this manner, it can be considered as a point in $\mathbf{P}^1$. The homogeneous coordinates are given by

$$
\overline{\left(\begin{vmatrix} w_x & X_x \\ w_b & X_b \end{vmatrix} \cdot \begin{vmatrix} w_a & X_a \\ w_y & X_y \end{vmatrix}, \begin{vmatrix} w_a & X_a \\ w_x & X_x \end{vmatrix} \cdot \begin{vmatrix} w_y & X_y \\ w_b & X_b \end{vmatrix} \right)}. \tag{3.13}
$$

Chapter 4

Two-Sided Space

In the two-sided space, it is possible to treat oriented lines (or planes), signed angles, line segments and convex sets, which could not be treated in classical projective space, while still retaining the useful properties for geometric computations existing in classical projective space [1)].

Oriented projective geometry deals with two-sided space, which is obtained by replacing non-oriented space (or elements) of classical projective geometry by a pair of spaces (or elements) having opposite orientations [53]. The basic geometric elements of oriented projective geometry are called *flats*, including points, lines, planes, etc., all of which have orientations.

This chapter is largely a reiteration of Stolfi [53] [2)].

4.1 Definition by Vector Space

Two-sided space is defined not only by signed homogeneous coordinates as stated in Section 2.3, but also by vector space. We shall give this definition next.

Definition 4.1 (Two-sided space)
In $(\nu+1)$-dimensional numerical vector space on real field, define a vector space $^*\mathbf{R}^{\nu+1}$:

$$^*\mathbf{R}^{\nu+1} = \mathbf{R}^{\nu+1} - \{\mathbf{0}\}$$

and an equivalence relation $\sim$ between two vectors $\boldsymbol{P}$ and $\boldsymbol{Q}$ in the space such that

$$\boldsymbol{P} \sim \boldsymbol{Q} \Leftrightarrow \exists\lambda \in \mathbf{R}^1, \lambda > 0 : \boldsymbol{Q} = \lambda\boldsymbol{P}. \tag{4.1}$$

1) Since two-sided space is also a kind of projective space, when it is necessary in this book to distinguish it from the space represented by unsigned homogeneous coordinates, the term "classical projective space" is sometimes used to refer to the latter.

2) Although this chapter is almost a reiteration of Stolfi, the responsibility of the descriptions lies in the present author.

Denote the set of all of the equivalence classes derived by classifying $^*\mathbf{R}^{\nu+1}$ *by the equivalence relation* $\sim$, *such that*

$$\overline{\mathbf{R}}^{\nu+1} = {}^*\mathbf{R}^{\nu+1}/\sim . \tag{4.2}$$

We refer to $\overline{\mathbf{R}}^{\nu+1}$ *as* ν*-dimensional two-sided space and denote it by* $\mathbf{T}^\nu$. *The equivalence class which includes* $\boldsymbol{Q} \in {}^*\mathbf{R}^{\nu+1}$ *is a point in two-sided space and is denoted by* $\overline{\boldsymbol{Q}}$ *in this book. We shall call* $\mathbf{R}^{\nu+1}$ *associated vector space of* $\mathbf{T}^\nu$.

4.2 Models of Two-sided Space

In this section, the four models used previously to describe classical projective space are used once again to examine two-sided space. After describing the analytical, spherical and straight models, we then present the concept of orientation, and finally discuss the vector space model.

1. **The analytical model**

   In the analytical model for classical projective space, both positive and negative scalar multiples of homogeneous coordinates belong to the same equivalence class. In the analytical model for two-sided space, however, they are considered as belonging to different equivalence classes.

2. **The spherical model**

   The spherical model of $\mathbf{T}^\nu$ is the set of points on the surface of a unit sphere in $\mathbf{R}^{\nu+1}$, which is denoted by $\mathbf{S}^\nu$. Unlike classical projective space, antipodal points are considered to be distinct in two-sided space.

   The spherical model of $\mathbf{T}^1$ is a unit circle in $\mathbf{R}^2$, while that of $\mathbf{T}^2$ the surface of a unit sphere in $\mathbf{R}^3$ (Fig. 4.1).

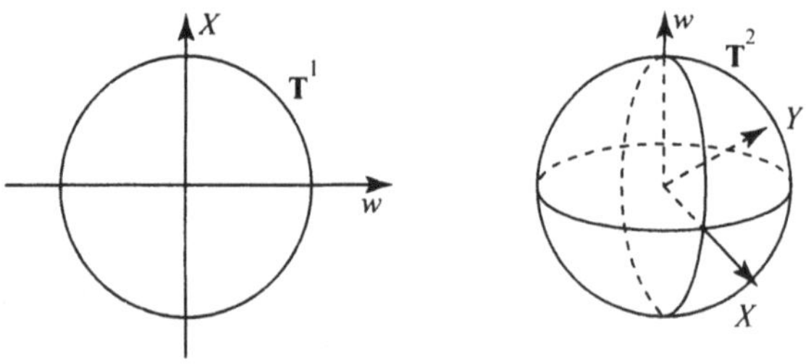

Figure 4.1: Spherical models of $\mathbf{T}^1$ and $\mathbf{T}^2$.

   Oriented projective geometry can be described as spherical geometry into which the concept of orientation has been introduced.

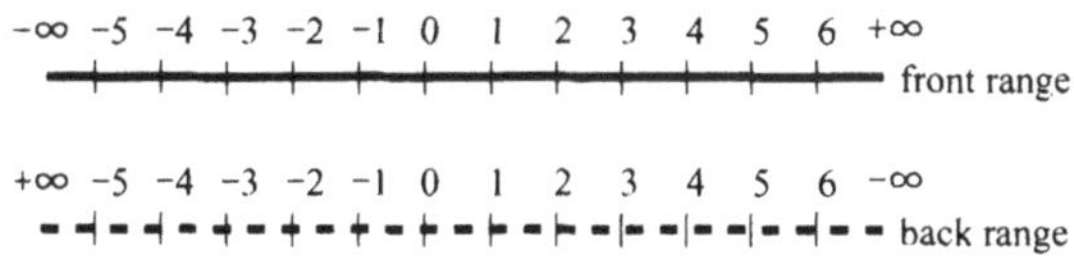

Figure 4.2: Straight model of $\mathbf{T}^1$.

3. **The straight model**

   The straight model of $\mathbf{T}^\nu$ is represented by two $\mathbf{R}^\nu$'s (i.e., *front* and *back ranges*) to which are added points at infinity $\boldsymbol{d}\infty$ lying in all directions $\boldsymbol{d}$ of $\mathbf{R}^\nu$. Here, $\boldsymbol{d}$ is a unit vector expressing direction.

   For example, the straight model of $\mathbf{T}^1$ consists of two real lines ($\mathbf{R}^1$'s) to which are added points at infinity, $+\infty$ and $-\infty$ (Fig. 4.2). Unlike classical projective space, the points at infinity having different orientations are considered to be distinct in two-sided space. As the figure shows, the two ranges connect with each other at $+\infty$ and $-\infty$.

   Note that points at infinity, $(+\boldsymbol{d})\infty$ and $(-\boldsymbol{d})\infty$ in $\mathbf{T}^\nu$, are expressed in reference to directions $\boldsymbol{d}$ and $-\boldsymbol{d}$ of the front range, in the discussion of this chapter.

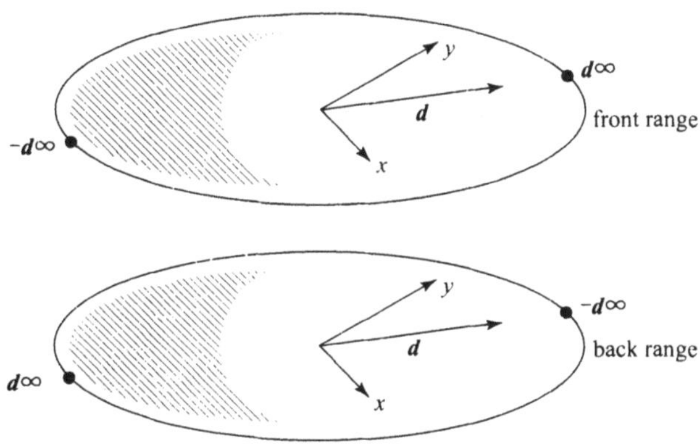

Figure 4.3: Straight model of $\mathbf{T}^2$.

Similarly, the straight model of $\mathbf{T}^2$ consists of two $\mathbf{R}^2$'s and points at infinity $(\boldsymbol{d})\infty$ at all directions $\boldsymbol{d}$ of $\mathbf{R}^2$. The front and back ranges can be thought of as parallel planes in three dimensional space (Fig. 4.3), or alternatively, they can be the two sides of a single plane. In Fig. 4.3, the front and back ranges are shown as two open unit disks. Note that $(+\boldsymbol{d})\infty$ and $(-\boldsymbol{d})\infty$ are distinct (whereas they are indistinguishable in classical projective space). The two points at infinity, $(+\boldsymbol{d})\infty$ and $(-\boldsymbol{d})\infty$, of the front range connect to points at infinity of the back range. Thus, $(\boldsymbol{d})\infty$ is the point at infinity in the direction $\boldsymbol{d}$ of the front range, which is also the point at infinity in the direction $-\boldsymbol{d}$ of the back range.

Fig. 4.4 shows the straight model of three dimensional two-sided space $\mathbf{T}^3$. The two ranges are represented by unit open balls, which connect to each other by a spherical surface representing the plane at infinity Ω_3 [3]. The point at infinity $(\boldsymbol{d})\infty$ is expressed as lying on this sphere in the $\boldsymbol{d}$ direction for the front range ball, and is also a point in the $-\boldsymbol{d}$ direction on the sphere corresponding to the back range ball.

Alternatively, the front and back ranges can be considered to be the sets of real and imaginary points, respectively. Each of the two ranges spreads over the entire $\mathbf{R}^3$, and connects at points at infinity.

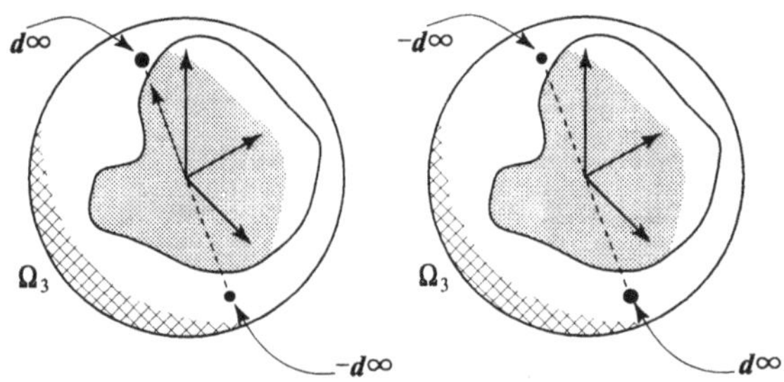

Figure 4.4: Straight model of $\mathbf{T}^3$.

4.3 Relations among Models

The relation among these models follows that for classical projective space; with the exception that for two-sided space, when $w > 0$, a point (w, X, Y) in $\mathbf{R}^3$ is centrally projected to the front range in the straight model, and to the upper half sphere in the spherical model, but when $w < 0$, it is centrally projected to the back range and lower half sphere in the respective models.

The projected coordinates are, for the straight model,

$$(x, y) = (\frac{X}{w}, \frac{Y}{w}),$$

and for the spherical model (Fig. 4.5),

$$\frac{(w, X, Y)}{\sqrt{w^2 + X^2 + Y^2}}.$$

We now look at the geometric relationship between the spherical and straight models for $\mathbf{T}^1$ in some detail (Fig. 4.6).

[3] We shall denote the line at infinity of $\mathbf{T}^2$ or the plane at infinity of $\mathbf{T}^3$ by Ω_2 or Ω_3 respectively in this chapter.

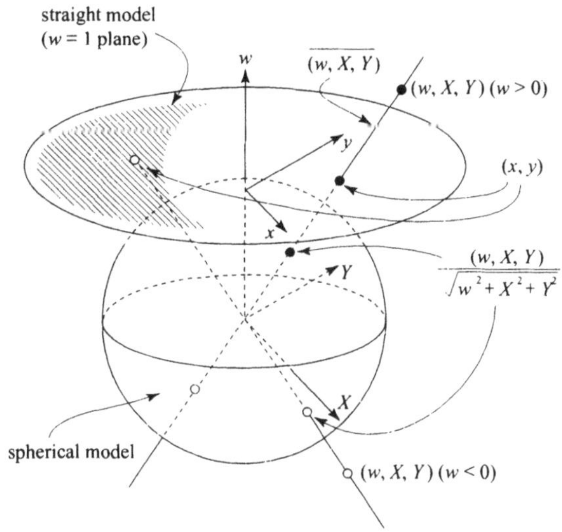

Figure 4.5: Relations among three models of $\mathbf{T}^2$.

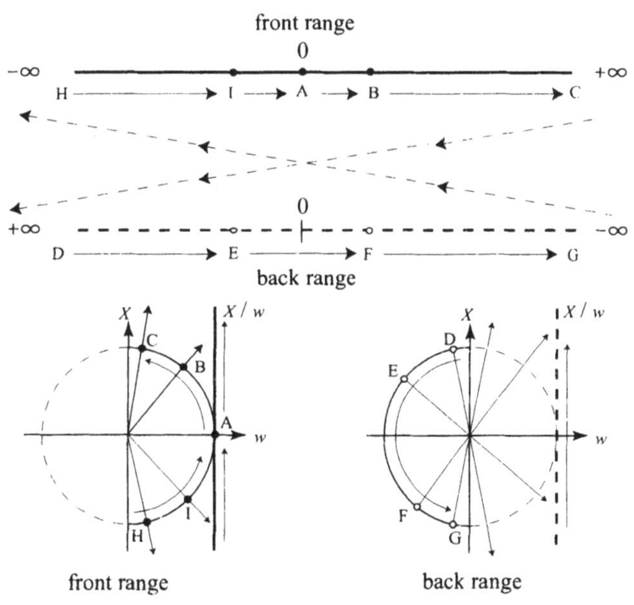

Figure 4.6: Relation between spherical and straight models of $\mathbf{T}^1$.

Let us begin at point A on the spherical model and move counter-clockwise. Since $w > 0$ at point A, it belongs to the front range, and is projected in the straight model to coordinate "0" on the real line for the front range.

Point B also satisfies $w > 0$ and so is projected to a positive point on the same real line; movement has taken place to the upward in the figure.

At point C, w is very small but still positive, so the point is projected to a positive coordinate point with a large magnitude on the front range.

At $w = 0$, the point reaches $+\infty$, beyond which (point D) $w < 0$, and the projected point jumps to a distant point in the negative direction of the back range (as stated, the $+, -$ signs in $+\infty$ and $-\infty$ refer to the directions in the front range). In other words, the point at infinity in the front range's positive direction is identical to that in the back range's negative direction, and this is where the two ranges meet.

If we continue moving counter-clockwise in the spherical model (points E and F), the projected point moves along the back range in the positive direction.

At point G on the spherical model, w is still negative but has a very small magnitude, so is projected to a distant point in the positive direction on the back range.

Moving further in the counter-clockwise direction, we reach $w = 0$, where the projected point passes the point at infinity in the back range's positive direction and instantaneously jumps to the point at infinity in the front range's negative direction; subsequent movement continues in the positive direction. The point at infinity in the front range's negative direction is identical to that in the back range's positive direction, and the two ranges meet here.

Moving further on the spherical model past points H and I, one returns to point A.

By looking at the central projection from a geometric standpoint, we see how the front and back ranges connect to form a closed space. Algebraically, the cut of the central projection of a point (w, X) in $\mathbf{R}^2$ is the point X/w. In two-sided space, however, X/w and $(-X)/(-w)$ are considered to be distinct points. In other words, the two points have the same coordinate value but lie on different ranges.

The relation between the spherical and straight models for $\mathbf{T}^2$ is similar to the case for $\mathbf{T}^1$ (Fig. 4.7). That is, a sphere of unit radius with its center at the origin of $\mathbf{R}^3$ is considered, with a light source at the origin. The upper and lower half spheres correspond to $w>0$ and $w<0$, respectively. A light ray passing the upper half sphere is projected to the front range of the straight model, while that directed at the lower half sphere is reflected back and projected to the back range.

We have presented three models of two-sided space above (the vector space model will be discussed in Section 4.5.3), and each has its advantages. The analytical model, for instance, is highly useful when performing computations or dealing with data structure. The straight model highlights the relationship between Euclidean space and two-sided space, since the front range is Euclidean space itself. Meanwhile, the spherical model demonstrates how two Euclidean

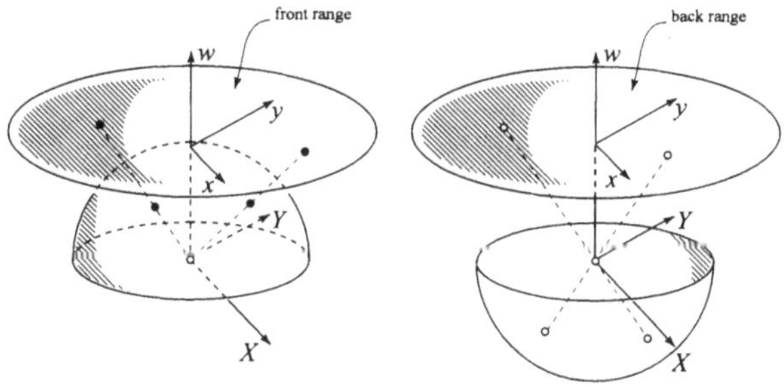

Figure 4.7: Relation between spherical and straight models of $\mathbf{T}^2$.

spaces connect to each other at points at infinity in two-sided space.

4.4 Flats

Definition 4.2 (Flat set and flat)
In the spherical model $\mathbf{S}^\nu$ of $\mathbf{T}^\nu$, a flat set represents a great sphere, that is, the intersection of $\mathbf{S}^\nu$ and some linear subspace of $\mathbf{R}^{\nu+1}$. A flat is a flat set which is given an orientation.

One-, two- and three-dimensional flats are called *lines*, *planes* and *three-spaces*, respectively. For an arbitrary flat A, there always exists $\neg A$. This consists of the same points as A and so represents the same great sphere, but has the opposite orientation and is therefore a distinct flat. For $\mathbf{T}^\nu$, there exist only two flats with ν dimensions. These are called *universes*, and denoted by Υ and $\neg\Upsilon$. A flat with $\nu-1$ dimensions is called a *hyperplane*. Empty sets to which orientations are given, which are special flats of -1 dimension, are called *vacuums* and denoted by Λ and $\neg\Lambda$.

When one is added to the number of dimensions, this is called *rank*; it is often used in place of dimensions. That is, a vacuum, point and line have ranks 0, 1 and 2 respectively. Oftentimes the use of ranks considerably simplifies mathematical formulas. Complementary rank or *coranks* are convenient when discussing such topics as *meet* operations, as we shall see later. A corank is defined as follows:

$$corank(A) = rank(\Upsilon) - rank(A) = dim(\Upsilon) - dim(A). \tag{4.3}$$

Thus, a universe and a hyperplane have coranks of 0 and 1 respectively.

In the discussion that follows, dimensions will be denoted by Greek letters such as κ, μ, ν, ρ, σ and τ, while rank will be denoted by the corresponding Roman letters, k, m, n, r, s and t. Thus,

$$k = \kappa + 1, m = \mu + 1, n = \nu + 1, r = \rho + 1, s = \sigma + 1, t = \tau + 1. \tag{4.4}$$

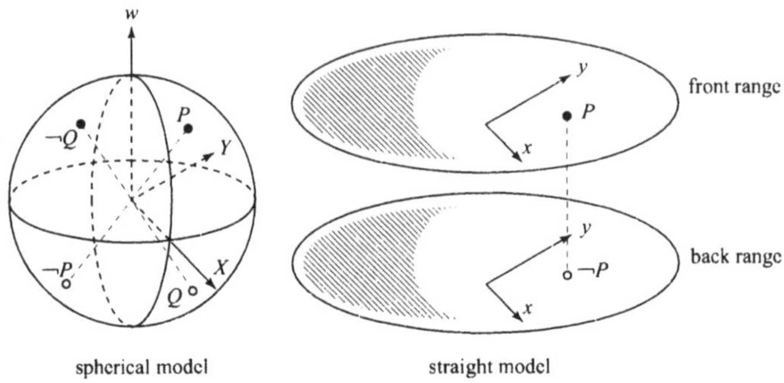

Figure 4.8: Antipodal points in the spherical and straight models.

4.4.1 Points

A flat set of zero dimension consists of two antipodal points on $\mathbf{S}^\nu$. As we will see in Section 4.5.2, orienting such a set means designating one of the two points as the "positive" one. Therefore, a flat of zero dimension is a point in $\mathbf{T}^\nu$.

In the spherical model, a point lies on the sphere's surface. Given a point P, $\neg P$ is its antipodal point (Fig. 4.8). In the straight model, points P and $\neg P$ have the same coordinates but lie on different ranges. In the analytical model, these points can be represented as $\overline{(w, X, Y)}$ and $\overline{(-w, -X, -Y)}$.

4.4.2 Lines

A line in $\mathbf{T}^\nu$ is expressed in the spherical model by an oriented great circle on the unit sphere $\mathbf{S}^\nu$. An arrow is used to indicate a line's orientation, with the arrow pointing in the positive orientation.

One-dimensional two-sided space $\mathbf{T}^1$ consists of a pair of lines with opposite orientations; these are the universes of $\mathbf{T}^1$. Using the spherical model, the positive universe is defined as the one oriented such that the route from $(1, 0)$ to $(0, 1)$ is the shortest, that is, counter-clockwise (Fig. 4.9) (see Section 4.5.2).

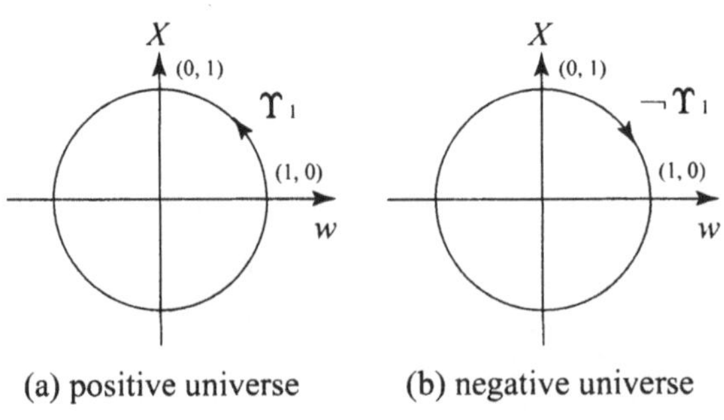

Figure 4.9: Spherical model of $\mathbf{T}^1$.

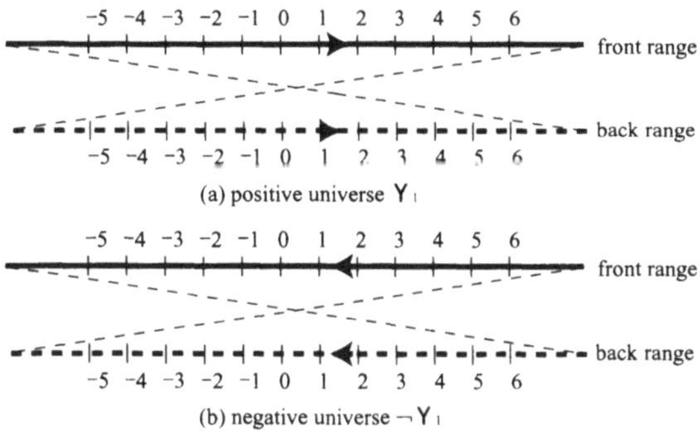

Figure 4.10: Straight model of $\mathbf{T}^1$.

Fig. 4.10 shows the straight model for $\mathbf{T}^1$. The front and back ranges of a line have the same orientation in the straight model.

Let us look at lines in spaces of higher dimensions. In the spherical model of $\mathbf{T}^2$, a line is expressed as an oriented great circle on a unit sphere in $\mathbf{R}^3$. Great circles for which $w \neq 0$ are *proper lines,* while that given by $w = 0$ is an *improper line*, i.e., the line at infinity that passes all points at infinity (Fig. 4.11).

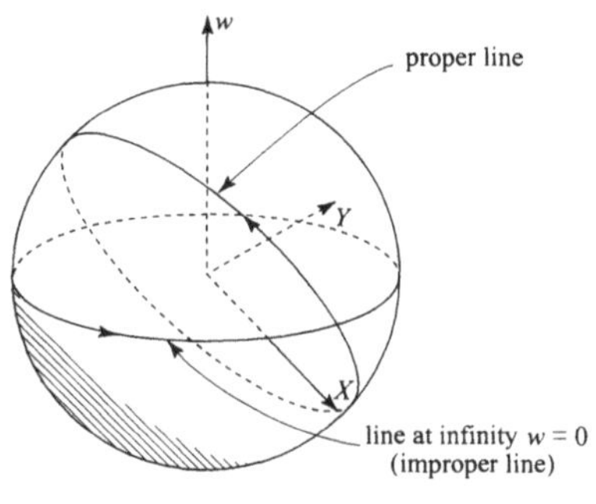

Figure 4.11: Lines in the spherical model of $\mathbf{T}^2$.

In the straight model, if one traces a proper line beginning at some point in the front range, it goes through a point at infinity to reach the back range; there, it continues on to the point at infinity which is antipodal to the one just mentioned, then returns to the front range, and finally to the original point (Fig. 4.12). It is thus a closed line.

A line is oriented in the same direction in both ranges. There are two lines at infinity (or horizons), which have the same location but different orientations. The line at infinity which has a counterclockwise orientation, when viewed on the front range, is denoted Ω_2.

Let us now look at lines in the straight model of $\mathbf{T}^3$ (Fig. 4.13). The surface of the unit sphere consists of points at infinity and so represents the plane at

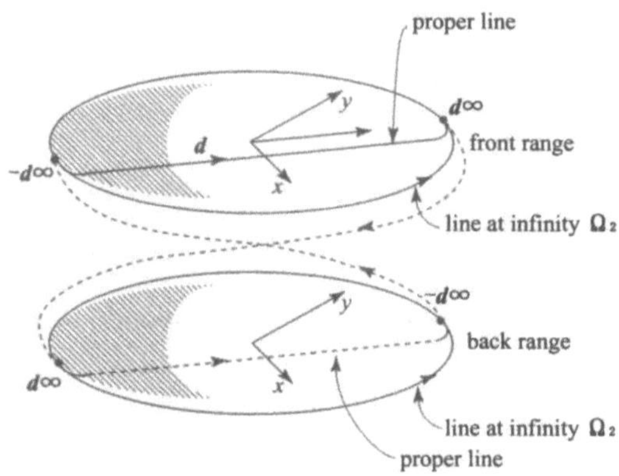

Figure 4.12: Proper line and line at infinity Ω_2 in the straight model of $\mathbf{T}^2$.

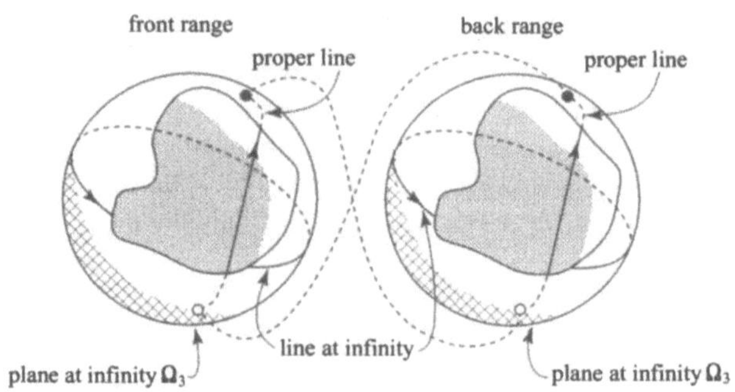

Figure 4.13: Lines in the straight model of $\mathbf{T}^3$.

infinity. That is, great circles on the unit sphere represent improper lines (i.e., lines at infinity). Unlike in $\mathbf{T}^2$, there are an infinite number of lines at infinity in $\mathbf{T}^3$.

Tracing a proper line from some point in the front range, one goes through a point at infinity to reach the back range, where one follows, in the same direction, a line consisting of points with the same coordinates as those of the front range line; then passing through the other point at infinity, one comes back to the front range, and finally to the original point. It thus forms a closed line.

4.4.3 Planes

$\mathbf{T}^2$ consists of a pair of planes with opposite orientations, which form universes Υ_2 and $\neg\Upsilon_2$. Using the spherical model, the positive universe Υ_2 is defined as the one oriented such that, when viewed from the point $(1,0,0)$, the angle from $(0,1,0)$ to $(0,0,1)$, is the smallest (see Section 4.5.2). Using a right-hand coordinate system for $\mathbf{R}^3$, Υ_2 and $\neg\Upsilon_2$ are shown in Fig. 4.14.

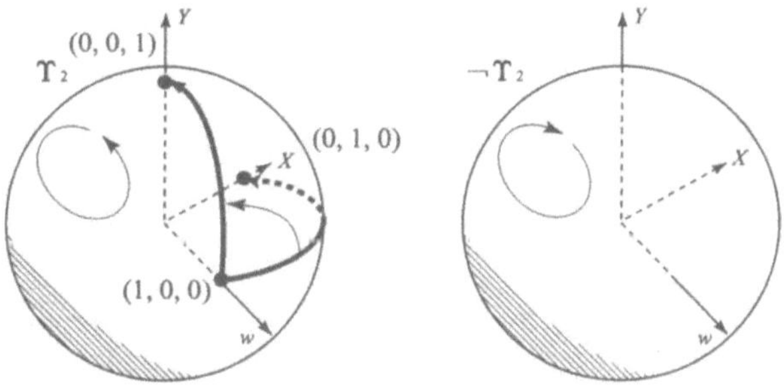

Figure 4.14: Two planes of $\mathbf{T}^2$.

The relation between two planes in the straight model is shown in Fig. 4.15. By centrally projecting the spherical model onto the straight model, one can see that the positive orientation of Υ_2 is counterclockwise in the front range, but clockwise in the back range.

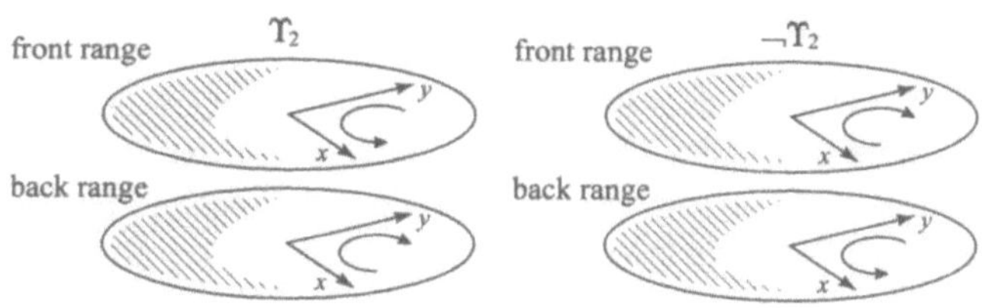

Figure 4.15: Two planes of $\mathbf{T}^2$ in the straight model.

In the straight model of $\mathbf{T}^3$, a proper plane appears as replicas of the Euclidean plane in the two ranges having opposite orientations (Fig. 4.16). The two planes connect to each other at points at infinity in all directions.

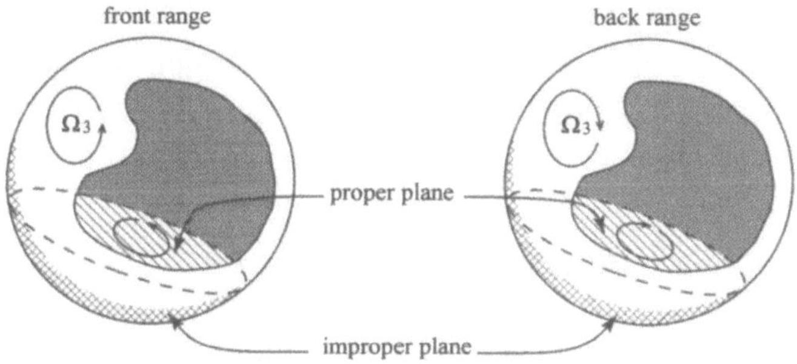

Figure 4.16: Planes in straight model of $\mathbf{T}^3$.

The improper plane (plane at infinity) is represented in the straight model by a pair of celestial spheres, which are topologically equivalent to two-dimensional spheres. The two spheres occupy the same location but with opposing orienta-

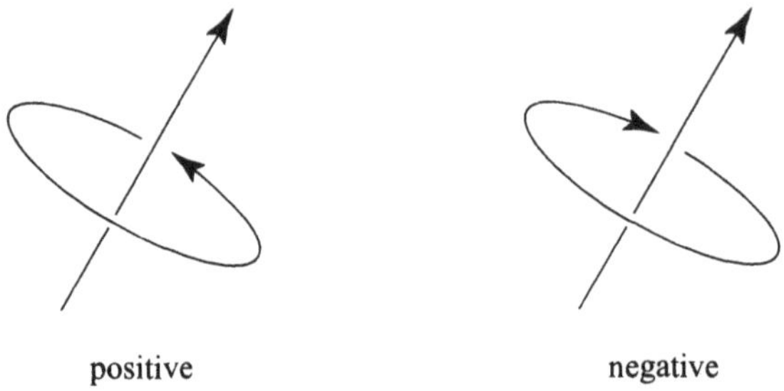

Figure 4.17: Orientation of three-space.

tions in the two ranges, and connect the ranges of $\mathbf{T}^3$.

The improper plane which has a clockwise orientation when viewed from the interior of the front range, and counterclockwise orientation from the back range, is denoted by Ω_3.

4.4.4 Three-space

A three-space (three-dimensional flat) is an oriented three-dimensional great sphere of $\mathbf{S}^{\nu}$. The orientation of a three-space can be expressed by combining a circular and a straight arrow (Fig. 4.17). The straight model for $\mathbf{T}^3$ consists of two $\mathbf{R}^3$'s and spherical surfaces representing the planes at infinity.

The orientation of a three-space is the same in both front and back ranges (Fig. 4.18) (since one can move from one range to the other through a point at infinity without changing the three-dimensional orientation).

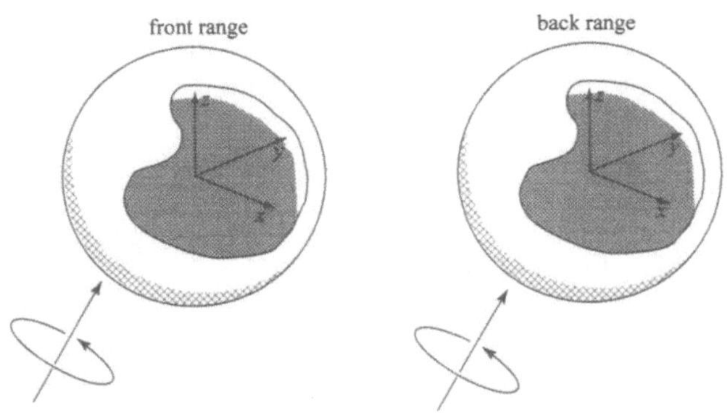

Figure 4.18: Universe Υ_3 of $\mathbf{T}^3$ in the straight model.

$\mathbf{T}^3$ consists of the standard universe Υ_3, and the universe $\neg\Upsilon_3$ with reverse orientation. The orientation of Υ_3 is defined as the one oriented such that, when the right-hand screw is turned and moved in the direction from the origin $(0,0,0)$ to the point $(0,0,1)$ in Euclidean coordinates, the angle from the point $(1,0,0)$ to $(0,1,0)$ is minimized (see Section 4.5.2).

Note that in the straight model the front and back ranges have the same orientation for $\mathbf{T}^1$ and $\mathbf{T}^3$, whereas the orientations for the two ranges are opposite in the case of $\mathbf{T}^2$.

4.5 Simplices and Orientation

4.5.1 Simplices

A *simplex* is a set of ordered points in $\mathbf{T}^\nu$ (Fig. 4.19). These points are sometimes referred to as *vertices*. In the spherical model, a simplex is a set of ordered unit vectors in $\mathbf{R}^{\nu+1}$; the simplex is said to be *proper* when the vectors are linearly independent, *improper* or *degenerate* when they are linearly dependent. Simplices are expressed as in $(V_0; V_1)$, $(V_0; V_1; V_2)$.

Given an arbitrary simplex s of $\mathbf{T}^\nu$, one can uniquely determine a flat set with the smallest dimension which contains s; this is called the *span* of s. The dimension of a simplex refers to that of its span.

Two simplices are said to be *equivalent* when, without causing changes in the spanned flat, one can be transformed in a continuous manner to coincide with the other (see Section 4.5.2).

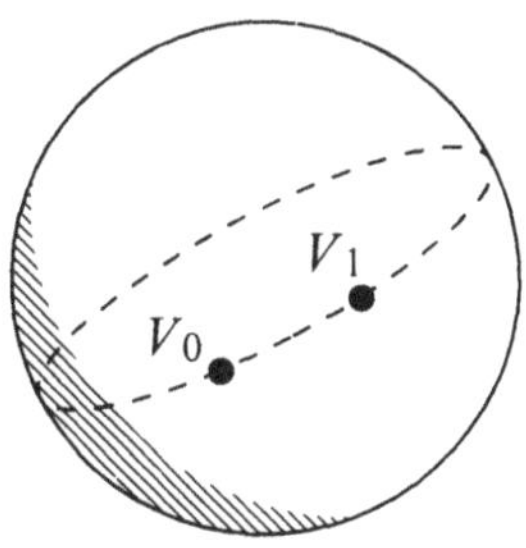

(a) A two-vertex simplex of $\mathbf{T}^2$

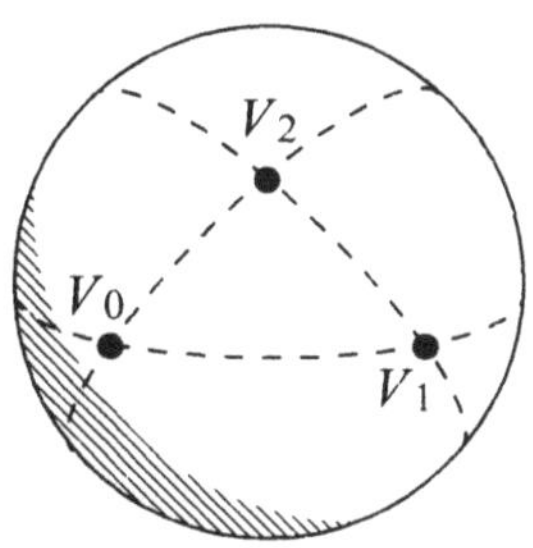

(b) A three-vertex simplex of $\mathbf{T}^2$

Figure 4.19: Simplices of $\mathbf{T}^2$.

4.5.2 Orientation of Simplices (Flats)

1. **Orientation of points**

   In the spherical model, zero-dimensional flats consist of a pair of antipodal points, one of which is designated as "positive."

2. **Orientation of two points (on a line)**

   Consider two proper simplices $(V_0; V_1)$ and $(V_0'; V_1')$ on the same great circle C. When V_0 and V_1 can be continuously shifted on C, without degenerating as a simplex, to V_0' and V_1' respectively, the two simplices are *equivalent*. For Fig. 4.20 (a), this operation is possible, so the two simplices are equivalent. In (b), however, the spans for the two simplices are the same, but they cannot be made to coincide by shifting in this manner. Thus, they are said to have different orientations.

The orientation of a simplex $(V_0; V_1)$ is defined as that from V_0 to V_1 when traced along the smallest distance, and is indicated by an arrow (Fig. 4.20 (c)).

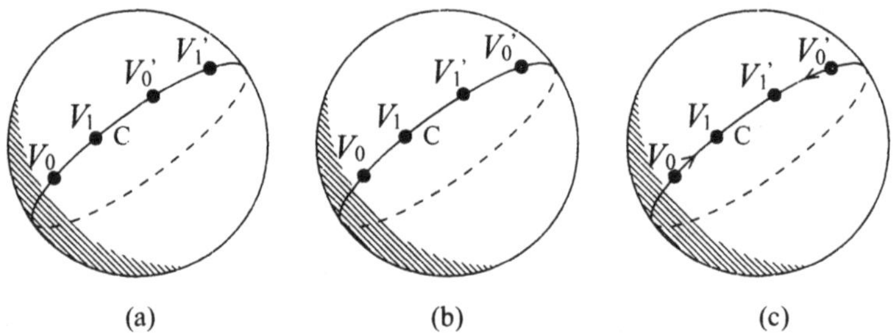

Figure 4.20: Two points on a line.

3. **Orientation of triangles**

Consider now a simplex with three vertices $(V_a; V_0; V_1)$ in $\mathbf{T}^2$. If this is a proper simplex, the three points span a two-dimensional great sphere, where they uniquely determine a triangle whose sides consist of the shortest arc lengths.

Assuming the triangles of Fig. 4.21 (a) and (b) to lie on the same sphere, it would not be possible to move V_a to V_a', V_0 to V_0' and V_1 to V_1', in a continuous manner while the vertices are kept on the sphere and without allowing the simplex to degenerate. Thus, two simplices $(V_a; V_0; V_1)$ and $(V_a'; V_0'; V_1')$ have opposite orientations.

The orientation of a simplex $(V_a; V_0; V_1)$ is defined as that from V_aV_0 to V_aV_1, through the smallest angle of rotation on the spherical surface, about V_a, and is indicated by an arced arrow.

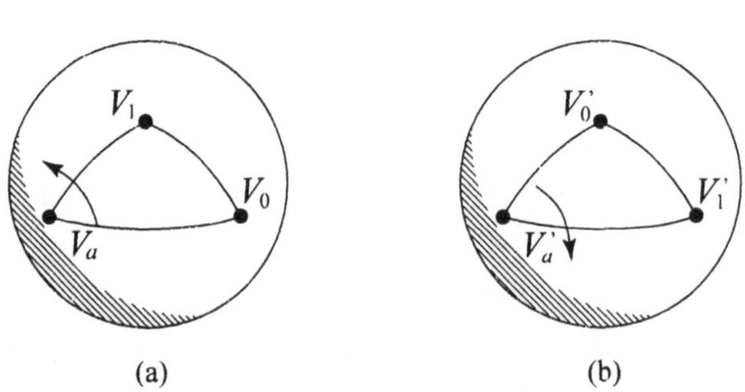

Figure 4.21: Orientation of two-dimensional simplices.

In Fig. 4.21, we define the triangle of (a) as a positive one, and that of (b) as a negative. The signs of a two-dimensional simplex $s = (V_a; V_0; V_1)$ in $\mathbf{T}^2$ are obtained by the following equation:

$$sign(V_a; V_0; V_1) = sign(\begin{vmatrix} w_a & X_a & Y_a \\ w_0 & X_0 & Y_0 \\ w_1 & X_1 & Y_1 \end{vmatrix}). \tag{4.5}$$

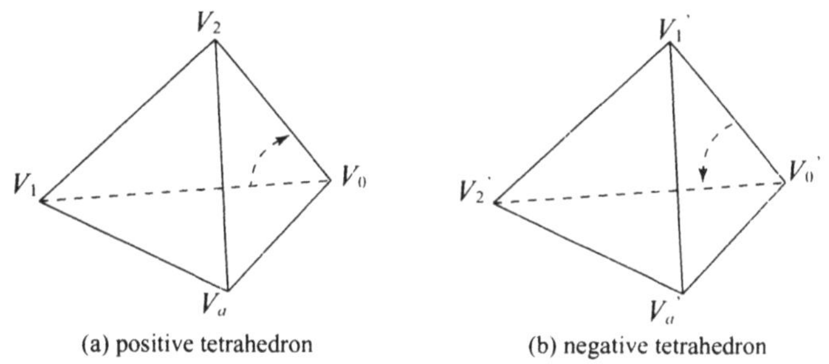

Figure 4.22: Orientation of three-dimensional simplices.

4. **Orientation of tetrahedra**

A proper three-dimensional simplex $s = (V_a; V_0; V_1; V_2)$ uniquely determines a tetrahedron whose sides consist of the smallest arc lengths.

In Fig. 4.22, it is impossible to make the tetrahedral vertices V_a, V_0, V_1 and V_2 of (a) coincide with V_a', V_0', V_1' and V_2' of (b), respectively, by continuous movement in the three-dimensional great sphere. Thus the two simplices have opposing orientations.

The orientation of a simplex $(V_a; V_0; V_1; V_2)$ is defined as the one where, taking the triangle $V_0V_1V_2$, a right-hand screw turned in the direction from the side V_0V_1 to the side V_0V_2 at the smallest angle will move V_a toward the triangle. This orientation can be expressed as in Fig. 4.23.

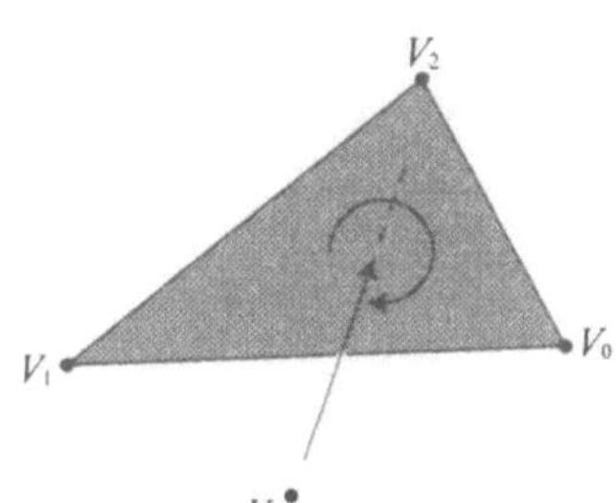

Figure 4.23: Indicating orientation of simplex $(V_a; V_0; V_1; V_2)$.

The signs of a three-dimensional simplex $s = (V_a; V_0; V_1; V_2)$ in $\mathbf{T}^3$ are given by the following equation:

$$sign(V_a; V_0; V_1; V_2) = sign(\begin{vmatrix} w_a & X_a & Y_a & Z_a \\ w_0 & X_0 & Y_0 & Z_0 \\ w_1 & X_1 & Y_1 & Z_1 \\ w_2 & X_2 & Y_2 & Z_2 \end{vmatrix}). \qquad (4.6)$$

5. **Orientation of universes**

   Orientations of the universes of $\mathbf{T}^1$, $\mathbf{T}^2$ and $\mathbf{T}^3$ were defined individually in Sections 4.4.2, 4.4.3 and 4.4.4. We now present general rules for determining the orientation of universes.

   To do so, we first define a *standard simplex.* Denoting the standard bases of $\mathbf{R}^{\nu+1}$ by E_0, ..., E_ν, the standard simplex e of $\mathbf{T}^\nu$ is defined as $e = (E_0; ...; E_\nu)$. $E_0 = (1, 0, ..., 0, 0)$ is the origin of the front range, while $E_1, ..., E_\nu$ represent the cardinal directions. The orientation of the universe Υ_ν of $\mathbf{T}^\nu$ can now be defined as that of the positive standard simplex.

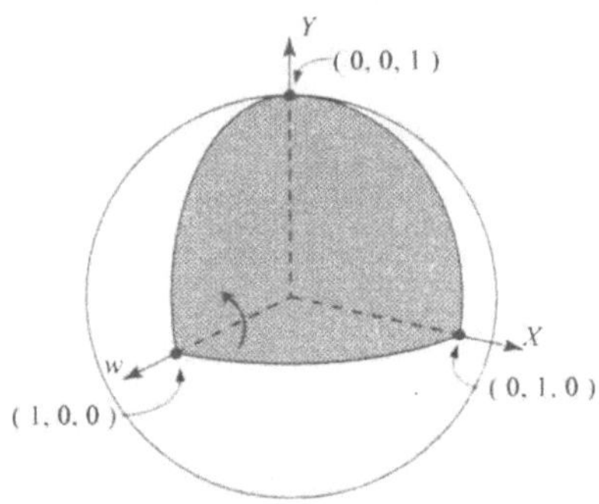

Figure 4.24: Standard simplex of $\mathbf{T}^2$.

   For instance, the positive universe of $\mathbf{T}^2$ is the one directed such that the simplex given by vertices $(1, 0, 0)$, $(0, 1, 0)$ and $(0, 0, 1)$ in this order has a positive orientation (Fig. 4.24).

   The straight model image of this simplex is given by the first quadrant of the front range, that is, the set of points consisting of the origin, the point at infinity in the x-axis direction and point at infinity in the y-axis direction, in this order.

4.5.3 Vector Space Model of $\mathbf{T}^\nu$

In the spherical model, all points are represented as vectors with unit length. This condition can at times be restrictive. By doing away with the condition

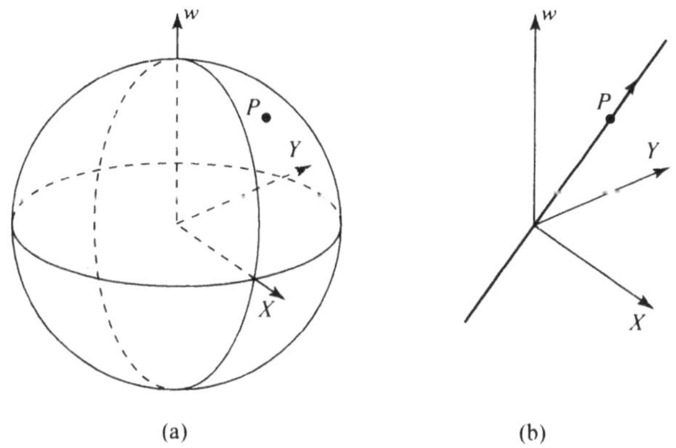

Figure 4.25: Points in spherical and vector space models.

of unit length, we obtain another model of $\mathbf{T}^{\nu}$, namely, a model of vector space $\mathbf{R}^{\nu+1}$ to which orientation is assigned, or oriented vector space.

In the vector space model of $\mathbf{T}^{\nu}$, a κ-dimensional flat is represented by a $(\kappa+1)$-dimensional oriented subspace in $\mathbf{R}^{\nu+1}$. For instance, a point, which is a zero-dimensional flat, is represented in $\mathbf{R}^{\nu+1}$ by an oriented line going through the origin [4)](Fig. 4.25).

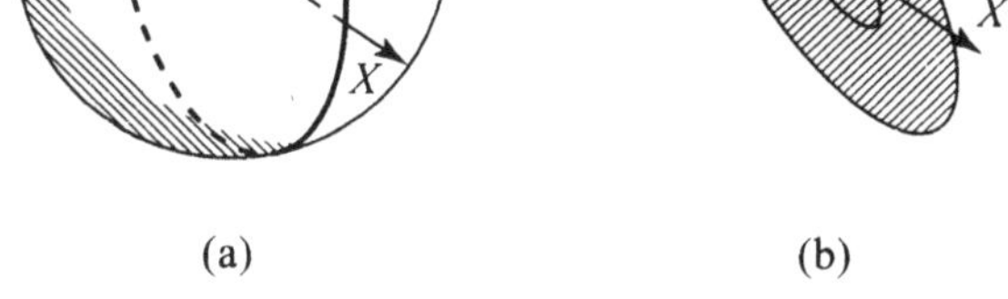

Figure 4.26: Lines in spherical and vector-space models.

A line in $\mathbf{T}^2$ is represented by an oriented two-dimensional subspace in $\mathbf{R}^3$, graphically expressed by an oriented plane containing the origin (Fig. 4.26 (b)). The orientation of the plane is in the same direction as that of the line in the spherical model.

[4)] Stolfi uses an oriented line as the vector space model of a point. In dealing with interference problems, however, it might be more convenient to use a half-line and half-plane as the vector space models of a point and line respectively.

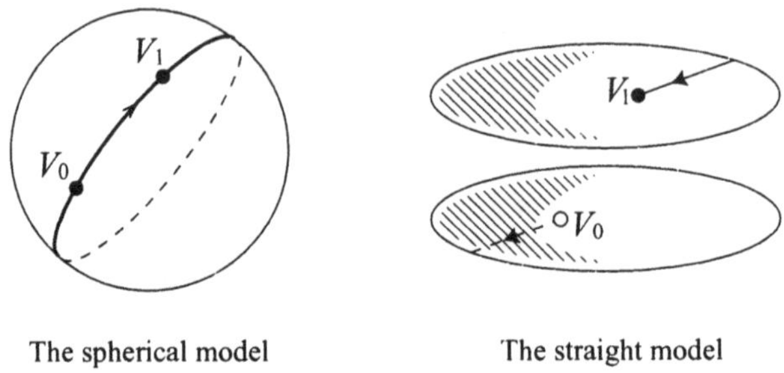

Figure 4.27: Line segment V_0V_1.

4.6 Position of Point in Relation to Simplex

The simplex $(V_0; V_1)$ was defined as a set of ordered points. This can also be defined as an oriented (open) line segment on the spherical model, having the shortest arc length (Fig. 4.27). The line segment V_0V_1 is an empty set, however, when $V_0 = V_1$ or $V_0 = \neg V_1$. Similarly, a simplex $(V_0; V_1; V_2)$ defines an oriented (open) triangle (Fig. 4.28).

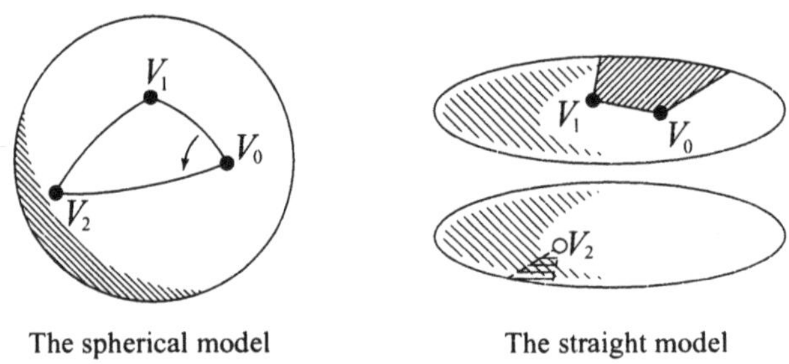

Figure 4.28: Triangle $V_0V_1V_2$.

Let us now look at how a point is positioned in relation to such geometric elements defined by simplices.

In the spherical model of Fig. 4.27, the condition for a point P on the line to lie on a (open) line segment V_0V_1 is that simplices $(V_0; P)$ and $(P; V_1)$ are both proper and equivalent to $(V_0; V_1)$.

Let us extend this method to simplices of higher dimension. Letting $s = (V_0; ...; V_\kappa)$ be a κ-dimensional simplex in $\mathbf{T}^\nu$, its interior is the set of points P such that any simplex obtained by replacing an arbitrary vertex of s by P is proper and equivalent to s. That is, P is in the interior of s if and only if the simplex $(V_0; ...; V_{i-1}; P; V_{i+1}; ...; V_\kappa)$ is both proper and equivalent to s for all i.

The discussion above can be further generalized. That is, if a point P lies on the flat spanned by a simplex $s = (V_0; ...; V_\kappa)$, the position of P can be classified according to regions in relation to s. To do so, replace each vertex of s by P and compare the orientation of the resulting simplex with that of s; if the orientation is the same, assign + (plus), if opposite, assign − (minus), and if a degenerate simplex results, assign 0 (zero). This procedure will produce a signature (series of signs) $\sigma_0\sigma_1....\sigma_\kappa$ for the point. Since 00...0 is excluded, there are $3^{\kappa+1}-1$ possible sign combinations or signatures.

For example, consider a proper simplex $(V_0; V_1; V_2)$ (Fig. 4.29). The $\mathbf{T}^2$ plane is divided by great circles defined by vertex pairs into $3^3 - 1 = 26$ regions: 8 open triangles, 12 open line segments and 6 isolated points. The signature $+++$ represents the interior of the triangle $V_0V_1V_2$, while $---$ is the interior of the antipodal triangle $\neg V_0 \neg V_1 \neg V_2$. Signatures $++0$, $+-0$, $--0$ and $-+0$ respectively represent open segments V_0V_1, $V_0\neg V_1$, $\neg V_0 \neg V_1$ and $\neg V_0 V_1$. $+00$ is the vertex V_0, while -00 represents its antipodal point $\neg V_0$.

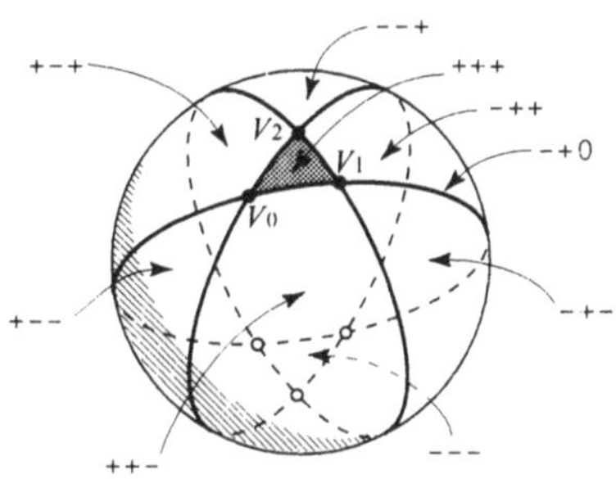

Figure 4.29: Signs of regions in relation to simplex $(V_0; V_1; V_2)$.

4.7 Join Operations

A *join* operation of two given flats yields the flat of the smallest dimension containing the given flats. The reader is reminded that in oriented projective geometry, attention must be paid to a flat's orientation.

4.7.1 Join Operation of Two Points

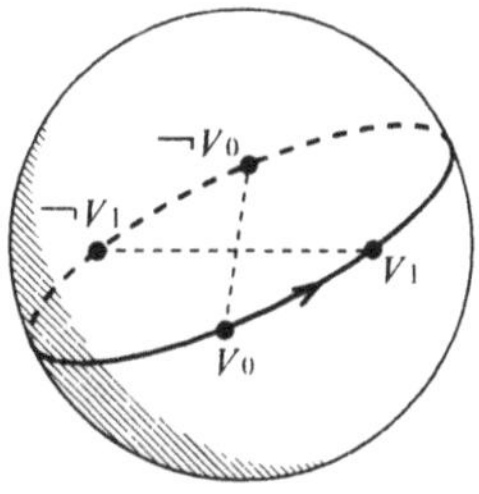

$V_0 \cup V_1$

Figure 4.30: Join of two points.

The join of two points V_0 and V_1 is the line having the same orientation as the line segment V_0V_1, that is, in the spherical model, a line oriented in the direction of the shortest arc from V_0 to V_1. It is denoted as $V_0 \cup V_1$ [5]. Fig. 4.30 shows the join of two points in the spherical model. Here, V_0 and V_1 must be distinct points, that is, $V_0 \neq V_1$ and $V_0 \neq \neg V_1$. Reversing the order of the operands will reverse the orientation of the join, or

$$V_1 \cup V_0 = \neg(V_0 \cup V_1). \tag{4.7}$$

As clearly seen from Fig. 4.30,

$$V_0 \cup (\neg V_1) = \neg(V_0 \cup V_1) = (\neg V_0) \cup V_1. \tag{4.8}$$

4.7.2 Join Operation of Point and Line

Letting L be a line and V_0 some point not on L, the join of V_0 with respect to L, $V_0 \cup L$, is a plane containing V_0 and L, with its orientation given by the rotation about V_0 produced by "turning" L in the positive orientation (Fig. 4.31). Clearly the following holds:

$$V_0 \cup (\neg L) = (\neg V_0) \cup L = \neg(V_0 \cup L). \tag{4.9}$$

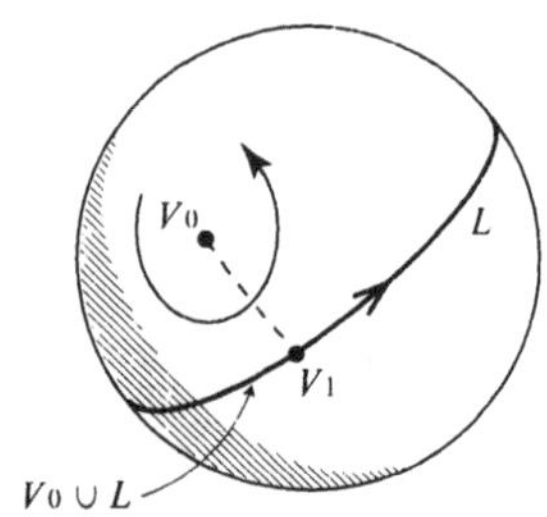

Figure 4.31: Join of V_0 with respect to L, $V_0 \cup L$.

4.7.3 Join Operation of Two Flats

As we saw above, the join of two points, V_0 and V_1, is defined as a line that contains both points, having the same orientation as the simplex $(V_0; V_1)$. Meanwhile, the join of a point V_0 with respect to a line L, when $(V_1; V_2)$ is a positive simplex of L, is a plane that contains V_0 and L, having the same orientation as $(V_0; V_1; V_2)$.

By generalizing, we can define join operations of arbitrary flats.

---

[5] $A \cup B$ is read "A cup B" or "A join B."

Definition 4.3 (Join operation)
Letting A and B be two flats determined from simplices a and b, respectively, and writing them as $(A_0; \cdots; A_\kappa)$ and $(B_0; \cdots; B_\mu)$, the join operation of A and B is defined as follows:

$$(A_0; \cdots; A_\kappa) \cup (B_0; \cdots; B_\mu) = (A_0; \cdots; A_\kappa; B_0; \cdots; B_\mu), \tag{4.10}$$

where A and B are proper flats with no points in common, i.e., they are disjoint flats. The resulting join is a proper simplex. When A and B have points in common, their join is undefined.

We shall also agree that

$$\Lambda \cup A = A = A \cup \Lambda,$$
$$(\neg\Lambda) \cup A = \neg A = A \cup (\neg\Lambda). \tag{4.11}$$

Although no join is defined when A and B have common points, we formally write as follows:

$$A \cup B = \mathbf{0}^{rank(A)+rank(B)},$$

assuming that a null object $\mathbf{0}$ is generated (see eq.(4.12)).

4.7.4 Properties of Join Operations

Join operations have the following properties:

1. **Rank**

   Given that $A \cup B$ is defined,

   $$rank(A \cup B) = rank(A) + rank(B) \tag{4.12}$$

   and

   $$(\neg A) \cup B = A \cup (\neg B) = \neg(A \cup B). \tag{4.13}$$

2. **Associativity**

   For arbitrary flats A, B and C,

   $$A \cup (B \cup C) = (A \cup B) \cup C, \tag{4.14}$$

   assuming that both sides of the equation can be defined.

3. **Commutativity**

   When any two vertices of a simplex are interchanged, the resulting simplex will have the reverse orientation. To transform the simplex $(A_0; \cdots; A_\kappa; B_0; \cdots; B_\mu)$ into $(B_0; \cdots; B_\mu; A_0; \cdots; A_\kappa)$, the number of vertex interchange required is $(\kappa+1) \times (\mu+1)$. Thus, the following holds for two flats A and B:

   $$A \cup B = \neg^{rank(A)rank(B)}(B \cup A). \tag{4.15}$$

   Thus, $B \cup A$ is identical to $A \cup B$ when at least one of the operands has even rank, but equal to $\neg(A \cup B)$ when both operands have odd ranks.

We have the following important theorem regarding joins.

Theorem 4.1 (Complementary flat)
Given an arbitrary subflat P of a flat F, there exists a flat Q such that $P \cup Q = F$.

Here, Q is called the right complement of P in F. Conversely, P is the left complement of Q in F. Except in special cases, the right and left complements are not uniquely determined.

4.8 Meet Operations

The *meet* operation of two given flats yields the intersecting flat of the given flats. The orientation of the flat must also be determined.

4.8.1 Meet Operation of Two Lines

Two lines A and B in $\mathbf{T}^2$ intersect at two antipodal points (Fig. 4.32). Of these, the *meet* of A and B, $A \cap B$, [6] is that intersecting point of A and B, about which the turning of A towards B through the smallest angle coincides with the positive orientation of the universe. $A \cap B$ is undefined when $A = B$ or $A = \neg B$.

Just as the join of two points is anticommutative, so is the meet of two lines. That is

$$B \cap A = \neg(A \cap B), \tag{4.16}$$

$$(\neg A) \cap B = A \cap (\neg B) = \neg(A \cap B). \tag{4.17}$$

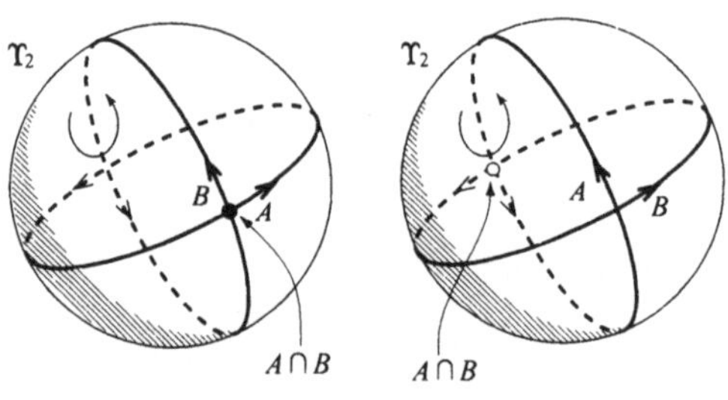

Figure 4.32: Intersection of two lines in $\mathbf{T}^2$ (1).

Note that the intersection V_1 of two lines, $A = (V_0; V_1)$ and $B = (V_1; V_2)$, in $\mathbf{T}^2$ can be expressed as follows (Fig. 4.33):

$$\begin{cases} V_0 \cup V_1 \cup V_2 = \Upsilon_2, \\ V_0 \cup V_1 = A, \\ V_1 \cup V_2 = B, \\ V_1 = A \cap B = (V_0 \cup V_1) \cap (V_1 \cup V_2). \end{cases} \tag{4.18}$$

[6] $A \cap B$ reads "A cap B" or "A *meet* B."

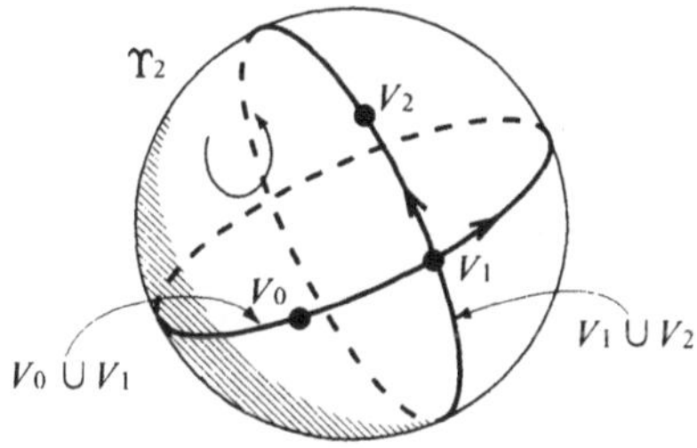

Figure 4.33: Intersection of two lines in $\mathbf{T}^2$ (2).

4.8.2 General Meet Operations

Based on eq.(4.18), the meet of two flats of arbitrary rank is defined as follows.

Definition 4.4 (Meet operation)
Letting U be the flat of the smallest rank containing flats A and B, the meet of A and B in U is the flat Q that satisfies the following relation:

$$\begin{aligned} P \cup Q \cup R &= U, \\ P \cup Q &= A, \\ Q \cup R &= B. \end{aligned} \tag{4.19}$$

We denote Q as $Q = A \cap_U B$.

From the definition above, we see that if U is not the smallest flat containing A and B, $A \cap_u B$ is not defined. The condition that U is indeed the smallest flat containing A and B is given by the following equation:

$$rank(A) + rank(B) - rank(A \cap B) = rank(U). \tag{4.20}$$

When U is not the smallest flat containing A and B, we formally write

$$A \cap_U B = \mathbf{0}^{rank(A)+rank(B)-rank(U)}.$$

It is shown that there always exists one and only one flat Q which satisfies eq.(4.19).

4.8.3 Properties of Meet Operations

The meet operation $A \cap B$ has the following properties.

1. **Orientation of meet**

   The orientation of the flat resulting from a meet operation is determined by the orientations not only of A and B but also of the reference flat U. That is,

$$A \cap_{(\neg U)} B = \neg(A \cap_U B). \tag{4.21}$$

The next relation exists as well:

$$(\neg A) \cap B = A \cap (\neg B) = \neg(A \cap B). \tag{4.22}$$

2. **Meet operation with universe**

   The reference flat Υ acts as a unit element in meet operations. That is, for any flat $A \subseteq \Upsilon$,

$$A \cap \Upsilon = A = \Upsilon \cap A,$$
$$A \cap (\neg\Upsilon) = \neg A = (\neg\Upsilon) \cap A.$$

3. **Meet operations in spaces of different dimensions**

   Let P, Q and U be flats such that $P \cup U \cup Q \neq \mathbf{0}$. For arbitrary flats A, $B \subseteq U$, the following equation holds:

$$(P \cup A) \cap_{P \cup U \cup Q} (B \cup Q) = A \cap_U B. \tag{4.23}$$

   In particular, if $P = \Lambda$ or $Q = \Lambda$, and $P \cup U \neq \mathbf{0}$, for arbitrary flats $A, B \subseteq U$, we have

$$(P \cup A) \cap_{P \cup U} B = A \cap_U B \tag{4.24}$$

   and

$$A \cap_{U \cup P} (B \cup P) = A \cap_U B. \tag{4.25}$$

   Eq. (4.24) or (4.25) shows how a meet operation in the reference flat U is carried out in a reference flat of higher dimension ($P \cup U$ or $U \cup P$).

4. **Rank and corank**

   From the definition of meet operations, we have

$$corank(A \cap B) = corank(A) + corank(B) \tag{4.26}$$

   and

$$rank(A \cap B) = rank(A) - corank(B) = rank(B) - corank(A). \tag{4.27}$$

5. **Commutativity**

   For all flats A and B,

$$B \cap A = \neg^{corank(A)corank(B)}(A \cap B), \tag{4.28}$$

   given that $A \cap B$ is defined. That is, commutativity holds unless both flats have odd coranks. For $\mathbf{T}^3$ and lesser spaces, commutativity does not hold for two points in $\mathbf{T}^1$, two lines in $\mathbf{T}^2$ and two planes in $\mathbf{T}^3$ as well as a point and a plane in $\mathbf{T}^3$.

6. **Associativity**

   Meet operations are associative. That is, for arbitrary flats A, B and C, we have

$$(A \cap B) \cap C = A \cap (B \cap C), \tag{4.29}$$

   given that both sides can be defined.

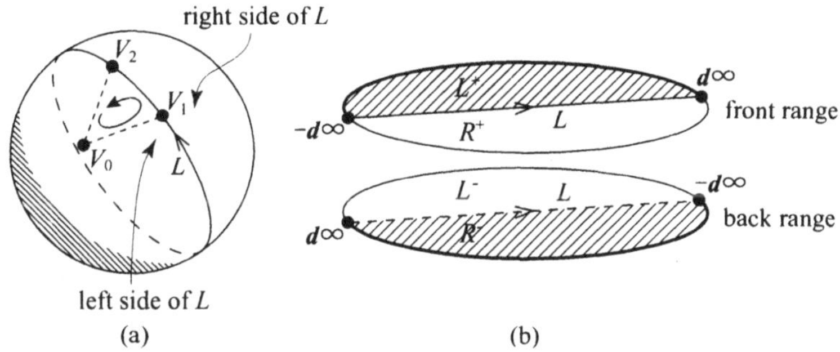

Figure 4.34: Two sides of line in spherical and straight models of $\mathbf{T}^2$.

4.9 Relative Orientation

A major feature of oriented projective space, i.e., two-sided space, which distinguishes it from classical projective space is that a line on a plane or a plane in three-space has two distinct sides (half-spaces). This can be expressed in terms of join or meet operations.

4.9.1 Two Sides of a Line

A line L separates the spherical model of the two-sided plane into two sides: left (positive) and right (negative) (Fig. 4.34(a)). Specifically, letting $(V_1; V_2)$ denote a simplex on the given line L, and V_0 a point on the sphere, V_0 lies on the left (positive) side of L when the simplex $(V_0; V_1; V_2)$ is a positive triangle in $\mathbf{T}^2$, and the right (negative) side of L when $(V_0; V_1; V_2)$ a negative triangle. This can be expressed in terms of join or meet operations as follows:

(1) If V_0 lies on the left side of L, $V_0 \cup L = \Upsilon_2$ (or $V_0 \cap L = \Lambda$),
(2) If V_0 lies on L, $V_0 \cup L = \mathbf{0}^3$ (or $V_0 \cap L = \mathbf{0}^0$),
(3) If V_0 lies on the right side of L, $V_0 \cup L = \neg\Upsilon_2$ (or $V_0 \cap L = \neg\Lambda$).

Let us examine this relation using the straight model.

If line L (with direction $\boldsymbol{d}$) is the line at infinity, that is, $L = \Omega_2$, its left and right sides are the front and back ranges, respectively, of $\mathbf{T}^2$. For $L = \neg\Omega_2$, the relation is reversed.

Consider next the case when L is a proper line. Of the half-planes formed by L, denote the left and right sides on the front range as L^+ and R^+, respectively, and their antipodal images on the back range as L^- and R^-. The left side of L is then the sum of L^+, R^- and all points at infinity from direction $+\boldsymbol{d}$ to $-\boldsymbol{d}$ as traced in the counterclockwise direction. Meanwhile, the right side of L is the sum of R^+, L^- and points on the remaining line at infinity (Fig. 4.34(b)).

Given a line $L = (V_0; V_1)$ in $\mathbf{T}^2$, and letting $\boldsymbol{V} = \boldsymbol{V}_0 \times \boldsymbol{V}_1$, whether a point V_a lies in the positive or negative half-spaces of the line, or on the line itself can be evaluated, referring to Fig. 4.35, by the following equation (see Section C.3):

$$S_{a01} = \boldsymbol{V}_a \cdot \boldsymbol{V} = \begin{vmatrix} w_a & X_a & Y_a \\ w_0 & X_0 & Y_0 \\ w_1 & X_1 & Y_1 \end{vmatrix}, \tag{4.30}$$

$$S_{a01} \begin{cases} > 0 & \cdots \text{ Point } V_a \text{ lies in the positive half-space of the line,} \\ = 0 & \cdots \text{ Point } V_a \text{ lies on the line,} \\ < 0 & \cdots \text{ Point } V_a \text{ lies in the negative half-space of the line.} \end{cases} \tag{4.31}$$

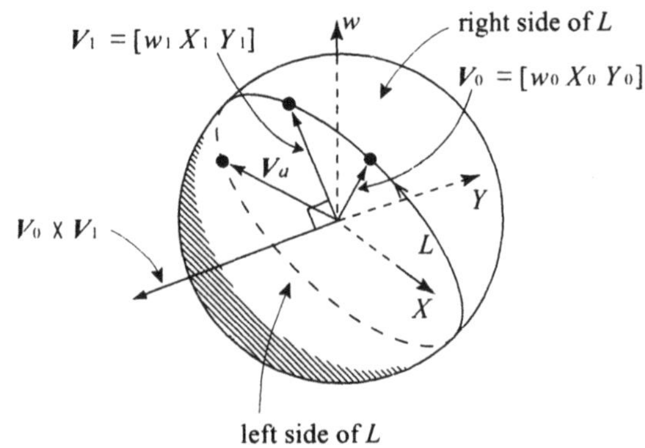

Figure 4.35: Derivation of S_{a01}.

4.9.2 Relative Orientation of an Arbitrary Flat

It is possible to evaluate the half-spaces formed by an arbitrary hyperplane in $\mathbf{T}^\nu$ by extending the method of previous section.

Generalizing further, letting A and B be two flats in $\mathbf{T}^\nu$ whose ranks when summed equal n $(=\nu+1)$, the *relative orientation*, $A \diamond B$, of A and B is defined as follows:

$$A \diamond B = \begin{cases} +1 & (A \cup B = \Upsilon_\nu), \\ 0 & (A \cup B = \mathbf{0}^n), \\ -1 & (A \cup B = \neg\Upsilon_\nu). \end{cases} \tag{4.32}$$

Using meet operators, this is expressed as follows:

$$A \diamond B = \begin{cases} +1 & (A \cap B = \Lambda), \\ 0 & (A \cap B = \mathbf{0}^0), \\ -1 & (A \cap B = \neg\Lambda). \end{cases} \tag{4.33}$$

When $A \diamond B = +1$, we say that "A is positively oriented relative to B" or "the pair A, B has a positive orientation." $A \diamond B$ is defined only when A and B are complementary flats, that is, when rank(A)+rank(B)=rank(Υ). Furthermore, $A \diamond B = 0$ only when A and B have points in common. Note that $A \diamond B$ depends on the orientations of not only A and B, but Υ as well.

As in join operations, switching the operands will cause sign reversal only when both have odd rank, that is,

$$B \diamond A = (\neg)^{rank(A)rank(B)}(A \diamond B). \tag{4.34}$$

Because rank(A)+rank(B)=n, the only times when the ordering of operands becomes an issue are when the space has even rank (or odd dimension) and at least one of the operands has odd rank (even dimension). For the case of three or lesser dimensions, this occurs for two points on a line, or a point and a plane in three-space.

4.9.3 Two Sides of a Hyperplane

Letting V_a be a point and H a hyperplane, we say that "the point V_a is on the positive side of hyperplane H" when $V_a \diamond H = +1$.

1. **Two sides of a point**

   The positive side of a point (hyperplane) V_0 in $\mathbf{T}^1$ consists of the set of points V_a such that $V_a \diamond V_0 = +1$, that is, the open half-circle from $\neg V_0$ to V_0 when traced in the counterclockwise direction (Fig. 4.36).

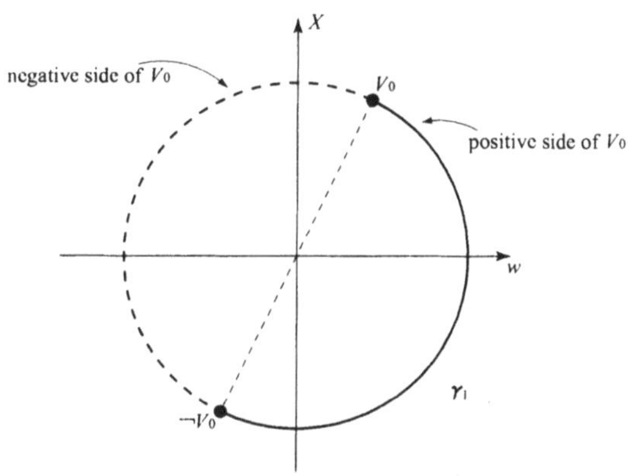

Figure 4.36: Half-spaces of $\mathbf{T}^1$.

Given a point V_0 in $\mathbf{T}^1$, and letting $\boldsymbol{V} = [X_0 \quad -w_0]$, whether a point V_a lies in the positive or negative half-space of V_0, or on V_0 itself can be evaluated, referring to Fig. 4.37, by the following equation:

$$S_{a0} = \boldsymbol{V}_a \cdot \boldsymbol{V} = \begin{vmatrix} w_a & X_a \\ w_0 & X_0 \end{vmatrix}. \tag{4.35}$$

$$S_{a0} \begin{cases} > 0 & \cdots\ V_a \text{ lies in the positive half-space of } V_0, \\ = 0 & \cdots\ V_a \text{ is identical with either } V_0 \text{ or } \neg V_0, \\ < 0 & \cdots\ V_a \text{ lies in the negative half-space of } V_0. \end{cases} \tag{4.36}$$

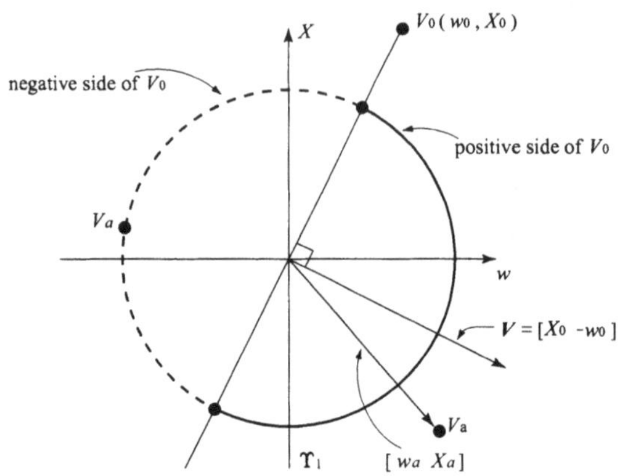

Figure 4.37: Derivation of S_{a0}.

2. **Two sides of a plane**

A plane Π divides $\mathbf{T}^3$ into two half-spaces. The set of points V_a such that $V_a \diamond \Pi = +1$, that is $V_a \cup \Pi = \Upsilon_3$, constitutes the positive side of Π, while that such that $V_a \cup \Pi = \neg\Upsilon_3$ constitutes the negative side.

Geometrically, this can be stated as follows: letting $(V_0; V_1; V_2)$ be a simplex on plane Π, V_a is on the positive side of Π when the simplex $(V_a; V_0; V_1; V_2)$ is a positive tetrahedron in $\mathbf{T}^3$ (Fig. 4.38).

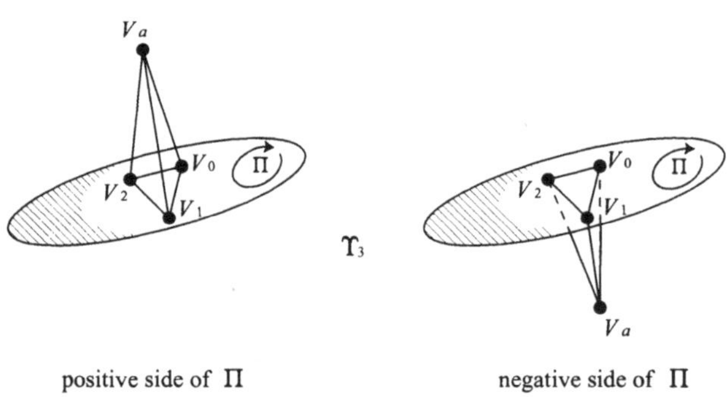

Figure 4.38: Geometric relation of half-spaces in $\mathbf{T}^3$.

Let us examine the half-spaces of $\mathbf{T}^3$ using the straight model. As we saw earlier, a proper plane Π, which is not the plane at infinity, is represented by planes Π^+ and Π^- in the front and back ranges, respectively, the two being identical copies of each other (see Section 4.4.3). Denoting by L^+ and R^+ the half-spaces of $\mathbf{R}^3$ formed by Π^+ in the front range, and by L^- and R^- those formed by Π^- in the back range, the half-spaces formed by plane Π are $L^+ \cup R^-$ and $R^+ \cup L^-$ to each of which are added suitable points at infinity (Fig. 4.39). Intuitively, the positive side of plane Π in $\mathbf{T}^3$ is that side from which the arrowed orientation of Π appears clockwise.

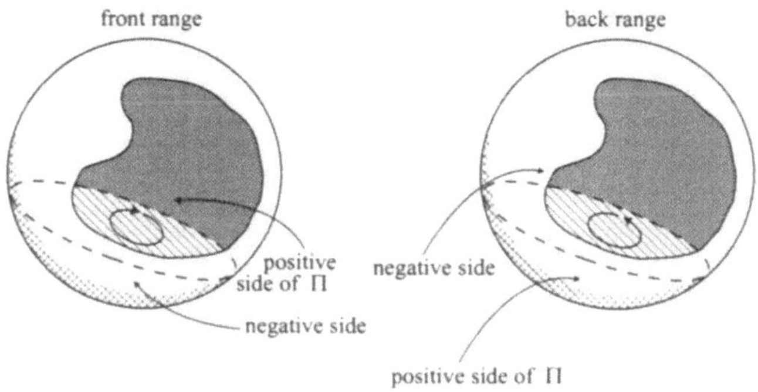

Figure 4.39: Half spaces of $\mathbf{T}^3$.

Since a plane and a point both have odd rank, $V_a \cup \Pi = \neg(\Pi \cup V_a)$, and so attention must be paid to the ordering of operands.

Of the planes consisting of points at infinity, the one which has the origin of the front range lying on its positive side is Ω_3.

Given a plane $H = (V_0; V_1; V_2)$ in $\mathbf{T}^3$, whether a point V_a lies in the positive or negative half-space of the plane, or on the plane itself can be evaluated, inferred from the cases of $\mathbf{T}^1$ and $\mathbf{T}^2$, by the following equation (see Chapter 13):

$$S_{a012} = \begin{vmatrix} w_a & X_a & Y_a & Z_a \\ w_0 & X_0 & Y_0 & Z_0 \\ w_1 & X_1 & Y_1 & Z_1 \\ w_2 & X_2 & Y_2 & Z_2 \end{vmatrix}. \tag{4.37}$$

$$S_{a012} \begin{cases} > 0 & \cdots V_a \text{ lies in the positive half-space of the plane,} \\ = 0 & \cdots V_a \text{ lies on the plane,} \\ < 0 & \cdots V_a \text{ lies in the negative half-space of the plane.} \end{cases} \tag{4.38}$$

4.10 Separation Theorem

The separation theory of Euclidean geometry states that "two distinct points on the plane can be separated by a line." For two-sided space, this is expressed as "Given two distinct points, V_0 and V_1 in $\mathbf{T}^2$, there exists a line L such that $V_0 \diamond L = \neg V_1 \diamond L$." This can be further generalized to the following theorem:

Theorem 4.2 (Separation)
Two flats A and B of the same rank are distinct if and only if there exists a complementary flat Q in universe Υ such that $A \diamond Q = -(B \diamond Q)$.

4.11 Polar Complements

In the spherical model, when two vectors, each expressing a point, are normal, the two points are said to *have a polar relation.* Generalizing, we say that two flats A and B are *polar* when every point of the flat A is polar to every point in the flat B. We denote this as $A \perp B$. We are now ready to define *polar complements.*

Definition 4.5 (Polar complement)
The right polar complement of a flat A is a flat $A^{\vdash}$ such that

$$\begin{cases} A \perp A^{\vdash}, \\ A \diamond A^{\vdash} = +1. \end{cases} \tag{4.39}$$

Similarly, the left polar complement is the flat $A^{\dashv}$ such that

$$\begin{cases} A^{\dashv} \perp A, \\ A^{\dashv} \diamond A = +1. \end{cases} \tag{4.40}$$

It is known that $A^{\vdash}$ and $A^{\dashv}$ always exist, that they are uniquely determined, are disjoint from A, are continuous functions of A, and have the following ranks:

$$rank(A^{\vdash}) = rank(A^{\dashv}) = corank(A). \tag{4.41}$$

Clearly, from the definition,

$$(A^{\vdash})^{\dashv} = A = (A^{\dashv})^{\vdash}. \tag{4.42}$$

$\vdash$ and $\dashv$ are thus inverses of each other.

Denoting the ranks of A and its universe by r and n, respectively, we have the following relation:

$$A^{\vdash} = \neg^{r(n-r)} A^{\dashv}. \tag{4.43}$$

For $\mathbf{T}^2$ ($n=3$), $r(n-r)$ is an even number for all r, so $A^{\vdash}$ and $A^{\dashv}$ represent the same function.

For $\mathbf{T}^3$ ($n=4$), $A^{\vdash} = A^{\dashv}$ when A has even rank, and $A^{\vdash} = \neg A^{\dashv}$ when A has odd rank. Thus, the right and left polar complements of a point or a plane have opposite orientations, whereas those of a line are identical.

We now look at some examples in two and three dimensions.

1. **Examples in $\mathbf{T}^2$**

   Because the right and left polar complements are the same ($A^{\vdash} = A^{\dashv}$), we write $A^{\perp}$.

   Given a line, that is, a great circle A, in the spherical model, its polar complement is the polar point on the left half-sphere as seen from A. Conversely, given a point on the sphere, its polar complement is the great circle, or line, from which that point is seen as a pole to the left (Fig. 4.40(a)).

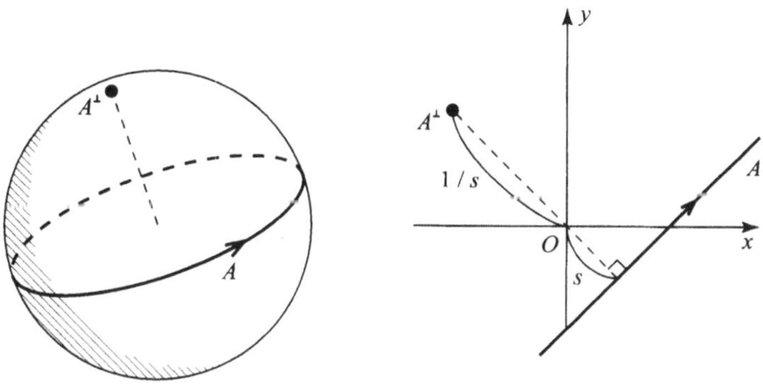

(a) The spherical model

(b) The straight model

Figure 4.40: A point and a line form polar complements in $\mathbf{T}^2$.

Consider this now in the straight model (Fig. 4.40(b)). Let a line A be expressed by the following equation:

$$aw + bX + cY = 0. \tag{4.44}$$

Since $w=1$ in the straight model, we have

$$a + bx + cy = 0. \tag{4.45}$$

Denoting by s the normal distance from the origin, then we have

$$s = \frac{a}{\sqrt{b^2 + c^2}}. \tag{4.46}$$

Vector $[a\ b\ c]$ is normal to vector $[w\ X\ Y]$ of a point on line eq.(4.44), and intersects $w=1$ plane at a point $(b/a, c/a)$ in the straight model. The distance from the origin to this point in the straight model is given by

$$\frac{\sqrt{b^2 + c^2}}{a} = \frac{1}{s}. \tag{4.47}$$

Note that in Fig. 4.40(b) the polar complement $A^\perp$ of line A lies to its left, which results from the relative orientation adopted in the definitions of eqs.(4.39) and (4.40).

If the line A passes the origin in the straight model, $A^\perp$ is the point at infinity in the 90° direction turning counterclockwise from the line's direction.

Conversely, the polar complement of the line at infinity Ω_2 is the origin of the front range. The polar complement of the line at infinity $\neg\Omega_2$ is the origin of the back range.

2. **Examples in $\mathbf{T}^3$**

Let us look at the polar complement of a point in three-space $\mathbf{T}^3$. Basically the situation is very similar to the two-dimensional case discussed above. Substituting $r=1$ and $n=4$ in eq.(4.43), we have $A^{\vdash} = \neg A^{\dashv}$.

Given a point P in the front range located at a distance $s > 0$ from the origin in the straight model, its polar complement $P^{\vdash}$ is the plane normal to the vector $\overrightarrow{\mathrm{OP}}$, located opposite the origin at a normal distance of $1/s$ from the origin (Fig. 4.41). It has a clockwise orientation as viewed from P.

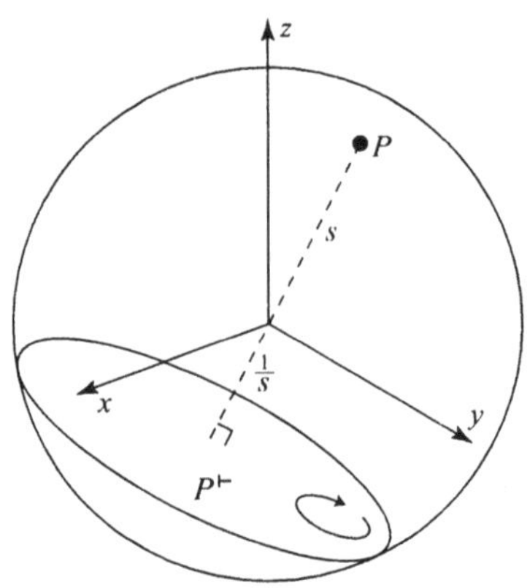

Figure 4.41: Polar complement of a point in $\mathbf{T}^3$ (straight model).

If P is at the origin of the front range O, its polar complement is one of the two planes at infinity. The same holds when P is at the origin of the back range $\neg O$.

If P is a point at infinity, its polar complement is a plane containing the origin, lying normal to the direction of P. Since $P \diamond P^{\vdash} = +1$, the plane is oriented such that P lies on its positive side, that is, it has a clockwise orientation as viewed from P.

We now examine polar complements using the analytical model for $\mathbf{T}^3$. In the vector space model, the right polar complement of a point $\overline{\boldsymbol{V}}$ is a hyperplane of $\mathbf{T}^3$ normal to the vector $\boldsymbol{V}$, represented by a three-dimensional linear subspace in $\mathbf{R}^4$. The homogeneous coefficients of the hyperplane are the coordinates of a properly oriented vector normal to the linear subspace, i.e., either $\boldsymbol{V}$ or $-\boldsymbol{V}$ (or any multiple thereof). Let us consider this problem.

From the definition of polar complements, we have

$$\overline{\boldsymbol{V}} \diamond \overline{\boldsymbol{V}}^{\vdash} = +1 \tag{4.48}$$

and

$$\overline{\boldsymbol{V}} \diamond \overline{\gamma} = \overline{[w\ X\ Y\ Z]} \diamond \overline{\begin{bmatrix} a \\ b \\ c \\ d \end{bmatrix}}$$
$$= sign(aw + bX + cY + dZ). \tag{4.49}$$

From eqs.(4.48) and (4.49), we have

$$\overline{\boldsymbol{V}}^{\vdash} = \overline{[w\ X\ Y\ Z]}^{\vdash} = \overline{\begin{bmatrix} w \\ X \\ Y \\ Z \end{bmatrix}}. \tag{4.50}$$

Meanwhile, corresponding to eqs.(4.48) and (4.49) (from eq.(4.34)), we have

$$\overline{\gamma} \diamond \overline{\gamma}^{\vdash} = +1 \tag{4.51}$$

and

$$\overline{\gamma} \diamond \overline{\boldsymbol{V}} = \neg \overline{\boldsymbol{V}} \diamond \overline{\gamma}$$
$$= \neg sign(aw + bX + cY + dZ). \tag{4.52}$$

From eqs.(4.48) and (4.52), then,

$$\overline{\gamma}^{\vdash} = \overline{\begin{bmatrix} a \\ b \\ c \\ d \end{bmatrix}}^{\vdash} = \neg \overline{[a\ b\ c\ d]}. \tag{4.53}$$

Eqs.(4.50) and (4.53) show the relations for right polar complements.

The relations for left polar complements, considering eq.(4.43), are given by

$$\overline{\boldsymbol{V}}^{\dashv} = \overline{[w\ X\ Y\ Z]}^{\dashv} = \neg \overline{\begin{bmatrix} w \\ X \\ Y \\ Z \end{bmatrix}} \tag{4.54}$$

and

$$\overline{\gamma}^{\dashv} = \overline{\begin{bmatrix} a \\ b \\ c \\ d \end{bmatrix}}^{\dashv} = \overline{[a\ b\ c\ d]}. \tag{4.55}$$

It is important that polar complement functions satisfy the following relations:

$$\begin{cases} (A \cup B)^{\vdash} = A^{\vdash} \cap B^{\vdash}, & (A \cup B)^{\dashv} = A^{\dashv} \cap B^{\dashv}, \\ (A \cap B)^{\vdash} = A^{\vdash} \cup B^{\vdash}, & (A \cap B)^{\dashv} = A^{\dashv} \cup B^{\dashv}. \end{cases} \tag{4.56}$$

Chapter 5

Processing in Projective Spaces

From the discussion of Chapter 1, we concluded that *"the division operation is the root cause of all evil."* In order to dispense with the detrimental division operations, we considered to use homogeneous coordinates instead of Euclidean coordinates.

As stated, ordinary homogeneous coordinates, i.e., unsigned homogeneous coordinates represent a space called classical projective space. It is true that some of the problems caused by division operations, pointed out in Chapter 1 are resolved by playing in the projective space, but at the same time we found that the projective space has some peculiar properties that differ from those of Euclidean space, with which most of us are familiar. If we play in the projective space, these properties could be obstacles of the processing in computer aided geometric design environment.

We list up some of these problems below:

1. **Line segment definition problem**
2. **No concept of convexity**

   In the classical projective geometry, a line segment is meaningless. In other words, given two points in the classical projective space it is not possible to define a line segment connecting the two points in a consistent manner.

   Two points divide the line passing those points into two arcs (Fig. 5.1). Yet, these two arcs can not be distinguished without employing some specific point (a point at infinity, for instance).

   A line segment is, however, an essential and fundamental geometric element in computer aided geometric design.

   Because the definition of convexity is based on that of a line segment, and the latter is difficult in projective space as stated above, the concept of convexity does not exist in classical projective space in a strict sense.

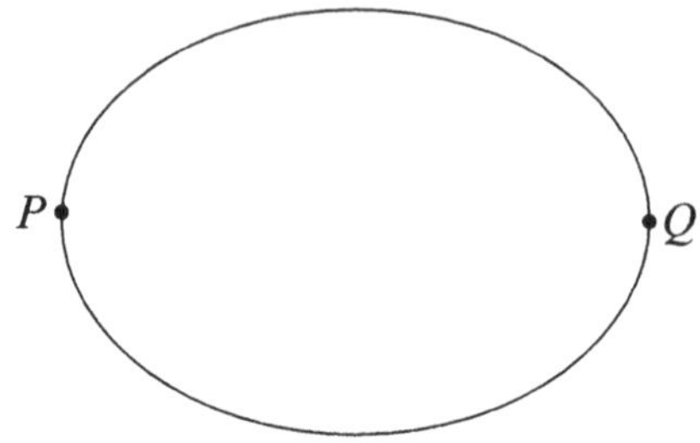

Figure 5.1: Two arcs determined by two points in $\mathbf{P}^1$.

3. **One-sidedness of lines and planes**
4. **Non-halfspace property**

   A line in $\mathbf{P}^2$ or a plane in $\mathbf{P}^3$ has only a single side. When a line is excluded from the projective plane, what remains is a single set of connected points that is topologically equivalent to a disk. Therefore, the question "on which side of a line does a point exist?" has no meaning [53].

   If one begins at some point and travels along a line (which is closed) on the projective plane while facing one's left side, one will eventually return to the original position but this time facing one's right [53].

   The line in $\mathbf{P}^2$ or plane in $\mathbf{P}^3$ does not have the property of half space.

5. **Non-orientability**

   A line in $\mathbf{P}^2$ or $\mathbf{P}^3$ has no orientation. Letting V_0 and V_1 be two points on a line, the point at infinity in the direction $V_0 \to V_1$ is also that in the direction $V_1 \to V_0$.

   As for plane, it is not possible to define orientation, either of clockwise or counter-clockwise rotation, consistently for the entire projective plane (see Definition 3). Thus, a triangle's orientation, for instance, can not be defined on the projective plane.

   If one starts out with a certain orientation and travels continuously on the projective plane, one eventually may return to the original position but with the orientation reversed [53].

   A line in $\mathbf{P}^2$ or $\mathbf{P}^3$, or plane in $\mathbf{P}^3$ does not have orientation.

6. **Vector operation problem**

   As stated in 7. of Section 2.2, vector addition does not hold in homogeneous coordinates. This means that projective space does not possess a vector space structure.

   If we cannot make use of vector algebra, the geometric processing capabilities in the space will be limited to a great extent.

Although some of the problems listed above can be avoided by taking the line at infinity as a reference, this necessarily removes from consideration special cases such as a line segment having a point at infinity as one end.

Jorge Stolfi proposed to use signed homogeneous coordinates instead of conventional unsigned homogeneous coordinates (see Chapter 4). The signed homogeneous coordinates represent another type of projective space, that is, two-sided space (or oriented projective space). He showed that the geometric modeling in two-sided space resolved many of the problems inherent in classical projective space [53].

There are still some difficulties, however, when we play in the two-sided space:

1. **Vector operation problem**

   As in the classical projective space, we have also vector operation problems because of the non-uniqueness of homogeneous coordinate representation, as long as we play in the two-sided space itself.

   This means that geometric elements can not be defined in terms of *points* in either classical projective space or two-sided space, although they can in terms of points in Euclidean space with the condition of partition of unity attached (see Section 10.1, Appendices A.2 and A.4).

In conclusion, we must look for some alternative technique to get over the difficulties above.

In Part II, we shall show a solution where we can solve many of the problems that we encountered so far. Before proceeding to Part II, however, we shall need to study transformations which we encounter in computer aided geometric design environment and also to learn a requirement from the transformations.

Chapter 6

Transformations

In considering and evaluating a processing paradigm of computer aided geometric design, it would be very important to ask what types of transformations are involved in the processing because we desire that all the theories, algorithms, geometry definitions, geometric computations and numerical data are not badly influenced by the transformations, in other words, invariant under these transformations.[1)]

6.1 Transformations in CAD

Transformations are frequently used in computer aided geometric design. Broadly speaking, there are three cases requiring transformations.

The first case is when a geometric model is to be defined. A geometric model generally consists of multiple elements. In order to define these elements, we must first establish suitable coordinate systems regarding each element. Meanwhile, the space in which the entire geometric model is defined is called the *world coordinate system*. To define a geometric model then, we must describe the relations that exist between the *local coordinate systems* for the individual elements and the overall world coordinate system. These relations can be expressed as transformations.

Transformations are also used to define movements of a geometric model.

Furthermore, in the set operations of solid modeling, a transformation is needed at the outset to properly position the operand solids before a set operation can take place; this is called *modeling transformation*. Since this information concerning a geometric model's spatial arrangement can be considered as part of its definition, we include modeling transformation in our first case.

---

1) The term "invariant under affine (or projective) transformation"or "affine (or projective) invariance"ordinarily applies to the case where a geometric representation holds under affine (or projective) transformation [16](see Sections 8.2, 10.4, A.2 and A.4). In this book, however, it is used with broader senses as described above, which include the ordinary definition.

The second case involves transformations for displaying a geometric model on a computer monitor, or for inputting geometric data using some input device. To display a geometric figure on screen, the relationship between the world coordinate system and the *screen coordinate system* set up for the computer monitor must be specified. This relationship is expressed by a transformation. When inputting a geometric figure's data from an input device as well, the relation between the world and *input device coordinate systems* is specified in terms of a transformation.

The third case is when a figure is being projected. While geometric models are usually three-dimensional, their display generally takes place on a two-dimensional screen. As a result, data with regard to one dimension are compressed, and the mathematical process for this is *projection*. There are several types of projections, including *perspective* and *isometric projections*, and any of these can be treated as a transformation.

Regular Linear Transformation

The most basic transformation used in computer aided geometric design is *regular linear transformation*. Scalings and rotations, when they are centered at the coordinate origin, are all represented by regular linear transformations. By using homogeneous coordinate vectors of points, two-dimensional regular linear transformations are represented as follows:

$$\overline{[1\ x\ y]\begin{bmatrix}1 & 0 & 0\\ 0 & a & b\\ 0 & c & d\end{bmatrix}} = \overline{[1\ x^*\ y^*]}, \quad \begin{vmatrix}a & b\\ c & d\end{vmatrix} \neq 0, \tag{6.1}$$

where a, d represent scalings in x- and y-directions respectively, and c, b shearings in x- and y-directions respectively.

Similarly, three-dimensional regular linear transformation is represented as

$$\overline{[1\ x\ y\ z]\begin{bmatrix}1 & 0 & 0 & 0\\ 0 & a & b & c\\ 0 & d & e & f\\ 0 & g & h & i\end{bmatrix}} = \overline{[1\ x^*\ y^*\ z^*]}, \tag{6.2}$$

$$\begin{vmatrix}a & b & c\\ d & e & f\\ g & h & i\end{vmatrix} \neq 0, \tag{6.3}$$

where, as in two-dimensional transformation case, diagonal elements a, e, i represent scalings and non-diagonal ones shearings.

Although regular linear transformations are easily treated mathematically, the transformational capabilities are severely limited. That is, the origin of the coordinate system is stationary under the transformation.

Regular Affine Transformation

Regular affine transformations are more general and include regular linear transformations, the only difference being that the former includes translation as well:

$$\overline{[1\ x\ y]\begin{bmatrix} 1 & t_x & t_y \\ 0 & a & b \\ 0 & c & d \end{bmatrix}} = \overline{[1\ x^*\ y^*]}, \quad \begin{vmatrix} a & b \\ c & d \end{vmatrix} \neq 0, \tag{6.4}$$

where t_x and t_y represent translations in x- and y-directions respectively.

Similarly, three-dimensional regular affine transformation is represented as

$$\overline{[1\ x\ y\ z]\begin{bmatrix} 1 & t_x & t_y & t_z \\ 0 & a & b & c \\ 0 & d & e & f \\ 0 & g & h & i \end{bmatrix}} = \overline{[1\ x^*\ y^*\ z^*]}, \tag{6.5}$$

$$\begin{vmatrix} a & b & c \\ d & e & f \\ g & h & i \end{vmatrix} \neq 0, \tag{6.6}$$

where t_x, t_y and t_z represent translations in x-, y- and z-directions respectively.

Thus with regular affine transformation, it is possible to scale or rotate a geometric figure about any arbitrary point.

Properties of Regular Affine Transformations

1. The transformation is one-to-one and the inverse transformation is also an affine transformation.

2. An affine transformation from $\mathbf{E}^2$ to $\mathbf{E}^2$ is uniquely determined by a non-degenerate triangle and its image, and one from $\mathbf{E}^3$ to $\mathbf{E}^3$ by a non-degenerate tetrahedron and its image.

3. A line or plane is affinely transformed to another line or plane, respectively.

4. An affine transformation preserves the divided ratio by a point on a line segment.

   Properties 3. and 4. are often used for the definition of affine transformations. That is, a transformation that transforms a line into a line while preserving the length ratio is an affine transformation.

5. An affine transformation preserves the parallelism of lines and planes.

6. The area A of a two-dimensional figure, and the volume V of a solid are affinely transformed as follows:

$$A^* = \begin{vmatrix} a & b \\ c & d \end{vmatrix} \times A, \tag{6.7}$$

$$V^* = \begin{vmatrix} a & b & c \\ d & e & f \\ g & h & i \end{vmatrix} \times V. \tag{6.8}$$

Regular Projective Transformation

Regular projective transformations, being more generalized, include affine transformation as its subset (see Fig. 6.1) and are defined as follows:

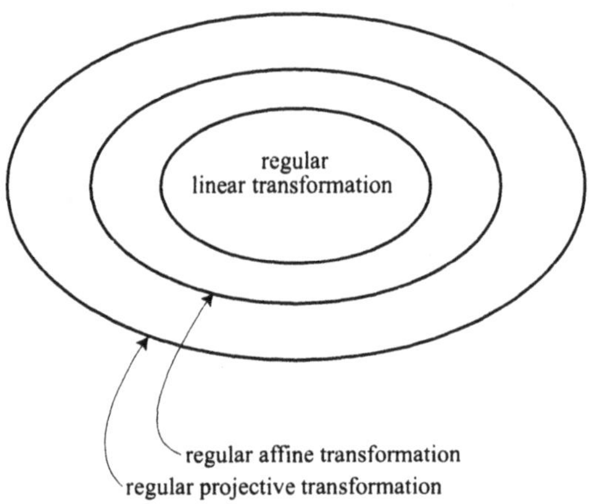

Figure 6.1: Transformations appearing in CAD (1).

$$\overline{[w\ X\ Y] \begin{bmatrix} s & t_x & t_y \\ p & a & b \\ q & c & d \end{bmatrix}} = \overline{[w^*\ X^*\ Y^*]}, \quad \begin{vmatrix} s & t_x & t_y \\ p & a & b \\ q & c & d \end{vmatrix} \neq 0, \tag{6.9}$$

$$\overline{[w\ X\ Y\ Z] \begin{bmatrix} s & t_x & t_y & t_z \\ p & a & b & c \\ q & d & e & f \\ r & g & h & i \end{bmatrix}} = \overline{[w^*\ X^*\ Y^*\ Z^*]}, \tag{6.10}$$

$$\begin{vmatrix} s & t_x & t_y & t_z \\ p & a & b & c \\ q & d & e & f \\ r & g & h & i \end{vmatrix} \neq 0. \tag{6.11}$$

A program possessing regular projective transformation capability would satisfy most applications encountered in computer aided geometric design.

Regular projective transformations are highly important in connection with generating perspective images. We shall discuss these themes in Sections 6.2 and 6.4.

Below, we shall give a formal definition of the regular projective transformation for the sake of discussions later [53]:

Definition 6.1 (Regular projective transformation)
Let S and T be two flats of $\mathbf{P}^{\nu}(\mathbf{T}^{\nu})$, represented in the vector space model by subspaces U and V. A function M from the points of S to those of T is a regular projective transformation if it takes (positive) simplices of S to (positive) simplices of T, and there is an invertible linear transformation $\boldsymbol{M}$ from U to V such that, for all $\boldsymbol{P} \in U$,

$$M(\overline{\boldsymbol{P}}) = \overline{\boldsymbol{P}\boldsymbol{M}}. \tag{6.12}$$

We can say that the linear transformation $\boldsymbol{M}$ above "induces" the projective transformation M, and denote that by $\overline{\boldsymbol{M}} = M$.

Properties of Regular Projective Transformations

1. The transformation is one-to-one, and the inverse transformation is also a projective transformation.

2. A line and a plane are projectively transformed to a line and a plane, respectively. Note that this line-preserving property is often used as the definition of projective transformation, and thus the projective transformation is sometimes called *collineation*.

3. In general, the divided ratio by a point on a line segment is not preserved.

4. The intersection of two lines, when projectively transformed, becomes the intersection of the two lines transformed.

5. Parallelism between two lines or planes is not necessarily preserved under projective transformation.

6. The cross ratio of four points lying on a single line is preserved in projective transformations (see Fig. 3.15).

7. A convex figure is projectively transformed to a convex figure (i.e., convexity is preserved).

Let us consider the meaning of projective transformation above, taking the two-dimensional relation, eq.(6.9), as an example.

The transformation of eq.(6.9) expresses a three-dimensional linear transformation in wXY-space. As long as two-dimensional projective transformations are thought to be operations taking place strictly within two-dimensional Euclidean space, their processing is not an easy one. That is, the two-dimensional projective transformation relation in two-dimensional Euclidean plane is expressed as:

$$[x^* \; y^*] = \frac{[x \; y] \begin{bmatrix} a & b \\ c & d \end{bmatrix} + [t_x \; t_y]}{px + qy + s}. \tag{6.13}$$

Similarly, the three-dimensional projective transformation relation in three-dimensional Euclidean space is expressed as:

$$[x^* \; y^* \; z^*] = \frac{[x \; y \; z] \begin{bmatrix} a & b & c \\ d & e & f \\ g & h & i \end{bmatrix} + [t_x \; t_y \; t_z]}{px + qy + rz + s}. \tag{6.14}$$

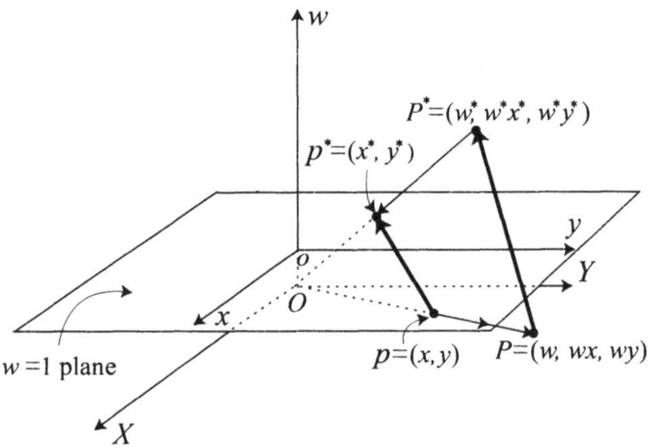

Figure 6.2: Linearization of projective transformation.

Recall here that the two-dimensional Euclidean space is $w=1$ plane in the more general three-dimensional wXY-space (see Fig. 6.2). To move p to p^* within this plane, the transformation must take place in the Euclidean plane, which is not an easy operation as seen from eq.(6.13).

Now a point (x, y) on the two-dimensional Euclidean plane is also the point $(1, x, y)$ in the wXY-space. What eq.(6.9) means is that a two-dimensional projective transformation on the Euclidean plane can be considered as a linear transformation in three-dimensional wXY-space. That is, by viewing a point in two-dimensional Euclidean space as a point in wXY-space, it can be linearly transformed using a 3×3 matrix, thus considerably simplifying the operation. In other words, moving p directly to p^* is troublesome, but it is much easier to take the path $p \rightarrow P \rightarrow P^* \rightarrow p^*$.

The same approach can be extended to three-dimensional transformations. That is, three-dimensional projective transformations can be simplified as four-dimensional linear transformations using 4×4 matrices.

The transformation technique above

1. expresses various types (linear, affine and projective) of transformations by means of a single representation,
2. applies to all points including points at infinity and,
3. being a linear transformation, is easy to carry out.

Projective Transformations of 2-D Lines and Planes

Denote by γ and γ^*, homogeneous coefficient vectors of a line (or plane) before and after transformation, respectively. That is, for a two-dimensional line,

$$\gamma = \begin{bmatrix} a \\ b \\ c \end{bmatrix}, \quad \gamma^* = \begin{bmatrix} a^* \\ b^* \\ c^* \end{bmatrix},$$

or for a plane,

$$\gamma = \begin{bmatrix} a \\ b \\ c \\ d \end{bmatrix}, \quad \gamma^* = \begin{bmatrix} a^* \\ b^* \\ c^* \\ d^* \end{bmatrix}.$$

The two-dimensional line, or plane is then expressed by the following equation:

$$\boldsymbol{P}\gamma = 0. \tag{6.15}$$

The equation after transformation is given by:

$$\boldsymbol{P}^*\gamma^* = 0. \tag{6.16}$$

We denote by $\boldsymbol{H}$ 3×3 (or 4×4) transformation matrix for two-dimensional lines (or planes). Then a point P on the two-dimensional line (or plane) is transformed to P^*, or:

$$\boldsymbol{P}\boldsymbol{H} = \boldsymbol{P}^*, \quad \text{so} \quad \boldsymbol{P} = \boldsymbol{P}^*\boldsymbol{H}^{-1}. \tag{6.17}$$

Substituting this into eq.(6.15), we have:

$$\boldsymbol{P}^*\boldsymbol{H}^{-1}\gamma = 0. \tag{6.18}$$

By comparing eqs.(6.16) and (6.18), we obtain the relation:

$$\overline{\gamma^*} = \overline{\boldsymbol{H}^{-1}\gamma}. \tag{6.19}$$

This represents the homogeneous coefficients of the line (or plane) after transformation.

If we denote the adjoint matrix [2] of $\boldsymbol{H}$ by $\boldsymbol{H}^a$, then:

$$\boldsymbol{H}^a = |\boldsymbol{H}|\boldsymbol{H}^{-1}.$$

So eq.(6.19) can also be written as:

$$\overline{\gamma^*} = \overline{\boldsymbol{H}^a\gamma}. \tag{6.20}$$

Since $\boldsymbol{H}^a$ is easier to obtain than $\boldsymbol{H}^{-1}$ and, in addition, requires no division, eq.(6.20) is often used in practice.

6.2 Perspective Projection and Transformation

Let us consider drawing on a plane a picture of a solid as it is seen.

Against a solid that exists in the negative z-region, assume that you are at a point $(0, 0, h)$ looking at a point $p(x, y, z)$ on a solid (see Fig. 6.3). In Fig. 6.3, denote by $p^*(x^*, y^*, z^*)$ the point at which your line of view intersects the xy-plane. The coordinates of p and p^* are then expressed by the following relations:

$$x^* = \frac{hx}{h-z}, \quad y^* = \frac{hy}{h-z}, \quad z^* = 0. \tag{6.21}$$

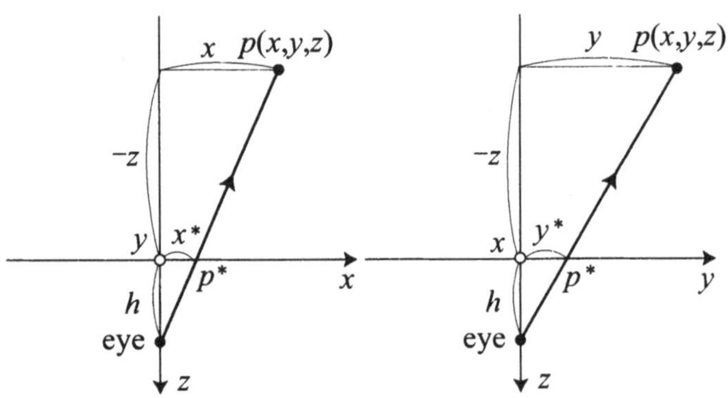

Figure 6.3: Perspective projection.

This set of equations transforms three-dimensional data into two-dimensional data, and represents a *perspective projection* in $\mathbf{E}^3$. If we vary p so that it assumes all points on the solid's surface, the figure appearing on the xy-plane is what you would see from your viewing position. p^* is therefore a *perspective*

[2] For matrix $\boldsymbol{M} = [m_{ij}]$, let M_{ij} denote the cofactor of m_{ji}. Then the adjoint $\boldsymbol{M}^a$ of $\boldsymbol{M}$ is the matrix $[M_{ij}]$. If $\boldsymbol{M}$ is a regular (i.e., nonsingular) matrix, then

$$\boldsymbol{M}^a = |\boldsymbol{M}|\boldsymbol{M}^{-1}.$$

drawing of point p. The viewer's position is called the *center of projection*, and the plane (xy-plane in this case) on which the two-dimensional drawing appears is called the *projection plane* or *image plane.*

Note that a line is transformed to another line, that is, linearity is preserved under perspective projection.

Note also that the perspective projection is not one-to-one, since it transforms all the points in the line of view to the same point of the projection plane.

Now, consider the following transformation:

$$\overline{[w\ X\ Y\ Z]\begin{bmatrix} 1 & 0 & 0 & 0 \\ 0 & 1 & 0 & 0 \\ 0 & 0 & 1 & 0 \\ -\frac{1}{h} & 0 & 0 & 1 \end{bmatrix}} = \overline{[w^*\ X^*\ Y^*\ Z^*]}, \tag{6.22}$$

or

$$x^* = \frac{hx}{h-z}, \quad y^* = \frac{hy}{h-z}, \quad z^* = \frac{hz}{h-z}. \tag{6.23}$$

If the vertices of some solid are projectively transformed by eq.(6.22) or (6.23), the new solid formed by the transformed vertices will have changed its shape. Note that the expressions for x^* and y^* in eq.(6.23) are the same as those in eq.(6.21). What this means is that if one views the transformed solid along lines parallel to z-axis, it will be identical with the perspective drawing. In this sense, the projective transformation expressed by eqs.(6.22) or (6.23) is called a *perspective transformation* of points in $\mathbf{E}^3$.

If we put zeros in all the fourth column elements in eq.(6.22), it turns out to be eq.(6.21), that is, the perspective projection:

$$\overline{[w\ X\ Y\ Z]\begin{bmatrix} 1 & 0 & 0 & 0 \\ 0 & 1 & 0 & 0 \\ 0 & 0 & 1 & 0 \\ -\frac{1}{h} & 0 & 0 & 0 \end{bmatrix}} = \overline{[w^*\ X^*\ Y^*\ Z^*]}. \tag{6.24}$$

Since

$$\begin{bmatrix} 1 & 0 & 0 & 0 \\ 0 & 1 & 0 & 0 \\ 0 & 0 & 1 & 0 \\ -\frac{1}{h} & 0 & 0 & 0 \end{bmatrix} = \begin{bmatrix} 1 & 0 & 0 & 0 \\ 0 & 1 & 0 & 0 \\ 0 & 0 & 1 & 0 \\ -\frac{1}{h} & 0 & 0 & 1 \end{bmatrix} \begin{bmatrix} 1 & 0 & 0 & 0 \\ 0 & 1 & 0 & 0 \\ 0 & 0 & 1 & 0 \\ 0 & 0 & 0 & 0 \end{bmatrix}, \tag{6.25}$$

the perspective projection of eq.(6.24) is the result of a parallel projection along z-axis after the perspective transformation of eq.(6.22).

Let us see how eq.(6.22) transforms the viewer's position (or center of projection). That is,

$$\begin{aligned} \overline{[w^*\ X^*\ Y^*\ Z^*]} &= \overline{[1\ 0\ 0\ h]\begin{bmatrix} 1 & 0 & 0 & 0 \\ 0 & 1 & 0 & 0 \\ 0 & 0 & 1 & 0 \\ -\frac{1}{h} & 0 & 0 & 1 \end{bmatrix}} \\ &= \overline{[0\ 0\ 0\ h]}. \end{aligned} \tag{6.26}$$

This shows that the viewer's position has been transformed to a point at infinity in the positive z-direction (in the two-sided space sense). This is why, after perspective transformation, the line of sight is parallel to z-axis.

How then does the perspective transformation change the z-coordinates of various points?

For points lying on the projection plane, i.e., $z = 0$, we see from the third equation in eq.(6.23) that z^* also is zero.

What about a point far removed from the viewer's position? Let us consider the extreme case of a point at infinity in the negative z-direction. We transform the point $\overline{(0,0,0,-1)}$ using eq.(6.22), or

$$\overline{[0\;0\;0\;-1]\begin{bmatrix} 1 & 0 & 0 & 0 \\ 0 & 1 & 0 & 0 \\ 0 & 0 & 1 & 0 \\ -\frac{1}{h} & 0 & 0 & 1 \end{bmatrix}} = \overline{[w^*\;X^*\;Y^*\;Z^*]},$$

so

$$z^* = \frac{Z^*}{w^*} = \frac{-1}{\frac{1}{h}} = -h. \tag{6.27}$$

This means that, from the viewer, all points lying beyond the projection plane $(-\infty \leq z \leq 0)$ are transformed so that their z^*-coordinates will fall within the range $-h \leq z^* \leq 0$.

Let us now see what happens to two points p_0 and p_1 with different z-coordinates. Assume that $z_0 \geq z_1$, that is, p_0 is closer to the viewer than p_1. We can rewrite the third equation of eq.(6.23) as follows:

$$z^* = \frac{hz}{h-z} = -h + \frac{h^2}{h-z}.$$

So,

$$z_0^* = -h + \frac{h^2}{h-z_0}, \quad z_1^* = -h + \frac{h^2}{h-z_1}.$$

Thus

$$z_0^* \geq z_1^*. \tag{6.28}$$

That is, a perspective transformation preserves the relative depths of points (i.e., their depth order) as seen from the viewer.

Upon perspective transformation of a solid, the xy-figure will show the perspective drawing, while its relative depth will be preserved. This means that, we can perform hidden line and surface elimination by placing the viewer (or center of projection) at a point at infinity in the perspectively transformed space.

6.3 Generalized Projective Transformation

For the sake of discussions later, we define the perspective projection using join and meet operations [53]:

Definition 6.2 (Perspective projection)
Let E and H be a point and a hyperplane in $\mathbf{P}^\nu(\mathbf{T}^\nu)$, respectively. Then the perspective projection P^* of a point P is:

$$P^* = (E \cup P) \cap H. \tag{6.29}$$

In connection with generating a perspective image, we have so far discussed two types of transformations, i.e., perspective transformation and perspective projection. While the former is a type of regular projective transformations, the latter, a perspective projection, is not according to Definition 6.1 because the latter is many-to-one and thus not invertible.

The perspective projection is not one-to-one, but has the important line-preserving property that Definition 6.1 means (see 2. of page 75). Therefore it would be natural to generalize the projective transformation such that it includes the perspective projection, by dropping the requirement in Definition 6.1 that the linear transformation $\boldsymbol{M}$ be invertible [53]:

Definition 6.3 (Generalized projective transformation(see Fig. 6.4))
Let S and T be two flats of $\mathbf{P}^\nu(\mathbf{T}^\nu)$, not necessarily of the same rank, represented in the vector space model by subspaces U and V. A function M from the points of S to those of T is a generalized projective transformation if there is a linear transformation $\boldsymbol{M}$ from U to V such that, for all $\boldsymbol{P} \in \mathbf{R}^{\nu+1}$,

$$M(\overline{\boldsymbol{P}}) = \overline{\boldsymbol{PM}}. \tag{6.30}$$

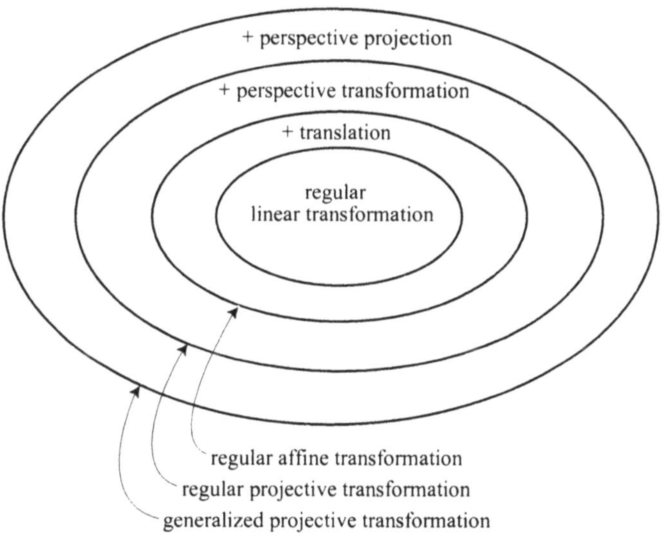

Figure 6.4: Transformations appearing in CAD (2).

We understand that the perspective projection is a special case of the generalized projective transformation.

6.4 Generalized Projective Invariance

We shall show that in computer aided geometric design we very frequently come across performing many types of perspective transformations and perspective projections, besides the time when in the very end of all process displaying pictures to human being.

1. A parametric circular segment in the first quadrant is expressed as follows:

$$\overline{[1\ t^2\ t]\begin{bmatrix}1 & 0 & 1\\ 1 & 0 & -1\\ 0 & 2 & 0\end{bmatrix}} = \overline{[w\ X\ Y]}, \quad (0 \le t \le 1), \tag{6.31}$$

or

$$x = \frac{X}{w} = \frac{2t}{1+t^2}, \quad y = \frac{Y}{w} = \frac{1-t^2}{1+t^2}, \quad (0 \le t \le 1). \tag{6.32}$$

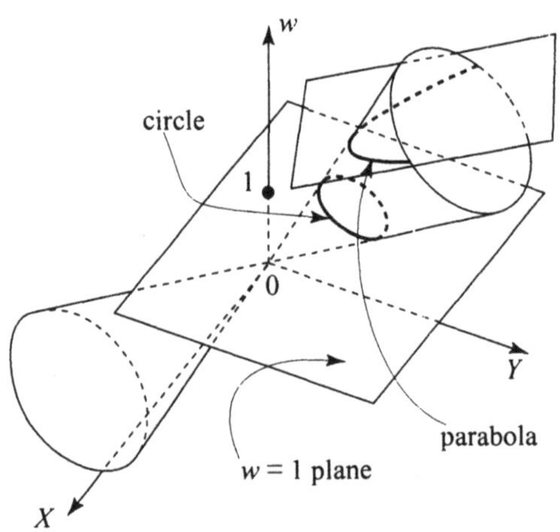

Figure 6.5: Perspective projection of a parabola.

Eq.(6.31) means that after a three-dimensional linear transformation the parabola $[1\ x\ y] = [1\ t^2\ t]$ is finally perspectively projected into the origin and a circular segment is generated on $w = 1$ plane (see Fig. 6.5). Changing the elements of the 3×3 matrix on the left side of eq.(6.31) generates conic sections or rational quadratic curves. This is a perspective transformation of points in $\mathbf{E}^2$. The last operation can be considered a perspective projection of a plane in $\mathbf{E}^3$ onto the $w = 1$ plane.

Similarly, a rational cubic curve is generated by first linearly transforming the curve $[1\ x\ y\ z] = [1\ t^3\ t^2\ t]$, then perspectively projecting it into the origin and finally cutting it by the $w=1$ hyperplane [58]:

$$\overline{[1\ t^3\ t^2\ t]\begin{bmatrix} s & t_x & t_y & t_z \\ p & a & b & c \\ q & d & e & f \\ r & g & h & i \end{bmatrix}} = \overline{[w\ X\ Y\ Z]}, \quad (0 \le t \le 1). \tag{6.33}$$

This is a perspective transformation of points in $\mathbf{E}^3$. The last operation can be considered a perspective projection of a three-space in $\mathbf{E}^4$ onto the $w=1$ hyperplane.

2. Let us consider the simple computations repetitively done in the pentagon problem presented in Section 1.1:

$$a_0 + b_0 x + c_0 y = 0,$$
$$a_1 + b_1 x + c_1 y = 0,$$

$$\Delta = \begin{vmatrix} b_0 & c_0 \\ b_1 & c_1 \end{vmatrix}, \quad \Delta_x = \begin{vmatrix} -a_0 & c_0 \\ -a_1 & c_1 \end{vmatrix}, \quad \Delta_y = \begin{vmatrix} b_0 & -a_0 \\ b_1 & -a_1 \end{vmatrix}, \tag{6.34}$$

$$x = \frac{\Delta_x}{\Delta}, \quad y = \frac{\Delta_y}{\Delta}. \tag{6.35}$$

From eq.(6.29), eq.(6.35) can be considered a perspective projection of points in $\mathbf{E}^3$.

Next, let us consider the computations for defining a face of a polyhedron in terms of vertex coordinates presented in Section 1.1:

$$a_0 + b_0 x + c_0 y + d_0 z = 0,$$
$$a_1 + b_1 x + c_1 y + d_1 z = 0,$$
$$a_2 + b_2 x + c_2 y + d_2 z = 0,$$

$$\Delta = \begin{vmatrix} b_0 & c_0 & d_0 \\ b_1 & c_1 & d_1 \\ b_2 & c_2 & d_2 \end{vmatrix}, \quad \Delta_x = \begin{vmatrix} -a_0 & c_0 & d_0 \\ -a_1 & c_1 & d_1 \\ -a_2 & c_2 & d_2 \end{vmatrix},$$

$$\Delta_y = \begin{vmatrix} b_0 & -a_0 & d_0 \\ b_1 & -a_1 & d_1 \\ b_2 & -a_2 & d_2 \end{vmatrix}, \Delta_z = \begin{vmatrix} b_0 & c_0 & -a_0 \\ b_1 & c_1 & -a_1 \\ b_2 & c_2 & -a_2 \end{vmatrix},$$

$$x = \frac{\Delta_x}{\Delta}, \quad y = \frac{\Delta_y}{\Delta}, \quad z = \frac{\Delta_z}{\Delta}. \tag{6.36}$$

From eq.(6.29), eq.(6.36) can be considered a perspective projection of points in $\mathbf{E}^4$.

Last, we shall consider performing a simple division operation a/b. This can be considered geometrically a perspective projection of points in $\mathbf{E}^2$ from a point (a, b) to a point (b/a) (Fig. 6.6).

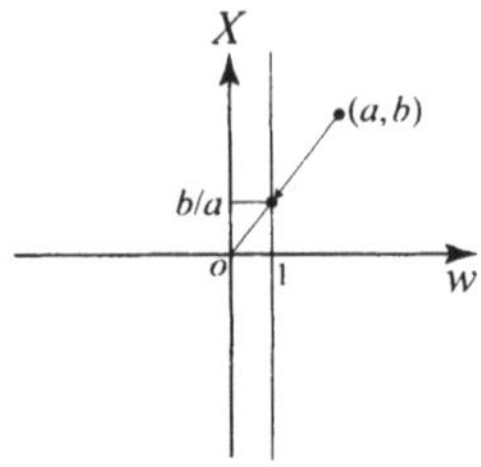

Figure 6.6: Performing a division is a perspective projection of a point in $\mathbf{E}^2$.

We are inclined to think that a perspective projection appears only when we generate pictures in the very end of all process. As understood in the descriptions above, however, we very often come across the generalized projective transformations.

Therefore we desire that all the theories, algorithms, geometry definitions and computations are not badly influenced, and furthermore all the numerical data are not deteriorated under the generalized projective transformations in computer aided geometric design. This can be considered another expression of dispensing with division operations or perspective projections.

Part II

Presentation of a Solution –Four-dimensional Processing–

Chapter 7

A Solution

As a solution of resolving the various problems encountered in Part I, we shall propose "Totally Four-dimensional Geometric Processing," or "Four-dimensional Processing" in short. In Part II, we shall describe the various techniques of this processing method in detail.

In this chapter we give an introduction to the Totally Four-dimensional Geometric Processing.

7.1 Definition of Four-dimensional Processing

In this section we shall define the concept of the Four-dimensional Processing. It is summarized as follows:

1. **Geometric definitions**

   Geometric elements are defined as ones in either classical projective space $\mathbf{P}^3$ or two-sided space $\mathbf{T}^3$ [1]. They are, however, defined, not by points in a projective space, but vectors in its associated vector space [2].

2. **Playground and processing**

   These vector space models are processed consistently in its associated vector space $\mathbf{R}^4$ throughout the whole processing,[3] where no division is ordinarily supposed to be done except in the very end where the results of the computations are finally to be interfaced to human being (see Chapter 27).

3. **Normalizations**

   Normalizations of homogeneous coordinate or coefficient data are preferably done frequently although division operations are not usually performed (see Sections 2.4 and 16.5).

---

1) For choosing these spaces appropriately, see Chapter 24.

2) In case of integer arithmetic, the notion of vector space must be generalized. See Section 16.3.

3) Note that the playground of the Four-dimensional Processing is not $^*\mathbf{R}^4$, but $\mathbf{R}^4$. The processing makes the most use of zero vector [0 0 0 0] (see Section 14.2, for example).

4. **Generalized projective invariances**

   Generalized projective invariances are pursued with respect to all the theories, algorithms, geometry definitions, computations and numerical data (see Sections 6.3 and 6.4).

5. **Duality**

   The principle of duality is made the most of both in geometry definitions and computations, and also in topology definitions and operations (see Section 7.4).

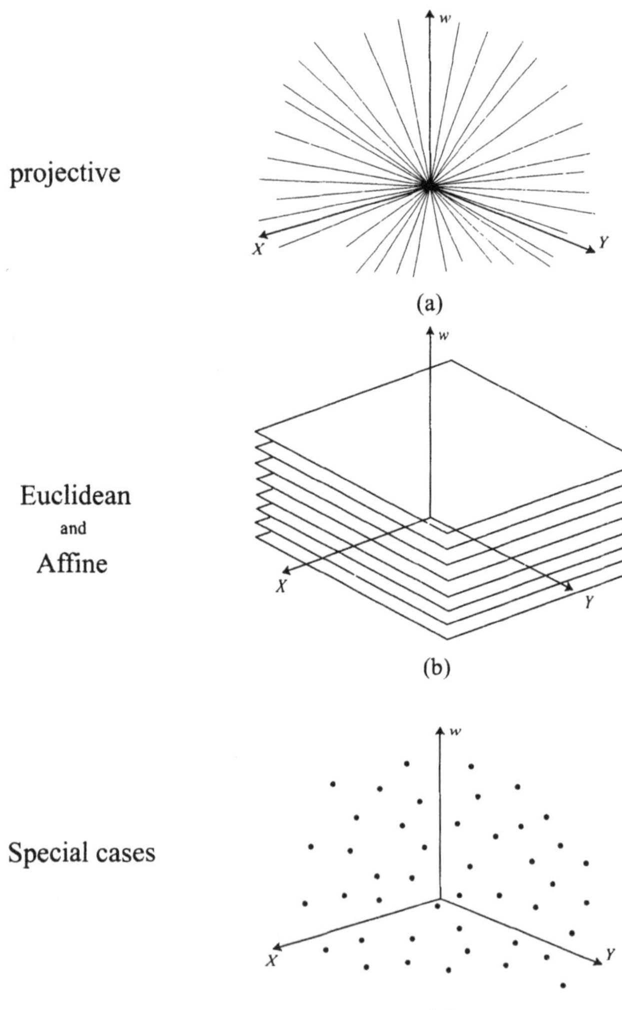

Figure 7.1: Various uses of $\mathbf{R}^4$ space ($Z=0$ section).

For the processing which is considered projective, it is done, supposing $\mathbf{R}^4$ is a set of lines passing through the origin, i.e., bundle (see Fig. 7.1(a)). Many geometric computations fall into this category.

On the other hand, for the processing which is considered Euclidean or affine, it is done, supposing $\mathbf{R}^4$ is a set of sections that represents Euclidean spaces $\mathbf{E}^3$ of different scales (see Fig. 7.1(b) and Chapter 19).

In some cases $\mathbf{R}^4$ is considered a set of points (see Fig. 7.1(c)). For example, a "simple curve" is defined by using the set of points (see Section 9.5).

The playground for the Four-dimensional Processing is not a projective space itself, but the associated vector space of the projective space. Therefore the Four-dimensional Processing is, in this respect, different from the approaches proposed by Stolfi [53] or described by Farin [17]. That is, every geometric element in the Four-dimensional Processing is defined not by points in a projective space, but by vectors in the associated vector space.

The relations among Euclidean, projective and vector spaces are shown in Fig. 7.2.

Throughout the present book, the expression "Four-dimensional Processing," which employs pre-division coordinates (i.e., homogeneous coordinates) is used in contradistinction to the conventional "Euclidean Processing" which employs post-division coordinates (i.e., Euclidean coordinates).

7.2 Theoretical Background

It seems strange that homogeneous coordinate technique has not extensively been used as expected in computer aided geometric design although it has been successfully applied to transformations [50] and clipping problems [54],[4]. The reason seems mainly to lie in the peculiar properties of the classical projective space we encounter if we play in the projective space itself (see Chapter 5).

It seems that the conventional approaches to geometric processing using homogeneous coordinates was either that some played in a projective space itself, or, that others used homogeneous coordinates without making the theoretical basis clear. Therefore, when we deal with geometric figures defined in a projective space, we must make it clear how to cope with these peculiar properties inherent particularly in the classical projective space listed in Chapter 5.

Because in the proposed processing paradigm we treat projective geometric elements, not in a projective space itself, but in the associated vector space of the projective space, we can get over most of these difficulties, as stated below:

1. **Line segment definition problem**

   As stated in Chapter 5, it is difficult to define a line segment connecting two points in a consistent manner in the classical projective geometry environment.

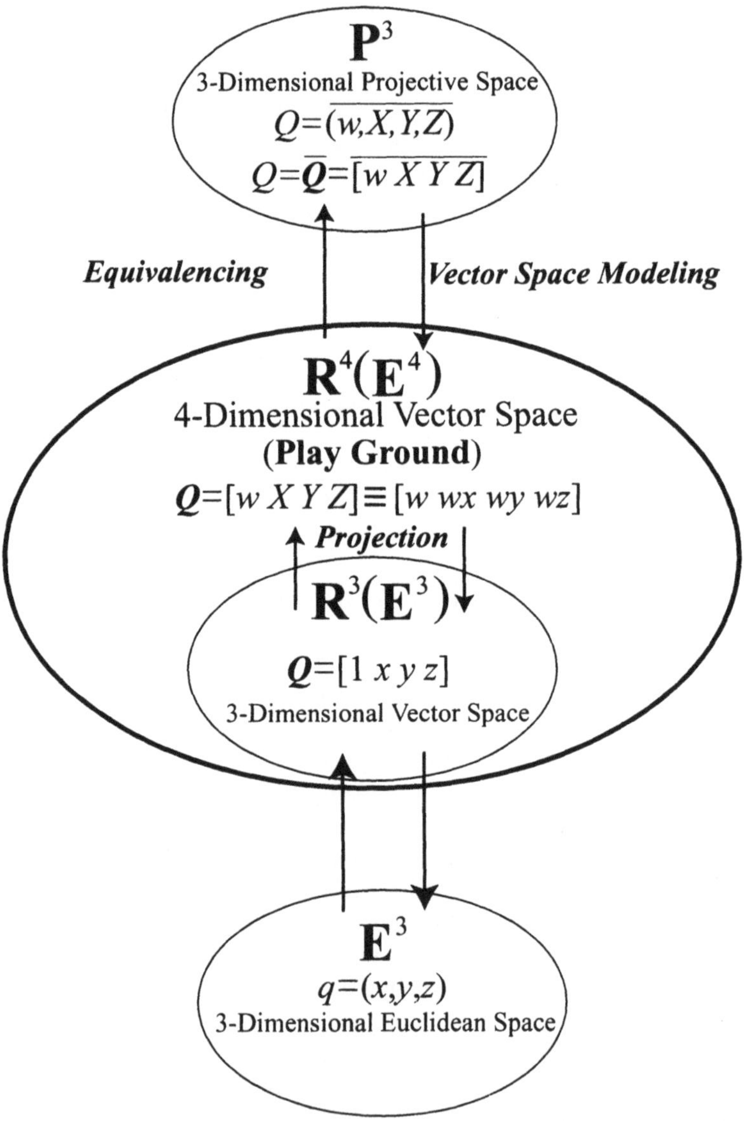

Figure 7.2: Relations among Euclidean, projective and vector spaces.

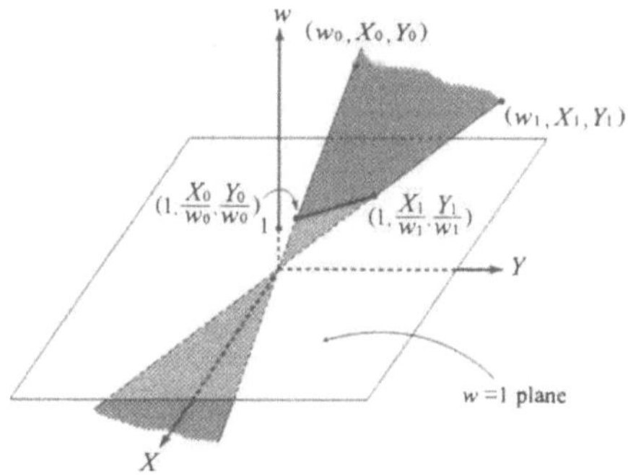

(a) internal line segment

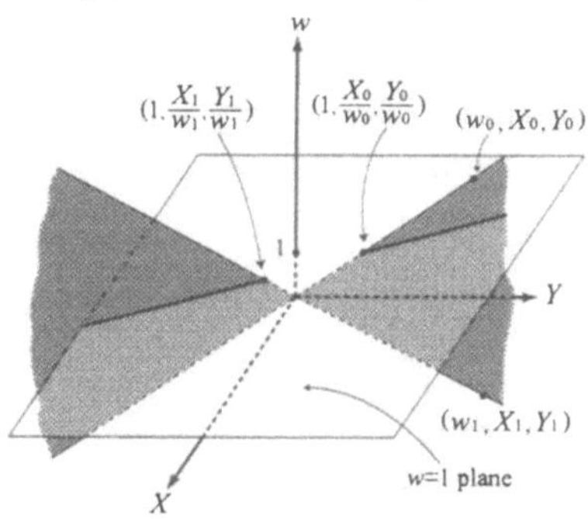

(b) external line segment

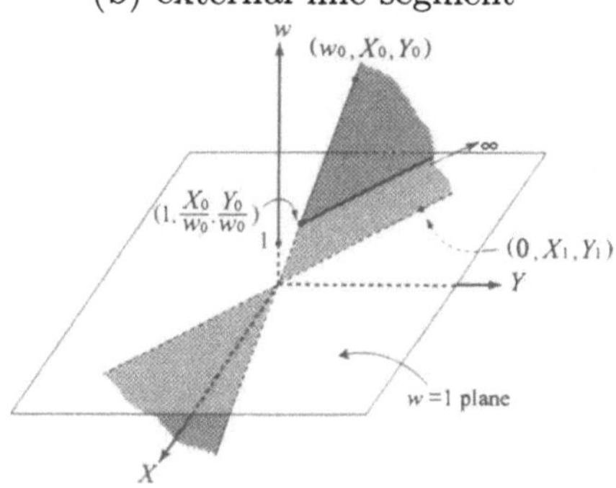

(c) half line

Figure 7.3: Definitions of three types of homogeneous line segments.

We can, however, define a line segment in classical projective space by giving two vectors $\boldsymbol{V}_0, \boldsymbol{V}_1$ corresponding to each endpoint and by making a convex combination with these vectors as shown below:

$$\overline{\boldsymbol{V}} = \overline{\xi_0 \boldsymbol{V}_0 + \xi_1 \boldsymbol{V}_1}, \ \xi_0, \xi_1 \geq 0 \ \text{ or } \ \xi_0, \xi_1 \leq 0, \ (\xi_0, \xi_1) \neq (0,0). \qquad (7.1)$$

The homogeneous line segment above passes through point $\overline{\boldsymbol{V}_0 + \boldsymbol{V}_1}$ and represents the three types of line segments depending on the signs of the weights of $\boldsymbol{V}_0$ and $\boldsymbol{V}_1$ (Fig. 7.3) [4].

In the Four-dimensional Processing, we can deal with either a line segment defined in classical projective space or in two-sided space.

2. **Non-halfspace property**

In Euclidean space a hyperplane separates the space into a region with a given point and one without it. The same is true in two-sided space. The classical projective space does not, however, possess such a half space property.

In the proposed processing approach a point V_a in classical projective plane $\mathbf{P}^2$ can be separated in $\mathbf{R}^3$ as shown below (Fig. 7.4):

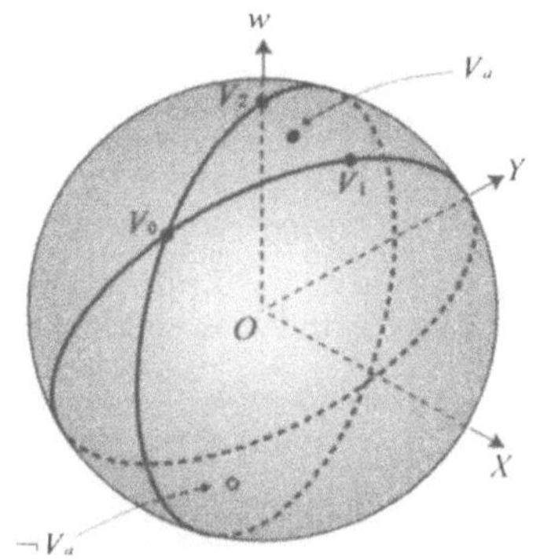

Figure 7.4: Separation of classical projective space by two hyperplanes.

In the vector space model, first, a plane (V_0, V_1, origin) is specified. At this stage the line (V_a, origin), the vector space model of V_a, exists in both

[4] As discussed in 1. of page 67, the projective line segment definition by using points V_0 and V_1 in projective space:

$$V = \xi_0 V_0 + \xi_1 V_1 \qquad (7.2)$$

does not make sense because it can not distinguish between the two arcs (see Fig. 5.1). Specification of an additional condition, for example, point at infinity, would resolve the ambiguity. This method may not be consistent, however, when one of the end points coincides with the point at infinity (half-line definition case).

On the other hand, eq.(7.1) defines a line segment in classical projective space. It is different from eq.(7.2) in that it specifies the magnitudes as well as the directions which correspond to the end points in projective space.

sides of the plane. Then we specify another plane (V_0, V_2, origin). These two planes separate the projective space into a region with the line (V_a, origin) and one without it. That is, in the spherical model of $\mathbf{R}^3$, the two lines separate the projective space into a region with the point V_a and one without it [5].

It is necessary to specify two hyperplanes to separate the classical projective space into a region with a point and one without it [1], [4].

3. **Non-orientability**

(1) While a geometric element in classical projective space does not possess its orientation (see Chapter 5), the interference detection in the proposed processing paradigm applies the concept of orientation to the vector space model (see Chapter 14).

The reason this processing is possible follows below:

The condition that a geometric element P interferes with another element Q is that there exist two such points, $V_P = \overline{(w_P, X_P, Y_P, Z_P)}$ in P and $V_Q = \overline{(w_Q, X_Q, Y_Q, Z_Q)}$ in Q as satisfy:

$$V_P = kV_Q, \quad k \neq 0. \tag{7.3}$$

The relation above is equivalent to:

$$\boldsymbol{V}_P = k\boldsymbol{V}_Q, \quad k \neq 0, \tag{7.4}$$

which expresses P and Q have a common line through the origin in the associated vector space. That is, the interference relation between geometric elements in classical projective space is equivalent to that between these vector space models (Fig. 7.5).

Therefore we can make use of the property of orientation of the associated vector space in interference detections between the vector space models of classical projective space.

(2) Note that the polygons and polyhedra defined in classical projective space in the proposed paradigm are orientable although the projective plane and projective three-space are not orientable respectively.

As discussed in Section 9.4, the polygons and polyhedra are defined in the paradigm such that they are orientable regions in the two types of divided regions in a projective plane or projective three-space respectively.

4. **Vector operation problem**

---

[5] The region with the point is expressed as follows:

$$(S_{a20}, S_{a01} \geq 0) \vee (S_{a20}, S_{a01} \leq 0).$$

As for S_{a20}, S_{a01}, see Section C.3.

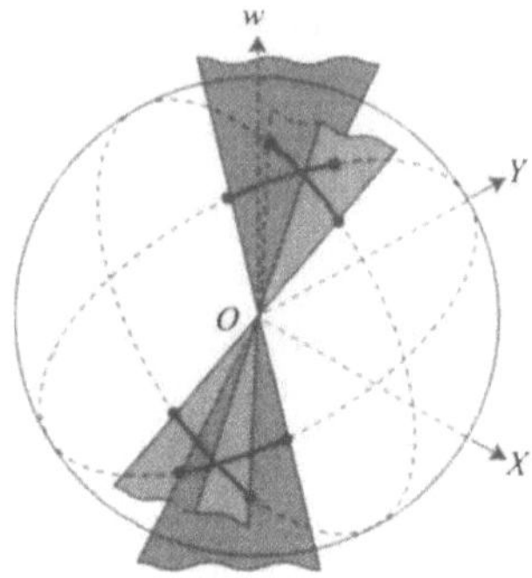

Figure 7.5: Geometric interference relationship.

Projective space does not possess a vector space structure. In the proposed Four-dimensional Processing, however, all types of geometric computations are done in the associated vector space $\mathbf{R}^4$, not in a projective space $\mathbf{P}^3$ or $\mathbf{T}^3$ itself. Therefore vector operations can be performed in the proposed processing paradigm. We can define homogeneous geometric elements by the use of the vector operation property as we can do Euclidean geometric elements (see Chapters 8 and 9).

7.3 Further Concepts of the Processing

Below we shall further explain the Four-dimensional Processing.

As we have seen in previous chapters, there are two kinds of homogeneous coordinates: signed and unsigned, representing classical projective space and two-sided space, respectively. Each has its advantages and disadvantages from the standpoint of computer aided geometric design, and they are both used accordingly depending on the specific application at hand (see Chapter 24). Consequently, there are basically two kinds of processing: one based on projective notions and properties existing in classical projective geometry, and one based on those in oriented projective geometry.

The author strongly advocates the Four-dimensional Processing in place of the conventional Euclidean processing if one wants to look for techniques for higher quality computer aided geometric design, and in this book, Four-dimensional Processing is taken to its logical conclusion, that is, "Totally" Four-dimensional Geometric Processing. By carrying out homogenization to its fullest extent, its maximum benefit can be derived. The expression "total" involves four aspects:

The first concerns the definitions of geometric elements:

1. Four-dimensional geometric elements expressed in vectors by homogeneous coordinates of points [6] and those expressed in vectors by homoge-

[6] Four-dimensional geometric elements include homogeneous lines, homogeneous line seg-

neous coefficients of planes (see Chapters 8 and 9) are dealt with. These two types of geometric elements form a dual relation.

2. Rational polynomial curves and surfaces are expressed in ordinary polynomial representation in terms of four-dimensional vectors (see Chapters 10 and 11). The representation includes that of ordinary polynomial curves or surfaces as special cases.

3. Homogenization is extended to parameters expressing curves and surfaces as well, i.e., homogeneous parameters are often used (see Sections 8.6 and 15.7).

The second concerns the topological representation of geometric figures [7]:

1. Three dimensional non-manifold solids are dealt with, in which the multiplicities of vertex- and edge-loops are allowed in addition to that of face-loops (see Sections 17.6, 18.3.3 and 20.5).

2. A new form of data structure called the quarter-edge data structure which is suited to dual processing is employed to represent incident relationships between elements in a geometric figure (see Section 18.3).

The geometric figures mentioned above are considered to be much more general than the Euclidean counterparts.

The third concerns geometric computations.

1. Computations are carried out consistently in four-dimensional space from beginning to end, i.e., from the first computational step, modeling, to the final step, generation of display data, and there is usually no computation in between that is performed in three-dimensional Euclidean space.

   Divisions are ordinarily carried out only when data are converted back to Euclidean ones at the very end after all other computations have been completed (see Chapter 27). This is illustrated in Fig. 7.6.

2. Curves and surfaces are processed in a unified manner whether rational or irrational; in other words, both ordinary and rational polynomial curves and surfaces are processed as homogeneous curves and surfaces represented in ordinary polynomial forms.

3. Transformations are performed by the homogeneous matrix method [8], while interference tests are performed by the homogeneous determinant

---

ments, homogeneous planes, homogeneous triangles, homogeneous polygons, homogeneous tetrahedra, homogeneous polyhedra, homogeneous curves and homogeneous surfaces.

[7] Geometric figures are considered to consist of geometric elements in this book.

[8] The technique of carrying out a three-dimensional projective transformation by taking the product of a four-dimensional homogeneous coordinate vector and 4×4 matrix has been employed in computer graphics from early on. That is,

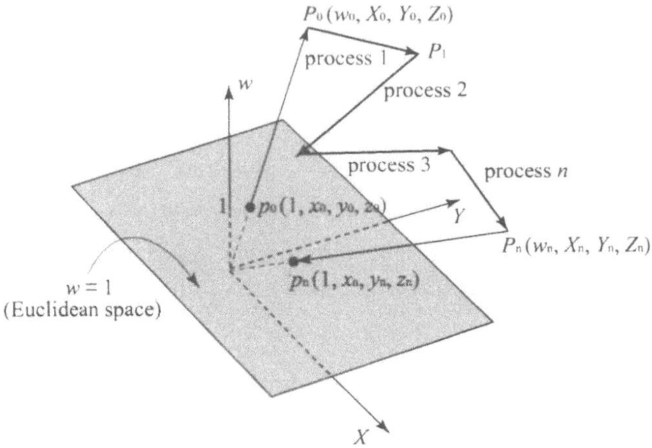

Figure 7.6: Processing is carried out consistently in $\mathbf{R}^4$ ($Z=0$ cross section).

method [9].

The fourth concerns topological operations of geometric figures.

1. Topological operations are based on the modified Euler formula, which is suited for dual processing (see Section 17.6).

2. Topological operations employ new dual Euler operators that make dual processing possible (see Chapter 18).

This book strongly argues the Four-dimensional Processing. Some problems may be nonetheless purely Euclidean. Determining the volume of a solid, for instance, is one such example. For dealing with Euclidean quantities or affine concepts, see Chapter 19.

$$\overline{[w\ X\ Y\ Z]\begin{bmatrix} s & t_x & t_y & t_z \\ p & a & b & c \\ q & d & e & f \\ r & g & h & i \end{bmatrix}} = \overline{[w^*\ X^*\ Y^*\ Z^*]}.$$

For a detailed discussion, see Section 6.1.

[9] The homogeneous determinant method is a method that employs 2×2, 3×3 and 4×4 determinants to carry out geometric computations such as interference tests. For example, the 4×4 determinants consist of type-S, based on the homogeneous coordinates of four points V_0, V_1, V_2 and V_3, and type-T, based on homogeneous coefficients of four planes, γ_0, γ_1, γ_2 and γ_3; the two types form a dual relation. The type-S and -T are shown below.

$$S_{0123} = \begin{vmatrix} w_0 & X_0 & Y_0 & Z_0 \\ w_1 & X_1 & Y_1 & Z_1 \\ w_2 & X_2 & Y_2 & Z_2 \\ w_3 & X_3 & Y_3 & Z_3 \end{vmatrix}, \qquad T_{0123} = \begin{vmatrix} a_0 & a_1 & a_2 & a_3 \\ b_0 & b_1 & b_2 & b_3 \\ c_0 & c_1 & c_2 & c_3 \\ d_0 & d_1 & d_2 & d_3 \end{vmatrix}.$$

For a detailed discussion, see Chapters 13 and 14.

7.4 Principle of Duality

Classical projective space and two-sided space share the notable feature that the principle of duality holds in a strict sense.

Definition 7.1 (Principle of duality)
In classical projective space as well as two-sided space, if some given proposition is true, then the proposition which results by interchanging a point in the given proposition with a hyperplane, a hyperplane with a point, and any notion with its dual notion is also true. This property is called the principle of projective duality or, simply, the principle of duality.

Let us look at an example.
In projective plane, it holds that

"two distinct points define a line;"

meanwhile, its dual proposition:

"two distinct lines define a point,"

also holds.

In the Euclidean plane, however, while the first proposition holds, the second does not, since there is no intersecting point if the two lines are parallel.

Let us now examine duality in projective plane in terms of algebra. Let $V_0 = \overline{(w_0, X_0, Y_0)}$ and $V_1 = \overline{(w_1, X_1, Y_1)}$ be the homogeneous coordinates of two distinct points. The homogeneous coefficients of the line γ that passes these points are given by:

$$\gamma = \overline{(X_0Y_1 - X_1Y_0,\ Y_0w_1 - Y_1w_0,\ X_1w_0 - X_0w_1)^T}. \tag{7.5}$$

Meanwhile, let $\gamma_0 = \overline{(a_0, b_0, c_0)^T}$ and $\gamma_1 = \overline{(a_1, b_1, c_1)^T}$ be the homogeneous coefficients of two distinct lines. Then the homogeneous coordinates of the intersecting point of the two lines are given by:

$$V = \overline{(b_0c_1 - b_1c_0,\ c_0a_1 - c_1a_0,\ b_1a_0 - b_0a_1)}. \tag{7.6}$$

That is, equations (7.5) and (7.6) form a dual relationship. Note that (7.6) expresses as well the intersection point for two parallel lines when $b_0c_1 - b_1c_0 = 0$. That is, the intersection point is the point at infinity in the direction of the lines.

Two notions that form a dual are called *dual notions*. A notion that forms a dual with itself is called a *self-dual notion*. For example, the Euler operators **mvfls** and **kvfls** discussed in Chapter 18 are both self-dual operators. Table 7.1 presents a few dual notions.

In conventional Euclidean processing, the duality which seems to hold, either in geometric computations or topological operations, is an imperfect one. For

Table 7.1: Some examples of dual notions.

Examples of dual notions	**Duality**
Point $\Leftrightarrow$ Plane	$\overline{(w,X,Y,Z)} \Leftrightarrow \overline{(a,b,c,d)^T}$
Join $\Leftrightarrow$ Meet	$A \cup (\neg B) = \neg(A \cup B) \Leftrightarrow A \cap (\neg B) = \neg(A \cap B)$
Vacuum $\Leftrightarrow$ Universe	$\Lambda \cup A = A \Leftrightarrow \Upsilon \cap A = A$
Rank $\Updownarrow$ Corank	$rank(A \cup B) = rank(A) + rank(B)$ $\Updownarrow$ $corank(A \cap B) = corank(A) + corank(B)$
Coplanarity $\Leftrightarrow$ Concurrency	$S_{0123} = 0 \Leftrightarrow T_{0123} = 0$ (see Section 14.3)
Homogeneous line segment $\Updownarrow$ Dual homogeneous line segment	$\overline{\boldsymbol{V}} = \overline{\xi_0 \boldsymbol{V}_0 + \xi_1 \boldsymbol{V}_1}, \xi_0, \xi_1 \geq 0, (\xi_0, \xi_1) \neq (0,0)$ $\Updownarrow$ $\overline{\boldsymbol{\gamma}} = \overline{\xi_0 \boldsymbol{\gamma}_0 + \xi_1 \boldsymbol{\gamma}_1},\quad \xi_0, \xi_1 \geq 0,\ (\xi_0, \xi_1) \neq (0,0)$ (see Section 9.2)

this reason, there were few attempts to make active use of duality. The proposed Four-dimensional Processing, on the other hand, is notable in that duality holds strictly.

Thanks to duality, the derivation of a conditional expression or theoretical equation automatically carries with it the derivation of the conditional expression or theoretical equation for its dual problem as well. This means that, using duality, it is possible to construct a theoretical system that is more organized and more self-contained compared to conventional, non-dual ones.

Duality plays an important role in practical program development as well. For instance, geometric elements that form dual relations can be represented with identical memory sizes, while their memories can be managed by a common system.

Furthermore, in the Four-dimensional Processing, a single geometric algorithm can be used for two dual problems. By achieving complete duality, therefore, the number of programs can be cut down to approximately one-half.

Duality is thus highly useful in producing streamlined, highly structured and easy-to-understand systems in program development as well.

7.5 Projective Invariance of the Processing

From the discussion of Chapter 6, we desire that all the theories, algorithms, geometric definitions, computations and numerical data are invariant under the generalized projective transformations in our processing paradigm.

Generally speaking the present CAGD techniques are insufficient even in supporting ordinary projective invariance. Therefore much computations have to be carried out in some cases, or complexities of processing are invited in others.

In the following we outline the projective invariances of the Four-dimensional Processing in comparison to the invariances of the conventional Euclidean processing.

1. **Definition of line segment**

   An ordinary (or internal) line segment could be transformed into a half line or external line segment by a projective transformation as discussed before (Fig. 1.5). The conventional Euclidean equation can not represent such three types of line segments in a single, unified form. That is, it is not invariant under projective transformation.

   A line segment in the Four-dimensional Processing, on the other hand, is defined by a convex combination of two vectors, $\boldsymbol{V}_0$ and $\boldsymbol{V}_1$, corresponding to the homogeneous coordinates of two end points (see Section 8.6) (classical projective space case):

$$\overline{\boldsymbol{V}} = \overline{\xi_0 \boldsymbol{V}_0 + \xi_1 \boldsymbol{V}_1}, \quad (\xi_0, \xi_1 \geq 0) \vee (\xi_0, \xi_1 \leq 0), \quad (\xi_0, \xi_1) \neq (0, 0). \tag{7.7}$$

   Eq.(7.7) represents the three types of line segments depending on the combinations of the signs of w-components of $\boldsymbol{V}_0$ and $\boldsymbol{V}_1$.

   In the associated vector space, the line segment, which we call *homogeneous line segment*, represents a wedge-shaped region, whose cut by $w = 1$ plane represents a Euclidean line segment (Fig. 7.3). It is also evident from Fig. 7.3 that the shape of the wedge-shaped region is invariant under projective transformation while the cut of the region is not.

2. **Definition of curves**

   A rational curve is defined as follows:

$$\boldsymbol{p}(t) = [x(t)\ y(t)\ z(t)] = \frac{\sum A_{j,M}(t) w_j \boldsymbol{q}_j}{\sum A_{j,M}(t) w_j}, \quad \boldsymbol{q}_j = [x_j\ y_j\ z_j]. \tag{7.8}$$

   A rational curve is defined in Euclidean space in eq.(7.8) just as an ordinary curve. Since projective transformation of a Euclidean point is not linear, a rational curve as well as an ordinary curve does not enjoy projective invariance although they can do affine invariance.

This means that we cannot perspectively transform such a curve by perspectively transforming the control points in Euclidean way and then computing the curve. We must repeat to generate each point on the curve and to perspectively transform the point in Euclidean way, which would be computationally very expensive [16].

A curve in the Four-dimensional Processing, which we call *homogeneous curve*, on the other hand, is defined in four-dimensional associated vector space in an ordinary polynomial form such that

$$\overline{\boldsymbol{P}(t)} = \overline{[w(t)\ X(t)\ Y(t)\ Z(t)]} = \overline{\sum A_{j,M}(t)\boldsymbol{Q}_j}, \qquad (7.9)$$
$$\boldsymbol{Q}_j = [w_j\ X_j\ Y_j\ Z_j].$$

A homogeneous curve has the representational capability of a rational curve.

Since projective transformation of homogeneous coordinate vector is linear, a homogeneous curve enjoys the projective invariance without any condition (see Section 10.4).

This means that we can simplify the perspective transformation of a curve by first perspectively transforming the control vectors of the curve in the homogeneous way, and then computing the curve. This homogeneous process is more efficient than the conventional Euclidean approach.

3. **Interference tests**

   In the Euclidean Processing, geometric element definitions are not projectively invariant, and thus the interference detections using the definitions are not, either.

   In the Four-dimensional Processing, on the other hand, the interference detections are projectively invariant based on the projectively invariant geometric definitions. For example, the interference condition of two line segments is derived, using eq.(7.7):

$$(S_{01ab} = 0) \wedge (\boldsymbol{F}_{01a} \cdot \boldsymbol{F}_{01b},\ \boldsymbol{F}_{ab0} \cdot \boldsymbol{F}_{ab1} \leq 0), \qquad (7.10)$$

   where S_{01ab} is a 4×4 determinant by homogeneous coordinates of points V_0, V_1, V_a, V_b, which is Plücker coordinate of three-space. $\boldsymbol{F}_{01a}$ is a four dimensional vector whose components are 3×3 determinants by homogeneous coordinates of points V_0, V_1, V_a, which is a vector of Plücker coordinates of plane.

   Eq.(7.10) applies to the six cases of line segment intersections, shown in Fig. 7.7, in a unified way.

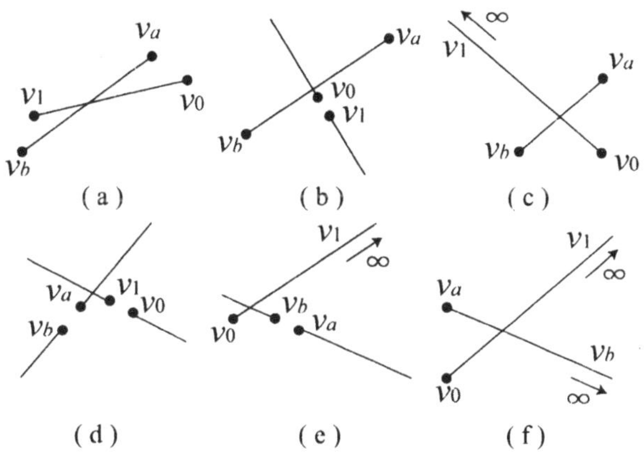

Figure 7.7: Six cases of line segment intersections.

In the Four-dimensional Processing, projective invariance is naturally satisfied, which is more general than affine invariance, while the affine invariance must be maintained with a condition attached in the conventional Euclidean Processing (see Section A.4).

In Section 6.3 we generalized the projective transformation such that it does not need to be invertible, i.e., it includes the perspective projections discussed in Section 6.4. Since there is no such perspective projections in the Four-dimensional Processing except at the very end of the whole processing, the Four-dimensional Processing can enjoy the generalized projective invariance.

7.6 Introductory Four-dimensional Processing

Prior to discussing, in detail, the Four-dimensional Processing in subsequent chapters, it would be better to explain here the basics of the processing in associated vector space $\mathbf{R}^3$ or $\mathbf{R}^4$.

In the Four-dimensional Processing, we deal with geometric elements defined either in classical projective space or two-sided space. For instance, a homogeneous line segment in classical projective space is defined as follows, by specifying three-, or four-dimensional vectors by the homogeneous coordinates of the end points, depending upon whether we are defining a planar or spatial line segment:

$$\overline{\boldsymbol{P}(\xi_0, \xi_1)} = \overline{\xi_0 \boldsymbol{Q}_0 + \xi_1 \boldsymbol{Q}_1}, \tag{7.11}$$

$$(\xi_0, \xi_1 \geq 0) \ \vee \ (\xi_0, \xi_1 \leq 0), \tag{7.12}$$

$$(\xi_0, \xi_1) \neq (0, 0). \tag{7.13}$$

Eq.(7.11) has two parameters, ξ_0 and ξ_1. That is, the line segment is homogenized not only with respect to the coordinate, but also to the parameter.

Eq.(7.12) represents the condition for a line segment of classical projective space while eq.(7.14) does the one for two-sided space:

$$\xi_0, \xi_1 \geq 0. \tag{7.14}$$

Eq.(7.13) represents that homogeneous coordinates and homogeneous parameters can not assume all zeros (see Definition 2.1).

Note that in eq.(7.11) a line segment is defined in terms of vectors, not points in classical projective space. As discussed repeatedly before, we can not define a line segment as below (see 7. of Section 2.2 and 1. in Chapter 5):

$$P(\xi_0, \xi_1) = \xi_0 Q_0 + \xi_1 Q_1. \tag{7.15}$$

The line segment definition in eq.(7.11) shows that homogeneous geometric elements are defined in terms of a vector operation in the associated vector space. Not only homogeneous geometric elements are defined thus, but their geometric processing is also carried out in the vector space associated with classical projective or two-sided space.

The associated vector space $\mathbf{R}^3$ or $\mathbf{R}^4$ is really the main playground in the proposed processing paradigm (see Fig. 7.2).

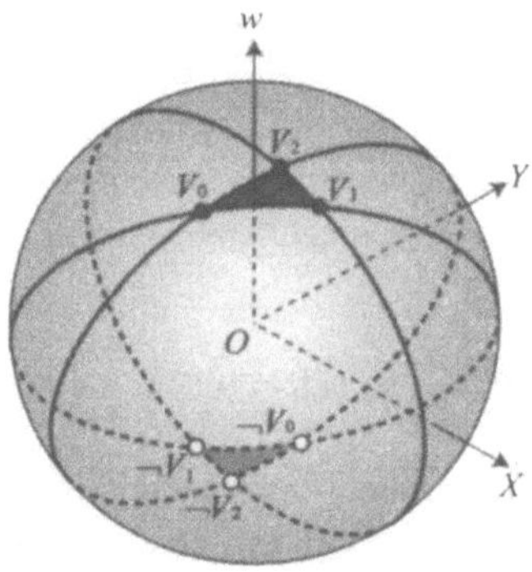

Figure 7.8: Antipodal element.

Suppose that some geometric element G has been defined in the spherical model. Then, the geometric element consisting of antipodal points to all points of G is called the *antipodal element* of G, and is denoted by $\neg G$ (see Fig. 7.8). The antipodal elements of line segment V_0V_1, triangle $V_0V_1V_2$ and tetrahedron $V_0V_1V_2V_3$ are denoted by $\neg V_0 \neg V_1$, $\neg V_0 \neg V_1 \neg V_2$ and $\neg V_0 \neg V_1 \neg V_2 \neg V_3$, respectively.

In classical projective space, no distinction is made between a geometric element G and its antipodal element $\neg G$, which are considered to be the same entity. In contrast, G and $\neg G$ are treated as different entities in two-sided space, where they belong to different ranges, one to the front and the other to the back ranges, respectively.

Another important difference between geometric elements in classical projective space and those in two-sided space is that the former has no orientation associated with them, whereas the latter does.

When dealing with a homogeneous geometric element one must take into account the differences between classical projective and two-sided spaces about how to deal with its orientation and antipodal element.

In classical projective space case, however, we have to be careful about how to deal with antipodal elements and the non-orientability. As stated above the main playground in the proposed processing paradigm is the associated vector space $\mathbf{R}^3$ or $\mathbf{R}^4$. These properties mentioned above are represented distinguishably in $\mathbf{R}^3$ or $\mathbf{R}^4$ although they are not finally distinguished in classical projective space.

Let us explain this by taking an example. Suppose that we partition a triangle $V_0V_1V_2$ by a point V_a on the plane of the triangle.

We must consider the following items:

1. We need to take the orientations of the triangle in $\mathbf{R}^3$ into account in testing whether V_a is contained in the triangle $V_0V_1V_2$ or $\neg V_0\neg V_1\neg V_2$ (see 1. of Section 14.4.1 and 1. of Section 14.4.3).

2. When V_a is found to be in the triangle, there are two possibilities: V_a is either in $V_0V_1V_2$ or in $\neg V_0\neg V_1\neg V_2$ in the associated vector space. Thus we need to take both $V_0V_1V_2$ and its antipodal triangle into account.

3. Considering subsequent processing will be done, it is advisable to use V_a as the partitioning point when V_a is in $V_0V_1V_2$, but to use $\neg V_a$ when in $\neg V_0\neg V_1\neg V_2$.

As shown in the example above, we need to take into account the orientations as well as antipodals of geometric elements in processing in $\mathbf{R}^3$ or $\mathbf{R}^4$ even if we deal with geometric elements defined in classical projective space.

Chapter 8

Geometric Definitions in General

Processing in computer aided geometric design involves various geometric elements, including straight lines, line segments, curves, curve segments, planes, triangles, polygons, curved surfaces, surface patches, polyhedra, etc.

We shall discuss five ways of representing these geometric elements mathematically.

8.1 Explicit Function Forms

A curve on the xy-plane is expressed in terms of an explicit function as $y = f(x)$. This representational method has the following disadvantages:

1. The equation is not symmetric with respect to x and y, and so they are not treated equally; that is, y is subordinate to x.

2. Wherever the curve's slope parallels the y-axis, dy/dx becomes infinity at that point, thereby complicating matters.

3. When a line parallel to the y-axis meets the curve at two or more points, $f(x)$ is multi-valued for a single x-value.

Due to such fundamental problems, explicit functions of the form $y = f(x)$ are not often used in computer aided geometric design.

8.2 Parametric Function Forms

The second method employs parameters. A point on a geometric element is represented by a vector, its components consisting of the positional coordinates of that point; each coordinate, in turn, is expressed as an explicit function (i.e., a polynomial) involving some parameter.

The reader is expected to understand from the descriptions of this section that the homogeneous geometric elements including homogeneous curves and surfaces, which are defined in the subsequent chapters, are natural extensions of Euclidean counterparts.

Let us consider a parametric function of a triangle. When three points $v_0(x_0, y_0, z_0)$, $v_1(x_1, y_1, z_1)$ and $v_2(x_2, y_2, z_2)$ are not collinear (i.e., are linearly independent), they define a plane (two-dimensional affine subspace). An arbitrary point $v(x, y, z)$ on the plane is represented by the following equation:

$$\boldsymbol{v} = \xi_0 \boldsymbol{v}_0 + \xi_1 \boldsymbol{v}_1 + \xi_2 \boldsymbol{v}_2, \tag{8.1}$$

$$\xi_0 + \xi_1 + \xi_2 = 1. \tag{8.2}$$

Eq.(8.1) indicates that v is the center of gravity with respect to the point set v_0, v_1, v_2, weighted by ξ_0, ξ_1, ξ_2 respectively. Points in the two-dimensional affine subspace have a 1-to-1 correspondence to the set of the three numbers:

$$(\xi_0, \xi_1, \xi_2), \quad \xi_0 + \xi_1 + \xi_2 = 1.$$

This set of numbers is called the *barycentric coordinates* (see Appendix A.3).

In eqs.(8.1) and (8.2), the set of points whose barycentric coordinates are non-negative makes up a triangle. In other words, the conditions that eq.(8.1) represents a triangle are given as:

$$\xi_0 + \xi_1 + \xi_2 = 1, \quad \xi_0 \geq 0, \ \xi_1 \geq 0, \ \xi_2 \geq 0. \tag{8.3}$$

In general, for $r+1$ linearly independent points [1], v_0, v_1, v_2, ..., v_r, in affine space, where points are respectively weighted by ξ_0, ξ_1, ξ_2, ..., ξ_r, the center of gravity v is given by:

$$\begin{cases} \boldsymbol{v} = \xi_0 \boldsymbol{v}_0 + \xi_1 \boldsymbol{v}_1 + \cdots + \xi_r \boldsymbol{v}_r, \\ \xi_0 + \xi_1 + \cdots + \xi_r = 1. \end{cases} \tag{8.4}$$

The set of all v forms an r-dimensional affine subspace. We now attach to eq.(8.4) the condition of non-negative barycentric coordinates:

$$\xi_0 \geq 0, \ \xi_1 \geq 0, \cdots, \xi_r \geq 0. \tag{8.5}$$

Under this condition, eq.(8.4) represents an r-dimensional simplex (r-simplex), for which v_0, v_1, ..., v_r are its vertices [2]. The relations described thus far are summarized in Tables 8.1 and 8.2.

By simply extending the definition of the simplex, we can now define a *convex polyhedron* as follows:

---

[1] As for linear independence of Euclidean points, see Section A.3.

[2] This definition of a simplex differs from that of Section 4.5.1. In the remainder of this book, we shall adopt the present definition.

Table 8.1: Affine subspaces by parametric functions.

Subspaces	Representations	Cond. on v_i	Cond. on coeff.
Line	$\boldsymbol{v} = \xi_0\boldsymbol{v}_0 + \xi_1\boldsymbol{v}_1$	Linearly independent	$\xi_0 + \xi_1 = 1$
Plane	$\boldsymbol{v} = \xi_0\boldsymbol{v}_0 + \xi_1\boldsymbol{v}_1 + \xi_2\boldsymbol{v}_2$	Linearly independent	$\xi_0 + \xi_1 + \xi_2 = 1$
3-space	$\boldsymbol{v} = \xi_0\boldsymbol{v}_0 + \cdots + \xi_3\boldsymbol{v}_3$	Linearly independent	$\xi_0 + \cdots + \xi_3 = 1$
r-space	$\boldsymbol{v} = \xi_0\boldsymbol{v}_0 + \cdots + \xi_r\boldsymbol{v}_r$	Linearly independent	$\xi_0 + \cdots + \xi_r = 1$

Table 8.2: Simplices expressed in parametric functions.

Simplices	Representations	Cond. on v_i	Cond. on coeff.
Line segment	$\boldsymbol{v} = \xi_0\boldsymbol{v}_0 + \xi_1\boldsymbol{v}_1$	Linearly independent	$\xi_0 + \xi_1 = 1$ $\xi_0, \xi_1 \geq 0$
Triangle	$\boldsymbol{v} = \xi_0\boldsymbol{v}_0 + \xi_1\boldsymbol{v}_1 + \xi_2\boldsymbol{v}_2$	Linearly independent	$\xi_0 + \xi_1 + \xi_2 = 1$ $\xi_0, \xi_1, \xi_2 \geq 0$
Tetrahedron	$\boldsymbol{v} = \xi_0\boldsymbol{v}_0 + \cdots + \xi_3\boldsymbol{v}_3$	Linearly independent	$\xi_0 + \cdots + \xi_3 = 1$ $\xi_0, \cdots, \xi_3 \geq 0$
r-simplex	$\boldsymbol{v} = \xi_0\boldsymbol{v}_0 + \cdots + \xi_r\boldsymbol{v}_r$	Linearly independent	$\xi_0 + \cdots + \xi_r = 1$ $\xi_0, \cdots, \xi_r \geq 0$

For v_0, v_1, v_2, ..., v_r, which are not necessarily linearly independent, consider

$$\begin{gathered} \boldsymbol{v} = \xi_0\boldsymbol{v}_0 + \xi_1\boldsymbol{v}_1 + \cdots + \xi_r\boldsymbol{v}_r, \\ \xi_0 + \xi_1 + \cdots + \xi_r = 1, \quad \xi_0 \geq 0,\ \xi_1 \geq 0, \cdots, \xi_r \geq 0. \end{gathered} \tag{8.6}$$

The set of all points, each given by the position vector $\boldsymbol{v}$ of eq.(8.6), is called the *convex polyhedron* or *convex hull* defined by $\boldsymbol{v}_0$, $\boldsymbol{v}_1$, ..., $\boldsymbol{v}_r$. A simplex is a convex polyhedron defined by linearly independent points. The vector $\boldsymbol{v}$ given by eq.(8.6) is called the *convex combination of vectors* $\boldsymbol{v}_0$, $\boldsymbol{v}_1$, ..., $\boldsymbol{v}_r$. The point v is called the *convex combination of points* v_0, v_1, ..., v_r.

The parametric representation of a curve segment is given by:

$$\begin{aligned} \boldsymbol{p}(t) &= [x(t)\ y(t)\ z(t)] \\ &= \boldsymbol{a}_n t^n + \cdots + \boldsymbol{a}_3 t^3 + \boldsymbol{a}_2 t^2 + \boldsymbol{a}_1 t + \boldsymbol{a}_0 \\ &= \sum_{j=0}^{n} \boldsymbol{a}_{n-j} t^{n-j}, \quad 0 \leq t \leq 1, \end{aligned} \tag{8.7}$$

where $\boldsymbol{a}_j = [a_{jx}\ a_{jy}\ a_{jz}]$. Curve segments are thus represented by a single parameter t.

A curve segment can be represented in the same form as a convex polyhedron, as:

$$\begin{aligned} \boldsymbol{p}(t) &= b_{0,n}(t)\boldsymbol{q}_0 + b_{1,n}(t)\boldsymbol{q}_1 + \cdots + b_{n,n}(t)\boldsymbol{q}_n \\ &= \sum_{j=0}^{n} b_{j,n}(t)\boldsymbol{q}_j, \end{aligned} \tag{8.8}$$

where

$$\sum_{j=0}^{n} b_{j,n}(t) \equiv 1, \quad b_{j,n}(t) \geq 0 \ (0 \leq t \leq 1). \tag{8.9}$$

Eq.(8.8) is known as the *Bézier curve segment* when the $b_{j,n}(t)$ represent Bernstein basis functions.

A surface patch is expressed by a polynomial of degree n for two parameters as:

$$\begin{aligned} \boldsymbol{p}(u,v) &= [x(u,v) \ y(u,v) \ z(u,v)] \\ &= \sum_{i=0}^{m}\sum_{j=0}^{n} \boldsymbol{a}_{m-i,n-j} u^{m-i} v^{n-j}, \quad 0 \leq u \leq 1, \ 0 \leq v \leq 1. \end{aligned} \tag{8.10}$$

Representing the surface patch in the same form as a convex polyhedron, we have:

$$\boldsymbol{p}(u,v) = \sum_{i=0}^{m}\sum_{j=0}^{n} b_{i,m}(u) b_{j,n}(v) \boldsymbol{q}_{ij}, \tag{8.11}$$

where

$$\sum_{i=0}^{m}\sum_{j=0}^{n} b_{i,m}(u)b_{j,n}(v) \equiv 1, \ b_{i,m}(u)b_{j,n}(v) \geq 0 \ (0 \leq u \leq 1, \ 0 \leq v \leq 1). \tag{8.12}$$

Eq.(8.11) is known as the *Bézier surface patch* when $b_{i,m}(u)$ and $b_{j,n}(v)$ represent Bernstein basis functions.

Above, we presented the convex polyhedron as an extension of the simplex, and the Bézier curve segment and Bézier surface patch as extensions of the convex polyhedron. This is summarized in Table 8.3.

Note in Tables 8.1 to 8.3 that the sum of coefficients for the linear combination of position vectors always equals unity. This is called the *condition of partition of unity* or *condition of affine invariance* (see Section 10 and Appendix A.2).

The parametric function of a curve segment can be considered to represent a mapping from a one-dimensional domain (t) onto three-dimensional space (x, y, z), while the parametric function of a surface patch represents a mapping from a two-dimensional domain (u, v) onto three-dimensional space (x, y, z).

The advantages of parametric functions are as follows:

Table 8.3: Generalization of geometric elements in parametric functions.

Elements	Representations	Cond. $\boldsymbol{v}_j$, $\boldsymbol{q}_j$, $\boldsymbol{q}_{ij}$	Cond. on coefficients
Convex polyhedron	$\boldsymbol{v} = \xi_0\boldsymbol{v}_0 + \cdots + \xi_r\boldsymbol{v}_r$	None	$\xi_0 + \cdots + \xi_r = 1$, $\xi_0, \cdots, \xi_r \geq 0$
Bézier segment	$\boldsymbol{p}(t) = \sum b_{j,n}(t)\boldsymbol{q}_j$	None	$\sum b_{j,n}(t) \equiv 1$, $b_{j,n}(t) \geq 0$
Bézier patch	$\boldsymbol{p}(\mathrm{u,v}) = \sum\sum b_{i,m}(u)b_{j,n}(v)\boldsymbol{q}_{ij}$	None	$\sum\sum b_{i,m}(u)b_{j,n}(v) \equiv 1$, $b_{i,m}(u)b_{j,n}(v) \geq 0$

1. Unlike the explicit functions discussed in Section 8.1, the coordinates are expressed on an equal basis.

2. Since the curve's slope is given by $dy/dx = \dot{y}/\dot{x}$, the direction parallel to the y-axis is simply $\dot{x} = 0$.

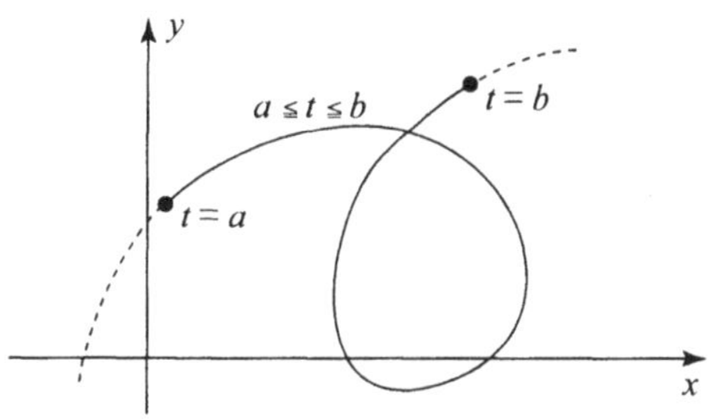

Figure 8.1: Specifying a range of a curve.

3. A range of a multi-valued curve can be indicated simply by specifying the parameter range (see Fig. 8.1). With other representational methods, however, it is generally extremely difficult to specify a range of a curve where it takes on multiple values.

4. Since each coordinate is given by an explicit function of the parameter, coordinates can be computed with ease when the parameter values are known. Parametric functions are thus suitable for displaying curves and surfaces.

5. Space curves can be expressed easily; they can be represented in the same form as planar curves by:

$$\boldsymbol{p}(t) = [x(t)\ y(t)\ z(t)].$$

In the case of space curves, $\boldsymbol{p}(\mathrm{t})$ must be of degree three or higher with respect to t. [3]

6. It is relatively easy to transform the equations of geometric elements. For example, a curve $\boldsymbol{p}^*(t)$ which has undergone affine transformation is given by:

$$\boldsymbol{p}^*(t) = \boldsymbol{p}(t) \begin{bmatrix} a & b & c \\ d & e & f \\ g & h & i \end{bmatrix} + [t_x \ t_y \ t_z]. \tag{8.13}$$

Because parametric representation has many advantages as we have seen above, parametric functions of curves and surfaces, such as Bézier curves and Bézier surfaces, are widely used in practice today.

It should be noted that conics, which are important in industrial applications, cannot be exactly represented using polynomials of the form employed above, i.e., ordinary polynomials. Thus, rational polynomials, by which conics can be expressed exactly and which has a wider expressional range, are often used. These are written as:

$$\begin{aligned} \boldsymbol{p}(t) &= [x(t) \ y(t) \ z(t)] \\ &= \frac{\boldsymbol{a}_n t^n + \cdots + \boldsymbol{a}_3 t^3 + \boldsymbol{a}_2 t^2 + \boldsymbol{a}_1 t + \boldsymbol{a}_0}{a_{nw} t^n + \cdots + a_{3w} t^3 + a_{2w} t^2 + a_{1w} t + a_{0w}}. \end{aligned} \tag{8.14}$$

In this book, however, rational curves are not treated in the form of eq.(8.14), but instead defined as ordinary polynomials using four-dimensional space vectors, as follows:

$$\begin{aligned} \boldsymbol{P}(t) &= [w(t) \ X(t) \ Y(t) \ Z(t)] \\ &= \boldsymbol{A}_n t^n + \cdots + \boldsymbol{A}_3 t^3 + \boldsymbol{A}_2 t^2 + \boldsymbol{A}_1 t + \boldsymbol{A}_0 \\ &= \sum_{j=0}^{n} \boldsymbol{A}_{n-j} t^{n-j}, \quad 0 \le t \le 1. \end{aligned} \tag{8.15}$$

where $\boldsymbol{A}_j = [a_{jw} \ a_{jx} \ a_{jy} \ a_{jz}]$ and $\boldsymbol{P}(t) = [w(t) \ X(t) \ Y(t) \ Z(t)]$ are vectors in four-dimensional vector space (for a detailed discussion, see Chapter 10).

In addition to rational curves, line segments, triangles and tetrahedra are consistently expressed by homogeneous coordinates throughout this book (see Section 9.2).

When line segments, triangles, curves and surfaces are all represented by a four-dimensional vector $\boldsymbol{P}(\mathrm{t})$, the affine transformation is given by:

$$\boldsymbol{P}^*(t) = \boldsymbol{P}(t) \begin{bmatrix} 1 & t_x & t_y & t_z \\ 0 & a & b & c \\ 0 & d & e & f \\ 0 & g & h & i \end{bmatrix}, \tag{8.16}$$

3) See, for example, p.41 of [58].

which is a simpler form than that of eq.(8.13).

Not only affine transformations, but the more general projective transformations can also be written in this simple form as:

$$\overline{\boldsymbol{P}^{4}(t)} = \boldsymbol{P}(t) \overline{\begin{bmatrix} s & t_x & t_y & t_z \\ p & a & b & c \\ q & d & e & f \\ r & g & h & i \end{bmatrix}}. \tag{8.17}$$

(see Section 6.1 for a discussion on transformations)

By using eq.(8.15) instead of rational polynomials, it is possible to carry out other types of geometric processing (besides transformations) in a unified scheme using ordinary polynomials in four-dimensional space, without having to distinguish between ordinary and rational polynomials. Furthermore, this avoids certain difficulties normally encountered with rational polynomials (see Chapter 10).

8.3 Implicit Function Forms

An implicit function of a planar curve is that expressed in the form $f(x, y) = 0$. For instance, $x^2 + y^2 - 1 = 0$ is an implicit function. We now discuss features of implicit functions [25].

1. They have a very general representational capability.

   Because the explicit functions discussed in Section 8.1 can be written as $f(x) - y = 0$, they are included in implicit functions, which constitute a more general class.

   Implicit functions also possess a higher generality than rational polynomials in the form of parametric functions, which are of highly general expressional forms in themselves. This is the most notable feature of implicit functions.

   In other words, for any arbitrary rational polynomial planar curve or surface written as a parametric function, there always exists an equivalent implicit function representation. Off-setting, blending or bisecting surfaces can be written as implicit functions, although they are represented only approximately with parametric functions.

2. It is easy to test whether a point exists inside or outside of a closed curve or surface.

   This is done by simply computing the function, and checking the sign of the result.

3. It is possible to express the space enclosed by a closed curve or surface.

Not only the curve or surface proper, but the enclosed space can be expressed as well, as follows:

$$\{(x, y, z) \mid f(x, y, z) \le 0\}.$$

Meanwhile, a shortcoming of implicit functions is that various formulas become complicated, making processing cumbersome. When displaying a curve, for instance, it is often necessary to compute square roots to determine the x- and y-values.

Furthermore, space curves must be defined as the intersection of two surfaces:

$$\phi_1(x, y, z) = 0, \ \phi_2(x, y, z) = 0,$$

which could be rather cumbersome.

Since they possess features that parametric functions are lacking, however, it is quite likely that implicit functions will see increased CAGD applications in the future.

Table 8.4: Flats in join and meet operation forms.

	Flats in join		**Flats in meet**
Line	$V_0 \cup V_1 = \overline{\begin{pmatrix} w_0 & X_0 & Y_0 & Z_0 \\ w_1 & X_1 & Y_1 & Z_1 \end{pmatrix}}$	Line	$\gamma_0 \cap \gamma_1 = \overline{\begin{pmatrix} a_0 & a_1 \\ b_0 & b_1 \\ c_0 & c_1 \\ d_0 & d_1 \end{pmatrix}}$
Plane	$V_0 \cup V_1 \cup V_2 = \overline{\begin{pmatrix} w_0 & X_0 & Y_0 & Z_0 \\ w_1 & X_1 & Y_1 & Z_1 \\ w_2 & X_2 & Y_2 & Z_2 \end{pmatrix}}$	Point	$\gamma_0 \cap \gamma_1 \cap \gamma_2 = \overline{\begin{pmatrix} a_0 & a_1 & a_2 \\ b_0 & b_1 & b_2 \\ c_0 & c_1 & c_2 \\ d_0 & d_1 & d_2 \end{pmatrix}}$
3-space	$V_0 \cup V_1 \cup V_2 \cup V_3 = \overline{\begin{pmatrix} w_0 & X_0 & Y_0 & Z_0 \\ w_1 & X_1 & Y_1 & Z_1 \\ w_2 & X_2 & Y_2 & Z_2 \\ w_3 & X_3 & Y_3 & Z_3 \end{pmatrix}}$	Vacuum	$\gamma_0 \cap \gamma_1 \cap \gamma_2 \cap \gamma_3 = \overline{\begin{pmatrix} a_0 & a_1 & a_2 & a_3 \\ b_0 & b_1 & b_2 & b_3 \\ c_0 & c_1 & c_2 & c_3 \\ d_0 & d_1 & d_2 & d_3 \end{pmatrix}}$

8.4 Join and Meet Operation Forms

Given a linearly independent set of points, a flat can be defined by *join* operations. Dually a flat can also be defined by *meet* operations, given a linearly independent set of homogeneous coefficients of planes. These definitions are summarized in Table 8.4. A more detailed discussion will be given in Section 9.1.3.

8.5 Plücker Coordinate, Coefficient Forms

Homogeneous coordinate representation is a coordinate system for describing points. Plücker (or Grassman) coordinates are generalized forms of homoge-

Table 8.5: Plücker coordinates and Plücker coefficients.

	Plücker coordinates		**Plücker coefficients**
Point	$V_0 = \overline{(w_0, X_0, Y_0, Z_0)}$	Plane	$\gamma_0 = \overline{(a_0, b_0, c_0, d_0)^T}$
Line	$L_{01} = \overline{(P_{01}, Q_{01}, R_{01}, S_{01}, T_{01}, U_{01})}$ $P_{01} = \begin{vmatrix} w_0 & X_0 \\ w_1 & X_1 \end{vmatrix}$ $Q_{01} = \begin{vmatrix} w_0 & Y_0 \\ w_1 & Y_1 \end{vmatrix}$ $R_{01} = \begin{vmatrix} w_0 & Z_0 \\ w_1 & Z_1 \end{vmatrix}$ $S_{01} = \begin{vmatrix} Y_0 & Z_0 \\ Y_1 & Z_1 \end{vmatrix}$ $T_{01} = \begin{vmatrix} Z_0 & X_0 \\ Z_1 & X_1 \end{vmatrix}$ $U_{01} = \begin{vmatrix} X_0 & Y_0 \\ X_1 & Y_1 \end{vmatrix}$	Line	$\lambda_{01} = \overline{(p_{01}, q_{01}, r_{01}, s_{01}, t_{01}, u_{01})}$ $p_{01} = \begin{vmatrix} a_0 & a_1 \\ b_0 & b_1 \end{vmatrix}$ $q_{01} = \begin{vmatrix} a_0 & a_1 \\ c_0 & c_1 \end{vmatrix}$ $r_{01} = \begin{vmatrix} a_0 & a_1 \\ d_0 & d_1 \end{vmatrix}$ $s_{01} = \begin{vmatrix} c_0 & c_1 \\ d_0 & d_1 \end{vmatrix}$ $t_{01} = \begin{vmatrix} d_0 & d_1 \\ b_0 & b_1 \end{vmatrix}$ $u_{01} = \begin{vmatrix} b_0 & b_1 \\ c_0 & c_1 \end{vmatrix}$
Plane	$F_{012} = \overline{(A_{012}, B_{012}, C_{012}, D_{012})^T}$ $A_{012} = \begin{vmatrix} X_0 & Y_0 & Z_0 \\ X_1 & Y_1 & Z_1 \\ X_2 & Y_2 & Z_2 \end{vmatrix}$ $B_{012} = \begin{vmatrix} w_0 & Z_0 & Y_0 \\ w_1 & Z_1 & Y_1 \\ w_2 & Z_2 & Y_2 \end{vmatrix}$ $C_{012} = \begin{vmatrix} w_0 & X_0 & Z_0 \\ w_1 & X_1 & Z_1 \\ w_2 & X_2 & Z_2 \end{vmatrix}$ $D_{012} = \begin{vmatrix} w_0 & Y_0 & X_0 \\ w_1 & Y_1 & X_1 \\ w_2 & Y_2 & X_2 \end{vmatrix}$	Point	$\pi_{012} = \overline{(w_{012}, x_{012}, y_{012}, z_{012})}$ $w_{012} = \begin{vmatrix} b_0 & b_1 & b_2 \\ c_0 & c_1 & c_2 \\ d_0 & d_1 & d_2 \end{vmatrix}$ $x_{012} = \begin{vmatrix} a_0 & a_1 & a_2 \\ d_0 & d_1 & d_2 \\ c_0 & c_1 & c_2 \end{vmatrix}$ $y_{012} = \begin{vmatrix} a_0 & a_1 & a_2 \\ b_0 & b_1 & b_2 \\ d_0 & d_1 & d_2 \end{vmatrix}$ $z_{012} = \begin{vmatrix} a_0 & a_1 & a_2 \\ c_0 & c_1 & c_2 \\ b_0 & b_1 & b_2 \end{vmatrix}$
Three-space	$U_{0123} = \overline{(S_{0123})}$ $S_{0123} = \begin{vmatrix} w_0 & X_0 & Y_0 & Z_0 \\ w_1 & X_1 & Y_1 & Z_1 \\ w_2 & X_2 & Y_2 & Z_2 \\ w_3 & X_3 & Y_3 & Z_3 \end{vmatrix}$	Vacuum	$\tau_{0123} = \overline{(T_{0123})}$ $T_{0123} = \begin{vmatrix} a_0 & a_1 & a_2 & a_3 \\ b_0 & b_1 & b_2 & b_3 \\ c_0 & c_1 & c_2 & c_3 \\ d_0 & d_1 & d_2 & d_3 \end{vmatrix}$

neous coordinates, that is, coordinates for flats of arbitrary rank. The Plücker coefficients are the duals of Plücker coordinates. Plücker coordinates and Plücker coefficients will play important roles in the Four-dimensional Processing proposed in this book.

The signs and orders assigned to Plücker coordinates and coefficients vary with authors, and the representation employed here is one among several methods.

Plücker coordinates and coefficients are shown in Table 8.5. A more detailed discussion will be given in Section 9.1.2.

8.6 Homogeneous Parameters

Various parametric, vector-valued functions shall be presented using line segments as an example.

The parametric function $\boldsymbol{v}(t)$ of a Euclidean line segment connecting two points v_0 and v_1 is given by:

$$\boldsymbol{v}(t) = (1-t)\boldsymbol{v}_0 + t\boldsymbol{v}_1, \quad 0 \le t \le 1. \tag{8.18}$$

Using homogeneous coordinate vector representation, this is:

$$\overline{\boldsymbol{V}(t)} = \overline{(1-t)\boldsymbol{V}_0 + t\boldsymbol{V}_1}, \quad 0 \le t \le 1. \tag{8.19}$$

Here, $\boldsymbol{V}_0$ and $\boldsymbol{V}_1$ are the vectors $[w_0\ X_0\ Y_0\ Z_0]$ and $[w_1\ X_1\ Y_1\ Z_1]$, corresponding to the endpoints V_0 and V_1 of the line segment, respectively.

Eq. (8.18) expresses an ordinary line segment connecting two points. On the other hand, eq. (8.19) is a line segment equation with the two points given in homogeneous coordinates, and depending on the combination of signs of the w values of the two vectors corresponding to the end points, expresses three types of line segments, as shown in Figs. 8.2 and 8.3. Fig. 8.2 shows line segments expressed in unsigned homogeneous coordinates, i.e., those in classical projective space, whereas those in Fig. 8.3 are given in signed homogeneous coordinates, i.e., they exist in two-sided space. In each figure, an internal line segment, external line segment and half-line are shown from left to right. Eq. (8.19) thus expresses what is called a *homogeneous line segment.*

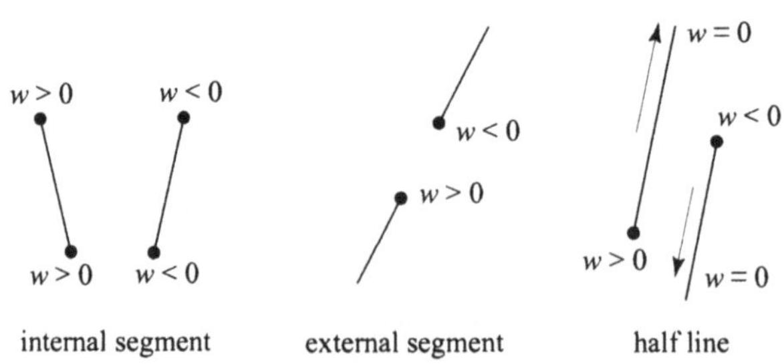

Figure 8.2: Homogeneous line segments defined in classical projective space.

The three line segment types and signs of w are related as follows (Fig. 8.4):

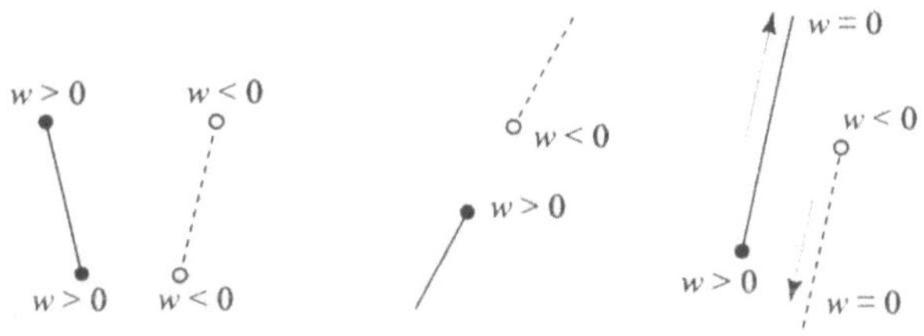

Figure 8.3: Homogeneous line segments defined in two sided space.

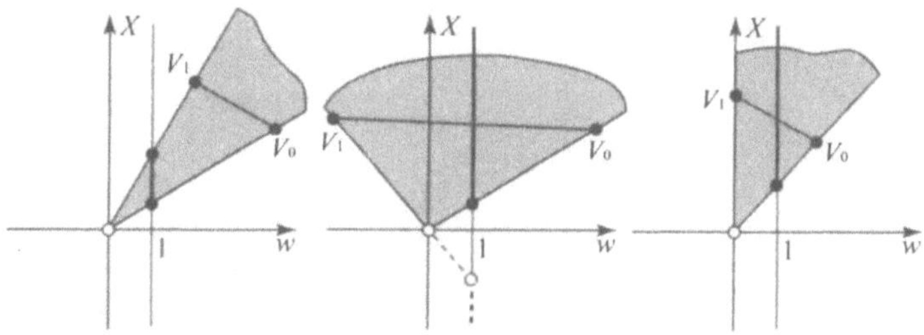

(a) internal segment (b) external segment (c) half line

Figure 8.4: Projections of homogeneous line segments (two-sided space).

- **Internal line segment**: the two vectors have w of the same sign (i.e., either both positive or both negative).
- **External line segment**: one vector has a positive w while the other has a negative.
- **Half line**: $w=0$ for one of the vectors (but not both).

Eq. (8.19) can be rewritten as follows:

$$\begin{aligned}\overline{\boldsymbol{V}(t)} &= \overline{(1-t)\boldsymbol{V}_0 + t\boldsymbol{V}_1} \\ &= \overline{(1-t)\{\boldsymbol{V}_0 + (t/(1-t))\boldsymbol{V}_1\}} \\ &= \overline{\boldsymbol{V}_0 + (t/(1-t))\boldsymbol{V}_1}, \quad 0 \le t \le 1. \end{aligned} \tag{8.20}$$

If we let $t/(1-t)$ be a new parameter and call this t instead, then

$$\overline{\boldsymbol{V}(t)} = \overline{\boldsymbol{V}_0 + t\boldsymbol{V}_1}, \quad 0 \le t \le \infty. \tag{8.21}$$

We now have an alternative parametric function with a different parameter range. Fig. 8.5 shows the parameter spaces for the two line segment equations, (8.19) and (8.21).

In addition to homogeneous coordinates of points, we are now ready to introduce homogeneous parameters [43], [56].

Figure 8.5: Two parameter ranges for a line segment.

1. **Homogeneous parameters "type-1"**

   If, in eq.(8.19), we substitute

$$t = s/h, \tag{8.22}$$

   then we have:

$$\begin{aligned} \overline{\boldsymbol{V}(t)} &= \overline{\boldsymbol{V}(h,s)} \\ &= \overline{\{1-(s/h)\}\boldsymbol{V}_0 + (s/h)\boldsymbol{V}_1} \\ &= \overline{(1/h)\{(h-s)\boldsymbol{V}_0 + s\boldsymbol{V}_1\}} \\ &= \overline{(h-s)\boldsymbol{V}_0 + s\boldsymbol{V}_1}, \end{aligned}$$

   where we assumed $h > 0$ in the last line of the equations above for the case of two-sided space.

   This is one form of homogeneous parametric functions of a homogeneous line segment; we shall call it "type-1." That is,

$$\overline{\boldsymbol{V}(h,s)} = \overline{(h-s)\boldsymbol{V}_0 + s\boldsymbol{V}_1}. \tag{8.23}$$

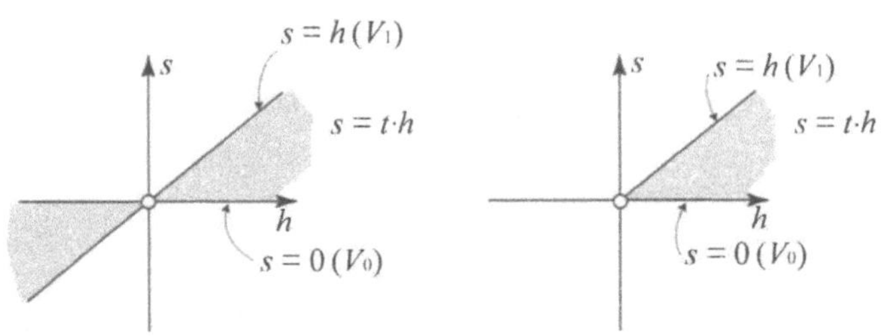

(a) parameters in projective space (b) parameters in two-sided space

Figure 8.6: Parameter spaces for homogeneous parameters "type-1."

   (a) **Homogeneous parameters for line segment in $\mathbf{P}^2$ or $\mathbf{P}^3$**

   By letting $h - s \geq 0, s \geq 0$ or $h - s \leq 0, s \leq 0$ in eq.(8.23), we have

$$(0 \leq s \leq h) \vee (h \leq s \leq 0), \tag{8.24}$$

   where $(h,s) \neq (0,0)$. The parameter space for this case is shown in Fig. 8.6(a).

(b) Homogeneous parameters for line segment in $\mathbf{T}^2$ or $\mathbf{T}^3$
By letting $h - s \geq 0, s \geq 0$ in eq.(8.23), we have

$$0 \leq s \leq h, \tag{8.25}$$

where $(h, s) \neq (0, 0)$. The parameter space for this case is shown in Fig. 8.6(b).

We now present another form of homogenous parameters.

2. **Homogeneous parameters "type-2"**
If, in eq. (8.23), we let

$$\eta = h - s, \quad \sigma = s, \tag{8.26}$$

then we have

$$\overline{\boldsymbol{V}(\eta, \sigma)} = \overline{\eta \boldsymbol{V}_0 + \sigma \boldsymbol{V}_1}. \tag{8.27}$$

We shall call this form "type-2" homogeneous parameters.
Eq. (8.27) can be rewritten as follows:

$$\begin{aligned} \overline{\boldsymbol{V}(\eta, \sigma)} &= \overline{\eta \boldsymbol{V}_0 + \sigma \boldsymbol{V}_1} \\ &= \overline{\frac{1}{\eta + \sigma}(\eta \boldsymbol{V}_0 + \sigma \boldsymbol{V}_1)} \\ &= \overline{(1 - \frac{\sigma}{\eta + \sigma})\boldsymbol{V}_0 + \frac{\sigma}{\eta + \sigma}\boldsymbol{V}_1}. \end{aligned} \tag{8.28}$$

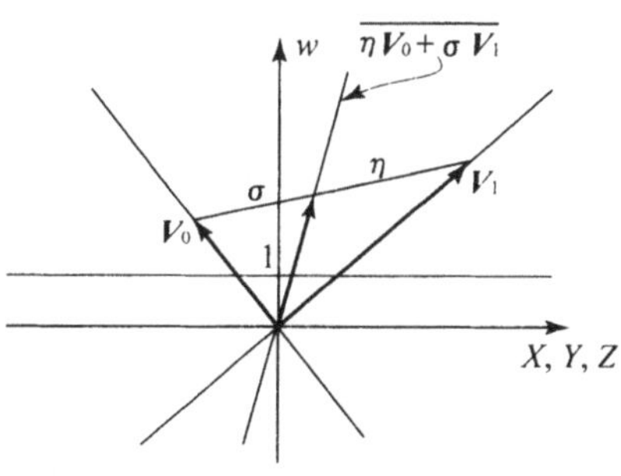

Figure 8.7: Geometric meaning of "type-2" parameters.

Note that in this derivation, we assumed $\eta + \sigma > 0$ for line segments in two-sided space.

By comparing eqs. (8.28) and (8.19), we have the relation:

$$t = \frac{\sigma}{\eta + \sigma}. \tag{8.29}$$

From a geometric viewpoint, $\overline{\boldsymbol{V}(\eta, \sigma)}$ of eq. (8.27) represents a point in projective space which corresponds in vector space to a vector that divides by the ratio $\sigma : \eta$ the line segment that connects the ends of vectors $\boldsymbol{V}_0$ and $\boldsymbol{V}_1$ (see Fig. 8.7).

(a) Homogeneous parameters for line segment in $\mathbf{P}^2$ or $\mathbf{P}^3$
By letting $h=\eta+\sigma$, $s=\sigma$ in eq. (8.24), we have

$$(\eta,\ \sigma \geq 0) \vee (\eta,\ \sigma \leq 0), \tag{8.30}$$

where $(\eta,\sigma) \neq (0,0)$.
The parameter space for this case is shown in Fig. 8.8(a).

(b) Homogeneous parameters for line segment in $\mathbf{T}^2$ or $\mathbf{T}^3$
By letting $h=\eta+\sigma$ and $s=\sigma$ in eq. (8.25), we have

$$\eta,\ \sigma \geq 0, \tag{8.31}$$

where $(\eta,\sigma) \neq (0,0)$.
The parameter space for this case is shown in Fig. 8.8(b).

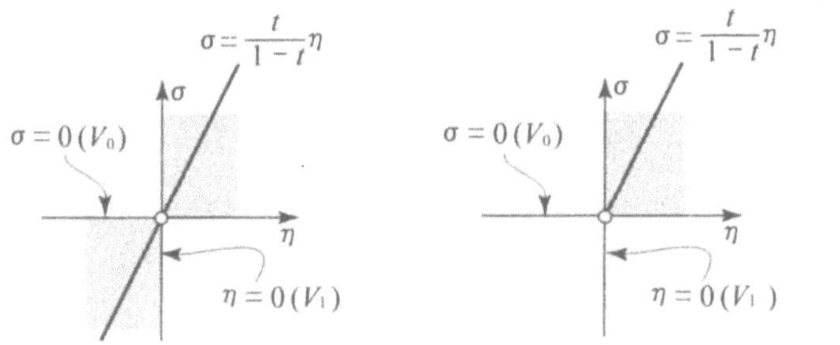

(a) parameters in projective space (b) parameters in two-sided space

Figure 8.8: Parameter spaces for homogeneous parameters "type-2."

The "type-2" homogeneous parameters are symmetric in form; another advantage is that it is possible to determine whether a point lies in the interior or exterior of a line segment, using only sign tests. Furthermore, with homogeneous parameters, it is possible to specify a point at $t=\infty$ using finite values.

In Fig. 8.9, ordinary parameter values t corresponding to homogeneous parameters are shown in both type-1 and type-2 cases. Note that the parametrizations are not uniform with respect to homogeneous parameter direction angle.

Homogeneous line segments using homogeneous parameters defined both in classical and two-sided projective spaces are shown in Fig. 8.10.

Let us examine the hyperbola given by the next equation (see Fig. 8.11):

$$\overline{\boldsymbol{P}(t)} = \overline{[w(t)\ X(t)\ Y(t)]} = \overline{[1-t^2\ \ \frac{1+t^2}{2}\ \ \sqrt{2}t]}, \tag{8.32}$$
$$(-\infty < t < +\infty).$$

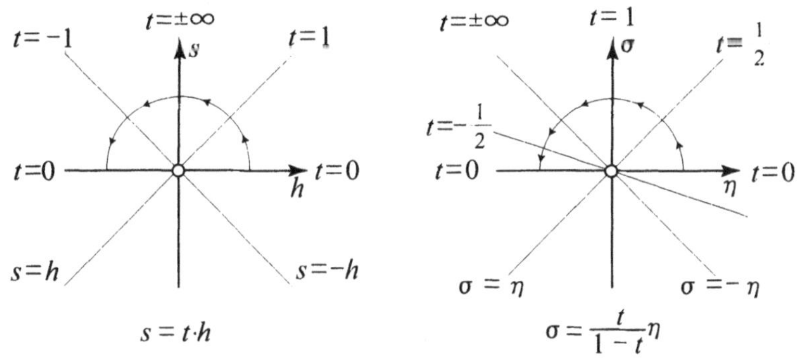

Figure 8.9: Ordinary parameter t corresponding to homogeneous parameters.

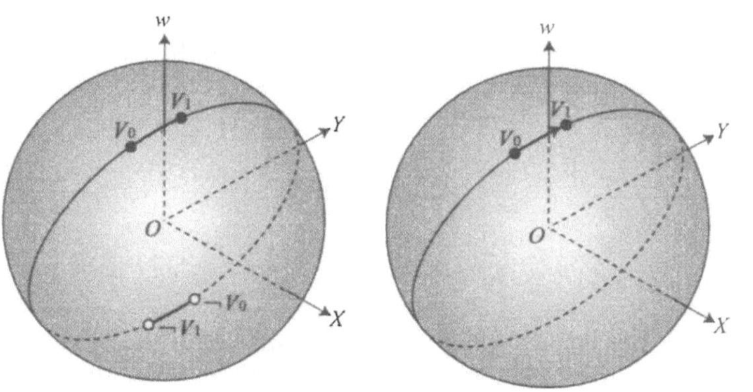

Figure 8.10: Line segments defined in classical and two-sided projective spaces.

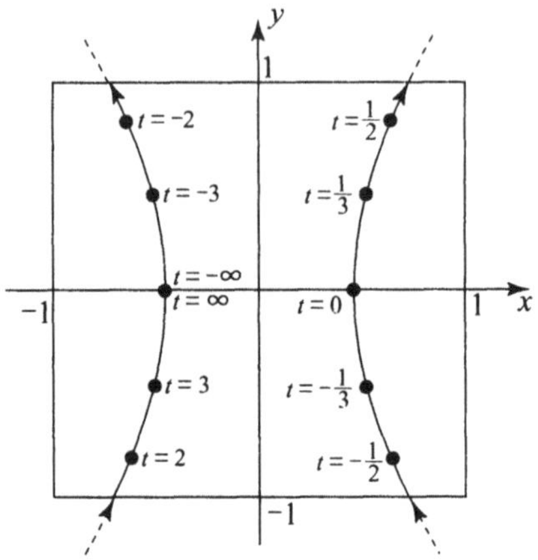

(b)

Figure 8.11: Parametric hyperbola.

By substituting the relation of eq. (8.29) to express this equation in homogeneous parameters, we obtain:

$$\begin{aligned}\overline{\boldsymbol{P}(t)} &= \overline{\boldsymbol{P}(\eta,\sigma)} \\ &= \overline{[2\eta(\eta+2\sigma) \quad (\eta+\sigma)^2+\sigma^2 \quad 2\sqrt{2}\sigma(\eta+\sigma)]}. \end{aligned} \tag{8.33}$$

From eq. (8.29), we see that $t = \infty$ is equivalent in homogeneous parameters to $\eta + \sigma = 0$. So the point on the curve for which $t = \infty$ is given, using eq. (8.33), by:

$$\begin{aligned} x &= \frac{X}{w} = \frac{\sigma^2}{-2\sigma^2} = -\frac{1}{2}, \\ y &= \frac{Y}{w} = \frac{0}{-2\sigma^2} = 0. \end{aligned}$$

The advantages of using homogeneous parameters are summarized below (note that they are much like the benefits derived from using homogeneous coordinates);

1. **Wide range of representable numbers**

   Very large and very small ordinary parameter value t can be expressed by homogeneous parameters. In particular, infinities can be treated in the same manner as finite numbers.

2. **Closed curves**

Any curve can be treated as a closed one since the parameter range can be selected as $\mathbf{P}^1$.

3. **Consistent, concise expressions of geometric elements**

   Geometric elements can be expressed in a mathematically consistent, concise manner by suitable homogeneous parameters. This is evident from the discussions in this chapter.

4. **Simplified geometric modeling**

   Containment test of a point can be done by a simple sign test when type-2 homogeneous parameters are used. This was seen earlier in this section.

5. **One degree of freedom**

   Homogeneous parameters give one degree of freedom. This property can be used for various purposes. As for an advantage of homogeneous parameters when applied to the geometric Newton-Raphson method, see Section 15.7.

6. **Exact arithmetic**

   Homogeneous parameters are useful in performing exact arithmetic. See the type-I homogenized NURBS in page 178.

Chapter 9

Geometric Element Definitions

In this chapter we discuss how to represent various types of geometric elements mathematically by using homogeneous coordinates and coefficients (more generally Plücker coordinates and coefficients). These types include flat sets [1], simplices, curves and surfaces, polygons and polyhedra. More detailed discussions on curves and surfaces will be given in Chapters 10 and 11 respectively.

These homogeneous geometric elements are defined such that they are natural extensions of Euclidean counterparts explained in the previous chapter.

9.1 Flat Sets

9.1.1 Implicit Function Forms

Two-dimensional Lines

We now determine the homogeneous coordinate representation of a line that passes two points, $V_0 = \overline{(w_0, X_0, Y_0)}$ and $V_1 = \overline{(w_1, X_1, Y_1)}$. A point is represented in the vector space model by a line going through the origin. Therefore, the line passing V_0 and V_1 is, in the vector space model, a plane that contains V_0, V_1 and the origin. If we denote by $V = \overline{(w, X, Y)}$ a point lying on the line that we seek, the line passing the origin and that point V lies on this plane. The necessary and sufficient condition for this is that three vectors, $\boldsymbol{V}$, $\boldsymbol{V}_0$ and $\boldsymbol{V}_1$, are linearly dependent (see Fig. 9.1), or

$$\begin{vmatrix} w & X & Y \\ w_0 & X_0 & Y_0 \\ w_1 & X_1 & Y_1 \end{vmatrix} = 0. \tag{9.1}$$

Eq.(9.1) is the equation of the line we seek.

[1] As for flat set, see Section 4.4.

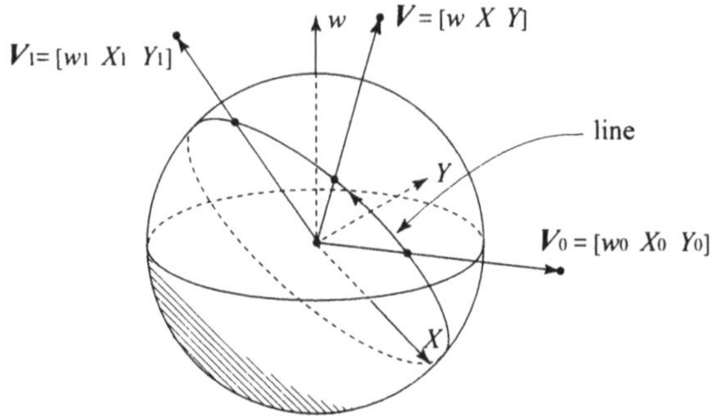

Figure 9.1: Three collinear points in the spherical and vector space models.

Alternatively, using homogeneous coefficients we have:

$$\begin{aligned} \gamma &= \overline{(a, b, c)^T} \\ &= \overline{\left(\begin{vmatrix} X_0 & Y_0 \\ X_1 & Y_1 \end{vmatrix}, - \begin{vmatrix} w_0 & Y_0 \\ w_1 & Y_1 \end{vmatrix}, \begin{vmatrix} w_0 & X_0 \\ w_1 & X_1 \end{vmatrix} \right)^T} \\ &\equiv \overline{(U_{01}, -Q_{01}, P_{01})^T}, \end{aligned} \tag{9.2}$$

where U_{01}, Q_{01}, P_{01} are Plücker coordinates of line (see Table C.1).

Or, in a determinant form,

$$\overline{\gamma} = \overline{\begin{vmatrix} \vec{i} & \vec{j} & \vec{k} \\ w_0 & X_0 & Y_0 \\ w_1 & X_1 & Y_1 \end{vmatrix}}. \tag{9.3}$$

When V_0 and V_1 are identical or antipodal points, clearly no line is defined. From eq.(9.2), we see that the homogeneous coefficients are all zero's in this case, that is:

$$\begin{vmatrix} X_0 & Y_0 \\ X_1 & Y_1 \end{vmatrix} = U_{01} = 0, \quad \begin{vmatrix} w_0 & Y_0 \\ w_1 & Y_1 \end{vmatrix} = Q_{01} = 0, \quad \begin{vmatrix} w_0 & X_0 \\ w_1 & X_1 \end{vmatrix} = P_{01} = 0. \tag{9.4}$$

Conversely, if the homogeneous coefficients are all zero's, then the two points are identical or antipodal.

Note eqs.(9.2) and (9.3) form duals with eqs.(12.2) and (12.3), respectively.

1. **Line going through point V_0 and parallel to line γ_0**

   A line that goes through the origin and that is parallel to the line $\gamma_0 = \overline{(a_0, b_0, c_0)^T}$ is given by:

$$[w\ X\ Y] \begin{bmatrix} 0 \\ b_0 \\ c_0 \end{bmatrix} = 0. \tag{9.5}$$

If this line is translated parallel-wise by moving the point corresponding to its origin to the point $V_0 = (w_0, X_0, Y_0)$, we obtain the following equation (see eq.(6.19)):

$$\boldsymbol{P} \cdot \gamma \equiv \boldsymbol{P} \cdot (\boldsymbol{T}^{-1} \begin{bmatrix} 0 \\ b_0 \\ c_0 \end{bmatrix}) = 0, \tag{9.6}$$

where

$$\boldsymbol{T} = \begin{bmatrix} w_0 & X_0 & Y_0 \\ 0 & w_0 & 0 \\ 0 & 0 & w_0 \end{bmatrix}. \tag{9.7}$$

So

$$\begin{aligned} \gamma \equiv \boldsymbol{T}^{-1} \begin{bmatrix} 0 \\ b_0 \\ c_0 \end{bmatrix} &= \begin{bmatrix} w_0 & -X_0 & -Y_0 \\ 0 & w_0 & 0 \\ 0 & 0 & w_0 \end{bmatrix} \begin{bmatrix} 0 \\ b_0 \\ c_0 \end{bmatrix} \\ &= \begin{bmatrix} -b_0 X_0 - c_0 Y_0 \\ b_0 w_0 \\ c_0 w_0 \end{bmatrix}. \end{aligned}$$

If the obtained line is expressed as a determinant, we have:

$$\begin{vmatrix} w & X & Y \\ w_0 & X_0 & Y_0 \\ 0 & c_0 & -b_0 \end{vmatrix} = 0. \tag{9.8}$$

The same result can be derived in the following manner.

The line γ_0 points in the direction given by a vector $[c_0 \ -b_0]$. Thus, the line we are looking for passes the point V_0 and the point at infinity $\overline{(0, c_0, -b_0)}$ in the direction of the vector $[c_0 \ -b_0]$. Therefore, eq.(9.1) directly gives us eq.(9.8).

2. **Line going through point V_0 and perpendicular to line γ_0**

   The line in question passes the point at infinity $\overline{(0, b_0, c_0)}$ in the direction of a vector $[b_0 \ c_0]$. So from eq.(9.1) we obtain:

$$\begin{vmatrix} w & X & Y \\ w_0 & X_0 & Y_0 \\ 0 & b_0 & c_0 \end{vmatrix} = 0. \tag{9.9}$$

Three-dimensional Lines

Expressing three-dimensional lines in homogeneous coordinates is not as simple as in the case of two-dimensional lines [3].

In general, three points $V_0 = \overline{(w_0, X_0, Y_0, Z_0)}$, $V_1 = \overline{(w_1, X_1, Y_1, Z_1)}$ and $V_2 = \overline{(w_2, X_2, Y_2, Z_2)}$ will define a plane, which we write $\gamma = \overline{(a, b, c, d)^T}$. This gives the following relation:

$$\overline{\begin{bmatrix} w_0 & X_0 & Y_0 & Z_0 \\ w_1 & X_1 & Y_1 & Z_1 \\ w_2 & X_2 & Y_2 & Z_2 \end{bmatrix} \begin{bmatrix} a \\ b \\ c \\ d \end{bmatrix}} = \overline{\begin{bmatrix} 0 \\ 0 \\ 0 \end{bmatrix}}. \tag{9.10}$$

We now consider a point $V_a = \overline{(w_a, X_a, Y_a, Z_a)}$, which does not lie on the plane defined by the three given points. The scalar product of the vector representing this point given in homogeneous coordinates, and the homogeneous coefficient vector of the plane is non-zero. Denoting it by q and incorporating into eq.(9.10), we have:

$$\overline{\begin{bmatrix} w_0 & X_0 & Y_0 & Z_0 \\ w_1 & X_1 & Y_1 & Z_1 \\ w_2 & X_2 & Y_2 & Z_2 \\ w_a & X_a & Y_a & Z_a \end{bmatrix} \begin{bmatrix} a \\ b \\ c \\ d \end{bmatrix}} \equiv \overline{\boldsymbol{M} \begin{bmatrix} a \\ b \\ c \\ d \end{bmatrix}} = \overline{\begin{bmatrix} 0 \\ 0 \\ 0 \\ q \end{bmatrix}}. \tag{9.11}$$

To determine $[a\ b\ c\ d]^T$ from eq.(9.11), we assume that $|\boldsymbol{M}| \neq 0$, and take the left product of the adjoint matrix $\boldsymbol{M}^a$ of $\boldsymbol{M}$ on both sides of eq.(9.11) (For adjoint matrix, see footnote of page 78).

$$\overline{|\boldsymbol{M}|\boldsymbol{M}^{-1}\boldsymbol{M} \begin{bmatrix} a \\ b \\ c \\ d \end{bmatrix}} = \overline{\boldsymbol{M}^a \begin{bmatrix} 0 \\ 0 \\ 0 \\ q \end{bmatrix}}. \tag{9.12}$$

Now,

$$\boldsymbol{M}^a = \begin{bmatrix} \text{cofactor of } w_0 & \text{cofactor of } w_1 & \text{cofactor of } w_2 & \text{cofactor of } w_a \\ \text{cofactor of } X_0 & \text{cofactor of } X_1 & \text{cofactor of } X_2 & \text{cofactor of } X_a \\ \text{cofactor of } Y_0 & \text{cofactor of } Y_1 & \text{cofactor of } Y_2 & \text{cofactor of } Y_a \\ \text{cofactor of } Z_0 & \text{cofactor of } Z_1 & \text{cofactor of } Z_2 & \text{cofactor of } Z_a \end{bmatrix}. \tag{9.13}$$

Therefore, eq.(9.12) turns out to be:

$$\overline{|\boldsymbol{M}| \begin{bmatrix} a \\ b \\ c \\ d \end{bmatrix}} = \overline{q \begin{bmatrix} \text{cofactor of } w_a \\ \text{cofactor of } X_a \\ \text{cofactor of } Y_a \\ \text{cofactor of } Z_a \end{bmatrix}}. \tag{9.14}$$

Because a plane is not affected when its homogeneous coefficient vector is multiplied by a non-zero scalar, we have:

$$\overline{\begin{bmatrix} a \\ b \\ c \\ d \end{bmatrix}} = \overline{\begin{bmatrix} \text{cofactor of } w_a \\ \text{cofactor of } X_a \\ \text{cofactor of } Y_a \\ \text{cofactor of } Z_a \end{bmatrix}} = \overline{\begin{vmatrix} w_0 & X_0 & Y_0 & Z_0 \\ w_1 & X_1 & Y_1 & Z_1 \\ w_2 & X_2 & Y_2 & Z_2 \\ \vec{\boldsymbol{I}} & \vec{\boldsymbol{J}} & \vec{\boldsymbol{K}} & \vec{\boldsymbol{L}} \end{vmatrix}}. \tag{9.15}$$

If, in the above derivation, $\boldsymbol{M}$ had been a singular matrix, i.e., $|\boldsymbol{M}| = 0$, then no solution exists.

Note here that

$$
\begin{aligned}
&|\boldsymbol{M}| \\
&= w_a \underbrace{\begin{vmatrix} Z_0 & Y_0 & X_0 \\ Z_1 & Y_1 & X_1 \\ Z_2 & Y_2 & X_2 \end{vmatrix}}_{\text{cofactor of } w_a} + X_a \underbrace{\begin{vmatrix} w_0 & Y_0 & Z_0 \\ w_1 & Y_1 & Z_1 \\ w_2 & Y_2 & Z_2 \end{vmatrix}}_{\text{cofactor of } X_a} \\
&+ Y_a \underbrace{\begin{vmatrix} w_0 & Z_0 & X_0 \\ w_1 & Z_1 & X_1 \\ w_2 & Z_2 & X_2 \end{vmatrix}}_{\text{cofactor of } Y_a} + Z_a \underbrace{\begin{vmatrix} w_0 & X_0 & Y_0 \\ w_1 & X_1 & Y_1 \\ w_2 & X_2 & Y_2 \end{vmatrix}}_{\text{cofactor of } Z_a} .
\end{aligned}
\tag{9.16}
$$

The cofactors of w_a, X_a, Y_a and Z_a are the homogeneous coefficients of the plane determined by the three points V_0, V_1 and V_2. Meanwhile, the point V_a exists outside of this plane. So $|\boldsymbol{M}| = 0$ occurs only when the three points do not form a plane, i.e., only when they are collinear, because if we assume they form a plane, $|\boldsymbol{M}|$ can not be zero, as shown in eq.(9.16), with respect to V_a not lying on the plane. When they are collinear, the four cofactors are all zero's (see Section 19.2.2). Clearly a, b, c and d obtained from eq.(9.15) are all zero's as well.

On the other hand, if a, b, c and d as computed from eq.(9.15) are all zero's, that is, if the four cofactors are all zero's in eq.(9.16), then $|\boldsymbol{M}| = 0$ and the three points must be collinear.

Note that this ($a=b=c=d=0$) is also the condition that the third point V_2 lies on a line determined by two given points V_0 and V_1 (see eq.(14.17)).

Thus, the condition that a point $V = \overline{(w, X, Y, Z)}$ lies on the line going through two points V_0 and V_1 is given from eq.(9.15) by:

$$
\overline{\begin{bmatrix} a \\ b \\ c \\ d \end{bmatrix}} = \overline{\begin{vmatrix} w_0 & X_0 & Y_0 & Z_0 \\ w_1 & X_1 & Y_1 & Z_1 \\ w & X & Y & Z \\ \vec{I} & \vec{J} & \vec{K} & \vec{L} \end{vmatrix}} = \overline{\begin{bmatrix} 0 \\ 0 \\ 0 \\ 0 \end{bmatrix}} .
\tag{9.17}
$$

Expansion of eq.(9.17) obtains:

$$
\begin{cases}
-X \begin{vmatrix} Y_0 & Z_0 \\ Y_1 & Z_1 \end{vmatrix} - Y \begin{vmatrix} Z_0 & X_0 \\ Z_1 & X_1 \end{vmatrix} - Z \begin{vmatrix} X_0 & Y_0 \\ X_1 & Y_1 \end{vmatrix} = 0, \\
+w \begin{vmatrix} Y_0 & Z_0 \\ Y_1 & Z_1 \end{vmatrix} - Y \begin{vmatrix} w_0 & Z_0 \\ w_1 & Z_1 \end{vmatrix} + Z \begin{vmatrix} w_0 & Y_0 \\ w_1 & Y_1 \end{vmatrix} = 0, \\
+w \begin{vmatrix} Z_0 & X_0 \\ Z_1 & X_1 \end{vmatrix} + X \begin{vmatrix} w_0 & Z_0 \\ w_1 & Z_1 \end{vmatrix} - Z \begin{vmatrix} w_0 & X_0 \\ w_1 & X_1 \end{vmatrix} = 0, \\
+w \begin{vmatrix} X_0 & Y_0 \\ X_1 & Y_1 \end{vmatrix} - X \begin{vmatrix} w_0 & Y_0 \\ w_1 & Y_1 \end{vmatrix} + Y \begin{vmatrix} w_0 & X_0 \\ w_1 & X_1 \end{vmatrix} = 0.
\end{cases}
\tag{9.18}
$$

Noting that the 2×2 determinants above are the Plücker coordinates of line (see Table 8.5), eq.(9.18) can be written as:

$$[w\ X\ Y\ Z]\boldsymbol{L} = [0\ 0\ 0\ 0], \tag{9.19}$$

$$\boldsymbol{L} = \begin{bmatrix} 0 & S_{01} & T_{01} & U_{01} \\ -S_{01} & 0 & R_{01} & -Q_{01} \\ -T_{01} & -R_{01} & 0 & P_{01} \\ -U_{01} & Q_{01} & -P_{01} & 0 \end{bmatrix}. \tag{9.20}$$

The anti-symmetric matrix $\boldsymbol{L}$ represents a three-dimensional line expressed in homogeneous coordinates of points. $\boldsymbol{L}$, when multiplied by an arbitrary non-zero scalar, will still represent the same line.

If we take the product of the homogeneous coordinate vector of a point and $\boldsymbol{L}$, and the resulting vector has zero's for all its components, then that point lies on the line.

If, on the other hand, the homogeneous coordinates of a point existing outside of the line are multiplied by $\boldsymbol{L}$, then from eq.(9.17), we obtain the homogeneous coefficient vector of the plane containing the point and $\boldsymbol{L}$, or:

$$\overline{\begin{bmatrix} a \\ b \\ c \\ d \end{bmatrix}} = \overline{\{[w\ X\ Y\ Z]\boldsymbol{L}\}^T}. \tag{9.21}$$

Since, in eq.(9.19), the scalar product of the homogeneous coordinate vector of an arbitrary point on the line and a column vector of $\boldsymbol{L}$ is zero, each column vector of $\boldsymbol{L}$ can be considered to be the homogeneous coefficient vector of a plane that contains the line. In other words, the line $\boldsymbol{L}$ consists of the homogeneous coefficients of four planes, each of which contains the line expressed by $\boldsymbol{L}$. We shall call this "*type-L representation* of line."

The line $\boldsymbol{L}$ derived above is a line going through two given points. The other definition of line is one determined by two given planes. We now discuss this case.

Using a similar method to the one we used earlier to determine the homogeneous coefficient vector of the plane equation defined by three points, we can find the homogeneous coordinates of the intersecting point of three given planes, $\gamma_0 = \overline{(a_0, b_0, c_0, d_0)^T}$, $\gamma_1 = \overline{(a_1, b_1, c_1, d_1)^T}$ and $\gamma_2 = \overline{(a_2, b_2, c_2, d_2)^T}$, to be:

$$\overline{[w\ X\ Y\ Z]} = \overline{\begin{vmatrix} a_0 & a_1 & a_2 & \boldsymbol{I} \\ b_0 & b_1 & b_2 & \boldsymbol{J} \\ c_0 & c_1 & c_2 & \boldsymbol{K} \\ d_0 & d_1 & d_2 & \boldsymbol{L} \end{vmatrix}}, \tag{9.22}$$

which corresponds to eq.(9.15).

Similar to when we derived eq.(9.15), if the four cofactors obtained in the process of deriving eq.(9.22) are all zero's, or if w, X, Y and Z computed in eq.(9.22) are all zero's, then the three planes are not intersecting at a point but instead they intersect at a single line. So if w, X, Y and Z are all found to be zero's when determining the intersection of three planes, then the three planes are collinear(see eq.(14.18)).

From the discussion above, we can write the condition that, given two planes, γ_0 and γ_1, a plane $\gamma = (a, b, c, d)^T$ contains the intersecting line of γ_0 and γ_1, to be:

$$\begin{vmatrix} a_0 & a_1 & a & \boldsymbol{I} \\ b_0 & b_1 & b & \boldsymbol{J} \\ c_0 & c_1 & c & \boldsymbol{K} \\ d_0 & d_1 & d & \boldsymbol{L} \end{vmatrix} = [0\ 0\ 0\ 0]. \tag{9.23}$$

Expansion of this equation gives:

$$\begin{cases} -b\begin{vmatrix} c_0 & c_1 \\ d_0 & d_1 \end{vmatrix} - c\begin{vmatrix} d_0 & d_1 \\ b_0 & b_1 \end{vmatrix} - d\begin{vmatrix} b_0 & b_1 \\ c_0 & c_1 \end{vmatrix} = 0, \\ +a\begin{vmatrix} c_0 & c_1 \\ d_0 & d_1 \end{vmatrix} - c\begin{vmatrix} a_0 & a_1 \\ d_0 & d_1 \end{vmatrix} + d\begin{vmatrix} a_0 & a_1 \\ c_0 & c_1 \end{vmatrix} = 0, \\ +a\begin{vmatrix} d_0 & d_1 \\ b_0 & b_1 \end{vmatrix} + b\begin{vmatrix} a_0 & a_1 \\ d_0 & d_1 \end{vmatrix} - d\begin{vmatrix} a_0 & a_1 \\ b_0 & b_1 \end{vmatrix} = 0, \\ +a\begin{vmatrix} b_0 & b_1 \\ c_0 & c_1 \end{vmatrix} - b\begin{vmatrix} a_0 & a_1 \\ c_0 & c_1 \end{vmatrix} + c\begin{vmatrix} a_0 & a_1 \\ b_0 & b_1 \end{vmatrix} = 0. \end{cases} \tag{9.24}$$

Expressing this in terms of matrices, we have:

$$\boldsymbol{K}'\begin{bmatrix} a \\ b \\ c \\ d \end{bmatrix} = \begin{bmatrix} 0 \\ 0 \\ 0 \\ 0 \end{bmatrix}, \tag{9.25}$$

$$\boldsymbol{K}' = \begin{bmatrix} 0 & -s_{01} & -t_{01} & -u_{01} \\ s_{01} & 0 & -r_{01} & q_{01} \\ t_{01} & r_{01} & 0 & -p_{01} \\ u_{01} & -q_{01} & p_{01} & 0 \end{bmatrix}, \tag{9.26}$$

where p_{01}, q_{01}, r_{01}, s_{01}, t_{01} and u_{01} represent Plücker coefficients of line (see Table 8.5).

$\boldsymbol{K}'$ is an anti-symmetric matrix. Eq.(9.25) represents a line in terms of the homogeneous coefficients of planes, i.e., as the intersecting line of two planes. $\boldsymbol{K}'$, when multiplied by an arbitrary non-zero scalar, will still represent the same line.

If we take the product of $\boldsymbol{K}'$ and the homogeneous coefficient vector of a plane, and the resulting vector has zero's for all of its components, then the plane contains that intersecting line.

If, on the other hand, the plane does not contain the intersecting line, the components of the product represent the homogeneous coordinates of the intersecting point for the line and plane, or

$$\overline{[w\ X\ Y\ Z]} = \overline{\left(\boldsymbol{K}' \begin{bmatrix} a \\ b \\ c \\ d \end{bmatrix} \right)^T} . \tag{9.27}$$

The scalar product between any row vector of $\boldsymbol{K}'$ and the homogeneous coefficient vector of an arbitrary plane containing the line is zero, so the row vectors of $\boldsymbol{K}'$ can be thought of as points on that line. In other words, $\boldsymbol{K}'$ consists of the homogeneous coordinates of four points lying on the line expressed by $\boldsymbol{K}'$. We shall call this "*type-K' representation* of line."

We now derive a few relations regarding Plücker coordinates and coefficients of lines. To this end, we determine an intersecting point of three planes, arbitrary but all of them containing line $\boldsymbol{L}$. Each column of eq.(9.20) represents a plane containing the line $\boldsymbol{L}$. Since they all intersect at a single line, the coordinates w, X, Y and Z of the intersecting point that we seek should all be zero's. Here we use the three planes given by the first three columns of eq.(9.20).

To determine the intersecting point, we proceed as follows. From eq.(9.22), we have

$$\begin{aligned} \overline{[w\ X\ Y\ Z]} &= \overline{\begin{vmatrix} 0 & S_{01} & T_{01} & \boldsymbol{I} \\ -S_{01} & 0 & R_{01} & \boldsymbol{J} \\ -T_{01} & -R_{01} & 0 & \boldsymbol{K} \\ -U_{01} & Q_{01} & -P_{01} & \boldsymbol{L} \end{vmatrix}} \\ &= (P_{01}S_{01} + Q_{01}T_{01} + R_{01}U_{01})\overline{[R_{01}\ T_{01}\ S_{01}\ 0]}. \end{aligned} \tag{9.28}$$

For $w = X = Y = Z = 0$ to hold in this equation, either $R_{01} = T_{01} = S_{01} = 0$ or

$$P_{01}S_{01} + Q_{01}T_{01} + R_{01}U_{01} = 0 \tag{9.29}$$

must hold. Since $w = X = Y = Z = 0$ must hold for any set of three planes of $\boldsymbol{L}$, however, we see that eq.(9.29) must hold. We now have a relation among the six Plücker coordinates for line.

In a similar manner, we can obtain a relation among Plücker coefficients, one that forms a dual with eq.(9.29):

$$p_{01}s_{01} + q_{01}t_{01} + r_{01}u_{01} = 0. \tag{9.30}$$

From eq.(9.29), we obtain the following equation (subscripts will be omitted from time to time for the sake of clarity, as done here):

$$\overbrace{\begin{bmatrix} 0 & -P & -Q & -R \\ P & 0 & -U & T \\ Q & U & 0 & -S \\ R & -T & S & 0 \end{bmatrix}}^{\boldsymbol{K}} \overbrace{\begin{bmatrix} 0 & S & T & U \\ -S & 0 & R & -Q \\ -T & -R & 0 & P \\ -U & Q & -P & 0 \end{bmatrix}}^{\boldsymbol{L}} = \begin{bmatrix} 0 & 0 & 0 & 0 \\ 0 & 0 & 0 & 0 \\ 0 & 0 & 0 & 0 \\ 0 & 0 & 0 & 0 \end{bmatrix} . \tag{9.31}$$

The second matrix is $\boldsymbol{L}$. The product of these two matrices is a matrix whose elements are all zero's. Columns of the matrix $\boldsymbol{L}$ each represent a homogeneous coefficient vector of a plane that contains the line $\boldsymbol{L}$. The scalar product between a row vector of the first matrix and any homogeneous coefficient vector of such a plane is zero, so the row vectors of the first matrix represent points on the line $\boldsymbol{L}$. Thus the first matrix consists of four points on the line, just as $\boldsymbol{K}'$ of eq.(9.26). Eq.(9.31) shows that a line corresponding to $\boldsymbol{K}'$ can be formed by using components of $\boldsymbol{L}$. We shall call this "*type-K representation* of line," for which:

$$\boldsymbol{K}\begin{bmatrix} a \\ b \\ c \\ d \end{bmatrix} = \begin{bmatrix} 0 \\ 0 \\ 0 \\ 0 \end{bmatrix}, \tag{9.32}$$

where

$$\boldsymbol{K} = \begin{bmatrix} 0 & -P_{01} & -Q_{01} & -R_{01} \\ P_{01} & 0 & -U_{01} & T_{01} \\ Q_{01} & U_{01} & 0 & -S_{01} \\ R_{01} & -T_{01} & S_{01} & 0 \end{bmatrix}. \tag{9.33}$$

Corresponding to eq.(9.27) (to give the intersecting point of the line $\boldsymbol{K}$ and a plane), we have:

$$\overline{[w\ X\ Y\ Z]} = \overline{\left(\boldsymbol{K}\begin{bmatrix} a \\ b \\ c \\ d \end{bmatrix}\right)^T}. \tag{9.34}$$

Now, a relation corresponding to eq.(9.31) can be obtained for Plücker coefficients as well, as follows:

$$\overbrace{\begin{bmatrix} 0 & -s & -t & -u \\ s & 0 & -r & q \\ t & r & 0 & -p \\ u & -q & p & 0 \end{bmatrix}}^{\boldsymbol{K}'}\overbrace{\begin{bmatrix} 0 & p & q & r \\ -p & 0 & u & -t \\ -q & -u & 0 & s \\ -r & t & -s & 0 \end{bmatrix}}^{\boldsymbol{L}'} = \begin{bmatrix} 0 & 0 & 0 & 0 \\ 0 & 0 & 0 & 0 \\ 0 & 0 & 0 & 0 \\ 0 & 0 & 0 & 0 \end{bmatrix}. \tag{9.35}$$

The row vectors of $\boldsymbol{K}'$ each represent coordinates for some point on the line, and so column vectors of $\boldsymbol{L}'$ each represent the homogeneous coefficients of a plane that contains this line. So we have the following line equation:

$$[w\ X\ Y\ Z]\boldsymbol{L}' = [0\ 0\ 0\ 0], \tag{9.36}$$

$$\boldsymbol{L}' = \begin{bmatrix} 0 & p_{01} & q_{01} & r_{01} \\ -p_{01} & 0 & u_{01} & -t_{01} \\ -q_{01} & -u_{01} & 0 & s_{01} \\ -r_{01} & t_{01} & -s_{01} & 0 \end{bmatrix}. \tag{9.37}$$

We shall call this "*type-L' representation* of line."

Table 9.1: Four types of three dimensional lines.

Type	**Data**	**Collinear data matrix**	**Line equation**
L	V_0, V_1	$\boldsymbol{L} = \begin{bmatrix} 0 & S_{01} & T_{01} & U_{01} \\ -S_{01} & 0 & R_{01} & -Q_{01} \\ -T_{01} & -R_{01} & 0 & P_{01} \\ -U_{01} & Q_{01} & -P_{01} & 0 \end{bmatrix}$ Each column plane is collinear with respect to line $\boldsymbol{L}$.	$[w\ X\ Y\ Z]\boldsymbol{L} = [0\ 0\ 0\ 0]$
L'	γ_0, γ_1	$\boldsymbol{L}' = \begin{bmatrix} 0 & p_{01} & q_{01} & r_{01} \\ -p_{01} & 0 & u_{01} & -t_{01} \\ -q_{01} & -u_{01} & 0 & s_{01} \\ -r_{01} & t_{01} & -s_{01} & 0 \end{bmatrix}$ Each column plane is collinear with respect to line $\boldsymbol{L}'$.	$[w\ X\ Y\ Z]\boldsymbol{L}' = [0\ 0\ 0\ 0]$
K	V_0, V_1	$\boldsymbol{K} = \begin{bmatrix} 0 & -P_{01} & -Q_{01} & -R_{01} \\ P_{01} & 0 & -U_{01} & T_{01} \\ Q_{01} & U_{01} & 0 & -S_{01} \\ R_{01} & -T_{01} & S_{01} & 0 \end{bmatrix}$ Each row point is collinear with respect to line $\boldsymbol{K}$.	$\boldsymbol{K} \begin{bmatrix} a \\ b \\ c \\ d \end{bmatrix} = \begin{bmatrix} 0 \\ 0 \\ 0 \\ 0 \end{bmatrix}$
K'	γ_0, γ_1	$\boldsymbol{K}' = \begin{bmatrix} 0 & -s_{01} & -t_{01} & -u_{01} \\ s_{01} & 0 & -r_{01} & q_{01} \\ t_{01} & r_{01} & 0 & -p_{01} \\ u_{01} & -q_{01} & p_{01} & 0 \end{bmatrix}$ Each row point is collinear with respect to line $\boldsymbol{K}'$.	$\boldsymbol{K}' \begin{bmatrix} a \\ b \\ c \\ d \end{bmatrix} = \begin{bmatrix} 0 \\ 0 \\ 0 \\ 0 \end{bmatrix}$

When the coordinates of a point that does not lie on the line are substituted into the left-hand side of eq.(9.36), we obtain the homogeneous coefficients of a plane containing that point and the line, that is:

$$\overline{\begin{bmatrix} a \\ b \\ c \\ d \end{bmatrix}} = \overline{\{[w\ X\ Y\ Z]\boldsymbol{L}'\}^T}. \tag{9.38}$$

The four types of three dimensional lines expressed in homogeneous coordinates or homogeneous coefficients are summarized in Table 9.1.

Planes

We now determine the homogeneous coordinate representation of a plane that contains three points, $V_0 = \overline{(w_0, X_0, Y_0, Z_0)}$, $V_1 = \overline{(w_1, X_1, Y_1, Z_1)}$ and $V_2 = \overline{(w_2, X_2, Y_2, Z_2)}$. Similar to the case of Section 9.1.1 (two-dimensional lines), this can be expressed as the condition that four points, $V = \overline{(w, X, Y, Z)}$, V_0, V_1 and V_2, are linearly dependent, or:

$$\begin{vmatrix} w & X & Y & Z \\ w_0 & X_0 & Y_0 & Z_0 \\ w_1 & X_1 & Y_1 & Z_1 \\ w_2 & X_2 & Y_2 & Z_2 \end{vmatrix} = 0. \tag{9.39}$$

The homogeneous coefficients of the plane equation is:

$$\overline{\begin{bmatrix} a \\ b \\ c \\ d \end{bmatrix}} = \overline{\begin{bmatrix} A_{012} \\ B_{012} \\ C_{012} \\ D_{012} \end{bmatrix}} = \overline{\begin{vmatrix} \vec{I} & \vec{J} & \vec{K} & \vec{L} \\ w_0 & X_0 & Y_0 & Z_0 \\ w_1 & X_1 & Y_1 & Z_1 \\ w_2 & X_2 & Y_2 & Z_2 \end{vmatrix}}. \tag{9.40}$$

The right-hand side of eq.(9.40) expresses a generalization, obtained by extending the vector product of two vectors in three-dimensional vector space, to the case of four-space [2)].

Eq.(9.40) forms a dual with eq.(12.8). If A_{012}, B_{012}, C_{012} and D_{012} are all found to be zero's, the three points are collinear (see Sections 12.2 and 14.3).

1. **Plane containing two points and one direction**

   Let $V_0 = \overline{(w_0, X_0, Y_0, Z_0)}$ and $V_1 = \overline{(w_1, X_1, Y_1, Z_1)}$ denote the two points. A plane containing a direction vector $[l\ m\ n]$ is one that contains the point

2) The vector product of $\boldsymbol{V}_0 = [w_0\ X_0\ Y_0]$ and $\boldsymbol{V}_1 = [w_1\ X_1\ Y_1]$ in three dimensional associated vector space defines a line γ and is written as:

$$\gamma = \overline{\begin{bmatrix} a \\ b \\ c \end{bmatrix}} = \overline{\begin{vmatrix} \vec{i} & \vec{j} & \vec{k} \\ w_0 & X_0 & Y_0 \\ w_1 & X_1 & Y_1 \end{vmatrix}}. \tag{9.41}$$

As for the generalization of vector product, refer to pp. 124-125 of [28].

at infinity in that direction. So from eq.(9.39), we have:

$$\begin{vmatrix} w & X & Y & Z \\ w_0 & X_0 & Y_0 & Z_0 \\ w_1 & X_1 & Y_1 & Z_1 \\ 0 & l & m & n \end{vmatrix} = 0. \tag{9.42}$$

2. **Plane containing one point and two directions**

Let $V_0 = \overline{(w_0, X_0, Y_0, Z_0)}$ denote the point. A plane containing two directions $\underline{[l_1\ m_1\ n_1]}$ and $\underline{[l_2\ m_2\ n_2]}$ is one that contains points at infinity, $\overline{(0, l_1, m_1, n_1)}$ and $\overline{(0, l_2, m_2, n_2)}$. So from eq.(9.39), we have:

$$\begin{vmatrix} w & X & Y & Z \\ w_0 & X_0 & Y_0 & Z_0 \\ 0 & l_1 & m_1 & n_1 \\ 0 & l_2 & m_2 & n_2 \end{vmatrix} = 0. \tag{9.43}$$

3. **Plane containing a point and parallel to plane γ_0**

The plane parallel to a plane $\gamma_0 = \overline{(a_0, b_0, c_0, d_0)^T}$ and which contains the origin is given by:

$$[w\ X\ Y\ Z] \begin{bmatrix} 0 \\ b_0 \\ c_0 \\ d_0 \end{bmatrix} = 0. \tag{9.44}$$

If the point on this plane corresponding to the origin is translated to point $V_0 = \overline{(w_0, X_0, Y_0, Z_0)}$, we obtain the plane equation:

$$\boldsymbol{P} \cdot \boldsymbol{\gamma} \equiv \boldsymbol{P} \cdot (\boldsymbol{T}^{-1} \begin{bmatrix} 0 \\ b_0 \\ c_0 \\ d_0 \end{bmatrix}) = 0,$$

where

$$\boldsymbol{T} = \begin{bmatrix} w_0 & X_0 & Y_0 & Z_0 \\ 0 & w_0 & 0 & 0 \\ 0 & 0 & w_0 & 0 \\ 0 & 0 & 0 & w_0 \end{bmatrix}. \tag{9.45}$$

So

$$\begin{aligned} \boldsymbol{\gamma} &\equiv \boldsymbol{T}^{-1} \begin{bmatrix} 0 \\ b_0 \\ c_0 \\ d_0 \end{bmatrix} \\ &= \begin{bmatrix} w_0 & -X_0 & -Y_0 & -Z_0 \\ 0 & w_0 & 0 & 0 \\ 0 & 0 & w_0 & 0 \\ 0 & 0 & 0 & w_0 \end{bmatrix} \begin{bmatrix} 0 \\ b_0 \\ c_0 \\ d_0 \end{bmatrix} \end{aligned}$$

$$
= \begin{bmatrix} -b_0X_0 - c_0Y_0 - d_0Z_0 \\ b_0w_0 \\ c_0w_0 \\ d_0w_0 \end{bmatrix}.
$$

Expressing this plane as a determinant, we have:

$$
\begin{vmatrix} w & X & Y & Z \\ w_0 & X_0 & Y_0 & Z_0 \\ 0 & 0 & -d_0 & c_0 \\ 0 & -d_0 & 0 & b_0 \end{vmatrix} = 0. \tag{9.46}
$$

This can also be derived as follows: on the plane γ_0, we take two independent vectors, $[0 \;\; -d_0 \;\; c_0]$ and $[-d_0 \;\; 0 \;\; b_0]$. Since the normal vector to the plane γ_0 is $[b_0 \; c_0 \; d_0]$, we can check to see whether these vectors do indeed exist on the plane as follows:

$$
[b_0 \; c_0 \; d_0] \begin{bmatrix} 0 \\ -d_0 \\ c_0 \end{bmatrix} = 0, \quad [b_0 \; c_0 \; d_0] \begin{bmatrix} -d_0 \\ 0 \\ b_0 \end{bmatrix} = 0.
$$

So a plane parallel to the plane γ_0 contains points at infinity, $\overline{(0, 0, -d_0, c_0)}$ and $\overline{(0, -d_0, 0, b_0)}$. Eq.(9.46) thus follows directly using eq.(9.39).

4. **Plane containing a point and a three-dimensional line $\boldsymbol{L}$**

   Given a point $V_0 = \overline{(w_0, X_0, Y_0, Z_0)}$ and a type-L line:

$$
\boldsymbol{L} = \begin{bmatrix} 0 & S_{01} & T_{01} & U_{01} \\ -S_{01} & 0 & R_{01} & -Q_{01} \\ -T_{01} & -R_{01} & 0 & P_{01} \\ -U_{01} & Q_{01} & -P_{01} & 0 \end{bmatrix},
$$

   the plane $\gamma = \overline{(a, b, c, d)^T}$ which contains V_0 and the line $\boldsymbol{L}$ is given, from eq.(9.21), as:

$$
\gamma = \overline{\begin{bmatrix} a \\ b \\ c \\ d \end{bmatrix}} = \boldsymbol{L}^T \overline{\begin{bmatrix} w_0 \\ X_0 \\ Y_0 \\ Z_0 \end{bmatrix}}. \tag{9.47}
$$

9.1.2 Plücker Coordinate or Coefficient Forms

Flat Sets in Plücker Coordinates

Points

Since the homogeneous coordinates of point represent a special case of Plücker coordinates, the Plücker coordinate representation V_0 of a point is:

$$
V_0 = \overline{(w_0, X_0, Y_0, Z_0)}. \tag{9.48}
$$

Lines

The Plücker coordinate representation, L_{01}, of a line passing through two points, V_0 and V_1, is:

$$L_{01} = \overline{(P_{01}, Q_{01}, R_{01}, S_{01}, T_{01}, U_{01})}, \tag{9.49}$$

where

$$\begin{cases} P_{01} = \begin{vmatrix} w_0 & X_0 \\ w_1 & X_1 \end{vmatrix} = w_0X_1 - X_0w_1, & Q_{01} = \begin{vmatrix} w_0 & Y_0 \\ w_1 & Y_1 \end{vmatrix} = w_0Y_1 - Y_0w_1, \\ R_{01} = \begin{vmatrix} w_0 & Z_0 \\ w_1 & Z_1 \end{vmatrix} = w_0Z_1 - Z_0w_1, & S_{01} = \begin{vmatrix} Y_0 & Z_0 \\ Y_1 & Z_1 \end{vmatrix} = Y_0Z_1 - Z_0Y_1, \\ T_{01} = \begin{vmatrix} Z_0 & X_0 \\ Z_1 & X_1 \end{vmatrix} = Z_0X_1 - X_0Z_1, & U_{01} = \begin{vmatrix} X_0 & Y_0 \\ X_1 & Y_1 \end{vmatrix} = X_0Y_1 - Y_0X_1. \end{cases} \tag{9.50}$$

Here, we examine the geometric meanings of the Plücker coordinates for line, assuming $w_0, w_1 \neq 0$.

With respect to P_{01}, Q_{01} and R_{01},

$$[P_{01}\ Q_{01}\ R_{01}] = w_0w_1[x_1 - x_0\ \ y_1 - y_0\ \ z_1 - z_0]. \tag{9.51}$$

Eq.(9.51) shows $[P_{01}\ Q_{01}\ R_{01}]$ represents a direction vector of the line V_0V_1, pointing from V_0 to V_1 if $w_0w_1 > 0$ (see Fig. 9.2).

This can also be confirmed by determining the intersection point of the line V_0V_1 with the plane at infinity. That is, from eq.(9.34), we have:

$$\overline{\left(\begin{bmatrix} 0 & -P_{01} & -Q_{01} & -R_{01} \\ P_{01} & 0 & -U_{01} & T_{01} \\ Q_{01} & U_{01} & 0 & -S_{01} \\ R_{01} & -T_{01} & S_{01} & 0 \end{bmatrix} \begin{bmatrix} 1 \\ 0 \\ 0 \\ 0 \end{bmatrix} \right)^T} = \overline{[0\ P_{01}\ Q_{01}\ R_{01}]}.$$

The result above shows that the line intersects the plane at infinity at $(0, P_{01}, Q_{01}, R_{01})$ and thus its direction vector is $[P_{01}\ Q_{01}\ R_{01}]$.

Next, with respect to S_{01}, T_{01} and U_{01},

$$\begin{aligned} [S_{01}\ T_{01}\ U_{01}] &= w_0w_1[y_0z_1 - z_0y_1\ \ z_0x_1 - x_0z_1\ \ x_0y_1 - y_0x_1] \\ &= w_0w_1 \begin{vmatrix} \boldsymbol{i} & \boldsymbol{j} & \boldsymbol{k} \\ x_0 & y_0 & z_0 \\ x_1 & y_1 & z_1 \end{vmatrix} \\ &= w_0w_1\boldsymbol{v}_0 \times \boldsymbol{v}_1. \end{aligned} \tag{9.52}$$

Eq.(9.52) shows that the vector $[S_{01}\ T_{01}\ U_{01}]$ represents the normal vector to the plane that contains the origin and that line (see Fig. 9.2).

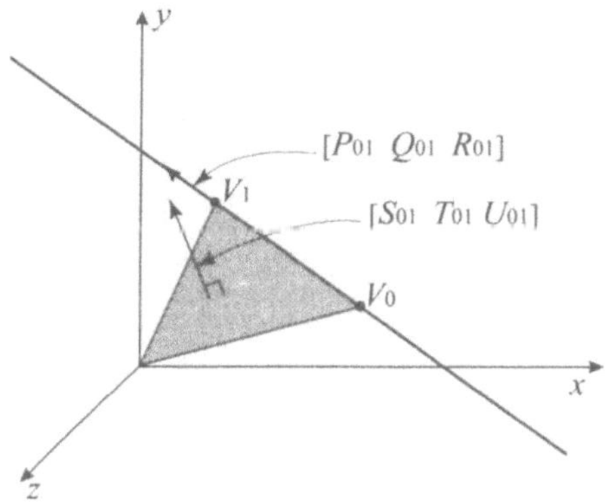

Figure 9.2: Geometric meaning of Plücker coordinates of line.

This can also be confirmed by determining the plane containing the origin and the line V_0V_1. From eq.(9.21), we have the plane:

$$\overline{\left([1\ 0\ 0\ 0] \begin{bmatrix} 0 & S_{01} & T_{01} & U_{01} \\ -S_{01} & 0 & R_{01} & -Q_{01} \\ -T_{01} & -R_{01} & 0 & P_{01} \\ -U_{01} & Q_{01} & -P_{01} & 0 \end{bmatrix} \right)^T} = \overline{\begin{bmatrix} 0 \\ S_{01} \\ T_{01} \\ U_{01} \end{bmatrix}}.$$

The result above shows that the normal vector of the plane containing the origin and the line is $[S_{01}\ T_{01}\ U_{01}]$.

The two vectors, $[P_{01}\ Q_{01}\ R_{01}]$ and $[S_{01}\ T_{01}\ U_{01}]$, obtained above are perpendicular, so their scalar product is zero. Note that this is equivalent to eq.(9.29), which expresses an identical relation among the six Plücker coodinates.

Planes

The Plücker coordinate representation, F_{012}, of plane containing three points, V_0, V_1 and V_2, is given by:

$$F_{012} = \overline{(A_{012}, B_{012}, C_{012}, D_{012})^T}, \tag{9.53}$$

where

$$A_{012} = \begin{vmatrix} X_0 & Y_0 & Z_0 \\ X_1 & Y_1 & Z_1 \\ X_2 & Y_2 & Z_2 \end{vmatrix},\ B_{012} = \begin{vmatrix} w_0 & Z_0 & Y_0 \\ w_1 & Z_1 & Y_1 \\ w_2 & Z_2 & Y_2 \end{vmatrix},$$

$$C_{012} = \begin{vmatrix} w_0 & X_0 & Z_0 \\ w_1 & X_1 & Z_1 \\ w_2 & X_2 & Z_2 \end{vmatrix},\ D_{012} = \begin{vmatrix} w_0 & Y_0 & X_0 \\ w_1 & Y_1 & X_1 \\ w_2 & Y_2 & X_2 \end{vmatrix}. \tag{9.54}$$

These are simply the homogeneous coefficients of the plane containing the three points.

As for the geometric meanings of $A_{012}, B_{012}, C_{012}$ and D_{012}, see Section 19.2.2.

Three-space

The Plücker coordinate representation, U_{0123}, of the three-space determined by four points, V_0, V_1, V_2 and V_3, is given by:

$$U_{0123} = \overline{(S_{0123})}, \tag{9.55}$$

where

$$S_{0123} = \begin{vmatrix} w_0 & X_0 & Y_0 & Z_0 \\ w_1 & X_1 & Y_1 & Z_1 \\ w_2 & X_2 & Y_2 & Z_2 \\ w_3 & X_3 & Y_3 & Z_3 \end{vmatrix}. \tag{9.56}$$

As for the geometric meaning of S_{0123}, see Section 13.2.2.

As shown above, Plücker coordinates can be defined by homogeneous coordinates whether they are signed or unsigned. Any non-zero scalar multiples of Plücker coordinates are equivalent in the case of unsigned homogeneous coordinates. Similarly, any positive scalar multiples are equivalent in the case of signed homogeneous coordinates.

Flat Sets in Plücker Coefficients

Planes

Since the homogeneous coefficients of plane represent a special case of Plücker coefficients, the Plücker coefficient representation, γ_0, of plane is:

$$\gamma_0 = \overline{(a_0, b_0, c_0, d_0)^T}. \tag{9.57}$$

Lines

In three-dimensional space, the Plücker coefficient representation, λ_{01}, of the intersecting line of two planes, γ_0 and γ_1, is:

$$\lambda_{01} = \overline{(p_{01}, q_{01}, r_{01}, s_{01}, t_{01}, u_{01})}, \tag{9.58}$$

$$\begin{cases} p_{01} = \begin{vmatrix} a_0 & a_1 \\ b_0 & b_1 \end{vmatrix}, & q_{01} = \begin{vmatrix} a_0 & a_1 \\ c_0 & c_1 \end{vmatrix}, \\ r_{01} = \begin{vmatrix} a_0 & a_1 \\ d_0 & d_1 \end{vmatrix}, & s_{01} = \begin{vmatrix} c_0 & c_1 \\ d_0 & d_1 \end{vmatrix}, \\ t_{01} = \begin{vmatrix} d_0 & d_1 \\ b_0 & b_1 \end{vmatrix}, & u_{01} = \begin{vmatrix} b_0 & b_1 \\ c_0 & c_1 \end{vmatrix}. \end{cases} \tag{9.59}$$

In geometric terms, the Plücker coefficients eq.(9.59) of line have the following meaning.

We first determine the direction of the line as its intersection with the plane at infinity. From eq.(9.27), we have:

$$\overline{\left(\begin{bmatrix} 0 & -s_{01} & -t_{01} & -u_{01} \\ s_{01} & 0 & -r_{01} & q_{01} \\ t_{01} & r_{01} & 0 & -p_{01} \\ u_{01} & -q_{01} & p_{01} & 0 \end{bmatrix}\begin{bmatrix} 1 \\ 0 \\ 0 \\ 0 \end{bmatrix}\right)^T} = \overline{[0\ s_{01}\ t_{01}\ u_{01}]}. \tag{9.60}$$

Thus we see that $[s_{01}\ t_{01}\ u_{01}]$ represents the direction vector of the line.

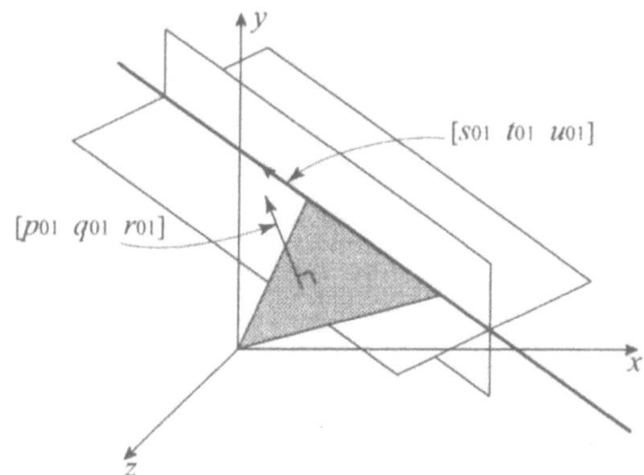

Figure 9.3: Geometric meaning of Plücker coefficients of line.

Next we determine the plane containing the origin and the line.
From eq.(9.38), we have:

$$\overline{\left([1\ 0\ 0\ 0]\begin{bmatrix} 0 & p_{01} & q_{01} & r_{01} \\ -p_{01} & 0 & u_{01} & -t_{01} \\ -q_{01} & -u_{01} & 0 & s_{01} \\ -r_{01} & t_{01} & -s_{01} & 0 \end{bmatrix}\right)^T} = \overline{\begin{bmatrix} 0 \\ p_{01} \\ q_{01} \\ r_{01} \end{bmatrix}}. \tag{9.61}$$

So $[p_{01}\ q_{01}\ r_{01}]$ represents the normal vector to the plane that contains the origin and that line (see Fig. 9.3).

Note that the reverse situation occurs for Plücker coefficients and Plücker coordinates in relation to geometric quantities. Since the vectors, $[p_{01}\ q_{01}\ r_{01}]$ and $[s_{01}\ t_{01}\ u_{01}]$, are perpendicular, their scalar product is zero. This is equivalent to eq.(9.30), which expresses an identical relation among the six Plücker coefficients.

Points

The Plücker coefficient representation, π_{012}, of the intersecting point of three planes, γ_0, γ_1 and γ_2, is given by:

$$\pi_{012} = \overline{(w_{012}, x_{012}, y_{012}, z_{012})}, \tag{9.62}$$

where

$$w_{012} = \begin{vmatrix} b_0 & b_1 & b_2 \\ c_0 & c_1 & c_2 \\ d_0 & d_1 & d_2 \end{vmatrix}, \; x_{012} = \begin{vmatrix} a_0 & a_1 & a_2 \\ d_0 & d_1 & d_2 \\ c_0 & c_1 & c_2 \end{vmatrix},$$

$$y_{012} = \begin{vmatrix} a_0 & a_1 & a_2 \\ b_0 & b_1 & b_2 \\ d_0 & d_1 & d_2 \end{vmatrix}, \; z_{012} = \begin{vmatrix} a_0 & a_1 & a_2 \\ c_0 & c_1 & c_2 \\ b_0 & b_1 & b_2 \end{vmatrix}. \tag{9.63}$$

These are simply the homogeneous coordinates of the intersecting point of three planes (see eq.(12.7)).

Vacuum

The Plücker coefficient representation, τ_{0123}, of the vacuum determined by four planes, γ_0, γ_1, γ_2 and γ_3, is given by:

$$\tau_{0123} = \overline{(T_{0123})}, \tag{9.64}$$

$$T_{0123} = \begin{vmatrix} a_0 & a_1 & a_2 & a_3 \\ b_0 & b_1 & b_2 & b_3 \\ c_0 & c_1 & c_2 & c_3 \\ d_0 & d_1 & d_2 & d_3 \end{vmatrix}. \tag{9.65}$$

Any non-zero scalar multiples of Plücker coefficients are equivalent in the case of unsigned homogeneous coefficients. Similarly, any positive scalar multiples are equivalent in the case of signed homogeneous coefficients.

9.1.3 Join or Meet Operation Forms

The description below follows Stolfi [53].

Flat Sets in Join Operations

Lines

A linearly independent point set [3], (V_0, V_1), can be considered to represent a line, when a *join* operation of the points is assumed. That is, a matrix which has as its row elements the homogeneous coordinates of V_0 and V_1, or

$$\begin{pmatrix} w_0 & X_0 & Y_0 & Z_0 \\ w_1 & X_1 & Y_1 & Z_1 \end{pmatrix}$$

represents a line.

[3] Points $V_0, V_1, \ldots, V_r$ in a projective space are linearly independent if the corresponding vectors $\boldsymbol{V}_0, \boldsymbol{V}_1, \ldots, \boldsymbol{V}_r$ are linearly independent.
Note the difference of the definition from that of Euclidean points (see Section A.3).

Let two matrices, $\boldsymbol{A}$ and $\boldsymbol{B}$, respectively represent lines a and b, defined as above by a point set. If a 2×2 matrix $\boldsymbol{K}$ satisfying the following relation exists, where $\det(\boldsymbol{K})\neq 0$:

$$\boldsymbol{A} = \boldsymbol{K}\boldsymbol{B}, \tag{9.66}$$

then matrices $\boldsymbol{A}$ and $\boldsymbol{B}$ represent the same line, assuming a and b are defined in classical projective space. As in the case for homogeneous coordinates, we will use an overline to express the equivalence class of the result of the *join* operation.

A line can then be written as follows:

$$V_0 \cup V_1 = \overline{\begin{pmatrix} w_0 & X_0 & Y_0 & Z_0 \\ w_1 & X_1 & Y_1 & Z_1 \end{pmatrix}}. \tag{9.67}$$

For two-sided space, the condition such that $\boldsymbol{A}$ and $\boldsymbol{B}$ represent the same line is given by $\det(\boldsymbol{K})>0$.

Planes

A linearly independent point set (V_0, V_1, V_2) defines a plane, which can then be written as:

$$V_0 \cup V_1 \cup V_2 = \overline{\begin{pmatrix} w_0 & X_0 & Y_0 & Z_0 \\ w_1 & X_1 & Y_1 & Z_1 \\ w_2 & X_2 & Y_2 & Z_2 \end{pmatrix}}. \tag{9.68}$$

Take two planes, a and b, each given by a 3×4 matrix in terms of the homogeneous coordinates of three points. If a 3×3 matrix $\boldsymbol{K}$ satisfying the relation of eq.(9.66) exists, where $\det(\boldsymbol{K}) \neq 0$, then matrices $\boldsymbol{A}$ and $\boldsymbol{B}$ represent the same plane, assuming these planes are defined in classical projective space. For two-sided space, the condition such that a and b represent the same plane is given by $\det(\boldsymbol{K})>0$.

Three-space

A linearly independent point set (V_0, V_1, V_2, V_3) defines a three-space, which can then be written as:

$$V_0 \cup V_1 \cup V_2 \cup V_3 = \overline{\begin{pmatrix} w_0 & X_0 & Y_0 & Z_0 \\ w_1 & X_1 & Y_1 & Z_1 \\ w_2 & X_2 & Y_2 & Z_2 \\ w_3 & X_3 & Y_3 & Z_3 \end{pmatrix}}. \tag{9.69}$$

There is only one three-space in classical projective space.

For two-sided space, take two three-spaces, a and b, each given by a 4×4 matrix in terms of the homogeneous coordinates of four points. If a 4×4 matrix $\boldsymbol{K}$ satisfying the relation of eq.(9.66) exists, where $\det(\boldsymbol{K}) > 0$, then matrices $\boldsymbol{A}$ and $\boldsymbol{B}$ represent the same three-space.

When flat sets are represented by a combination of a point set and *join* operations, the *join* operations between these flat sets are very simple, that is, one just joins the rows of the two matrices representing the two flat sets. Other operations, however, are not quite so simple.

Above we defined flat sets in terms of a point set. In classical projective space, where geometric elements have no orientation, the signs of homogeneous coordinates and the order of rows have no bearing on the outcome of an operation. When dealing with two-sided space, however, it becomes necessary to pay attention to such matters since they will directly affect the results.

Flat Sets in Meet Operations

Forming duals to flat sets expressed in *join* operations, we can also define flat sets in terms of *meet* operations of homogeneous coefficients of planes.

Lines

The combination of a linearly independent plane coefficient set, (γ_0, γ_1), and their *meet* expresses a line. That is, the matrix which has as its column elements the homogeneous coefficients of γ_0 and γ_1, or

$$\begin{pmatrix} a_0 & a_1 \\ b_0 & b_1 \\ c_0 & c_1 \\ d_0 & d_1 \end{pmatrix}$$

represents a line when its *meet* is also assumed.

Given two such matrices, $\boldsymbol{A}$ and $\boldsymbol{B}$, representing lines, if a 2×2 matrix $\boldsymbol{K}$ satisfying the following relation exists, where $\det(\boldsymbol{K}) \neq 0$:

$$\boldsymbol{B} = \boldsymbol{A}\boldsymbol{K}, \tag{9.70}$$

then matrices $\boldsymbol{A}$ and $\boldsymbol{B}$ represent the same line, assuming these lines are defined in classical projective space. As before, we will use an overline to express the equivalence class of the result of a *meet* operation. A line can then be written as follows:

$$\gamma_0 \cap \gamma_1 = \overline{\begin{pmatrix} a_0 & a_1 \\ b_0 & b_1 \\ c_0 & c_1 \\ d_0 & d_1 \end{pmatrix}}. \tag{9.71}$$

For two-sided space, the condition such that $\boldsymbol{A}$ and $\boldsymbol{B}$ represent the same line is given by $\det(\boldsymbol{K}) > 0$.

Points

A linearly independent plane coefficient set $(\gamma_0, \gamma_1, \gamma_2)$ defines a point, which can then be written as:

$$\gamma_0 \cap \gamma_1 \cap \gamma_2 = \overline{\begin{pmatrix} a_0 & a_1 & a_2 \\ b_0 & b_1 & b_2 \\ c_0 & c_1 & c_2 \\ d_0 & d_1 & d_2 \end{pmatrix}}. \tag{9.72}$$

Take two points, a and b, each given by a 4×3 matrix in terms of the homogeneous coefficients of three planes. If a 3×3 matrix $\boldsymbol{K}$ satisfying the relation of eq.(9.70) exists, where $\det(\boldsymbol{K}) \neq 0$, then matrices $\boldsymbol{A}$ and $\boldsymbol{B}$ represent the same point, assuming a and b are defined in classical projective space. For two-sided space, the condition such that $\boldsymbol{A}$ and $\boldsymbol{B}$ represent the same point is given by $\det(\boldsymbol{K}) > 0$.

Vacuum

A linearly independent plane coefficient set $(\gamma_0, \gamma_1, \gamma_2, \gamma_3)$ defines a vacuum, which can then be written as:

$$\gamma_0 \cap \gamma_1 \cap \gamma_2 \cap \gamma_3 = \overline{\begin{pmatrix} a_0 & a_1 & a_2 & a_3 \\ b_0 & b_1 & b_2 & b_3 \\ c_0 & c_1 & c_2 & c_3 \\ d_0 & d_1 & d_2 & d_3 \end{pmatrix}}. \tag{9.73}$$

There is only one vacuum in classical projective space.

For two-sided space, take two vacuums, a and b, each given by a 4×4 matrix in terms of the homogeneous coefficients of four planes. If a 4×4 matrix $\boldsymbol{K}$ satisfying the relation of eq.(9.70) exists, where $\det(\boldsymbol{K}) > 0$, then matrices $\boldsymbol{A}$ and $\boldsymbol{B}$ represent the same vacuum.

Vacuums in two-sided space have orientations. When the sign given by the following expression:

$$sign(\begin{vmatrix} a_0 & a_1 & a_2 & a_3 \\ b_0 & b_1 & b_2 & b_3 \\ c_0 & c_1 & c_2 & c_3 \\ d_0 & d_1 & d_2 & d_3 \end{vmatrix}) \tag{9.74}$$

is positive, then the vacuum in question is a positive one, Λ; conversely, a negative sign indicates a negative vacuum, $\neg\Lambda$.

We have now defined flat sets in terms of *meet* operations.

When flat sets are represented by a combination of a plane coefficient set and *meet* operations, the *meet* operations between these flat sets are quite simple, that is, one just attaches together the columns of the two matrices representing the two flat sets. Other operations, however, are not so simple.

With flat sets defined with *meet* operations as well, geometric elements in classical projective space have no orientation, and so the signs of homogeneous coefficients and the order of columns have no effect on the outcome of an operation, but in two-sided space, one must pay attention to such matters.

9.2 Homogeneous Simplices

We shall first define homogeneously expressed simplices as natural extensions of simplices in Euclidean space [42] (see Section 8.2). These will consist of homogeneous simplices, defined using homogeneous coordinates of points, and their duals, that is, dual homogeneous simplices, defined in terms of homogeneous coefficients of planes. They can also be divided into simplices in classical projective space and those in two-sided space.

Table 9.2: Homogeneous simplices and dual homogeneous simplices

Homogeneous simplices	**Dual homogeneous simplices**
1. Homogeneous line segment A homogeneous line segment can be defined by homogeneous parameters as a convex combination of two linearly independent homogeneous point vectors, $\boldsymbol{V}_0$ and $\boldsymbol{V}_1$ (see Figs. 8.2 and 8.3), as follows: $\overline{\boldsymbol{V}} = \overline{\xi_0 \boldsymbol{V}_0 + \xi_1 \boldsymbol{V}_1}$, $(\xi_0, \xi_1) \neq (0, 0)$, $(\xi_0, \xi_1 \geq 0) \vee (\xi_0, \xi_1 \leq 0)$....classical, $\xi_0, \xi_1 \geq 0$...............two-sided.	**1'. Dual homogeneous line segment** A dual homogeneous line segment can be defined by homogeneous parameters as a convex combination of two linearly independent homogeneous coefficient vectors, $\boldsymbol{\gamma}_0$ and $\boldsymbol{\gamma}_1$ (see Fig. 9.4), as follows: $\overline{\boldsymbol{\gamma}} = \overline{\xi_0 \boldsymbol{\gamma}_0 + \xi_1 \boldsymbol{\gamma}_1}$, $(\xi_0, \xi_1) \neq (0, 0)$, $(\xi_0, \xi_1 \geq 0) \vee (\xi_0, \xi_1 \leq 0)$....classical, $\xi_0, \xi_1 \geq 0$...............two-sided.
2. Homogeneous triangle A homogeneous triangle can be defined by homogeneous parameters as a convex combination of three linearly independent homogeneous point vectors, $\boldsymbol{V}_0$, $\boldsymbol{V}_1$ and $\boldsymbol{V}_2$ (see Figs. 9.5 and 9.6), as follows: $\overline{\boldsymbol{V}} = \overline{\xi_0 \boldsymbol{V}_0 + \xi_1 \boldsymbol{V}_1 + \xi_2 \boldsymbol{V}_2}$, $(\xi_0, \xi_1, \xi_2) \neq (0, 0, 0)$, $(\xi_0, \xi_1, \xi_2 \geq 0) \vee (\xi_0, \xi_1, \xi_2 \leq 0)$ ....classical, $\xi_0, \xi_1, \xi_2 \geq 0$.......two-sided.	**2'. Dual homogeneous triangle** A dual homogeneous triangle can be defined by homogeneous parameters as a convex combination of three linearly independent homogeneous coefficient vectors, $\boldsymbol{\gamma}_0$, $\boldsymbol{\gamma}_1$ and $\boldsymbol{\gamma}_2$, as follows: $\overline{\boldsymbol{\gamma}} = \overline{\xi_0 \boldsymbol{\gamma}_0 + \xi_1 \boldsymbol{\gamma}_1 + \xi_2 \boldsymbol{\gamma}_2}$, $(\xi_0, \xi_1, \xi_2) \neq (0, 0, 0)$, $(\xi_0, \xi_1, \xi_2 \geq 0) \vee (\xi_0, \xi_1, \xi_2 \leq 0)$ ....classical, $\xi_0, \xi_1, \xi_2 \geq 0$.......two-sided.
3. Homogeneous tetrahedron A homogeneous tetrahedron can be defined by homogeneous parameters as a convex combination of four linearly independent homogeneous point vectors, $\boldsymbol{V}_0$, $\boldsymbol{V}_1$, $\boldsymbol{V}_2$ and $\boldsymbol{V}_3$ (see Figs. 9.7 and 9.8), as follows: $\overline{\boldsymbol{V}} = \overline{\xi_0 \boldsymbol{V}_0 + \xi_1 \boldsymbol{V}_1 + \xi_2 \boldsymbol{V}_2 + \xi_3 \boldsymbol{V}_3}$, $(\xi_0, \xi_1, \xi_2, \xi_3) \neq (0, 0, 0, 0)$, $(\xi_0, \xi_1, \xi_2, \xi_3 \geq 0) \vee (\xi_0, \xi_1, \xi_2, \xi_3 \leq 0)$ .....classical, $\xi_0, \xi_1, \xi_2, \xi_3 \geq 0$.....two-sided.	**3'. Dual homogeneous tetrahedron** A dual homogeneous tetrahedron can be defined by homogeneous parameters as a convex combination of four linearly independent homogeneous coefficient vectors, $\boldsymbol{\gamma}_0$, $\boldsymbol{\gamma}_1$, $\boldsymbol{\gamma}_2$ and $\boldsymbol{\gamma}_3$, as follows: $\overline{\boldsymbol{\gamma}} = \overline{\xi_0 \boldsymbol{\gamma}_0 + \xi_1 \boldsymbol{\gamma}_1 + \xi_2 \boldsymbol{\gamma}_2 + \xi_3 \boldsymbol{\gamma}_3}$, $(\xi_0, \xi_1, \xi_2, \xi_3) \neq (0, 0, 0, 0)$, $(\xi_0, \xi_1, \xi_2, \xi_3 \geq 0) \vee (\xi_0, \xi_1, \xi_2, \xi_3 \leq 0)$ .....classical, $\xi_0, \xi_1, \xi_2, \xi_3 \geq 0$.....two-sided.

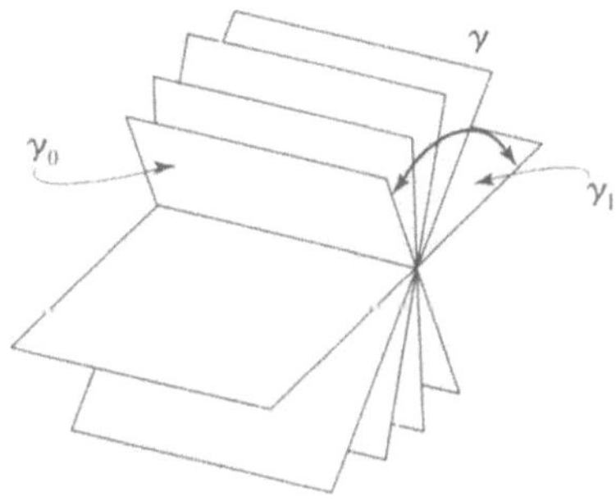

Figure 9.4: A dual homogeneous line segment.

Homogeneous simplices and dual homogeneous simplices are shown in Table 9.2. Note that these simplices are natural extensions of the Euclidean ones listed in Table 8.2. Note also that there is no such condition as the partition of unity, that exists in Euclidean representations (see Section 8.2). This property makes the Four-dimensional Processing more simplified and generalized.

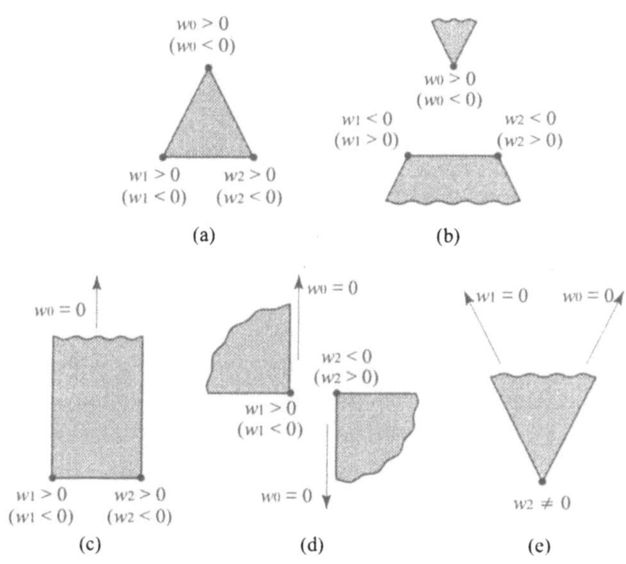

Figure 9.5: Homogeneous triangles (classical projective space).

With an ordinary line segment, an external line segment or half-line can occur when it is perspectively transformed or when a rational polynomial curve is linearly approximated. That is, a half-line results when $w=0$ plane contains an end point of the line segment, an external line segment occurs when it cuts the line segment, and a line segment at infinity occurs (which does not appear in Euclidean space), when it contains the whole segment (see Fig. 8.2 and 8.3).

One example of a dual homogeneous line segment is shown in Fig. 9.4.

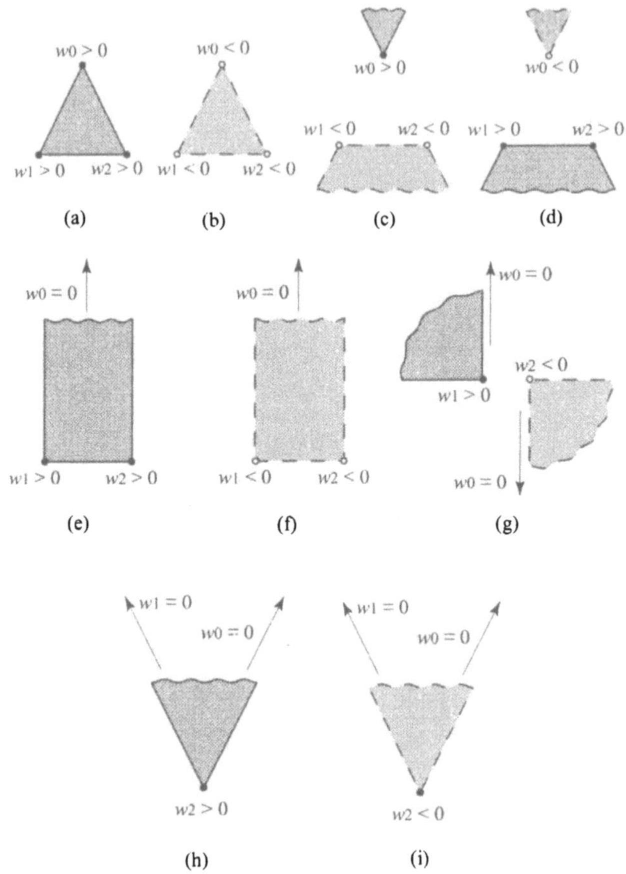

Figure 9.6: Homogeneous triangles (two-sided space).

An ordinary triangle can have various images in Euclidean space, as shown in Figs. 9.5 and 9.6, when it is perspectively transformed, or when a rational polynomial surface is triangularly approximated.

We shall look at the projective space case (see Fig. 9.5). Here, (b) is when $w = 0$ plane cuts two edges of the triangle; (c) when $w = 0$ plane contains a single vertex of the triangle; (d) when $w=0$ plane contains a single vertex and, at the same time, cuts the opposing edge; (e) is when $w=0$ plane contains two vertices along with the in-between edge.

When the entire triangular plane is contained in $w = 0$ plane, a triangular face at infinity results, which does not appear in Euclidean space.

When a tetrahedron is perspectively transformed, or when a tetrahedral form is produced by approximating a rational polynomial surface by triangles, various images in Euclidean space, as shown in Figs. 9.7 and 9.8, can result.

Again, we look at the classical projective space case (see Fig. 9.7). That is, (b) is when $w = 0$ plane cuts three edges of the tetrahedron; (c) when it cuts

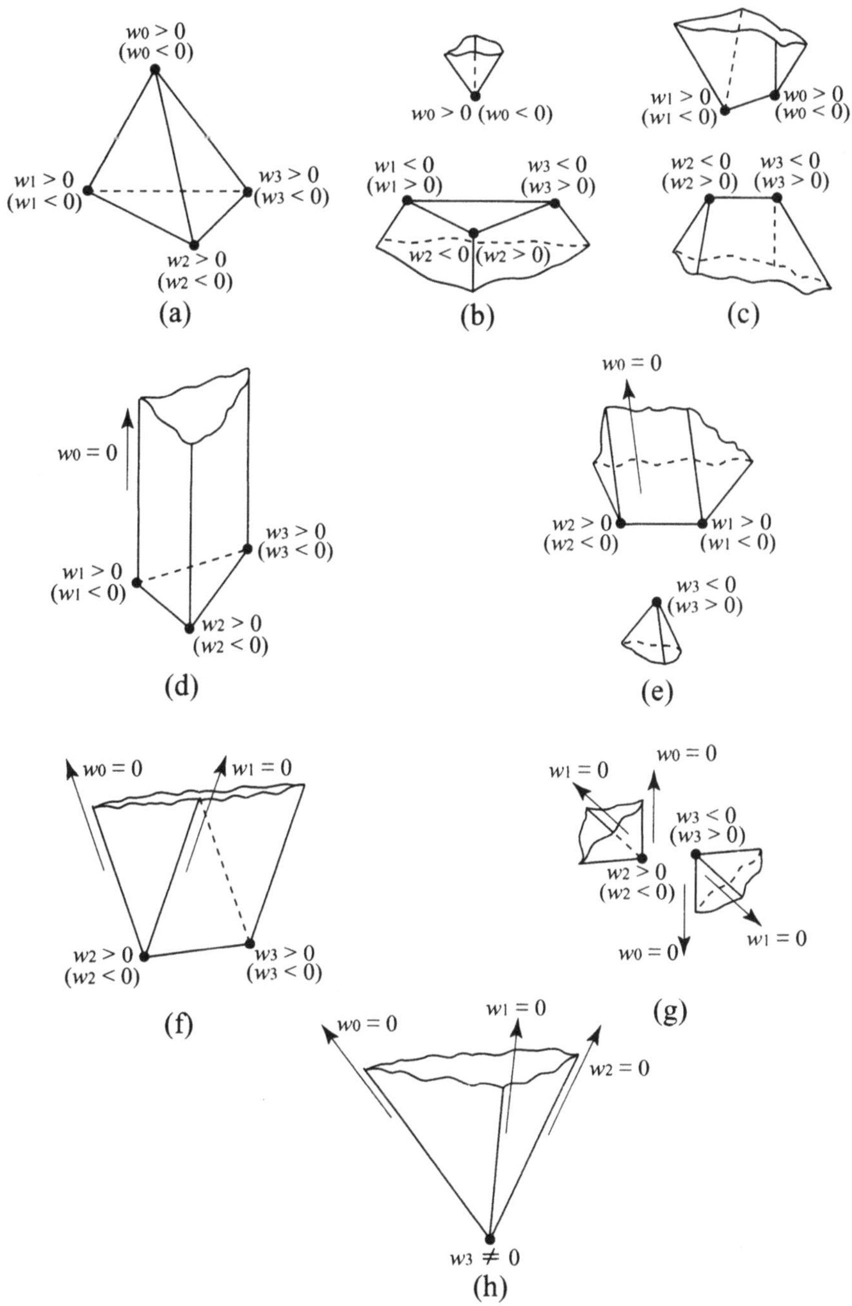

Figure 9.7: Homogeneous tetrahedra (classical projective space).

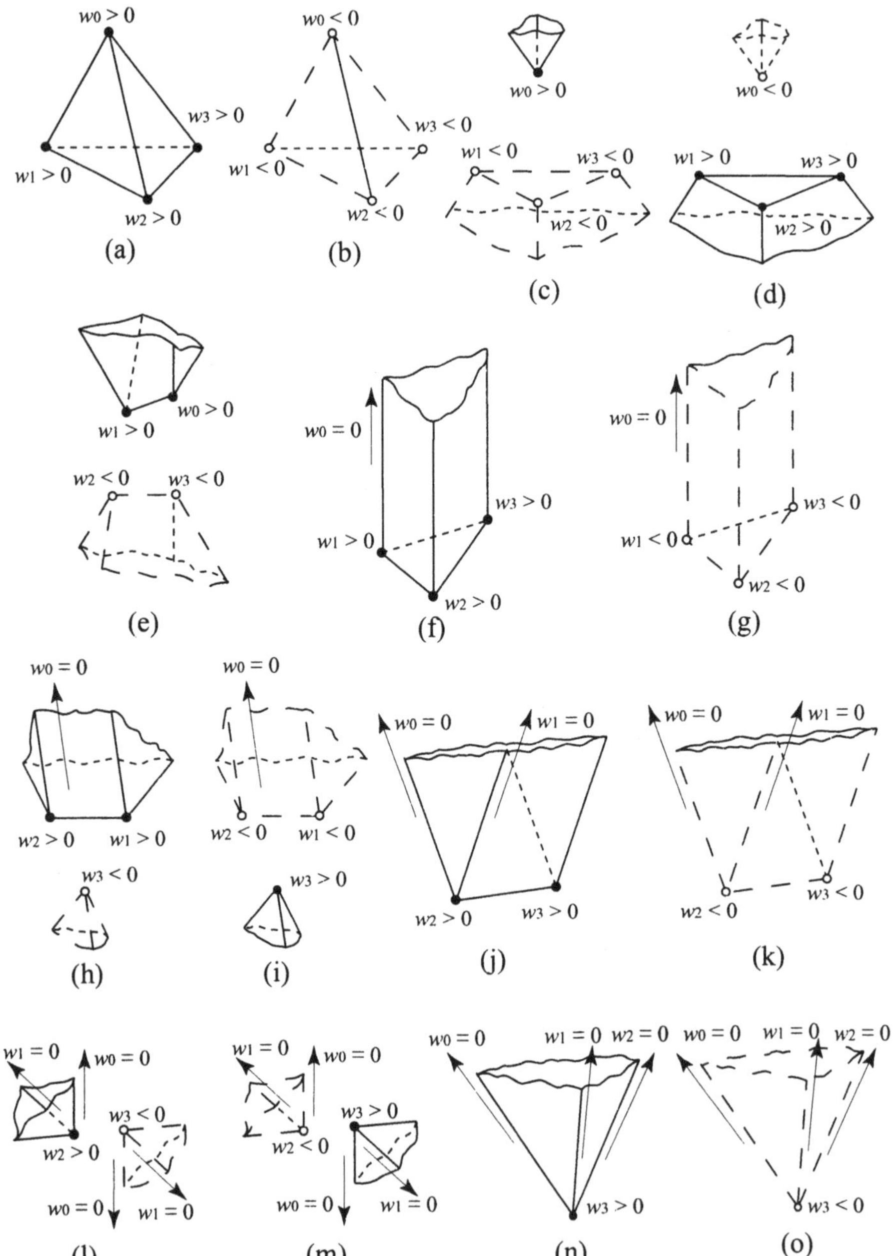

Figure 9.8: Homogeneous tetrahedra (two-sided space).

four edges; (d) when it contains a single vertex; (e) when it contains one vertex and, at the same time, cuts the two edges of the opposing triangle; (f) is when $w = 0$ plane contains two vertices and the edge in between; (g) when $w = 0$ plane contains two vertices and cuts the opposing edge; while (h) shows the case when one of the triangular faces of the tetrahedron is entirely contained in $w=0$ plane.

When $w = 0$ for all four vertices of the tetrahedron, the vertices all lie in the plane at infinity, and the tetrahedron is degenerate; this does not appear in Euclidean space.

The homogeneous simplices defined above are compared to Euclidean simplices in Table 9.3. The reader will note here that, in the case of homogeneous equations, there is no requirement that the sum of coefficients must equal unity, and that projective invariance holds for arbitrary coefficients (see Sections 6.4 and 10.4).

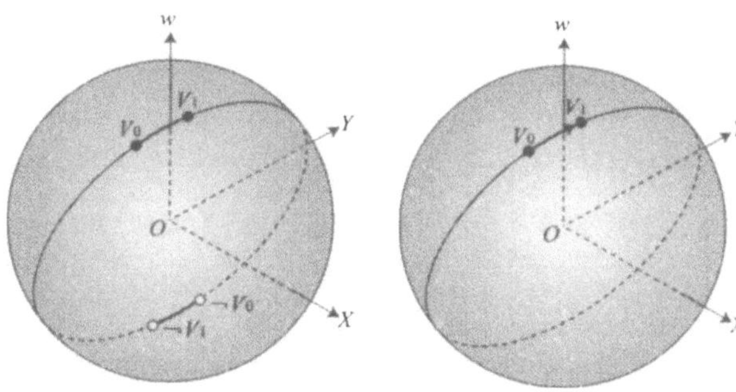

(a) Classical projective space (b) Two-sided space

Figure 9.9: Spherical models of line segments.

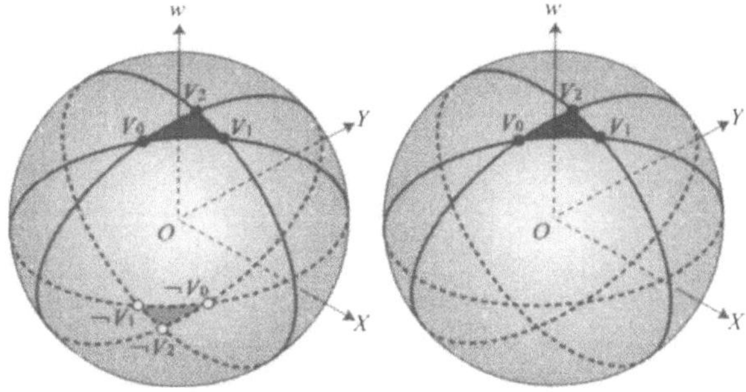

(a) Classical Projective Space (b) Two-sided Space

Figure 9.10: Spherical models of triangles.

Using the spherical model, Fig. 9.9 and 9.10 show a line segment and triangle, respectively, in classical projective and two-sided spaces. Recall that, in

Table 9.3: Comparison of Euclidean and homogeneous simplices.

Elements	Euclidean	Homogeneous
Line segment	$\boldsymbol{v} = \xi_0 \boldsymbol{v}_0 + \xi_1 \boldsymbol{v}_1$	$\overline{\boldsymbol{V}} = \overline{\xi_0 \boldsymbol{V}_0 + \xi_1 \boldsymbol{V}_1}$
	$\xi_0 + \xi_1 = 1$	none
	$\xi_0, \xi_1 \geq 0$	$(\xi_0, \xi_1 \geq 0) \vee (\xi_0, \xi_1 \leq 0)$ or $\xi_0, \xi_1 \geq 0$
	v_0, v_1: linearly independent	V_0, V_1: linearly independent
Triangle	$\boldsymbol{v} = \xi_0 \boldsymbol{v}_0 + \xi_1 \boldsymbol{v}_1 + \xi_2 \boldsymbol{v}_2$	$\overline{\boldsymbol{V}} = \overline{\xi_0 \boldsymbol{V}_0 + \xi_1 \boldsymbol{V}_1 + \xi_2 \boldsymbol{V}_2}$
	$\xi_0 + \xi_1 + \xi_2 = 1$	none
	$\xi_0, \xi_1, \xi_2 \geq 0$	$(\xi_0, \xi_1, \xi_2 \geq 0) \vee (\xi_0, \xi_1, \xi_2 \leq 0)$ or $\xi_0, \xi_1, \xi_2 \geq 0$
	v_0, v_1, v_2: linearly independent	V_0, V_1, V_2: linearly independent
Tetrahedron	$\boldsymbol{v} = \xi_0 \boldsymbol{v}_0 + \cdots + \xi_3 \boldsymbol{v}_3$	$\overline{\boldsymbol{V}} = \overline{\xi_0 \boldsymbol{V}_0 + \cdots + \xi_3 \boldsymbol{V}_3}$
	$\xi_0 + \cdots + \xi_3 = 1$	none
	$\xi_0, \cdots, \xi_3 \geq 0$	$(\xi_0, \cdots, \xi_3 \geq 0) \vee (\xi_0, \cdots, \xi_3 \leq 0)$ or $\xi_0, \cdots, \xi_3 \geq 0$
	$v_0, \cdots, v_3$: linearly independent	$V_0, \cdots, V_3$: linearly independent

classical projective space, a geometric element and its antipodal element are considered to be the same, and with no orientation. In two-sided space, however, a geometric element is different from its antipodal element and always possesses an orientation.

9.3 Curves and Surfaces

9.3.1 Implicit Function Forms

Here, we only show the simplest implicit curve and surface, that is, quadratic curve and surface.

Quadratic Curve

The general expression of the quadratic curve in x and y is given by:

$$ax^2 + 2hxy + by^2 + 2gx + 2fy + c = 0.$$

The homogeneous coordinate representation of the quadratic curve is given by:

$$[w\ X\ Y]\begin{bmatrix} c & g & f \\ g & a & h \\ f & h & b \end{bmatrix}\begin{bmatrix} w \\ X \\ Y \end{bmatrix} = 0, \tag{9.75}$$

or

$$\boldsymbol{P}\boldsymbol{B}\boldsymbol{P}^T = 0, \tag{9.76}$$

where

$$\boldsymbol{B} = \begin{bmatrix} c & g & f \\ g & a & h \\ f & h & b \end{bmatrix}, \quad \boldsymbol{P} = [w\ X\ Y]. \tag{9.77}$$

Quadratic Surface

The general expression of the quadratic surface in x, y and z is given by:

$$ax^2 + by^2 + cz^2 + 2fyz + 2gzx + 2hxy + 2lx + 2my + 2nz + d = 0.$$

The homogeneous coordinate representation of the quadratic surface is given by:

$$[w\ X\ Y\ Z]\begin{bmatrix} d & l & m & n \\ l & a & h & g \\ m & h & b & f \\ n & g & f & c \end{bmatrix}\begin{bmatrix} w \\ X \\ Y \\ Z \end{bmatrix} = 0, \tag{9.78}$$

or

$$\boldsymbol{P}\boldsymbol{B}\boldsymbol{P}^T = 0, \tag{9.79}$$

where

$$\boldsymbol{B} = \begin{bmatrix} d & l & m & n \\ l & a & h & g \\ m & h & b & f \\ n & g & f & c \end{bmatrix}, \quad \boldsymbol{P} = [w\ X\ Y\ Z]. \tag{9.80}$$

9.3.2 Parametric Function Forms

In Section 9.2, we defined homogeneous simplices as natural extensions of Euclidean ones. While, for Euclidean simplices, the sum of parameters (coefficients) must equal unity for an equation to remain valid under affine transformation, or:

$$\sum \xi_j = 1, \tag{9.81}$$

we found that no such requirement exists in the case of equations for homogeneous simplices, for which invariance holds for projective transformations, including affine transformations.

In Euclidean space, convex polyhedra are extended forms of Euclidean simplices. A convex polyhedron can be obtained when we remove the requirement regarding simplices that their defining points must be linearly independent. Thus, by replacing Euclidean vectors with vectors in $\mathbf{R}^4$ we can produce homogeneous convex polyhedra. The condition for convexity regarding parameters is that they are either all non-negative or all non-positive, that is:

$$\overline{\boldsymbol{V}} = \overline{\xi_0 \boldsymbol{V}_0 + \xi_1 \boldsymbol{V}_1 + \cdots + \xi_r \boldsymbol{V}_r}, \tag{9.82}$$

$$\xi_0, \xi_1, \cdot\cdot, \xi_r \geq 0, \quad \text{or} \quad \xi_0, \xi_1, \cdot\cdot, \xi_r \leq 0,$$
$$(\xi_0, \xi_1, \cdot\cdot, \xi_r) \neq (0, 0, \cdot\cdot, 0).$$

Curves and surfaces in Euclidean space can be defined as scalar functions of parameters which are obtained by generalizing the parameters of convex polyhedra. That is, a homogeneous curve can be defined as follows:

$$\overline{\boldsymbol{P}(t)} = \overline{\sum_{j=0}^{n} A_j(t) \boldsymbol{Q}_j}, \tag{9.83}$$

$$\text{For all } j, \quad A_j(t) \geq 0, \quad \text{or} \quad A_j(t) \leq 0,$$
$$(A_0(t), A_1(t), \cdots, A_n(t)) \neq (0, 0, \cdots, 0).$$

Note that projective invariance holds here also regardless of the coefficient functions. The relations so far discussed are summarized in Table 9.4.

Equations in homogeneous parameters (type-2 representation) for homogeneous Bézier curve segments and homogeneous Bézier surface patches, and their duals – dual homogeneous Bézier curve segments and dual homogeneous Bézier surface patches – are given in Table 9.5. The equations are defined in classical projective space (see Chapter 24).

9.4 Polygons and Polyhedra

9.4.1 Homogeneous Polygons

We begin our discussion with homogeneous polygons in classical projective space. A closed loop consisting of homogeneous line segments can be defined as follows: using homogeneous coordinates, first assign a cyclic order to a series of vertices lying on the same plane, then let the homogeneous coordinates

Table 9.4. Comparison of Euclidean and homogeneous curves and surfaces.

Elements	**Euclidean**	**Homogeneous**
Convex polyhedron	$\boldsymbol{v} = \xi_0 \boldsymbol{v}_0 + \cdots + \xi_r \boldsymbol{v}_r$	$\overline{\boldsymbol{V}} = \overline{\xi_0 \boldsymbol{V}_0 + \cdots + \xi_r \boldsymbol{V}_r}$
	$\xi_0 + \cdots + \xi_r = 1$	none
	$\xi_0, \cdots, \xi_r \geq 0$	$(\xi_0, \cdots, \xi_r \geq 0) \vee (\xi_0, \cdots, \xi_r \leq 0)$ or $(\xi_0, \cdots, \xi_r \geq 0)$
	$\boldsymbol{v}_0, \cdots, \boldsymbol{v}_r$: arbitrary	$\boldsymbol{V}_0, \cdots, \boldsymbol{V}_r$: arbitrary
Curve	$\boldsymbol{p}(t) = \sum_{j=0}^{n} a_j(t) \boldsymbol{q}_j$	$\overline{\boldsymbol{P}(t)} = \overline{\sum_{j=0}^{n} A_j(t) \boldsymbol{Q}_j}$
	$\sum_{j=0}^{n} a_j(t) \equiv 1$	none
	$a_j(t) \geq 0$ for all j	$(A_j(t) \geq 0$ for all $j)$ $\vee\ (A_j(t) \leq 0$ for all $j)$
	$\boldsymbol{q}_j$: arbitrary	$\boldsymbol{Q}_j$: arbitrary
Surface	$\boldsymbol{p}(u, v) =$ $\sum_{i=0}^{m} \sum_{j=0}^{n} a_i(u) a_j(v) \boldsymbol{q}_{ij}$	$\overline{\boldsymbol{P}(u, v)} =$ $\overline{\sum_{i=0}^{m} \sum_{j=0}^{n} A_i(u) A_j(v) \boldsymbol{Q}_{ij}}$
	$\sum_{i=0}^{m} \sum_{j=0}^{n} a_i(u) a_j(v) \equiv 1$	none
	$a_i(u) a_j(v) \geq 0$ for all i, j	$(A_i(u) A_j(v) \geq 0$ for all $i, j)$ $\vee\ (A_i(u) A_j(v) \leq 0$ for all $i, j)$
	$\boldsymbol{q}_{ij}$: arbitrary	$\boldsymbol{Q}_{ij}$: arbitrary

Table 9.5: Homogeneous and dual homogeneous Bézier curves and surfaces.

Homogeneous	Dual homogeneous
1. Homogeneous segment A homogeneous Bézier curve segment of degree n can be defined with $n+1$ sequentially ordered, point coordinate vectors, $\boldsymbol{Q}_0, \boldsymbol{Q}_1, \ldots, \boldsymbol{Q}_n$, in $\mathbf{R}^4$ as follows: $\overline{\boldsymbol{HP}(\eta,\sigma)} = \overline{\sum_{j=0}^{n} \binom{n}{j} \eta^{n-j}\sigma^j \boldsymbol{Q}_j}$ $\eta, \sigma \geq 0$ or $\eta, \sigma \leq 0$, where $(\eta,\sigma) \neq (0,0)$.	**1'. Dual homogeneous segment** A dual homogeneous Bézier curve segment of degree n can be defined with $n+1$ sequentially ordered, plane coefficient vectors, $\boldsymbol{\gamma}_0, \boldsymbol{\gamma}_1, \ldots, \boldsymbol{\gamma}_n$, in $\mathbf{R}^4$, as follows: $\overline{\boldsymbol{H\beta}(\eta,\sigma)} = \overline{\sum_{j=0}^{n} \binom{n}{j} \eta^{n-j}\sigma^j \boldsymbol{\gamma}_j}$ $\eta, \sigma \geq 0$ or $\eta, \sigma \leq 0$, where $(\eta,\sigma) \neq (0,0)$.
2. Homogeneous surface patch A homogeneous Bézier triangular surface patch can be defined with triangularly ordered, point coordinate vectors, $\boldsymbol{Q}_{ijk}$ in $\mathbf{R}^4$ as follows : $\overline{\boldsymbol{HP}(\xi_0,\xi_1,\xi_2)} = \overline{\sum_{i+j+k=n} \frac{n!}{i!j!k!} \xi_0^i \xi_1^j \xi_2^k \boldsymbol{Q}_{ijk}}$ $\xi_0, \xi_1, \xi_2 \geq 0$ or $\xi_0, \xi_1, \xi_2 \leq 0$, where $(\xi_0, \xi_1, \xi_2) \neq (0,0,0)$.	**2'. Dual homogeneous surface patch** A dual homogeneous Bézier triangular surface patch can be defined with triangularly ordered, plane coefficient vectors, $\boldsymbol{\gamma}_{ijk}$, in $\mathbf{R}^4$ as follows: $\overline{\boldsymbol{H\beta}(\xi_0,\xi_1,\xi_2)} = \overline{\sum_{i+j+k=n} \frac{n!}{i!j!k!} \xi_0^i \xi_1^j \xi_2^k \boldsymbol{\gamma}_{ijk}}$ $\xi_0, \xi_1, \xi_2 \geq 0$ or $\xi_0, \xi_1, \xi_2 \leq 0$, where $(\xi_0, \xi_1, \xi_2) \neq (0,0,0)$.

of two consecutive vertices define a homogeneous line segment, including that between the final and first vertices. The resulting closed loop of homogeneous line segments divides the plane into two regions. Since a plane expressed in homogeneous coordinates is topologically equivalent to the classical projective plane, one region of the plane is topologically a disc while the remaining region a Möbius band (see Section 3.4). The region equivalent to a disc and its boundary are called a *homogeneous polygon in classical projective space* [42]. Figure 9.11 shows an example of a homogeneous polygon. Since any homogeneous polygon is topologically the same as a disc, they are orientable and can be triangulated. When the w-values of the homogeneous coordinates of vertices all have the same sign, the homogeneous polygon is the same as an ordinary Euclidean one.

In two-sided space $\mathbf{T}^3$, a homogeneous polygon is defined as follows: when a closed simple polygonal line existing on a plane in $\mathbf{T}^3$ does not intersect with some other line on that plane, of the two planar parts divided by the closed simple polygonal line, that region which does not contain that line is called a *homogeneous polygon in two-side space* [42] (see Fig. 9.12). Normally, points on the closed simple polygonal line are included in the polygon.

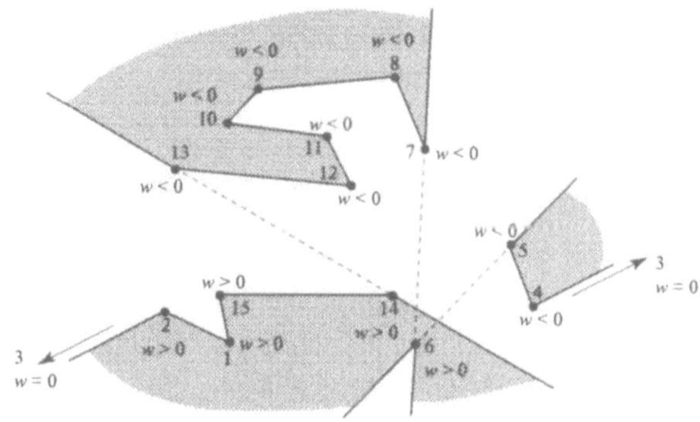

Figure 9.11: Homogeneous polygon defined in classical projective space.

A polygon in Euclidean space can be considered to have positive scale factors, w, for its vertex coordinates. So a polygon in Euclidean space will still satisfy the definition of a polygon after being embedded in $\mathbf{T}^3$, as it will after any projective transformation.

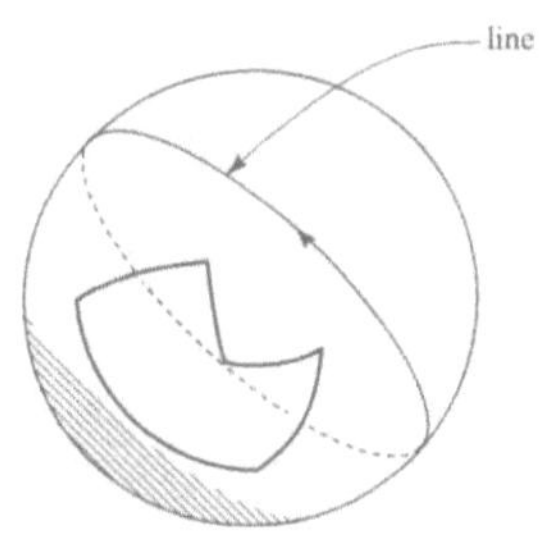

Figure 9.12: Homogeneous polygon defined in two-sided space.

9.4.2 Homogeneous Polyhedra

In consideration of the fact that classical projective space $\mathbf{P}^n$ is orientable if n is odd [47], a homogeneous polyhedron in the space can be defined in the following manner.

Assume that several homogeneous polygons exist in $\mathbf{P}^3$, that each one connects to other homogeneous polygons at all of its edges, and no polygon intersects with another. This set of homogeneous polygons will divide $\mathbf{P}^3$ into two orientable regions. One of these regions, along with its boundary, is defined as a *homogeneous polyhedron in classical projective space.*

Similarly, a homogeneous polyhedron in two-sided space can be defined by a natural extension of homogeneous polygons in two-sided space. Assume that several homogeneous polygons exist in $\mathbf{T}^3$, that each one connects to another homogeneous polygon at all of its edges, and no polygon intersects with another. This set of homogeneous polygons will divide $\mathbf{T}^3$ into two regions. There exists some plane in this space with which this set of homogeneous polygons does not intersect; the region that does not contain this plane is defined as a *homogeneous polyhedron in two-sided space* [42].

9.5 Homogeneous and Simple Curve Segments

In the Four-dimensional Processing a curve segment is defined in projective space, given several vectors determined by homogeneous coordinates:

$$\overline{\boldsymbol{P}(t)} = \overline{\sum_{j=0}^{n} A_j(t)\boldsymbol{Q}_j}. \tag{9.84}$$

We call such a curve segment $\overline{\boldsymbol{P}(t)}$ "homogeneous curve segment" as explained before.

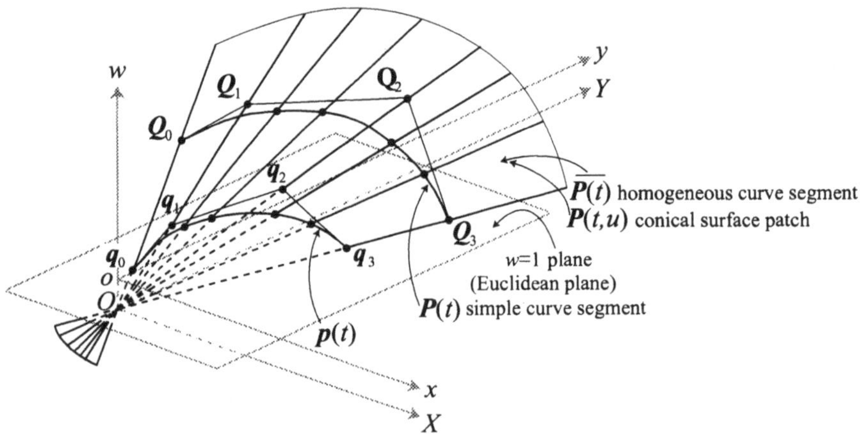

Figure 9.13: Homogeneous curve and simple curve segments in vector space.

The homogeneous curve segment is dealt with, however, not in projective space itself, but in the associated vector space, and its vector space model is the object of geometric processing in the Four-dimensional Processing paradigm. The vector space model of the curve segment is, in reality, represented as a four-dimensional conical surface $\boldsymbol{P}(t,u)$ with two parameters t and u, as seen in eq.(9.85), whose apex is at the origin (Fig. 9.13):

$$\boldsymbol{P}(t,u) = u\sum_{j=0}^{n} A_j(t)\boldsymbol{Q}_j, \quad u \neq 0. \tag{9.85}$$

Considering u is constant, we have a curve segment. We shall call the curve segment "simple curve segment" in contradistinction to a homogeneous curve segment. Ordinarily, u is put as unity:

$$\boldsymbol{P}(t,1) = \boldsymbol{P}(t) = \sum_{j=0}^{n} A_j(t)\boldsymbol{Q}_j, \quad u \neq 0. \tag{9.86}$$

In vector space a rational curve segment $\boldsymbol{p}(t)$ is the cut of its corresponding homogeneous curve segment $\overline{\boldsymbol{P}(t)}$ by $w = 1$ hyper-plane. Alternatively, it is considered to be the projection of its corresponding simple curve segment $\boldsymbol{P}(t)$ into $w=1$ hyper-plane.

As for surface, we deal with a homogeneous surface patch in vector space:

$$\begin{aligned} \overline{\boldsymbol{P}(u,v)} &= \overline{[w(u,v)\ X(u,v)\ Y(u,v)\ Z(u,v)]} \\ &= \overline{\sum_{i=0}^{m}\sum_{j=0}^{n} A_{i,m}(u)A_{j,n}(v)\boldsymbol{Q}_{ij}}, \\ \boldsymbol{Q}_{ij} &= [w_{ij}\ X_{ij}\ Y_{ij}\ Z_{ij}]. \end{aligned} \tag{9.87}$$

The vector space model of the surface patch is, in reality, represented as a hyper-conical body. In contradistinction to a homogeneous surface patch we shall call $\boldsymbol{P}(u, v)$ "simple surface patch."

In vector space a rational surface patch $\boldsymbol{p}(u, v)$ is the cut of its corresponding homogeneous surface patch $\overline{\boldsymbol{P}(u, v)}$ by $w = 1$ hyper-plane. Alternatively, it is considered to be the projection of its corresponding simple surface patch $\boldsymbol{P}(u, v)$ into $w=1$ hyper-plane.

9.6 Conversion from Parametric to Implicit

Consider a planar curve given by the following parametric rational equations:

$$x(t) = \frac{X(t)}{w(t)}, \quad y(t) = \frac{Y(t)}{w(t)}.$$

By multiplying by the denominator and rearranging, we have:

$$\begin{cases} x \cdot w(t) - X(t) = 0, \\ y \cdot w(t) - Y(t) = 0. \end{cases} \tag{9.88}$$

Since this is a set of polynomials with three variables, x, y and t, we can obtain an implicit function for x and y by eliminating t.

Similarly, consider a surface given by the following parametric rational equations:

$$x(u,v) = \frac{X(u,v)}{w(u,v)}, \quad y(u,v) = \frac{Y(u,v)}{w(u,v)} \quad z(u,v) = \frac{Z(u,v)}{w(u,v)}.$$

By multiplying by the denominator and rearranging, we have:

$$\begin{cases} x \cdot w(u,v) - X(u,v) = 0, \\ y \cdot w(u,v) - Y(u,v) = 0, \\ z \cdot w(u,v) - Y(u,v) = 0. \end{cases} \tag{9.89}$$

Since this is a set of polynomials with five variables, x, y, z, u and v, we can obtain an implicit function for x, y and z by eliminating u and v.

Thus, any parametric planar curve or parametric surface, whether it is in an ordinary or rational form, can be expressed as an implicit function. There are several known methods for transforming parametric functions into implicit functions, for example, one that uses resultants, one that employs Gröbner bases, the Wu-Ritt method, etc [25].

Sylvester's elimination method
Given two algebraic equations:

$$f(x) = a_n x^n + a_{n-1}x^{n-1} + \cdots + a_0, \quad (a_n \neq 0),$$
$$g(x) = b_m x^m + b_{m-1}x^{m-1} + \cdots + b_0, \quad (b_m \neq 0),$$

if their common root exists, then:

$$\overbrace{\begin{vmatrix} a_n & a_{n-1} & \dots & a_0 & 0 & \dots & 0 \\ 0 & a_n & \dots & a_1 & a_0 & \dots & 0 \\ & & \dots & \dots & \dots & & \\ 0 & \dots & \dots & a_n & \dots & \dots & a_0 \\ b_m & b_{m-1} & \dots & b_0 & 0 & \dots & 0 \\ 0 & b_m & \dots & b_1 & b_0 & \dots & 0 \\ & & \dots & \dots & \dots & & \\ 0 & \dots & b_m & b_{m-1} & \dots & \dots & b_0 \end{vmatrix}}^{m+n \ columns} = 0. \tag{9.90}$$

The reverse also holds. This equation can be used to eliminate variables; this is called *Sylvester's elimination method.* The determinant on the left-hand side is called the *Sylvester resultant* for $f(x)$ and $g(x)$.

Using the following parametric circle equation as an example:

$$x = \frac{2t}{1+t^2}, \quad y = \frac{1-t^2}{1+t^2}, \tag{9.91}$$

let us transform it into an implicit function using the Sylvester's elimination method.

This equation can be rewritten as:

$$xt^2 - 2t + x = 0, \quad (y+1)t^2 + y - 1 = 0. \tag{9.92}$$

Setting the Sylvester resultant equal to zero, we have:

$$\begin{vmatrix} x & -2 & x & 0 \\ 0 & x & -2 & x \\ y+1 & 0 & y-1 & 0 \\ 0 & y+1 & 0 & y-1 \end{vmatrix} = 4(x^2 + y^2 - 1) = 0.$$

Sometimes, unnecessary factors can arise when using the Sylvester resultant to eliminate parameters, and finding and removing such factors involves a tedious procedure. No such factors arise in the above example, but this problem commonly occurs when multiple variables must be eliminated, as for a surface [25].

Chapter 10

Homogeneous Curves

10.1 Rational Polynomial Curve Segment

A rational polynomial curve segment is usually defined by the following expressions:

$$\begin{aligned}
\boldsymbol{p}(t) &= [x(t)\ y(t)\ z(t)] = [\frac{X(t)}{w(t)}\ \frac{Y(t)}{w(t)}\ \frac{Z(t)}{w(t)}] \\
&= \frac{\sum_{j=0}^{n} a_j(t) w_j \boldsymbol{q}_j}{\sum_{i=0}^{n} a_i(t) w_i}, \quad (0 \leq t \leq 1), && (10.1) \\
\boldsymbol{q}_j &= [x_j\ y_j\ z_j], \\
&(a_j(t) \geq 0 \text{ for all } j) \vee (a_j(t) \leq 0 \text{ for all } j), && (10.2) \\
&(w_j > 0 \text{ for all } j) \vee (w_j < 0 \text{ for all } j), && (10.3)
\end{aligned}$$

where w_j are called *weights*.

Alternatively, a rational curve segment can be defined as follows [43]:

$$\boldsymbol{p}(t) = [1\ x(t)\ y(t)\ z(t)] = \frac{\sum_{j=0}^{n} a_j(t) w_j \boldsymbol{q}_j}{\sum_{i=0}^{n} a_i(t) w_i} = \frac{\boldsymbol{P}(t)}{w(t)}, \quad (0 \leq t \leq 1), \quad (10.4)$$

$$\begin{aligned}
\boldsymbol{q}_j &= [1\ x_j\ y_j\ z_j], \\
&(a_j(t) \geq 0 \text{ for all } j) \vee (a_j(t) \leq 0 \text{ for all } j), && (10.5) \\
&(w_j > 0 \text{ for all } j) \vee (w_j < 0 \text{ for all } j). && (10.6)
\end{aligned}$$

Next, we shall examine some important properties of a rational polynomial curve segment.

Affine Invariance

A rational polynomial curve segment eq.(10.1) can be expressed as:

$$\boldsymbol{p}(t) = \sum_{j=0}^{n} \left(\frac{a_j(t) w_j}{\sum_{i=0}^{n} a_i(t) w_i} \right) \boldsymbol{q}_j \equiv \sum_{j=0}^{n} \phi_j(t) \boldsymbol{q}_j, \tag{10.7}$$

where

$$\phi_j(t) = \frac{a_j(t) w_j}{\sum_{i=0}^{n} a_i(t) w_i}. \tag{10.8}$$

It is clear that

$$\sum_{j=0}^{n} \left(\frac{a_j(t) w_j}{\sum_{i=0}^{n} a_i(t) w_i} \right) = \sum_{j=0}^{n} \phi_j(t) \equiv 1. \tag{10.9}$$

Eq.(10.9) shows that unlike an ordinary polynomial curve segment, a rational polynomial curve segment eq.(10.1) is invariant under affine transformations, independently of the basis functions $a_j(t)$ (see Appendix A.4).

Convex Hull Property

Since the basis functions, $\phi_j(t)$, are not negative under the conditions of (10.2) and (10.3), the rational polynomial curve segment, eq.(10.1), enjoys the convex hull property. That is, the curve segment always lies within the convex hull made by the defining vertices, q_j.

Rational polynomial curve segments have superior representational capabilities and, unlike ordinary polynomial ones, they can be used to exactly represent circles and other conics.

NURBS (Non-Uniform Rational B-Spline) curves and rational Bézier curves, both widely employed in current CAD systems, are typical rational polynomial curves. Yet, certain problems exist with these curves because of the rational representations (see next section).

10.2 Problems of Rational Representations

Taking rational polynomial curve segment, eq.(10.1), as an example, we list up and explain below some problems which are inherent in rational representations.

Lack of Projective Invariance

As stated in Section 6.4, we desire our curve representations to be projectively invariant.

In the rational polynomial curve segment of eq.(10.7), projective invariance requires, assuming a projective transformation ψ is applied (see eq.(6.14)):

$$\psi(\boldsymbol{p}(t)) = \sum_j \phi_j(t)\psi(\boldsymbol{q}_j), \tag{10.10}$$

or

$$\frac{\boldsymbol{p}(t)\boldsymbol{L} + [t_x\ t_y\ t_z]}{\boldsymbol{p}(t)\begin{bmatrix} p \\ q \\ r \end{bmatrix} + s} = \sum_j \phi_j(t)\left(\frac{\boldsymbol{q}_j\boldsymbol{L} + [t_x\ t_y\ t_z]}{\boldsymbol{q}_j\begin{bmatrix} p \\ q \\ r \end{bmatrix} + s}\right), \tag{10.11}$$

where $\boldsymbol{L}$ is a 3×3 matrix representing three-dimensional linear transformation.

Unfortunately, the equation above does not hold. That is, the rational polynomial curve segment, eq.(10.1), does not enjoy projective invariance. A perspective transformation is a type of projective ones which is neither a linear, nor an affine transformation. Perspective transformations are used in a computer aided design system, for example, when an object is to be rendered realistically.

In perspectively transforming a rational polynomial curve eq.(10.1), tranforming the control points and then computing the curve does not give its correct projected image [16] ! One must perspectively transform each generated point on the curve.

Non-exactness

In ordinary polynomial curves, the basis functions $a_j(t)$ contain many fractional coefficients. These division operations can create a small amount of error.

With rational polynomial curves, it is possible with a simple technique to avoid the problem mentioned above in which the coefficients of the basis functions are given in fractional representation; however, in actual computations, exactness is lost in computing points on the curve because the divisions of the rational curve form must be carried out. In some particular applications such as set operations in solid modeling, this small amount of error could affect the reliability of the algorithm.

Although a rational quadratic curve exactly expresses a conic, one cannot generally determine the exact coordinates of points on the curve in actual computations.

Non-robustness

When the geometric Newton-Raphson method is applied to a rational polynomial curve for intersection computation with some geometric element, the parameter value could diverge to an extremely big number, thus causing to halt the algorithm. This non-robustness problem can occur occasionally and could cause a serious trouble because it may decrease the reliability of the CAD system. One such example was shown in Section 1.2.

This problem is inherent in rational polynomial curves, never occurring when ordinary polynomial curves are used. As for the details of this problem, see Chapter 15.

Formulas and Algorithms

Some formulas are applicable only to ordinary polynomials, but not to rational ones. One such example is calculus of finite differences (see Section 10.7), and another the Sturm's theorem (see Section 20.6).

In general, formulas and algorithms on rational polynomial curves are considerably more complex than those for ordinary polynomial ones. Some of such examples include projective transformations of a curve equation, and de Casteljau's subdivision algorithm that are also more complex for the case of rational polynomial curves.

Representational Capabilities

In rational polynomial curves, the weights w_j must all be of the same sign (see eq.(10.3)); this ensures that the curve will have a convex hull property, thus making it easier to carry out interference processing and other operations.

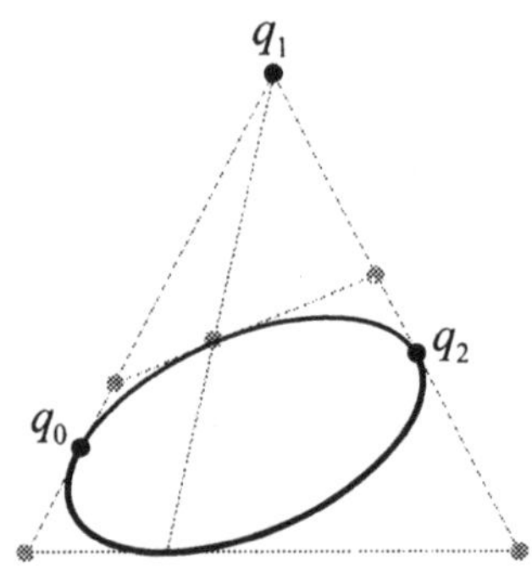

Figure 10.1: Quadratic Bézier curve and its complementary segment.

Now, consider that the complementary segment of a quadratic rational Bézier curve can be obtained by simply reversing the sign of w_1, which is the weight of the second control point, q_1 (see Fig. 10.1). Because of the above restriction in the signs of w_j, however, this complementary segment is excluded from processing.

This seems to indicate that there may lie a fundamental problem in the conventional processing of rational polynomial curves. We expect some other processing approach which enables us to exploit the high representational capability that the rational polynomial curves possess.

We have so far presented various problems that exist in the use of rational polynomial curves. It is the author's belief that these problems arise because the rational polynomial curves are defined in Euclidean space. We thus propose in their place the use of homogeneous curves defined through vector operations in the associated vector space of classical projective space.

10.3 The Homogeneous Curves

10.3.1 Simply-homogenized Curve Segment

The ordinary polynomial curves are free from the problems pointed out in the previous section. These problems exist only in the rational representations, which are considered to produce the data after division operations.

Therefore in incubating a curve form, we take the same approach that we took in defining other types of geometric elements. That is, we note the data before division operations, not the data after division operations. We look upon the data set before division operations, $w(t), X(t), Y(t)$ and $Z(t)$, as a vector $\boldsymbol{P}(t) = [w(t)\ X(t)\ Y(t)\ Z(t)] = [w(t)\ w(t)x(t)\ w(t)y(t)\ w(t)z(t)]$ $(w(t) \neq 0)$ in a space of dimension higher by one (four-space), and we define the vector $\boldsymbol{P}(t)$ as a convex combination of vectors $\boldsymbol{Q}_j = [w_j\ X_j\ Y_j\ Z_j] = [w_j\ w_jx_j\ w_jy_j\ w_jz_j]$ $(w_j \neq 0)$ in four-space (see Section 9.3.2):

$$\begin{aligned}
\overline{\boldsymbol{P}(t)} &= \overline{[w(t)\ X(t)\ Y(t)\ Z(t)]} \\
&= \overline{[w(t)\ w(t)x(t)\ w(t)y(t)\ w(t)z(t)]} \quad (w(t) \neq 0) \\
&= \overline{\sum_{j=0}^{n} A_j(t)\boldsymbol{Q}_j}, \quad (0 \leq t \leq 1),
\end{aligned} \tag{10.12}$$

$$\begin{aligned}
\boldsymbol{Q}_j &= [w_j\ X_j\ Y_j\ Z_j] \\
&= [w_j\ w_jx_j\ w_jy_j\ w_jz_j], \quad (w_j \neq 0),
\end{aligned}$$

$$(A_j(t) \geq 0 \text{ for all } j) \vee (A_j(t) \leq 0 \text{ for all } j), \tag{10.13}$$

$$w_j \text{ can take arbitrary signs including zero.}$$

We stipulate $\overline{\boldsymbol{P}(t)}$ to be defined in classical projective space, not in two-sided space because of the reason mentioned in Chapter 24.

We shall call $\overline{\boldsymbol{P}(t)}$ *a homogeneous curve segment* (or *a projective curve segment*). Because it is obtained by simply homogenizing the rational polynomial curve segment, that is, by homogenizing only the coordinates of the curve, we shall call it *simply-homogenized curve segment*, or *type-S homogeneous curve segment*.

In the four-space, the vector space model of $\overline{\boldsymbol{P}(t)}$ creates in reality a four-dimensional conical surface, $\boldsymbol{P}(t,u)$, of which the apex is at the origin (see Section 9.5 and Fig. 10.2). The cut of the conical surface by $w=1$ hyper-plane coincides with the rational polynomial curve, $\boldsymbol{p}(\mathrm{t})$ in eq.(10.1).

Note that a homogeneous curve is defined as an ordinary polynomial by some vectors, not by some points (see Section 9.3.2) [1].

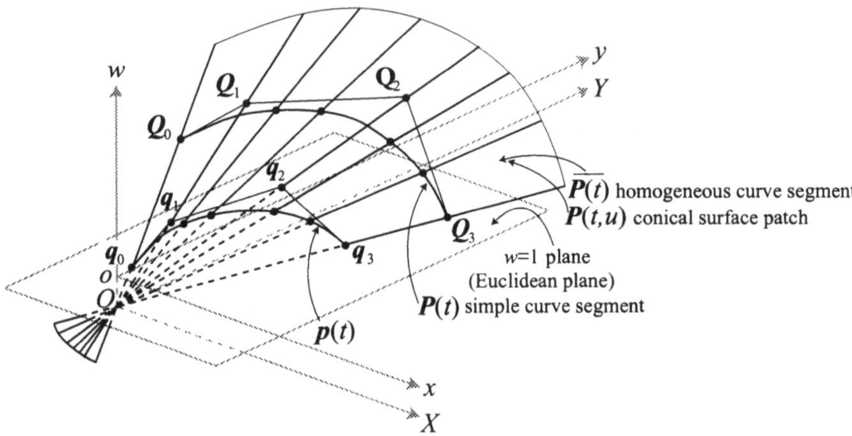

Figure 10.2: $\overline{\boldsymbol{P}(t)}$ defines a conical surface $\boldsymbol{P}(t,u)$.

10.3.2 Doubly-homogenized Curve Segment

The parameter of a homogeneous curve segment can also be homogenized by using two parameters (see Section 8.6). We shall call this *doubly-homogenized curve segment* or *type-D homogeneous curve segment* because it is obtained by doubly homogenizing the curve, that is, by homogenizing the parameter as well as the coordinates of the curve.

We shall discuss two types of type-D homogeneous curve segments according to two types of homogeneous parameters presented in Section 8.6.

Type-D1 Homogeneous Curve Segment

$$\begin{aligned}\boldsymbol{P}(t) &= \sum_{j=0}^{n} A_j(t)\boldsymbol{Q}_j \\ &= \boldsymbol{P}(\frac{s}{h})\end{aligned}$$

---

[1] Note that a projective curve definition by using <u>points</u> Q_j in projective space does not make sense because it is indefinite (see 7. of Section 2.2):

$$P(t) = \overline{\sum_{j=0}^{n} A_j(t)Q_j}. \tag{10.14}$$

See also the footnote of page 92.

$$
\begin{aligned}
&= \sum_{j=0}^{n} A_j(\frac{s}{h})\boldsymbol{Q}_j \\
&= \frac{1}{h^m} \sum_{j=0}^{n} HA_j(h,s)\boldsymbol{Q}_j \\
&\equiv \frac{1}{h^m} \boldsymbol{HP}(h,s),
\end{aligned}
\tag{10.15}
$$

where m is the degree of $A_j(t)$.

Thus we define the type-D1 homogeneous curve segment as below:

$$
\begin{aligned}
\overline{\boldsymbol{HP}(h,s)} &= \overline{[w(h,s)\ X(h,s)\ Y(h,s)\ Z(h,s)]} \\
&= \overline{\sum_{j=0}^{n} HA_j(h,s)\boldsymbol{Q}_j},
\end{aligned}
\tag{10.16}
$$

where

$$
HA_j(h,s) = h^m A_j(\frac{s}{h}). \tag{10.17}
$$

Type-D2 Homogeneous Curve Segment

$$
\begin{aligned}
\boldsymbol{P}(t) &= \sum_{j=0}^{n} A_j(t)\boldsymbol{Q}_j \\
&= \boldsymbol{P}(\frac{\sigma}{\eta+\sigma}) \\
&= \sum_{j=0}^{n} A_j(\frac{\sigma}{\eta+\sigma})\boldsymbol{Q}_j \\
&= \frac{1}{(\eta+\sigma)^m} \sum_{j=0}^{n} HA_j(\eta,\sigma)\boldsymbol{Q}_j \\
&\equiv \frac{1}{(\eta+\sigma)^m} \boldsymbol{HP}(\eta,\sigma).
\end{aligned}
\tag{10.18}
$$

Thus we define the type-D2 homogeneous curve segment as below:

$$
\begin{aligned}
\overline{\boldsymbol{HP}(\eta,\sigma)} &= \overline{[w(\eta,\sigma)\ X(\eta,\sigma)\ Y(\eta,\sigma)\ Z(\eta,\sigma)]} \\
&= \overline{\sum_{j=0}^{n} HA_j(\eta,\sigma)\boldsymbol{Q}_j},
\end{aligned}
\tag{10.19}
$$

where

$$
HA_j(\eta,\sigma) = (\eta+\sigma)^m A_j(\frac{\sigma}{\eta+\sigma}). \tag{10.20}
$$

The following relations (Euler's relation) exist:

$$m\boldsymbol{HP}(h,s) = h\boldsymbol{HP}_h(h,s) + s\boldsymbol{HP}_s(h,s), \tag{10.21}$$

$$m\boldsymbol{HP}(\eta,\sigma) = \eta\boldsymbol{HP}_\eta(\eta,\sigma) + \sigma\boldsymbol{HP}_\sigma(\eta,\sigma). \tag{10.22}$$

10.3.3 Continuity

In the Four-dimensional Processing, every processing is done in the associated vector space $\mathbf{R}^4$ of a projective space. The continuity problem between two homogeneous curve segments is also dealt with in the space with respect to the vector space models of the curve segments.

In the vector space a homogeneous curve segment is expressed as a triangular part of a conical surface of which the appex is at the origin (Fig. 10.3). Thus the continuity problem of two homogeneous curve segments means that of two conical surface patches in the vector space.

Let us consider the conditions that two homogeneous curve segments, $P_0(t)$ and $P_1(t)$, are position-continuous in Euclidean space at $t=t_0$ and $t=t_1$ respectively.

C^0 Continuity

This is the condition that the 0-th derivative vectors of the "simple" curve segments, $\boldsymbol{P}_0(t)$ and $\boldsymbol{P}_1(t)$, are continuous in vector space mathematically (as for simple curves, see Section 9.5):

$$\boldsymbol{P}_1(t_1) = \boldsymbol{P}_0(t_0). \tag{10.23}$$

If the condition above is satisfied, the positions of the homogeneous curve segments are continuous in Euclidean space, but it is too strong.

G^0 Continuity

This is the condition that the positions of the homogeneous curve segments, $\overline{\boldsymbol{P}_0(t)}$, $\overline{\boldsymbol{P}_1(t)}$ are continuous in Euclidean space:

$$\overline{\boldsymbol{P}_1(t_1)} = \overline{\boldsymbol{P}_0(t_0)}, \tag{10.24}$$

or

$$\boldsymbol{P}_1(t_1) = k\boldsymbol{P}_0(t_0), \tag{10.25}$$

where k is an arbitrary scalar. Eq.(10.24) or (10.25) shows that the simple curve segments $\boldsymbol{P}_0(t)$ and $\boldsymbol{P}_1(t)$ do not have to connect at $t=t_0$ and $t=t_1$ respectively, in order for the position of the homogeneous curve segments to be continuous in Euclidean space. The G^0 continuity condition is that the endpoints of the simple curve segments have a common line through the origin in the associated vector space (Fig. 10.3).

Next, let us consider the conditions that the two homogeneous curve segments, $P_0(t)$ and $P_1(t)$, are slope-continuous in Euclidean space at $t=t_0$ and $t=t_1$ respectively.

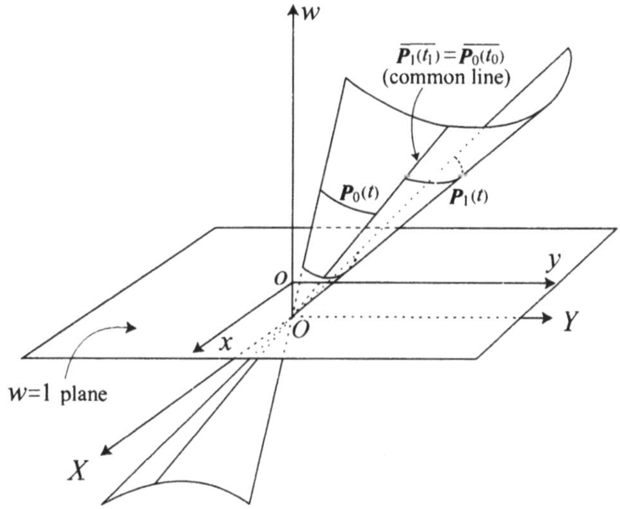

Figure 10.3: G^0 continuity.

C^1 Continuity

We assume the condition eq.(10.23) holds. Then the C^1 continuity condition is that the 1-st derivative vectors of the simple curve segments are continuous in vector space mathematically:

$$\dot{\boldsymbol{P}}_1(t_1) = \dot{\boldsymbol{P}}_0(t_0). \tag{10.26}$$

If the condition above is satisfied, the slopes of the homogeneous curve segments are continuous in Euclidean space, but it is too strong.

G^1 Continuity

This is the condition that the slopes of the homogeneous curve segments, $P_0(t)$, $P_1(t)$ are continuous in Euclidean space.

First, we assume $\boldsymbol{P}_1(t_1) = k\boldsymbol{P}_0(t_0)$, where k is an arbitrary scalar, but assumed positive for simplicity.

Next, we postulate that the two conical surface patches have a common tangent plane at the connecting line (Fig. 10.4):

$$\dot{\boldsymbol{P}}_1(t_1) \times \boldsymbol{P}_0(t_0) = \alpha\dot{\boldsymbol{P}}_0(t_0) \times \boldsymbol{P}_0(t_0), \tag{10.27}$$

where α is an arbitrary positive scalar. From eq.(10.27), we have:

$$\dot{\boldsymbol{P}}_1(t_1) = \alpha\dot{\boldsymbol{P}}_0(t_0) + \beta\boldsymbol{P}_0(t_0), \tag{10.28}$$

where β is an arbitrary scalar.

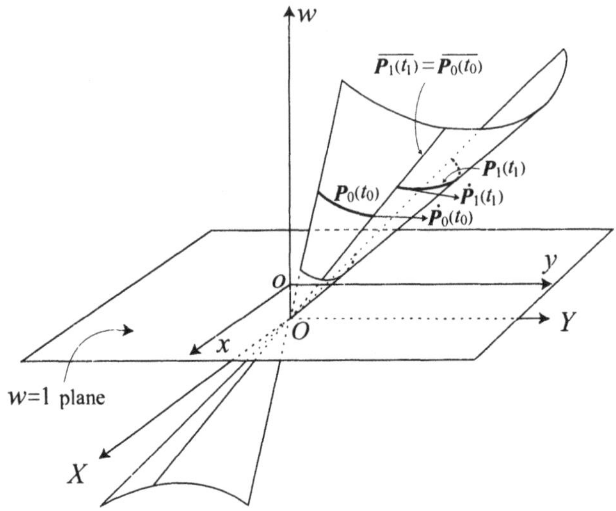

Figure 10.4: G^1 continuity.

Note that the simple curve segments $\boldsymbol{P}_0(t)$ and $\boldsymbol{P}_1(t)$ on the conical surface do not have to be slope-continuous at $t = t_0$ and $t = t_1$ respectively. The slope continuity condition is that the two conical surface patches (i.e., homogeneous curve segments) have, at $t = t_0$ and $t = t_1$ respectively, a common tangent plane.

10.4 Features of the Homogeneous Curve

Below we discuss the features of the homogeneous curves as compared to the problems with rational polynomial curves.

Projective Invariance without Condition

We consider the homogeneous curve, eq.(10.12).

Let us derive the condition that a projective transformation ψ can be applied to eq.(10.12). The relation for the condition is expressed below:

$$\overline{\psi(\boldsymbol{P}(t))} = \overline{\sum A_j(t)\psi(\boldsymbol{Q}_j)}. \tag{10.29}$$

Now, since a projective transformation is expressed linearly with respect to a homogeneous coordinate vector $\boldsymbol{Q}_j$ and a homogeneous transformation matrix $\boldsymbol{T}$,

$$\begin{aligned}\sum A_j(t)\psi(\boldsymbol{Q}_j) &= \sum A_j(t)(\boldsymbol{Q}_j\boldsymbol{T}) \\ &= (\sum A_j(t)\boldsymbol{Q}_j)\boldsymbol{T} \\ &= \psi(\boldsymbol{P}(t)).\end{aligned}$$

We have found that eq.(10.29) exists without any condition under any projective transformation [43].

As discussed before, the form of eq.(10.1) is not projectively invariant. If we deal with it, however, in the form of the homogeneous curve, eq.(10.12), it enjoys projective invariance without any condition for the basis functions $A_j(t)$. Projective invariance is, of course, more general than affine invariance.

Exactness

From the property of projective space, the point $\overline{\boldsymbol{P}(t)}$ of eq.(10.12) is identical to the point $\overline{\lambda \boldsymbol{P}(t)}$, obtained by multiplication by an arbitrary non-zero scalar λ, and furthermore the homogeneous curve does not have to be barycentrically combined (see Appendix A.4).

From these properties, whenever the right-hand side of eq.(10.12) contains fractions, we can remove them by multiplying the entire equation by the least common multiple of their denominators.

Suppose the parameter is transformed into a rational number form. Since this will produce a polynomial expressed in integers only and containing no fractions, the computations of $\overline{\boldsymbol{P}(t)}$ can be carried out exactly (see type-I homogenized NURBS curve in Sections 10.6 and 25.1.3).

Robustness

We pointed out some non-robustness with the geometric Newton-Raphson method, which could occur when it is applied to a rational polynomial curve and, which cannot when it is applied to an ordinary one.

Since the homogeneous curve is represented and treated as an ordinary polynomial, the geometric Newton-Raphson method, when it is applied to the homogeneous curve, does not exhibit the type of non-robustness that is inherent in rational representations.

The geometric Newton-Raphson method for the homogeneous curves is much more robust than the one for rational curves. For details, see Chapter 15 and Section 25.2.1.

Formulas and Algorithms

Many formulas are applicable to ordinary polynomials even if they are not to rational ones (see Sections 10.7 and 20.6).

As stated before, the Four-dimensional Processing is done, in vector space, with respect to vector space models of projective geometric elements, and not, in the projective space itself, with respect to projective geometric elements. Because the vector space model of a projective geometric element is an element of a linear subspace, various operations to the model tend to be simplified.

Representational Capabilities

As stated before, there exists a restriction in a rational polynomial curve that all w_j must have the same sign for reasonable processing in Euclidean space because many inconveniences will arise if the restriction is not observed. One such inconvenience is that convex hull property does not exist in such a mixed sign situation.

On the other hand, there is no such restriction in the homogeneous curve.

Here, we define the homogeneous convex hull as follows [56]:

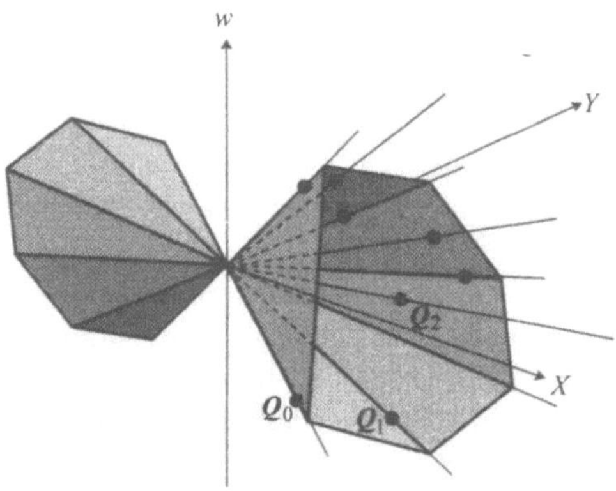

Figure 10.5: Homogeneous convex hull in vector space.

Definition 10.1 (Homogeneous convex hull)
Given r+1 non-zero, four-dimensional vectors, $\boldsymbol{Q}_0, \boldsymbol{Q}_1, \ldots, \boldsymbol{Q}_r$, the homogeneous convex hull, $\overline{\boldsymbol{P}}$, is defined as a homogeneous convex polyhedron:

$$\overline{\boldsymbol{P}} = \overline{\xi_0 \boldsymbol{Q}_0 + \xi_1 \boldsymbol{Q}_1, \ldots, \xi_r \boldsymbol{Q}_r}, \tag{10.30}$$

$$\xi_0, \xi_1, \ldots, \xi_r \geq 0 \ \ or \ \ \xi_0, \xi_1, \ldots, \xi_r \leq 0, \tag{10.31}$$

$$where\ (\xi_0, \xi_1, \ldots, \xi_r) \neq (0, 0, \ldots, 0).$$

Note in the definition above that the homogeneous convex hull is defined by vectors, not by points.

The vector space model of a homogeneous curve is always enclosed by a convex pyramid formed by the origin and control vectors in the associated vector space as shown in Fig. 10.5.

Fig. 10.6 shows various convex hulls (shaded area) projected onto the Euclidean plane. While the homogeneous convex hull coincides with the Euclidean one in case (a), the one in case (b) is separated in the Euclidean plane and looks completely different from an ordinary convex hull. Case (c) shows a special homogeneous convex hull, which turns out to be the whole Euclidean plane.

The homogeneous convex hull property holds in a homogeneous curve regardless of the signs of w_j, which means that w_j can be chosen freely without

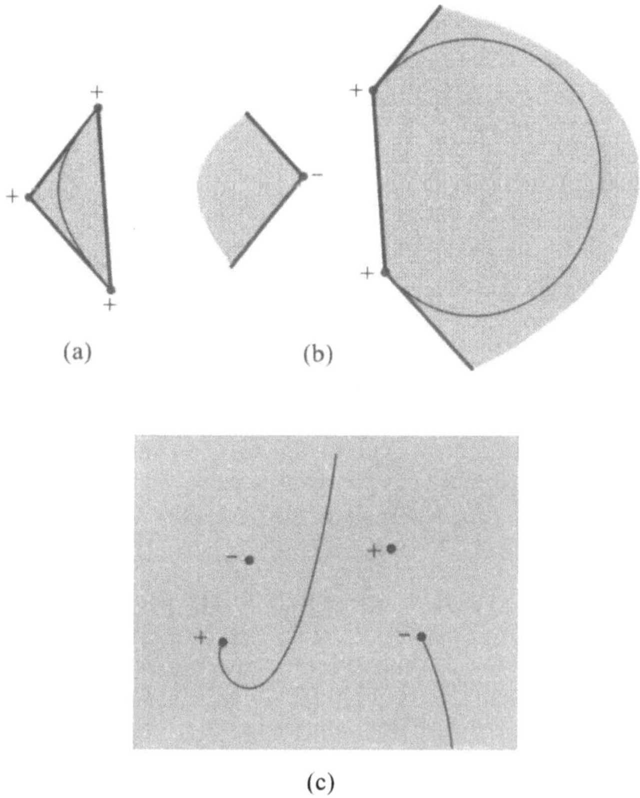

Figure 10.6: Homogeneous convex hulls (sign denotes that of vertex weight).

any restriction. This also makes it possible to process the complementary segment of a curve which could not be dealt with in a rational curve approach processed in Euclidean space (see Section 10.2).

Furthermore, we can manipulate homogeneous control vectors which correspond to points at infinity. This can, for example, enables us to define a half circle with the homogeneous curve (Fig. 10.7).

By dealing with the homogeneous curve form, we will have a possibility of exploiting the full representational capabilities that a rational representation essentially possesses.

Efficiency

Since the homogeneous curve is expressed in an ordinary polynomial form and thus is simpler than a rational polynomial curve, higher efficiency would generally be attained for its processing.

For instance, successive points on a homogeneous curve are generated very efficiently by difference calculus (see Sections 10.7 and 25.1.3).

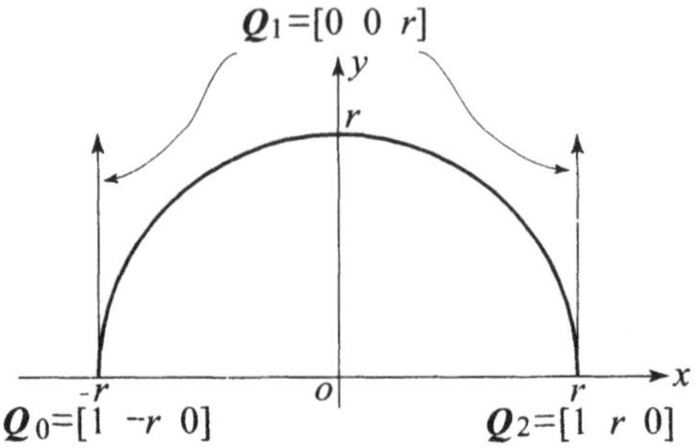

Figure 10.7: Half circle.

Note that in a homogeneous curve, $\boldsymbol{Q}_0, \boldsymbol{Q}_1, \ldots, \boldsymbol{Q}_n$ make a homogeneous polygon (see Section 9.4) and thus we must take care to clip the curve and the control polygon correctly for the display (see Sections 10.9 and 23.6).

10.5 Homogeneous Bézier Curve Segments

So far we have pointed out various problems with rational polynomial curves, and at the same time superior characteristics with homogeneous curves. Thus we now propose homogeneous Bézier curves in place of the conventionally used rational ones.

We first review the rational Bézier curve.

10.5.1 Rational Bézier Curve Segment

The following expression represents the rational Bézier curve segment.

Given $n+1$ points, $\boldsymbol{q}_j = [x_j \ y_j \ z_j]$, and their corresponding weights w_j,

$$\begin{aligned}\boldsymbol{p}(t) &= [x(t) \ y(t) \ z(t)] \\ &= \frac{\displaystyle\sum_{j=0}^{n} b_{j,n}(t) w_j \boldsymbol{q}_j}{\displaystyle\sum_{i=0}^{n} b_{i,n}(t) w_i}, \quad (0 \le t \le 1),\end{aligned} \tag{10.32}$$

$$b_{j,n}(t) = \binom{n}{j} (1-t)^{n-j} t^j, \tag{10.33}$$

where $b_{j,n}(t)$ are Bernstein basis functions of degree n [58].

The Bernstein basis functions have such an important property as satisfies the following recursion:

$$b_{j,n}(t) = (1-t) b_{j,n-1}(t) + t b_{j-1,n-1}(t). \tag{10.34}$$

10.5.2 Homogeneous Bézier Curve Segments

Simply-homogenized Bézier Curve Segment

Simply-homogenized Bézier curve segment or type-S homogeneous Bézier curve segment is obtained by simply homogenizing the rational Bézier curve, that is, by homogenizing only the coordinates of the curve [43].

This can be expressed as follows [2]):

$$\begin{aligned}\overline{\boldsymbol{P}(t)} &= \overline{[w(t)\ X(t)\ Y(t)\ Z(t)]}\\ &= \overline{\sum_{j=0}^{n}} B_{j,n}(t)\boldsymbol{Q}_j, \quad (0 \le t \le 1), \qquad (10.35)\\ \boldsymbol{Q}_j &= [w_j\ X_j\ Y_j\ Z_j].\end{aligned}$$

Because type-S homogeneous Bézier curve segment is an ordinary polynomial, there is no worry of a denominator becoming zero during processing. This results in a much more robust processing than the conventionally used rational Bézier curve when it is used in the Newton-Raphson method (see Chapter 15 and Section 25.2).

Doubly-homogenized Bézier Curve Segment

Doubly-homogenized Bézier curve segment or type-D homogeneous Bézier curve segment is obtained by doubly homogenizing the rational Bézier curve, that is, by homogenizing the parameter as well as the coordinates of the curve segment.

We define two types of type-D homogeneous Bézier curve segments corresponding to two types of homogeneous parameters (see Section 8.6).

Type-D1 homogeneous Bézier curve segment

The parameter homogenization is accomplished by placing $t = s/h$ in $B_{j,n}(t)$ of eq.(10.33) and by using the scalar multiple property of homogeneous coordinates.

Then type-D1 homogeneous Bézier curve segment is defined as follows:

$$\begin{aligned}\overline{\boldsymbol{HP}(h,s)} &= \overline{[w(h,s)\ X(h,s)\ Y(h,s)\ Z(h,s)]}\\ &= \overline{\sum_{j=0}^{n}} HB1_{j,n}(h,s)\boldsymbol{Q}_j, \qquad (10.36)\\ HB1_{j,n}(h,s) &= \binom{n}{j}(h-s)^{n-j}s^j, \qquad (10.37)\\ \boldsymbol{Q}_j &= [w_j\ X_j\ Y_j\ Z_j].\end{aligned}$$

The parameter range for the curve segment above is: (Fig. 10.8)

$$(0 \le s \le h) \vee (h \le s \le 0), \quad (h,s) \ne (0,0). \qquad (10.38)$$

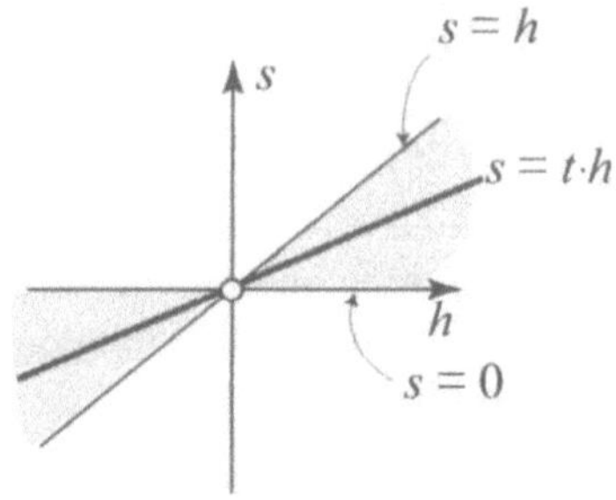

Figure 10.8: Parameter range for type-1 homogeneous parameters.

The homogeneous Bernstein polynomial $HB1_{j,n}(h,s)$ has the following recursion property:

$$\begin{aligned} HB1_{j,n}(h,s) &= \binom{n}{j}(h-s)^{n-j}s^j \\ &= \binom{n-1}{j}(h-s)^{n-j}s^j + \binom{n-1}{j-1}(h-s)^{n-j}s^j \\ &= (h-s)HB1_{j,n-1}(h,s) + sHB1_{j-1,n-1}(h,s). \end{aligned} \tag{10.39}$$

Type-D2 homogeneous Bézier curve segment

The parameter homogenization in this case is accomplished by placing $t = \sigma/(\eta+\sigma)$ in $B_{j,n}(t)$ of eq.(10.33) and by using the scalar multiple property of homogeneous coordinates.

Then the type-D2 homogeneous Bézier curve segment is defined as follows:

$$\begin{aligned} \overline{\boldsymbol{HP}(\eta,\sigma)} &= \overline{[w(\eta,\sigma)\ X(\eta,\sigma)\ Y(\eta,\sigma)\ Z(\eta,\sigma)]} \\ &= \overline{\sum_{j=0}^{n} HB2_{j,n}(\eta,\sigma)\boldsymbol{Q}_j}, \end{aligned} \tag{10.40}$$

$$HB2_{j,n}(\eta,\sigma) = \binom{n}{j}\eta^{n-j}\sigma^j, \tag{10.41}$$

$$\boldsymbol{Q}_j = [w_j\ X_j\ Y_j\ Z_j].$$

The parameter range for the curve segment above is: (Fig. 10.9)

$$(\eta,\ \sigma \geq 0) \vee (\eta,\ \sigma \leq 0), \quad (\eta,\sigma) \neq (0,0). \tag{10.42}$$

The homogeneous Bernstein polynomial $HB2_{j,n}(\eta,\sigma)$ has the following recursion property:

$$HB2_{j,n}(\eta,\sigma) = \eta HB2_{j,n-1}(\eta,\sigma) + \sigma HB2_{j-1,n-1}(\eta,\sigma). \tag{10.43}$$

[2] For the Bernstein basis function, the author denotes it by $B_{j,n}(t)$ in the homogeneous Bézier cases, not by $b_{j,n}(t)$ as he does it in the Euclidean Bézier cases.

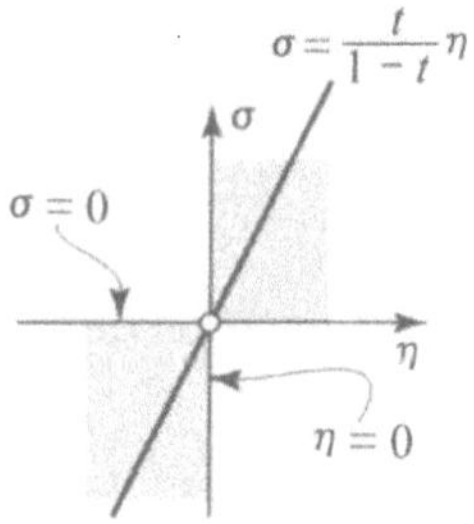

Figure 10.9: Parameter range for type-2 homogeneous parameters.

Type-D2 homogeneous Bézier curve segments show much superior characteristics to type-S homogeneous ones when they are used for computing intersection points by the geometric Newton-Raphson method (see Sections 15.7 and 25.2.1).

Furthermore, type-D1 homogeneous Bézier curve segments make it possible to attain exact computations of points on the curves coupled with integer arithmetic when rational parametric values are given.

Unlike a rational Bézier curve, a homogeneous Bézier curve does not have any restrictions on the signs of weights w_j.

10.6 Homogenized NURBS Curves

Nowadays, NURBS curves are considered to be the most versatile in their expressive capabilities among free form curves. NURBS curves, however, are represented in a rational polynomial form and so harbor those problems presented earlier in Section 10.2.

The author thus proposes three types of homogenized NURBS curves, which result from the homogenizations of NURBS curves.

10.6.1 Conventional NURBS Curve

The following expression represents the conventional NURBS curve.

Given $n+1$ vectors, $\boldsymbol{q}_j = [x_j \ y_j \ z_j]$, their corresponding weights w_j and a knot vector $[t_0, \ldots, t_{n+M}]$, determine all $N_{j,M}(t)$ $(j = 0, 1, \ldots, n)$ according to:

$$
\begin{aligned}
N_{j,1}(t) &= \begin{cases} N_{i,1}(t) = 1 & (t_i \leq t < t_{i+1}), \\ N_{i,1}(t) = 0 & \text{(outside above range)}, \end{cases} \\
N_{j,M}(t) &= \frac{t - t_j}{t_{j+M-1} - t_j} N_{j,M-1}(t) + \frac{t_{j+M} - t}{t_{j+M} - t_{j+1}} N_{j+1,M-1}(t),
\end{aligned}
\tag{10.44}
$$

where $N_{j,M}(t)$ is a normalized B-spline basis function of order M defined by $M+1$ consecutive knots beginning with t_j. Note here that i is an integer satisfying $t_i \leq t < t_{i+1}$. The relation eq.(10.44) is called *the de-Boor recurrence relation.*

Then the conventional NURBS curve is defined as follows:

$$\begin{aligned} \boldsymbol{p}(t) &= [x(t)\ y(t)\ z(t)] \\ &= \frac{\sum_{j=0}^{n} N_{j,M}(t) w_j \boldsymbol{q}_j}{\sum_{j=0}^{n} N_{j,M}(t) w_j}. \end{aligned} \tag{10.45}$$

10.6.2 Homogenized NURBS Curves

Simply-homogenized NURBS Curve

The simply-homogenized NURBS curve or type-S homogenized NURBS curve is obtained by simply homogenizing the conventional NURBS curve, that is, by homogenizing only the coordinates of the curve.

The following expression represents the type-S homogenized NURBS curve.

Given $n+1$ four-dimensional vectors, $\boldsymbol{Q}_j = [w_j\ X_j\ Y_j\ Z_j]$, and a knot vector $[t_0, \ldots, t_{n+M}]$, then type-S homogenized NURBS curve is defined as follows:

$$\begin{aligned} \overline{\boldsymbol{P}(t)} &= \overline{[w(t)\ X(t)\ Y(t)\ Z(t)]} \\ &= \sum_{j=0}^{n} N_{j,M}(t) \boldsymbol{Q}_j. \end{aligned} \tag{10.46}$$

Because type-S homogenized NURBS curve is an ordinary polynomial, there is no worry of a denominator becoming zero during processing. This results in a much more robust processing than the conventional NURBS curve when it is used in the Newton-Raphson method (see Chapter 15 and Section 25.2).

Doubly-homogenized NURBS Curve

The doubly-homogenized NURBS curve or type-D homogenized NURBS curve is obtained by doubly homogenizing the conventional NURBS curve, that is, by homogenizing the parameter as well as the coordinates of the curve.

We define two types of type-D homogenized NURBS curves corresponding to two types of homogeneous parameters (see Section 8.6).

Type-D1 homogenized NURBS curve

The parameter homogenization is accomplished by placing $t = s/h$ in $N_{j,M}(t)$ of eq.(10.44).

Then we have:

$$N_{j,M}(\frac{s}{h}) = \frac{\frac{s}{h} - t_j}{t_{j+M-1} - t_j} N_{j,M-1}(\frac{s}{h}) + \frac{t_{j+M} - \frac{s}{h}}{t_{j+M} - t_{j+1}} N_{j+1,M-1}(\frac{s}{h})$$
$$= \frac{1}{h}\left\{ \frac{s - ht_j}{t_{j+M-1} - t_j} N_{j,M-1}(\frac{s}{h}) + \frac{ht_{j+M} - s}{t_{j+M} - t_{j+1}} N_{j+1,M-1}(\frac{s}{h}) \right\}. \tag{10.47}$$

Now, since we are dealing with homogeneous coordinates, we can delete the common h in the denominators of eq.(10.47) to simplify the relation. We define $HN1_{j,M}(h,s)$ as below:

$$HN1_{j,M}(h,s) = \frac{s - ht_j}{t_{j+M-1} - t_j} HN1_{j,M-1}(h,s) + \frac{ht_{j+M} - s}{t_{j+M} - t_{j+1}} HN1_{j+1,M-1}(h,s).$$

The next expression represents the type-D1 homogenized NURBS curve.

Given $n+1$ four-dimensional vectors, $\boldsymbol{Q}_j = [w_j\ X_j\ Y_j\ Z_j]$, and a knot vector $[t_0, \ldots, t_{n+M}]$, determine all $HN1_{j,M}(h,s)$ $(j = 0, 1, \ldots, n)$ according to:

$$HN1_{j,1}(h,s) = \begin{cases} HN1_{i,1}(h,s) = 1 & (t_i \leq t = \frac{s}{h} < t_{i+1}), \\ HN1_{i,1}(h,s) = 0 & \text{(outside above range)}, \end{cases} \tag{10.48}$$

$$HN1_{j,M}(h,s) = \frac{s - ht_j}{t_{j+M-1} - t_j} HN1_{j,M-1}(h,s) + \frac{ht_{j+M} - s}{t_{j+M} - t_{j+1}} HN1_{j+1,M-1}(h,s). \tag{10.49}$$

Note here that i is an integer satisfying $t_i \leq t = \frac{s}{h} < t_{i+1}$.

Then the type-D1 homogenized NURBS curve is defined as follows:

$$\overline{\boldsymbol{HP}(h,s)} = \overline{[w(h,s)\ X(h,s)\ Y(h,s)\ Z(h,s)]}$$
$$= \overline{\sum_{j=0}^{n} HN1_{j,M}(h,s)\boldsymbol{Q}_j}. \tag{10.50}$$

The parameter range is shown in eq.(10.38) and Fig. 10.8.

Type-D2 homogenized NURBS curve

The parameter homogenization in this case is accomplished by placing $t = \sigma/(\eta + \sigma)$ in $N_{j,M}(t)$ of eq.(10.44).

Then we have $HN2_{j,M}(\eta,\sigma)$, as follows:

$$HN2_{j,M}(\eta,\sigma) = \frac{\sigma - (\eta+\sigma)t_j}{t_{j+M-1} - t_j} HN2_{j,M-1}(\eta,\sigma) + \frac{(\eta+\sigma)t_{j+M} - \sigma}{t_{j+M} - t_{j+1}} HN2_{j+1,M-1}(\eta,\sigma).$$

The next expression represents the type-D2 homogenized NURBS curve.

Given $n+1$ four-dimensional vectors, $\boldsymbol{Q}_j = [w_j\ X_j\ Y_j\ Z_j]$, and a knot vector $[t_0, \ldots, t_{n+M}]$, determine all $HN2_{j,M}(\eta,\sigma)$ $(j = 0, 1, \ldots, n)$ according to:

$$HN2_{j,1}(\eta,\sigma) = \begin{cases} HN2_{i,1}(\eta,\sigma) = 1 & (t_i \leq t = \frac{\sigma}{\eta+\sigma} < t_{i+1}), \\ HN2_{i,1}(\eta,\sigma) = 0 & \text{(outside above range)}, \end{cases} \tag{10.51}$$

$$HN2_{j,M}(\eta,\sigma) = \frac{\sigma - (\eta+\sigma)t_j}{t_{j+M-1} - t_j} HN2_{j,M-1}(\eta,\sigma) + \frac{(\eta+\sigma)t_{j+M} - \sigma}{t_{j+M} - t_{j+1}} HN2_{j+1,M-1}(\eta,\sigma). \tag{10.52}$$

Note here that i is an integer satisfying $t_i \le t = \frac{\sigma}{\eta+\sigma} < t_{i+1}$.

Then the type-D2 homogenized NURBS curve is defined as follows:

$$\begin{aligned}\overline{\boldsymbol{HP}(\eta,\sigma)} &= \overline{[w(\eta,\sigma)\ X(\eta,\sigma)\ Y(\eta,\sigma)\ Z(\eta,\sigma)]} \\ &= \overline{\sum_{j=0}^{n} HN2_{j,M}(\eta,\sigma)\boldsymbol{Q}_j}.\end{aligned} \tag{10.53}$$

The parameter range is shown in eq.(10.42) and Fig. 10.9.

The type-D homogenized NURBS curves show much superior characteristics when they are used for computing intersection points by the geometric Newton-Raphson method (see Sections 15.7 and 25.2.1).

Integrally-homogenized NURBS Curve

Given rational knots,

$$[t_0\ t_1 \ldots t_k \ldots\ t_{n+M}] = [s_0/h_0\ s_1/h_1 \ldots s_k/h_k \ldots s_{n+M}/h_{n+M}], \tag{10.54}$$

the integrally-homogenized NURBS curve, or type-I homogenized NURBS curve is obtained by integerizing all the coefficients of the basis functions of the type-D1 homogenized NURBS curve.

Introducing the rational knots above into eq.(10.49) yields:

$$\begin{aligned}HN1_{j,M}(h,s) = &\frac{h_{j+M-1}(h_j s - s_j h)}{s_{j+M-1}h_j - s_j h_{j+M-1}} HN1_{j,M-1}(h,s) \\ &+ \frac{h_{j+1}(s_{j+M}h - h_{j+M}s)}{s_{j+M}h_{j+1} - s_{j+1}h_{j+M}} HN1_{j+1,M-1}(h,s).\end{aligned} \tag{10.55}$$

Now, when $t_i = \frac{s_i}{h_i} \le t = \frac{s}{h} < t_{i+1} = \frac{s_{i+1}}{h_{i+1}}$, non-zero B-spline functions, $HN1_{j,M}(h,s)$, of order M in eq.(10.55) are (see Fig. 10.10):

$$HN1_{i-M+1,M}(h,s) = \frac{h_{i-M+2}(s_{i+1}h - h_{i+1}s)}{s_{i+1}h_{i-M+2} - s_{i-M+2}h_{i+1}} HN1_{i-M+2,M-1}(h,s),$$

$$\begin{aligned}HN1_{i-M+2,M}(h,s) = &\frac{h_{i+1}(h_{i-M+2}s - s_{i-M+2}h)}{s_{i+1}h_{i-M+2} - s_{i-M+2}h_{i+1}} HN1_{i-M+2,M-1}(h,s) \\ &+ \frac{h_{i-M+3}(s_{i+2}h - h_{i+2}s)}{s_{i+2}h_{i-M+3} - s_{i-M+3}h_{i+2}} HN1_{i-M+3,M-1}(h,s),\end{aligned}$$

$$\begin{aligned}HN1_{i-M+3,M}(h,s) = &\frac{h_{i+2}(h_{i-M+3}s - s_{i-M+3}h)}{s_{i+2}h_{i-M+3} - s_{i-M+3}h_{i+2}} HN1_{i-M+3,M-1}(h,s) \\ &+ \frac{h_{i-M+4}(s_{i+3}h - h_{i+3}s)}{s_{i+3}h_{i-M+4} - s_{i-M+4}h_{i+3}} HN1_{i-M+4,M-1}(h,s),\end{aligned}$$

$$\ldots = \ldots \tag{10.56}$$

$$HN1_{i-1,M}(h,s) = \frac{h_{i+M-2}(h_{i-1}s - s_{i-1}h)}{s_{i+M-2}h_{i-1} - s_{i-1}h_{i+M-2}} HN1_{i-1,M-1}(h,s) + \frac{h_i(s_{i+M-1}h - h_{i+M-1}s)}{s_{i+M-1}h_i - s_ih_{i+M-1}} HN1_{i,M-1}(h,s),$$

$$HN1_{i,M}(h,s) = \frac{h_{i+M-1}(h_is - s_ih)}{s_{i+M-1}h_i - s_ih_{i+M-1}} HN1_{i,M-1}(h,s).$$

$HN1_{i,1}$

$\swarrow \searrow$

$C_2 \times$ .... $HN1_{i-1,2}$ $HN1_{i,2}$

$\swarrow \searrow \quad \swarrow \searrow$

$C_3 \times$ .... $HN1_{i-2,3}$ $HN1_{i-1,3}$ $HN1_{i,3}$

....

$C_{M-1} \times$ .... $HN1_{i-M+2,M-1}$ $HN1_{i-M+3,M-1}$........ $HN1_{i,M-1}$

$\swarrow \quad \searrow \quad \swarrow$ .... $\searrow$

$C_M \times$ .... $HN1_{i-M+1,M}$ $HN1_{i-M+2,M}$............................... $HN1_{i,M}$

Figure 10.10: Hierarchy of non-zero B-splines.

Let C_M be the least common multiple of the denominators of the coefficients of the non-zero B-splines of order M, shown in eq.(10.56).

In order to accomplish the integerizations of B-splines, we multiply eq.(10.55) by the product of all the least common multiples C_k from order 2 to M:

$$\prod_{k=2}^{M} C_k = \prod_{k=2}^{M} \prod_{b=i-k+1}^{i-1} (s_{b+k}h_{b+1} - s_{b+1}h_{b+k}),$$

where

$$C_k = \prod_{b=i-k+1}^{i-1} (s_{b+k}h_{b+1} - s_{b+1}h_{b+k})$$

and define B-splines $HI_{j,M}(h,s)$ such that:

$$HI_{j,M}(h,s) = \{\prod_{k=2}^{M} C_k\} HN1_{j,M}(h,s). \tag{10.57}$$

From eq.(10.55),

$$HI_{j,M}(h,s) = \{\prod_{k=2}^{M} C_k\} HN1_{j,M}(h,s)$$

$$= \frac{h_{j+M-1}(h_j s - s_j h)}{s_{j+M-1}h_j - s_j h_{j+M-1}}\{C_M \prod_{k=2}^{M-1} C_k\} HN1_{j,M-1}(h,s)$$

$$+ \frac{h_{j+1}(s_{j+M}h - h_{j+M}s)}{s_{j+M}h_{j+1} - s_{j+1}h_{j+M}}\{C_M \prod_{k=2}^{M-1} C_k\} HN1_{j+1,M-1}(h,s)$$

$$= \frac{h_{j+M-1}(h_j s - s_j h)}{s_{j+M-1}h_j - s_j h_{j+M-1}} C_M HI_{j,M-1}(h,s)$$

$$+ \frac{h_{j+1}(s_{j+M}h - h_{j+M}s)}{s_{j+M}h_{j+1} - s_{j+1}h_{j+M}} C_M HI_{j+1,M-1}(h,s)$$

$$= \frac{h_{j+M-1}(h_j s - s_j h)}{s_{j+M-1}h_j - s_j h_{j+M-1}}\Big(\prod_{b=i-M+1}^{i-1}(s_{b+M}h_{b+1} - s_{b+1}h_{b+M})\Big) HI_{j,M-1}(h,s)$$

$$+ \frac{h_{j+1}(s_{j+M}h - h_{j+M}s)}{s_{j+M}h_{j+1} - s_{j+1}h_{j+M}}\Big(\prod_{b=i-M+1}^{i-1}(s_{b+M}h_{b+1} - s_{b+1}h_{b+M})\Big) HI_{j+1,M-1}(h,s)$$

$$= h_{j+M-1}(h_j s - s_j h)\Big(\prod_{\substack{b=i-M+1 \\ b\neq j-1}}^{i-1}(s_{b+M}h_{b+1} - s_{b+1}h_{b+M})\Big) HI_{j,M-1}(h,s)$$

$$+ h_{j+1}(s_{j+M}h - h_{j+M}s)\Big(\prod_{\substack{b=i-M+1 \\ b\neq j}}^{i-1}(s_{b+M}h_{b+1} - s_{b+1}h_{b+M})\Big) HI_{j+1,M-1}(h,s).$$

Then, the following is the type-I homogenized NURBS curve representation.

Given $n+1$ four-dimensional vectors, $\boldsymbol{Q}_j = [w_j\ X_j\ Y_j\ Z_j]$, and a knot vector $[t_0, \ldots, t_{n+M}]$, determine all $HI_{j,M}(h,s)$ $(j = 0, 1, \ldots, n)$ according to:

$$HI_{j,1}(h,s) = \begin{cases} HI_{i,1}(h,s) = 1 & (t_i = \frac{s_i}{h_i} \leq t = \frac{s}{h} < t_{i+1} = \frac{s_{i+1}}{h_{i+1}}), \\ HI_{i,1}(h,s) = 0 & \text{(outside above range)}, \end{cases} \tag{10.58}$$

$$HI_{j,M}(h,s) = h_{j+M-1}(h_j s - s_j h)\Big(\prod_{\substack{b=i-M+1 \\ b\neq j-1}}^{i-1}(s_{b+M}h_{b+1} - s_{b+1}h_{b+M})\Big) HI_{j,M-1}(h,s)$$

$$+ h_{j+1}(s_{j+M}h - h_{j+M}s)\Big(\prod_{\substack{b=i-M+1 \\ b\neq j}}^{i-1}(s_{b+M}h_{b+1} - s_{b+1}h_{b+M})\Big) HI_{j+1,M-1}(h,s), \tag{10.59}$$

where factor "0" in the difference products above is considered to be unity. Note here that i is an integer satisfying $t_i = \frac{s_i}{h_i} \leq t = \frac{s}{h} < t_{i+1} = \frac{s_{i+1}}{h_{i+1}}$.

Then the type-I homogenized NURBS curve is defined as follows:

$$\overline{\boldsymbol{HP}(h,s)} = \overline{\sum_{j=0}^{n} HI_{j,M}(h,s)\boldsymbol{Q}_j}. \tag{10.60}$$

The coefficients and parameters of the basis functions $HI_{j,M}(h,s)$ of the type-I homogenized NURBS curve can all be expressed in integers. The coordinates of points on the curve can be determined with strict accuracy.

In order to generate $n{+}1$ points on the curve between $t=a=\frac{s_a}{h_a}$ and $t=b=\frac{s_b}{h_b}$, we set such that (see Fig. 10.11)

$$h = nh_a h_b, \quad D = h_a s_b - h_b s_a, \quad s = nh_b s_a + j \cdot D \ (j = 0, 1, \cdots, n). \qquad (10.61)$$

For more efficient computations of the points on the type I homogenized NURBS curve, see Section 10.7.

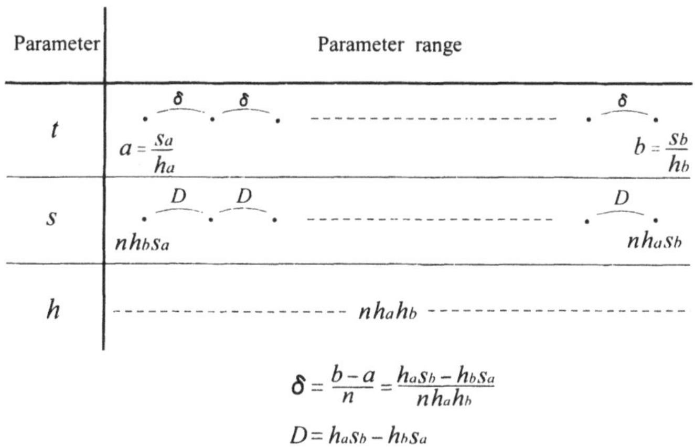

Figure 10.11: Relation between ordinary and homogeneous parameters.

10.6.3 Knot Insertion

The knot insertion technique enables us to increase the number of segments by adding a new knot, maintaining the shape of the curve [6]. We shall apply it to the type-S homogenized NURBS curve as an example.

We assume a type-S homogenized NURBS curve of order M is defined on a knot vector $\boldsymbol{T}=[t_0\ t_1\ \ldots\ t_k\ t_{k+1}\ \ldots\ t_{n+M}]$:

$$\overline{\boldsymbol{P}(t)} = \overline{\sum_j N_{j,M}(t)\boldsymbol{Q}_j}.$$

We add a new knot t_l between t_k and t_{k+1} ($t_k < t_l \leq t_{k+1}$) and create a new knot vector $\hat{\boldsymbol{T}}$. The relation between the old and new knots is shown in Fig. 10.12.

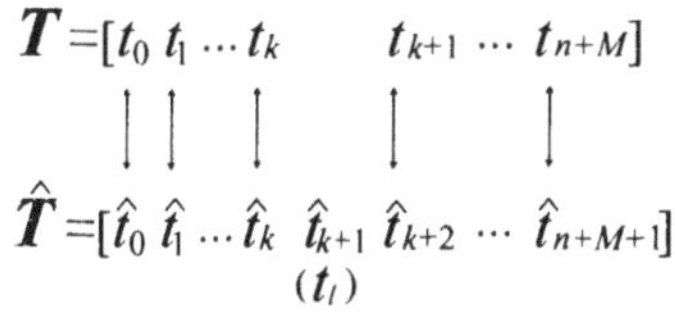

Figure 10.12: Relation between old and new knots.

We place the condition that the shape of the curve is maintained after the insertion. Then the old and new curves are respectively represented as:

$$\overline{\boldsymbol{P}(t)} = \overline{\sum_{j=k-M+1}^{k} N_{j,M}(t)\boldsymbol{Q}_j \quad (t_k \leq t < t_{k+1})} \tag{10.62}$$

and

$$\overline{\boldsymbol{P}(t)} = \overline{\sum_{j=k-M+1}^{k+1} \hat{N}_{j,M}(t)\hat{\boldsymbol{Q}}_j \quad (t_k \leq t < t_{k+1})}. \tag{10.63}$$

We shall derive new curve defining vectors $\hat{\boldsymbol{Q}}_j$, which define the same shape that the original curve represents.

With respect to M+2 knots including t_k, t_l, t_{k+1}:

$$t_j, \ldots, t_k, t_l, t_{k+1}, \ldots, t_{j+M} \quad (k - M + 1 \leq j \leq k),$$

the following divided difference relation holds [3]:

$$(t_j - t_{j+M})M[t; t_j, \ldots, t_{j+M}] + (t_l - t_j)M[t; t_j, \ldots, t_{j+M-1}, t_l] \\ +(t_{j+M} - t_l)M[t; t_l, t_{j+1}, \ldots, t_{j+M}] = 0. \tag{10.68}$$

This equation can be easily understood from the divided difference relations:

$$M[t; t_j, \ldots, t_{j+M}] \\ = \frac{1}{t_{j+M} - t_j}(M[t; t_{j+1}, \ldots, t_{j+M}] - M[t; t_j, \ldots, t_{j+M-1}]),$$

$$M[t; t_j, \ldots, t_{j+M-1}, t_l] \\ = \frac{1}{t_l - t_j}(M[t; t_{j+1}, \ldots, t_{j+M-1}, t_l] - M[t; t_j, \ldots, t_{j+M-1}]),$$

---

[3] In the following two variable functions of t and u:

$$M(t; u) = (u - t)_+^{M-1} \\ = \begin{cases} (u - t)^{M-1} & (u \geq t), \\ 0 & (u < t), \end{cases} \tag{10.64}$$

define an M-th order divided difference function $M_{j,M}(t)$ with respect to the variable u based on knots $t_0, t_1, \ldots,$:

$$M_{j,M}(t) \equiv M[t; t_j, t_{j+1}, \ldots, t_{j+M}]. \tag{10.65}$$

The function $M_{j,M}(t)$ in eq.(10.65) is called a B-spline function of order M.

The B-spline functions used in practical applications are the normalized B-splines $N_{j,M}(t)$. $N_{j,M}(t)$ is given by the following formula:

$$N_{j,M}(t) = (t_{j+M} - t_j)M_{j,M}(t) \tag{10.66}$$

$$= M[t; t_{j+1}, \ldots, t_{j+M}] - M[t; t_j, \ldots, t_{j+M-1}]. \tag{10.67}$$

Note that the values of the divided differences are invariant no matter how the order of the arguments is interchanged. For details of divided difference, see pages 67-71 of [58].

$$M[t;t_l,t_{j+1},\ldots,t_{j+M}]$$
$$=\frac{1}{t_{j+M}-t_l}(M[t;t_{j+1},\ldots,t_{j+M}]-M[t;t_l,t_{j+1},\ldots,t_{j+M-1}]).$$

Now, rearranging eq.(10.68) into a B-spline function relation gives:

$$(t_{j+M}-t_j)M_{j,M}(t)=(t_l-t_j)\hat{M}_{j,M}(t)+(t_{j+M}-t_l)\hat{M}_{j+1,M}(t),$$
$$(k-M+1\leq j\leq k).$$

This can be expressed as a relation among the normalized B-spline functions:

$$N_{j,M}(t)=\frac{t_l-t_j}{\hat{t}_{j+M}-\hat{t}_j}\hat{N}_{j,M}(t)+\frac{t_{j+M}-t_l}{\hat{t}_{j+M+1}-\hat{t}_{j+1}}\hat{N}_{j+1,M}(t). \tag{10.69}$$
$$(k-M+1\leq j\leq k).$$

Note that $t_j=\hat{t}_j$ and $t_{j+M}=\hat{t}_{j+M+1}$. Thus

$$N_{j,M}(t)=\frac{t_l-\hat{t}_j}{\hat{t}_{j+M}-\hat{t}_j}\hat{N}_{j,M}(t)+\frac{\hat{t}_{j+M+1}-t_l}{\hat{t}_{j+M+1}-\hat{t}_{j+1}}\hat{N}_{j+1,M}(t),$$
$$(k-M+1\leq j\leq k). \tag{10.70}$$

If j has a different value than the above we have:

$$\left.\begin{aligned}N_{j,M}(t)&=\hat{N}_{j,M}(t), &&(j\leq k-M),\\ N_{j,M}(t)&=\hat{N}_{j+1,M}(t), &&(j\geq k+1).\end{aligned}\right\} \tag{10.71}$$

Substituting $N_{j,M}(t)$ from eq.(10.70) into eq.(10.62) gives:

$$\begin{aligned}\boldsymbol{P}(t)&=\sum_{j=k-M+1}^{k}N_{j,M}(t)\boldsymbol{Q}_j\\
&=\sum_{j=k-M+1}^{k}\left(\frac{t_l-\hat{t}_j}{\hat{t}_{j+M}-\hat{t}_j}\boldsymbol{Q}_j\hat{N}_{j,M}(t)+\frac{\hat{t}_{j+M+1}-t_l}{\hat{t}_{j+M+1}-\hat{t}_{j+1}}\boldsymbol{Q}_j\hat{N}_{j+1,M}(t)\right)\\
&=\sum_{j=k-M+1}^{k+1}\left(\frac{t_l-\hat{t}_j}{\hat{t}_{j+M}-\hat{t}_j}\boldsymbol{Q}_j\hat{N}_{j,M}(t)+\frac{\hat{t}_{j+M}-t_l}{\hat{t}_{j+M}-\hat{t}_j}\boldsymbol{Q}_{j-1}\hat{N}_{j,M}(t)\right),\\
&(t_k\leq t<t_{k+1})\end{aligned} \tag{10.72}$$

because the first term at $j=k+1$ and the second term at $j=k-M+1$ are both zeros, owing to $t_l=\hat{t}_{k+1}$. Eq.(10.72) follows below:

$$=\sum_{j=k-M+1}^{k+1}\hat{N}_{j,M}(t)\left[\frac{t_l-\hat{t}_j}{\hat{t}_{j+M}-\hat{t}_j}\boldsymbol{Q}_j+\left(1-\frac{t_l-\hat{t}_j}{\hat{t}_{j+M}-\hat{t}_j}\right)\boldsymbol{Q}_{j-1}\right], \tag{10.73}$$
$$(t_k\leq t<t_{k+1}).$$

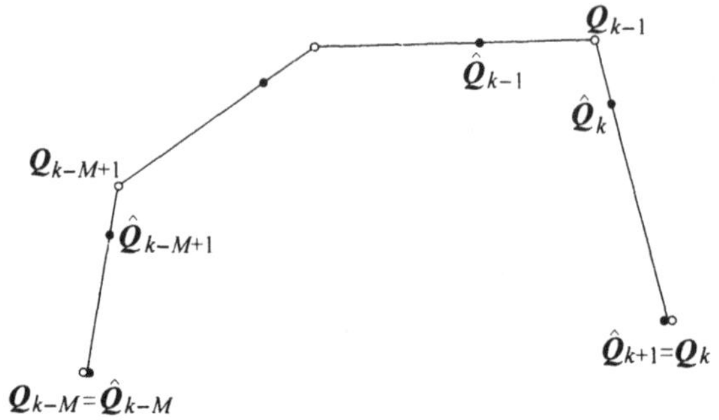

Figure 10.13: Relation between old-curve and new-curve defining vectors.

Comparing this equation with eq.(10.63) gives:

$$\hat{\boldsymbol{Q}}_j = (1-\alpha_j)\boldsymbol{Q}_{j-1} + \alpha_j \boldsymbol{Q}_j, \tag{10.74}$$

where:

$$\alpha_j = \begin{cases} 1 & (j \le k-M) \\ \frac{t_l - \hat{t}_j}{\hat{t}_{j+M} - \hat{t}_j} = \frac{t_l - t_j}{t_{j+M-1} - t_j} & (k-M+1 \le j \le k) \\ 0 & (j \ge k+1) \end{cases} . \tag{10.75}$$

Eq.(10.74) means that the new curve defining vectors $\hat{\boldsymbol{Q}}_j$ divide the line segments $\boldsymbol{Q}_{j-1}\boldsymbol{Q}_j$ in the ratio of $\alpha_j : 1-\alpha_j$. This relation is shown in Fig. 10.13.

The knot insertion relation of the homogenized NURBS curve shows exactly the same form as that of an ordinary B-spline curve.

10.7 Generation of Successive Points on Curve

An ordinary polynomial curve $\boldsymbol{p}(t)$ enables us to generate successive points on the curve very efficiently by using calculus of finite differences. Below we shall explain this method with respect to a cubic polynomial curve.

Assume that

$$\boldsymbol{p}(t) = \boldsymbol{a}t^3 + \boldsymbol{b}t^2 + \boldsymbol{c}t + \boldsymbol{d}, \quad (0 \le t \le 1), \tag{10.76}$$

then the 0-th, 1-st, 2-nd and 3-rd order forward differences are as follows:

$$\begin{aligned} \boldsymbol{p}(t) &= \boldsymbol{a}t^3 + \boldsymbol{b}t^2 + \boldsymbol{c}t + \boldsymbol{d}, \\ \Delta\boldsymbol{p}(t) &= \boldsymbol{p}(t+\delta) - \boldsymbol{p}(t) \\ &= 3\boldsymbol{a}\delta t^2 + (3\boldsymbol{a}\delta^2 + 2\boldsymbol{b}\delta)t + \boldsymbol{a}\delta^3 + \boldsymbol{b}\delta^2 + \boldsymbol{c}\delta, \\ \Delta^2\boldsymbol{p}(t) &= \Delta\boldsymbol{p}(t+\delta) - \Delta\boldsymbol{p}(t) \\ &= \boldsymbol{p}(t+2\delta) - 2\boldsymbol{p}(t+\delta) + \boldsymbol{p}(t) \\ &= 6\boldsymbol{a}\delta^2 t + 6\boldsymbol{a}\delta^3 + 2\boldsymbol{b}\delta^2, \end{aligned} \tag{10.77}$$

$$\begin{aligned}\Delta^3 \boldsymbol{p}(t) &= \Delta^2 \boldsymbol{p}(t+\delta) - \Delta^2 \boldsymbol{p}(t) \\ &= \boldsymbol{p}(t+3\delta) - 3\boldsymbol{p}(t+2\delta) + 3\boldsymbol{p}(t+\delta) - \boldsymbol{p}(t) \\ &= 6\boldsymbol{a}\delta^3,\end{aligned}$$

where δ is a small increment of t. The equations above show that the 3-rd order forward difference is a constant vector irrespective of t. In general the m-th order forward difference is constant in an m-th degree polynomial.

If we denote the forward differences by $\boldsymbol{p}_0, \Delta\boldsymbol{p}_0, \Delta^2\boldsymbol{p}_0, \Delta^3\boldsymbol{p}_0$ and $\boldsymbol{p}_i$, $\Delta\boldsymbol{p}_i$, $\Delta^2\boldsymbol{p}_i$, $\Delta^3\boldsymbol{p}_i$ at $t=0$ and $t=i\cdot\delta$ $(i=1,2,\ldots)$, respectively, then the differences at $t=\delta$ are simply computed as:

$$\begin{aligned}\boldsymbol{p}_1 &= \boldsymbol{p}_0 + \Delta\boldsymbol{p}_0, \\ \Delta\boldsymbol{p}_1 &= \Delta\boldsymbol{p}_0 + \Delta^2\boldsymbol{p}_0, \\ \Delta^2\boldsymbol{p}_1 &= \Delta^2\boldsymbol{p}_0 + \Delta^3\boldsymbol{p}_0, \\ \Delta^3\boldsymbol{p}_1 &= \Delta^3\boldsymbol{p}_0.\end{aligned}$$

If the computations above are repeated, points $\boldsymbol{p}_i$ on the curve are successively generated very efficiently by only additions. There is neither multiplication nor division involved. Prior to the computations all we have to do is to generate 0-th, 1-st, ..., m-th order forward differences (m is the degree of the polynomial curve) at the initial point. As estimated from eq.(10.77), the i-th order forward difference is represented below:

$$\Delta^i \boldsymbol{p}(t) = \sum_{j=0}^{i} (-1)^{i-j} \binom{i}{j} \boldsymbol{p}(t+j\delta). \tag{10.78}$$

Let us consider applying the difference calculus method above to the generation of successive points on the homogeneous curves, which are represented in ordinary polynomial forms. It is interesting to note that exact computations might be possible in the cases of type-I homogenized NURBS curve because they are totally represented in integer. We shall explain this below.

Consider the parameter range shown in eq.(10.61) and Fig. 10.11. Parameter h is set to nh_ah_b, and the other parameter s is changed from nh_bs_a to nh_as_b. This parameter change corresponds to that from $t=a=s_a/h_a$ to $t=b=s_b/h_b$. Therefore we generate all the forward differences from 0-th to $(M-1)$-th orders at the initial point $s=nh_bs_a$. We denote these forward differences by $\boldsymbol{HP}_0$, $\Delta\boldsymbol{HP}_0$, $\Delta^2\boldsymbol{HP}_0$, ..., $\Delta^{M-1}\boldsymbol{HP}_0$, which can be obtained from eq.(10.78).

Then the computations of difference calculus are done as follows:

$$\begin{aligned}\boldsymbol{HP}_1 &= \boldsymbol{HP}_0 + \Delta\boldsymbol{HP}_0, \\ \Delta\boldsymbol{HP}_1 &= \Delta\boldsymbol{HP}_0 + \Delta^2\boldsymbol{HP}_0, \\ \Delta^2\boldsymbol{HP}_1 &= \Delta^2\boldsymbol{HP}_0 + \Delta^3\boldsymbol{HP}_0, \\ \cdots\cdots & \quad \cdots\cdots \\ \Delta^{M-1}\boldsymbol{HP}_1 &= \Delta^{M-1}\boldsymbol{HP}_0.\end{aligned}$$

As for the test results, see Sections 25.1.3 and 25.3.1.

10.8 Homogeneous Quadratic Curves

Quadratic curves are the simplest and used frequently in industrial applications. Quadratic Bézier and NURBS curves are the two typical representations of them.

10.8.1 Relation of Bézier and NURBS Curves

Here we investigate the relation of the homogenized quadratic NURBS curve to homogeneous quadratic Bézier curve segment, after reviewing that of the B-spline curve to the Bézier curve [32].

Now, we write the quadratic Bézier curve segment, $\boldsymbol{p}(t)=[x(t)\ y(t)]$, as:

$$\begin{aligned} \boldsymbol{p}(t) &= B_{0,2}(t)\boldsymbol{q}_0 + B_{1,2}(t)\boldsymbol{q}_1 + B_{2,2}(t)\boldsymbol{q}_2, \\ B_{j,2}(t) &= \binom{2}{j}(1-t)^{2-j}t^j, \qquad j = 0,1,2 \end{aligned} \tag{10.79}$$

and write the quadratic B-spline curve, $\boldsymbol{p}_k(u)=[x(u)\ y(u)]$, as:

$$\boldsymbol{p}_k(u) = \sum_{j=0}^{2} N_{k+j-2,3}(u)\boldsymbol{q}_{k+j-2}, \tag{10.80}$$

$$\begin{aligned} N_{j,1}(u) &= \begin{cases} N_{i,1}(u) = 1 & (u_i \le u < u_{i+1}), \\ N_{i,1}(u) = 0 & (\text{outside above range}), \end{cases} \\ N_{j,M}(u) &= \frac{u-u_j}{u_{j+M-1}-u_j}N_{j,M-1}(u) + \frac{u_{j+M}-u}{u_{j+M}-u_{j+1}}N_{j+1,M-1}(u). \end{aligned} \tag{10.81}$$

We shall represent equivalent Bézier control points of $\boldsymbol{p}_k(u)$ in terms of B-spline control points.

In the range $u_k \le u < u_{k+1}$, B-spline curve, $\boldsymbol{p}_k(u)$, is expressed as:

$$\boldsymbol{p}_k(u) = N_{k-2,3}(u)\boldsymbol{q}_{k-2} + N_{k-1,3}(u)\boldsymbol{q}_{k-1} + N_{k,3}(u)\boldsymbol{q}_k. \tag{10.82}$$

From the relation of eq.(10.81), we have:

$$\begin{aligned} \boldsymbol{p}_k(u) = {} & \frac{(u_{k+1}-u)^2}{(u_{k+1}-u_{k-1})(u_{k+1}-u_k)}\boldsymbol{q}_{k-2} + \left\{ \frac{(u_{k+1}-u)(u-u_{k-1})}{(u_{k+1}-u_{k-1})(u_{k+1}-u_k)} \right. \\ & \left. + \frac{(u_{k+2}-u)(u-u_k)}{(u_{k+2}-u_k)(u_{k+1}-u_k)} \right\} \boldsymbol{q}_{k-1} + \frac{(u-u_k)^2}{(u_{k+2}-u_k)(u_{k+1}-u_k)}\boldsymbol{q}_k. \end{aligned} \tag{10.83}$$

We put:

$$u_k - u_{k-1} = \delta_{k-1},\ u_{k+1} - u_k = \delta_k,\ u_{k+2} - u_{k+1} = \delta_{k+1},\ t = (u-u_k)/\delta_k, \tag{10.84}$$

then eq.(10.83) becomes:

$$\boldsymbol{p}_k(t) = \frac{\delta_k(1-t)^2}{\delta_{k-1}+\delta_k}\boldsymbol{q}_{k-2} + \left\{1 - \frac{\delta_k(1-t)^2}{\delta_{k-1}+\delta_k} - \frac{\delta_k t^2}{\delta_k+\delta_{k+1}}\right\}\boldsymbol{q}_{k-1} + \frac{\delta_k t^2}{\delta_k+\delta_{k+1}}\boldsymbol{q}_k. \tag{10.85}$$

That is,

$$\boldsymbol{p}_k(t) = (1-t)^2\boldsymbol{q}^*_{k-2} + 2t(1-t)\boldsymbol{q}_{k-1} + t^2\boldsymbol{q}^*_k, \tag{10.86}$$

where

$$\boldsymbol{q}^*_{k-2} = \frac{\delta_k\boldsymbol{q}_{k-2}+\delta_{k-1}\boldsymbol{q}_{k-1}}{\delta_k+\delta_{k-1}}, \quad \boldsymbol{q}^*_k = \frac{\delta_{k+1}\boldsymbol{q}_{k-1}+\delta_k\boldsymbol{q}_k}{\delta_{k+1}+\delta_k}. \tag{10.87}$$

Eq.(10.86) represents a quadratic Bézier curve segment of which the control points are $\boldsymbol{q}^*_{k-2}$, $\boldsymbol{q}_{k-1}$ and $\boldsymbol{q}^*_k$.

From eq.(10.87), we understand that $\boldsymbol{q}^*_{k-2}$ and $\boldsymbol{q}^*_k$ are the position vectors which divide line segments $\boldsymbol{q}_{k-2}\boldsymbol{q}_{k-1}$ and $\boldsymbol{q}_{k-1}\boldsymbol{q}_k$ in the ratios of $\delta_{k-1} : \delta_k$ and $\delta_k : \delta_{k+1}$ respectively. These are the C^1 continuity conditions of Bézier curve segments in terms of B-spline control points (see Fig. 10.14).

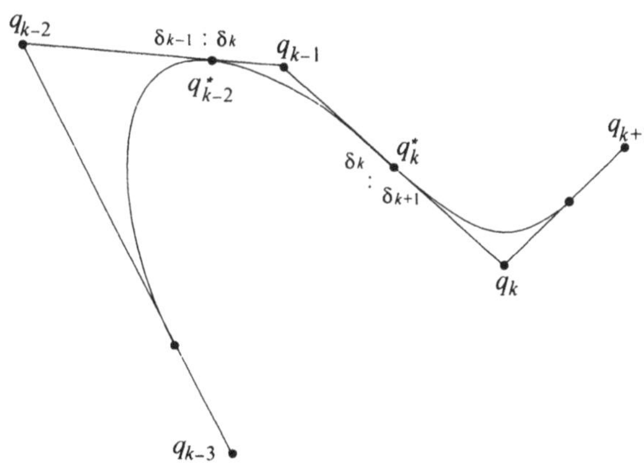

Figure 10.14: A C^1-continuous quadratic B-spline curve.

Following the process above, we shall derive the relation of the homogenized quadratic NURBS curve to the homogeneous quadratic Bézier curve segment.

We write the homogeneous quadratic Bézier curve, $\overline{\boldsymbol{P}(t)} = \overline{[w(t)\ X(t)\ Y(t)]}$, as:

$$\overline{\boldsymbol{P}(t)} = \overline{B_{0,2}(t)\boldsymbol{Q}_0 + B_{1,2}(t)\boldsymbol{Q}_1 + B_{2,2}(t)\boldsymbol{Q}_2}, \tag{10.88}$$

and write the homogenized quadratic type-S NURBS curve, $\overline{\boldsymbol{P}_k(u)} = \overline{[w(u)\ X(u)\ Y(u)]}$, as:

$$\overline{\boldsymbol{P}_k(u)} = \overline{\sum_{j=0}^{2} N_{k+j-2,3}(u)\boldsymbol{Q}_{k+j-2}}. \tag{10.89}$$

Then we have a corresponding result below to eq.(10.86) (see Fig. 10.15):

$$\overline{\boldsymbol{P}_k(t)} = \overline{(1-t)^2\boldsymbol{Q}^*_{k-2} + 2t(1-t)\boldsymbol{Q}_{k-1} + t^2\boldsymbol{Q}^*_k}, \tag{10.90}$$

where

$$\boldsymbol{Q}^*_{k-2} = \frac{\Delta_k \boldsymbol{Q}_{k-2} + \Delta_{k-1}\boldsymbol{Q}_{k-1}}{\Delta_k + \Delta_{k-1}}, \quad \boldsymbol{Q}^*_k = \frac{\Delta_{k+1}\boldsymbol{Q}_{k-1} + \Delta_k \boldsymbol{Q}_k}{\Delta_{k+1} + \Delta_k}. \tag{10.91}$$

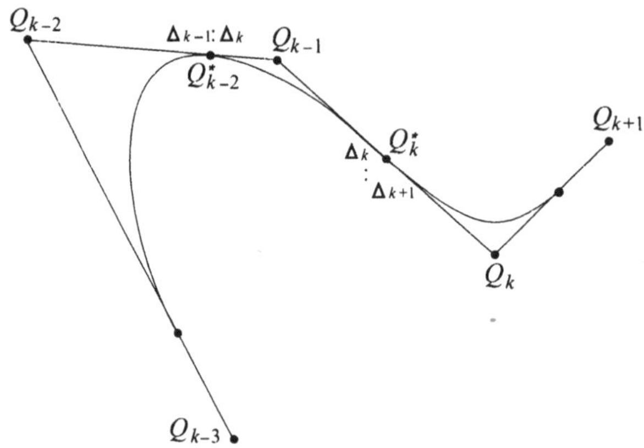

Figure 10.15: A C^1-continuous homogeneous quadratic B-spline curve.

10.8.2 Conversion to Implicit Representation

In the vector space, eq.(10.88) represents an elliptic cone whose apex is at the origin [32].

Now, we put:

$$t_0 = (1-t)^2, \quad t_1 = 2t(1-t), \quad t_2 = t^2.$$

Then eq.(10.88) becomes:

$$\begin{aligned} w &= w_0 t_0 + w_1 t_1 + w_2 t_2, \\ X &= X_0 t_0 + X_1 t_1 + X_2 t_2, \\ Y &= Y_0 t_0 + Y_1 t_1 + Y_2 t_2. \end{aligned} \tag{10.92}$$

If $\boldsymbol{Q}_0, \boldsymbol{Q}_1$ and $\boldsymbol{Q}_2$ are linearly independent, eq.(10.92) has a unique solution:

$$t_0 = D_0/D, \quad t_1 = D_1/D, \quad t_2 = D_2/D,$$

where

$$D = \begin{vmatrix} w_0 & X_0 & Y_0 \\ w_1 & X_1 & Y_1 \\ w_2 & X_2 & Y_2 \end{vmatrix}, \quad D_0 = \begin{vmatrix} w & X & Y \\ w_1 & X_1 & Y_1 \\ w_2 & X_2 & Y_2 \end{vmatrix},$$

$$D_1 = \begin{vmatrix} w & X & Y \\ w_2 & X_2 & Y_2 \\ w_0 & X_0 & Y_0 \end{vmatrix}, \quad D_2 = \begin{vmatrix} w & X & Y \\ w_0 & X_0 & Y_0 \\ w_1 & X_1 & Y_1 \end{vmatrix}.$$

By noting the relation, $t_1^2 = 4t_0t_2$, we have an implicit representation of the general quadratic curve:

$$\begin{vmatrix} w & X & Y \\ w_2 & X_2 & Y_2 \\ w_0 & X_0 & Y_0 \end{vmatrix}^2 = 4 \begin{vmatrix} w & X & Y \\ w_1 & X_1 & Y_1 \\ w_2 & X_2 & Y_2 \end{vmatrix} \begin{vmatrix} w & X & Y \\ w_0 & X_0 & Y_0 \\ w_1 & X_1 & Y_1 \end{vmatrix}. \tag{10.93}$$

Eq.(10.93) can be used for the containment test of a point in a crescent area made by a quadratic curve segment and a line segment (Fig. 10.16).

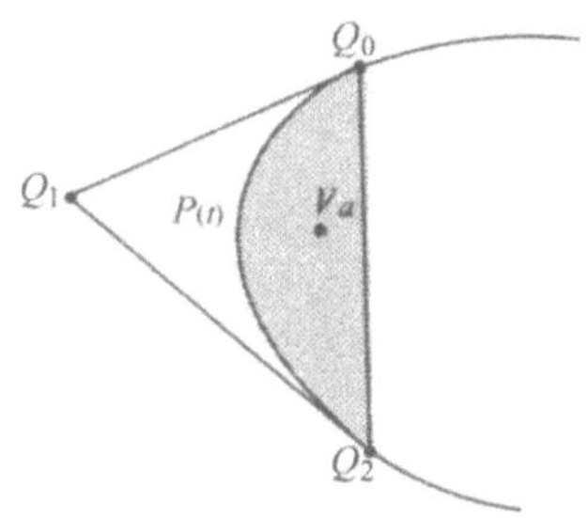

Figure 10.16: Containment test of a point in a crescent area.

Let $V_a(w_a, X_a, Y_a)$ be a test point for the containment. We put as below [4]:

$$\begin{aligned} C &= 4 \begin{vmatrix} w_a & X_a & Y_a \\ w_1 & X_1 & Y_1 \\ w_2 & X_2 & Y_2 \end{vmatrix} \begin{vmatrix} w_a & X_a & Y_a \\ w_0 & X_0 & Y_0 \\ w_1 & X_1 & Y_1 \end{vmatrix} - \begin{vmatrix} w_a & X_a & Y_a \\ w_2 & X_2 & Y_2 \\ w_0 & X_0 & Y_0 \end{vmatrix}^2 \\ &\equiv 4S_{a12}S_{a01} - S_{a20}^2, \end{aligned} \tag{10.94}$$

where

$$S_{a12} \equiv \begin{vmatrix} w_a & X_a & Y_a \\ w_1 & X_1 & Y_1 \\ w_2 & X_2 & Y_2 \end{vmatrix}, \quad S_{a01} \equiv \begin{vmatrix} w_a & X_a & Y_a \\ w_0 & X_0 & Y_0 \\ w_1 & X_1 & Y_1 \end{vmatrix}, \quad S_{a20} \equiv \begin{vmatrix} w_a & X_a & Y_a \\ w_2 & X_2 & Y_2 \\ w_0 & X_0 & Y_0 \end{vmatrix}.$$

Then the point is judged to be inside, outside or on the boundary, of the area enclosed by the quadratic curve, corresponding to whether the sign of C is positive, negative or zero, respectively.

Now, substituting $\neg V_a$ in place of V_a in eq.(10.94) creates the same result. This means that the test using eq.(10.94) is the one for a point in classical projective space.

In order for the point to be contained in the crescent area, the following two conditions must be satisfied:

---

[4] For $S_{a12}, \ldots$, see Appendix C.

1. Containment condition of V_a in the triangle $Q_0Q_1Q_2$ (see eq.(C.26)),

$$(S_{a12}, S_{a20}, S_{a01} \geq 0) \vee (S_{a12}, S_{a20}, S_{a01} \leq 0),$$

2. Containment condition of V_a in the area enclosed by the quadratic curve,

$$C = 4S_{a12}S_{a01} - S_{a20}^2 \geq 0.$$

10.8.3 Classification

We shall classify the general homogeneous quadratic curve eq.(10.93) [32]. We assume three points Q_0, Q_1 and Q_2 are linearly independent. Then the polynomial represents an irreducible quadratic curve.

If $w_0, w_1, w_2 \neq 0$, then eq.(10.93) can be rewritten as:

$$\begin{vmatrix} w & X & Y \\ 1 & x_2 & y_2 \\ 1 & x_0 & y_0 \end{vmatrix}^2 = 4\omega \begin{vmatrix} w & X & Y \\ 1 & x_1 & y_1 \\ 1 & x_2 & y_2 \end{vmatrix} \begin{vmatrix} w & X & Y \\ 1 & x_0 & y_0 \\ 1 & x_1 & y_1 \end{vmatrix}, \tag{10.95}$$

where

$$\omega = \frac{w_1^2}{w_0 w_2}. \tag{10.96}$$

Changing the value of w_0, w_1 or w_2 generally causes shape modification of the curve. If the condition, eq.(10.96), is observed, however, the shape is invariant. ω is thus called *shape invariance* of the rational quadratic curve, or homogeneous quadratic curve.

The quadratic curves in Euclidean space or conic sections are the cuts of elliptic cone, eq.(10.95), by $w = 1$ plane. We can classify the conic sections according to the number of intersection lines of the elliptic cone with the plane at infinity, $w=0$. Putting $w=0$ in eq.(10.95) yields:

$$(\alpha + \beta)^2 = 4\omega\alpha\beta, \tag{10.97}$$

where

$$\alpha = \begin{vmatrix} X & Y \\ x_1 - x_2 & y_1 - y_2 \end{vmatrix}, \quad \beta = \begin{vmatrix} X & Y \\ x_0 - x_1 & y_0 - y_1 \end{vmatrix}. \tag{10.98}$$

Solving for α in eq.(10.97) yields the intersection line equation below:

$$\alpha = (2\omega - 1 \pm 2\sqrt{\omega(\omega - 1)})\beta. \tag{10.99}$$

According to eq.(10.99), we classify the conic sections:

1. ${w_1}^2 > w_0 w_2$:

   There are two intersection lines. The conic section is a hyperbola.

2. ${w_1}^2 = w_0 w_2$:

   There is one intersection line. The conic section is a parabola.

3. ${w_1}^2 < w_0 w_2$:

   There is no intersection line. The conic section is an ellipse.

The classification criterion above applies also to the cases where either of w_0, w_1 or w_2 is zero. For example, when $w = w_1 = 0$, eq.(10.93) turns out to be:

$$w_0 w_2 \left\{ \begin{vmatrix} X & Y \\ x_2 & y_2 \end{vmatrix} - \begin{vmatrix} X & Y \\ x_0 & y_0 \end{vmatrix} \right\}^2 = -4 \begin{vmatrix} X & Y \\ X_1 & Y_1 \end{vmatrix}^2, \tag{10.100}$$

which represents intersection lines of the elliptic cone with $w = 0$ plane when $w_1 = 0$. Putting $w_1 = 0$ in the classification criterion above yields the same number of intersection lines as that produced in eq.(10.100).

The classification criterion above is applicable to the homogeneous quadratic curve as well.

10.8.4 Circle and Circular Arc

We shall represent a full circle by homogenized NURBS [32].

A method of generating a full circle by the conventional NURBS curve is to set knot vector, control points and their weights as follows (Fig. 10.17):

$$\begin{aligned} \boldsymbol{p}(t) &= [x(t)\ y(t)] \\ &= \frac{\sum_{j=0}^{8} N_{j,3}(t) w_j \boldsymbol{q}_j}{\sum_{j=0}^{8} N_{j,3}(t) w_j}, \quad (0 \le t \le 4), \qquad (10.101) \\ \boldsymbol{T} &= [0\ 0\ 0\ 1\ 1\ 2\ 2\ 3\ 3\ 4\ 4\ 4], \end{aligned}$$

$$(w_0, w_1, w_2, w_3, w_4, w_5, w_6, w_7, w_8) = (1, \frac{1}{\sqrt{2}}, 1, \frac{1}{\sqrt{2}}, 1, \frac{1}{\sqrt{2}}, 1, \frac{1}{\sqrt{2}}, 1).$$

The circle above can be considered to be composed of four rational quadratic Bézier segments whose weights are $1, \frac{1}{\sqrt{2}}, 1$.

By keeping the shape invariance same, we can choose other weight sequences. One such example is shown below:

$$(w_0, w_1, w_2, w_3, w_4, w_5, w_6, w_7, w_8) = (2, 1, 1, 1, 2, 1, 1, 1, 2). \tag{10.102}$$

Under the weight sequence of eq.(10.102), we homogenize the control vectors to represent the circle by a type-S homogenized NURBS such that

$$\boldsymbol{Q}'_j = [w_j\ w_j \boldsymbol{q}_j], \quad j = 0, 1, \ldots, 8, \tag{10.103}$$

where $[w_j\ w_j \boldsymbol{q}_j]$ is a shorthand notation for $[w_j\ w_j x_j\ w_j y_j]$ with $\boldsymbol{q}_j = [x_j\ y_j]$. Considering eq.(10.91) and Fig. 10.15, we can omit $\boldsymbol{Q}'_2$ and $\boldsymbol{Q}'_6$. We renumber

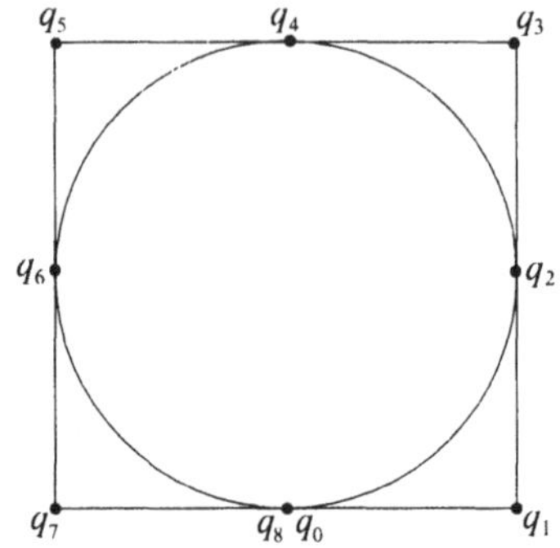

Figure 10.17: A full circle by a conventional NURBS.

the control vectors such that (Fig. 10.18):

$$\boldsymbol{Q}'_0 \rightarrow \boldsymbol{Q}_0, \quad \boldsymbol{Q}'_1 \rightarrow \boldsymbol{Q}_1, \quad \boldsymbol{Q}'_3 \rightarrow \boldsymbol{Q}_2, \quad \boldsymbol{Q}'_4 \rightarrow \boldsymbol{Q}_3,$$
$$\boldsymbol{Q}'_5 \rightarrow \boldsymbol{Q}_4, \quad \boldsymbol{Q}'_7 \rightarrow \boldsymbol{Q}_5, \quad \boldsymbol{Q}'_8 \rightarrow \boldsymbol{Q}_6.$$

Then we represent the full circle by a quadratic type-S homogenized NURBS curve as follows:

$$\overline{\boldsymbol{P}(t)} = \overline{\sum_{j=0}^{6} N_{j,3}(t)\boldsymbol{Q}_j}, \quad (0 \leq t \leq 4), \tag{10.104}$$
$$\boldsymbol{T} = [0\ 0\ 0\ 1\ 2\ 2\ 3\ 4\ 4\ 4].$$

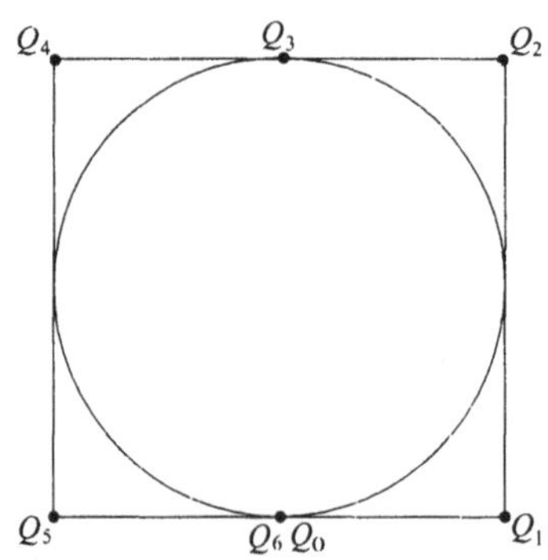

Figure 10.18: A full circle by a homogenized NURBS.

Example

By using the homogeneous quadratic type-S NURBS curve, eq.(10.104), let us generate a unit circle of which the center is at the origin.

We set the control vectors as follows:

$$\boldsymbol{Q}_0 = [2\ 0\ -2],\quad \boldsymbol{Q}_1 = [1\ 1\ -1],\quad \boldsymbol{Q}_2 = [1\ 1\ 1],\quad \boldsymbol{Q}_3 = [2\ 0\ 2],$$
$$\boldsymbol{Q}_4 = [1\ -1\ 1],\quad \boldsymbol{Q}_5 = [1\ -1\ -1],\quad \boldsymbol{Q}_6 = [2\ 0\ -2].$$

Knots and their values are shown below:

$$\begin{matrix} t_0 & t_1 & t_2 & t_3 & t_4 & t_5 & t_6 & t_7 & t_8 & t_9 \\ 0 & 0 & 0 & 1 & 2 & 2 & 3 & 4 & 4 & 4\,. \end{matrix}$$

$\underline{t_2 = 0 \le t < t_3 = 1}$

In the parameter range above, the type-S NURBS curve is represented as:

$$\overline{\boldsymbol{P}(t)} = \overline{N_{0,3}(t)\boldsymbol{Q}_0 + N_{1,3}(t)\boldsymbol{Q}_1 + N_{2,3}(t)\boldsymbol{Q}_2}.$$

Since

$$N_{0,3}(t) = (1-t)^2,\quad N_{1,3}(t) = \frac{-3t^2+4t}{2},\quad N_{2,3}(t) = \frac{t^2}{2},$$

then

$$w = t^2 - 2t + 2,\quad X = -t^2 + 2t,\quad Y = 2t - 2.$$

The relations above represent a circular arc because

$$\left(\frac{X}{w}\right)^2 + \left(\frac{Y}{w}\right)^2 = \left(\frac{-t^2+2t}{t^2-2t+2}\right)^2 + \left(\frac{2t-2}{t^2-2t+2}\right)^2 = 1.$$

$\underline{t_3 = 1 \le t < t_4 = 2}$

In the parameter range above, the type-S NURBS curve is represented as:

$$\overline{\boldsymbol{P}(t)} = \overline{N_{1,3}(t)\boldsymbol{Q}_1 + N_{2,3}(t)\boldsymbol{Q}_2 + N_{3,3}(t)\boldsymbol{Q}_3}.$$

Since

$$N_{1,3}(t) = \frac{(2-t)^2}{2},\quad N_{2,3}(t) = \frac{(2-t)(3t-2)}{2},\quad N_{3,3}(t) = (t-1)^2,$$

then

$$w = t^2 - 2t + 2,\quad X = -t^2 + 2t,\quad Y = 2t - 2, \tag{10.105}$$

which are the same as those for the range $t_2 = 0 \le t < t_3 = 1$. This means that eq.(10.105) represents a semi-circular arc.

$\underline{t_5 = 2 \le t < t_6 = 3}$

In the parameter range above, the type-S NURBS curve is represented as:

$$\overline{\boldsymbol{P}(t)} = \overline{N_{3,3}(t)\boldsymbol{Q}_3 + N_{4,3}(t)\boldsymbol{Q}_4 + N_{5,3}(t)\boldsymbol{Q}_5}.$$

Since

$$N_{3,3}(t) = (t-3)^2,\quad N_{4,3}(t) = \frac{(t-2)(10-3t)}{2},\quad N_{5,3}(t) = \frac{(t-2)^2}{2},$$

then

$$w = t^2 - 6t + 10, \quad X = t^2 - 6t + 8, \quad Y = -2t + 6. \tag{10.106}$$

The relations above represent a circle because

$$\left(\frac{X}{w}\right)^2 + \left(\frac{Y}{w}\right)^2 = \left(\frac{t^2 - 6t + 8}{t^2 - 6t + 10}\right)^2 + \left(\frac{-2t + 6}{t^2 - 6t + 10}\right)^2 = 1.$$

$\underline{t_6 = 3 \leq t < t_7 = 4}$

In the parameter range above, the type-S NURBS curve is represented as:

$$\overline{\boldsymbol{P}(t)} = \overline{N_{4,3}(t)\boldsymbol{Q}_4 + N_{5,3}(t)\boldsymbol{Q}_5 + N_{6,3}(t)\boldsymbol{Q}_6}.$$

Since

$$N_{4,3}(t) = \frac{(t-4)^2}{2}, \quad N_{5,3}(t) = \frac{(4-t)(3t-8)}{2}, \quad N_{6,3}(t) = (t-3)^2,$$

then

$$w = t^2 - 6t + 10, \quad X = t^2 - 6t + 8, \quad Y = -2t + 6, \tag{10.107}$$

which are the same as those for the range $t_5 = 2 \leq t < t_6 = 3$. This means that eq.(10.107) represents the other semi-circle.

Next, let us represent a circular arc by using the homogeneous quadratic Bézier curve, $\overline{\boldsymbol{P}(t)} = \overline{[w(t)\ X(t)\ Y(t)]}$ (Fig. 10.19):

$$\overline{\boldsymbol{P}(t)} = \overline{B_{0,2}(t)\boldsymbol{Q}_0 + B_{1,2}(t)\boldsymbol{Q}_1 + B_{2,2}(t)\boldsymbol{Q}_2}.$$

We set the control vectors as follows:

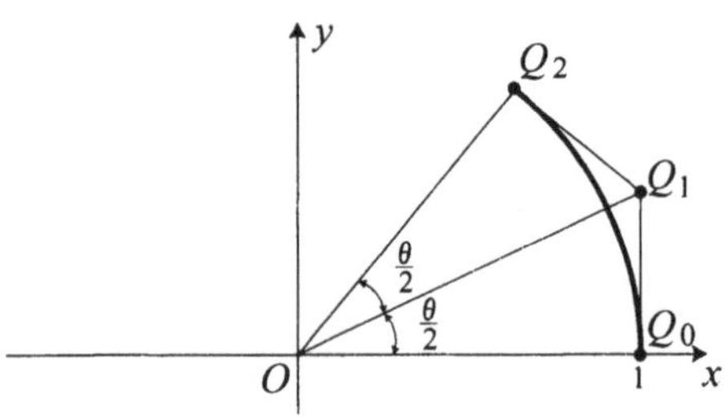

Figure 10.19: A circular arc by a homogeneous Bézier curve.

$$\boldsymbol{Q}_0 = [1\ 1\ 0], \quad \boldsymbol{Q}_1 = [w_1\ w_1\ w_1 \tan\frac{\theta}{2}], \quad \boldsymbol{Q}_2 = [1\ \cos\theta\ \sin\theta].$$

Then we have:

$$\begin{aligned} w &= (1-t)^2 + 2t(1-t)w_1 + t^2, \\ X &= (1-t)^2 + 2t(1-t)w_1 + t^2\cos\theta, \\ Y &= 2t(1-t)w_1\tan\frac{\theta}{2} + t^2\sin\theta. \end{aligned}$$

The following condition holds:

$$\left(\frac{X}{w}\right)^2 + \left(\frac{Y}{w}\right)^2 = 1. \tag{10.108}$$

This yields

$$w_1 = \pm\cos\frac{\theta}{2}. \tag{10.109}$$

Therefore we have two circular arc representations. One is the circular arc that we seek, corresponding to $w_1 = +\cos\frac{\theta}{2}$ (Fig. 10.19):

$$\overline{\boldsymbol{P}(t)} = \overline{B_{0,2}(t)\boldsymbol{Q}_0 + B_{1,2}(t)\boldsymbol{Q}_1 + B_{2,2}(t)\boldsymbol{Q}_2}, \tag{10.110}$$
$$\boldsymbol{Q}_0 = [1\ 1\ 0],\quad \boldsymbol{Q}_1 = [\cos\frac{\theta}{2}\ \ \cos\frac{\theta}{2}\ \ \sin\frac{\theta}{2}],\quad \boldsymbol{Q}_2 = [1\ \ \cos\theta\ \ \sin\theta].$$

The other is the complementary circular arc that corresponds to $w_1 = -\cos\frac{\theta}{2}$ (Fig. 10.20):

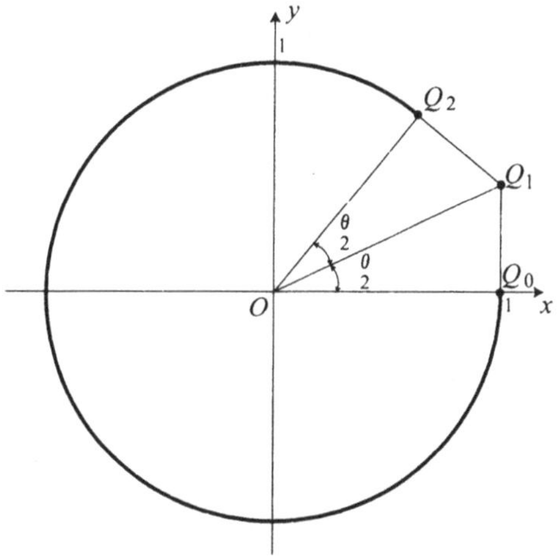

Figure 10.20: A complementary circular arc.

$$\overline{\boldsymbol{P}(t)} = \overline{B_{0,2}(t)\boldsymbol{Q}_0 + B_{1,2}(t)\boldsymbol{Q}_1 + B_{2,2}(t)\boldsymbol{Q}_2}, \tag{10.111}$$
$$\boldsymbol{Q}_0 = [1\ 1\ 0],\quad \boldsymbol{Q}_1 = [-\cos\frac{\theta}{2}\ \ -\cos\frac{\theta}{2}\ \ -\sin\frac{\theta}{2}],\quad \boldsymbol{Q}_2 = [1\ \ \cos\theta\ \ \sin\theta].$$

Note that putting $\theta = 180°$ in eq.(10.110) yields a semi-circle, which could not be represented in the rational curve processing (see Section 10.4).

Note also that the complementary circular arc can be processed just as an ordinary curve segment in the homogeneous processing while it can be derived in a similar manner in the conventional rational curve processing but can not be treated as an ordinary one because the signs of weights are mixed (see Section 10.2).

10.9 Shape Control

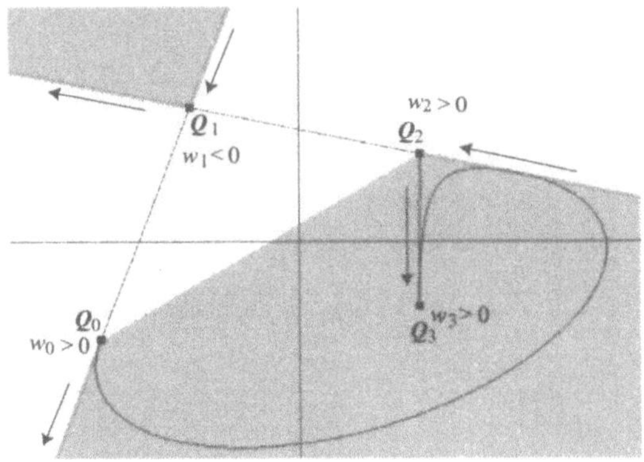

Figure 10.21: A homogeneous control polygon and a homogeneous curve.

Just as an ordinary Bézier curve or NURBS curve is displayed on a computer screen along with a control polygon, a homogeneous Bézier curve or homogenized NURBS curve is displayed along with a homogeneous control polygon. A homogeneous control polygon is a sequence of homogeneous line segments. Since a homogeneous line segment takes on three shapes, i.e., internal, external and half lines, the shape of a homogeneous control polygon looks a little complicated (Fig. 10.21).

In Fig. 10.21, the polygon $\boldsymbol{Q}_0\boldsymbol{Q}_1\boldsymbol{Q}_2\boldsymbol{Q}_3$ represents the homogeneous control polygon, where $\boldsymbol{Q}_0\boldsymbol{Q}_1$ and $\boldsymbol{Q}_1\boldsymbol{Q}_2$ are external line segments and $\boldsymbol{Q}_2\boldsymbol{Q}_3$ an internal line segment. The Euclidean image of the convex hull of homogeneous polygon $\boldsymbol{Q}_0\boldsymbol{Q}_1\boldsymbol{Q}_2\boldsymbol{Q}_3$ is detached and is shown shaded in the figure. We can see that the curve lies entirely in the convex hull. It is recommended that the projected area of homogeneous convex hull is also displayed along with the homogeneous control polygon in order for a man to understand and control the shape of the curve easily.

The shapes of the type-S homogenized NURBS curves (M=4) are shown in Fig. 10.22 with respect to various w_j values. When w_j values of all the control points are unity, then the curve turns out to be an ordinary polynomial curve (Fig. (a)). The effect on the projected curve of increasing w_j is to draw the curve nearer to the corresponding control point (Fig. (b)). If one of the weights w_j assumes the value 0, the curve shape near $\boldsymbol{Q}_j$ looks attracted to the direction of the vector $[X_j\ Y_j]$ although $\boldsymbol{Q}_j$ loses all influence on the curve in the case of a rational curve (Fig. (c)) [43]. Therefore the curve shape coincides with that of a rational curve when $[X_j\ Y_j] = [0\ 0]$ is also satisfied. If one of the w_j becomes negative, the curve appears repelled by the corresponding control point (Fig. (d)).

Lastly, we give the author's subjective evaluation of B-spline, conventional NURBS and homogenized NURBS in Table 10.1.

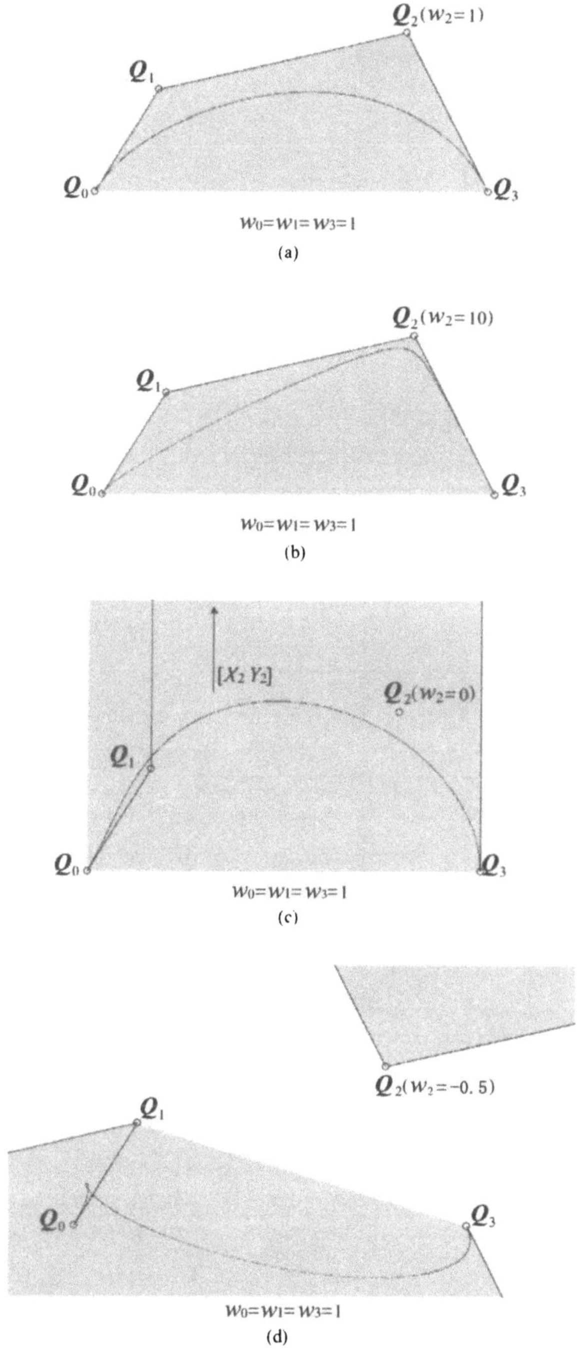

Figure 10.22: Shapes of homogenized NURBS curves against various w values.

Table 10.1: Comparison and evaluation of B-spline, NURBS and homogenized NURBS.

Items	**B-Spline**	**NURBS**	**Ord. par. H-NURBS** 1)	**Homo. par. H-NURBS** 2)
Transformation invariance	Affine (conditional)	Affine (no condition)	Projective (no condition)	Projective (no condition)
	3	4	5	5
Representation capability	no weights	limitation on weight's sign	no limitation on weight	no limitation on weight
	3	4	5	5
Processing robustness (Newton method)	robust	poorly robust	robust	robust and locally unique
	4	2	4	5
Processing simplicity (Various formula) 3)	good	not good	good	good
	5	3	5	4
Processing efficiency (Points-on-curve computation)	calculus of differences	de Boor-Cox algorithm	calculus of differences	calculus of differences
	5	4	5	5
Processing exactness	not exact	not exact	can be exact int. par. only	can be exact
	3	4	4.5	5
Unifiability	not unifiable	unifiable in rational form	unifiable in ordinary form	unifiable in ordinary form
	3	4	5	5
Total points	26/35	25/35	33.5/35	34/35

1): Ordinary parameter, homogenized NURBS (type-S).
2): Homogeneous-parameter, homogenized NURBS (type-D and -I).
3): Projective transformation, de Casteljau algorithm and so on.

Chapter 11

Homogeneous Surfaces

11.1 Rational Polynomial Surface Patch

A rational polynomial surface patch is usually defined by the following expressions:

$$\boldsymbol{p}(u,v) = [x(u,v)\ y(u,v)\ z(u,v)] = [\frac{X(u,v)}{w(u,v)}\ \frac{Y(u,v)}{w(u,v)}\ \frac{Z(u,v)}{w(u,v)}]$$

$$= \frac{\sum_{i=0}^{m}\sum_{j=0}^{n} a_i(u)a_j(v)w_{ij}\boldsymbol{q}_{ij}}{\sum_{k=0}^{m}\sum_{l=0}^{n} a_k(u)a_l(v)w_{kl}}, \quad (0 \le u, v \le 1), \tag{11.1}$$

$$\boldsymbol{q}_{ij} = [x_{ij}\ y_{ij}\ z_{ij}],$$

$$(a_i(u), a_j(v) \ge 0 \text{ for all } i,j) \vee (a_i(u), a_j(v) \le 0 \text{ for all } i,j), \tag{11.2}$$

$$(w_{ij} > 0 \text{ for all } i,j) \vee (w_{ij} < 0 \text{ for all } i,j), \tag{11.3}$$

where w_{ij} are called *weights*.

Alternatively, a rational surface patch can be defined as follows:

$$\boldsymbol{p}(u,v) = [1\ x(u,v)\ y(u,v)\ z(u,v)] = [1\ \frac{X(u,v)}{w(u,v)}\ \frac{Y(u,v)}{w(u,v)}\ \frac{Z(u,v)}{w(u,v)}]$$

$$= \frac{\sum_{i=0}^{m}\sum_{j=0}^{n} a_i(u)a_j(v)w_{ij}\boldsymbol{q}_{ij}}{\sum_{k=0}^{m}\sum_{l=0}^{n} a_k(u)a_l(v)w_{kl}}$$

$$= \frac{\boldsymbol{P}(u,v)}{w(u,v)}, \quad (0 \le u, v \le 1), \tag{11.4}$$

$$\boldsymbol{q}_{ij} = [1\ x_{ij}\ y_{ij}\ z_{ij}],$$

$$(a_i(u), a_j(v) \ge 0 \text{ for all } i,j) \vee (a_i(u), a_j(v) \le 0 \text{ for all } i,j),$$

$$(w_{ij} > 0 \text{ for all } i,j) \vee (w_{ij} < 0 \text{ for all } i,j).$$

Affine Invariance

A rational polynomial surface patch, eq.(11.1) or eq.(11.4), can be expressed as:

$$\boldsymbol{p}(u,v) = \sum_{i=0}^{m}\sum_{j=0}^{n}\left(\frac{a_i(u)a_j(v)w_{ij}}{\displaystyle\sum_{k=0}^{m}\sum_{l=0}^{n} a_k(u)a_l(v)w_{kl}}\right)\boldsymbol{q}_{ij} \equiv \sum_{i=0}^{m}\sum_{j=0}^{n}\phi_{ij}(u,v)\boldsymbol{q}_{ij}, \quad (11.5)$$

where

$$\phi_{ij}(u,v) = \frac{a_i(u)a_j(v)w_{ij}}{\displaystyle\sum_{k=0}^{m}\sum_{l=0}^{n} a_k(u)a_l(v)w_{kl}}. \quad (11.6)$$

It is clear that

$$\sum_{i=0}^{m}\sum_{j=0}^{n}\left(\frac{a_i(u)a_j(v)w_{ij}}{\displaystyle\sum_{k=0}^{m}\sum_{l=0}^{n} a_k(u)a_l(v)w_{kl}}\right) \equiv \sum_{i=0}^{m}\sum_{j=0}^{n}\phi_{ij}(u,v) \equiv 1. \quad (11.7)$$

Eq.(11.7) shows that unlike ordinary polynomial surfaces, a rational polynomial surface patch, eq.(11.1) or eq.(11.4), is invariant under affine transformations, independently of the basis functions $a_i(u)$, $a_j(v)$ (see Appendix A.4).

Convex Hull Property

Since the basis functions, $\phi_{ij}(u,v)$, are not negative under the conditions, (11.2) and (11.3), the rational polynomial surface patch, eq.(11.1) or eq.(11.4), enjoys the convex hull property. That is, the surface always lies within the convex hull made by the defining vertices, $\boldsymbol{q}_{ij}$.

Rational polynomial surfaces have more general representational capabilities than ordinary polynomial ones. NURBS surfaces and rational Bézier surfaces, both widely employed in current CAD systems, are typical rational polynomial surfaces. Yet, certain problems exist with these surfaces because of the rational representations.

In Chapter 10, we discussed the problems of rational curve representations. These problems are inherited in the rational surface representations as well. In the surface case these problems with rational representation can also be removed by the homogenization of the rational forms.

In the following sections, we present homogeneous Bézier surfaces and homogenized NURBS surfaces.

Just as in the homogeneous curves, we also stipulate that the homogeneous surfaces are defined in classical projective space, not in two-sided space because of the reason mentioned in Chapter 24.

11.2 Homogeneous Bézier Surface Patches

We now propose homogeneous Bézier surface patches in place of the conventionally used rational ones.

11.2.1 Rational Bézier Surface Patch

We first review the conventionally used rational Bézier surface patch. It is represented as follows:

Given $(m+1) \times (n+1)$ points, $\boldsymbol{q}_{ij} = [x_{ij}\ y_{ij}\ z_{ij}]$,

$$\boldsymbol{p}(u,v) = [x(u,v)\ y(u,v)\ z(u,v)]$$
$$= \frac{\sum_{i=0}^{m}\sum_{j=0}^{n} b_{i,m}(u) b_{j,n}(v) w_{ij} \boldsymbol{q}_{ij}}{\sum_{k=0}^{m}\sum_{l=0}^{n} b_{k,m}(u) b_{l,n}(v) w_{kl}}, \quad (0 \le u, v \le 1), \tag{11.8}$$

$$b_{i,m}(t) = \binom{m}{i}(1-t)^{m-i} t^i, \tag{11.9}$$

where $b_{i,m}(t)$ are Bernstein basis functions of degree m [58].

11.2.2 Homogeneous Bézier Surface Patches

Simply-homogenized Bézier Surface Patch

Simply-homogenized Bézier surface patch or type-S homogeneous Bézier surface patch is obtained by simply homogenizing the rational one, that is, by homogenizing only the coordinates of the rational Bézier surface patch.

This can be expressed as follows [1)]:

$$\overline{\boldsymbol{P}(u,v)} = \overline{[w(u,v)\ X(u,v)\ Y(u,v)\ Z(u,v)]}$$
$$= \overline{\sum_{i=0}^{m}\sum_{j=0}^{n} B_{i,m}(u) B_{j,n}(v) \boldsymbol{Q}_{ij}}, \tag{11.10}$$
$$\boldsymbol{Q}_{ij} = [w_{ij}\ X_{ij}\ Y_{ij}\ Z_{ij}].$$

Because type-S homogeneous Bézier surface patch is an ordinary polynomial, there is no worry of a denominator becoming zero during processing. This results in a much more robust processing than the conventionally used rational Bézier surface when it is used in the Newton-Raphson method (see Chapter 15 and Section 25.2).

[1)] For the Bernstein basis function, the author denotes it by $B_{j,n}(t)$ in the homogeneous Bézier cases, not by $b_{j,n}(t)$ as he does it in the Euclidean Bézier cases.

Doubly-homogenized Bézier Surface Patch

Doubly-homogenized Bézier surface patch or type-D homogeneous Bézier surface patch is obtained by doubly homogenizing the rational one, that is, by homogenizing the parameters as well as the coordinates of the rational Bézier surface patch.

We define two types of type-D homogeneous Bézier surface patches corresponding to the two types of homogeneous parameters (see Section 8.6).

Type-D1 homogeneous Bézier surface patch:

The parameter homogenization is accomplished by placing $u=r/h, v=s/h$ in $B_{i,m}(u)$ and $B_{j,n}(v)$ of eq.(11.10) and by using the scalar multiple property of homogeneous coordinates.

Then type-D1 homogeneous Bézier surface patch is defined as follows:

$$\begin{aligned}\overline{\boldsymbol{HP}(h,r,s)} &= \overline{[w(h,r,s)\ X(h,r,s)\ Y(h,r,s)\ Z(h,r,s)]} \\ &= \overline{\sum_{i=0}^{m}\sum_{j=0}^{n} HB1_{i,m}(h,r)HB1_{j,n}(h,s)\boldsymbol{Q}_{ij}}, \qquad (11.11) \\ \boldsymbol{Q}_{ij} &= [w_{ij}\ X_{ij}\ Y_{ij}\ Z_{ij}].\end{aligned}$$

Type-D2 homogeneous Bézier surface patch:

The parameter homogenization in this case is accomplished by placing $u=\rho/(\eta+\rho), v=\sigma/(\eta+\sigma)$ in $B_{i,m}(u), B_{j,n}(v)$ of eq.(11.10) respectively and by using the scalar multiple property of homogeneous coordinates.

Then type-D2 homogeneous Bézier surface patch is defined as follows:

$$\begin{aligned}\overline{\boldsymbol{HP}(\eta,\rho,\sigma)} &= \overline{[w(\eta,\rho,\sigma)\ X(\eta,\rho,\sigma)\ Y(\eta,\rho,\sigma)\ Z(\eta,\rho,\sigma)]} \\ &= \overline{\sum_{i=0}^{m}\sum_{j=0}^{n} HB2_{i,m}(\eta,\rho)HB2_{j,n}(\eta,\sigma)\boldsymbol{Q}_{ij}}, \qquad (11.12) \\ \boldsymbol{Q}_{ij} &= [w_{ij}\ X_{ij}\ Y_{ij}\ Z_{ij}].\end{aligned}$$

Type-D homogeneous Bézier surfaces show superior characteristics to type-S homogeneous ones when they are used for computing intersection points by the geometric Newton-Raphson method (see Sections 15.7 and 25.2.1).

Furthermore, type-D1 homogeneous Bézier surfaces make it possible to attain exact computations of points on the surfaces coupled with integer arithmetic when rational parametric values are given.

Homogeneous Bézier surface patches do not have any restrictions on the signs of weights w_{ij} as the rational Bézier surface patch does.

Note that in homogeneous Bézier surfaces, $\boldsymbol{Q}_{00}, \boldsymbol{Q}_{01}, \ldots, \boldsymbol{Q}_{mn}$ make a homogeneous net (see Section 9.4) and thus we must take care to clip the surface and the defining net correctly for the display (see Sections 23.6 and 10.9).

11.3 Homogenized NURBS Surfaces

The author proposes two types of homogenized NURBS surfaces, which result from the homogenizations of NURBS surfaces.

11.3.1 Conventional NURBS Surface

The following expression represents the conventional NURBS surface.

Given $(m+1) \times (n+1)$ points, $\boldsymbol{q}_{ij} = [x_{ij}\ y_{ij}\ z_{ij}]$, and knot vectors:

$$\boldsymbol{T}_u = [u_0, \ldots, u_{m+M}], \quad \boldsymbol{T}_v = [v_0, \ldots, v_{n+N}],$$

then the conventional NURBS surface is defined as follows:

$$\begin{aligned}\boldsymbol{p}(u,v) &= [x(u,v)\ y(u,v)\ z(u,v)] \\ &= \frac{\displaystyle\sum_{i=0}^{m}\sum_{j=0}^{n} N_{i,M}(u)N_{j,N}(v)w_{ij}\boldsymbol{q}_{ij}}{\displaystyle\sum_{k=0}^{m}\sum_{l=0}^{n} N_{k,M}(u)N_{l,N}(v)w_{ij}}, \quad (0 \le u, v \le 1),\end{aligned} \tag{11.13}$$

where $N_{i,M}(u)$ and $N_{j,N}(v)$ are normalized B-spline functions of orders M and N respectively (see eq.(10.44)).

11.3.2 Homogenized NURBS Surfaces

Simply-homogenized NURBS Surface

<u>S</u>imply-homogenized NURBS surface or type-S homogenized NURBS surface is obtained by simply homogenizing the conventional NURBS surface, that is, by homogenizing only the coordinates of the surface.

This can be expressed as follows:

$$\begin{aligned}\overline{\boldsymbol{P}(u,v)} &= \overline{[w(u,v)\ X(u,v)\ Y(u,v)\ Z(u,v)]} \\ &= \overline{\sum_{i=0}^{m}\sum_{j=0}^{n}} N_{i,M}(u)N_{j,M}(v)\boldsymbol{Q}_{ij}, \\ \boldsymbol{Q}_{ij} &= [w_{ij}\ X_{ij}\ Y_{ij}\ Z_{ij}].\end{aligned} \tag{11.14}$$

Because type-S homogenized NURBS surface is represented in an ordinary polynomial, there is no worry of a denominator becoming zero during processing. This results in a much more robust processing than the conventional NURBS surface when it is used in the Newton-Raphson method (see Chapter 15 and Section 25.2).

Doubly-homogenized NURBS Surface

Doubly-homogenized NURBS surface or type-D homogenized NURBS surface is obtained by doubly homogenizing the conventional NURBS surface, that is, by homogenizing the parameters as well as the coordinates of the surface.

We define two types of type-D homogenized NURBS surfaces corresponding to the two types of homogeneous parameters (see Section 8.6).

Type-D1 homogenized NURBS surface
Type-D1 homogenized NURBS surface is defined as follows:

$$\begin{aligned}\overline{\boldsymbol{HP}(h,r,s)} &= \overline{[w(h,r,s)\ X(h,r,s)\ Y(h,r,s)\ Z(h,r,s)]}\\ &= \sum_{i=0}^{m}\sum_{j=0}^{n} HN1_{i,M}(h,r)HN1_{j,M}(h,s)\boldsymbol{Q}_{ij}, \qquad (11.15)\\ \boldsymbol{Q}_{ij} &= [w_{ij}\ X_{ij}\ Y_{ij}\ Z_{ij}],\end{aligned}$$

$$HN1_{j,1}(h,r) = \begin{cases} HN1_{i,1}(h,r) = 1 & (u_i \le u = \frac{r}{h} < u_{i+1}), \\ HN1_{i,1}(h,r) = 0 & (\text{outside above range}), \end{cases} \qquad (11.16)$$

$$HN1_{j,M}(h,r) = \frac{r - hu_j}{u_{j+M-1} - u_j} HN1_{j,M-1}(h,r) + \frac{hu_{j+M} - r}{u_{j+M} - u_{j+1}} HN1_{j+1,M-1}(h,r). \qquad (11.17)$$

Note here that i is an integer satisfying $u_i \le u = \frac{r}{h} < u_{i+1}$.

Type-D2 homogenized NURBS surface
Type-D2 homogenized NURBS surface is defined as follows:

$$\begin{aligned}\overline{\boldsymbol{HP}(\eta,\rho,\sigma)} &= \overline{[w(\eta,\rho,\sigma)\ X(\eta,\rho,\sigma)\ Y(\eta,\rho,\sigma)\ Z(\eta,\rho,\sigma)]}\\ &= \sum_{i=0}^{m}\sum_{j=0}^{n} HN2_{i,M}(\eta,\rho)HN2_{j,M}(\eta,\sigma)\boldsymbol{Q}_{ij}, \qquad (11.18)\\ \boldsymbol{Q}_{ij} &= [w_{ij}\ X_{ij}\ Y_{ij}\ Z_{ij}],\end{aligned}$$

$$HN2_{j,1}(\eta,\rho) = \begin{cases} HN2_{i,1}(\eta,\rho) = 1 & (u_i \le u = \frac{\rho}{\eta+\rho} < u_{i+1}), \\ HN2_{i,1}(\eta,\rho) = 0 & (\text{outside above range}), \end{cases} \qquad (11.19)$$

$$HN2_{j,M}(\eta,\rho) = \frac{\rho - (\eta+\rho)u_j}{u_{j+M-1} - u_j} HN2_{j,M-1}(\eta,\rho) + \frac{(\eta+\rho)u_{j+M} - \rho}{u_{j+M} - u_{j+1}} HN2_{j+1,M-1}(\eta,\rho). \qquad (11.20)$$

Note here that i is an integer satisfying $u_i \le u = \frac{\rho}{\eta+\rho} < u_{i+1}$.

Type-D homogenized NURBS surface shows superior characteristics when it is used for computing intersection points by the geometric Newton-Raphson method (see Sections 15.7 and 25.2.1).

11.4 Shape Control

Just as an ordinary Bézier surface or NURBS surface is displayed on a computer screen along with a control net, a homogeneous Bézier surface or homogenized surface is displayed along with a homogeneous control net. A homogeneous control net is the one made of homogeneous line segments. Since a homogeneous line segment takes on three shapes, i.e., internal, external and half lines, the shape of a homogeneous control net looks a little complicated. Fig. 11.1 shows a case where Q_{11} is a point at infinity, i.e., $w_{11}=0$.

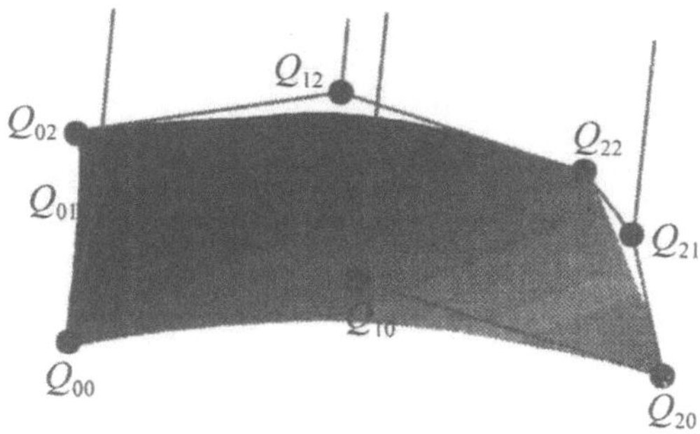

Figure 11.1: An example of homogeneous control net ($w_{11}=0$).

In addition to a homogeneous control net it is often helpful to display projections of homogeneous convex hulls on the screen (Fig. 11.2).

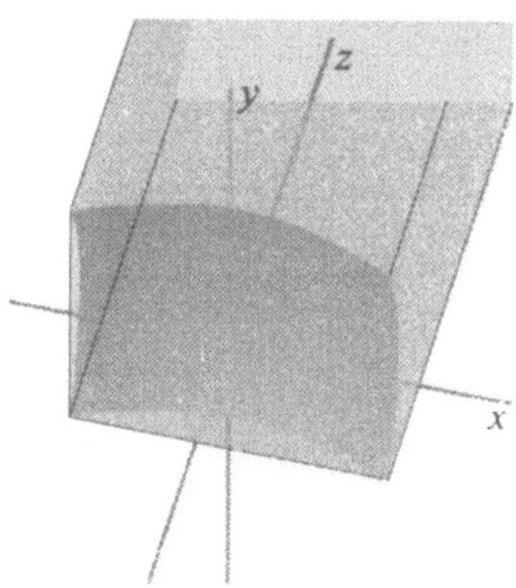

Figure 11.2: An example of projections of homogeneous convex hulls ($w_{11}=0$).

The shapes of bi-quadratic homogeneous surface patches with respect to various w_{11} values are shown in Fig. 11.3 ($w_{11}<0$ cases are not shown in the figure because of complicated shape). When w_{ij} values of all the control points are unity, then the patch turns out to be an ordinary polynomial patch (Case 1). The effect on the projected patch of increasing w_{ij} is to draw the patch nearer to the corresponding control point (Cases 2 and 3). If one of the weights w_{ij} assumes the value 0, the patch shape near $\boldsymbol{Q}_{ij}$ looks attracted to the direction of the vector $[X_{ij}\ Y_{ij}\ Z_{ij}]$ while $\boldsymbol{q}_{ij}$ loses all influence on the patch in the case of a rational surface patch. If one of the w_{ij} becomes negative, the patch appears repelled by the corresponding control point.

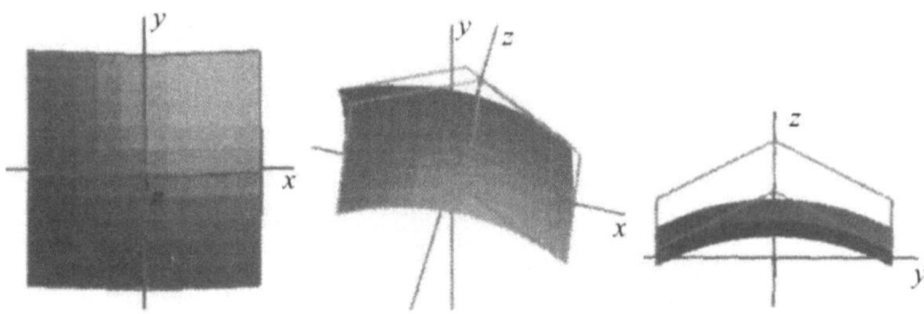

(a) z-direction (b) $(-1,-1,1)$-direction (c) x-direction

Case 1: $w_{11} = 1$

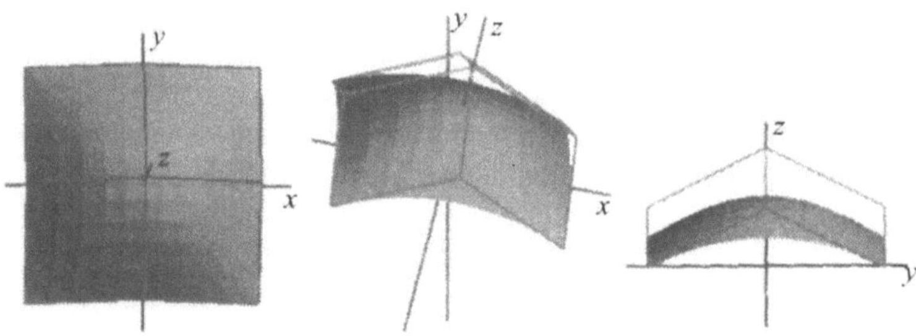

(a) z-direction (b) $(-1,-1,1)$-direction (c) x-direction

Case 2: $w_{11} = 2$

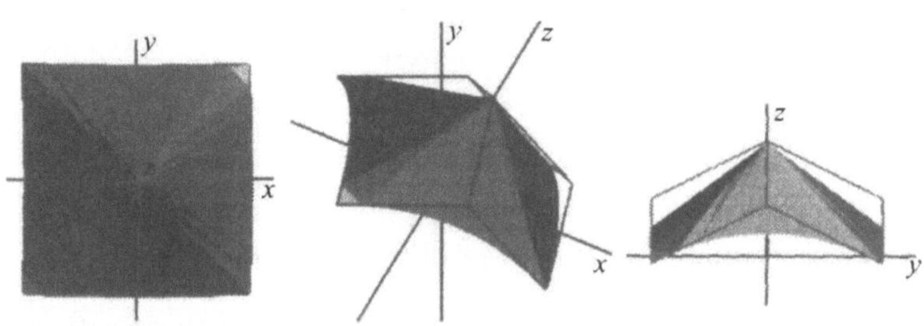

(a) z-direction (b) $(-1,-1,1)$-direction (c) x-direction

Case 3: $w_{11} = 50$

Figure 11.3: Bi-quadratic homogeneous surface patches.

Chapter 12

Basic Intersections

12.1 Intersection of 2-D Lines

1. When line equations are given:

   Consider two lines $\gamma_0 = \overline{(a_0, b_0, c_0)^T}$ and $\gamma_1 = \overline{(a_1, b_1, c_1)^T}$. In the wXY vector space, these lines represent two planes that pass the origin and are normal to vectors $\boldsymbol{\gamma}_0$ and $\boldsymbol{\gamma}_1$, respectively. If the line $\gamma = \overline{(a, b, c)^T}$ goes through the intersection of these two lines, then vector $\boldsymbol{\gamma}$ lies on the plane formed by $\boldsymbol{\gamma}_0$ and $\boldsymbol{\gamma}_1$. That is, $\boldsymbol{\gamma}$, $\boldsymbol{\gamma}_0$ and $\boldsymbol{\gamma}_1$ are linearly dependent. The necessary and sufficient condition for this is given by:

$$\begin{vmatrix} a & a_0 & a_1 \\ b & b_0 & b_1 \\ c & c_0 & c_1 \end{vmatrix} = 0. \tag{12.1}$$

   Evaluating this by the first column, we have:

$$\begin{vmatrix} b_0 & b_1 \\ c_0 & c_1 \end{vmatrix} a + \begin{vmatrix} c_0 & c_1 \\ a_0 & a_1 \end{vmatrix} b + \begin{vmatrix} a_0 & a_1 \\ b_0 & b_1 \end{vmatrix} c = 0.$$

   This expresses the pencil of lines passing the intersection of two lines γ_0 and γ_1 (eq.(12.1) forms a dual to line, eq.(9.1), that passes two points).

   The intersecting point V_c of the two lines is thus given by:

$$\begin{aligned} V_c &= \overline{(w_c, X_c, Y_c)} \\ &= \overline{\left(\begin{vmatrix} b_0 & b_1 \\ c_0 & c_1 \end{vmatrix}, -\begin{vmatrix} a_0 & a_1 \\ c_0 & c_1 \end{vmatrix}, \begin{vmatrix} a_0 & a_1 \\ b_0 & b_1 \end{vmatrix} \right)} \\ &\equiv \overline{(u_{01}, -q_{01}, p_{01})}, \end{aligned} \tag{12.2}$$

   where u_{01}, q_{01}, p_{01} are Plücker coefficients of line (see Table C.1).

Or, in a determinant form,

$$\overline{V_c} = \overline{\begin{vmatrix} \boldsymbol{i} & a_0 & a_1 \\ \boldsymbol{j} & b_0 & b_1 \\ \boldsymbol{k} & c_0 & c_1 \end{vmatrix}}. \tag{12.3}$$

(a) When γ_0 and γ_1 are either identical lines or have the reverse orientations (two-sided space case), clearly no intersecting point is defined. In this case, the homogeneous coordinates of eq.(12.2) all vanish. That is, $V_c = (0,0,0)$.

Conversely, if these homogeneous coordinates are all zeros, then the two lines are either identical or have the reverse orientation (two-sided space case).

(b) If $V_c \neq (0,0,0)$, there is an intersecting point.

i. When $w_c \neq 0$, V_c is a finite point.

ii. When $w_c = 0$, V_c is a point at infinity in the direction of vector $[X_c\ Y_c]$ in Euclidean plane. In this case the two lines are parallel.

Eqs.(12.2) and (12.3) form dual relationships to eqs.(9.2) and (9.3), respectively.

2. When the lines are each defined by two points:

Suppose that two lines L_{01} and L_{ab} are defined by the following points:

$$V_0 = \overline{(w_0, X_0, Y_0)}, \qquad V_1 = \overline{(w_1, X_1, Y_1)},$$

and

$$V_a = \overline{(w_a, X_a, Y_a)}, \qquad V_b = \overline{(w_b, X_b, Y_b)}.$$

Then, the intersecting point V_c is given as (see Appendix C):

$$\begin{aligned} V_c &= \overline{S_{01a}\boldsymbol{V}_b - S_{01b}\boldsymbol{V}_a} \\ &= \overline{\begin{vmatrix} w_0 & X_0 & Y_0 \\ w_1 & X_1 & Y_1 \\ w_a & X_a & Y_a \end{vmatrix} \boldsymbol{V}_b - \begin{vmatrix} w_0 & X_0 & Y_0 \\ w_1 & X_1 & Y_1 \\ w_b & X_b & Y_b \end{vmatrix} \boldsymbol{V}_a} \\ &= \overline{\left(\begin{vmatrix} \begin{vmatrix} w_a & X_a \\ w_b & X_b \end{vmatrix} & \begin{vmatrix} w_a & Y_a \\ w_b & Y_b \end{vmatrix} \\ \begin{vmatrix} w_0 & X_0 \\ w_1 & X_1 \end{vmatrix} & \begin{vmatrix} w_0 & Y_0 \\ w_1 & Y_1 \end{vmatrix} \end{vmatrix}, \begin{vmatrix} \begin{vmatrix} X_0 & Y_0 \\ X_1 & Y_1 \end{vmatrix} & \begin{vmatrix} w_0 & X_0 \\ w_1 & X_1 \end{vmatrix} \\ \begin{vmatrix} X_a & Y_a \\ X_b & Y_b \end{vmatrix} & \begin{vmatrix} w_a & X_a \\ w_b & X_b \end{vmatrix} \end{vmatrix}, \right.} \\ &\quad \overline{\left. \begin{vmatrix} \begin{vmatrix} X_0 & Y_0 \\ X_1 & Y_1 \end{vmatrix} & \begin{vmatrix} w_0 & Y_0 \\ w_1 & Y_1 \end{vmatrix} \\ \begin{vmatrix} X_a & Y_a \\ X_b & Y_b \end{vmatrix} & \begin{vmatrix} w_a & Y_a \\ w_b & Y_b \end{vmatrix} \end{vmatrix} \right)} \end{aligned}$$

$$= \overline{(P_{ab}Q_{01} - P_{01}Q_{ab}, U_{01}P_{ab} - U_{ab}P_{01}, U_{01}Q_{ab} - U_{ab}Q_{01})}. \tag{12.4}$$

12.2 Intersection of Three Planes

The intersecting point of three planes $\gamma_0 = \overline{(a_0, b_0, c_0, d_0)^T}$, $\gamma_1 = \overline{(a_1, b_1, c_1, d_1)^T}$ and $\gamma_2 = \overline{(a_2, b_2, c_2, d_2)^T}$, expressed in homogeneous coordinates, forms a dual to the plane, eq.(9.39), that passes three points, and thus is given by:

$$\begin{vmatrix} a & a_0 & a_1 & a_2 \\ b & b_0 & b_1 & b_2 \\ c & c_0 & c_1 & c_2 \\ d & d_0 & d_1 & d_2 \end{vmatrix} = 0. \tag{12.5}$$

Evaluating this by the first column, we have:

$$\begin{vmatrix} b_0 & b_1 & b_2 \\ c_0 & c_1 & c_2 \\ d_0 & d_1 & d_2 \end{vmatrix} a + \begin{vmatrix} a_0 & a_1 & a_2 \\ d_0 & d_1 & d_2 \\ c_0 & c_1 & c_2 \end{vmatrix} b + \begin{vmatrix} a_0 & a_1 & a_2 \\ b_0 & b_1 & b_2 \\ d_0 & d_1 & d_2 \end{vmatrix} c + \begin{vmatrix} a_0 & a_1 & a_2 \\ c_0 & c_1 & c_2 \\ b_0 & b_1 & b_2 \end{vmatrix} d = 0. \tag{12.6}$$

This expresses a pencil of planes that pass the intersecting point of the three planes.

The intersecting point $V_c = \overline{(w_c, X_c, Y_c, Z_c)}$ is therefore given by:

$$\begin{aligned} V_c &= \overline{(w_c, X_c, Y_c, Z_c)} \\ &= \overline{\left(\begin{vmatrix} b_0 & b_1 & b_2 \\ c_0 & c_1 & c_2 \\ d_0 & d_1 & d_2 \end{vmatrix}, \begin{vmatrix} a_0 & a_1 & a_2 \\ d_0 & d_1 & d_2 \\ c_0 & c_1 & c_2 \end{vmatrix}, \begin{vmatrix} a_0 & a_1 & a_2 \\ b_0 & b_1 & b_2 \\ d_0 & d_1 & d_2 \end{vmatrix}, \begin{vmatrix} a_0 & a_1 & a_2 \\ c_0 & c_1 & c_2 \\ b_0 & b_1 & b_2 \end{vmatrix} \right)} \\ &= \overline{(w_{012}, x_{012}, y_{012}, z_{012})}, \end{aligned} \tag{12.7}$$

where $w_{012}, x_{012}, y_{012}$ and z_{012} are Plücker coefficients of point.

Or, in a determinant form,

$$V_c = \overline{\begin{vmatrix} \boldsymbol{I} & a_0 & a_1 & a_2 \\ \boldsymbol{J} & b_0 & b_1 & b_2 \\ \boldsymbol{K} & c_0 & c_1 & c_2 \\ \boldsymbol{L} & d_0 & d_1 & d_2 \end{vmatrix}}. \tag{12.8}$$

Eq.(12.8) forms a dual to eq.(9.40). This is a generalization of the vector product of two vectors in three-dimensional vector space to the case of four-space.

1. When three planes γ_0, γ_1 and γ_2 are collinear, two planes are parallel and the other plane is at infinity, or at least two of the planes are coplanar, clearly no intersecting point is defined. In this case, the components of eq.(12.7) all vanish. That is, $V_c = (0, 0, 0, 0)$.

Conversely, if these homogeneous coordinates are all zeros, then the three planes are collinear, two planes are parallel and the other plane is at infinity, or at least two of the planes are coplanar.

2. If $V_c \neq (0,0,0,0)$, there is an intersecting point.

   (a) When $w_c \neq 0$, V_c is a finite point.

   (b) When $w_c = 0$, V_c is a point at infinity in the direction of vector $[X_c\ Y_c\ Z_c]$ in Euclidean plane. In this case at least two of the three planes are parallel.

12.3 Intersection of 3-D Lines

We now consider the intersection of two space lines defined in classical projective space [3].

Denoting by $\boldsymbol{K}_1$ the type-K representation of "line 1" and by $\boldsymbol{L}_2$ the type-L representation of "line 2," we make their product:

$$\boldsymbol{K}_1\boldsymbol{L}_2 \equiv \overbrace{\begin{bmatrix} 0 & -P_1 & -Q_1 & -R_1 \\ P_1 & 0 & -U_1 & T_1 \\ Q_1 & U_1 & 0 & -S_1 \\ R_1 & -T_1 & S_1 & 0 \end{bmatrix}}^{\boldsymbol{K}_1} \overbrace{\begin{bmatrix} 0 & S_2 & T_2 & U_2 \\ -S_2 & 0 & R_2 & -Q_2 \\ -T_2 & -R_2 & 0 & P_2 \\ -U_2 & Q_2 & -P_2 & 0 \end{bmatrix}}^{\boldsymbol{L}_2} = \boldsymbol{N}. \tag{12.9}$$

Because each row of $\boldsymbol{K}_1$ represents a point on "line 1," the corresponding row of $\boldsymbol{N}$, which is the product of this point and $\boldsymbol{L}_2$, represents a plane that contains this point on "line 1," and "line 2" (see eq.(9.21)). When "lines 1" and "2" intersect, these planes (represented by the rows of $\boldsymbol{N}$) are reduced to a single plane, namely, the one containing the two lines.

Similarly, each column of $\boldsymbol{L}_2$ represents a plane containing "line 2," so the corresponding column of $\boldsymbol{N}$, which is the product of $\boldsymbol{K}_1$ and this plane, represents the intersecting point of "line 1" and the plane containing "line 2" (see eq.(9.34)). When "lines 1" and "2" intersect, these points (represented by the columns of $\boldsymbol{N}$) are reduced to a single point, which is the intersecting point of the two lines.

Thus, when the two lines intersect, the rows of $\boldsymbol{N}$ each represent the homogeneous coefficients of the plane containing the two lines, while the columns each represent the homogeneous coordinates of the intersecting point of the two lines.

So $\boldsymbol{N}$ has the following form:

$$\boldsymbol{N} = \begin{bmatrix} w \\ X \\ Y \\ Z \end{bmatrix} [a\ \ b\ \ c\ \ d] = \begin{bmatrix} aw & bw & cw & dw \\ aX & bX & cX & dX \\ aY & bY & cY & dY \\ aZ & bZ & cZ & dZ \end{bmatrix}. \tag{12.10}$$

Because the intersecting point must always lie on the plane containing the two lines, the scalar product of the intersecting point and the plane is zero. This can be computed as the *trace* of $\boldsymbol{N}$. To compute its trace, we first obtain $\boldsymbol{N}$ as follows:

$$\boldsymbol{N} = \begin{bmatrix} 0 & -P_1 & -Q_1 & -R_1 \\ P_1 & 0 & -U_1 & T_1 \\ Q_1 & U_1 & 0 & -S_1 \\ R_1 & -T_1 & S_1 & 0 \end{bmatrix} \begin{bmatrix} 0 & S_2 & T_2 & U_2 \\ -S_2 & 0 & R_2 & -Q_2 \\ -T_2 & -R_2 & 0 & P_2 \\ -U_2 & Q_2 & -P_2 & 0 \end{bmatrix}$$

$$= \begin{bmatrix} P_1S_2 + Q_1T_2 + R_1U_2 & Q_1R_2 - R_1Q_2 & R_1P_2 - P_1R_2 & P_1Q_2 - Q_1P_2 \\ U_1T_2 - T_1U_2 & P_1S_2 + U_1R_2 + T_1Q_2 & P_1T_2 - T_1P_2 & P_1U_2 - U_1P_2 \\ S_1U_2 - U_1S_2 & Q_1S_2 - S_1Q_2 & Q_1T_2 + U_1R_2 + S_1P_2 & Q_1U_2 - U_1Q_2 \\ T_1S_2 - S_1T_2 & R_1S_2 - S_1R_2 & R_1T_2 - T_1R_2 & R_1U_2 + T_1Q_2 + S_1P_2 \end{bmatrix}. \tag{12.11}$$

So,

$$\text{trace}(\boldsymbol{N}) = 2\{(P_1S_2 + Q_1T_2 + R_1U_2) + (S_1P_2 + T_1Q_2 + U_1R_2)\}. \tag{12.12}$$

Therefore, the intersecting condition of two space lines $\boldsymbol{K}_1$ and $\boldsymbol{L}_2$ is:

$$P_1S_2 + Q_1T_2 + R_1U_2 + S_1P_2 + T_1Q_2 + U_1R_2 = 0. \tag{12.13}$$

Note the similarity between this expression and eq.(9.29), and also the relation between the left hand side of the equation above and the 4×4 determinant eq.(13.102).

When the two lines intersect, the intersecting point P and the plane γ containing the two lines are obtained as follows:

$$\begin{aligned} P &= \overline{(P_1S_2 + Q_1T_2 + R_1U_2,\ U_1T_2 - T_1U_2,\ S_1U_2 - U_1S_2,\ T_1S_2 - S_1T_2)} \\ &= \overline{(Q_1R_2 - R_1Q_2,\ P_1S_2 + U_1R_2 + T_1Q_2,\ Q_1S_2 - S_1Q_2,\ R_1S_2 - S_1R_2)} \\ &= \overline{(R_1P_2 - P_1R_2,\ P_1T_2 - T_1P_2,\ Q_1T_2 + U_1R_2 + S_1P_2,\ R_1T_2 - T_1R_2)} \\ &= \overline{(P_1Q_2 - Q_1P_2,\ P_1U_2 - U_1P_2,\ Q_1U_2 - U_1Q_2,\ R_1U_2 + T_1Q_2 + S_1P_2)}. \end{aligned} \tag{12.14}$$

$$\gamma = \overline{(P_1S_2 + Q_1T_2 + R_1U_2,\ Q_1R_2 - R_1Q_2,\ R_1P_2 - P_1R_2,\ P_1Q_2 - Q_1P_2)^T}$$

$$= \overline{(U_1T_2 - T_1U_2,\ P_1S_2 + U_1R_2 + T_1Q_2,\ P_1T_2 - T_1P_2,\ P_1U_2 - U_1P_2)^T}$$

$$= \overline{(S_1U_2 - U_1S_2,\ Q_1S_2 - S_1Q_2,\ Q_1T_2 + U_1R_2 + S_1P_2,\ Q_1U_2 - U_1Q_2)^T}$$

$$= \overline{(T_1S_2 - S_1T_2,\ R_1S_2 - S_1R_2,\ R_1T_2 - T_1R_2,\ R_1U_2 + T_1Q_2 + S_1P_2)^T}. \tag{12.15}$$

12.4 Intersection of Plane and Space Line

Given a plane $\gamma = \overline{(a_0, b_0, c_0, d_0)^T}$ and a line of type-K representation:

$$\boldsymbol{K} = \begin{bmatrix} 0 & -P & -Q & -R \\ P & 0 & -U & T \\ Q & U & 0 & -S \\ R & -T & S & 0 \end{bmatrix},$$

the intersection point $P_c = \overline{(w_c, X_c, Y_c, Z_c)}$ of the plane γ and the line $\boldsymbol{K}$ is given from eq.(9.34) as:

$$P_c = \overline{(w_c, X_c, Y_c, Z_c)} = \overline{\left(\boldsymbol{K}\begin{bmatrix} a_0 \\ b_0 \\ c_0 \\ d_0 \end{bmatrix}\right)^T}. \tag{12.16}$$

1. When the space line K is coplanar with the plane γ, clearly no intersecting point is defined. In this case, the homogeneous coordinates of eq.(12.16) all vanish. That is $V_c = (0, 0, 0, 0)$.

   Conversely, if these homogeneous coordinates are all zeros, then the line is coplanar with the plane.

2. If $V_c \neq (0, 0, 0, 0)$, there is an intersecting point.

   (a) When $w_c \neq 0$, V_c is a finite point.

   (b) When $w_c = 0$, V_c is a point at infinity in the direction of vector $[X_c\ Y_c\ Z_c]$ in Euclidean plane. In this case the space line and the plane are parallel.

12.5 Intersection of Two Planes

An intersection of two planes, $\gamma_0 = \overline{(a_0, b_0, c_0, d_0)^T}$ and $\gamma_1 = \overline{(a_1, b_1, c_1, d_1)^T}$, generally generates a space line. This is fully detailed in Sections 9.1.1 and 9.1.2. The summary follows:

1. **Plücker coefficient representation**

   The Plücker coefficient representation, λ_{01}, of the intersecting line of two planes, γ_0 and γ_1, is:

$$\lambda_{01} = \overline{(p_{01}, q_{01}, r_{01}, s_{01}, t_{01}, u_{01})}, \tag{12.17}$$

$$\begin{cases} p_{01} = \begin{vmatrix} a_0 & a_1 \\ b_0 & b_1 \end{vmatrix}, & q_{01} = \begin{vmatrix} a_0 & a_1 \\ c_0 & c_1 \end{vmatrix}, \\ r_{01} = \begin{vmatrix} a_0 & a_1 \\ d_0 & d_1 \end{vmatrix}, & s_{01} = \begin{vmatrix} c_0 & c_1 \\ d_0 & d_1 \end{vmatrix}, \\ t_{01} = \begin{vmatrix} d_0 & d_1 \\ b_0 & b_1 \end{vmatrix}, & u_{01} = \begin{vmatrix} b_0 & b_1 \\ c_0 & c_1 \end{vmatrix}. \end{cases} \tag{12.18}$$

2. **Equation representation**

   There exist two types of line representations, i.e., type-L' and type-K'.

   Type-L' representation

$$[w\ X\ Y\ Z]\boldsymbol{L}' = [0\ 0\ 0\ 0], \tag{12.19}$$

$$\boldsymbol{L}' = \begin{bmatrix} 0 & p_{01} & q_{01} & r_{01} \\ -p_{01} & 0 & u_{01} & -t_{01} \\ -q_{01} & -u_{01} & 0 & s_{01} \\ -r_{01} & t_{01} & -s_{01} & 0 \end{bmatrix}.$$

   Each column vector of $\boldsymbol{L}'$ represents the homogeneous coefficients of four planes containing the line expressed by $\boldsymbol{L}'$.

   Type-K' representation

$$\boldsymbol{K}' \begin{bmatrix} a \\ b \\ c \\ d \end{bmatrix} = \begin{bmatrix} 0 \\ 0 \\ 0 \\ 0 \end{bmatrix}, \tag{12.20}$$

$$\boldsymbol{K}' = \begin{bmatrix} 0 & -s_{01} & -t_{01} & -u_{01} \\ s_{01} & 0 & -r_{01} & q_{01} \\ t_{01} & r_{01} & 0 & -p_{01} \\ u_{01} & -q_{01} & p_{01} & 0 \end{bmatrix}.$$

Each row vector of $\boldsymbol{K}'$ represents the homogeneous coordinates of four points lying on the line expressed by $\boldsymbol{K}'$.

Chapter 13

4×4 Determinant Methods

13.1 Euclidean 4×4 Determinant Method

13.1.1 Type-s 4×4 Determinant Method

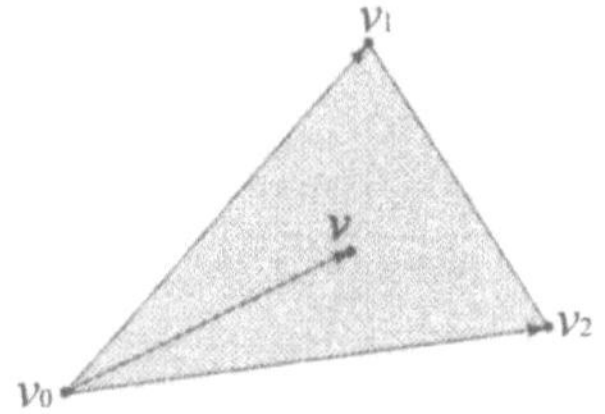

Figure 13.1: Plane defined by three points.

Three points $v_0(x_0, y_0, z_0), v_1(x_1, y_1, z_1)$ and $v_2(x_2, y_2, z_2)$ given in Euclidean space define a plane (Fig. 13.1). Let $v(x, y, z)$ be a point on this plane. Since three vectors $\boldsymbol{v}-\boldsymbol{v}_0$, $\boldsymbol{v}_1-\boldsymbol{v}_0$ and $\boldsymbol{v}_2-\boldsymbol{v}_0$ are linearly dependent, the following relation holds:

$$\begin{vmatrix} x - x_0 & y - y_0 & z - z_0 \\ x_1 - x_0 & y_1 - y_0 & z_1 - z_0 \\ x_2 - x_0 & y_2 - y_0 & z_2 - z_0 \end{vmatrix} = 0. \tag{13.1}$$

This can be rewritten as:

$$\begin{vmatrix} 1 & x & y & z \\ 1 & x_0 & y_0 & z_0 \\ 1 & x_1 & y_1 & z_1 \\ 1 & x_2 & y_2 & z_2 \end{vmatrix} = 0. \tag{13.2}$$

This is none other than the equation for the plane containing the three points v_0, v_1 and v_2. If we substitute the coordinates of some point $v_a(x_a, y_a, z_a)$ for x, y and z in the left-hand side of eq.(13.2), and denote this by s_{a012}, we have:

$$s_{a012} \equiv \begin{vmatrix} 1 & x_a & y_a & z_a \\ 1 & x_0 & y_0 & z_0 \\ 1 & x_1 & y_1 & z_1 \\ 1 & x_2 & y_2 & z_2 \end{vmatrix}. \tag{13.3}$$

This determinant is called the *Euclidean type-s* 4×4 *determinant.*

Evaluating this by the first row, we obtain:

$$s_{a012} = a_{012} + b_{012}x_a + c_{012}y_a + d_{012}z_a, \tag{13.4}$$

where

$$a_{012} = \begin{vmatrix} x_0 & y_0 & z_0 \\ x_1 & y_1 & z_1 \\ x_2 & y_2 & z_2 \end{vmatrix}, \quad b_{012} = \begin{vmatrix} 1 & z_0 & y_0 \\ 1 & z_1 & y_1 \\ 1 & z_2 & y_2 \end{vmatrix},$$

$$c_{012} = \begin{vmatrix} 1 & x_0 & z_0 \\ 1 & x_1 & z_1 \\ 1 & x_2 & z_2 \end{vmatrix}, \quad d_{012} = \begin{vmatrix} 1 & y_0 & x_0 \\ 1 & y_1 & x_1 \\ 1 & y_2 & x_2 \end{vmatrix}. \tag{13.5}$$

b_{012}, c_{012} and d_{012} can be further determined to be:

$$b_{012} = \begin{vmatrix} 1 & z_0 & y_0 \\ 1 & z_1 & y_1 \\ 1 & z_2 & y_2 \end{vmatrix} = \begin{vmatrix} 1 & 0 & 0 \\ 1 & z_1 - z_0 & y_1 - y_0 \\ 1 & z_2 - z_0 & y_2 - y_0 \end{vmatrix} = \begin{vmatrix} z_1 - z_0 & y_1 - y_0 \\ z_2 - z_0 & y_2 - y_0 \end{vmatrix},$$

$$c_{012} = \begin{vmatrix} 1 & x_0 & z_0 \\ 1 & x_1 & z_1 \\ 1 & x_2 & z_2 \end{vmatrix} = \begin{vmatrix} 1 & 0 & 0 \\ 1 & x_1 - x_0 & z_1 - z_0 \\ 1 & x_2 - x_0 & z_2 - z_0 \end{vmatrix} = \begin{vmatrix} x_1 - x_0 & z_1 - z_0 \\ x_2 - x_0 & z_2 - z_0 \end{vmatrix},$$

$$d_{012} = \begin{vmatrix} 1 & y_0 & x_0 \\ 1 & y_1 & x_1 \\ 1 & y_2 & x_2 \end{vmatrix} = \begin{vmatrix} 1 & 0 & 0 \\ 1 & y_1 - y_0 & x_1 - x_0 \\ 1 & y_2 - y_0 & x_2 - x_0 \end{vmatrix} = \begin{vmatrix} y_1 - y_0 & x_1 - x_0 \\ y_2 - y_0 & x_2 - x_0 \end{vmatrix}.$$

From this, we obtain:

$$\begin{bmatrix} b_{012} \\ c_{012} \\ d_{012} \end{bmatrix} = \{(\boldsymbol{v}_2 - \boldsymbol{v}_0) \times (\boldsymbol{v}_1 - \boldsymbol{v}_0)\}^T. \tag{13.6}$$

The vector $[b_{012}\ c_{012}\ d_{012}]$ is therefore an outward normal vector of triangle $v_0v_1v_2$ (the side from which rotation in the direction $v_0v_1v_2$ appears clockwise is the front, outward, or positive side; conversely, the side from which the rotation $v_0v_1v_2$ appears counterclockwise is the back, inward or negative side) (see Section 4.9.3) and its magnitude is equal to the area of the parallelogram formed by v_0,v_1,v_2. We denote this area by g_{012}.

Letting $v_p(x_p, y_p, z_p)$ be a point on this triangle's plane, eq.(13.4) can be further rewritten as:

$$\begin{aligned} s_{a012} &= a_{012} + b_{012}x_a + c_{012}y_a + d_{012}z_a \\ &= a_{012} + b_{012}x_a + c_{012}y_a + d_{012}z_a \\ &\quad - (a_{012} + b_{012}x_p + c_{012}y_p + d_{012}z_p) \\ &= [x_a - x_p\ \ y_a - y_p\ \ z_a - z_p] \cdot \begin{bmatrix} b_{012} \\ c_{012} \\ d_{012} \end{bmatrix} \\ &\equiv \boldsymbol{h} \cdot \boldsymbol{g}, \end{aligned} \tag{13.7}$$

where

$$h = [x_a - x_p \;\; y_a - y_p \;\; z_a - z_p] = (\boldsymbol{v}_a - \boldsymbol{v}_p), \tag{13.8}$$

$$\boldsymbol{g} = \begin{bmatrix} b_{012} \\ c_{012} \\ d_{012} \end{bmatrix} = \{(\boldsymbol{v}_2 - \boldsymbol{v}_0) \times (\boldsymbol{v}_1 - \boldsymbol{v}_0)\}^T. \tag{13.9}$$

Thus, we have:

$$s_{a012} = [\boldsymbol{v}_a - \boldsymbol{v}_p, \boldsymbol{v}_2 - \boldsymbol{v}_0, \boldsymbol{v}_1 - \boldsymbol{v}_0]. \tag{13.10}$$

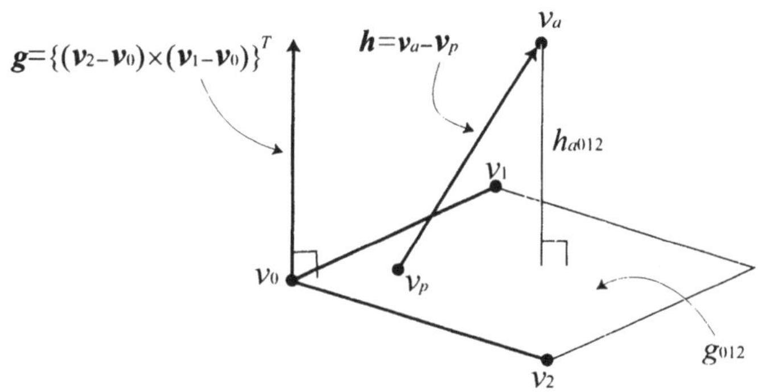

Figure 13.2: Geometric relationship of $s_{a012} = g_{012}h_{a012}$.

Let us now examine the geometric meaning of s_{a012}. From eqs.(13.7), (13.8) and (13.9), we see that s_{a012} is the scalar product of vectors $\boldsymbol{h} = \boldsymbol{v}_a - \boldsymbol{v}_p$ and $\boldsymbol{g} = \{(\boldsymbol{v}_2 - \boldsymbol{v}_0) \times (\boldsymbol{v}_1 - \boldsymbol{v}_0)\}^T$, that is, the scalar triple product of vectors $\boldsymbol{v}_a - \boldsymbol{v}_p$, $\boldsymbol{v}_2 - \boldsymbol{v}_0$ and $\boldsymbol{v}_1 - \boldsymbol{v}_0$ (Fig. 13.2). Denoting by h_{a012} the signed normal distance from point v_a to the triangle's plane (h_{a012} is positive when the sequence $v_0v_1v_2$ appears clockwise from v_a, negative when counterclockwise), we have:

$$s_{a012} = g_{012}h_{a012}. \tag{13.11}$$

Thus, s_{a012} is the signed volume of a parallelepiped with a base area of g_{012} and a height equal to the normal distance h_{a012} from point v_a to the triangle's plane (Fig. 13.3).

Furthermore, if in eq.(13.4) we substitute the coordinates of the origin $v_G(0,0,0)$ into v_a, we obtain:

$$s_{G012} = a_{012}. \tag{13.12}$$

So a_{012} represents the signed volume of the parallelepiped formed by the origin and three points v_0, v_1 and v_2.

A Euclidean type-s 4×4 determinant also represents a special case of eq.(4.6), that is, its sign represents the orientation of the simplex $(v_a; v_0; v_1; v_2)$ (see Section 4.5.2).

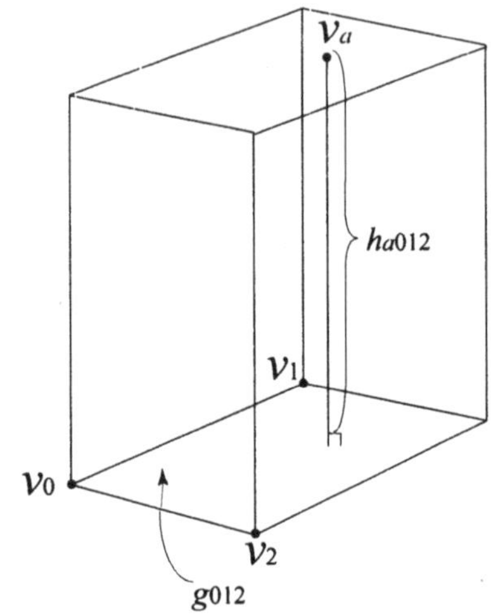

Figure 13.3: Geometric interpretation of a 4×4 determinant.

13.1.2 Properties of Type-s 4×4 Determinants

We now discuss the properties of Euclidean type-s 4×4 determinants.

Property 1

The sign of s_{a012} indicates the half space to which point v_a belongs with regard to the plane of triangle $v_0v_1v_2$. From eq.(13.7), s_{a012} is positive when the point v_a belongs to the half space from which the order of $v_0v_1v_2$ appears clockwise, but negative when it appears counterclockwise. When v_a lies on the plane of the triangle $v_0v_1v_2$, s_{a012} is zero. This sign property of s_{a012} is used in various geometric tests.

The sign of s_{a012} also shows the orientation of the simplex $(v_a; v_0; v_1; v_2)$. That is, when s_{a012} is positive, $(v_a; v_0; v_1; v_2)$ is a positively oriented tetrahedron, if negative, it is a negatively oriented one (Fig. 13.4).

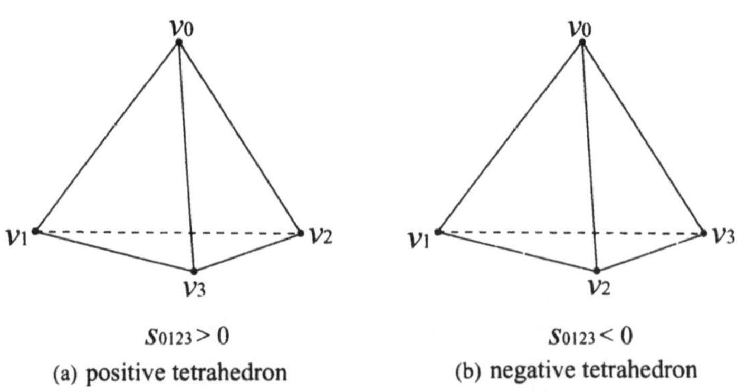

Figure 13.4: Orientation of simplex $(v_0; v_1; v_2; v_3)$.

Property 2
The magnitude of s_{a012} is proportional to the normal distance from the point v_a to the plane of the triangle $v_0v_1v_2$. This property is used to determine intersection points, where we employ the ratio of two determinants instead of their actual values.

Let us use this property to determine the formula for the intersection of the line segment v_av_b and triangle $v_0v_1v_2$, when they intersect at a single point. The distances from the points v_a and v_b to the plane of the triangle $v_0v_1v_2$ are proportional to s_{a012} and s_{b012}, respectively. s_{a012} and s_{b012} have different signs when the line segment v_av_b intersects with the plane of the triangle $v_0v_1v_2$ at a single point. Thus, the vector $\boldsymbol{v}$ for the intersection point is given by (Fig. 13.5):

$$\boldsymbol{v} = \boldsymbol{v}_a + \frac{s_{a012}}{s_{a012} - s_{b012}}(\boldsymbol{v}_b - \boldsymbol{v}_a). \tag{13.13}$$

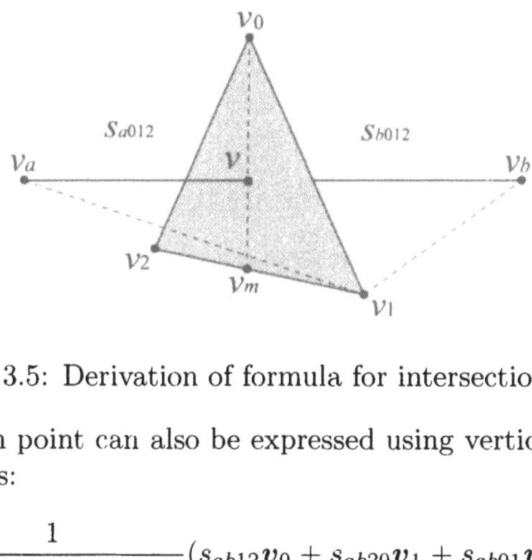

Figure 13.5: Derivation of formula for intersection point.

The intersection point can also be expressed using vertices v_0, v_1 and v_2 of a triangle as follows:

$$\boldsymbol{v} = \frac{1}{s_{ab12} + s_{ab20} + s_{ab01}}(s_{ab12}\boldsymbol{v}_0 + s_{ab20}\boldsymbol{v}_1 + s_{ab01}\boldsymbol{v}_2). \tag{13.14}$$

Eq.(13.14) can be derived as follows (Fig. 13.5):

From the formula eq.(13.13), we obtain the intersection point v_m of the line segment v_1v_2 and the plane of the triangle $v_0v_av_b$:

$$\begin{aligned}\boldsymbol{v}_m &= \boldsymbol{v}_1 + \frac{s_{10ab}}{s_{10ab} - s_{20ab}}(\boldsymbol{v}_2 - \boldsymbol{v}_1) \\ &= \frac{s_{10ab}}{s_{10ab} - s_{20ab}}\boldsymbol{v}_2 - \frac{s_{20ab}}{s_{10ab} - s_{20ab}}\boldsymbol{v}_1. \end{aligned} \tag{13.15}$$

Next, we determine the point v which is the intersection of the line segment v_0v_m and the plane of the triangle $v_1v_av_b$:

$$\boldsymbol{v} = \boldsymbol{v}_0 + \frac{s_{01ba}}{s_{01ba} - s_{m1ba}}(\boldsymbol{v}_m - \boldsymbol{v}_0). \tag{13.16}$$

Now, by using eq.(13.15) and the linearity property of a determinant, s_{m1ba} is represented as:

$$s_{m1ba} = \frac{s_{10ab}}{s_{10ab} - s_{20ab}} s_{21ba} - \frac{s_{20ab}}{s_{10ab} - s_{20ab}} s_{11ba}$$
$$= \frac{s_{10ab} s_{21ba}}{s_{10ab} - s_{20ab}}. \tag{13.17}$$

Then, by using eqs.(13.15) and (13.17) we obtain the intersection point v as follows:

$$\boldsymbol{v} = \boldsymbol{v}_0 + \frac{s_{01ba}}{s_{01ba} - s_{m1ba}} (\boldsymbol{v}_m - \boldsymbol{v}_0)$$
$$= \frac{1}{s_{ab12} + s_{ab20} + s_{ab01}} (s_{ab12}\boldsymbol{v}_0 + s_{ab20}\boldsymbol{v}_1 + s_{ab01}\boldsymbol{v}_2).$$

Property 3

The magnitude of vector $[b_{012}\ c_{012}\ d_{012}]^T$ is twice the area of the triangle $v_0v_1v_2$; meanwhile, s_{a012} is six times the volume of the tetrahedron formed by the points v_a, v_0, v_1 and v_2. These properties are used to calculate Euclidean geometric quantities (see Chapter 19).

13.1.3 Interferences between Simplices (1)

The Euclidean 4×4 determinant method uses Euclidean type-s 4×4 determinants to carry out various geometric tests and computations [57]. Such geometric tests and computations are based on the three properties of the Euclidean 4×4 determinants described in the previous section.

Tests based on (Property 1) base their principle on the properties of Euclidean half spaces. Here, only the signs of the 4×4 determinants are relevant instead of their actual values. This makes it possible to carry out adaptive processing efficiently (see Section 16.7).

After we use an intersection test to find that an intersecting point does indeed exist, it can be determined from eqs.(13.13) or (13.14). In this case, the ratio of two 4×4 determinants affects the intersection's accuracy.

Meanwhile, Euclidean geometric quantities such as a polygon's area or a polyhedron's surface area or volume are determined using (Property 3). Euclidean geometric quantities are discussed in Chapter 19. In these instances, the 4×4 determinants' actual values directly affect the accuracy of the Euclidean quantities.

In this section, we discuss geometric tests based on the Euclidean type-s 4×4 determinant method using some basic examples. We shall assume that the line segments, triangles and tetrahedra given below are defined by linearly independent points and thus nondegenerate (see Section 14.2).

Containment Test of a Point in a Tetrahedron

The condition that a point v_a exists inside a tetrahedron $v_0v_1v_2v_3$ can be derived as follows (Fig. 13.6).

After determining whether the tetrahedron is positive ($s_{0123}>0$) or negative ($s_{0123}<0$), the relation is established between the point and the half spaces for four faces $v_1v_2v_3$, $v_0v_3v_2$, $v_0v_1v_3$ and $v_0v_2v_1$.

For a positive tetrahedron, the point v_a exists inside the tetrahedron if it lies on the positive sides of all the four faces; for a negative tetrahedron, the point v_a must lie on the negative sides of the four faces. That is,

$$\begin{aligned}&((s_{0123} > 0) \wedge (s_{a123}, s_{a032}, s_{a013}, s_{a021} \geq 0))\\ &\vee ((s_{0123} < 0) \wedge (s_{a123}, s_{a032}, s_{a013}, s_{a021} \leq 0)).\end{aligned} \tag{13.18}$$

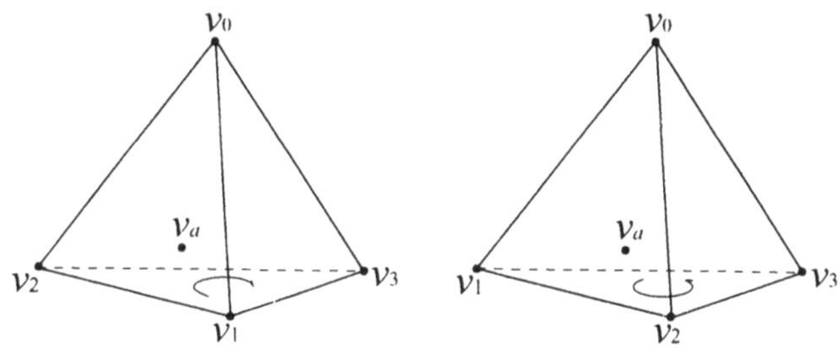

(a) positive tetrahedron (b) negative tetrahedron

Figure 13.6: Containment test of a point in a tetrahedron.

If we wish to find whether a point lies inside or outside of a triangle or line segment, these can be regarded as special cases of determining whether a point lies in a tetrahedron.

That is, to see whether a point v_a lies in a triangle $v_0v_1v_2$, we first establish some suitable point v_N that exists out of the plane of the triangle in order to form a tetrahedron, then add the condition that the point v_a lies on the plane of the triangle ($s_{a012}=0$); finally, we determine whether v_a lies in the tetrahedron (Fig. 13.7). That is,

$$\begin{aligned}&(s_{N012} \neq 0) \wedge (s_{a012} = 0)\\ &\wedge (((s_{N012} > 0) \wedge (s_{a21N}, s_{a02N}, s_{a10N} \geq 0))\\ &\vee ((s_{N012} < 0) \wedge (s_{a21N}, s_{a02N}, s_{a10N} \leq 0))).\end{aligned} \tag{13.19}$$

Meanwhile, to establish whether a point v_a lies in the interior of a line segment v_0v_1, we first set two arbitrary points v_M and v_N that form a tetrahedron with v_0 and v_1, add the condition that the point v_a lies on the line v_0v_1 ($s_{a01M}, s_{a01N}=0$), and then determine whether v_a lies in the tetrahedron $v_0v_1v_Mv_N$ (Fig. 13.8). That is,

$$\begin{aligned}&(s_{01MN} \neq 0) \wedge (s_{a01M}, s_{a01N} = 0)\\ &\wedge (((s_{01MN} > 0) \wedge (s_{a1MN}, s_{a0NM} \geq 0))\\ &\vee ((s_{01MN} < 0) \wedge (s_{a1MN}, s_{a0NM} \leq 0))).\end{aligned} \tag{13.20}$$

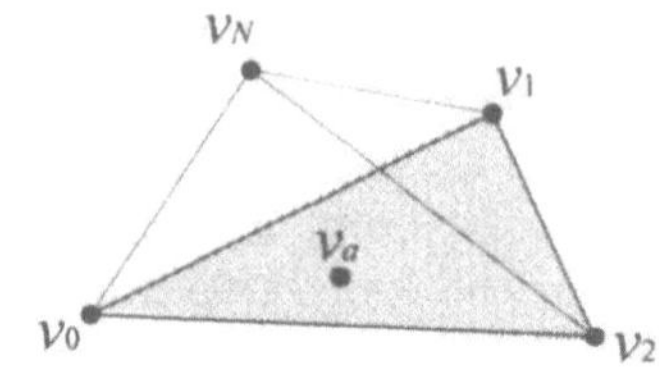

Figure 13.7: Containment test of a point in a triangle.

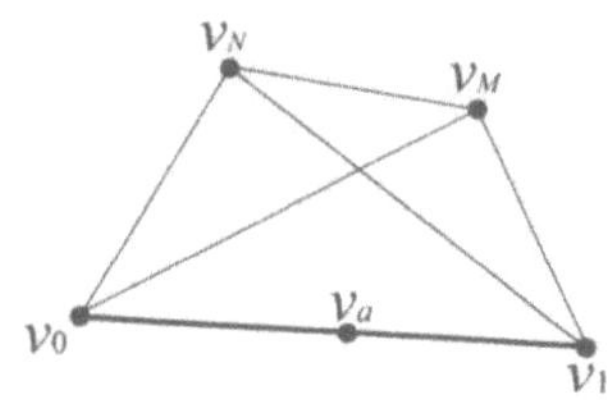

Figure 13.8: Containment test of a point in a line segment.

Intersection Test between a Line Segment and a Triangle

The condition for a line segment and triangle to intersect at a single point can be derived as follows (Fig. 13.9).

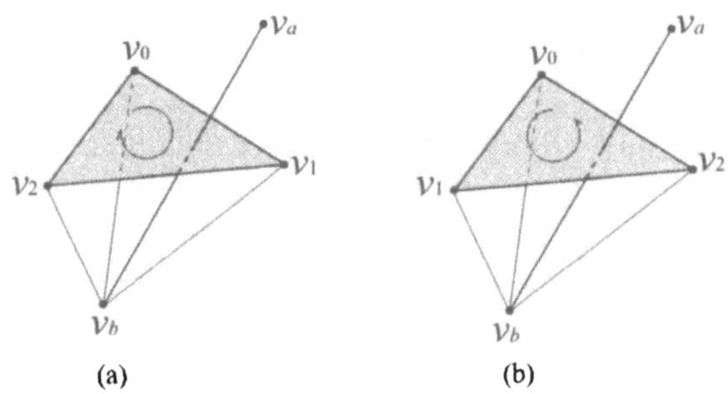

Figure 13.9: Intersection test between a line segment and a triangle.

For a line segment $v_a v_b$ and triangle $v_0 v_1 v_2$ to have a single intersecting point, at least one of the sets of points (v_a, v_0, v_1, v_2) and (v_b, v_0, v_1, v_2) must form a tetrahedron, or

$$(s_{a012}, s_{b012}) \neq (0, 0).$$

After determining whether the tetrahedron $v_a v_0 v_1 v_2$ is positive $(s_{a012} \geq 0 \wedge s_{b012} \leq 0)$ or negative $(s_{a012} \leq 0 \wedge s_{b012} \geq 0)$, the relations are established between v_a and the half spaces of the three faces $v_b v_1 v_2$, $v_b v_2 v_0$ and $v_b v_0 v_1$.

For the line segment and triangle to intersect at a single point, if tetrahedron $v_a v_0 v_1 v_2$ is positive, the point v_a must lie on the positive sides of the three faces above; if the tetrahedron is negative, the point v_a must be on the negative sides of the three faces. Thus, we have:

$$\begin{aligned}&((s_{a012}, s_{b012}) \neq (0,0))\\ \wedge\, &((s_{a012} \geq 0 \wedge s_{b012} \leq 0 \wedge s_{ab12}, s_{ab20}, s_{ab01} \geq 0)\\ \vee\, &(s_{a012} \leq 0 \wedge s_{b012} \geq 0 \wedge s_{ab12}, s_{ab20}, s_{ab01} \leq 0)).\end{aligned} \tag{13.21}$$

Once we find that there indeed exists a single intersecting point, it can be determined from eq.(13.13) using the 4×4 determinants (which we have already determined at the intersection test).

Finding whether two line segments intersect can be regarded as a special case of finding whether a line segment and triangle intersect (Fig. 13.10).

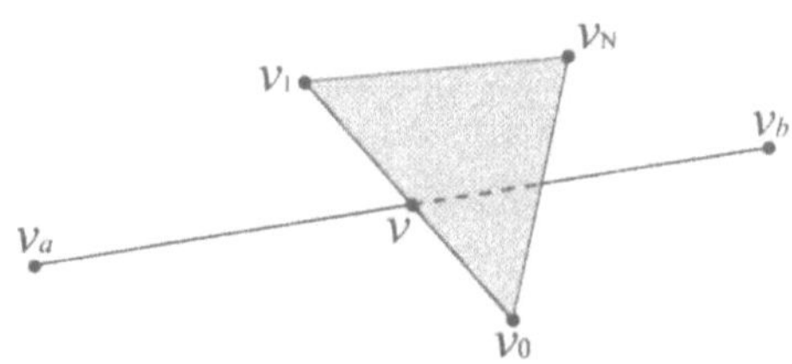

Figure 13.10: Intersection test of two line segments.

To determine whether line segments v_0v_1 and v_av_b intersect, therefore, we first establish an arbitrary point v_N that forms a tetrahedron with at least either three of the four points v_0, v_1, v_a and v_b. That is,

$$(s_{a01N}, s_{b01N}, s_{abN0}, s_{abN1}) \neq (0,0,0,0).$$

To this, we attach the condition that the two line segments lie on the same plane ($s_{01ab} = 0$), as well as the condition for the line segment v_av_b and the triangle $v_0v_1v_N$ to intersect, that is:

$$\begin{aligned}&((s_{a01N}, s_{b01N}, s_{abN0}, s_{abN1}) \neq (0,0,0,0)) \wedge (s_{01ab} = 0)\\ \wedge\, &((s_{a01N} \geq 0 \wedge s_{b01N} \leq 0 \wedge s_{0abN} \leq 0 \wedge s_{1abN} \geq 0)\\ \vee\, &(s_{a01N} \leq 0 \wedge s_{b01N} \geq 0 \wedge s_{0abN} \geq 0 \wedge s_{1abN} \leq 0)).\end{aligned} \tag{13.22}$$

13.1.4 Remarks

As we saw above, the Euclidean 4×4 determinant method makes it possible to unify geometric tests as computations involving 4×4 determinants. Geometric tests can thus be classified under an orderly scheme using simple expressions.

A few problems, however, exist.

Problem ①

Formulas (13.13) and (13.14) involve division operations. Thus, if the triangle is extremely small, or if the point v_a or v_b lies extremely close to the triangle's plane, the computed result for the intersection may contain large errors or instabilities. The use of division also makes it impossible to achieve a totally error-free computation of intersections.

Euclidean 4×4 determinants include only point coordinates, and so direction, of which the concept is distinguished from that of points in Euclidean space, is difficult to deal with. For this reason, geometric tests that involve direction (such as the convexity test of a polygon's vertex or of a polyhedron's edge) are troublesome within the framework of Euclidean 4×4 determinants.

As we saw in Chapter 9, when division is carried out for a perspective transformation or for rational equations, an "ordinary" line segment, triangle, or tetrahedron can change into various geometric shapes (Figs. 8.2, 8.3 and Figs. 9.5 through 9.8). The Euclidean 4×4 determinant method deals only with these "ordinary" elements and so is generally not applicable to geometric elements generated as a result of division. In other words, conditions used in the Euclidean 4×4 determinant method are not invariant under projective transformations (see Section 7.5).

The problems discussed here are all directly or indirectly related to division operations.

Problem ②

In the 4×4 determinant method, a tetrahedron is constructed from four points to conduct various tests and operations. Thus, if we wish to find out whether a point lies inside a triangle or a line segment, we must additionally set one or two points to form a tetrahedron. In practice, this could be a tedious step.

13.2 Homogeneous 4×4 Determinant Methods

13.2.1 Homogeneous 4×4 Determinants

Problem ① above can be avoided if we use 4×4 determinants in which the rows of the Euclidean 4×4 determinants are replaced by homogeneous coordinates of points (see Section 4.9.3) [57], [42]. The reader will recall that complete duality holds in classical projective space or two-sided space, i.e., the spaces which homogeneous coordinates represent. Thus, if a 4×4 determinant consisting of the homogeneous coordinates of four points has a meaning, then its dual, the 4×4 determinant consisting of the homogeneous coefficients of four planes, must also have a meaning. In the rest of this book, we shall call the former type "*homogeneous type-S* 4×4 *determinants*" and the latter "*homogeneous type-T* 4×4 *determinants*." The latter has as its columns the homogeneous coefficients of four planes.

Homogeneous Type-S Determinant

The homogeneous type-S 4×4 determinant S_{a012} is defined by the homogeneous coordinates of four points, $V_a = \overline{(w_a, X_a, Y_a, Z_a)}$, $V_0 = \overline{(w_0, X_0, Y_0, Z_0)}$, $V_1 =$

$\overline{(w_1, X_1, Y_1, Z_1)}$ and $V_2 = \overline{(w_2, X_2, Y_2, Z_2)}$ (Fig.13.11), as follows:

$$S_{a012} = \begin{vmatrix} w_a & X_a & Y_a & Z_a \\ w_0 & X_0 & Y_0 & Z_0 \\ w_1 & X_1 & Y_1 & Z_1 \\ w_2 & X_2 & Y_2 & Z_2 \end{vmatrix}. \tag{13.23}$$

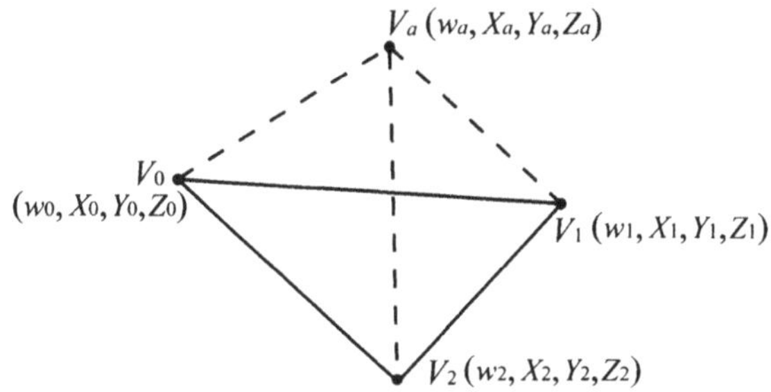

Figure 13.11: Defining data of type-S 4×4 determinant.

Homogeneous Type-T Determinant

The homogeneous type-T 4×4 determinant T_{a012} is defined by the homogeneous coefficients of four planes, $\gamma_a = \overline{(a_a, b_a, c_a, d_a)^T}$, $\gamma_0 = \overline{(a_0, b_0, c_0, d_0)^T}$, $\gamma_1 = \overline{(a_1, b_1, c_1, d_1)^T}$ and $\gamma_2 = \overline{(a_2, b_2, c_2, d_2)^T}$ (Fig.13.12), as follows:

$$T_{a012} = \begin{vmatrix} a_a & a_0 & a_1 & a_2 \\ b_a & b_0 & b_1 & b_2 \\ c_a & c_0 & c_1 & c_2 \\ d_a & d_0 & d_1 & d_2 \end{vmatrix}. \tag{13.24}$$

The homogeneous type-S 4×4 determinant is obtained by substituting the coordinates $\overline{(w_a, X_a, Y_a, Z_a)}$ of point V_a into the left-hand side of the homogeneous coordinate plane equation (9.39), which expresses the plane passing three points V_0, V_1 and V_2. Meanwhile, the homogeneous type-T 4×4 determinant is obtained by substituting the coefficients $\overline{(a_a, b_a, c_a, d_a)^T}$ of plane γ_a into the left-hand side of the homogeneous coefficient point equation eq.(12.5), which expresses the point at which three planes γ_0, γ_1 and γ_2 intersect.

13.2.2 Homogeneous Type-S 4×4 Determinant

Here we examine the geometric meaning of a homogeneous type-S 4×4 determinant in terms of their Euclidean image.

Evaluating eq.(13.23) by its first row, we obtain:

$$S_{a012} = A_{012}w_a + B_{012}X_a + C_{012}Y_a + D_{012}Z_a, \tag{13.25}$$

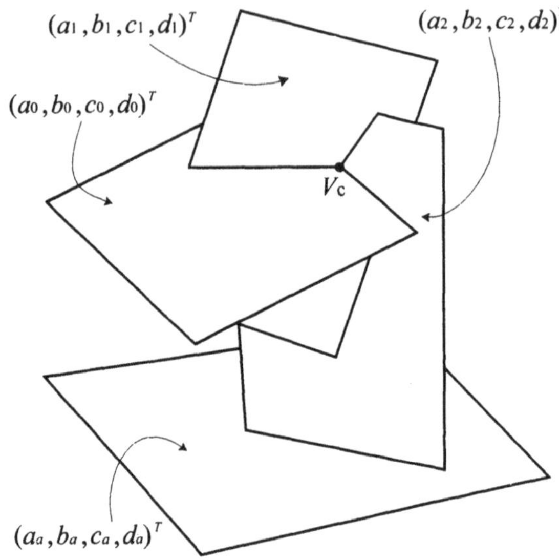

Figure 13.12: Defining data of type-T 4×4 determinant.

where

$$A_{012} = \begin{vmatrix} X_0 & Y_0 & Z_0 \\ X_1 & Y_1 & Z_1 \\ X_2 & Y_2 & Z_2 \end{vmatrix}, \ B_{012} = \begin{vmatrix} w_0 & Z_0 & Y_0 \\ w_1 & Z_1 & Y_1 \\ w_2 & Z_2 & Y_2 \end{vmatrix},$$

$$C_{012} = \begin{vmatrix} w_0 & X_0 & Z_0 \\ w_1 & X_1 & Z_1 \\ w_2 & X_2 & Z_2 \end{vmatrix}, D_{012} = \begin{vmatrix} w_0 & Y_0 & X_0 \\ w_1 & Y_1 & X_1 \\ w_2 & Y_2 & X_2 \end{vmatrix}. \tag{13.26}$$

$A_{012}, B_{012}, C_{012}$ and D_{012} are the homogeneous coefficients of the plane that passes the three points V_0, V_1 and V_2.

Letting $v_p(x_p, y_p, z_p)$ be a point on the plane of triangle $V_0V_1V_2$, eq.(13.25) can be further rewritten as:

$$\begin{aligned} S_{a012} &= A_{012}w_a + B_{012}X_a + C_{012}Y_a + D_{012}Z_a \\ &= A_{012}w_a + B_{012}X_a + C_{012}Y_a + D_{012}Z_a \\ &\quad - w_a(A_{012} + B_{012}x_p + C_{012}y_p + D_{012}z_p) \\ &= [X_a - w_a x_p \ \ Y_a - w_a y_p \ \ Z_a - w_a z_p] \cdot \begin{bmatrix} B_{012} \\ C_{012} \\ D_{012} \end{bmatrix} \\ &\equiv \boldsymbol{H} \cdot \boldsymbol{G}, \end{aligned} \tag{13.27}$$

where

$$\boldsymbol{H} = [X_a - w_a x_p \ \ Y_a - w_a y_p \ \ Z_a - w_a z_p], \ \ \boldsymbol{G} = \begin{bmatrix} B_{012} \\ C_{012} \\ D_{012} \end{bmatrix}. \tag{13.28}$$

Thus the homogeneous type-S 4×4 determinant can be expressed as the scalar product of vectors $\boldsymbol{H}$ and $\boldsymbol{G}$.

Let us now examine the meaning of these vectors, dividing them into the cases in which vertices are finite and in which they are points at infinity.

Vector H

1. When V_a is a finite point ($w_a \neq 0$)

$$\begin{aligned}\boldsymbol{H} &= [X_a - w_a x_p \;\; Y_a - w_a y_p \;\; Z_a - w_a z_p] \\ &= w_a[x_a - x_p \;\; y_a - y_p \;\; z_a - z_p] \\ &= w_a(\boldsymbol{v}_a - \boldsymbol{v}_p).\end{aligned} \tag{13.29}$$

   Hence, $\boldsymbol{H}$ is a vector pointing from an arbitrary point on the triangle's plane toward the point V_a with a magnitude w_a times the distance between these two points.

2. When V_a is a point at infinity ($w_a = 0$)

$$\begin{aligned}\boldsymbol{H} &= [X_a - w_a x_p \;\; Y_a - w_a y_p \;\; Z_a - w_a z_p] \\ &= [X_a \; Y_a \; Z_a].\end{aligned} \tag{13.30}$$

   To determine the equivalent vector $\boldsymbol{v}_a^*$ that corresponds to $\boldsymbol{v}_a$ in eq.(13.29), we put:

$$w_a^*(\boldsymbol{v}_a^* - \boldsymbol{v}_p) = [X_a \; Y_a \; Z_a].$$

   Letting $w_a^*=1$, we obtain:

$$\boldsymbol{v}_a^* = \boldsymbol{v}_p + [X_a \; Y_a \; Z_a]. \tag{13.31}$$

   When V_a is a point at infinity $\overline{(0, X_a, Y_a, Z_a)}$, therefore, the equivalent finite point v_a^* is located at the tip of vector $[X_a \; Y_a \; Z_a]$ when this vector is positioned so that its base coincides with an arbitrary point on the triangle's plane, that is, $v_a^* = (x_p + X_a, y_p + Y_a, z_p + Z_a)$. So we can write:

$$\boldsymbol{H} = \boldsymbol{v}_a^* - \boldsymbol{v}_p. \tag{13.32}$$

   Thus, $\boldsymbol{H}$ is a vector from an arbitrary point on the triangle's plane to point v_a^*. We shall hereafter denote by h_{a^*012} the normal distance from the point v_a^* to the triangle's plane.

Vector G

1. When V_0, V_1 and V_2 are all finite points ($w_0, w_1, w_2 \neq 0$)

   In this case, we have:

$$\begin{bmatrix} A_{012} \\ B_{012} \\ C_{012} \\ D_{012} \end{bmatrix} = w_0 w_1 w_2 \begin{bmatrix} a_{012} \\ b_{012} \\ c_{012} \\ d_{012} \end{bmatrix}.$$

Meanwhile, we know from eq.(13.6) that:

$$\begin{bmatrix} b_{012} \\ c_{012} \\ d_{012} \end{bmatrix} = \{(\boldsymbol{v}_2 - \boldsymbol{v}_0) \times (\boldsymbol{v}_1 - \boldsymbol{v}_0)\}^T.$$

Therefore,

$$\begin{aligned} \boldsymbol{G} &= \begin{bmatrix} B_{012} \\ C_{012} \\ D_{012} \end{bmatrix} \\ &= w_0 w_1 w_2 \begin{bmatrix} b_{012} \\ c_{012} \\ d_{012} \end{bmatrix} \\ &= w_0 w_1 w_2 \{(\boldsymbol{v}_2 - \boldsymbol{v}_0) \times (\boldsymbol{v}_1 - \boldsymbol{v}_0)\}^T. \end{aligned} \tag{13.33}$$

Thus, $\boldsymbol{G}$ is a normal vector in the positive direction of triangle $v_0 v_1 v_2$, with a magnitude $w_0 w_1 w_2$ times the area of the parallelogram formed by v_0, v_1 and v_2.

2. When one of the points V_0, V_1 and V_2 is a point at infinity (let us say $w_1 = 0;\ w_0, w_2 \neq 0$)

   In this case, we have:

$$\begin{bmatrix} A_{012} \\ B_{012} \\ C_{012} \\ D_{012} \end{bmatrix} = w_0 w_2 \begin{bmatrix} a_{01*2} \\ b_{01*2} \\ c_{01*2} \\ d_{01*2} \end{bmatrix},$$

$$\begin{cases} a_{01*2} = \begin{vmatrix} x_0 & y_0 & z_0 \\ x_0 + X_1 & y_0 + Y_1 & z_0 + Z_1 \\ x_2 & y_2 & z_2 \end{vmatrix}, & b_{01*2} = \begin{vmatrix} 1 & z_0 & y_0 \\ 1 & z_0 + Z_1 & y_0 + Y_1 \\ 1 & z_2 & y_2 \end{vmatrix}, \\ c_{01*2} = \begin{vmatrix} 1 & x_0 & z_0 \\ 1 & x_0 + X_1 & z_0 + Z_1 \\ 1 & x_2 & z_2 \end{vmatrix}, & d_{01*2} = \begin{vmatrix} 1 & y_0 & x_0 \\ 1 & y_0 + Y_1 & x_0 + X_1 \\ 1 & y_2 & x_2 \end{vmatrix}. \end{cases} \tag{13.34}$$

   That is, when V_1 is a point at infinity $\overline{(0, X_1, Y_1, Z_1)}$, its equivalent finite point v_1^* is located at the tip of vector $[X_1\ Y_1\ Z_1]$ when it is based at point v_0, i.e., $v_1^* = [x_0 + X_1\ y_0 + Y_1\ z_0 + Z_1]$.

   So:

$$\begin{bmatrix} b_{01*2} \\ c_{01*2} \\ d_{01*2} \end{bmatrix} = \{(\boldsymbol{v}_2 - \boldsymbol{v}_0) \times (\boldsymbol{v}_1^* - \boldsymbol{v}_0)\}^T$$

and

$$\begin{aligned} \boldsymbol{G} &= \begin{bmatrix} B_{012} \\ C_{012} \\ D_{012} \end{bmatrix} \\ &= w_0 w_2 \begin{bmatrix} b_{01*2} \\ c_{01*2} \\ d_{01*2} \end{bmatrix} \\ &= w_0 w_2 \{(\boldsymbol{v}_2 - \boldsymbol{v}_0) \times (\boldsymbol{v}_1^* - \boldsymbol{v}_0)\}^T. \end{aligned} \tag{13.35}$$

That is, if we denote by v_1^* the point at the tip of vector $[X_1\ Y_1\ Z_1]$ based at v_0, $\boldsymbol{G}$ is a normal vector in the positive direction of triangle $v_0 v_1^* v_2$, with a magnitude $w_0 w_2$ times the area (which we shall denote g_{01*2}) of the parallelogram formed by v_0, v_1^* and v_2.

3. When two of the points V_0, V_1 and V_2 are points at infinity (let us say $w_1 = w_2 = 0;\ w_0 \neq 0$).

   In this case, we have:

$$\begin{bmatrix} A_{012} \\ B_{012} \\ C_{012} \\ D_{012} \end{bmatrix} = w_0 \begin{bmatrix} a_{01*2*} \\ b_{01*2*} \\ c_{01*2*} \\ d_{01*2*} \end{bmatrix},$$

$$\begin{cases} a_{01*2*} = \begin{vmatrix} x_0 & y_0 & z_0 \\ x_0 + X_1 & y_0 + Y_1 & z_0 + Z_1 \\ x_0 + X_2 & y_0 + Y_2 & z_0 + Z_2 \end{vmatrix}, \quad b_{01*2*} = \begin{vmatrix} 1 & z_0 & y_0 \\ 1 & z_0 + Z_1 & y_0 + Y_1 \\ 1 & z_0 + Z_2 & y_0 + Y_2 \end{vmatrix}, \\ c_{01*2*} = \begin{vmatrix} 1 & x_0 & z_0 \\ 1 & x_0 + X_1 & z_0 + Z_1 \\ 1 & x_0 + X_2 & z_0 + Z_2 \end{vmatrix}, \quad d_{01*2*} = \begin{vmatrix} 1 & y_0 & x_0 \\ 1 & y_0 + Y_1 & x_0 + X_1 \\ 1 & y_0 + Y_2 & x_0 + X_2 \end{vmatrix}. \end{cases} \tag{13.36}$$

   That is, when V_1 and V_2 are points at infinity $\overline{(0, X_1, Y_1, Z_1)}$ and $\overline{(0, X_2, Y_2, Z_2)}$, respectively, their equivalent finite points v_1^* and v_2^* are located at the tips of vectors $[X_1\ Y_1\ Z_1]$ and $[X_2\ Y_2\ Z_2]$, respectively, when they are based at point v_0, i.e., $v_1^* = (x_0{+}X_1, y_0{+}Y_1, z_0{+}Z_1)$ and $v_2^* = (x_0{+}X_2, y_0{+}Y_2, z_0{+}Z_2)$.

   So:

$$\begin{bmatrix} b_{01*2*} \\ c_{01*2*} \\ d_{01*2*} \end{bmatrix} = \{(\boldsymbol{v}_2^* - \boldsymbol{v}_0) \times (\boldsymbol{v}_1^* - \boldsymbol{v}_0)\}^T$$

   and:

$$\begin{aligned} \boldsymbol{G} &= \begin{bmatrix} B_{012} \\ C_{012} \\ D_{012} \end{bmatrix} \\ &= w_0 \begin{bmatrix} b_{01*2*} \\ c_{01*2*} \\ d_{01*2*} \end{bmatrix} \end{aligned}$$

$$= w_0\{(\boldsymbol{v}_2^* - \boldsymbol{v}_0) \times (\boldsymbol{v}_1^* - \boldsymbol{v}_0)\}^T. \tag{13.37}$$

That is, if we denote by v_1^* and v_2^* the points at the tips of vectors $[X_1\ Y_1\ Z_1]$ and $[X_2\ Y_2\ Z_2]$, respectively, when both vectors are based at v_0, $\boldsymbol{G}$ is a normal vector in the positive direction of triangle $v_0v_1^*v_2^*$, with a magnitude w_0 times the area (which we shall denote $g_{01^*2^*}$) of the parallelogram formed by v_0, v_1^* and v_2^*.

We saw from eq.(13.27) that the homogeneous 4×4 determinant S_{a012} can be expressed as the scalar product of vectors $\boldsymbol{H}$ and $\boldsymbol{G}$. While these vectors differ – $\boldsymbol{H}$ depending on whether V_a is a finite point or point at infinity, and $\boldsymbol{G}$ on whether V_0, V_1 and V_2 are finite points or points at infinity – , in all cases, $\boldsymbol{G}$ represents a normal vector on the plane of the triangle $V_0V_1V_2$ with a magnitude of a scalar times the area of the parallelogram, while $\boldsymbol{H}$ is the vector from some point on the plane of the triangle $V_0V_1V_2$ pointing toward V_a with a magnitude of a scalar times the distance between the two points. Therefore, S_{a012} represents the volume of a parallelepiped with a base area G_{012}, which is a scalar times the parallelogram's area, and a height H_{a012}, which is a scalar times the normal distance from point V_a to the plane of the triangle. That is:

$$S_{a012} = H_{a012}G_{012}, \tag{13.38}$$

where

1. when V_a is a finite point;

$$H_{a012} = w_a h_{a012},$$

2. when V_a is a point at infinity;

$$H_{a012} = h_{a^*012}$$

and

1. when V_0, V_1 and V_2 are all finite points;

$$G_{012} = w_0 w_1 w_2 g_{012},$$

2. when one of the points V_0, V_1 and V_2 is a point at infinity (say, $w_1 = 0; w_0, w_2 \neq 0$);

$$G_{012} = w_0 w_2 g_{01^*2},$$

3. when two of the points V_0, V_1 and V_2 are points at infinity (say, $w_1 = w_2 = 0; w_0 \neq 0$);

$$G_{012} = w_0 g_{01^*2^*}.$$

It is also possible to interpret the 4×4 determinant S_{a012} in another light. That is, from eq.(13.102) we have:

$$\begin{aligned} S_{a012} &= S_{a0}P_{12} + T_{a0}Q_{12} + U_{a0}R_{12} + P_{a0}S_{12} + Q_{a0}T_{12} + R_{a0}U_{12} \\ &= \boldsymbol{K}_{a0} \cdot \boldsymbol{L}_{12}, \end{aligned} \tag{13.39}$$

where

$$\boldsymbol{K}_{a0} \equiv [S_{a0}\ T_{a0}\ U_{a0}\ P_{a0}\ Q_{a0}\ R_{a0}\ ],$$

$$\boldsymbol{L}_{12} \equiv [P_{12}\ Q_{12}\ R_{12}\ S_{12}\ T_{12}\ U_{12}].$$

This shows that S_{a012} can be expressed as the scalar product of two six-dimensional vectors which have as their components the Plücker coordinates of lines.

Eq.(13.39) can also be rewritten, using eqs.(12.12) and (19.30), as:

$$S_{a012} = \sqrt{P_0^2 + Q_0^2 + R_0^2} \cdot l_c, \tag{13.40}$$

where

$$[P_0\ \ Q_0\ \ R_0] = [P_{a0}\ \ Q_{a0}\ \ R_{a0}] \times [P_{12}\ \ Q_{12}\ \ R_{12}],$$

and l_c is the length of the common perpendicular between two lines V_aV_0 and V_1V_2. So the 4×4 determinant S_{a012} can be thought of as the length of the common perpendicular between two lines V_aV_0 and V_1V_2 multiplied by a scalar.

13.2.3 Homogeneous Type-T 4×4 Determinant

The homogeneous type-T 4×4 determinant:

$$T_{a012} = \begin{vmatrix} a_a & a_0 & a_1 & a_2 \\ b_a & b_0 & b_1 & b_2 \\ c_a & c_0 & c_1 & c_2 \\ d_a & d_0 & d_1 & d_2 \end{vmatrix}$$

represents the dual of eq.(4.6), that is, the orientation of a vacuum. Thus there is no relation to a geometric entity as in the case of the type-S determinant.

The homogeneous type-T determinant forms a complete dual to the homogeneous type-S determinant. Therefore, geometric conditions for a problem expressed in terms of type-S determinants become those for its dual when S is replaced by T (see Sections 14.4.2 and 14.4.4).

13.2.4 Homogeneous Intersection Formulas

In this section we derive homogeneous intersection formulas, that is, equations for the intersection points when a homogeneous line segment V_aV_b and a homogeneous triangle $V_0V_1V_2$ are given.

From Table 9.2, a homogeneous line segment and a homogeneous triangle are expressed as:

Homogeneous line segment $V_a V_b$

$$\overline{\boldsymbol{V}} = \overline{\xi_a \boldsymbol{V}_a + \xi_b \boldsymbol{V}_b}, \qquad (13.41)$$
$$(\xi_a, \xi_b) \neq (0,0),$$

where

$$(\xi_a, \xi_b \geq 0) \vee (\xi_a, \xi_b \leq 0) \text{.......... projective space,} \qquad (13.42)$$
$$\xi_a, \xi_b \geq 0 \qquad \text{.......... two-sided space.} \qquad (13.43)$$

Homogeneous triangle $V_0 V_1 V_2$

$$\overline{\boldsymbol{V}} = \overline{\xi_0 \boldsymbol{V}_0 + \xi_1 \boldsymbol{V}_1 + \xi_2 \boldsymbol{V}_2}, \qquad (13.44)$$
$$(\xi_0, \xi_1, \xi_2) \neq (0,0,0),$$

where

$$(\xi_0, \xi_1, \xi_2 \geq 0) \vee (\xi_0, \xi_1, \xi_2 \leq 0) \text{....... projective space,} \qquad (13.45)$$
$$\xi_0, \xi_1, \xi_2 \geq 0 \qquad \text{....... two-sided space.} \qquad (13.46)$$

Intersection Conditions

We have:

$$\xi_0 \boldsymbol{V}_0 + \xi_1 \boldsymbol{V}_1 + \xi_2 \boldsymbol{V}_2 - \xi_a \boldsymbol{V}_a - \xi_b \boldsymbol{V}_b = 0. \qquad (13.47)$$

For eq.(13.47) to have a single nontrivial solution, the 4×5 matrix formed by V_0, V_1, V_2, V_a and V_b must have rank 4. This means that at least one of the following determinants:

$$S_{a012}, \ S_{b012}, \ S_{ab12}, \ S_{ab20}, \ S_{ab01}$$

must be non-zero.

Solving for $\xi_0, \xi_1, \xi_2, \xi_a$ and ξ_b assuming $S_{a012} \neq 0$ yields:

$$(\xi_a, \xi_b) = \left(\frac{-\xi_b S_{b012}}{S_{a012}}, \xi_b \right) = \frac{\xi_b}{S_{a012}} (-S_{b012}, S_{a012}), \qquad (13.48)$$

$$(\xi_0, \xi_1, \xi_2) = \left(\frac{\xi_b S_{ab12}}{S_{a012}}, \frac{\xi_b S_{ab20}}{S_{a012}}, \frac{\xi_b S_{ab01}}{S_{a012}} \right) = \frac{\xi_b}{S_{a012}} \left(S_{ab12}, S_{ab20}, S_{ab01} \right). \qquad (13.49)$$

Then intersection conditions of a line segment and a triangle are derived from eqs.(13.42), (13.45)(projective space case), and (13.43), (13.46)(two-sided space case) respectively:

Projective space condition

$$((S_{a012} \geq 0 \wedge S_{b012} \leq 0) \vee (S_{a012} \leq 0 \wedge S_{b012} \geq 0)) \\ \wedge ((S_{ab12}, S_{ab20}, S_{ab01} \geq 0) \vee (S_{ab12}, S_{ab20}, S_{ab01} \leq 0)), \tag{13.50}$$

Two-sided space condition

$$((S_{a012} \geq 0 \wedge S_{b012} \leq 0) \wedge (S_{ab12}, S_{ab20}, S_{ab01} \geq 0)) \\ \vee ((S_{a012} \leq 0 \wedge S_{b012} \geq 0) \wedge (S_{ab12}, S_{ab20}, S_{ab01} \leq 0)). \tag{13.51}$$

Intersection Point Formula A

From eqs.(13.41) and (13.48),

$$\begin{aligned} \overline{\boldsymbol{V}} &= \overline{\xi_a \boldsymbol{V}_a + \xi_b \boldsymbol{V}_b} \\ &= \overline{\frac{-S_{b012}}{S_{a012}} \xi_b \boldsymbol{V}_a + \xi_b \boldsymbol{V}_b} \\ &= \overline{\frac{-S_{b012}}{S_{a012}} \boldsymbol{V}_a + \boldsymbol{V}_b}. \end{aligned} \tag{13.52}$$

In order for the line segment and the triangle to intersect, S_{a012} and S_{b012} must be of different signs from eqs.(13.50) and (13.51). Thus:

$$\frac{S_{a012}}{S_{a012} - S_{b012}} \geq 0. \tag{13.53}$$

Eq.(13.53) holds whether the line segment and the triangle are defined in classical projective space or in two-sided space.

By using eq.(13.53), we obtain:

$$\begin{aligned} \overline{\boldsymbol{V}} &= \overline{\frac{-S_{b012}}{S_{a012}} \boldsymbol{V}_a + \boldsymbol{V}_b} \\ &= \overline{\frac{S_{a012}}{S_{a012} - S_{b012}} (\frac{-S_{b012}}{S_{a012}} \boldsymbol{V}_a + \boldsymbol{V}_b)} \\ &= \overline{\boldsymbol{V}_a + \frac{S_{a012}}{S_{a012} - S_{b012}} (\boldsymbol{V}_b - \boldsymbol{V}_a)}. \end{aligned}$$

We call the next equation "*Intersection Point Formula A*," which corresponds to the formula (13.13) in Euclidean processing case:

$$\overline{\boldsymbol{V}} = \overline{\boldsymbol{V}_a + \frac{S_{a012}}{S_{a012} - S_{b012}} (\boldsymbol{V}_b - \boldsymbol{V}_a)}. \tag{13.54}$$

Intersection Point Formula B

We derive "*Intersection Point Formula B*," which is a variation of "Intersection Point Formula A." From eq.(13.54), we have:

$$\begin{aligned}\overline{\boldsymbol{V}} &= \overline{\boldsymbol{V}_a + \frac{S_{a012}}{S_{a012} - S_{b012}}(\boldsymbol{V}_b - \boldsymbol{V}_a)} \\ &= \overline{\frac{1}{S_{a012} - S_{b012}}(S_{a012}\boldsymbol{V}_b - S_{b012}\boldsymbol{V}_a)}.\end{aligned} \tag{13.55}$$

Therefore

Projective space case

$$\overline{\boldsymbol{V}} = \overline{S_{a012}\boldsymbol{V}_b - S_{b012}\boldsymbol{V}_a}, \tag{13.56}$$

or

$$\overline{\boldsymbol{V}} = \overline{S_{b012}\boldsymbol{V}_a - S_{a012}\boldsymbol{V}_b}. \tag{13.57}$$

Two-sided space case

$$\overline{\boldsymbol{V}} = \begin{cases} \overline{S_{a012}\boldsymbol{V}_b - S_{b012}\boldsymbol{V}_a}, & (S_{a012} \geq 0 \wedge S_{b012} \leq 0), \\ \overline{S_{b012}\boldsymbol{V}_a - S_{a012}\boldsymbol{V}_b}, & (S_{a012} \leq 0 \wedge S_{b012} \geq 0). \end{cases} \tag{13.58}$$

Intersection Point Formula C

By using eqs.(13.44), (13.48) and (13.49), we have:

$$\begin{aligned}\overline{\boldsymbol{V}} &= \overline{\xi_0\boldsymbol{V}_0 + \xi_1\boldsymbol{V}_1 + \xi_2\boldsymbol{V}_2} \\ &= \overline{\frac{S_{ab12}}{S_{a012}}\xi_b\boldsymbol{V}_0 + \frac{S_{ab20}}{S_{a012}}\xi_b\boldsymbol{V}_1 + \frac{S_{ab01}}{S_{a012}}\xi_b\boldsymbol{V}_2} \\ &= \overline{\frac{S_{ab12}}{S_{a012}}\boldsymbol{V}_0 + \frac{S_{ab20}}{S_{a012}}\boldsymbol{V}_1 + \frac{S_{ab01}}{S_{a012}}\boldsymbol{V}_2}.\end{aligned} \tag{13.59}$$

In order for the line segment and the triangle to intersect in two-sided space, S_{a012} and $S_{ab12}, S_{ab20}, S_{ab01}$ must be of a same sign as shown in eq.(13.51). Thus:

$$\frac{S_{a012}}{S_{ab12} + S_{ab20} + S_{ab01}} \geq 0. \tag{13.60}$$

By using eq.(13.60), we obtain the next equations irrespective of classical projective or two-sided space cases. That is,

$$\overline{\boldsymbol{V}} = \overline{\frac{S_{ab12}}{S_{a012}}\boldsymbol{V}_0 + \frac{S_{ab20}}{S_{a012}}\boldsymbol{V}_1 + \frac{S_{ab01}}{S_{a012}}\boldsymbol{V}_2}$$

$$= \overline{\frac{S_{a012}}{S_{ab12}+S_{ab20}+S_{ab01}}(\frac{S_{ab12}}{S_{a012}}\boldsymbol{V}_0+\frac{S_{ab20}}{S_{a012}}\boldsymbol{V}_1+\frac{S_{ab01}}{S_{a012}}\boldsymbol{V}_2)}$$

$$= \overline{\frac{1}{S_{ab12}+S_{ab20}+S_{ab01}}(S_{ab12}\boldsymbol{V}_0+S_{ab20}\boldsymbol{V}_1+S_{ab01}\boldsymbol{V}_2)}.$$

We call the next equation "*Intersection Point Formula C*," which corresponds to the formula eq.(13.14) in Euclidean processing case:

$$\overline{\boldsymbol{V}} = \overline{\frac{1}{S_{ab12}+S_{ab20}+S_{ab01}}(S_{ab12}\boldsymbol{V}_0+S_{ab20}\boldsymbol{V}_1+S_{ab01}\boldsymbol{V}_2)}. \qquad (13.61)$$

Intersection Point Formula D

We derive "*Intersection Point Formula D*" which is a variation of "Intersection Point Formula C." From eq.(13.61), we have:

Projective space case

$$\overline{\boldsymbol{V}} = \overline{S_{ab12}\boldsymbol{V}_0+S_{ab20}\boldsymbol{V}_1+S_{ab01}\boldsymbol{V}_2}, \qquad (13.62)$$

or

$$\overline{\boldsymbol{V}} = \overline{-S_{ab12}\boldsymbol{V}_0-S_{ab20}\boldsymbol{V}_1-S_{ab01}\boldsymbol{V}_2}. \qquad (13.63)$$

Two-sided space case

$$\overline{\boldsymbol{V}} = \begin{cases} \overline{S_{ab12}\boldsymbol{V}_0+S_{ab20}\boldsymbol{V}_1+S_{ab01}\boldsymbol{V}_2}, & (S_{ab12}, S_{ab20}, S_{ab01} \geq 0), \\ \overline{-S_{ab12}\boldsymbol{V}_0-S_{ab20}\boldsymbol{V}_1-S_{ab01}\boldsymbol{V}_2}, & (S_{ab12}, S_{ab20}, S_{ab01} \leq 0). \end{cases} \qquad (13.64)$$

In the above we derived four types of intersection point formulas, or common point formulas, given a line segment and a triangle defined in terms of homogeneous coordinates. What is dual to finding a common point between a line segment and a triangle is finding a common plane, given a dual line segment and a dual triangle defined in terms of homogeneous coefficients. Therefore the derivation of common plane formulas from the common point formulas is straightforward.

The followings are common plane formulas corresponding to common point ones. Suppose that a dual line segment $\gamma_a\gamma_b$ and a dual triangle $\gamma_0\gamma_1\gamma_2$ are given.

Common Plane Formula A

$$\overline{\gamma} = \overline{\gamma_a + \frac{T_{a012}}{T_{a012}-T_{b012}}(\gamma_b-\gamma_a)}. \qquad (13.65)$$

Common Plane Formula B

Projective space case

$$\overline{\gamma} = \overline{T_{a012}\gamma_b - T_{b012}\gamma_a}, \tag{13.66}$$

or

$$\overline{\gamma} = \overline{T_{b012}\gamma_a - T_{a012}\gamma_b}. \tag{13.67}$$

Two-sided space case

$$\overline{\gamma} = \begin{cases} \overline{T_{a012}\gamma_b - T_{b012}\gamma_a}, & (T_{a012} \geq 0 \wedge T_{b012} \leq 0), \\ \overline{T_{b012}\gamma_a - T_{a012}\gamma_b}, & (T_{a012} \leq 0 \wedge T_{b012} \geq 0). \end{cases} \tag{13.68}$$

Common Plane Formula C

$$\overline{\gamma} = \overline{\frac{1}{T_{ab12} + T_{ab20} + T_{ab01}}(T_{ab12}\gamma_0 + T_{ab20}\gamma_1 + T_{ab01}\gamma_2)}. \tag{13.69}$$

Common Plane Formula D

Projective space case

$$\overline{\gamma} = \overline{T_{ab12}\gamma_0 + T_{ab20}\gamma_1 + T_{ab01}\gamma_2} \tag{13.70}$$

or

$$\overline{\gamma} = \overline{-T_{ab12}\gamma_0 - T_{ab20}\gamma_1 - T_{ab01}\gamma_2}. \tag{13.71}$$

Two-sided space case

$$\overline{\gamma} = \begin{cases} \overline{T_{ab12}\gamma_0 + T_{ab20}\gamma_1 + T_{ab01}\gamma_2}, & (T_{ab12}, T_{ab20}, T_{ab01} \geq 0), \\ \overline{-T_{ab12}\gamma_0 - T_{ab20}\gamma_1 - T_{ab01}\gamma_2}, & (T_{ab12}, T_{ab20}, T_{ab01} \leq 0). \end{cases} \tag{13.72}$$

Some Comments on Formulas above

1. The Formulas A and C for intersection points have the same form as the formulas (13.13) and (13.14) in Euclidean space, respectively.

2. The Formulas A and C for both intersection points and common planes apply to geometric elements in both classical projective and two-sided spaces.

3. In the Formulas A and B for intersection points, the homogeneous line segment V_aV_b is split into two homogeneous line segments V_aV and VV_b by the intersection point V, and the point V is expressed by the end points of the original line segment.

   The Formula A is convenient for dealing with theoretical mathematical expressions, while B is often used in practice because it is simple and requires no division.

4. In the Formulas C and D for intersection points, the homogeneous triangle $V_0V_1V_2$ is divided into three homogeneous triangles V_0V_1V, V_1V_2V and V_2V_0V by the intersection point V, and the point V is expressed by the three vertices of the original triangle. The Formulas C and D for intersection points are sometimes used to split up homogeneous polygons.

   The Formula C is convenient for dealing with theoretical mathematical expressions; meanwhile, the Formula D is often used in practice because it is simple and requires no division.

5. In the Formulas B and D for intersection points and for common planes, when the intersecting point or common plane in classical projective space is multiplied by a negative scalar, the result will still correspond to the same Euclidean geometric element. When subsequent processing is required, however, the signs of the end points (end planes) and intersection point coordinates (common plane coefficients) had better be kept consistent in $\mathbf{R}^4$. The author advises to use the formulas for two-sided space.

Here, we further study a property of the intersection point formulas using the Formula B, eq.(13.56), which is given by:

$$\overline{\boldsymbol{V}} = V = \overline{S_{a012}\boldsymbol{V}_b - S_{b012}\boldsymbol{V}_a}. \tag{13.73}$$

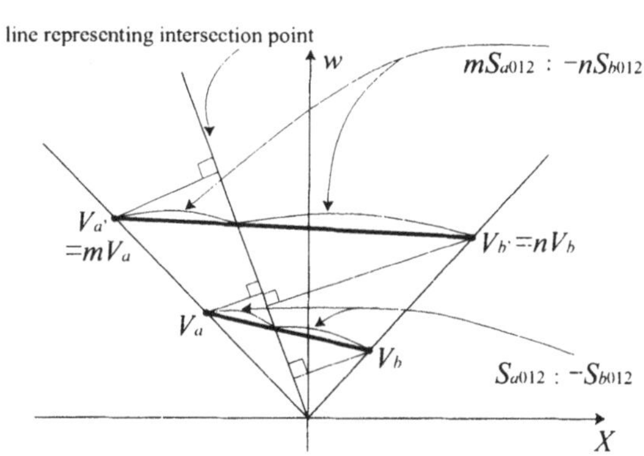

Figure 13.13: Examination of intersection point formula ($Y=Z=0$ section).

When the triangle $V_0V_1V_2$ and the line segment V_aV_b intersect at point V, we denote by V' the intersecting point of the triangle, and the line segment whose defining endpoint vectors $\boldsymbol{V}_a$ and $\boldsymbol{V}_b$ are multiplied by m and n respectively (where m and n are non-zero scalars):

$$\boldsymbol{V}_{a'} = m\boldsymbol{V}_a, \quad \boldsymbol{V}_{b'} = n\boldsymbol{V}_b.$$

Then we shall show $V' = V$ as below:

$$\begin{aligned} V' &= \overline{S_{a'012}\boldsymbol{V}_{b'} - S_{b'012}\boldsymbol{V}_{a'}} \\ &= \overline{mS_{a012}\boldsymbol{V}_{b'} - nS_{b012}\boldsymbol{V}_{a'}} \\ &= \overline{mnS_{a012}\boldsymbol{V}_b - mnS_{b012}\boldsymbol{V}_a} \\ &= \overline{mn(S_{a012}\boldsymbol{V}_b - S_{b012}\boldsymbol{V}_a)} \\ &= \overline{mn\boldsymbol{V}} \\ &= V. \end{aligned}$$

In terms of geometry, this can be explained as follows:

In vector space, the intersecting point before scalar multiplication divides the line segment that connects the ends of $\boldsymbol{V}_a$ and $\boldsymbol{V}_b$ by a ratio $S_{a012} : -S_{b012}$ (Fig. 13.13). From the figure, we see that for $V' = V$ to hold, the scaled (i.e., after scalar multiplication) intersecting point in vector space must divide the line segment between the ends of V_a' and V_b' by the ratio $mS_{a012} : -nS_{b012}$.

In the formula for the scaled intersection point, or

$$V' = \overline{S_{a'012}\boldsymbol{V}_{b'} - S_{b'012}\boldsymbol{V}_{a'}},$$

we have $S_{a'012} = mS_{a012}$ and $S_{b'012} = nS_{b012}$, so that the parameter ratio is $mS_{a012} : -nS_{b012}$, showing that the intersection point is the same as that before scalar multiplication.

13.2.5 Interferences between Simplices (2)

In the Four-dimensional Processing there are two spaces where geometric elements are defined, that is, classical projective space and two-sided space.

Followings are the results of deriving algebraically the conditions of various interference tests between simplices defined both in classical projective space and in two-sided space. The derivation processes are omitted for simplicity [62].

We assume that all the simplices in the following are defined by linearly independent homogeneous coordinate vectors.

Geometric Elements Defined in Classical Projective Space

1. **Containment of point V_a in tetrahedron $V_0V_1V_2V_3$**

   The condition that a homogeneous point V_a is contained in a homogeneous tetrahedron $V_0V_1V_2V_3$ is expressed as:

$$(S_{a123}, S_{a032}, S_{a013}, S_{a021} \geq 0) \vee (S_{a123}, S_{a032}, S_{a013}, S_{a021} \leq 0). \quad (13.74)$$

2. **Containment of point V_a in triangle $V_0V_1V_2$**

   The condition that a homogeneous point V_a is contained in a homogeneous triangle $V_0V_1V_2$ is expressed as:

$$(S_{N012} \neq 0) \wedge (S_{a012} = 0)$$
$$\wedge\, ((S_{a21N}, S_{a02N}, S_{a10N} \geq 0) \vee (S_{a21N}, S_{a02N}, S_{a10N} \leq 0)), \quad (13.75)$$

   where V_N is an arbitrary point which is not coplanar with the triangle plane.

3. **Containment of point V_a in line segment V_0V_1**

   The condition that a homogeneous point V_a is contained in a homogeneous line segment V_0V_1 is expressed as:

$$(S_{01MN} \neq 0) \wedge (S_{a01M}, S_{a01N} = 0)$$
$$\wedge\, ((S_{a1MN}, S_{a0NM} \geq 0) \vee (S_{a1MN}, S_{a0NM} \leq 0)), \quad (13.76)$$

   where V_M and V_N are arbitrary distinct points which are not collinear with the line segment.

4. **Coincidence of two points V_a and V_0**

   The condition that a homogeneous point V_a coincides with another homogeneous point V_0 is expressed as:

$$(S_{0LMN}, S_{aLMN} \neq 0) \wedge (S_{a0LM}, S_{a0MN}, S_{a0NL} = 0), \quad (13.77)$$

   where V_L, V_M and V_N are arbitrary distinct points which constitute a tetrahedron with V_0. This is too expensive compared with the condition eq.(14.9).

5. **Intersection of line segment V_aV_b and triangle $V_0V_1V_2$**

   The condition that a homogeneous line segment V_aV_b intersects a homogeneous triangle $V_0V_1V_2$ is expressed as:

$$((S_{a012}, S_{b012}) \neq (0,0))$$
$$\wedge\, ((S_{a012} \geq 0 \wedge S_{b012} \leq 0) \;\vee\; (S_{a012} \leq 0 \wedge S_{b012} \geq 0)) \quad (13.78)$$
$$\wedge\, ((S_{ab12}, S_{ab20}, S_{ab01} \geq 0) \;\vee\; (S_{ab12}, S_{ab20}, S_{ab01} \leq 0)).$$

   From the reason mentioned in page p.237, only the expressions of intersection points for two-sided space are shown in the following.

   Intersection point in terms of V_a and V_b

$$V = \begin{cases} \overline{S_{a012}\boldsymbol{V}_b - S_{b012}\boldsymbol{V}_a}, & (S_{a012} \geq 0 \wedge S_{b012} \leq 0), \\ \overline{S_{b012}\boldsymbol{V}_a - S_{a012}\boldsymbol{V}_b}, & (S_{a012} \leq 0 \wedge S_{b012} \geq 0). \end{cases} \quad (13.79)$$

Intersection point in terms of V_0, V_1 and V_2

$$V = \begin{cases} \overline{S_{ab12}\boldsymbol{V}_0 + S_{ab20}\boldsymbol{V}_1 + S_{ab01}\boldsymbol{V}_2}, & (S_{ab12}, S_{ab20}, S_{ab01} \geq 0), \\ \overline{-S_{ab12}\boldsymbol{V}_0 - S_{ab20}\boldsymbol{V}_1 - S_{ab01}\boldsymbol{V}_2}, & (S_{ab12}, S_{ab20}, S_{ab01} \leq 0). \end{cases} \tag{13.80}$$

6. **Intersection of two line segments V_aV_b and V_0V_1**

   The condition that two homogeneous line segments V_aV_b and V_0V_1 intersect is expressed as:

$$\begin{aligned} &((S_{a01N}, S_{b01N}, S_{abN0}, S_{abN1}) \neq (0,0,0,0)) \wedge (S_{01ab} = 0) \\ &\wedge ((S_{0abN} \geq 0 \wedge S_{1abN} \leq 0) \vee (S_{0abN} \leq 0 \wedge S_{1abN} \geq 0)) \\ &\wedge ((S_{a01N} \geq 0 \wedge S_{b01N} \leq 0) \vee (S_{a01N} \leq 0 \wedge S_{b01N} \geq 0)). \end{aligned} \tag{13.81}$$

   From the reason mentioned in page p.237, only the expressions of intersection points for two-sided space are shown in the following.

   Intersection point in terms of V_a and V_b

$$V = \begin{cases} \overline{S_{a01N}\boldsymbol{V}_b - S_{b01N}\boldsymbol{V}_a}, & (S_{a01N} \geq 0 \wedge S_{b01N} \leq 0), \\ \overline{S_{b01N}\boldsymbol{V}_a - S_{a01N}\boldsymbol{V}_b}, & (S_{a01N} \leq 0 \wedge S_{b01N} \geq 0). \end{cases} \tag{13.82}$$

   Intersection point in terms of V_0 and V_1

$$V = \begin{cases} \overline{S_{0abN}\boldsymbol{V}_1 - S_{1abN}\boldsymbol{V}_0}, & (S_{0abN} \geq 0 \wedge S_{1abN} \leq 0), \\ \overline{S_{1abN}\boldsymbol{V}_0 - S_{0abN}\boldsymbol{V}_1}, & (S_{0abN} \leq 0 \wedge S_{1abN} \geq 0). \end{cases} \tag{13.83}$$

Geometric Elements Defined in Two-sided Space

1. **Containment of point V_a in tetrahedron $V_0V_1V_2V_3$**

   The condition that a homogeneous point V_a is contained in a homogeneous tetrahedron $V_0V_1V_2V_3$ is expressed as:

$$\begin{aligned} &((S_{0123} > 0) \wedge (S_{a123}, S_{a032}, S_{a013}, S_{a021} \geq 0)) \\ &\vee ((S_{0123} < 0) \wedge (S_{a123}, S_{a032}, S_{a013}, S_{a021} \leq 0)). \end{aligned} \tag{13.84}$$

2. **Containment of point V_a in triangle $V_0V_1V_2$**

The condition that a homogeneous point V_a is contained in a homogeneous triangle $V_0V_1V_2$ is expressed as:

$$\begin{aligned}&(S_{N012} \neq 0) \wedge (S_{a012} = 0)\\ \wedge\,&(((S_{N012} > 0) \wedge (S_{a21N}, S_{a02N}, S_{a10N} \geq 0))\\ \vee\,&((S_{N012} < 0) \wedge (S_{a21N}, S_{a02N}, S_{a10N} \leq 0))),\end{aligned} \tag{13.85}$$

where V_N is an arbitrary point which is not coplanar with the triangle plane.

3. **Containment of point V_a in line segment V_0V_1**

The condition that a homogeneous point V_a is contained in a homogeneous line segment V_0V_1 is expressed as:

$$\begin{aligned}&(S_{01MN} \neq 0) \wedge (S_{a01M}, S_{a01N} = 0)\\ \wedge\,&(((S_{01MN} > 0) \wedge (S_{a1MN}, S_{a0NM} \geq 0))\\ \vee\,&((S_{01MN} < 0) \wedge (S_{a1MN}, S_{a0NM} \leq 0))),\end{aligned} \tag{13.86}$$

where V_M and V_N are arbitrary distinct points which are not collinear with the line segment.

4. **Coincidence of two points V_a and V_0**

The condition that a homogeneous point V_a coincides with another homogeneous point V_0 is expressed as:

$$\begin{aligned}&(S_{0LMN}, S_{aLMN} \neq 0) \wedge (S_{a0LM}, S_{a0MN}, S_{a0NL} = 0)\\ \wedge\,&((S_{0LMN}, S_{aLMN} > 0) \vee (S_{0LMN}, S_{aLMN} < 0)),\end{aligned} \tag{13.87}$$

where V_L, V_M and V_N are arbitrary distinct points which constitute a tetrahedron with V_0. This is too expensive compared with condition eq.(14.9).

5. **Intersection of line segment V_aV_b and triangle $V_0V_1V_2$**

The condition that a homogeneous line segment V_aV_b intersects a homogeneous triangle $V_0V_1V_2$ is expressed as:

$$\begin{aligned}&((S_{a012}, S_{b012}) \neq (0,0))\\ \wedge\,&((S_{a012} \geq 0 \wedge S_{b012} \leq 0 \wedge S_{ab12}, S_{ab20}, S_{ab01} \geq 0)\\ \vee\,&(S_{a012} \leq 0 \wedge S_{b012} \geq 0 \wedge S_{ab12}, S_{ab20}, S_{ab01} \leq 0)).\end{aligned} \tag{13.88}$$

Intersection point in terms of V_a and V_b

$$V = \begin{cases} \overline{S_{a012}\boldsymbol{V}_b - S_{b012}\boldsymbol{V}_a}, & (S_{a012} \geq 0 \wedge S_{b012} \leq 0),\\ \overline{S_{b012}\boldsymbol{V}_a - S_{a012}\boldsymbol{V}_b}, & (S_{a012} \leq 0 \wedge S_{b012} \geq 0).\end{cases} \tag{13.89}$$

Intersection point in terms of V_0, V_1 and V_2

$$V = \begin{cases} \overline{S_{ab12}\boldsymbol{V}_0 + S_{ab20}\boldsymbol{V}_1 + S_{ab01}\boldsymbol{V}_2}, & (S_{ab12}, S_{ab20}, S_{ab01} \geq 0), \\ \overline{-S_{ab12}\boldsymbol{V}_0 - S_{ab20}\boldsymbol{V}_1 - S_{ab01}\boldsymbol{V}_2}, & (S_{ab12}, S_{ab20}, S_{ab01} \leq 0). \end{cases} \tag{13.90}$$

6. **Intersection of two line segments V_aV_b and V_0V_1**

   The condition that two homogeneous line segments V_aV_b and V_0V_1 intersect is expressed as:

$$\begin{aligned} &((S_{a01N}, S_{b01N}, S_{abN0}, S_{abN1}) \neq (0,0,0,0)) \wedge (S_{01ab} = 0) \\ &\wedge ((S_{a01N} \geq 0 \wedge S_{b01N} \leq 0 \wedge S_{0abN} \leq 0 \wedge S_{1abN} \geq 0) \\ &\vee (S_{a01N} \leq 0 \wedge S_{b01N} \geq 0 \wedge S_{0abN} \geq 0 \wedge S_{1abN} \leq 0)). \end{aligned} \tag{13.91}$$

Intersection point in terms of V_a and V_b

$$V = \begin{cases} \overline{S_{a01N}\boldsymbol{V}_b - S_{b01N}\boldsymbol{V}_a}, & (S_{a01N} \geq 0 \wedge S_{b01N} \leq 0), \\ \overline{S_{b01N}\boldsymbol{V}_a - S_{a01N}\boldsymbol{V}_b}, & (S_{a01N} \leq 0 \wedge S_{b01N} \geq 0). \end{cases} \tag{13.92}$$

Intersection point in terms of V_0 and V_1

$$V = \begin{cases} \overline{S_{0abN}\boldsymbol{V}_1 - S_{1abN}\boldsymbol{V}_0}, & (S_{0abN} \geq 0 \wedge S_{1abN} \leq 0), \\ \overline{S_{1abN}\boldsymbol{V}_0 - S_{0abN}\boldsymbol{V}_1}, & (S_{0abN} \leq 0 \wedge S_{1abN} \geq 0). \end{cases} \tag{13.93}$$

13.2.6 Some Properties of Determinants

Since the 4×4 determinant method makes extensive use of 4×4 determinants, their properties are very important. This subject is discussed below:

1. **Interchange of rows or columns**

   When two rows (or two columns) of a determinant are interchanged, the sign of the determinant changes.

2. **Multiplication of row or column by a negative scalar**

   When a row or column of a determinant is multiplied by a negative scalar, the determinant's sign changes. Thus, if, for example, one of the rows of a type-S determinant is replaced by the homogeneous coordinates of its antipodal point, the determinant's sign changes.

3. **Cyclic permutation of row or column**

   When all rows (or all columns) of a determinant are cyclically permuted once, the sign of an odd-order determinant is unchanged while that of an even-order determinant is reversed [1]. For example, $S_{a01} = S_{01a} = S_{1a0}$ for a 3×3 determinant, while $S_{a012} = -S_{012a} = -S_{2a01} = S_{12a0}$ for a 4×4 determinant.

4. **Projective transformations**

   Denoting by S^*_{a012} the 4×4 determinant of points V_a, V_0, V_1 and V_2 after they have been projectively transformed by $\boldsymbol{M}$, we have:

$$
\begin{aligned}
S^*_{a012} &= det \begin{bmatrix} \boldsymbol{V}_a\boldsymbol{M} \\ \boldsymbol{V}_0\boldsymbol{M} \\ \boldsymbol{V}_1\boldsymbol{M} \\ \boldsymbol{V}_2\boldsymbol{M} \end{bmatrix} \\
&= det \left(\begin{bmatrix} \boldsymbol{V}_a \\ \boldsymbol{V}_0 \\ \boldsymbol{V}_1 \\ \boldsymbol{V}_2 \end{bmatrix} \boldsymbol{M} \right) \\
&= det \begin{bmatrix} \boldsymbol{V}_a \\ \boldsymbol{V}_0 \\ \boldsymbol{V}_1 \\ \boldsymbol{V}_2 \end{bmatrix} \cdot det(\boldsymbol{M}) \\
&= S_{a012} \cdot det(\boldsymbol{M}).
\end{aligned}
\qquad (13.94)
$$

   Thus, the determinant's sign is unchanged for a positive projective transformation, i.e., when $\det(\boldsymbol{M}) > 0$, but reversed for a negative projective transformation, i.e., $\det(\boldsymbol{M}) < 0$. Negative projective transformation matrices can occur when transforming a coordinate system's orientation.

5. **Maximum value**

   Hadamard's inequality can be used to determine the maximum value of a determinant when the range of values of its components is known. Hadamard's inequality for a determinant $\Delta = det(a_{ij})$ of n-th degree is given by:

$$|\Delta| \leq n^{n/2} M^n \quad \text{if } |a_{ij}| \leq M. \qquad (13.95)$$

   Thus for $n = 4$,

$$|\Delta| \leq 16 M^4 \quad \text{if } |a_{ij}| \leq M. \qquad (13.96)$$

13.2.7 Computation of a 4×4 Determinant

1. **Method #1**

   Evaluating the 4×4 determinant S_{a012} by the first row, we have:

$$S_{a012} = \begin{vmatrix} w_a & X_a & Y_a & Z_a \\ w_0 & X_0 & Y_0 & Z_0 \\ w_1 & X_1 & Y_1 & Z_1 \\ w_2 & X_2 & Y_2 & Z_2 \end{vmatrix}$$

[1] This is because to carry out a single cyclic permutation of a row (or column) with n elements, one must interchange its elements $(n-1)$ times.

$$= w_a \begin{vmatrix} X_0 & Y_0 & Z_0 \\ X_1 & Y_1 & Z_1 \\ X_2 & Y_2 & Z_2 \end{vmatrix} + X_a \begin{vmatrix} w_0 & Z_0 & Y_0 \\ w_1 & Z_1 & Y_1 \\ w_2 & Z_2 & Y_2 \end{vmatrix}$$

$$+ Y_a \begin{vmatrix} w_0 & X_0 & Z_0 \\ w_1 & X_1 & Z_1 \\ w_2 & X_2 & Z_2 \end{vmatrix} + Z_a \begin{vmatrix} w_0 & Y_0 & X_0 \\ w_1 & Y_1 & X_1 \\ w_2 & Y_2 & X_2 \end{vmatrix} \quad (13.97)$$

$$= A_{012} w_a + B_{012} X_a + C_{012} Y_a + D_{012} Z_a \quad (13.98)$$

$$= \boldsymbol{V}_a \cdot \boldsymbol{F}_{012}, \quad (13.99)$$

where

$$\boldsymbol{V}_a = [w_a \; X_a \; Y_a \; Z_a],$$
$$\boldsymbol{F}_{012} = [A_{012} \; B_{012} \; C_{012} \; D_{012}]^T.$$

To compute eq.(13.97) in a straightforward manner, the cofactors A_{012}, B_{012}, C_{012} and D_{012}, together require 48 multiplications and 20 additions/subtractions, so computation of S_{a012} requires 52 multiplications and 23 additions/subtractions.

Here we obtain the cofactors along with the determinant.

2. **Method #2**

One of the 3×3 determinants above, say A_{012}, can be evaluated as follows:

$$A_{012} = \begin{vmatrix} X_0 & Y_0 & Z_0 \\ X_1 & Y_1 & Z_1 \\ X_2 & Y_2 & Z_2 \end{vmatrix}$$

$$= X_0(Y_1 Z_2 - Z_1 Y_2) + Y_0(Z_1 X_2 - X_1 Z_2) + Z_0(Y_1 X_2 - X_1 Y_2). \quad (13.100)$$

A 3×3 determinant can thus be computed by 9 multiplications and 5 additions/subtractions, so computation of S_{a012} requires 40 multiplications and 23 additions/subtractions.

This method also yields cofactors at the same time.

3. **Method #3**

S_{a012} can also be written as follows:

$$S_{a012} = w_a \begin{vmatrix} X_0 & Y_0 & Z_0 \\ X_1 & Y_1 & Z_1 \\ X_2 & Y_2 & Z_2 \end{vmatrix} + X_a \begin{vmatrix} w_0 & Z_0 & Y_0 \\ w_1 & Z_1 & Y_1 \\ w_2 & Z_2 & Y_2 \end{vmatrix}$$

$$+ Y_a \begin{vmatrix} w_0 & X_0 & Z_0 \\ w_1 & X_1 & Z_1 \\ w_2 & X_2 & Z_2 \end{vmatrix} + Z_a \begin{vmatrix} w_0 & Y_0 & X_0 \\ w_1 & Y_1 & X_1 \\ w_2 & Y_2 & X_2 \end{vmatrix}$$

$$
\begin{aligned}
&= w_a(X_0(Y_1Z_2 - Z_1Y_2) + Y_0(Z_1X_2 - X_1Z_2) \\
&\quad +Z_0(X_1Y_2 - Y_1X_2)) \\
&\quad +X_a(-w_0(Y_1Z_2 - Z_1Y_2) - Z_0(w_1Y_2 - Y_1w_2) \\
&\quad +Y_0(w_1Z_2 - Z_1w_2)) \\
&\quad +Y_a(-w_0(Z_1X_2 - X_1Z_2) - X_0(w_1Z_2 - w_2Z_1) \\
&\quad +Z_0(w_1X_2 - w_2X_1)) \\
&\quad +Z_a(-w_0(X_1Y_2 - Y_1X_2) - Y_0(w_1X_2 - X_1w_2) \\
&\quad +X_0(w_1Y_2 - Y_1w_2)) \\
&= \quad (Y_aZ_0 - Z_aY_0) \times (w_1X_2 - X_1w_2) \\
&\quad +(Z_aX_0 - Z_0X_a) \times (w_1Y_2 - Y_1w_2) \\
&\quad +(X_aY_0 - X_0Y_a) \times (w_1Z_2 - Z_1w_2) \\
&\quad +(w_aX_0 - w_0X_a) \times (Y_1Z_2 - Z_1Y_2) \\
&\quad +(w_aY_0 - w_0Y_a) \times (Z_1X_2 - X_1Z_2) \\
&\quad +(w_aZ_0 - w_0Z_a) \times (X_1Y_2 - Y_1X_2). \qquad (13.101)
\end{aligned}
$$

Here the number of multiplications and additions/subtractions are respectively reduced to 30 and 17.

In this method, however, the cofactors (i.e., the Plücker coordinates A_{012}, B_{012}, C_{012} and D_{012} of plane) are not obtained.

Eq.(13.101) can be expressed as the scalar product of two 6-dimensional vectors:

$$
\begin{aligned}
S_{a012} &= S_{a0}P_{12} + T_{a0}Q_{12} + U_{a0}R_{12} + P_{a0}S_{12} + Q_{a0}T_{12} + R_{a0}U_{12} \\
&= \boldsymbol{K}_{a0} \cdot \boldsymbol{L}_{12}, \qquad (13.102)
\end{aligned}
$$

where

$$\boldsymbol{K}_{a0} \equiv [S_{a0}\ T_{a0}\ U_{a0}\ P_{a0}\ Q_{a0}\ R_{a0}\ ], \qquad (13.103)$$

$$\boldsymbol{L}_{12} \equiv [P_{12}\ Q_{12}\ R_{12}\ S_{12}\ T_{12}\ U_{12}]. \qquad (13.104)$$

P_{12}, Q_{12}, R_{12}, S_{12}, T_{12} and U_{12} are Plücker coordinates of line.

4. **Method #4**

We now present our fourth and final method. The cofactors A_{012}, B_{012}, C_{012} and D_{012} are expressed as in Method #2 above, then arranged as follows:

$$
\left\{
\begin{aligned}
A_{012} &= +S_{01}X_2 + T_{01}Y_2 + U_{01}Z_2, \\
B_{012} &= -S_{01}w_2 + R_{01}Y_2 - Q_{01}Z_2, \\
C_{012} &= -T_{01}w_2 - R_{01}X_2 + P_{01}Z_2, \\
D_{012} &= -U_{01}w_2 + Q_{01}X_2 - P_{01}Y_2.
\end{aligned}
\right. \qquad (13.105)
$$

In matrix form, this is written:

$$\begin{bmatrix} A_{012} \\ B_{012} \\ C_{012} \\ D_{012} \end{bmatrix} = \begin{bmatrix} 0 & S_{01} & T_{01} & U_{01} \\ -S_{01} & 0 & R_{01} & -Q_{01} \\ -T_{01} & -R_{01} & 0 & P_{01} \\ -U_{01} & Q_{01} & -P_{01} & 0 \end{bmatrix} \begin{bmatrix} w_2 \\ X_2 \\ Y_2 \\ Z_2 \end{bmatrix}$$
$$= \boldsymbol{L}\boldsymbol{V}_2^T, \qquad (13.106)$$

where $\boldsymbol{L}$ represents a type-L three-dimensional line (see Section 9.1.1).

P_{01}, Q_{01}, R_{01}, S_{01}, T_{01} and U_{01} each appear twice in eq.(13.105). Thus, by storing the results, we can reduce the number of computational operations for a 4×4 determinant to 28 multiplications and 17 additions/subtractions. The cofactors A_{012}, B_{012}, C_{012} and D_{012} are also obtained simultaneously. Since all of the Plücker coordinates are obtained as well, this method seems to be the most suitable one for the determinant method.

Hacker states that the minimum number of multiplications needed for an $n\times n$ determinant is given by the formula $n(2^{n-1}-1)$ [22]. Substituting $n=4$, we thus obtain 28 as the minimum number of multiplications.

13.2.8 Remarks

The Euclidean 4×4 determinant method made it possible to conduct all geometric tests as 4×4 determinant operations, where the test conditions were described in simple terms. At the same time, however, it lacked generality in terms of its applicable geometric elements, was rather restricted in the type of applicable tests, and harbored the problems that stemmed from division operations.

In comparison, the homogeneous 4×4 determinant method covers a wider range of geometric tests as well as a much more general class of geometric elements, including dual homogeneous geometric elements. Also, directions can be treated in the same way as points using the homogeneous 4×4 determinants.

In addition, the homogeneous 4×4 determinant method is free from problems of Euclidean processing that stem from division operations, and further has the major feature that complete duality holds in its test conditions.

However, Problem ②, which was pointed out with regard to the Euclidean 4×4 determinant method in Section 13.1.4, still remains for the homogeneous 4×4 determinant method. To solve this problem while retaining the advantages of the homogeneous 4×4 determinant method, we propose the homogeneous determinant method in Chapter 14 as an extension of the homogeneous 4×4 determinant method.

Chapter 14

The Homogeneous Determinant Method

14.1 Projectively Invariant Geometric Test

When geometric elements are processed, they undergo various projective transformations. This was discussed in detail in Chapter 6. Sometimes the shape of a geometric element will undergo significant changes upon projective transformation.

Let us illustrate this by taking two line segments, V_0V_1 and V_aV_b, which intersect in projective space, where:

$$V_0 = \overline{(1,0,0)},\quad V_1 = \overline{(1,1,1)},$$
$$V_a = \overline{(1,0,1)},\quad V_b = \overline{(1,1,0)}$$

and transform them by the following projective transformation matrix (Fig. 14.1 (a)):

$$\begin{bmatrix} 3 & 0 & 0 \\ -2 & 1 & 0 \\ -2 & 0 & 1 \end{bmatrix}.$$

The four end points of the two line segments are transformed as follows:

$$\begin{matrix} V_0 \\ V_1 \\ V_a \\ V_b \end{matrix} \begin{bmatrix} 1 & 0 & 0 \\ 1 & 1 & 1 \\ 1 & 0 & 1 \\ 1 & 1 & 0 \end{bmatrix} \begin{bmatrix} 3 & 0 & 0 \\ -2 & 1 & 0 \\ -2 & 0 & 1 \end{bmatrix} = \begin{bmatrix} 3 & 0 & 0 \\ -1 & 1 & 1 \\ 1 & 0 & 1 \\ 1 & 1 & 0 \end{bmatrix} \begin{matrix} V_0^* \\ V_1^* \\ V_a^* \\ V_b^* \end{matrix} \Rightarrow \begin{bmatrix} 0 & 0 \\ -1 & -1 \\ 0 & 1 \\ 1 & 0 \end{bmatrix} \begin{matrix} v_0^* \\ v_1^* \\ v_a^* \\ v_b^* \end{matrix}. \quad (14.1)$$

When the transformed end points are connected directly, the line segments would be as in Fig. 14.1(b).

Because both end points of the line segment V_aV_b have positive homogeneous w-coordinate values after transformation, we know that it is an "internal line

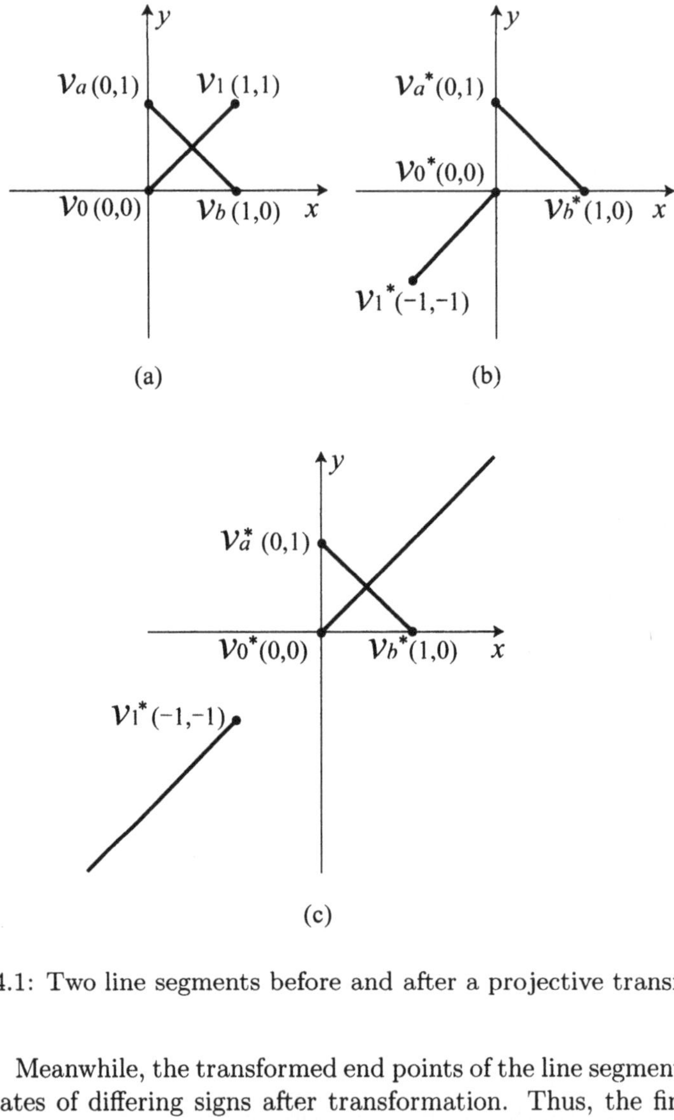

Figure 14.1: Two line segments before and after a projective transformation.

segment." Meanwhile, the transformed end points of the line segment V_0V_1 have w-coordinates of differing signs after transformation. Thus, the finally transformed line segment $v_0^*v_1^*$ passes a point at infinity as shown by the "external line segment" of Fig. 14.1(c). Such special types of line segments also occur in the linear approximation of rational curves or surfaces [1)].

Note the intersection point of two lines, when projectively transformed, becomes the intersection of the two lines transformed (see 4. of properties of projective transformations in Section 6.1).

We have seen above that a geometric test criterion, if it is to be projectively invariant, must apply universally to an internal line segment, external line segment and half line. Moreover, for tests based on determinants, the test criterion

[1)] Determining a point on a rational curve or surface involves a perspective projection (see Section 6.4).

must remain valid even when the determinant changes its sign, which occurs when it is multiplied by a projective transformation matrix with a negative determinant (see Section 13.2.6) [42].

14.2 Linearly Independent Conditions

We have seen that homogeneous geometric elements and their dual counterparts are defined in terms of homogeneous coordinates of points and homogeneous coefficients of planes, respectively. For example, a homogeneous plane or triangle is defined by the homogeneous coordinates of three linearly independent points. If the three points are not linearly independent, neither plane nor triangle can be defined. Before conducting a geometric test, therefore, we often first check to see whether the given geometric element is indeed linearly independent. If it is found not to be so, i.e., it is degenerate, then one must take some corresponding action.

In this section, we present the linearly independent conditions of homogeneous geometric elements defined in terms of Plücker coordinates and Plücker coefficients [63].

1. **3-D homogeneous lines and homogeneous line segments**

   Given two points V_0 and V_1 expressed in four-dimensional homogeneous coordinates, a three-dimensional homogeneous line can be expressed by the following six-dimensional Plücker coordinates (see Section 9.1.2):

   $$\overline{(P_{01}, Q_{01}, R_{01}, S_{01}, T_{01}, U_{01})}. \tag{14.2}$$

   If the two points are identical or antipodal, in which cases no line is formed, in other words, if $V_0 = kV_1$ (k is an arbitrary nonzero scalar), then all components of eq.(14.2) are zeros.

   Conversely, if all components of eq.(14.2) are zeros, then the two points are identical or antipodal.

   Thus, the condition such that the two points V_0 and V_1 are linearly independent and thus define a three-dimensional line or line segment is expressed as follows:

   $$[P_{01}\ Q_{01}\ R_{01}\ S_{01}\ T_{01}\ U_{01}] \neq [0\ 0\ 0\ 0\ 0\ 0]. \tag{14.3}$$

   If eq.(14.3) does not hold, then a three-dimensional homogeneous line or homogeneous line segment cannot be defined.

2. **Homogeneous planes and homogeneous triangles**

   Given three points V_0, V_1 and V_2, expressed in four-dimensional homogeneous coordinates, a homogeneous plane can be expressed by the following four-dimensional Plücker coordinates (i.e., homogeneous coefficients of plane) (see Section 9.1.2):

   $$\overline{(A_{012}, B_{012}, C_{012}, D_{012})}. \tag{14.4}$$

If the three points do not form a plane, i.e., if they lie on a single line, then all components of eq.(14.4) are zeros.

Conversely, if all components of eq.(14.4) are zeros, then the three points lie on a single line (see Section 9.1.1).

Thus, the condition such that the three points V_0, V_1 and V_2 are linearly independent and thus define a homogeneous plane or homogeneous triangle is expressed as follows:

$$[A_{012}\ B_{012}\ C_{012}\ D_{012}] \neq [0\ 0\ 0\ 0]. \tag{14.5}$$

If eq.(14.5) does not hold, then homogeneous plane or homogeneous triangle cannot be defined.

3. **Homogeneous three-space and homogeneous tetrahedra**

   Given four points V_0, V_1, V_2 and V_3, expressed in four-dimensional homogeneous coordinates, a homogeneous tetrahedron, or three-space, can be expressed by the following one-dimensional Plücker coordinate (which is none other than a type-S 4×4 determinant) (see Section 9.1.2):

$$\overline{(S_{0123})}. \tag{14.6}$$

   If the four points do not form a tetrahedron, i.e., if they lie on a single plane, then the component of eq.(14.6) is zero.

   Conversely, if the component of eq.(14.6) is zero, then the four points lie on a single plane.

   Thus, the condition such that the four points V_0, V_1, V_2 and V_3 are linearly independent and thus define a homogeneous tetrahedron or three-space is expressed as follows:

$$[S_{0123}] \neq [0]. \tag{14.7}$$

   If eq.(14.7) does not hold, then a homogeneous tetrahedron or three-space cannot be defined.

The results above are summarized in Table 14.1 along with the dual ones.

14.3 Basic Geometric Relations

We first define the terms "coplanarity," "concurrency" and "collinearity."

Coplanarity: When one or more geometric elements lie on a single plane, these are said to be *coplanar.*

Concurrency: When one or more geometric elements have a single point in common, these are said to be *concurrent.*

Collinearity: When one or more geometric elements have a single line in common, these are said to be *collinear.*

Table 14.1: Linearly independent conditions for geometric elements.

Elements	Conditions	Dual elements	Conditions
Line Line segment	$\boldsymbol{L}_{01} =$ $[P_{01}\ Q_{01}\ R_{01}\ S_{01}\ T_{01}\ U_{01}]$ $\neq [0\ 0\ 0\ 0\ 0\ 0]$	Line Line segment	$\boldsymbol{\lambda}_{01} =$ $[p_{01}\ q_{01}\ r_{01}\ s_{01}\ t_{01}\ u_{01}]$ $\neq [0\ 0\ 0\ 0\ 0\ 0]$
Plane Triangle	$\boldsymbol{F}_{012} =$ $[A_{012}\ B_{012}\ C_{012}\ D_{012}]^T$ $\neq [0\ 0\ 0\ 0]^T$	Point	$\boldsymbol{\pi}_{012} =$ $[w_{012}\ x_{012}\ y_{012}\ z_{012}]$ $\neq [0\ 0\ 0\ 0]$
Three-space Tetrahedron	$\boldsymbol{U}_{0123} = [S_{0123}] \neq [0]$	Vacuum	$\boldsymbol{\tau}_{0123} = [T_{0123}] \neq [0]$

Below we describe the conditions in which two or more elements are coincident (identical, antipodal or reverse-oriented), coplanar, concurrent and collinear [63].

1. **Conditions for coincident (identical,antipodal,reverse) elements**

Coincident points

The Plücker coordinates of a line that passes two points $V_0 = \overline{(w_0, X_0, Y_0, Z_0)}$ and $V_1 = \overline{(w_1, X_1, Y_1, Z_1)}$ are given by:

$$\overline{(P_{01}, Q_{01}, R_{01}, S_{01}, T_{01}, U_{01})}. \tag{14.8}$$

When the two points V_0 and V_1 are either identical or antipodal, that is, $V_0 = kV_1$ $(k \neq 0)$, then:

$$[P_{01}\ Q_{01}\ R_{01}\ S_{01}\ T_{01}\ U_{01}] = \boldsymbol{L}_{01} = [0\ 0\ 0\ 0\ 0\ 0]. \tag{14.9}$$

Conversely, if eq.(14.9) holds, then eq.(14.8) does not represent a line, that is, the two points V_0 and V_1 are either identical or antipodal to each other.

Thus, eq.(14.9) expresses the condition for the two points V_0 and V_1 in three-space to be either identical or antipodal.

When V_0 and V_1 satisfy eq.(14.9):

- they are identical points if V_0 and V_1 are points in classical projective space;

- the following test is needed if they are points in two-sided space:
  - · $\boldsymbol{V}_0 \cdot \boldsymbol{V}_1 > 0 \cdots V_0$ and V_1 are identical points;
  - · $\boldsymbol{V}_0 \cdot \boldsymbol{V}_1 < 0 \cdots V_0$ and V_1 are antipodal and thus distinct.

Coincident planes

The condition for two planes $\gamma_0 = \overline{(a_0, b_0, c_0, d_0)^T}$ and $\gamma_1 = \overline{(a_1, b_1, c_1, d_1)^T}$ to be coincident is derived in the exactly same manner as, but forming a dual relationship to, the condition for two coincident points. That is, the necessary and sufficient condition for the two planes γ_0 and γ_1 to be identical or to have reverse orientations can be expressed by the dual equation to eq.(14.9), or:

$$[p_{01}\ q_{01}\ r_{01}\ s_{01}\ t_{01}\ u_{01}] = [0\ 0\ 0\ 0\ 0\ 0]. \tag{14.10}$$

When γ_0 and γ_1 satisfy eq.(14.10):

- they are identical planes if γ_0 and γ_1 are planes in classical projective space;
- the following test is needed if they are planes in two-sided space:
  - · $\boldsymbol{\gamma}_0 \cdot \boldsymbol{\gamma}_1 > 0 \cdots \gamma_0$ and γ_1 are identical planes;
  - · $\boldsymbol{\gamma}_0 \cdot \boldsymbol{\gamma}_1 < 0 \cdots \gamma_0$ and γ_1 are reversely oriented and thus distinct.

Coincident lines

Line $L_{01} = \overline{(P_{01}, Q_{01}, R_{01}, S_{01}, T_{01}, U_{01})}$ defined by two points V_0 and V_1 and line $L_{ab} = \overline{(P_{ab}, Q_{ab}, R_{ab}, S_{ab}, T_{ab}, U_{ab})}$ defined by two points V_a and V_b are either identical or have reverse orientations when (see Section 9.1.2):

$$L_{01} = kL_{ab}, \quad k \neq 0. \tag{14.11}$$

This represents the condition for the two three-dimensional lines L_{01} and L_{ab} to be either identical or have reverse orientations.

When L_{01} and L_{ab} satisfy eq.(14.11):

- they are identical lines if L_{01} and L_{ab} are lines in classical projective space;
- the following test is needed if they are lines in two-sided space:
  - · $\boldsymbol{L}_{01} \cdot \boldsymbol{L}_{ab} > 0 \cdots L_{01}$ and L_{ab} are identical lines;
  - · $\boldsymbol{L}_{01} \cdot \boldsymbol{L}_{ab} < 0 \cdots L_{01}$ and L_{ab} are reversely oriented and thus distinct.

The condition for a line $\lambda_{01} = \overline{(p_{01}, q_{01}, r_{01}, s_{01}, t_{01}, u_{01})}$ defined by two planes λ_0 and λ_1 and a line $\lambda_{ab} = \overline{(p_{ab}, q_{ab}, r_{ab}, s_{ab}, t_{ab}, u_{ab})}$ defined by two planes λ_a and λ_b to be either identical or have reverse orientations forms a dual relationship to eq.(14.11), that is:

$$\lambda_{01} = k\lambda_{ab}, \quad k \neq 0. \tag{14.12}$$

When λ_{01} and λ_{ab} satisfy eq.(14.12):

- they are identical lines if λ_{01} and λ_{ab} are lines in classical projective space;
- the following test is needed if they are lines in two-sided space:
  - $\boldsymbol{\lambda}_{01} \cdot \boldsymbol{\lambda}_{ab} > 0 \cdots \lambda_{01}$ and γ_{ab} are identical lines;
  - $\boldsymbol{\lambda}_{01} \cdot \boldsymbol{\lambda}_{ab} < 0 \cdots \lambda_{01}$ and λ_{ab} are reversely oriented and thus distinct.

2. **Conditions for coplanar and concurrent elements**

Four coplanar points

The condition for four points V_0, V_1, V_2 and V_3 to be coplanar is that the vectors formed by their homogeneous coordinates are linearly dependent, or:

$$\begin{vmatrix} w_0 & X_0 & Y_0 & Z_0 \\ w_1 & X_1 & Y_1 & Z_1 \\ w_2 & X_2 & Y_2 & Z_2 \\ w_3 & X_3 & Y_3 & Z_3 \end{vmatrix} = S_{0123} = 0. \tag{14.13}$$

Four concurrent planes

The condition for four planes γ_0, γ_1, γ_2 and γ_3 to be concurrent is given by the dual to eq.(14.13), that is:

$$\begin{vmatrix} a_0 & a_1 & a_2 & a_3 \\ b_0 & b_1 & b_2 & b_3 \\ c_0 & c_1 & c_2 & c_3 \\ d_0 & d_1 & d_2 & d_3 \end{vmatrix} = T_{0123} = 0. \tag{14.14}$$

3. **Conditions for collinear elements**

Three points

The plane that passes points $V_0 = \overline{(w_0, X_0, Y_0, Z_0)}$, $V_1 = \overline{(w_1, X_1, Y_1, Z_1)}$ and $V_2 = \overline{(w_2, X_2, Y_2, Z_2)}$ is given from eq.(9.39) as:

$$\begin{vmatrix} w & X & Y & Z \\ w_0 & X_0 & Y_0 & Z_0 \\ w_1 & X_1 & Y_1 & Z_1 \\ w_2 & X_2 & Y_2 & Z_2 \end{vmatrix} = A_{012}w + B_{012}X + C_{012}Y + D_{012}Z = 0, \tag{14.15}$$

where A_{012}, B_{012}, C_{012} and D_{012} are the Plücker coordinates of the plane.

Now if we substitute into the left-hand side of eq.(14.15) the coordinates of some point $V_a = \overline{(w_a, X_a, Y_a, Z_a)}$ that lies out of the plane, we have:

$$\begin{vmatrix} w_a & X_a & Y_a & Z_a \\ w_0 & X_0 & Y_0 & Z_0 \\ w_1 & X_1 & Y_1 & Z_1 \\ w_2 & X_2 & Y_2 & Z_2 \end{vmatrix} = A_{012}w_a + B_{012}X_a + C_{012}Y_a + D_{012}Z_a. \tag{14.16}$$

If V_0, V_1 and V_2 are collinear, then (see Section 19.2.2):

$$[A_{012}\ B_{012}\ C_{012}\ D_{012}]^T = \boldsymbol{F}_{012} = [0\ 0\ 0\ 0]^T. \tag{14.17}$$

Conversely, if we assume the condition of eq.(14.17), eq.(14.16) is always equal to zero. But since the point V_a lies outside the plane, eq.(14.16) is nonzero as long as the other three points form a plane. Therefore, eq.(14.17) must mean that the three points are collinear and unable to form a plane.

We therefore conclude that eq.(14.17) expresses the necessary and sufficient condition for three points to be collinear.

Three planes

The condition for three planes $\gamma_0 = \overline{(a_0, b_0, c_0, d_0)^T}$, $\gamma_1 = \overline{(a_1, b_1, c_1, d_1)^T}$ and $\gamma_2 = \overline{(a_2, b_2, c_2, d_2)^T}$ to be collinear is derived in the exactly same manner as, but forming a dual relationship to, the condition for three collinear points. That is, the necessary and sufficient condition for the three planes γ_0, γ_1 and γ_2 to be collinear can be expressed by the dual equation to eq.(14.17), or:

$$[w_{012}\ x_{012}\ y_{012}\ z_{012}] = \boldsymbol{\pi}_{012} = [0\ 0\ 0\ 0]. \tag{14.18}$$

The above results are summarized in Table 14.2.

14.4 Interferences between Simplices (3)

The 4×4 determinant method described in Chapter 13 was a computational method that enabled three-dimensional geometric operations (except transformations) under a uniform scheme, that is, by using 4×4 determinants. For this purpose, it was necessary, when dealing with elements with two dimensions or less, to make it into a three-dimensional problem by adding suitable auxiliary points, after which it could be treated using 4×4 determinants.

For example, in determining whether a triangle in space contains a point, as soon as the point is found to lie on the plane of the triangle, the test becomes essentially a two-dimensional problem. One must then set up an auxiliary point outside the plane of the triangle. One of the easiest way to determine the point is to choose a point at infinity in the direction of the normal vector of the triangle. This is not projectively invariant, however. This could, therefore, present a problem if we require the choice of the point to be projectively invariant.

In this section, we derive interference conditions between homogeneous simplices without the introduction of auxiliary points [63]. The derived conditions are projectively invariant. That is, they apply even when geometric elements are subjected to general projective transformations and are transformed into anomalous shapes as mentioned in Section 9.2.

We assume here that homogeneous line segments, homogeneous triangles and homogeneous tetrahedra as well as their dual counterparts (i.e., dual homogeneous line segments, dual homogeneous triangles and dual homogeneous

Table 14.2: Conditions for geometric elements to be coincident, coplanar, concurrent and collinear.

Coincidence conditions for homogeneous elements	**Coincidence conditions for dual homogeneous elements**
1. Two Points The condition for two points V_0 and V_1 to be either identical or antipodal is given by: $P_{01} = Q_{01} = R_{01} = S_{01} = T_{01} = U_{01} = 0.$	**1'. Two planes** The condition for two planes γ_0 and γ_1 to be identical or to have reverse orientations is given by: $p_{01} = q_{01} = r_{01} = s_{01} = t_{01} = u_{01} = 0.$
2. Two lines The condition for two lines L_{01} and L_{ab} to be identical or have reverse orientations is given by: $L_{01} = kL_{ab}, \quad k \neq 0.$	**2'. Two lines** The condition for two lines λ_{01} and λ_{ab} to be identical or have reverse orientations is given by: $\lambda_{01} = k\lambda_{ab}, \quad k \neq 0.$

Coplanarity conditions	**Concurrency conditions**
Four points The condition for four points V_0, V_1, V_2 and V_3 to be coplanar is given by: $S_{0123} = 0.$	**Four planes** The condition for four planes γ_0, γ_1, γ_2 and γ_3 to be concurrent is given by: $T_{0123} = 0.$

Collinearity conditions for homogeneous elements	**Collinearity conditions for dual homogeneous elements**
Three points The condition for three points V_0, V_1 and V_2 to be collinear is given by: $A_{012} = B_{012} = C_{012} = D_{012} = 0.$	**Three planes** The condition for three planes γ_0, γ_1 and γ_2 to be collinear is given by: $w_{012} = x_{012} = y_{012} = z_{012} = 0.$

tetrahedra) are all defined by linearly independent point vectors or plane coefficient vectors (see Section 14.2 for the linearly independent conditions of geometric elements).

Note that in the test conditions derived below, the faces, edges and vertices of a simplex are considered to be "inside" the simplex. This also holds for dual simplices.

14.4.1 Simplices in Classical Projective Space

1. **Containment of a point in a tetrahedron**

We now derive the condition in classical projective space for a homogeneous point V_a to lie inside a homogeneous tetrahedron $V_0V_1V_2V_3$.

Geometric derivation

Prior to considering this problem, let us first consider a problem in plane geometry, i.e., the containment of a point V_a in a triangle $V_0V_1V_2$ (see 2. of C.5.1). The condition in this case is in the spherical model of $\mathbf{R}^3$:

$$(V_a \text{ is in } V_0V_1V_2) \vee (V_a \text{ is in } \neg V_0\neg V_1\neg V_2).$$

Note here that conditions ($\neg V_a$ is in $V_0V_1V_2$) and ($\neg V_a$ is in $\neg V_0\neg V_1\neg V_2$) are not included in the condition above because the former is the same as (V_a is in $\neg V_0\neg V_1\neg V_2$) and the latter the same as (V_a is in $V_0V_1V_2$) (see Fig. 14.2).

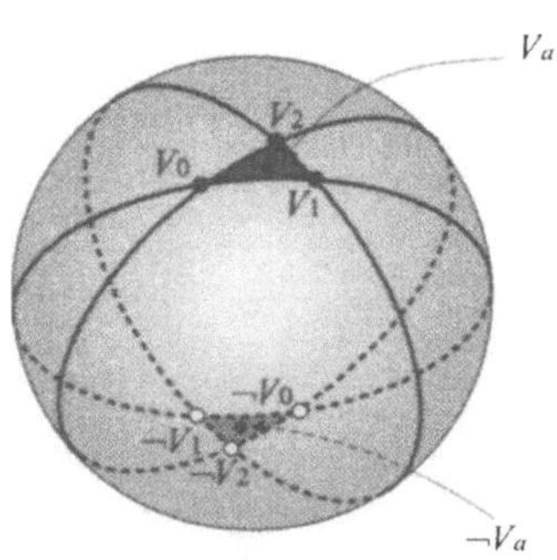

Figure 14.2: Containment test of point in 2-D triangle (projective space).

Let us assume temporarily the triangle is oriented positively.

The first condition above is that V_a exists in the left (positive) half-spaces of all three oriented lines V_1V_2, V_2V_0 and V_0V_1 and the second one is that it exists in the right (negative) half-spaces of these lines (Fig. 14.2).

Now, if we take a point V on the triangle $V_0V_1V_2$ and a point V' on the antipodal triangle $\neg V_0\neg V_1\neg V_2$, and denote some arbitrary edge of these

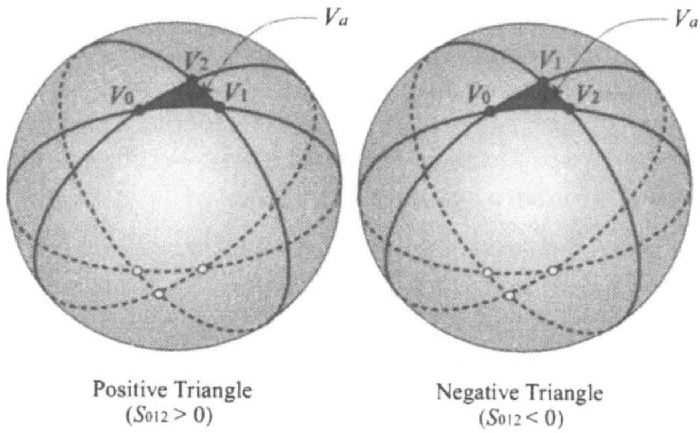

Figure 14.3: Orientations of triangle and containment test (projective space).

triangles by V_iV_j, we know that the following relation exists:

$$\operatorname{sign}\left(\begin{vmatrix} \boldsymbol{V} \\ \boldsymbol{V}_i \\ \boldsymbol{V}_j \end{vmatrix}\right) = -\operatorname{sign}\left(\begin{vmatrix} \boldsymbol{V}' \\ \boldsymbol{V}_i \\ \boldsymbol{V}_j \end{vmatrix}\right). \tag{14.19}$$

By using the relation (14.19), we have the containment condition of V_a in $V_0V_1V_2$:

$$(S_{a12}, S_{a20}, S_{a01} \geq 0) \vee (S_{a12}, S_{a20}, S_{a01} \leq 0). \tag{14.20}$$

Now, let us consider the effect of triangle's orientations.

The containment condition of V_a in a negative triangle is the same as that of V_a in the antipode of a positive one, and the condition of V_a in the antipode of a negative triangle is the same as that of V_a in a positive one (Fig. 14.3). This means that the orientations of a triangle do not affect the final condition, eq.(14.20).

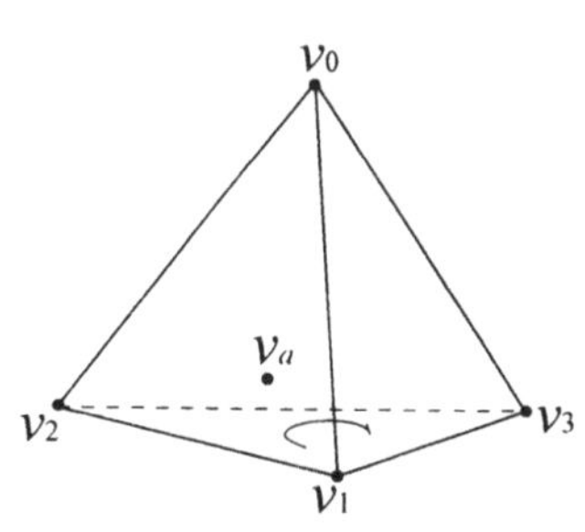

Figure 14.4: Containment test of point in tetrahedron.

Analogously to the plane geometry case above, the containment condition of V_a in $V_0V_1V_2V_3$ is in the spherical model of $\mathbf{R}^4$:

$$(V_a \text{ is in } V_0V_1V_2V_3) \vee (V_a \text{ is in } \neg V_0\neg V_1\neg V_2\neg V_3).$$

The first condition above is that V_a exists in the positive half-spaces of all four oriented planes $V_1V_2V_3$, $V_0V_3V_2$, $V_0V_1V_3$ and $V_0V_2V_1$ and the second one is that it exists in the negative half-spaces of these planes, when we consider the tetrahedron is positively oriented (Fig. 14.4).

Now, as in the plane geometry case above, if we take a point V within the tetrahedron $V_0V_1V_2V_3$ and a point V' within the antipode $\neg V_0\neg V_1\neg V_2\neg V_3$, and denote some arbitrary plane of the former tetrahedron by $V_iV_jV_k$, we have the following relation:

$$\text{sign}\left(\begin{vmatrix} \boldsymbol{V} \\ \boldsymbol{V}_i \\ \boldsymbol{V}_j \\ \boldsymbol{V}_k \end{vmatrix}\right) = -\,\text{sign}\left(\begin{vmatrix} \boldsymbol{V}' \\ \boldsymbol{V}_i \\ \boldsymbol{V}_j \\ \boldsymbol{V}_k \end{vmatrix}\right). \tag{14.21}$$

By using the relation (14.21), we have the containment condition of V_a in $V_0V_1V_2V_3$:

$$(S_{a123}, S_{a032}, S_{a013}, S_{a021} \geq 0) \vee (S_{a123}, S_{a032}, S_{a013}, S_{a021} \leq 0). \tag{14.22}$$

Algebraic derivation

A homogeneous tetrahedron $V_0V_1V_2V_3$ in classical projective space can be expressed by homogeneous parameters as follows (see Section 9.2):

$$\overline{\boldsymbol{V}} = \overline{\xi_0\boldsymbol{V}_0 + \xi_1\boldsymbol{V}_1 + \xi_2\boldsymbol{V}_2 + \xi_3\boldsymbol{V}_3},$$
$$(\xi_0, \xi_1, \xi_2, \xi_3 \geq 0) \vee (\xi_0, \xi_1, \xi_2, \xi_3 \leq 0).$$

Thus, the condition for V_a to lie inside the homogeneous tetrahedron is given by:

$$\overline{\xi_0\boldsymbol{V}_0 + \xi_1\boldsymbol{V}_1 + \xi_2\boldsymbol{V}_2 + \xi_3\boldsymbol{V}_3} = \overline{\boldsymbol{V}_a},$$
$$(\xi_0, \xi_1, \xi_2, \xi_3 \geq 0) \vee (\xi_0, \xi_1, \xi_2, \xi_3 \leq 0),$$

or,

$$\xi_0\boldsymbol{V}_0 + \xi_1\boldsymbol{V}_1 + \xi_2\boldsymbol{V}_2 + \xi_3\boldsymbol{V}_3 = \boldsymbol{V}_a, \tag{14.23}$$
$$(\xi_0, \xi_1, \xi_2, \xi_3 \geq 0) \vee (\xi_0, \xi_1, \xi_2, \xi_3 \leq 0). \tag{14.24}$$

Eq.(14.23) expresses a set of four simultaneous linear equations with variables, ξ_0, ξ_1, ξ_2 and ξ_3 [2)].

Since V_0, V_1, V_2 and V_3 are assumed to be linearly independent, we have:

$$S_{0123} \neq 0.$$

[2)] Eq.(14.23) might be written as follows:

$$\xi_0\boldsymbol{V}_0 + \xi_1\boldsymbol{V}_1 + \xi_2\boldsymbol{V}_2 + \xi_3\boldsymbol{V}_3 = k\boldsymbol{V}_a, \quad k \neq 0. \tag{14.25}$$

Since the homogeneous parameters play the role of k, it is omitted for simplicity. The same simplification is taken throughout.

Thus, eq.(14.23) has a unique solution for ξ_0, ξ_1, ξ_2 and ξ_3, as given by:

$$(\xi_0, \xi_1, \xi_2, \xi_3) = \left(\frac{S_{a123}}{S_{0123}}, \frac{S_{0a23}}{S_{0123}}, \frac{S_{01a3}}{S_{0123}}, \frac{S_{012a}}{S_{0123}} \right)$$
$$= \frac{1}{S_{0123}} (S_{a123}, S_{a032}, S_{a013}, S_{a021}). \tag{14.26}$$

From eq.(14.24), therefore, we have the same condition as eq.(14.22):

$$(S_{a123}, S_{a032}, S_{a013}, S_{a021} \geq 0) \vee (S_{a123}, S_{a032}, S_{a013}, S_{a021} \leq 0). \tag{14.27}$$

The interference condition in $\mathbf{R}^4$ is expressed as the sum of the condition for the point V_a to lie inside the tetrahedron $V_0V_1V_2V_3$ and the one inside its antipodal tetrahedron $\neg V_0 \neg V_1 \neg V_2 \neg V_3$ (see eq.(C.26)). While there is no distinction between these two tetrahedra in classical projective space, they are processed separately in $\mathbf{R}^4$, as shown above.

Partition

Now, let us consider partitioning the tetrahedron using the point V_a, when it is found to lie in the tetrahedron.

In $\mathbf{R}^4$, the orientations of geometric elements are treated distinguishably: That is, we have a positive tetrahedron when $S_{0123} > 0$ and a negative tetrahedron when $S_{0123} < 0$.

Thus, from eqs.(14.24) and (14.26), the condition for V_a to be in $V_0V_1V_2V_3$ is:

$$\begin{array}{l} (S_{0123} > 0 \ \wedge \ S_{a123}, S_{a032}, S_{a013}, S_{a021} \geq 0) \\ \vee \ (S_{0123} < 0 \ \wedge \ S_{a123}, S_{a032}, S_{a013}, S_{a021} \leq 0), \end{array} \tag{14.28}$$

and the condition for V_a to be in $\neg V_0 \neg V_1 \neg V_2 \neg V_3$ is:

$$\begin{array}{l} (S_{0123} > 0 \ \wedge \ S_{a123}, S_{a032}, S_{a013}, S_{a021} \leq 0) \\ \vee \ (S_{0123} < 0 \ \wedge \ S_{a123}, S_{a032}, S_{a013}, S_{a021} \geq 0). \end{array} \tag{14.29}$$

Therefore it is advisable to use the following vector $\boldsymbol{V}$ for the partitioning to maintain consistency in the vector signs between the tetrahedron vertices and a partitioning point (see 2. of C.5.1):

$$\left\{ \begin{array}{l} \textbf{If } (S_{0123} > 0 \ \wedge \ S_{a123}, S_{a032}, S_{a013}, S_{a021} \geq 0) \\ \ \vee \ (S_{0123} < 0 \ \wedge \ S_{a123}, S_{a032}, S_{a013}, S_{a021} \leq 0) \\ \qquad\qquad \textbf{then } \boldsymbol{V} = \boldsymbol{V}_a \\ \qquad\qquad\qquad \textbf{else} \\ \textbf{if } (S_{0123} > 0 \ \wedge \ S_{a123}, S_{a032}, S_{a013}, S_{a021} \leq 0) \\ \ \vee \ (S_{0123} < 0 \ \wedge \ S_{a123}, S_{a032}, S_{a013}, S_{a021} \geq 0) \\ \qquad\qquad \textbf{then } \boldsymbol{V} = -\boldsymbol{V}_a. \end{array} \right. \tag{14.30}$$

2. **Containment of a point in a triangle**

We now derive the condition in classical projective space for a homogeneous point V_a to lie inside a homogeneous triangle $V_0V_1V_2$.

First, we add the condition that the point V_a and the triangle $V_0V_1V_2$ are coplanar, which is:

$$S_{a012} = 0. \tag{14.31}$$

Geometric derivation

The condition for the point V_a to be contained in the coplanar triangle $V_0V_1V_2$ is expressed in the spherical model as the condition for V_a to be contained in the triangle $V_0V_1V_2$ or its antipodal triangle $\neg V_0\neg V_1\neg V_2$ (see Fig. 14.5). Referring to Fig. 4.29, this condition can be expressed using vectors defined by Plücker coordinates of plane as follows:

$$\begin{aligned}&(\boldsymbol{F}_{012}\cdot\boldsymbol{F}_{a12}\geq 0\ \wedge\ \boldsymbol{F}_{012}\cdot\boldsymbol{F}_{0a2}\geq 0\ \wedge\ \boldsymbol{F}_{012}\cdot\boldsymbol{F}_{01a}\geq 0)\\ \vee\ &(\boldsymbol{F}_{012}\cdot\boldsymbol{F}_{a12}\leq 0\ \wedge\ \boldsymbol{F}_{012}\cdot\boldsymbol{F}_{0a2}\leq 0\ \wedge\ \boldsymbol{F}_{012}\cdot\boldsymbol{F}_{01a}\leq 0).\end{aligned} \tag{14.32}$$

Together with the coplanarity condition above, this is written as follows:

$$\begin{aligned}&(S_{a012}=0)\ \wedge\\ &((\boldsymbol{F}_{012}\cdot\boldsymbol{F}_{a12}\geq 0\ \wedge\ \boldsymbol{F}_{012}\cdot\boldsymbol{F}_{a20}\geq 0\ \wedge\ \boldsymbol{F}_{012}\cdot\boldsymbol{F}_{a01}\geq 0)\\ \vee\ &(\boldsymbol{F}_{012}\cdot\boldsymbol{F}_{a12}\leq 0\ \wedge\ \boldsymbol{F}_{012}\cdot\boldsymbol{F}_{a20}\leq 0\ \wedge\ \boldsymbol{F}_{012}\cdot\boldsymbol{F}_{a01}\leq 0)).\end{aligned} \tag{14.33}$$

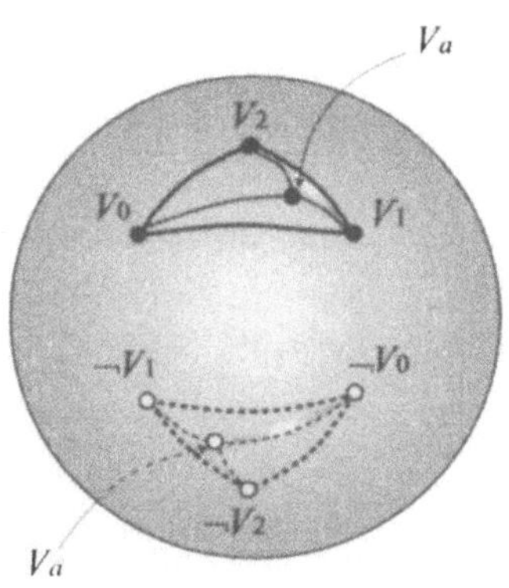

Figure 14.5: Containment test of point in triangle (projective space).

Algebraic derivation

The condition for the point V_a to lie inside the triangle $V_0V_1V_2$ is given by (see Section 9.2):

$$\xi_0\boldsymbol{V}_0+\xi_1\boldsymbol{V}_1+\xi_2\boldsymbol{V}_2=\boldsymbol{V}_a, \tag{14.34}$$

$$(\xi_0,\xi_1,\xi_2\geq 0)\vee(\xi_0,\xi_1,\xi_2\leq 0). \tag{14.35}$$

Note here that when the homogeneous equation (14.34), consisting of four simultaneous equations, is solved for the three variables, ξ_0, ξ_1 and ξ_2, four solution sets are possible depending on which equations are chosen.

We shall let f_{012} represent one of the four Plücker coordinates of the plane defined by the three points:

$$F_{012} = \overline{(A_{012}, B_{012}, C_{012}, D_{012})^T},$$

that is,

$$f_{012} \in \{A_{012}, B_{012}, C_{012}, D_{012}\}. \tag{14.36}$$

Since the triangle is assumed to be linearly independent:

$$(A_{012}, B_{012}, C_{012}, D_{012}) \neq (0,0,0,0),$$

we can obtain ξ_0, ξ_1 and ξ_2 using the notation above. We assume

$$f_{012} \neq 0. \tag{14.37}$$

Then

$$\begin{aligned}(\xi_0, \xi_1, \xi_2) &= \left(\frac{f_{a12}}{f_{012}}, \frac{f_{0a2}}{f_{012}}, \frac{f_{01a}}{f_{012}}\right) \\ &= \frac{1}{f_{012}}(f_{a12}, f_{a20}, f_{a01}).\end{aligned} \tag{14.38}$$

From eq.(14.35), therefore, we have:

$$(f_{a12}, f_{a20}, f_{a01} \geq 0) \vee (f_{a12}, f_{a20}, f_{a01} \leq 0). \tag{14.39}$$

Together with eqs.(14.31) and (14.37), we have:

$$\begin{gathered}\text{With respect to } f_{012} \neq 0 \ (\in \{A_{012}, B_{012}, C_{012}, D_{012}\}), \\ (S_{a012} = 0) \wedge \\ (f_{a12}, f_{a20}, f_{a01} \geq 0 \ \vee \ f_{a12}, f_{a20}, f_{a01} \leq 0).\end{gathered} \tag{14.40}$$

This expression represents eq.(14.33) in terms of its vector components.

Partition

In $\mathbf{R}^4$, the orientations of geometric elements are distinguished. That is, we have oriented triangles in the space.

Thus, from eqs.(14.35) and (14.38), the condition for V_a to be in $V_0V_1V_2$ is:

$$\begin{aligned}&(f_{012} > 0 \ \wedge \ f_{a12}, f_{a20}, f_{a01} \geq 0) \\ \vee \ &(f_{012} < 0 \ \wedge \ f_{a12}, f_{a20}, f_{a01} \leq 0),\end{aligned} \tag{14.41}$$

and the condition for V_a to be in $\neg V_0 \neg V_1 \neg V_2$ is:

$$\begin{aligned}&(f_{012} > 0 \ \wedge \ f_{a12}, f_{a20}, f_{a01} \leq 0) \\ \vee \ &(f_{012} < 0 \ \wedge \ f_{a12}, f_{a20}, f_{a01} \geq 0).\end{aligned} \tag{14.42}$$

These cases are shown in (a),(b) (corresponding to eq.(14.41)) and (c),(d) (corresponding to eq.(14.42)) in Fig. 14.6.

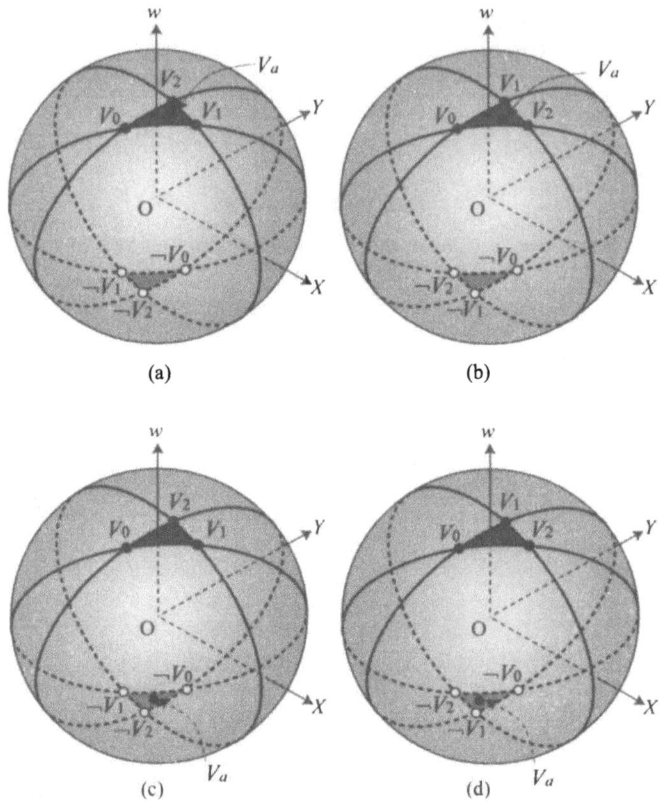

Figure 14.6: Partitioning triangle $V_0V_1V_2$ using point V_a (projective space).

Therefore it is advisable to use the following vector $\boldsymbol{V}$ for the partitioning to maintain consistency in the vector signs between the triangle vertices and a partitioning point:

$$\left\{\begin{array}{l} \text{With respect to } f_{012} \neq 0 \ (\in \{A_{012}, B_{012}, C_{012}, D_{012}\}), \\ \qquad \textbf{If } (f_{012} > 0 \ \wedge \ f_{a12}, f_{a20}, f_{a01} \geq 0) \\ \qquad \vee \ (f_{012} < 0 \ \wedge \ f_{a12}, f_{a20}, f_{a01} \leq 0) \\ \qquad\qquad \textbf{then } \boldsymbol{V} = \boldsymbol{V}_a \\ \qquad\qquad \textbf{else} \\ \qquad \textbf{if } (f_{012} > 0 \ \wedge \ f_{a12}, f_{a20}, f_{a01} \leq 0) \\ \qquad \vee \ (f_{012} < 0 \ \wedge \ f_{a12}, f_{a20}, f_{a01} \geq 0) \\ \qquad\qquad \textbf{then } \boldsymbol{V} = -\boldsymbol{V}_a. \end{array}\right. \tag{14.43}$$

3. **Containment of a point in a line segment**

   We derive the condition in classical projective space for a homogeneous point V_a to lie on a homogeneous line segment V_0V_1.

First, we add the condition such that the point V_a and the line segment V_0V_1 are collinear, which is given by:

$$\boldsymbol{F}_{a01} = \boldsymbol{0}. \tag{14.44}$$

Geometric derivation

The condition for the point V_a to be contained in the collinear line segment V_0V_1 is expressed in the spherical model as the condition for V_a to be contained in the line segment V_0V_1 or its antipodal line segment $\neg V_0 \neg V_1$ (see Fig. 14.7).

Referring to Section 4.6, this condition can be expressed using vectors defined by Plücker coordinates of line as follows:

$$(\boldsymbol{L}_{01} \cdot \boldsymbol{L}_{0a},\ \boldsymbol{L}_{01} \cdot \boldsymbol{L}_{a1} \geq 0) \ \vee \ (\boldsymbol{L}_{01} \cdot \boldsymbol{L}_{0a},\ \boldsymbol{L}_{01} \cdot \boldsymbol{L}_{a1} \leq 0). \tag{14.45}$$

This is simplified to:

$$\boldsymbol{L}_{a0} \cdot \boldsymbol{L}_{a1} \leq 0. \tag{14.46}$$

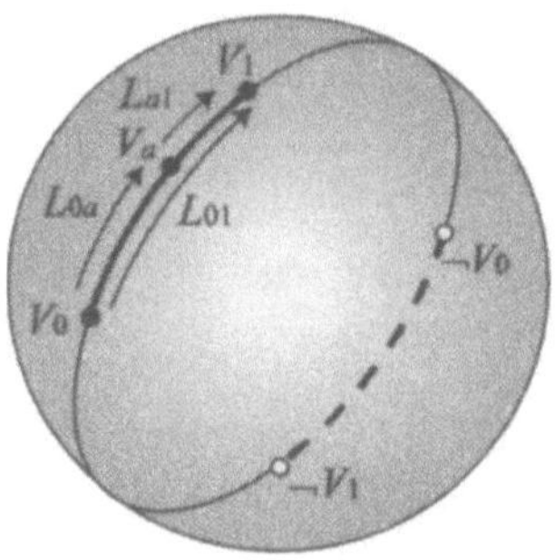

Figure 14.7: Containment of point in line segment (projective space).

Together with the collinearity condition above, the final condition is written as follows:

$$(\boldsymbol{F}_{a01} = \boldsymbol{0}) \ \wedge \ (\boldsymbol{L}_{a0} \cdot \boldsymbol{L}_{a1} \leq 0). \tag{14.47}$$

Algebraic derivation

The condition for the point V_a to be contained in the line segment V_0V_1 is expressed as follows (see Section 9.2):

$$\xi_0 \boldsymbol{V}_0 + \xi_1 \boldsymbol{V}_1 = \boldsymbol{V}_a, \tag{14.48}$$

$$(\xi_0, \xi_1 \geq 0) \vee (\xi_0, \xi_1 \leq 0). \tag{14.49}$$

Note here that when the homogeneous equation (14.48), consisting of four simultaneous equations, is solved for the two variables, ξ_0 and ξ_1, six solution sets are possible depending on which equations are chosen.

We shall let l_{01} represent one of the six Plücker coordinates of the line defined by the two points:

$$L_{01} = \overline{(P_{01}, Q_{01}, R_{01}, S_{01}, T_{01}, U_{01})},$$

that is,

$$l_{01} \in \{P_{01}, Q_{01}, R_{01}, S_{01}, T_{01}, U_{01}\}. \tag{14.50}$$

Since the line segment is assumed to be linearly independent:

$$(P_{01}, Q_{01}, R_{01}, S_{01}, T_{01}, U_{01}) \neq (0, 0, 0, 0, 0, 0),$$

we can obtain ξ_0 and ξ_1 using the notation above. We assume $l_{01} \neq 0$. Then

$$(\xi_0, \xi_1) = (\frac{l_{a1}}{l_{01}}, \frac{l_{0a}}{l_{01}}). \tag{14.51}$$

From eq.(14.49), we have:

$$(l_{a1} \geq 0 \ \wedge \ l_{0a} \geq 0) \ \vee \ (l_{a1} \leq 0 \ \wedge \ l_{0a} \leq 0). \tag{14.52}$$

This is simplified as:

$$l_{a0} \cdot l_{a1} \leq 0. \tag{14.53}$$

Combining the relation above with the collinearity condition gives the final result:

$$\begin{array}{c}\text{With respect to } l_{01} \neq 0 \ (\in \{P_{01}, Q_{01}, R_{01}, S_{01}, T_{01}, U_{01}\}), \\ (\boldsymbol{F}_{a01} = \mathbf{0}) \wedge (l_{a0} \cdot l_{a1} \leq 0).\end{array} \tag{14.54}$$

This expression represents eq.(14.47) in terms of its vector components.

Partition

Now, let us consider partitioning the line segment V_0V_1 using the point V_a, when it is found to lie in the line segment.

In $\mathbf{R}^4$, the orientations of geometric elements are distinguished. That is, we have oriented lines.

Thus, from eqs.(14.49) and (14.51), the condition for the point V_a to be in the line segment V_0V_1 is:

$$\begin{array}{c}(l_{01} > 0 \wedge l_{a0} \leq 0 \wedge l_{a1} \geq 0) \\ \vee \ (l_{01} < 0 \wedge l_{a0} \geq 0 \wedge l_{a1} \leq 0),\end{array} \tag{14.55}$$

and the condition for V_a to be in $\neg V_0 \neg V_1$ is:,

$$\begin{array}{c}(l_{01} > 0 \wedge l_{a0} \geq 0 \wedge l_{a1} \leq 0) \\ \vee \ (l_{01} < 0 \wedge l_{a0} \leq 0 \wedge l_{a1} \geq 0).\end{array} \tag{14.56}$$

Therefore it is advisable to use the following vector $\boldsymbol{V}$ for the partitioning to maintain consistency in the vector signs between the line segment vertices and a partitioning point:

$$\left\{\begin{array}{l}\text{With respect to } l_{01} \neq 0\ (\in \{P_{01}, Q_{01}, R_{01}, S_{01}, T_{01}, U_{01}\}),\\ \qquad \textbf{If } (l_{01} > 0 \wedge l_{a0} < 0 \wedge l_{a1} \geq 0)\\ \qquad \vee\ (l_{01} < 0 \wedge l_{a0} \geq 0 \wedge l_{a1} \leq 0)\\ \qquad\qquad \textbf{then } \boldsymbol{V} = \boldsymbol{V}_a\\ \qquad\qquad \textbf{else}\\ \qquad \textbf{if } (l_{01} > 0 \wedge l_{a0} \geq 0 \wedge l_{a1} \leq 0)\\ \qquad \vee\ (l_{01} < 0 \wedge l_{a0} \leq 0 \wedge l_{a1} \geq 0)\\ \qquad\qquad \textbf{then } \boldsymbol{V} = -\boldsymbol{V}_a.\end{array}\right. \tag{14.57}$$

4. **Intersection of a line segment and a triangle**

Here we derive the condition in classical projective space for a homogeneous line segment V_aV_b and a homogeneous triangle $V_0V_1V_2$ to intersect at a single point.

We attach the condition:

$$(S_{a012},\ S_{b012}) \neq (0,0) \tag{14.58}$$

for the line segment and the triangle not to be coplanar.

Geometric derivation

First, in $\mathbf{R}^4$ we require the endpoints of the line segment lie in the opposite half spaces of the triangle plane $V_0V_1V_2$. There are two cases; one is where V_a is in the positive half space of the plane and the other where V_a is in the negative half space. These are expressed as follows:

$$(S_{a012} \geq 0 \wedge S_{b012} \leq 0)\ \vee\ (S_{a012} \leq 0 \wedge S_{b012} \geq 0). \tag{14.59}$$

Second, we must further require that the line segment intersects the interior of the triangle.

Now, let us consider a triangular pyramid $V_aV_0V_1V_2$ (Fig. 14.8). According to the discussion in 1. of this section, the condition that V_b is included in the pyramid is in the spherical model of $\mathbf{R}^4$:

$$(V_b \text{ is in pyramid } V_aV_0V_1V_2) \vee (V_b \text{ is in pyramid } \neg V_a\neg V_0\neg V_1\neg V_2).$$

Thus, the condition is expressed as below:

$$(S_{ba21}, S_{ba02}, S_{ba10} \geq 0)\ \vee\ (S_{ba21}, S_{ba02}, S_{ba10} \leq 0). \tag{14.60}$$

Combining eqs.(14.58), (14.59) and (14.60) yields:

$$\begin{array}{c}((S_{a012}, S_{b012}) \neq (0,0))\\ \wedge\ ((S_{a012} \geq 0 \wedge S_{b012} \leq 0)\ \vee\ (S_{a012} \leq 0 \wedge S_{b012} \geq 0))\\ \wedge\ ((S_{ab12}, S_{ab20}, S_{ab01} \geq 0)\ \vee\ (S_{ab12}, S_{ab20}, S_{ab01} \leq 0)).\end{array} \tag{14.61}$$

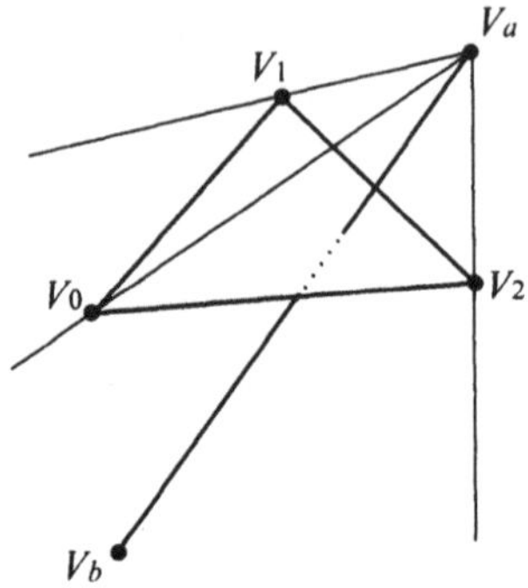

Figure 14.8: Intersection test of line segment and triangle (projective space).

Algebraic derivation

For the line segment and the triangle to have a common intersecting point, the following set of simultaneous homogeneous equations must be satisfied:

$$\xi_0 \boldsymbol{V}_0 + \xi_1 \boldsymbol{V}_1 + \xi_2 \boldsymbol{V}_2 - \xi_a \boldsymbol{V}_a - \xi_b \boldsymbol{V}_b = 0, \tag{14.62}$$
$$(\xi_0, \xi_1, \xi_2 \geq 0 \vee \xi_0, \xi_1, \xi_2 \leq 0) \ \wedge \ (\xi_a, \xi_b \geq 0 \vee \xi_a, \xi_b \leq 0). \tag{14.63}$$

For eq.(14.62) to have a single nontrivial solution, the 4×5 matrix formed by V_0, V_1, V_2, V_a and V_b must have rank 4. This means that at least one of the following determinants:

$$S_{a012}, \ S_{b012}, \ S_{ab12}, \ S_{ab20}, \ S_{ab01}$$

must be non-zero. We already have condition (14.58). Thus eq.(14.62) has a single nontrivial solution, which follows (we assume $S_{012a} \neq 0$):

$$(\xi_0, \xi_1, \xi_2) = \left(\frac{\xi_b S_{b12a}}{S_{012a}}, \frac{\xi_b S_{0b2a}}{S_{012a}}, \frac{\xi_b S_{01ba}}{S_{012a}} \right) = \frac{\xi_b}{S_{012a}} \left(S_{b12a}, S_{0b2a}, S_{01ba} \right), \tag{14.64}$$

$$(\xi_a, \xi_b) = \left(\frac{-\xi_b S_{012b}}{S_{012a}}, \xi_b \right) = \frac{\xi_b}{S_{012a}} (-S_{012b}, S_{012a}). \tag{14.65}$$

Using these results, condition (14.63) can be rewritten as:

$$\begin{aligned} &(S_{b12a}, S_{0b2a}, S_{01ba} \geq 0 \vee S_{b12a}, S_{0b2a}, S_{01ba} \leq 0) \\ &\wedge (-S_{012b}, S_{012a} \geq 0 \vee -S_{012b}, S_{012a} \leq 0). \end{aligned} \tag{14.66}$$

Rearranging and attaching the condition (14.58), we obtain the following condition:

$$\begin{aligned} &((S_{a012}, S_{b012}) \neq (0,0)) \\ \wedge &((S_{a012} \geq 0 \wedge S_{b012} \leq 0) \ \vee \ (S_{a012} \leq 0 \wedge S_{b012} \geq 0)) \\ \wedge &((S_{ab12}, S_{ab20}, S_{ab01} \geq 0) \ \vee \ (S_{ab12}, S_{ab20}, S_{ab01} \leq 0)). \end{aligned} \tag{14.67}$$

Intersection Point

As we stated in the discussion for Section 13.2.4, it is advisable to maintain consistency in the signs to facilitate subsequent processing in $\mathbf{R}^4$, and so we present below only the intersecting point that corresponds to the positive conditions of eq.(14.63).

The intersecting point V can be expressed either as a point on the homogeneous line segment $V_a V_b$ or that on the homogeneous triangle $V_0 V_1 V_2$, as follows:

Expression in terms of V_a and V_b:

$$V = \begin{cases} \overline{S_{a012}\boldsymbol{V}_b - S_{b012}\boldsymbol{V}_a}, & (S_{a012} \geq 0 \wedge S_{b012} \leq 0), \\ \overline{S_{b012}\boldsymbol{V}_a - S_{a012}\boldsymbol{V}_b}, & (S_{a012} \leq 0 \wedge S_{b012} \geq 0). \end{cases} \tag{14.68}$$

Expression in terms of V_0, V_1 and V_2:

$$V = \begin{cases} \overline{S_{ab12}\boldsymbol{V}_0 + S_{ab20}\boldsymbol{V}_1 + S_{ab01}\boldsymbol{V}_2}, & (S_{ab12}, S_{ab20}, S_{ab01} \geq 0), \\ \overline{-S_{ab12}\boldsymbol{V}_0 - S_{ab20}\boldsymbol{V}_1 - S_{ab01}\boldsymbol{V}_2}, & (S_{ab12}, S_{ab20}, S_{ab01} \leq 0). \end{cases} \tag{14.69}$$

5. **Intersection of two line segments**

We now derive the condition in classical projective space for two homogeneous line segments, V_0V_1 and V_aV_b, to intersect.

First we attach the condition:

$$S_{01ab} = 0$$

for the two lines to lie on a same plane.

Geometric derivation

To determine whether the two line segments intersect, we employ the sign zones relative to a triangle discussed in Section 4.6 (see Fig. 14.9), using here the triangle $V_0V_1V_a$.

We see that the line segment V_aV_b intersects with V_0V_1 when V_b lies in the $++-$ zone (see Fig.14.9(a)), while it intersects with $\neg V_0 \neg V_1$ when V_b lies in the $---$ zone (see Fig. 14.9(b)).

Using vectors defined by Plücker coordinates, this is expressed as follows:

$$\begin{aligned} &(S_{01ab} = 0) \wedge \\ &((\boldsymbol{F}_{01a} \cdot \boldsymbol{F}_{b1a} \geq 0 \wedge \boldsymbol{F}_{01a} \cdot \boldsymbol{F}_{0ba} \geq 0 \wedge \boldsymbol{F}_{01a} \cdot \boldsymbol{F}_{01b} \leq 0) \\ &\vee (\boldsymbol{F}_{01a} \cdot \boldsymbol{F}_{b1a} \leq 0 \wedge \boldsymbol{F}_{01a} \cdot \boldsymbol{F}_{0ba} \leq 0 \wedge \boldsymbol{F}_{01a} \cdot \boldsymbol{F}_{01b} \leq 0)), \end{aligned} \tag{14.70}$$

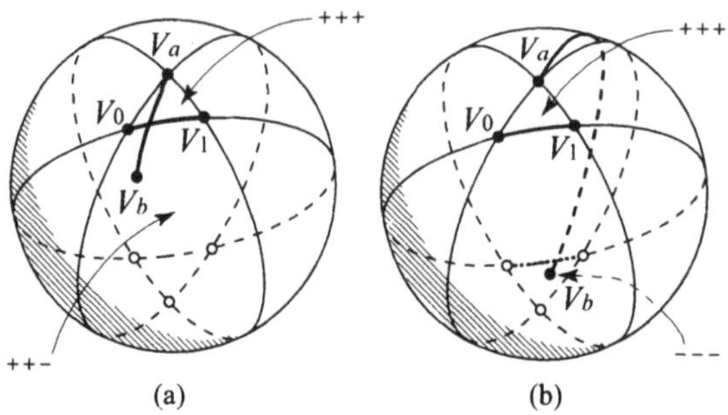

Figure 14.9: Intersections of two line segments.

which can be simplified as:

$$(S_{01ab} = 0) \wedge (\boldsymbol{F}_{01a} \cdot \boldsymbol{F}_{01b},\ \boldsymbol{F}_{ab0} \cdot \boldsymbol{F}_{ab1} \leq 0). \tag{14.71}$$

Algebraic derivation

The same condition can also be derived by solving the following equation:

$$\boldsymbol{V} = \xi_0 \boldsymbol{V}_0 + \xi_1 \boldsymbol{V}_1 = \xi_a \boldsymbol{V}_a + \xi_b \boldsymbol{V}_b, \tag{14.72}$$

$$(\xi_0, \xi_1 \geq 0 \vee \xi_0, \xi_1 \leq 0)\ \wedge\ (\xi_a, \xi_b \geq 0 \vee \xi_a, \xi_b \leq 0). \tag{14.73}$$

Note here that when the homogeneous equation (14.72), consisting of four simultaneous equations, is solved for the three variables, ξ_0, ξ_1 and ξ_a, four solution sets are possible depending on which equations are chosen.

We shall let f_{012} represent one of the four Plücker coordinates of the plane defined by the three points:

$$F_{012} = \overline{(A_{012}, B_{012}, C_{012}, D_{012})},$$

that is,

$$f_{012} \in \{A_{012}, B_{012}, C_{012}, D_{012}\}. \tag{14.74}$$

Using this notation, we obtain the following ratio for ξ_0, ξ_1, ξ_a and ξ_b:

$$\xi_0 : \xi_1 : \xi_a : \xi_b = f_{b1a} : f_{0ba} : -f_{01b} : f_{01a}. \tag{14.75}$$

Substituting this into eq.(14.73), we obtain the following result:

$$\begin{gathered}((f_{01a} \geq 0, f_{01b} \leq 0) \vee (f_{01a} \leq 0, f_{01b} \geq 0)) \\ \wedge\ ((f_{ab0} \geq 0, f_{ab1} \leq 0) \vee (f_{ab0} \leq 0, f_{ab1} \geq 0)).\end{gathered} \tag{14.76}$$

By attaching to this the coplanarity condition above, we have the final condition for the two line segments to intersect as follows:

With respect to $f_{01a}, f_{01b}, f_{ab0}, f_{ab1}$ which include at least one non-zero element,

$$
\begin{gathered}
(S_{01ab} = 0) \wedge \\
(((f_{01a} \geq 0, f_{01b} \leq 0) \vee (f_{01a} \leq 0, f_{01b} \geq 0)) \\
\wedge ((f_{ab0} \geq 0, f_{ab1} \leq 0) \vee (f_{ab0} \leq 0, f_{ab1} \geq 0))).
\end{gathered}
\tag{14.77}
$$

In this expression, the vectors of eq.(14.71) are represented by their components. In other words, vectors $\boldsymbol{F}_{01a}$ and $\boldsymbol{F}_{01b}$ represent the same plane but have reverse orientations; and similarly for vectors $\boldsymbol{F}_{ab0}$ and $\boldsymbol{F}_{ab1}$. So the two vectors representing the same plane have components of opposite signs, which is expressed by eq.(14.77).

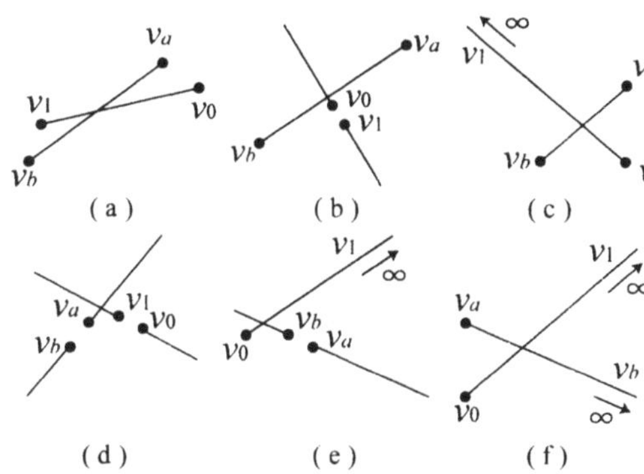

Figure 14.10: Various intersection cases of two line segments (classical projective space).

Intersection Point

As we stated in the discussion for Section 13.2.4, it is advisable to maintain consistency in the signs to facilitate subsequent processing in $\mathbf{R}^4$, and so we present below only the intersection point that corresponds to the positive conditions of eq.(14.73).

Expression in terms of V_0 and V_1:

$$
V = \begin{cases} \overline{f_{ab0}\boldsymbol{V}_1 - f_{ab1}\boldsymbol{V}_0}, & (f_{ab0} \geq 0 \wedge f_{ab1} \leq 0), \\ \overline{f_{ab1}\boldsymbol{V}_0 - f_{ab0}\boldsymbol{V}_1}, & (f_{ab0} \leq 0 \wedge f_{ab1} \geq 0). \end{cases} \tag{14.78}
$$

Expression in terms of V_a and V_b:

$$
V = \begin{cases} \overline{f_{01a}\boldsymbol{V}_b - f_{01b}\boldsymbol{V}_a}, & (f_{01a} \geq 0 \wedge f_{01b} \leq 0), \\ \overline{f_{01b}\boldsymbol{V}_a - f_{01a}\boldsymbol{V}_b}, & (f_{01a} \leq 0 \wedge f_{01b} \geq 0). \end{cases} \tag{14.79}
$$

Eqs.(14.71) and (14.77) each applies in a simple, unified form, to various intersecting cases as shown in Fig. 14.10.

14.4.2 Dual Simplices in Classical Projective Space

The interference conditions between dual homogeneous simplices in classical projective space form a dual relationship to those between homogeneous simplices in classical projective space.

1. **Containment of a plane in a dual tetrahedron**

   The condition in classical projective space for a dual homogeneous tetrahedron $\gamma_0\gamma_1\gamma_2\gamma_3$ to contain a homogeneous plane γ_a and the condition for a homogeneous tetrahedron to contain a homogeneous point form a dual relationship.

   From eq.(14.27), therefore, we have:

$$(T_{a123}, T_{a032}, T_{a013}, T_{a021} \geq 0) \vee (T_{a123}, T_{a032}, T_{a013}, T_{a021} \leq 0). \quad (14.80)$$

   When partitioning up a dual homogeneous tetrahedron using the homogeneous plane γ_a, it is advisable to use the following vector $\boldsymbol{\gamma}$ instead of vector $\boldsymbol{\gamma}_a$ to maintain consistency in the vector signs:

$$\begin{cases} \textbf{If } ((T_{0123} > 0) \wedge (T_{a123}, T_{a032}, T_{a013}, T_{a021} \geq 0)) \\ \vee((T_{0123} < 0) \wedge (T_{a123}, T_{a032}, T_{a013}, T_{a021} \leq 0)) \\ \qquad \textbf{then } \boldsymbol{\gamma} = \boldsymbol{\gamma}_a \\ \qquad \textbf{else} \\ \textbf{if } ((T_{0123} > 0) \wedge (T_{a123}, T_{a032}, T_{a013}, T_{a021} \leq 0)) \\ \vee((T_{0123} < 0) \wedge (T_{a123}, T_{a032}, T_{a013}, T_{a021} \geq 0)) \\ \qquad \textbf{then } \boldsymbol{\gamma} = -\boldsymbol{\gamma}_a. \end{cases} \quad (14.81)$$

2. **Containment of a plane in a dual triangle**

   The condition in classical projective space for a dual homogeneous triangle $\gamma_0\gamma_1\gamma_2$ to contain a homogeneous plane γ_a and the condition for a homogeneous triangle to contain a homogeneous point form a dual relationship.

   From eq.(14.33), therefore, we have:

$$\begin{gathered} (T_{a012} = 0) \wedge \\ ((\boldsymbol{\pi}_{012} \cdot \boldsymbol{\pi}_{a12} \geq 0 \ \wedge \ \boldsymbol{\pi}_{012} \cdot \boldsymbol{\pi}_{a20} \geq 0 \ \wedge \ \boldsymbol{\pi}_{012} \cdot \boldsymbol{\pi}_{a01} \geq 0) \\ \vee \ (\boldsymbol{\pi}_{012} \cdot \boldsymbol{\pi}_{a12} \leq 0 \ \wedge \ \boldsymbol{\pi}_{012} \cdot \boldsymbol{\pi}_{a20} \leq 0 \ \wedge \ \boldsymbol{\pi}_{012} \cdot \boldsymbol{\pi}_{a01} \leq 0)). \end{gathered} \quad (14.82)$$

3. **Containment of a plane in a dual line segment**

   The condition in classical projective space for a dual homogeneous line segment $\gamma_0\gamma_1$ to contain a homogeneous plane γ_a and the condition for a homogeneous line segment to contain a homogeneous point form a dual relationship.

   From eq.(14.47), therefore, we have:

$$(\boldsymbol{\pi}_{a01} = \mathbf{0}) \wedge (\boldsymbol{\lambda}_{a0} \cdot \boldsymbol{\lambda}_{a1} \leq 0). \quad (14.83)$$

4. **Containment of a common plane in a dual line segment and a dual triangle**

   The condition for a dual homogeneous line segment $\gamma_a\gamma_b$ and a dual homogeneous triangle $\gamma_0\gamma_1\gamma_2$ in classical projective space to have a single common homogeneous plane, and the condition for a homogeneous line segment and a homogeneous triangle to have a single intersection point form a dual relationship.

   From eq.(14.67), therefore, we have:

$$\begin{array}{c} ((T_{a012}, T_{b012}) \neq (0,0)) \\ \wedge\ ((T_{a012} \geq 0 \wedge T_{b012} \leq 0)\ \vee\ (T_{a012} \leq 0 \wedge T_{b012} \geq 0)) \\ \wedge\ ((T_{ab12}, T_{ab20}, T_{ab01} \geq 0)\ \vee\ (T_{ab12}, T_{ab20}, T_{ab01} \leq 0)). \end{array} \tag{14.84}$$

   The common homogeneous plane γ can be expressed either in terms of γ_a and γ_b or in terms of γ_0, γ_1 and γ_2. It is advisable to use the following common plane from the reason mentioned before:

   Homogeneous plane in terms of γ_a and γ_b

$$\gamma = \begin{cases} \overline{T_{a012}\gamma_b - T_{b012}\gamma_a}, & (T_{a012} \geq 0 \wedge T_{b012} \leq 0), \\ \overline{T_{b012}\gamma_a - T_{a012}\gamma_b}, & (T_{a012} \leq 0 \wedge T_{b012} \geq 0). \end{cases} \tag{14.85}$$

   Homogeneous plane in terms of γ_0, γ_1 and γ_2

$$\gamma = \begin{cases} \overline{T_{ab12}\gamma_0 + T_{ab20}\gamma_1 + T_{ab01}\gamma_2}, & (T_{ab12}, T_{ab20}, T_{ab01} \geq 0), \\ \overline{-T_{ab12}\gamma_0 - T_{ab20}\gamma_1 - T_{ab01}\gamma_2}, & (T_{ab12}, T_{ab20}, T_{ab01} \leq 0). \end{cases} \tag{14.86}$$

5. **Containment of a common plane in two dual line segments**

   The condition for two dual homogeneous line segments $\gamma_a\gamma_b$ and $\gamma_0\gamma_1$ in classical projective space to have a common homogeneous plane, and the condition for two homogeneous line segments V_0V_1 and V_aV_b to intersect, form a dual relationship (see Fig. 14.11).

   From eq.(14.71), therefore, we have:

$$(T_{01ab} = 0)\ \wedge (\boldsymbol{\pi}_{01a} \cdot \boldsymbol{\pi}_{01b},\ \boldsymbol{\pi}_{ab0} \cdot \boldsymbol{\pi}_{ab1} \leq 0). \tag{14.87}$$

   Also, from eq.(14.77), we have:

   With respect to $p_{01a}, p_{01b}, p_{ab0}, p_{ab1}$ which include at least one non-zero element,

$$\begin{array}{c} (T_{01ab} = 0)\ \wedge \\ (((p_{01a} \geq 0, p_{01b} \leq 0) \vee (p_{01a} \leq 0, p_{01b} \geq 0)) \\ \wedge\ ((p_{ab0} \geq 0, p_{ab1} \leq 0) \vee (p_{ab0} \leq 0, p_{ab1} \geq 0))). \end{array} \tag{14.88}$$

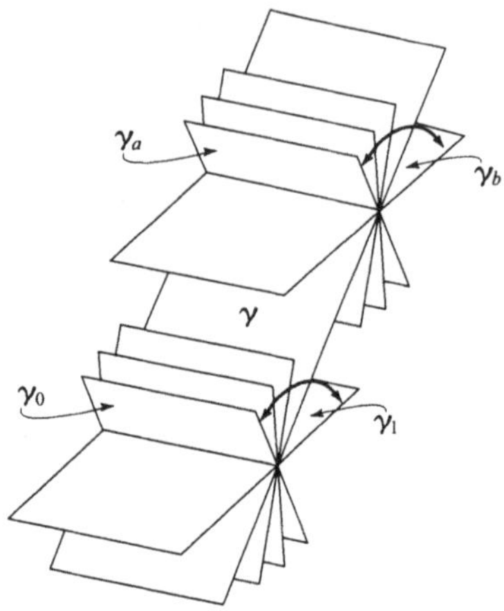

Figure 14.11: Common plane of two dual homogeneous line segments.

Here, p_{012} represents one of the four Plücker coefficients of the point defined by the three planes:

$$\pi_{012} = \overline{(w_{012}, x_{012}, y_{012}, z_{012})},$$

that is,

$$p_{012} \in \{w_{012}, x_{012}, y_{012}, z_{012}\}. \tag{14.89}$$

It is advisable to use the common plane γ between the two dual homogeneous line segments $\gamma_a\gamma_b$ and $\gamma_0\gamma_1$ from the reason mentioned before:

Expression in terms of γ_0 and γ_1

$$\gamma = \begin{cases} \overline{p_{ab0}\gamma_1 - p_{ab1}\gamma_0}, & (p_{ab0} \geq 0 \wedge p_{ab1} \leq 0), \\ \overline{p_{ab1}\gamma_0 - p_{ab0}\gamma_1}, & (p_{ab0} \leq 0 \wedge p_{ab1} \geq 0). \end{cases} \tag{14.90}$$

Expression in terms of γ_a and γ_b

$$\gamma = \begin{cases} \overline{p_{01a}\gamma_b - p_{01b}\gamma_a}, & (p_{01a} \geq 0 \wedge p_{01b} \leq 0), \\ \overline{p_{01b}\gamma_a - p_{01a}\gamma_b}, & (p_{01a} \leq 0 \wedge p_{01b} \geq 0). \end{cases} \tag{14.91}$$

14.4.3 Simplices in Two-sided Space

1. **Containment of a point in a tetrahedron**

   We now derive the condition in two-sided space for a homogeneous point V_a to lie inside a homogeneous tetrahedron $V_0V_1V_2V_3$.

Geometric derivation

Prior to considering this problem, let us first consider a problem in plane geometry, i.e., the containment of a point V_a in a triangle $V_0V_1V_2$ (see 2. of C.5.2).

The condition in this case is, in the spherical model of $\mathbf{R}^3$, simply the one for V_a to be contained in $V_0V_1V_2$. It is expressed, depending on the orientations of the triangle, as:

$$\begin{aligned}&(S_{012} > 0 \wedge S_{a12}, S_{a20}, S_{a01} \geq 0)\\ \vee\ &(S_{012} < 0 \wedge S_{a12}, S_{a20}, S_{a01} \leq 0).\end{aligned} \tag{14.92}$$

The second term of the first line above is that V_a exists in the positive half-spaces of all the three oriented lines V_1V_2, V_2V_0 and V_0V_1, and the second term of the second line above is that it exists in the negative half-spaces of these lines.

Analogously to the two-dimensional case above, the containment condition of V_a in the tetrahedron $V_0V_1V_2V_3$ is in the spherical model of $\mathbf{R}^4$, simply the one for V_a to be in the tetrahedron $V_0V_1V_2V_3$. This is broken down into as follows:

$$\begin{aligned}&((V_0V_1V_2V_3 \text{ is positive}) \wedge (V_a \text{ is in the positive tetrahedron}))\\ \vee\ &((V_0V_1V_2V_3 \text{ is negative}) \wedge (V_a \text{ is in the negative tetrahedron})).\end{aligned}$$

The second term of the first line above is that V_a exists in the positive half-spaces of all the four oriented planes $V_1V_2V_3$, $V_0V_3V_2$, $V_0V_1V_3$ and $V_0V_2V_1$, and the second term of the second line above is that it exists in the negative half-spaces of these planes.

Refering to eq.(14.21), we have:

$$\begin{aligned}&(S_{0123} > 0 \wedge S_{a123}, S_{a032}, S_{a013}, S_{a021} \geq 0)\\ \vee\ &(S_{0123} < 0 \wedge S_{a123}, S_{a032}, S_{a013}, S_{a021} \leq 0).\end{aligned} \tag{14.93}$$

Algebraic derivation

The condition for V_a to lie inside the tetrahedron is given by [3]:

$$\xi_0 \boldsymbol{V}_0 + \xi_1 \boldsymbol{V}_1 + \xi_2 \boldsymbol{V}_2 + \xi_3 \boldsymbol{V}_3 = \boldsymbol{V}_a, \tag{14.95}$$

$$\xi_0, \xi_1, \xi_2, \xi_3 \geq 0. \tag{14.96}$$

Since V_0, V_1, V_2 and V_3 are assumed to be linearly independent, we have:

$$S_{0123} \neq 0.$$

[3] Eq.(14.95) must be written as follows:

$$\xi_0 \boldsymbol{V}_0 + \xi_1 \boldsymbol{V}_1 + \xi_2 \boldsymbol{V}_2 + \xi_3 \boldsymbol{V}_3 = k\boldsymbol{V}_a, \quad k > 0. \tag{14.94}$$

Since the homogeneous parameters play the role of k, it is omitted for simplicity. The same simplification is taken throughout.

Thus, eq.(14.95) has a unique solution for ξ_0, ξ_1, ξ_2 and ξ_3, as given by:

$$(\xi_0, \xi_1, \xi_2, \xi_3) = \left(\frac{S_{a123}}{S_{0123}}, \frac{S_{0a23}}{S_{0123}}, \frac{S_{01a3}}{S_{0123}}, \frac{S_{012a}}{S_{0123}} \right). \tag{14.97}$$

By comparing eqs.(14.96) and (14.97), we have:

$$\left(\frac{S_{a123}}{S_{0123}}, \frac{S_{0a23}}{S_{0123}}, \frac{S_{01a3}}{S_{0123}}, \frac{S_{012a}}{S_{0123}} \right) \geq 0. \tag{14.98}$$

Thus, the final result is given by:

$$\begin{aligned} &(S_{0123} > 0 \wedge S_{a123}, S_{a032}, S_{a013}, S_{a021} \geq 0) \\ \vee\ &(S_{0123} < 0 \wedge S_{a123}, S_{a032}, S_{a013}, S_{a021} \leq 0). \end{aligned} \tag{14.99}$$

The first line is the condition for the point V_a to lie inside a positive tetrahedron (Fig. 14.12(a)), while the second line is that for the point V_a to lie inside a negative tetrahedron (Fig. 14.12(b)).

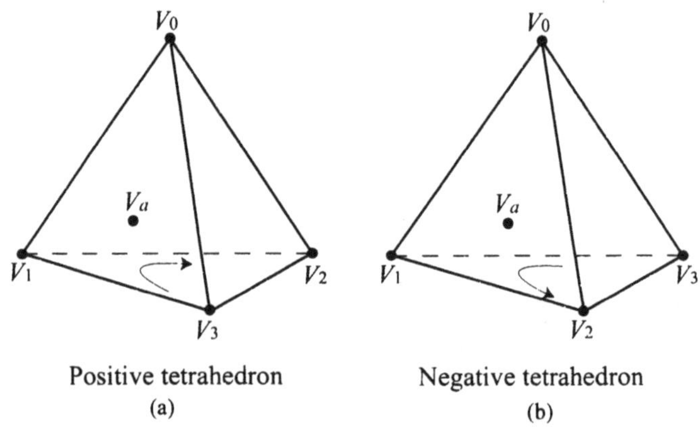

Figure 14.12: Containment test of point in tetrahedron (two-sided space).

Partition

In the case of two-sided space, we can partition the tetrahedron by simply using V_a as a partitioning point.

2. **Containment of a point in a triangle**

   We now derive the condition in two-sided space for a homogeneous point V_a to lie inside a homogeneous triangle $V_0V_1V_2$.

   First, we add the condition such that V_a and $V_0V_1V_2$ are coplanar, which is:

$$S_{a012} = 0. \tag{14.100}$$

Geometric derivation

The condition for the point V_a to be contained in the coplanar triangle $V_0V_1V_2$ is expressed in the spherical model simply as the condition for V_a to be contained in the triangle $V_0V_1V_2$ (see Fig. 14.13).

Referring to Fig. 4.29, this condition can be expressed using vectors defined by Plücker coordinates of plane as follows:

$$\boldsymbol{F}_{012} \cdot \boldsymbol{F}_{a12},\ \boldsymbol{F}_{012} \cdot \boldsymbol{F}_{a20},\ \boldsymbol{F}_{012} \cdot \boldsymbol{F}_{a01} \geq 0. \tag{14.101}$$

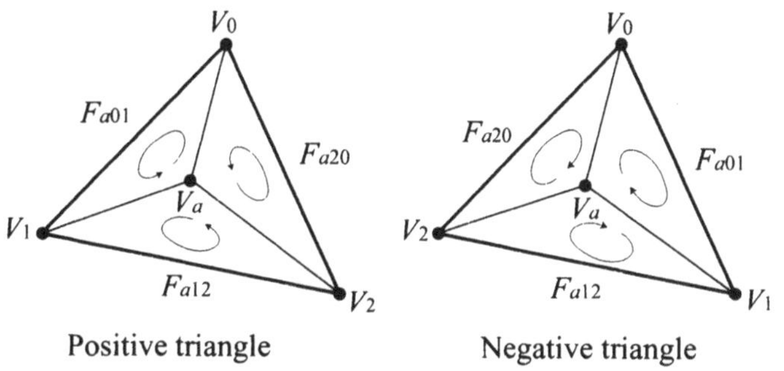

Figure 14.13: Containment test of point in triangle (1) (two-sided space).

Together with the coplanarity condition, the final condition is written as follows:

$$\begin{array}{c}(S_{a012} = 0) \wedge \\ (\boldsymbol{F}_{012} \cdot \boldsymbol{F}_{a12},\ \boldsymbol{F}_{012} \cdot \boldsymbol{F}_{a20},\ \boldsymbol{F}_{012} \cdot \boldsymbol{F}_{a01} \geq 0).\end{array} \tag{14.102}$$

This condition holds regardless of whether the triangle is positive or negative (see Fig. 14.13). Note also that, unlike the case in classical projective space, the interior points of the antipodal triangle $\neg V_0 \neg V_1 \neg V_2$ are excluded (see Fig. 14.14).

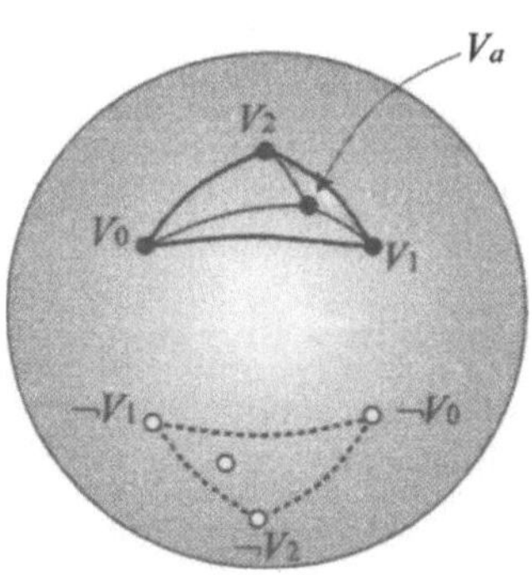

Figure 14.14: Containment test of a point in a triangle (2) (two-sided space).

Algebraic derivation

The condition for the point V_a to lie inside the triangle $V_0V_1V_2$ is given by (see Section 9.2):

$$\xi_0 \boldsymbol{V}_0 + \xi_1 \boldsymbol{V}_1 + \xi_2 \boldsymbol{V}_2 = \boldsymbol{V}_a, \tag{14.103}$$

$$\xi_0, \xi_1, \xi_2 \geq 0. \tag{14.104}$$

We shall let f_{012} represent one of the four Plücker coordinates of the plane defined by the three points.

Since

$$(A_{012}, B_{012}, C_{012}, D_{012}) \neq (0,0,0,0),$$

we can obtain ξ_0, ξ_1 and ξ_2 using the notation above. We assume

$$f_{012} \neq 0. \tag{14.105}$$

Then

$$\begin{aligned}(\xi_0, \xi_1, \xi_2) &= \left(\frac{f_{a12}}{f_{012}}, \frac{f_{0a2}}{f_{012}}, \frac{f_{01a}}{f_{012}}\right) \\ &= \frac{1}{f_{012}}(f_{a12}, f_{a20}, f_{a01}).\end{aligned} \tag{14.106}$$

From eq.(14.104), therefore, we have:

$$\begin{aligned}&(f_{012} > 0 \wedge f_{a12}, f_{a20}, f_{a01} \geq 0) \\ \vee\ &(f_{012} < 0 \wedge f_{a12}, f_{a20}, f_{a01} \leq 0).\end{aligned} \tag{14.107}$$

Together with eqs.(14.100) and (14.105), we have:

$$\begin{aligned}&\text{With respect to } f_{012} \neq 0\ (\in \{A_{012}, B_{012}, C_{012}, D_{012}\}), \\ &(S_{a012} = 0) \wedge \\ &((f_{012} > 0\ \wedge\ f_{a12}, f_{a20}, f_{a01} \geq 0) \\ &\vee\ (f_{012} < 0\ \wedge\ f_{a12}, f_{a20}, f_{a01} \leq 0)).\end{aligned} \tag{14.108}$$

This expression represents eq.(14.102) in terms of its vector components.

Partition

In the case of two-sided space, we can partition the triangle by simply using V_a as a partitioning point.

3. **Containment of a point in a line segment**

We derive the condition in two-sided space for a homogeneous point V_a to lie on a homogeneous line segment V_0V_1.

First, we add the condition that the point V_a and the line segment V_0V_1 are collinear, which is given by:

$$\boldsymbol{F}_{a01} = \boldsymbol{0}.$$

Geometric derivation

The condition for the point V_a to be contained in the collinear line segment V_0V_1 is expressed in the spherical model as the condition for the two line segments V_0V_a and V_aV_1 to have the same orientation as the line segment V_0V_1 (see Fig. 14.15):

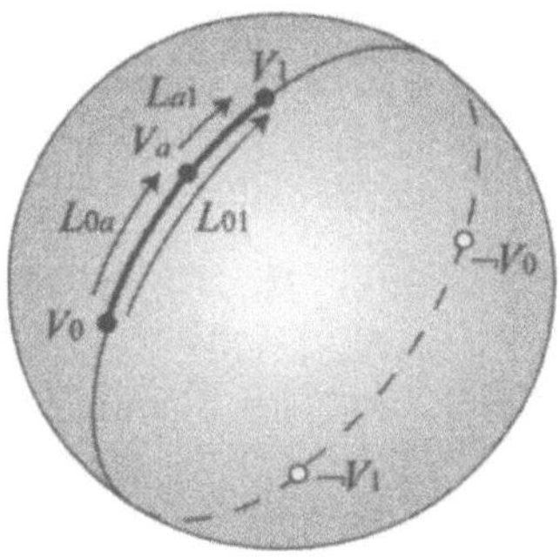

Figure 14.15: Containment test of point in line segment (two-sided space).

$$\boldsymbol{L}_{01} \cdot \boldsymbol{L}_{0a} \geq 0 \ \wedge \ \boldsymbol{L}_{01} \cdot \boldsymbol{L}_{a1} \geq 0. \tag{14.109}$$

Together with the collinearity condition above, the final condition is written as follows:

$$(\boldsymbol{F}_{a01} = \boldsymbol{0}) \wedge (\boldsymbol{L}_{01} \cdot \boldsymbol{L}_{a0} \leq 0) \wedge (\boldsymbol{L}_{01} \cdot \boldsymbol{L}_{a1} \geq 0). \tag{14.110}$$

Note here that, unlike in classical projective space, the interior points of antipodal line segment $\neg V_0 \neg V_1$ are excluded.

Algebraic derivation

The condition for the point V_a to be contained in the line segment V_0V_1 is expressed as follows (see Section 9.2):

$$\xi_0 \boldsymbol{V}_0 + \xi_1 \boldsymbol{V}_1 = \boldsymbol{V}_a, \tag{14.111}$$

$$\xi_0, \xi_1 \geq 0. \tag{14.112}$$

Note here that when the homogeneous equation (14.111), consisting of four simultaneous equations, is solved for the two variables, ξ_0 and ξ_1, six solution sets are possible depending on which equations are chosen.

We shall let l_{01} represent one of the six Plücker coordinates of the line defined by the two points.

Since

$$(P_{01}, Q_{01}, R_{01}, S_{01}, T_{01}, U_{01}) \neq (0,0,0,0,0,0),$$

we can obtain ξ_0 and ξ_1 using the notation above. We assume

$$l_{01} \neq 0. \tag{14.113}$$

Then

$$(\xi_0, \xi_1) = (\frac{l_{a1}}{l_{01}}, \frac{l_{0a}}{l_{01}}). \tag{14.114}$$

From eq.(14.112), we have:

$$\begin{aligned} &(l_{01} > 0 \wedge l_{0a} \geq 0 \wedge l_{a1} \geq 0) \\ \vee\ &(l_{01} < 0 \wedge l_{0a} \leq 0 \wedge l_{a1} \leq 0). \end{aligned} \tag{14.115}$$

Combining eqs.(14.115) and (14.113) with the collinearity condition above gives the final result:

$$\begin{aligned} &\text{With respect to } l_{01} \neq 0\ (\in \{P_{01}, Q_{01}, R_{01}, S_{01}, T_{01}, U_{01}\}), \\ &\qquad (\boldsymbol{F}_{a01} = \mathbf{0}) \\ &\wedge\ ((l_{01} > 0 \wedge l_{a0} \leq 0 \wedge l_{a1} \geq 0) \\ &\vee\ \ (l_{01} < 0 \wedge l_{a0} \geq 0 \wedge l_{a1} \leq 0)). \end{aligned} \tag{14.116}$$

This expression represents eq.(14.110) in terms of its vector components.

Partition

In the case of two-sided space, we can partition the line segment by simply using V_a as a partitioning point.

4. **Intersection of a line segment and a triangle**

Here we derive the condition in two-sided space for a homogeneous line segment V_aV_b and a homogeneous triangle $V_0V_1V_2$ to intersect at a single point.

We attach the condition:

$$(S_{a012},\ S_{b012}) \neq (0, 0) \tag{14.117}$$

for the line segment and the triangle not to be coplanar.

Geometric derivation

First, in $\mathbf{R}^4$ we require the endpoints of the line segment lie in the opposite half spaces of the triangle plane $V_0V_1V_2$. There are two cases; where the triangle is oriented two-way (Fig. 14.16). These conditions are expressed as follows:

$$(S_{a012} \geq 0 \wedge S_{b012} \leq 0)\ \vee\ (S_{a012} \leq 0 \wedge S_{b012} \geq 0). \tag{14.118}$$

Second, we must further require that the line segment intersects the interior of the triangle.

Now, let us consider a triangular pyramid $V_aV_0V_1V_2$ with respect to each case expressed in eq.(14.118). For the line segment to intersect the interior of the triangle, V_b must be in the pyramid. There are two types of

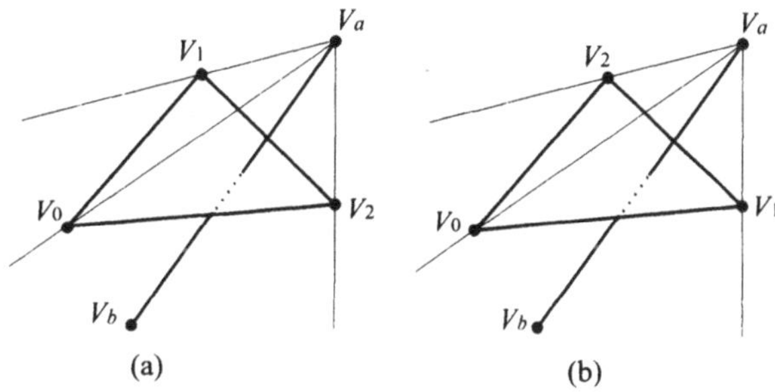

Figure 14.16: Intersection test of line segment with triangle (two-sided space).

pyramids; positive and negative. Thus, the containment condition of V_b in these pyramids is expressed as follows:

$$\begin{aligned} &(S_{a012} \geq 0 \wedge S_{b012} \leq 0 \wedge S_{ba21}, S_{ba02}, S_{ba10} \geq 0) \\ \vee\ &(S_{a012} \leq 0 \wedge S_{b012} \geq 0 \wedge S_{ba21}, S_{ba02}, S_{ba10} \leq 0). \end{aligned} \tag{14.119}$$

Attaching eq.(14.117) to eq.(14.119) and rearranging yields:

$$\begin{aligned} &((S_{a012},\ S_{b012}) \neq (0,0)) \\ \wedge\ &((S_{a012} \geq 0 \wedge S_{b012} \leq 0 \wedge S_{ab12}, S_{ab20}, S_{ab01} \geq 0) \\ \vee\ &(S_{a012} \leq 0 \wedge S_{b012} \geq 0 \wedge S_{ab12}, S_{ab20}, S_{ab01} \leq 0)). \end{aligned} \tag{14.120}$$

Algebraic derivation

For the line segment and the triangle to have an intersecting point, the following equation must be satisfied:

$$\xi_0 \boldsymbol{V}_0 + \xi_1 \boldsymbol{V}_1 + \xi_2 \boldsymbol{V}_2 - \xi_a \boldsymbol{V}_a - \xi_b \boldsymbol{V}_b = 0, \tag{14.121}$$

$$(\xi_0, \xi_1, \xi_2 \geq 0) \wedge (\xi_a, \xi_b \geq 0). \tag{14.122}$$

For eq.(14.121) to have a single nontrivial solution, the 4×5 matrix formed by V_0, V_1, V_2, V_a and V_b must have rank 4. This means that at least one of the following determinants:

$$S_{a012},\ S_{b012},\ S_{ab12},\ S_{ab20},\ S_{ab01}$$

must be non-zero. We already have condition (14.117). Thus eq.(14.121) has a single nontrivial solution, which follows (we assume $S_{012a} \neq 0$):

$$(\xi_0, \xi_1, \xi_2) = \left(\frac{\xi_b S_{b12a}}{S_{012a}}, \frac{\xi_b S_{0b2a}}{S_{012a}}, \frac{\xi_b S_{01ba}}{S_{012a}} \right) = \frac{\xi_b}{S_{012a}} (S_{b12a}, S_{0b2a}, S_{01ba}), \tag{14.123}$$

$$(\xi_a, \xi_b) = \left(\frac{-\xi_b S_{012b}}{S_{012a}}, \xi_b \right) = \frac{\xi_b}{S_{012a}} (-S_{012b}, S_{012a}). \tag{14.124}$$

Using these results, eq.(14.122) can be rewritten as:

$$\begin{aligned}&(-S_{012b}, S_{012a} \geq 0 \wedge S_{b12a}, S_{0b2a}, S_{01ba} \geq 0)\\ \vee\ &(-S_{012b}, S_{012a} \leq 0 \wedge S_{b12a}, S_{0b2a}, S_{01ba} \leq 0).\end{aligned} \tag{14.125}$$

Rearranging and attaching the condition (14.117), we obtain the following condition:

$$\begin{aligned}&((S_{a012}, S_{b012}) \neq (0,0))\\ \wedge\ &((S_{a012} \geq 0 \wedge S_{b012} \leq 0 \wedge S_{ab12}, S_{ab20}, S_{ab01} \geq 0)\\ \vee\ &\ (S_{a012} \leq 0 \wedge S_{b012} \geq 0 \wedge S_{ab12}, S_{ab20}, S_{ab01} \leq 0)),\end{aligned} \tag{14.126}$$

which is exactly the same as eq.(14.120).

Intersection Point

The intersection point V can be expressed either in terms of V_a and V_b or in terms of V_0, V_1 and V_2, as follows:

Expression in terms of V_a and V_b

$$V = \begin{cases} \overline{S_{a012}\boldsymbol{V}_b - S_{b012}\boldsymbol{V}_a}, & (S_{a012} \geq 0 \wedge S_{b012} \leq 0),\\[2ex] \overline{S_{b012}\boldsymbol{V}_a - S_{a012}\boldsymbol{V}_b}, & (S_{a012} \leq 0 \wedge S_{b012} \geq 0). \end{cases} \tag{14.127}$$

Expression in terms of V_0, V_1 and V_2

$$V = \begin{cases} \overline{S_{ab12}\boldsymbol{V}_0 + S_{ab20}\boldsymbol{V}_1 + S_{ab01}\boldsymbol{V}_2}, & (S_{ab12}, S_{ab20}, S_{ab01} \geq 0),\\[2ex] \overline{-S_{ab12}\boldsymbol{V}_0 - S_{ab20}\boldsymbol{V}_1 - S_{ab01}\boldsymbol{V}_2}, & (S_{ab12}, S_{ab20}, S_{ab01} \leq 0). \end{cases} \tag{14.128}$$

5. **Intersection of two line segments**

We now derive the condition for two homogeneous line segments, V_0V_1 and V_aV_b, in two-sided space to intersect.

We attach the coplanarity condition:

$$S_{01ab} = 0$$

for the two lines to lie on the same plane.

Geometric derivation

To determine whether the two line segments intersect, we employ the sign zones relative to a triangle in the spherical model, discussed in Section 4.6 (see Fig. 14.17). We see that the line segment V_aV_b intersects V_0V_1 when V_b lies in the $++-$ zone. Using vectors defined by Plücker coordinates of plane, this is expressed as follows:

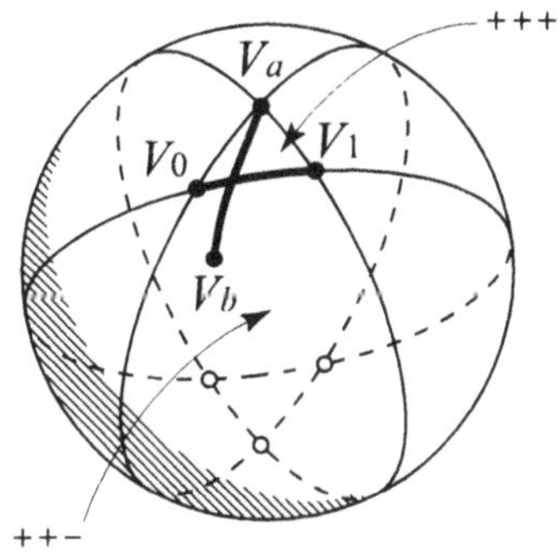

Figure 14.17: Intersection of two line segments (two-sided space).

$$(\boldsymbol{F}_{01a} \cdot \boldsymbol{F}_{b1a} \geq 0) \wedge (\boldsymbol{F}_{01a} \cdot \boldsymbol{F}_{0ba} \geq 0) \wedge (\boldsymbol{F}_{01a} \cdot \boldsymbol{F}_{01b} \leq 0). \qquad (14.129)$$

From the first term, we can substitute $\boldsymbol{F}_{b1a}$ for $\boldsymbol{F}_{01a}$ in the second term to obtain:

$$(\boldsymbol{F}_{01a} \cdot \boldsymbol{F}_{b1a} \geq 0) \wedge (\boldsymbol{F}_{b1a} \cdot \boldsymbol{F}_{0ba} \geq 0) \wedge (\boldsymbol{F}_{01a} \cdot \boldsymbol{F}_{01b} \leq 0).$$

From the second term above, we can substitute $\boldsymbol{F}_{0ba}$ for $\boldsymbol{F}_{b1a}$ in the first term, and then rearrange in a symmetrical manner to obtain:

$$(\boldsymbol{F}_{01a} \cdot \boldsymbol{F}_{01b} \leq 0) \wedge (\boldsymbol{F}_{ab0} \cdot \boldsymbol{F}_{ab1} \leq 0) \wedge (\boldsymbol{F}_{01a} \cdot \boldsymbol{F}_{ab0} \leq 0). \qquad (14.130)$$

To this, we attach the coplanarity condition for the two line segments to obtain the final condition:

$$(S_{01ab} = 0) \wedge (\boldsymbol{F}_{01a} \cdot \boldsymbol{F}_{01b},\ \boldsymbol{F}_{ab0} \cdot \boldsymbol{F}_{ab1},\ \boldsymbol{F}_{01a} \cdot \boldsymbol{F}_{ab0} \leq 0). \qquad (14.131)$$

The first term is the coplanarity condition, and the second and third terms express the condition for two line segments in classical projective space to intersect (see eq.(14.71)).

Note that the condition up to this point does not exclude the case where the antipodal element to a line segment intersects with the other line segment (see Fig. 14.18). We need the fourth term to exclude this possibility.

In Fig. 14.18(a), the orientations of $V_0V_1V_a$ and $V_aV_bV_0$ are both counterclockwise, and those of the same vertices also both clockwise in Fig. 14.18 (b). These cases are rejected by the fourth term of eq.(14.131).

Algebraic derivation

Let us take a different approach to derive the condition for two line segments to intersect. The same condition can be derived by solving the

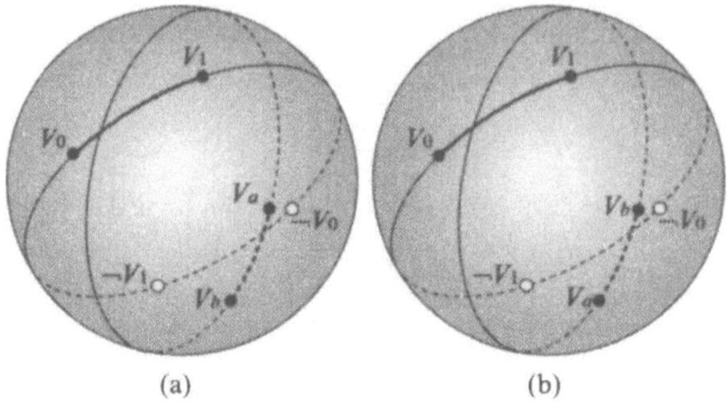

Figure 14.18: Excluding intersection of antipodal line segment.

following equation:

$$\boldsymbol{V} = \xi_0 \boldsymbol{V}_0 + \xi_1 \boldsymbol{V}_1 = \xi_a \boldsymbol{V}_a + \xi_b \boldsymbol{V}_b, \tag{14.132}$$
$$(\xi_0, \xi_1 \geq 0) \wedge (\xi_a, \xi_b \geq 0). \tag{14.133}$$

When the homogeneous equation (14.132), consisting of four simultaneous equations, is solved for the three variables, ξ_0, ξ_1 and ξ_a, four solution sets are possible depending on which equations are chosen.

We shall let f_{012} represent one of the four Plücker coordinates of the plane defined by the three points. Using this notation, we obtain the following relationship among ξ_0, ξ_1, ξ_a and ξ_b:

$$\xi_0 : \xi_1 : \xi_a : \xi_b = f_{b1a} : f_{0ba} : -f_{01b} : f_{01a}. \tag{14.134}$$

Substituting this into eq.(14.133), we obtain the following result:

$$\begin{array}{l}(f_{01a} \geq 0 \wedge f_{01b} \leq 0 \wedge f_{ab0} \leq 0 \wedge f_{ab1} \geq 0) \\ \vee\ (f_{01a} \leq 0 \wedge f_{01b} \geq 0 \wedge f_{ab0} \geq 0 \wedge f_{ab1} \leq 0).\end{array} \tag{14.135}$$

By attaching to this the coplanarity condition for the two line segments, we have the final condition for two line segments to intersect as follows:

With respect to $f_{01a}, f_{01b}, f_{ab0}, f_{ab1}$ which include at least one non-zero element,

$$\begin{array}{c}(S_{01ab} = 0) \wedge \\ ((f_{01a} \geq 0 \wedge f_{01b} \leq 0 \wedge f_{ab0} \leq 0 \wedge f_{ab1} \geq 0) \\ \vee\ (f_{01a} \leq 0 \wedge f_{01b} \geq 0 \wedge f_{ab0} \geq 0 \wedge f_{ab1} \leq 0)).\end{array} \tag{14.136}$$

The vectors of eq.(14.131) are represented in this expression by their components. In other words, vectors $\boldsymbol{F}_{01a}$ and $\boldsymbol{F}_{01b}$ represent the same plane but have reverse orientations; and similarly for vectors $\boldsymbol{F}_{ab0}$ and $\boldsymbol{F}_{ab1}$, and vectors $\boldsymbol{F}_{01a}$ and $\boldsymbol{F}_{ab0}$. So the two vectors representing the same plane have components of opposite signs, which is expressed by eq.(14.136).

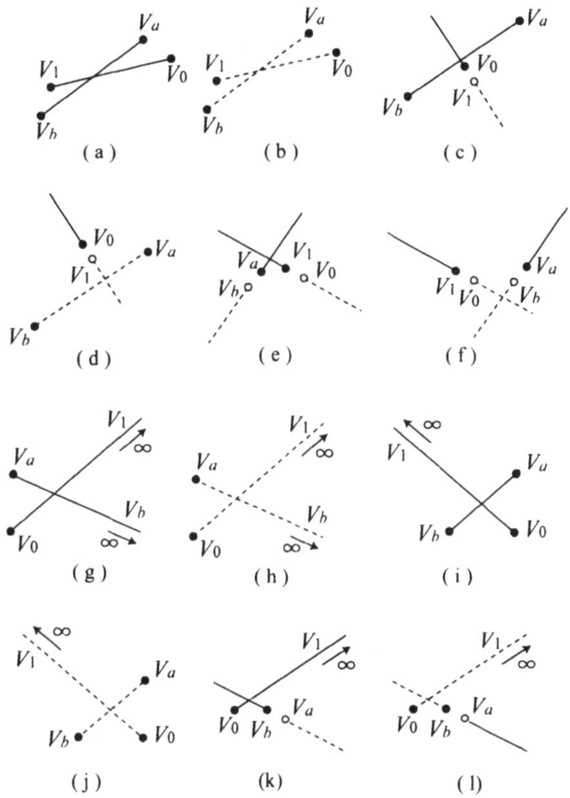

Figure 14.19: Various intersection cases of two line segments (two-sided space).

Note that the condition eq.(14.136) excludes the cases shown in Fig. 14.18.

Intersection Point

We present below the intersection point V.

Expression in terms of V_0 and V_1

$$V = \begin{cases} \overline{f_{ab0}\boldsymbol{V}_1 - f_{ab1}\boldsymbol{V}_0}, & (f_{ab0} \geq 0 \wedge f_{ab1} \leq 0), \\ \overline{f_{ab1}\boldsymbol{V}_0 - f_{ab0}\boldsymbol{V}_1}, & (f_{ab0} \leq 0 \wedge f_{ab1} \geq 0). \end{cases} \tag{14.137}$$

Expression in terms of V_a and V_b

$$V = \begin{cases} \overline{f_{01a}\boldsymbol{V}_b - f_{01b}\boldsymbol{V}_a}, & (f_{01a} \geq 0 \wedge f_{01b} \leq 0), \\ \overline{f_{01b}\boldsymbol{V}_a - f_{01a}\boldsymbol{V}_b}, & (f_{01a} \leq 0 \wedge f_{01b} \geq 0). \end{cases} \tag{14.138}$$

Eqs.(14.131) and (14.136) each applies in a simple, unified form, to various intersecting conditions as shown in Fig. 14.19.

14.4.4 Dual Simplices in Two-sided Space

The interference conditions between dual homogeneous simplices in two-sided space form a dual relationship to those between homogeneous simplices in two-sided space.

1. **Containment of a plane in a dual tetrahedron**

   The condition for a dual homogeneous tetrahedron $\gamma_0\gamma_1\gamma_2\gamma_3$ to contain a homogeneous plane γ_a and the condition for a homogeneous tetrahedron to contain a homogeneous point form a dual relationship.

   So from eq.(14.99), we have:

$$\begin{aligned} &(T_{0123} > 0 \wedge T_{a123}, T_{a032}, T_{a013}, T_{a021} \geq 0) \\ \vee\ &(T_{0123} < 0 \wedge T_{a123}, T_{a032}, T_{a013}, T_{a021} \leq 0). \end{aligned} \tag{14.139}$$

2. **Containment of a plane in a dual triangle**

   The condition in two-sided space for a dual homogeneous triangle $\gamma_0\gamma_1\gamma_2$ to contain a homogeneous plane γ_a and the condition for a homogeneous triangle to contain a homogeneous point form a dual relationship.

   So from eq.(14.102), we have:

$$\begin{gathered} (T_{a012} = 0) \wedge \\ (\boldsymbol{\pi}_{012} \cdot \boldsymbol{\pi}_{a12},\ \boldsymbol{\pi}_{012} \cdot \boldsymbol{\pi}_{a20},\ \boldsymbol{\pi}_{012} \cdot \boldsymbol{\pi}_{a01} \geq 0). \end{gathered} \tag{14.140}$$

3. **Containment of a plane in a dual line segment**

   The condition in two-sided space for a dual homogeneous line segment $\gamma_0\gamma_1$ to contain a homogeneous plane γ_a and the condition for a homogeneous line segment to contain a homogeneous point form a dual relationship.

   From eq.(14.110), therefore, we have:

$$(\boldsymbol{\pi}_{a01} = \mathbf{0}) \ \wedge \ (\boldsymbol{\lambda}_{01} \cdot \boldsymbol{\lambda}_{a0} \leq 0 \wedge \boldsymbol{\lambda}_{01} \cdot \boldsymbol{\lambda}_{a1} \geq 0). \tag{14.141}$$

4. **Containment of a common plane in a dual line segment and a dual triangle**

   The condition for a dual homogeneous line segment $\gamma_a\gamma_b$ and a dual homogeneous triangle $\gamma_0\gamma_1\gamma_2$ in two-sided space to have a single common homogeneous plane, and the condition for a homogeneous line segment and a homogeneous triangle to have a single intersecting point form a dual relationship.

From eq.(14.126), therefore, we have:

$$\begin{aligned} &((T_{a012}, T_{b012}) \neq (0,0)) \\ \wedge\ &((T_{a012} \geq 0 \wedge T_{b012} \leq 0 \wedge T_{ab12}, T_{ab20}, T_{ab01} \geq 0) \\ \vee\ &(T_{a012} \leq 0 \wedge T_{b012} \geq 0 \wedge T_{ab12}, T_{ab20}, T_{ab01} \leq 0)). \end{aligned} \tag{14.142}$$

The common homogeneous plane γ can be expressed either in terms of γ_a and γ_b or in terms of γ_0, γ_1 and γ_2, as follows:

Expression in terms of γ_a and γ_b

$$\gamma = \begin{cases} \overline{T_{a012}\gamma_b - T_{b012}\gamma_a}, & (T_{a012} \geq 0 \wedge T_{b012} \leq 0), \\ \overline{T_{b012}\gamma_a - T_{a012}\gamma_b}, & (T_{a012} \leq 0 \wedge T_{b012} \geq 0). \end{cases} \tag{14.143}$$

Expression in terms of γ_0, γ_1 and γ_2

$$\gamma = \begin{cases} \overline{T_{ab12}\gamma_0 + T_{ab20}\gamma_1 + T_{ab01}\gamma_2}, & (T_{ab12}, T_{ab20}, T_{ab01} \geq 0), \\ \overline{-T_{ab12}\gamma_0 - T_{ab20}\gamma_1 - T_{ab01}\gamma_2}, & (T_{ab12}, T_{ab20}, T_{ab01} \leq 0). \end{cases} \tag{14.144}$$

5. **Containment of a common plane in two dual line segments**

   The condition for two dual homogeneous line segments $\gamma_a\gamma_b$ and $\gamma_0\gamma_1$ in two-sided space to have a common homogeneous plane, and the condition for two homogeneous line segments V_0V_1 and V_aV_b to intersect, form a dual relationship (see Fig. 14.20).

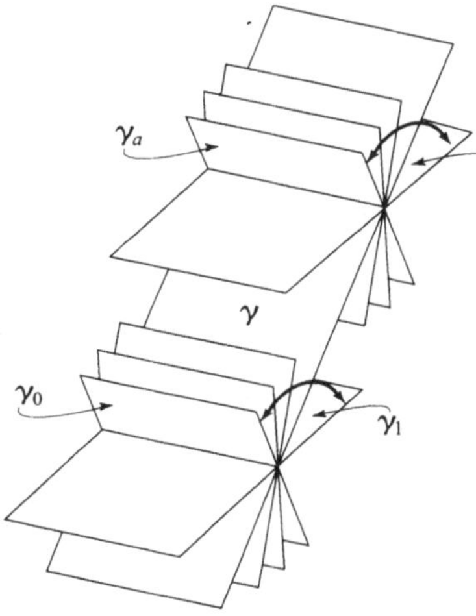

Figure 14.20: Common homogeneous plane of two dual line segments.

From eq.(14.131), therefore, we have:

$$(T_{01ab} = 0) \ \wedge \ (\boldsymbol{\pi}_{01a} \cdot \boldsymbol{\pi}_{01b}, \ \boldsymbol{\pi}_{ab0} \cdot \boldsymbol{\pi}_{ab1}, \ \boldsymbol{\pi}_{01a} \cdot \boldsymbol{\pi}_{ab0} \leq 0). \qquad (14.145)$$

Also, from eq.(14.136), we have:

With respect to $p_{01a}, p_{01b}, p_{ab0}, p_{ab1}$ which include at least one non-zero element,

$$\begin{array}{c}(T_{01ab} = 0) \wedge \\ ((p_{01a} \geq 0 \wedge p_{01b} \leq 0 \wedge p_{ab0} \leq 0 \wedge p_{ab1} \geq 0) \\ \vee \ (p_{01a} \leq 0 \wedge p_{01b} \geq 0 \wedge p_{ab0} \geq 0 \wedge p_{ab1} \leq 0)).\end{array} \qquad (14.146)$$

The common homogeneous plane γ is given as follows:

Expression in terms of γ_0 and γ_1

$$\gamma = \begin{cases} \overline{p_{ab0}\gamma_1 - p_{ab1}\gamma_0}, & (p_{ab0} \geq 0 \wedge p_{ab1} \leq 0), \\ \overline{p_{ab1}\gamma_0 - p_{ab0}\gamma_1}, & (p_{ab0} \leq 0 \wedge p_{ab1} \geq 0). \end{cases} \qquad (14.147)$$

Expression in terms of γ_a and γ_b

$$\gamma = \begin{cases} \overline{p_{01a}\gamma_b - p_{01b}\gamma_a}, & (p_{01a} \geq 0 \wedge p_{01b} \leq 0), \\ \overline{p_{01b}\gamma_a - p_{01a}\gamma_b}, & (p_{01a} \leq 0 \wedge p_{01b} \geq 0). \end{cases} \qquad (14.148)$$

It should be emphasized here that the conditions presented above apply not only to homogeneous simplices, which in themselves constitute a very general class of geometric elements, but, in their dual forms, to dual homogeneous simplices as well.

For instance, the condition (14.131) can be applied to see whether two line segments intersect for all of the cases given in Fig.14.19, while eq.(14.145), which is obtained by replacing S and $\boldsymbol{F}$ of eq.(14.131) by T and $\boldsymbol{\pi}$, respectively, expresses the condition for two dual homogeneous line segments to have a common homogeneous plane. In other words, a single program written to test some geometric condition can serve two purposes at the same time.

Interference test conditions between simplices mentioned so far are summarized in Table 14.3.

14.5 Tests for Polygons and Polyhedra

14.5.1 Convexity Test for Vertices and Edges

Here we limit our discussion to testing the convexity of a vertex of a polygon and edge of a polyhedron, both defined in Euclidean space, using homogeneous

Table 14.3: Test conditions of interferences between simplices.

Test type	**Space**	**Test conditions**
Point-in-tetrahedron	classical	$(S_{a123}, S_{a032}, S_{a013}, S_{a021} \geq 0)$ $\vee(S_{a123}, S_{a032}, S_{a013}, S_{a021} \leq 0)$
	two-sided	$(S_{0123} > 0 \wedge S_{a123}, S_{a032}, S_{a013}, S_{a021} \geq 0)$ $\vee\ (S_{0123} < 0 \wedge S_{a123}, S_{a032}, S_{a013}, S_{a021} \leq 0)$
Point-in-triangle	classical	$(S_{a012} = 0)\wedge$ $((\boldsymbol{F}_{012} \cdot \boldsymbol{F}_{a12} \geq 0 \wedge \boldsymbol{F}_{012} \cdot \boldsymbol{F}_{a20} \geq 0 \wedge \boldsymbol{F}_{012} \cdot \boldsymbol{F}_{a01} \geq 0)$ $\vee(\boldsymbol{F}_{012} \cdot \boldsymbol{F}_{a12} \leq 0 \wedge \boldsymbol{F}_{012} \cdot \boldsymbol{F}_{a20} \leq 0 \wedge \boldsymbol{F}_{012} \cdot \boldsymbol{F}_{a01} \leq 0))$.
	two-sided	$(S_{a012} = 0) \wedge$ $(\boldsymbol{F}_{012} \cdot \boldsymbol{F}_{a12},\ \boldsymbol{F}_{012} \cdot \boldsymbol{F}_{a20},\ \boldsymbol{F}_{012} \cdot \boldsymbol{F}_{a01} \geq 0)$
Point-in-line segment	classical	$(\boldsymbol{F}_{a01} = \mathbf{0})\ \wedge\ (\boldsymbol{L}_{a0} \cdot \boldsymbol{L}_{a1} \leq 0)$
	two-sided	$(\boldsymbol{F}_{a01} = \mathbf{0}) \wedge (\boldsymbol{L}_{01} \cdot \boldsymbol{L}_{a0} \leq 0) \wedge (\boldsymbol{L}_{01} \cdot \boldsymbol{L}_{a1} \geq 0)$
Intersect. of line segment and triangle	classical	$((S_{a012}, S_{b012}) \neq (0,0))$ $\wedge\ ((S_{a012} \geq 0 \wedge S_{b012} \leq 0)\ \vee\ (S_{a012} \leq 0 \wedge S_{b012} \geq 0))$ $\wedge\ ((S_{ab12}, S_{ab20}, S_{ab01} \geq 0) \vee\ (S_{ab12}, S_{ab20}, S_{ab01} \leq 0))$
	two-sided	$((S_{a012},\ S_{b012}) \neq (0,0))$ $\wedge\ ((S_{a012} \geq 0 \wedge S_{b012} \leq 0 \wedge S_{ab12}, S_{ab20}, S_{ab01} \geq 0)$ $\vee\ (S_{a012} \leq 0 \wedge S_{b012} \geq 0 \wedge S_{ab12}, S_{ab20}, S_{ab01} \leq 0))$
Intersect. of two line segments	classical	$(S_{01ab} = 0) \wedge (\boldsymbol{F}_{01a} \cdot \boldsymbol{F}_{01b},\ \boldsymbol{F}_{ab0} \cdot \boldsymbol{F}_{ab1} \leq 0)$
	two-sided	$(S_{01ab} = 0) \wedge (\boldsymbol{F}_{01a} \cdot \boldsymbol{F}_{01b},\ \boldsymbol{F}_{ab0} \cdot \boldsymbol{F}_{ab1},\ \boldsymbol{F}_{01a} \cdot \boldsymbol{F}_{ab0} \leq 0)$

coordinates, rather than that of a homogeneous polygon or polyhedron defined in classical projective or two-sided space.

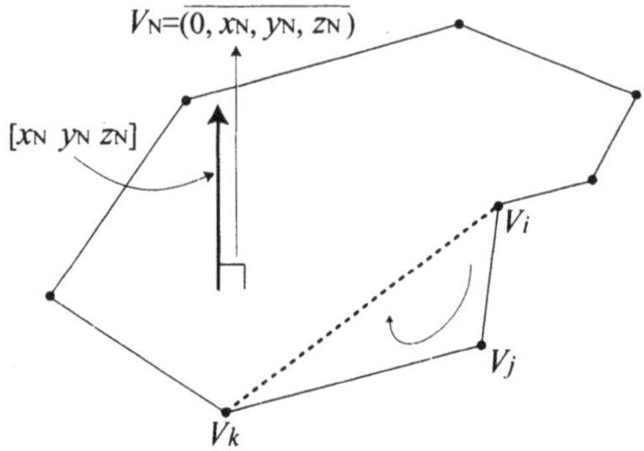

Figure 14.21: Convexity of vertex V_j.

We denote by $V_i = \overline{(w_i, X_i, Y_i, Z_i)}$, $V_j = \overline{(w_j, X_j, Y_j, Z_j)}$ and $V_k = \overline{(w_k, X_k, Y_k, Z_k)}$, three successive vertices lying in the clockwise direction when the polygon is viewed from outside, and by V_N the point at infinity in the direction of the outward normal vector (see Fig. 14.21). If we denote the outward normal vector by $\boldsymbol{n} = [x_N \; y_N \; z_N]$, then $V_N = \overline{(0, x_N, y_N, z_N)}$.

The convexity/concavity of the vertex V_j can be determined from the sign of S_{Nijk}. That is, assuming that $w_i > 0$, $w_j > 0$ and $w_k > 0$, we have:

$$S_{Nijk} \begin{cases} > 0 & \cdots V_j \text{ is a convex vertex,} \\ \leq 0 & \cdots V_j \text{ is a concave vertex.} \end{cases} \tag{14.149}$$

Let us now derive this condition. The conventional test usually uses the sign of the scalar triple product:

$$[\boldsymbol{v}_k - \boldsymbol{v}_i, \boldsymbol{v}_j - \boldsymbol{v}_i, \boldsymbol{n}] \equiv \begin{vmatrix} x_k - x_i & y_k - y_i & z_k - z_i \\ x_j - x_i & y_j - y_i & z_j - z_i \\ x_N & y_N & z_N \end{vmatrix}.$$

That is,

$$[\boldsymbol{v}_k - \boldsymbol{v}_i, \boldsymbol{v}_j - \boldsymbol{v}_i, \boldsymbol{n}] \begin{cases} > 0 & \cdots V_j \text{ is a convex vertex,} \\ \leq 0 & \cdots V_j \text{ is a concave vertex.} \end{cases}$$

We now modify this scalar triple product as follows:

$$\begin{aligned} [\boldsymbol{v}_k - \boldsymbol{v}_i, \boldsymbol{v}_j - \boldsymbol{v}_i, \boldsymbol{n}] &= \begin{vmatrix} x_k - x_i & y_k - y_i & z_k - z_i \\ x_j - x_i & y_j - y_i & z_j - z_i \\ x_N & y_N & z_N \end{vmatrix} \\ &= \begin{vmatrix} 1 & 0 & 0 & 0 \\ 1 & x_k - x_i & y_k - y_i & z_k - z_i \\ 1 & x_j - x_i & y_j - y_i & z_j - z_i \\ 0 & x_N & y_N & z_N \end{vmatrix} \end{aligned}$$

$$= \begin{vmatrix} 1 & x_i & y_i & z_i \\ 1 & x_k & y_k & z_k \\ 1 & x_j & y_j & z_j \\ 0 & x_N & y_N & z_N \end{vmatrix}$$

$$= \frac{1}{w_i w_j w_k} \begin{vmatrix} 0 & x_N & y_N & z_N \\ w_i & X_i & Y_i & Z_i \\ w_j & X_j & Y_j & Z_j \\ w_k & X_k & Y_k & Z_k \end{vmatrix}$$

$$= \frac{1}{w_i w_j w_k} S_{Nijk}. \tag{14.150}$$

So the scalar triple product and S_{Nijk} have the same sign if w_i, w_j, $w_k > 0$. In geometric terms, this means that, when the triangle $V_i V_j V_k$ is viewed from point V_N, V_j is convex if the three vertices are traced clockwise (in which case $S_{Nijk} > 0$), but concave otherwise (i.e., $S_{Nijk} \leq 0$).

Let us now determine the convexity of a polyhedron's edge. We denote by $\boldsymbol{m} = [x_M \; y_M \; z_M]$ and $\boldsymbol{n} = [x_N \; y_N \; z_N]$, the outward normal vectors of the faces on the left and right sides, respectively, of the edge $V_i V_j$ when viewed in the direction $V_i \rightarrow V_j$ from outside of the polyhedron (see Fig. 14.22). We denote by $V_M = \overline{(0, x_M, y_M, z_M)}$ and $V_N = \overline{(0, x_N, y_N, z_N)}$ the two points at infinity in both directions, respectively.

The convexity/concavity of the edge $V_i V_j$ can be determined from the sign of S_{MNij}. That is, assuming that $w_i > 0$ and $w_j > 0$, we have:

$$S_{MNij} \begin{cases} > 0 & \cdots V_i V_j \text{ is a convex edge,} \\ \leq 0 & \cdots V_i V_j \text{ is a concave edge.} \end{cases} \tag{14.151}$$

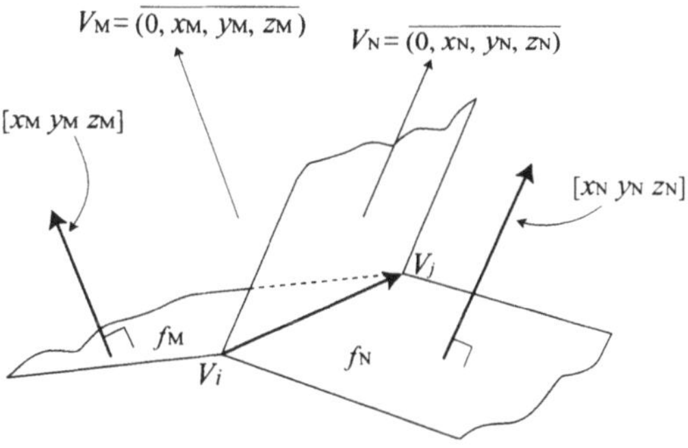

Figure 14.22: Convexity of edge $V_i V_j$.

Let us derive this. The conventional geometric test uses the sign of the scalar triple product:

$$[\boldsymbol{m}, \boldsymbol{n}, \boldsymbol{v}_j - \boldsymbol{v}_i] = \begin{vmatrix} x_M & y_M & z_M \\ x_N & y_N & z_N \\ x_j - x_i & y_j - y_i & z_j - z_i \end{vmatrix}.$$

Thus,

$$[\boldsymbol{m}, \boldsymbol{n}, \boldsymbol{v}_j - \boldsymbol{v}_i] \begin{cases} > 0 & \cdots V_iV_j \text{ is a convex edge,} \\ \leq 0 & \cdots V_iV_j \text{ is a concave edge.} \end{cases}$$

We now modify the scalar triple product above:

$$\begin{aligned}
[\boldsymbol{m}, \boldsymbol{n}, \boldsymbol{v}_j - \boldsymbol{v}_i] &= \begin{vmatrix} x_M & y_M & z_M \\ x_N & y_N & z_N \\ x_j - x_i & y_j - y_i & z_j - z_i \end{vmatrix} \\
&= \begin{vmatrix} 1 & 0 & 0 & 0 \\ 0 & x_M & y_M & z_M \\ 0 & x_N & y_N & z_N \\ 1 & x_j - x_i & y_j - y_i & z_j - z_i \end{vmatrix} \\
&= \begin{vmatrix} 1 & x_i & y_i & z_i \\ 0 & x_M & y_M & z_M \\ 0 & x_N & y_N & z_N \\ 1 & x_j & y_j & z_j \end{vmatrix} \\
&= \frac{1}{w_iw_j} \begin{vmatrix} 0 & X_M & Y_M & Z_M \\ 0 & X_N & Y_N & Z_N \\ w_i & X_i & Y_i & Z_i \\ w_j & X_j & Y_j & Z_j \end{vmatrix} \\
&= \frac{1}{w_iw_j} S_{MNij}. \qquad (14.152)
\end{aligned}$$

So the scalar triple product and S_{MNij} have the same sign if w_i, $w_j > 0$.

In geometric terms, this means that, when triangle $V_NV_iV_j$ is viewed from point V_M, V_iV_j is convex if the triangle's three vertices are traced clockwise (in which case $S_{MNij} > 0$), but concave otherwise (i.e., $S_{MNij} \leq 0$).

As this shows, points at infinity (like V_M and V_N) can be treated as ordinary points.

14.5.2 Point-In-Polygon Tests

A Method of Using a Reference Point

We first discuss in this section how to determine whether a point lies in or out of a polygon by using a reference point [4].

We denote by V_i, V_j and V_k, three consecutive clockwise vertices when the polygon is viewed from outside. The fan-shaped zone formed by the extensions of the edges V_iV_j and V_jV_k can be classified according to whether $\theta < 180°$, $\theta > 180°$ or $\theta = 180°$, where θ is the interior angle of the vertex V_j (Fig. 14.23). We shall call these convex, concave and straight-line zones, respectively.

Now, let us consider a situation where there is an infinitely extending sheet of paper on which a polygon is drawn. At each vertex, whether it is convex or concave, its zone, or some part of the zone is deleted if it has existed, and

[4] This method is included for an introduction to the method of not using a reference point discussed later.

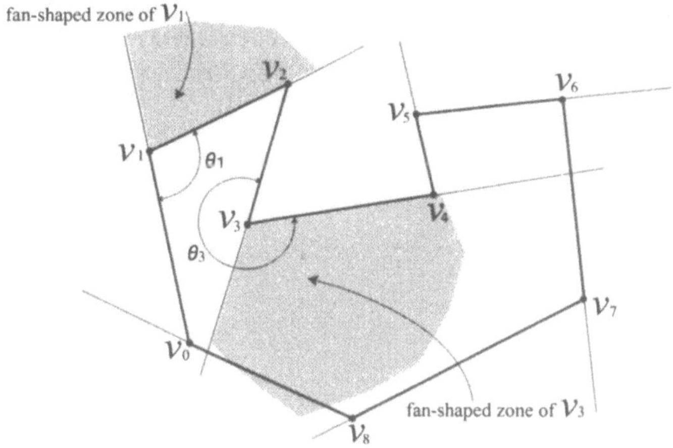

Figure 14.23: Fan-shaped zones.

appended if it has not. That is, this operation reverses the status of the "point set" in the zone under consideration. If this operation is performed with respect to all the vertices of the polygon, then this algorithm creates the polygon. This process is illustrated in Figs. 14.24 and 14.25.

In Fig. 14.24, the algorithm starts at vertex V_0, and it completes the processing at vertices V_0 and V_1 in figure (1). Figure (2) shows the status after the processing at V_2. At V_3 the algorithm recovers its zone which was once deleted. This status is shown in figure (3). At V_4 the algorithm recovers its zone as well, as shown in figure (4). In Figure (6) the originally drawn polygon has been generated.

A more complicated case is shown in Fig. 14.25.

The algorithm below is based on the observation explained above.

We let V_N be the point at infinity in the direction of the outward normal vector (although it can be any arbitrary point lying outside the plane of the polygon), so:

$$\boldsymbol{V}_N = [0 \; x_N \; y_N \; z_N].$$

We assume the signs of w-coordinates of all the vertices are positive. In this case,

$$S_{Nijk} \begin{cases} > 0 & \cdots \text{ the zone is convex,} \\ < 0 & \cdots \text{ the zone is concave,} \\ = 0 & \cdots \text{ the zone is straight-line.} \end{cases} \tag{14.153}$$

The extensions of the edges V_iV_j and V_jV_k are called virtual edges.

To determine whether the point V_a lies in or out of the polygon, we first initialize the test point status to TRUE (because V_a is on the infinitely extending paper), then see whether the point lies inside or outside of the fan-shaped zone corresponding to each vertex of the polygon, adjusting the status as we move from one vertex to the next. That is:

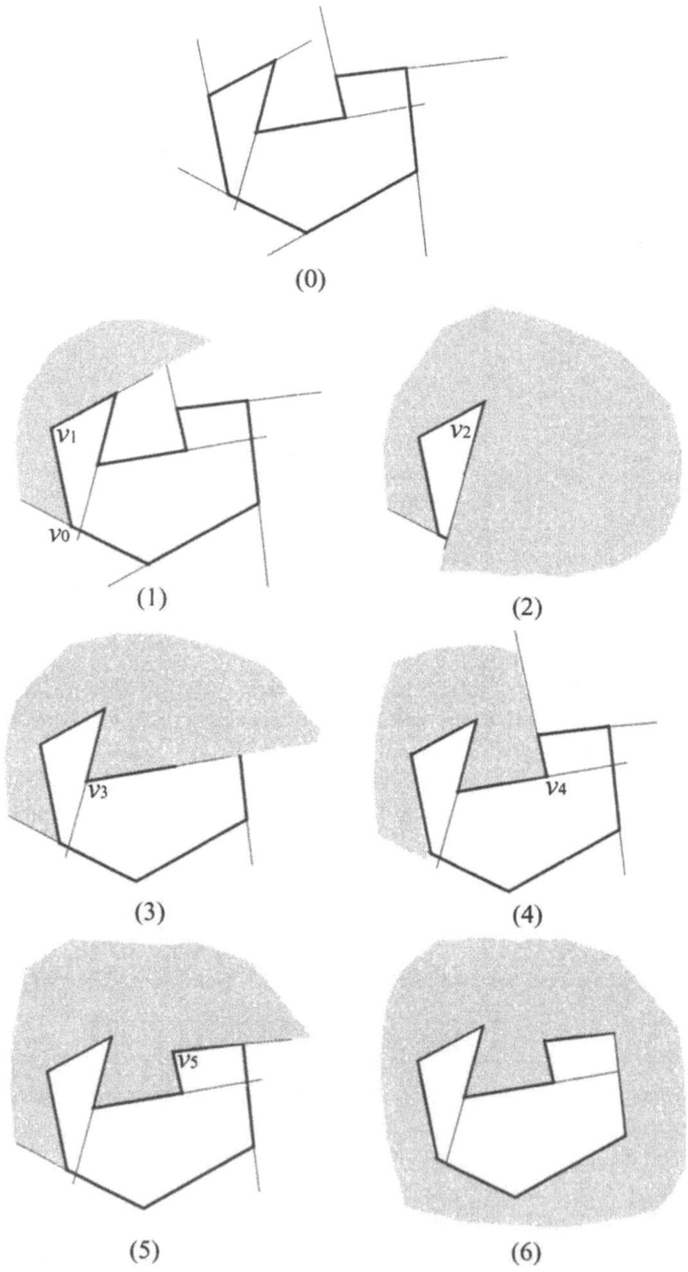

Figure 14.24: Creating a polygon from a sheet of paper (1).

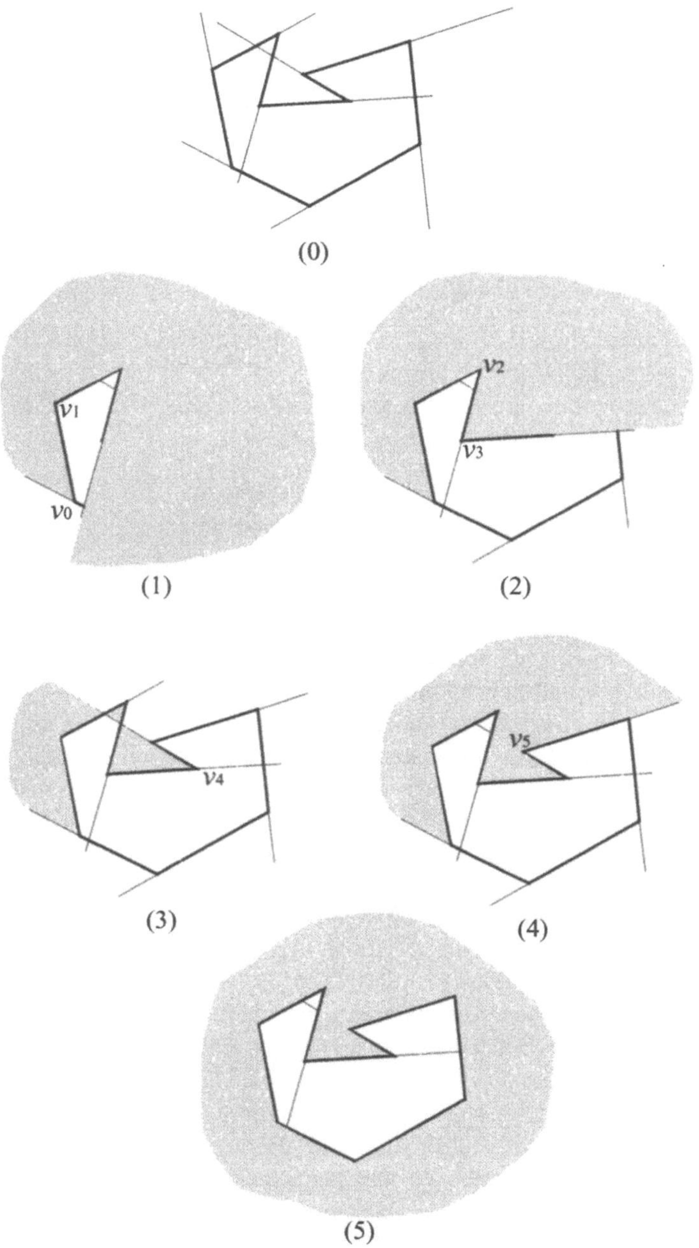

Figure 14.25: Creating a polygon from a sheet of paper (2).

1) reverse the status value if V_a lies within a concave or convex zone,

2) skip and move to the next vertex if V_a lies on a straight-line zone.

After repeating this procedure until all vertices are covered, we can determine such that the point lies inside the polygon if the final status value is TRUE, but lies outside of the polygon if FALSE.

Whether the point V_a lies within a convex or concave zone is determined by the following criterion:

$$\begin{cases} (S_{aijN} < 0) \wedge (S_{ajkN} > 0) & \cdots V_a \text{ is in a convex zone,} \\ (S_{aijN} > 0) \wedge (S_{ajkN} < 0) & \cdots V_a \text{ is in a concave zone.} \end{cases} \tag{14.154}$$

In order to avoid double-counting for the virtual edges, appropriate equality signs must be included in the program.

A program of this algorithm is shown in Fig. 14.26. This algorithm will be refined in the next method.

A Method of not Using a Reference Point

In the algorithm discussed above, we employed an auxiliary point V_N to determine whether a point lies inside or outside of a polygon. This extra point was necessary to treat a planar geometric element in three dimensional space by the homogeneous 4×4 determinant method, which determines the positional relationship between four points. Thus, it was necessary for V_N to lie outside of the plane of the polygon being tested.

In practice, we often choose as V_N the point at infinity in the direction of the normal vector of the polygon or some suitable basis vector of the homogeneous coordinate system. Yet, finding a suitable point for V_N is often tedious. For example, one cannot use a point at infinity in the normal vector direction if the polygon plane is to be transformed onto the plane at infinity. Or, when using a basis vector, we may have to test for all four basis vectors until we find one that will work. In other words, much effort is spent on processing that has no direct bearing on the test, which is to establish the geometric relationship between a point and a polygon.

Instead of employing 4×4 determinants for all processing, we can use the Plücker coordinates of line or plane, for processing that does not have to take place in three dimensional space. This method, i.e., homogeneous determinant method, allows us to determine whether a point lies in or out of a polygon without having to introduce an auxiliary point. The algorithm in this case compares the relative orientations of signed Plücker coordinate vectors of planes.

Let us denote by V_i, V_j and V_k three consecutive vertices of a polygon, and by $\boldsymbol{F}_{ijk} = [A_{ijk}\ B_{ijk}\ C_{ijk}\ D_{ijk}]^T$ the vector consisting of the homogeneous coefficients, i.e., the Plücker coordinates, of the plane defined by these three points.

We wish to test a point V_a. To determine whether it lies inside the polygon, we compare the three planes, F_{ijk}, F_{aij} and F_{ajk}, which can either be identical, have the reverse orientation or be a null object. Instead of a function that

[**program** ①]

```
extern double s_value(double[4], double[4], double[4],
                      double[4]);

#define TRUE 1
#define FALSE 0
#define not(x) ((x==FALSE) ? TRUE : FALSE)
#define sign(x) ((x > 0. 0) ? 1 : ((x < 0. 0) ? (-1) : 0))

int point_in_polygon_test(va, v, m, vn)
double va[4]; /*test point*/
double v[][4]; /*polygon vertices*/
int m; /*number of polygon vertices*/
double vn[4]; /*point at infinity in direction normal to polygon
plane*/
int i,j,k;
int Saijn, Sajkn, Snijk;
int status; /*status value*/

{
status = TRUE;
i = m - 2; j = m - 1;
Saijn = sign(s_value(va, v[i], v[j], vn));
for (k = 0; k < m; k++) {
        Sajkn = sign(s_value(va, v[j], v[k], vn));
        Snijk = sign(s_value(vn, v[i], v[j], v[k]));
        if (((Snijk > 0) && (Saijn <= 0) && (Sajkn > 0))
          || ((Snijk < 0) && (Saijn > 0) && (Sajkn <= 0))) {
        status = not(status);
        }
        Saijn = Sajkn; i = j; j = k;
        }
return status;
}
```

Figure 14.26: Program No.1 for Point-In-Polygon test (C language).

[**program** ②]

```
status0 = status1 = TRUE;
i = nm -2; j = nm -1;
Faij = f(va, v[i], v[j]);
for (k = 0; k < nm; k++) {
        Fajk = f(va, v[j], v[k]); Fijk = f(v[i], v[j], v[k]);
        if (Fijk < 0) {
                if ((Faij ≤ 0) && (Fajk > 0))
                        status0 = not(status0);
                if ((Faij < 0) && (Fajk ≥ 0))
                        status1 = not(status1);
        }
        else if (Fijk > 0) {
                if ((Faij > 0) && (Fajk ≤ 0))
                        status0=not(status0);
                if ((Faij ≥ 0) && (Fajk < 0))
                        status1 = not(status1);
                }
        Faij = Fajk; i = j; j = k;
}
if (status0 != status1) {
        return BOUNDARY;
}
else if (status0 == TRUE) {
        return INSIDE;
}
else {
        return OUTSIDE;
}
```

Figure 14.27: Program No.2 for Point-In-Polygon test (C language).

determines a determinant's sign, we employ here a function $f()$ into which the homogeneous coordinate vectors of the three points are inputted, and which determines whether that plane is identical or in reverse orientation to a reference plane; if they are identical, the function outputs $+1$, if reversely oriented -1. The initially inputted plane is used as the reference plane. Thus, $f()$ needs only to establish a sign which represents the relative orientation of a homogeneous coefficient vector of a plane with respect to that of the reference plane.

The algorithm, written in C language, is shown in Fig. 14.27, where the variable nm denotes the number of vertices of the polygon and "not ()" is a function that reverses the argument (TRUE/FALSE).

This program can test whether a point lies on a polygon's edge or vertex by comparing the signs of the signed Plücker coordinates. If all components of a vector $\boldsymbol{F}$ defined by the test point and two adjacent vertices of a polygon are zero, then the test point is collinear to the corresponding edge (see eq.(14.17)).

The features of the algorithm presented above are summarized below.

1. **Simplicity**

   The algorithm is quite simple, and makes it possible to determine whether any arbitrary point lies within a polygon. Since the algorithm is simple, it can easily be built into hardware.

2. **Computational quantities**

   Two types of four dimensional vectors, $\boldsymbol{F}_{ijk}$ and $\boldsymbol{F}_{aij}$ (which are nothing but plane coefficient vectors with 3×3 determinant components), must be computed in this algorithm. Since a single 3×3 determinant requires 9 multiplications and 5 additions/subtractions (see Method # 2 of Section 13.2.7), a single vector does 36 multiplications and 20 additions/subtractions. Therefore 72 multiplications and 40 additions/subtra -ctions are needed for the sign tests with respect to an edge.

   $\boldsymbol{F}_{ijk}$ are needed for the convexity test of each vertex, so these computations are not required if the vertex convexities are known in advance.

   As for $\boldsymbol{F}_{aij}$, the components are represented as below (see eq.(13.105)):

$$\begin{cases} A_{aij} = +S_{ij}X_a + T_{ij}Y_a + U_{ij}Z_a, \\ B_{aij} = -S_{ij}w_a + R_{ij}Y_a - Q_{ij}Z_a, \\ C_{aij} = -T_{ij}w_a - R_{ij}X_a + P_{ij}Z_a, \\ D_{aij} = -U_{ij}w_a + Q_{ij}X_a - P_{ij}Y_a. \end{cases} \tag{14.155}$$

   Accordingly, if the Plücker coordinates $\overline{(P_{ij}, Q_{ij}, R_{ij}, S_{ij}, T_{ij}, U_{ij})}$ of each edge line are known in advance, 12 multiplications and 8 additions/subtractions are needed for the sign tests with respect to an edge, supposing $\boldsymbol{F}_{ijk}$ are known in advance.

3. **Accuracy**

   By using the exact arithmetic described in Chapter 16, it is possible to determine whether a point lies in or out of a polygon without error.

Chapter 15

Geometric Newton-Raphson Method

15.1 Geometric Newton-Raphson Method

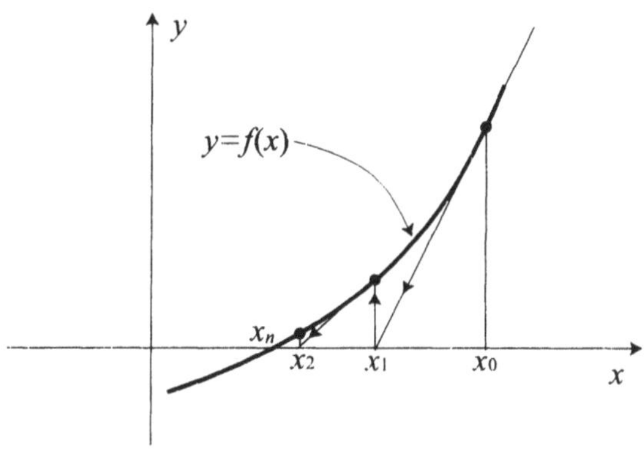

Figure 15.1: Newton-Raphson method.

Given an equation $y = f(x)$, the Newton-Raphson method employs successive approximations to determine the roots of the equation $f(x) = 0$.

Denoting the successive approximate solutions as follows:

$$x_0, x_1, \ldots, x_i, x_{i+1}, \ldots,$$

we can write

$$x_{i+1} = x_i + \delta x, \tag{15.1}$$

where δx can be determined from the first two terms of the Taylor expansion of $f(x_{i+1})$:

$$f(x_{i+1}) = f(x_i + \delta x) = f(x_i) + \frac{\dot{f}(x_i)}{1!}\delta x + \frac{\ddot{f}(x_i)}{2!}(\delta x)^2 + \dots. \tag{15.2}$$

Setting $f(x_{i+1})=0$ yields:

$$\delta x = -\frac{f(x_i)}{\dot{f}(x_i)}. \tag{15.3}$$

Thus,

$$x_{i+1} = x_i - \frac{f(x_i)}{\dot{f}(x_i)}. \tag{15.4}$$

Determination of the roots of an equation using eq.(15.4) is called the *Newton-Raphson method* (Fig. 15.1). Highly accurate solutions can be obtained efficiently with this method.

The application of the Newton-Raphson method to determination of intersections between geometric elements is often called the *geometric Newton-Raphson method*, which we are dealing with in this chapter.

15.2 Conventional Euclidean Approach

To illustrate the conventional geometric Newton-Raphson method, where processing takes place in Euclidean space, we consider the problem of finding the intersection point between a plane curve and a line segment. We shall consider the cases for ordinary and rational polynomial curves separately.

Ordinary Polynomial Curve Case

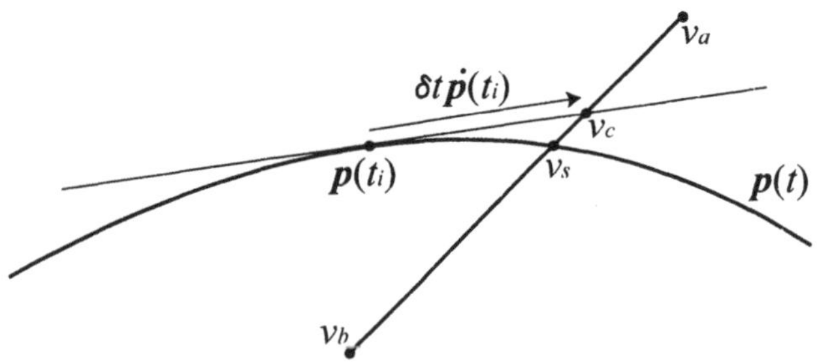

Figure 15.2: Determining intersection point of curve and line segment.

We use the Newton-Raphson method to find the intersection of an ordinary parametric polynomial plane curve (Fig. 15.2):

$$\boldsymbol{p}(t) = [x(t) \;\; y(t)]$$

and a line segment $v_a v_b$, where

$$\boldsymbol{v}_a = [x_a \;\; y_a], \quad \boldsymbol{v}_b = [x_b \;\; y_b].$$

The basic algorithm is as follows:

1. Specify $i = 0$ and an approximate parameter $t = t_0$ to the intersection point.
2. Determine the tangent at $p(t_i)$ on the curve and then find its intersection point with the other geometric element.
3. An increment δt is determined from the intersection point.
4. Increase the parameter t_i by δt, and return to step 2.

The tangent line of the curve at $p(t_i)$ is given by:

$$-\dot{y}(t_i)x + \dot{x}(t_i)y + x(t_i)\dot{y}(t_i) - \dot{x}(t_i)y(t_i) = 0. \tag{15.5}$$

Meanwhile, the line equation for the line segment $v_a v_b$ is given by:

$$(y_a - y_b)x - (x_a - x_b)y + x_a y_b - x_b y_a = 0. \tag{15.6}$$

The intersection point v_c of these two lines is then obtained as:

$$x_c = \frac{\begin{vmatrix} \dot{x}(t_i) & x(t_i)\dot{y}(t_i) - \dot{x}(t_i)y(t_i) \\ x_b - x_a & x_a y_b - x_b y_a \end{vmatrix}}{\begin{vmatrix} \dot{x}(t_i) & \dot{y}(t_i) \\ x_b - x_a & y_b - y_a \end{vmatrix}},$$

$$y_c = \frac{\begin{vmatrix} \dot{y}(t_i) & x(t_i)\dot{y}(t_i) - \dot{x}(t_i)y(t_i) \\ y_b - y_a & x_a y_b - x_b y_a \end{vmatrix}}{\begin{vmatrix} \dot{x}(t_i) & \dot{y}(t_i) \\ x_b - x_a & y_b - y_a \end{vmatrix}}. \tag{15.7}$$

Now, $\boldsymbol{v}_c$, $\boldsymbol{p}(t_i)$, $\dot{\boldsymbol{p}}(t_i)$ and the parameter increment δt have the following relation:

$$\boldsymbol{v}_c - \boldsymbol{p}(t_i) = \delta t \dot{\boldsymbol{p}}(t_i). \tag{15.8}$$

So we can determine the increment δt from either the expression for x- or y-coordinate above as:

$$\delta t = -\frac{\begin{vmatrix} x(t_i) - x_a & y(t_i) - y_a \\ x_b - x_a & y_b - y_a \end{vmatrix}}{\begin{vmatrix} \dot{x}(t_i) & \dot{y}(t_i) \\ x_b - x_a & y_b - y_a \end{vmatrix}}. \tag{15.9}$$

There is another more general, simpler method to determine δt, which will be useful in later discussions.

First we express the line segment in a parametric form as:

$$\boldsymbol{v}(u) = (1 - u)\boldsymbol{v}_a + u\boldsymbol{v}_b, \quad 0 \leq u \leq 1. \tag{15.10}$$

If an intersection exists between the curve and line segment, then the following is satisfied at that point:

$$\boldsymbol{p}(t) = \boldsymbol{v}(u).$$

Now, if t_i and u_i are sufficiently close to the intersection point, then there exist δt and δu such that the following equation holds:

$$\boldsymbol{p}(t_i + \delta t) = \boldsymbol{v}(u_i + \delta u). \tag{15.11}$$

Applying the Taylor expansion to both sides and extracting up to the first-order term, we obtain:

$$\begin{aligned}\boldsymbol{p}(t_i) + \delta t\dot{\boldsymbol{p}}(t_i) &\doteqdot \boldsymbol{v}(u_i) + \delta u\dot{\boldsymbol{v}}(u_i)\\ &= (1 - u_i - \delta u)\boldsymbol{v}_a + (u_i + \delta u)\boldsymbol{v}_b.\end{aligned} \tag{15.12}$$

This shows that $\boldsymbol{p}(t_i)+\delta t\dot{\boldsymbol{p}}(t_i)$, $\boldsymbol{v}_a$ and $\boldsymbol{v}_b$ are linearly dependent, so:

$$\begin{vmatrix} 1 & x(t_i) + \delta t\dot{x}(t_i) & y(t_i) + \delta t\dot{y}(t_i) \\ 1 & x_a & y_a \\ 1 & x_b & y_b \end{vmatrix} = 0. \tag{15.13}$$

Solving this for δt yields the same expression as eq.(15.9).

Rational Polynomial Curve Case

Consider now a rational curve given by:

$$\boldsymbol{p}(t) = [x(t)\ \ y(t)] = [\frac{X(t)}{w(t)}\ \ \frac{Y(t)}{w(t)}]. \tag{15.14}$$

From this, the expression for δt can be obtained in the same manner as for the ordinary polynomial curve above, or:

$$\delta t = -\frac{\begin{vmatrix} \frac{X(t_i)}{w(t_i)} - x_a & \frac{Y(t_i)}{w(t_i)} - y_a \\ x_b - x_a & y_b - y_a \end{vmatrix}}{\begin{vmatrix} \frac{\dot{X}(t_i)w(t_i)-X(t_i)\dot{w}(t_i)}{w(t_i)^2} & \frac{\dot{Y}(t_i)w(t_i)-Y(t_i)\dot{w}(t_i)}{w(t_i)^2} \\ x_b - x_a & y_b - y_a \end{vmatrix}}. \tag{15.15}$$

If we let $w(t_i)=1$ above, we obtain the same expression as eq.(15.9).

We now rewrite eq.(15.15) using 3×3 determinants as follows:

$$\delta t = -\frac{\begin{vmatrix} 1 & x_a & y_a \\ 0 & \frac{X(t_i)}{w(t_i)} - x_a & \frac{Y(t_i)}{w(t_i)} - y_a \\ 0 & x_b - x_a & y_b - y_a \end{vmatrix}}{\begin{vmatrix} 1 & x_a & y_a \\ 0 & \frac{\dot{X}(t_i)w(t_i)-X(t_i)\dot{w}(t_i)}{w(t_i)^2} & \frac{\dot{Y}(t_i)w(t_i)-Y(t_i)\dot{w}(t_i)}{w(t_i)^2} \\ 0 & x_b - x_a & y_b - y_a \end{vmatrix}}$$

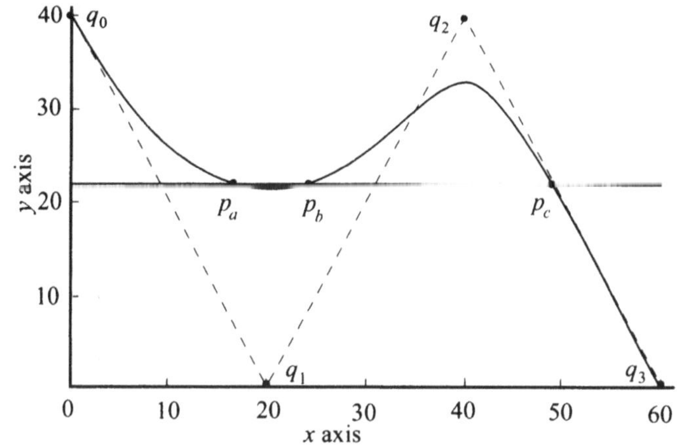

$$\boldsymbol{q}_0 = [0 \quad 40], \quad \boldsymbol{q}_1 = [20 \quad 0], \quad \boldsymbol{q}_2 = [40 \quad 40], \quad \boldsymbol{q}_3 = [60 \quad 0],$$
$$w_0 = 1, \qquad w_1 = 3, \qquad w_2 = 9, \qquad w_3 = 1.$$

Figure 15.3: Intersection of curve and line segment.

$$= -\frac{\begin{vmatrix} 1 & \frac{X(t_i)}{w(t_i)} & \frac{Y(t_i)}{w(t_i)} \\ w_a & X_a & Y_a \\ w_b & X_b & Y_b \end{vmatrix}}{\begin{vmatrix} 0 & \frac{\dot{X}(t_i)w(t_i)-X(t_i)\dot{w}(t_i)}{w(t_i)^2} & \frac{\dot{Y}(t_i)w(t_i)-Y(t_i)\dot{w}(t_i)}{w(t_i)^2} \\ w_a & X_a & Y_a \\ w_b & X_b & Y_b \end{vmatrix}}. \tag{15.16}$$

15.3 Problems with Euclidean Approach

Problems arise when the conventional method, based on eq.(15.16), is used to process rational polynomial curves. These are now discussed.

A non-robust example was given in Section 1.2 (Fig. 15.3). As Table 15.1 shows for this case, the parameter converges when given the initial value of 0.5, but diverges out to infinity from an initial value of, say, 0.7. That is, the robustness of the algorithm is lost. Convergence to the roots depends on initial values.

Note that this non-robust phenomenon does not arise when the geometric Newton-Raphson method is applied to an ordinary polynomial curve, and that the non-robustness occurs even when the w-values of the control points of the

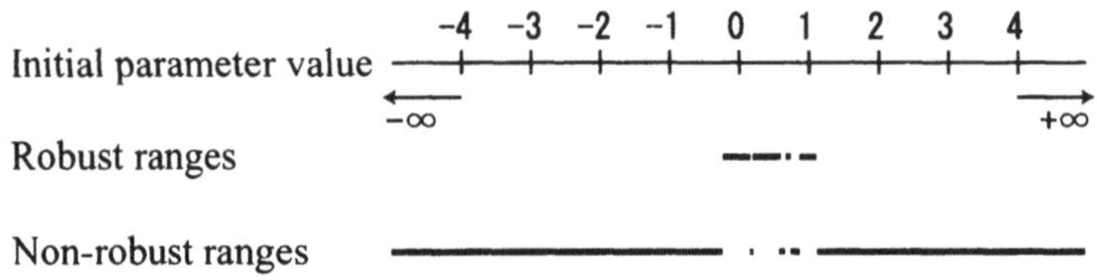

Figure 15.4: Robust and non-robust ranges of parameter initial values.

Table 15.1: Convergence robustness depends on initial values.

Iteration cycle	**Initial value:** 0.5	**Initial value:** 0.7
0	0.50000000000000	0.70000000000000
1	0.16936274509804	-0.88040815211995
2	0.34229003494887	-2.0737146408332
3	0.22792555017231	-8.6191804840474
4	0.21765691304635	-124.86741441742
5	0.21713144078115	-24983.420641812
6	0.21712987883649	-996854619.52794
7	0.21712987882260	-1.5870292685864e+018
8	...	-8.7803503746756e+032
9	...	8.9074699540767e+047
10	...	-1.0733480293644e+063
11	...	1.8161797552409e+078
12	...	$-\infty$

rational curve are all positive. The results over a wide range of initial parameters are again shown in Fig. 15.4.

There is another type of problems with the conventional Newton-Raphson method. That is, assigning as the initial value a parameter value relatively close to a root often fails to converge to that root, but to another. We say that the *local uniqueness* of generated points with respect to initial parameter values is lost in this case. The local uniqueness is defined as such a property that the initial parameter values corresponding to a solution are in a unique continuous range.

15.4 Type-S Homogeneous Method

We have seen how the processing of rational polynomial curves using the geometric Newton-Raphson method in Euclidean space can lead to non-robustness. In the paradigm proposed in this book, the processing takes place not in Euclidean space, but in the associated vector space of a projective space. In dealing with curves and surfaces, however, these are stipulated to be defined only in classical projective space, not in two-side space (see Section 10.3.1 and Chapter 24).

Consider now the type-S homogeneous curve, which represents the capability of a rational polynomial plane curve:

$$\overline{\boldsymbol{P}(t)} = \overline{[w(t) \quad X(t) \quad Y(t)]}$$

and the homogeneous line segment defined by two homogeneous points V_a and V_b (Fig. 15.5):

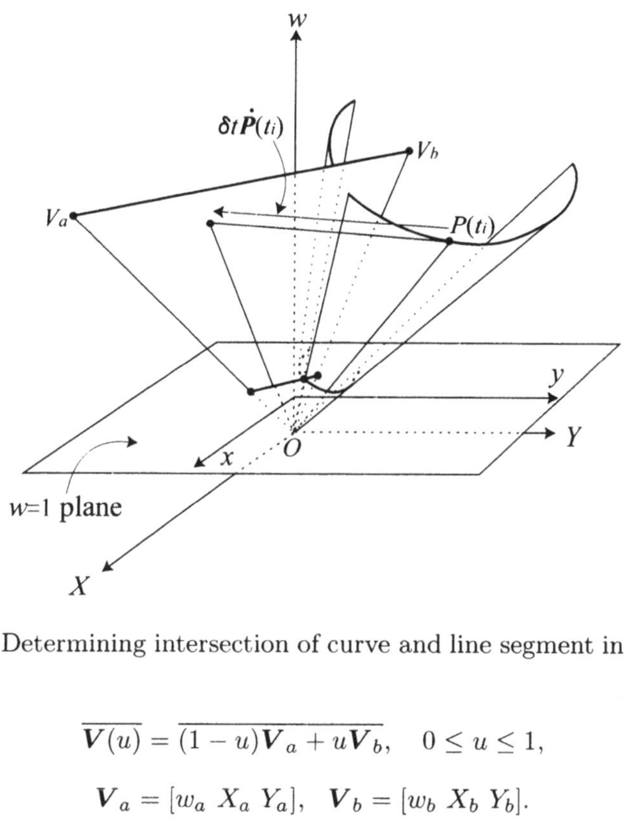

Figure 15.5: Determining intersection of curve and line segment in wXY space.

$$\overline{\boldsymbol{V}(u)} = \overline{(1-u)\boldsymbol{V}_a + u\boldsymbol{V}_b}, \quad 0 \le u \le 1,$$

$$\boldsymbol{V}_a = [w_a \ X_a \ Y_a], \quad \boldsymbol{V}_b = [w_b \ X_b \ Y_b].$$

If an intersection point exists between the homogeneous curve and homogeneous line segment, then the following is satisfied at that point:

$$\boldsymbol{P}(t) = \alpha \boldsymbol{V}(u), \quad \alpha \neq 0,$$

where α is a non-zero scalar.

Now, if $\boldsymbol{P}(t_i)$ and $\boldsymbol{V}(u_i)$ are sufficiently close to the intersection point, then there exist δt and δu such that the following equation holds:

$$\boldsymbol{P}(t_i + \delta t) = \alpha \boldsymbol{V}(u_i + \delta u). \tag{15.17}$$

Applying the Taylor expansion to both sides and extracting up to the first-order term, we obtain:

$$\begin{aligned} \boldsymbol{P}(t_i) + \delta t\dot{\boldsymbol{P}}(t_i) &\doteqdot \alpha\{\boldsymbol{V}(u_i) + \delta u\dot{\boldsymbol{V}}(u_i)\} \\ &= \alpha\{(1-(u_i+\delta u))\boldsymbol{V}_a + (u_i+\delta u)\boldsymbol{V}_b\}. \end{aligned} \tag{15.18}$$

This shows that vector $\boldsymbol{P}(t_i)+\delta t\dot{\boldsymbol{P}}(t_i)$ is linearly dependent on $\boldsymbol{V}_a$ and $\boldsymbol{V}_b$, so we have:

$$\begin{vmatrix} w(t_i)+\delta t\dot{w}(t_i) & X(t_i)+\delta t\dot{X}(t_i) & Y(t_i)+\delta t\dot{Y}(t_i) \\ w_a & X_a & Y_a \\ w_b & X_b & Y_b \end{vmatrix} = 0. \tag{15.19}$$

Solving this for δt yields the following:

$$\delta t = -\frac{\begin{vmatrix} w(t_i) & X(t_i) & Y(t_i) \\ w_a & X_a & Y_a \\ w_b & X_b & Y_b \end{vmatrix}}{\begin{vmatrix} \dot{w}(t_i) & \dot{X}(t_i) & \dot{Y}(t_i) \\ w_a & X_a & Y_a \\ w_b & X_b & Y_b \end{vmatrix}}. \tag{15.20}$$

As for the example shown in Section 15.3, the results of the homogeneous method are shown in Fig. 15.6, along with that of the Euclidean one. Note that there is no non-robust range in the homogeneous method.

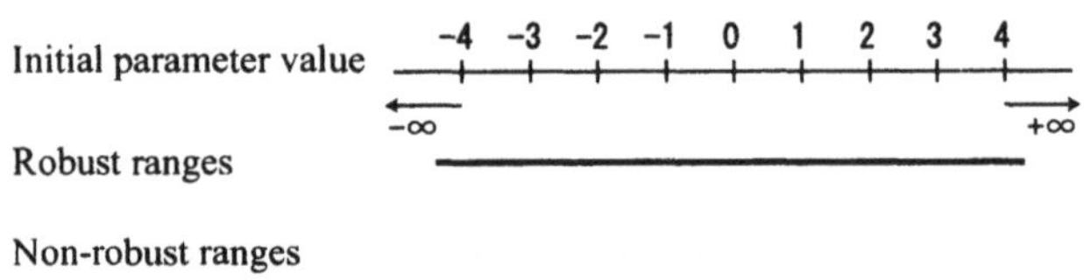

(a) Homogeneous geometric Newton-Raphson method

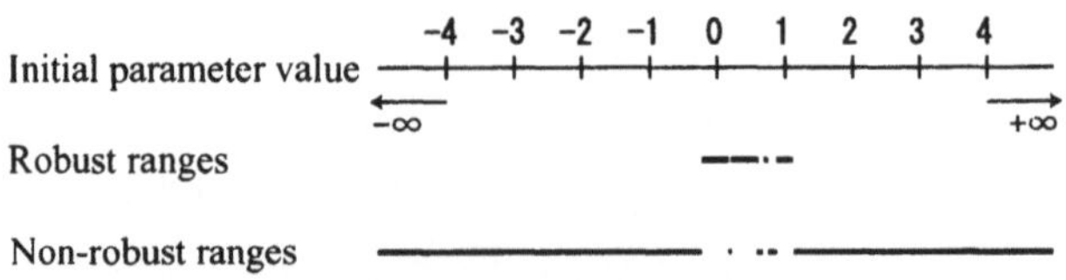

(b) Ordinary geometric Newton-Raphson method

Figure 15.6: Robustness of the homogeneous approach in comparison to the Euclidean one.

15.5 Comparison of Both Approaches

In this section, we compare the characteristics between the geometric Newton-Raphson method based on the ordinary Euclidean processing and that based on the homogeneous processing from geometric and algebraic viewpoints. See Section 25.2.1 for detailed experimental results.

Geometric Comparison

In the conventional geometric Newton-Raphson method, a rational polynomial curve $\boldsymbol{p}(t)$ is processed in Euclidean space. The rational polynomial curve $\boldsymbol{p}(t) = [X(t)/w(t)\ \ Y(t)/w(t)]$ is, in wXY-space, the cut that appears on the $w = 1$ plane when the "simple" polynomial curve $\boldsymbol{P}(t) = [w(t)\ \ X(t)\ \ Y(t)]$ is centrally projected toward the origin. Whenever the curve $\boldsymbol{P}(t)$ passes $w = 0$ plane, the projected rational curve $\boldsymbol{p}(t)$ will have an asymptote (Fig. 15.7). It is anticipated that when $\boldsymbol{p}(t)$ has an asymptote, normal processing might be disturbed by the asymptote.

The homogeneous method, however, processes the rational curve (in the Euclidean plane) as a conical surface made by an ordinary polynomial curve in wXY-space, with an additional dimension, thus avoiding any problems arising from asymptotes.

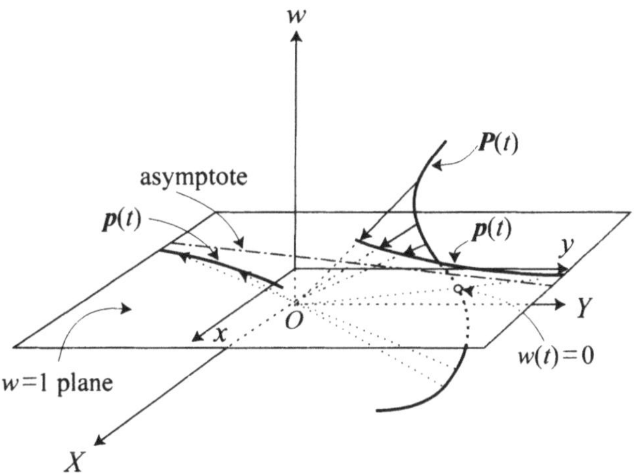

Figure 15.7: A "simple curve" $\boldsymbol{P}(t)$ passing $w = 0$ plane causes an asymptote.

Algebraic Comparison

In eqs.(15.16) and (15.20) we shall introduce the following notations:

$$F(t) = \begin{vmatrix} w(t) & X(t) & Y(t) \\ w_a & X_a & Y_a \\ w_b & X_b & Y_b \end{vmatrix}, \tag{15.21}$$

$$f(t) = \frac{F(t)}{w(t)}. \tag{15.22}$$

- For the homogeneous case, since

$$\dot{F}(t) = \begin{vmatrix} \dot{w}(t) & \dot{X}(t) & \dot{Y}(t) \\ w_a & X_a & Y_a \\ w_b & X_b & Y_b \end{vmatrix}, \tag{15.23}$$

thus eq.(15.20) is expressed as:

$$\delta t = -\frac{\begin{vmatrix} w(t_i) & X(t_i) & Y(t_i) \\ w_a & X_a & Y_a \\ w_b & X_b & Y_b \end{vmatrix}}{\begin{vmatrix} \dot{w}(t_i) & \dot{X}(t_i) & \dot{Y}(t_i) \\ w_a & X_a & Y_a \\ w_b & X_b & Y_b \end{vmatrix}} = -\frac{F(t_i)}{\dot{F}(t_i)}. \tag{15.24}$$

- For the Euclidean case, since

$$f(t) = \begin{vmatrix} 1 & \frac{X(t)}{w(t)} & \frac{Y(t)}{w(t)} \\ w_a & X_a & Y_a \\ w_b & X_b & Y_b \end{vmatrix} \tag{15.25}$$

and

$$\dot{f}(t) = \begin{vmatrix} 0 & \frac{\dot{X}(t)w(t)-X(t)\dot{w}(t)}{w(t)^2} & \frac{\dot{Y}(t)w(t)-Y(t)\dot{w}(t)}{w(t)^2} \\ w_a & X_a & Y_a \\ w_b & X_b & Y_b \end{vmatrix}, \tag{15.26}$$

thus

$$\delta t = -\frac{\begin{vmatrix} 1 & \frac{X(t_i)}{w(t_i)} & \frac{Y(t_i)}{w(t_i)} \\ w_a & X_a & Y_a \\ w_b & X_b & Y_b \end{vmatrix}}{\begin{vmatrix} 0 & \frac{\dot{X}(t_i)w(t_i)-X(t_i)\dot{w}(t_i)}{w(t_i)^2} & \frac{\dot{Y}(t_i)w(t_i)-Y(t_i)\dot{w}(t_i)}{w(t_i)^2} \\ w_a & X_a & Y_a \\ w_b & X_b & Y_b \end{vmatrix}} = -\frac{f(t_i)}{\dot{f}(t_i)}. \tag{15.27}$$

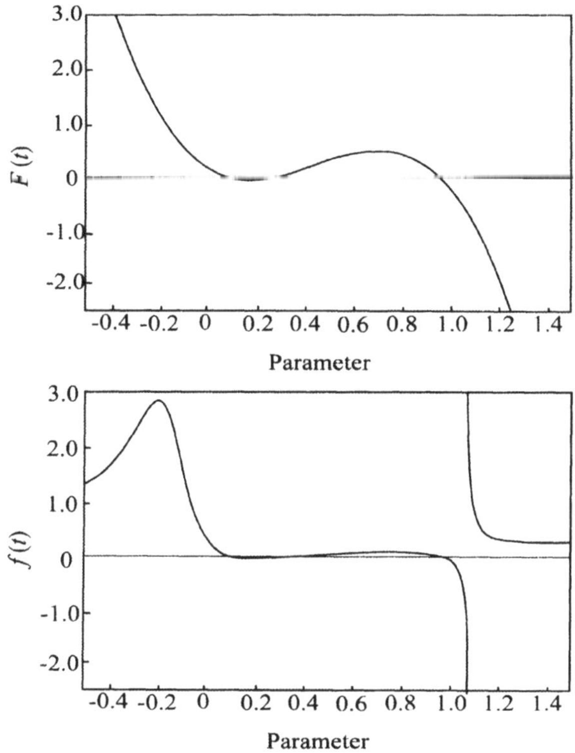

Figure 15.8: Equivalent functions $F(t)$ and $f(t)$.

As we see in eqs.(15.24) and (15.27), in the method based on the homogeneous processing, finding an intersection is equivalent to solving the roots of the algebraic equation $F(t)=0$. On the other hand, in the conventional geometric Newton-Raphson method, finding an intersection is equivalent to solving the roots of the algebraic equation $f(t)=0$.

Note that while $f(t)$ is rational, $F(t)$ is not (Fig. 15.8). In Fig. 15.8 $f(t)$ has a horizontal asymptote as well as a vertical one while $F(t)$ does not have any. Note also that when the algorithm determines a point on a curve along the horizontal asymptote, $\dot{f}(t)$ tends to become smaller and smaller, and thus δt larger and larger, finally t becoming overflowed (eq.(15.27)).

We write the function $f(t)$ as below:

$$f(t) = \frac{a_n t^n + \cdots + a_3 t^3 + a_2 t^2 + a_1 t + a_0}{a_{nw} t^n + \cdots + a_{3w} t^3 + a_{2w} t^2 + a_{1w} t + a_{0w}}. \tag{15.28}$$

Then

$$\lim_{t \to \pm\infty} f(t) = \frac{a_n}{a_{nw}}. \tag{15.29}$$

That is, when we apply the conventional geometric Newton-Raphson method to a rational curve, we have always a horizontal asymptote in the equivalent function and thus have always the possibility of the algorithm breakdown.

Because of a vertical asymptote, furthermore, the parameter value suddenly jumps to another curve range and thus the local uniqueness property of the algorithm is badly damaged.

On the other hand, in the homogeneous processing we deal with a rational curve in the form of an ordinary polynomial curve of dimension higher by one and therefore do not come across such a trouble inherent in rational representation.

As for the aspect of computational quantities, by comparing eqs.(15.21) with (15.25), and eqs.(15.23) with (15.26), we can see that the expressions for the Euclidean processing are considerably more complex than those for the homogeneous processing. If we compare the steps involved for computing δt, the Euclidean processing requires 6 more multiplications and 4 more divisions than the homogeneous processing.

15.6 Other Cases of Intersections

Our discussion on the homogeneous geometric Newton-Raphson method has so far been limited to finding the intersection of a homogeneous curve and homogeneous line segment. In this section, we apply the homogeneous geometric Newton-Raphson method to determine intersections of other geometric elements.

15.6.1 Intersection of Two Curves

Consider two planar homogeneous curves that represent rational polynomial curves:

$$\overline{\boldsymbol{P}(t)} = \overline{[w(t) \;\; X(t) \;\; Y(t)]},$$

and

$$\overline{\boldsymbol{Q}(s)} = \overline{[w(s) \;\; X(s) \;\; Y(s)]}.$$

If $\overline{\boldsymbol{P}(t_i)}$ and $\overline{\boldsymbol{Q}(s_i)}$ are sufficiently close to the intersection point, then there exist δt and δs such that the following equation holds:

$$\boldsymbol{P}(t_i + \delta t) = \alpha \boldsymbol{Q}(s_i + \delta s), \quad \alpha \neq 0. \tag{15.30}$$

Applying the Taylor expansion to both sides and extracting up to the first-order term, we obtain:

$$\boldsymbol{P}(t_i) + \delta t \dot{\boldsymbol{P}}(t_i) \doteqdot \alpha\{\boldsymbol{Q}(s_i) + \delta s \dot{\boldsymbol{Q}}(s_i)\}. \tag{15.31}$$

This shows that $\boldsymbol{P}(t_i)+\delta t\dot{\boldsymbol{P}}(t_i)$ is linearly dependent on $\boldsymbol{Q}(s_i)$ and $\dot{\boldsymbol{Q}}(s_i)$, and that $\boldsymbol{Q}(s_i)+\delta s\dot{\boldsymbol{Q}}(s_i)$ is linearly dependent on $\boldsymbol{P}(t_i)$ and $\dot{\boldsymbol{P}}(t_i)$, so we have:

$$\delta t = -\begin{vmatrix} w(t_i) & X(t_i) & Y(t_i) \\ w(s_i) & X(s_i) & Y(s_i) \\ \dot{w}(s_i) & \dot{X}(s_i) & \dot{Y}(s_i) \end{vmatrix} \Bigg/ \begin{vmatrix} \dot{w}(t_i) & \dot{X}(t_i) & \dot{Y}(t_i) \\ w(s_i) & X(s_i) & Y(s_i) \\ \dot{w}(s_i) & \dot{X}(s_i) & \dot{Y}(s_i) \end{vmatrix}, \tag{15.32}$$

$$\delta s = -\begin{vmatrix} w(s_i) & X(s_i) & Y(s_i) \\ w(t_i) & X(t_i) & Y(t_i) \\ \dot{w}(t_i) & \dot{X}(t_i) & \dot{Y}(t_i) \end{vmatrix} \Bigg/ \begin{vmatrix} \dot{w}(s_i) & \dot{X}(s_i) & \dot{Y}(s_i) \\ w(t_i) & X(t_i) & Y(t_i) \\ \dot{w}(t_i) & \dot{X}(t_i) & \dot{Y}(t_i) \end{vmatrix}. \tag{15.33}$$

We then repeat the substitutions $t_{i+1} = t_i + \delta t$ and $s_{i+1} = s_i + \delta s$ to obtain parameter values for the intersection point.

15.6.2 Intersection of Surface and Line Segment

Let $\overline{\boldsymbol{P}(u,v)}$ be a homogeneous surface patch representing a rational quadrilateral patch and $\overline{\boldsymbol{V}(t)}$ a homogeneous line segment:

$$\overline{\boldsymbol{P}(u,v)} = \overline{[w(u,v) \;\; X(u,v) \;\; Y(u,v) \;\; Z(u,v)]},$$

$$\overline{\boldsymbol{V}(t)} = \overline{(1-t)\boldsymbol{V}_a + t\boldsymbol{V}_b},$$

$$\boldsymbol{V}_a = [w_a \;\; X_a \;\; Y_a \;\; Z_a], \quad \boldsymbol{V}_b = [w_b \;\; X_b \;\; Y_b \;\; Z_b].$$

If $\overline{\boldsymbol{P}(u_i,v_i)}$ and $\overline{\boldsymbol{V}(t_i)}$ are sufficiently close to the intersection point, then there exist δu, δv and δt such that the following equation holds:

$$\boldsymbol{P}(u_i+\delta u, v_i+\delta v) = \alpha \boldsymbol{V}(t_i+\delta t), \quad \alpha \neq 0. \tag{15.34}$$

Applying the Taylor expansion to both sides and extracting up to the first-order term, we obtain:

$$\boldsymbol{P}(u_i,v_i) + \delta u \boldsymbol{P}_u(u_i,v_i) + \delta v \boldsymbol{P}_v(u_i,v_i) \doteqdot \alpha\{(1-t_i-\delta t)\boldsymbol{V}_a + (t_i+\delta t)\boldsymbol{V}_b\}. \tag{15.35}$$

This shows that $\boldsymbol{P}(u_i,v_i)+\delta u \boldsymbol{P}_u(u_i,v_i)$ is linearly dependent on $\boldsymbol{P}_v(u_i,v_i)$, $\boldsymbol{V}_a$ and $\boldsymbol{V}_b$, and that $\boldsymbol{P}(u_i,v_i)+\delta v \boldsymbol{P}_v(u_i,v_i)$ is linearly dependent on $\boldsymbol{P}_u(u_i,v_i)$, $\boldsymbol{V}_a$ and $\boldsymbol{V}_b$, so we have:

$$\delta u = -\begin{vmatrix} w(u_i,v_i) & X(u_i,v_i) & Y(u_i,v_i) & Z(u_i,v_i) \\ w_v(u_i,v_i) & X_v(u_i,v_i) & Y_v(u_i,v_i) & Z_v(u_i,v_i) \\ w_a & X_a & Y_a & Z_a \\ w_b & X_b & Y_b & Z_b \end{vmatrix} \Bigg/ \begin{vmatrix} w_u(u_i,v_i) & X_u(u_i,v_i) & Y_u(u_i,v_i) & Z_u(u_i,v_i) \\ w_v(u_i,v_i) & X_v(u_i,v_i) & Y_v(u_i,v_i) & Z_v(u_i,v_i) \\ w_a & X_a & Y_a & Z_a \\ w_b & X_b & Y_b & Z_b \end{vmatrix}. \tag{15.36}$$

$$\delta v = -\begin{vmatrix} w(u_i,v_i) & X(u_i,v_i) & Y(u_i,v_i) & Z(u_i,v_i) \\ w_u(u_i,v_i) & X_u(u_i,v_i) & Y_u(u_i,v_i) & Z_u(u_i,v_i) \\ w_a & X_a & Y_a & Z_a \\ w_b & X_b & Y_b & Z_b \end{vmatrix} \Bigg/ \begin{vmatrix} w_v(u_i,v_i) & X_v(u_i,v_i) & Y_v(u_i,v_i) & Z_v(u_i,v_i) \\ w_u(u_i,v_i) & X_u(u_i,v_i) & Y_u(u_i,v_i) & Z_u(u_i,v_i) \\ w_a & X_a & Y_a & Z_a \\ w_b & X_b & Y_b & Z_b \end{vmatrix}. \tag{15.37}$$

15.6.3 Intersection of Surface and Curve

Let $\overline{\boldsymbol{P}(u,v)}$ be a homogeneous surface patch representing a rational quadrilateral patch and $\overline{\boldsymbol{Q}(t)}$ a homogeneous curve representing a rational curve:

$$\overline{\boldsymbol{P}(u,v)} = \overline{[w(u,v) \;\; X(u,v) \;\; Y(u,v) \;\; Z(u,v)]},$$
$$\overline{\boldsymbol{Q}(t)} = \overline{[w(t) \;\; X(t) \;\; Y(t) \;\; Z(t)]}.$$

If $\overline{\boldsymbol{P}(u_i,v_i)}$ and $\overline{\boldsymbol{Q}(t_i)}$ are sufficiently close to the intersection point, then there exist δu, δv and δt such that the following equation holds:

$$\boldsymbol{P}(u_i+\delta u, v_i+\delta v) = \alpha \boldsymbol{Q}(t_i+\delta t), \quad \alpha \neq 0. \tag{15.38}$$

Applying the Taylor expansion to both sides and extracting up to the first-order term, we obtain:

$$\boldsymbol{P}(u_i,v_i) + \delta u \boldsymbol{P}_u(u_i,v_i) + \delta v \boldsymbol{P}_v(u_i,v_i) \doteqdot \alpha\{\boldsymbol{Q}(t_i) + \delta t \dot{\boldsymbol{Q}}(t_i)\}, \quad \alpha \neq 0. \tag{15.39}$$

This shows that $\boldsymbol{P}(u_i,v_i)+\delta u \boldsymbol{P}_u(u_i,v_i)$ is linearly dependent on $\boldsymbol{P}_v(u_i,v_i)$, $\boldsymbol{Q}(t_i)$ and $\dot{\boldsymbol{Q}}(t_i)$; that $\boldsymbol{P}(u_i,v_i)+\delta v \boldsymbol{P}_v(u_i,v_i)$ is linearly dependent on $\boldsymbol{P}_u(u_i,v_i)$, $\boldsymbol{Q}(t_i)$ and $\dot{\boldsymbol{Q}}(t_i)$; and that $\boldsymbol{Q}(t_i)+\delta t \dot{\boldsymbol{Q}}(t_i)$ on $\boldsymbol{P}(u_i,v_i)$, $\boldsymbol{P}_u(u_i,v_i)$ and $\boldsymbol{P}_v(u_i,v_i)$, so we have:

$$\delta u = -\begin{vmatrix} w(u_i,v_i) & X(u_i,v_i) & Y(u_i,v_i) & Z(u_i,v_i) \\ w_v(u_i,v_i) & X_v(u_i,v_i) & Y_v(u_i,v_i) & Z_v(u_i,v_i) \\ w(t_i) & X(t_i) & Y(t_i) & Z(t_i) \\ \dot{w}(t_i) & \dot{X}(t_i) & \dot{Y}(t_i) & \dot{Z}(t_i) \end{vmatrix} \Bigg/ \begin{vmatrix} w_u(u_i,v_i) & X_u(u_i,v_i) & Y_u(u_i,v_i) & Z_u(u_i,v_i) \\ w_v(u_i,v_i) & X_v(u_i,v_i) & Y_v(u_i,v_i) & Z_v(u_i,v_i) \\ w(t_i) & X(t_i) & Y(t_i) & Z(t_i) \\ \dot{w}(t_i) & \dot{X}(t_i) & \dot{Y}(t_i) & \dot{Z}(t_i) \end{vmatrix}, \tag{15.40}$$

$$\delta v = -\begin{vmatrix} w(u_i,v_i) & X(u_i,v_i) & Y(u_i,v_i) & Z(u_i,v_i) \\ w_u(u_i,v_i) & X_u(u_i,v_i) & Y_u(u_i,v_i) & Z_u(u_i,v_i) \\ w(t_i) & X(t_i) & Y(t_i) & Z(t_i) \\ \dot{w}(t_i) & \dot{X}(t_i) & \dot{Y}(t_i) & \dot{Z}(t_i) \end{vmatrix} \Bigg/ \begin{vmatrix} w_v(u_i,v_i) & X_v(u_i,v_i) & Y_v(u_i,v_i) & Z_v(u_i,v_i) \\ w_u(u_i,v_i) & X_u(u_i,v_i) & Y_u(u_i,v_i) & Z_u(u_i,v_i) \\ w(t_i) & X(t_i) & Y(t_i) & Z(t_i) \\ \dot{w}(t_i) & \dot{X}(t_i) & \dot{Y}(t_i) & \dot{Z}(t_i) \end{vmatrix}, \tag{15.41}$$

$$\delta t = -\begin{vmatrix} w(t_i) & X(t_i) & Y(t_i) & Z(t_i) \\ w(u_i,v_i) & X(u_i,v_i) & Y(u_i,v_i) & Z(u_i,v_i) \\ w_u(u_i,v_i) & X_u(u_i,v_i) & Y_u(u_i,v_i) & Z_u(u_i,v_i) \\ w_v(u_i,v_i) & X_v(u_i,v_i) & Y_v(u_i,v_i) & Z_v(u_i,v_i) \end{vmatrix} \Bigg/ \begin{vmatrix} \dot{w}(t_i) & \dot{X}(t_i) & \dot{Y}(t_i) & \dot{Z}(t_i) \\ w(u_i,v_i) & X(u_i,v_i) & Y(u_i,v_i) & Z(u_i,v_i) \\ w_u(u_i,v_i) & X_u(u_i,v_i) & Y_u(u_i,v_i) & Z_u(u_i,v_i) \\ w_v(u_i,v_i) & X_v(u_i,v_i) & Y_v(u_i,v_i) & Z_v(u_i,v_i) \end{vmatrix}. \tag{15.42}$$

15.6.4 Intersection of Two Surfaces

Let us now use the homogeneous geometric Newton-Raphson method to determine a point that lies on the intersecting curve of two homogeneous surfaces $\overline{\boldsymbol{P}(u,v)}$ and $\overline{\boldsymbol{Q}(s,t)}$:

$$\overline{\boldsymbol{P}(u,v)} = \overline{[w(u,v) \;\; X(u,v) \;\; Y(u,v) \;\; Z(u,v)]},$$

$$\overline{\boldsymbol{Q}(s,t)} = \overline{[w(s,t) \;\; X(s,t) \;\; Y(s,t) \;\; Z(s,t)]}.$$

If the points $\overline{\boldsymbol{P}(u_i,v_i)}$ and $\overline{\boldsymbol{Q}(s_i,t_i)}$ are sufficiently close to the intersecting curve, then there exist δu, δv, δs and δt such that the following equation holds:

$$\boldsymbol{P}(u_i+\delta u, v_i+\delta v) = \alpha \boldsymbol{Q}(s_i+\delta s, t_i+\delta t), \quad \alpha \neq 0. \tag{15.43}$$

Applying the Taylor expansion to both sides and extracting up to the first-order term, we obtain:

$$\begin{aligned} &\boldsymbol{P}(u_i,v_i) + \delta u \boldsymbol{P}_u(u_i,v_i) + \delta v \boldsymbol{P}_v(u_i,v_i) \\ &\doteqdot \alpha\{\boldsymbol{Q}(s_i,t_i) + \delta s \boldsymbol{Q}_s(s_i,t_i) + \delta t \boldsymbol{Q}_t(s_i,t_i)\}. \end{aligned} \tag{15.44}$$

Eq.(15.44) cannot be solved in this form because it comprises four equations but

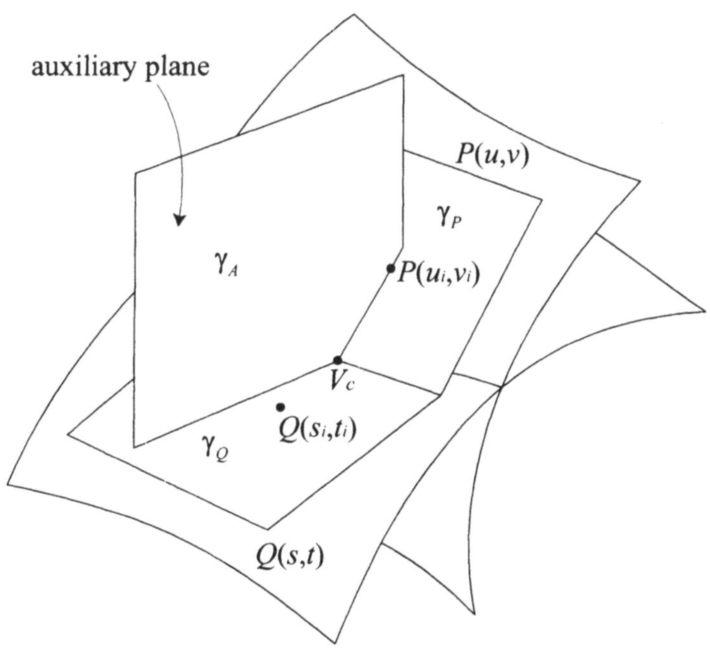

Figure 15.9: Determination of a point on intersecting curve of two surfaces.

contains five unknowns. The equation represents the intersection of a tangent plane at point $P(u_i,v_i)$ (let it be $\gamma_P = \overline{(a_P, b_P, c_P, d_P)^T}$) and a tangent plane at point $Q(s_i,t_i)$ (let it be $\gamma_Q = \overline{(a_Q, b_Q, c_Q, d_Q)^T}$).

Consider now the plane $\gamma_a = \overline{(a_A, b_A, c_A, d_A)^T}$, which is normal to these two planes, γ_P, γ_Q, and contains point $P(u_i, v_i)$. Let the intersecting point of these three planes be V_c (Fig. 15.9). Then the point V_c is expressed as:

$$\begin{aligned}\overline{\boldsymbol{V}_c} &= \overline{[w_c \ \ X_c \ \ Y_c \ \ Z_c]} \\ &= \overline{\boldsymbol{P}(u_i, v_i) + \delta u \boldsymbol{P}_u(u_i, v_i) + \delta v \boldsymbol{P}_v(u_i, v_i)},\end{aligned} \tag{15.45}$$

and from eqs.(9.36) and (9.37) we have:

$$[w_c \ \ X_c \ \ Y_c \ \ Z_c] \begin{bmatrix} 0 & p_{AQ} & q_{AQ} & r_{AQ} \\ -p_{AQ} & 0 & u_{AQ} & -t_{AQ} \\ -q_{AQ} & -u_{AQ} & 0 & s_{AQ} \\ -r_{AQ} & t_{AQ} & -s_{AQ} & 0 \end{bmatrix} = [0 \ \ 0 \ \ 0 \ \ 0]. \tag{15.46}$$

Now, eq.(15.46) can also be written as:

$$\begin{aligned} &\boldsymbol{P}(u_i, v_i) \begin{bmatrix} 0 & p_{AQ} & q_{AQ} & r_{AQ} \\ -p_{AQ} & 0 & u_{AQ} & -t_{AQ} \\ -q_{AQ} & -u_{AQ} & 0 & s_{AQ} \\ -r_{AQ} & t_{AQ} & -s_{AQ} & 0 \end{bmatrix} \\ &+ \delta u \boldsymbol{P}_u(u_i, v_i) \begin{bmatrix} 0 & p_{AQ} & q_{AQ} & r_{AQ} \\ -p_{AQ} & 0 & u_{AQ} & -t_{AQ} \\ -q_{AQ} & -u_{AQ} & 0 & s_{AQ} \\ -r_{AQ} & t_{AQ} & -s_{AQ} & 0 \end{bmatrix} \\ &+ \delta v \boldsymbol{P}_v(u_i, v_i) \begin{bmatrix} 0 & p_{AQ} & q_{AQ} & r_{AQ} \\ -p_{AQ} & 0 & u_{AQ} & -t_{AQ} \\ -q_{AQ} & -u_{AQ} & 0 & s_{AQ} \\ -r_{AQ} & t_{AQ} & -s_{AQ} & 0 \end{bmatrix} \\ &= [0 \ 0 \ 0 \ 0]. \end{aligned} \tag{15.47}$$

We first eliminate δv in order to find δu.

The third term expresses the plane that contains point $P_v(u_i, v_i)$ and the intersecting line of two planes γ_A and γ_Q (eq.(9.38)). Thus, by taking the scalar product of eq.(15.47) and vector $\boldsymbol{P}_v(u_i, v_i)$ which lies on that plane, we can eliminate the third term, and hence δv as well.

From eq.(15.46), we obtain:

$$\begin{bmatrix} -X_c p_{AQ} - Y_c q_{AQ} - Z_c r_{AQ} \\ w_c p_{AQ} - Y_c u_{AQ} + Z_c t_{AQ} \\ w_c q_{AQ} + X_c u_{AQ} - Z_c s_{AQ} \\ w_c r_{AQ} - X_c t_{AQ} + Y_c s_{AQ} \end{bmatrix}^T = [0 \ \ 0 \ \ 0 \ \ 0]. \tag{15.48}$$

Taking the scalar product of eq.(15.48) and $\boldsymbol{P}_v(u_i, v_i)$ and rearranging, we obtain:

$$\begin{aligned} &(w_c X_v(u_i, v_i) - X_c w_v(u_i, v_i)) p_{AQ} + (w_c Y_v(u_i, v_i) - Y_c w_v(u_i, v_i)) q_{AQ} \\ &+ (w_c Z_v(u_i, v_i) - Z_c w_v(u_i, v_i)) r_{AQ} + (Y_c Z_v(u_i, v_i) - Z_c Y_v(u_i, v_i)) s_{AQ} \\ &+ (Z_c X_v(u_i, v_i) - X_c Z_v(u_i, v_i)) t_{AQ} + (X_c Y_v(u_i, v_i) - Y_c X_v(u_i, v_i)) u_{AQ} = 0. \end{aligned}$$

When eq.(15.45) is substituted into this, δv is eliminated and we have the following equation:

$$\begin{aligned}
&(w(u_i,v_i)X_v(u_i,v_i) - X(u_i,v_i)w_v(u_i,v_i))p_{AQ}\\
&+ (w(u_i,v_i)Y_v(u_i,v_i) - Y(u_i,v_i)w_v(u_i,v_i))q_{AQ}\\
&+ (w(u_i,v_i)Z_v(u_i,v_i) - Z(u_i,v_i)w_v(u_i,v_i))r_{AQ}\\
&+ (Y(u_i,v_i)Z_v(u_i,v_i) - Z(u_i,v_i)Y_v(u_i,v_i))s_{AQ}\\
&+ (Z(u_i,v_i)X_v(u_i,v_i) - X(u_i,v_i)Z_v(u_i,v_i))t_{AQ}\\
&+ (X(u_i,v_i)Y_v(u_i,v_i) - Y(u_i,v_i)X_v(u_i,v_i))u_{AQ}\\
&+ \delta u\{(w_u(u_i,v_i)X_v(u_i,v_i) - X_u(u_i,v_i)w_v(u_i,v_i))p_{AQ}\\
&+ (w_u(u_i,v_i)Y_v(u_i,v_i) - Y_u(u_i,v_i)w_v(u_i,v_i))q_{AQ}\\
&+ (w_u(u_i,v_i)Z_v(u_i,v_i) - Z_u(u_i,v_i)w_v(u_i,v_i))r_{AQ}\\
&+ (Y_u(u_i,v_i)Z_v(u_i,v_i) - Z_u(u_i,v_i)Y_v(u_i,v_i))s_{AQ}\\
&+ (Z_u(u_i,v_i)X_v(u_i,v_i) - X_u(u_i,v_i)Z_v(u_i,v_i))t_{AQ}\\
&+ (X_u(u_i,v_i)Y_v(u_i,v_i) - Y_u(u_i,v_i)X_v(u_i,v_i))u_{AQ}\} = 0.
\end{aligned} \tag{15.49}$$

To write this in a clearer form, we introduce the following notations which correspond to the Plücker coordinates for line:

$$\begin{aligned}
&[P_{ppv}\ \ Q_{ppv}\ \ R_{ppv}\ \ S_{ppv}\ \ T_{ppv}\ \ U_{ppv}]\\
&= \left[\begin{vmatrix} w(u_i,v_i) & X(u_i,v_i)\\ w_v(u_i,v_i) & X_v(u_i,v_i)\end{vmatrix}\ \begin{vmatrix} w(u_i,v_i) & Y(u_i,v_i)\\ w_v(u_i,v_i) & Y_v(u_i,v_i)\end{vmatrix}\ \begin{vmatrix} w(u_i,v_i) & Z(u_i,v_i)\\ w_v(u_i,v_i) & Z_v(u_i,v_i)\end{vmatrix}\right.\\
&\left.\begin{vmatrix} Y(u_i,v_i) & Z(u_i,v_i)\\ Y_v(u_i,v_i) & Z_v(u_i,v_i)\end{vmatrix}\ \begin{vmatrix} Z(u_i,v_i) & X(u_i,v_i)\\ Z_v(u_i,v_i) & X_v(u_i,v_i)\end{vmatrix}\ \begin{vmatrix} X(u_i,v_i) & Y(u_i,v_i)\\ X_v(u_i,v_i) & Y_v(u_i,v_i)\end{vmatrix}\right],
\end{aligned} \tag{15.50}$$

$$\begin{aligned}
&[P_{pupv}\ \ Q_{pupv}\ \ R_{pupv}\ \ S_{pupv}\ \ T_{pupv}\ \ U_{pupv}]\\
&= \left[\begin{vmatrix} w_u(u_i,v_i) & X_u(u_i,v_i)\\ w_v(u_i,v_i) & X_v(u_i,v_i)\end{vmatrix}\ \begin{vmatrix} w_u(u_i,v_i) & Y_u(u_i,v_i)\\ w_v(u_i,v_i) & Y_v(u_i,v_i)\end{vmatrix}\ \begin{vmatrix} w_u(u_i,v_i) & Z_u(u_i,v_i)\\ w_v(u_i,v_i) & Z_v(u_i,v_i)\end{vmatrix}\right.\\
&\left.\begin{vmatrix} Y_u(u_i,v_i) & Z_u(u_i,v_i)\\ Y_v(u_i,v_i) & Z_v(u_i,v_i)\end{vmatrix}\ \begin{vmatrix} Z_u(u_i,v_i) & X_u(u_i,v_i)\\ Z_v(u_i,v_i) & X_v(u_i,v_i)\end{vmatrix}\ \begin{vmatrix} X_u(u_i,v_i) & Y_u(u_i,v_i)\\ X_v(u_i,v_i) & Y_v(u_i,v_i)\end{vmatrix}\right].
\end{aligned} \tag{15.51}$$

Solving eq.(15.49) for δu, we thus obtain:

$$\delta u = -\frac{P_{ppv}p_{AQ} + Q_{ppv}q_{AQ} + R_{ppv}r_{AQ} + S_{ppv}s_{AQ} + T_{ppv}t_{AQ} + U_{ppv}u_{AQ}}{P_{pupv}p_{AQ} + Q_{pupv}q_{AQ} + R_{pupv}r_{AQ} + S_{pupv}s_{AQ} + T_{pupv}t_{AQ} + U_{pupv}u_{AQ}}. \tag{15.52}$$

δv, δs and δt are found in a similar manner as:

$$\delta v = -\frac{P_{ppu}p_{AQ} + Q_{ppu}q_{AQ} + R_{ppu}r_{AQ} + S_{ppu}s_{AQ} + T_{ppu}t_{AQ} + U_{ppu}u_{AQ}}{P_{pupv}p_{AQ} + Q_{pupv}q_{AQ} + R_{pupv}r_{AQ} + S_{pupv}s_{AQ} + T_{pupv}t_{AQ} + U_{pupv}u_{AQ}}, \tag{15.53}$$

$$\delta s = -\frac{P_{ppt}p_{AQ} + Q_{ppt}q_{AQ} + R_{ppt}r_{AQ} + S_{ppt}s_{AQ} + T_{ppt}t_{AQ} + U_{ppt}u_{AQ}}{P_{pspt}p_{AQ} + Q_{pspt}q_{AQ} + R_{pspt}r_{AQ} + S_{pspt}s_{AQ} + T_{pspt}t_{AQ} + U_{pspt}u_{AQ}}, \tag{15.54}$$

$$\delta t = -\frac{P_{pps}p_{AQ} + Q_{pps}q_{AQ} + R_{pps}r_{AQ} + S_{pps}s_{AQ} + T_{pps}t_{AQ} + U_{pps}u_{AQ}}{P_{pspt}p_{AQ} + Q_{pspt}q_{AQ} + R_{pspt}r_{AQ} + S_{pspt}s_{AQ} + T_{pspt}t_{AQ} + U_{pspt}u_{AQ}}. \tag{15.55}$$

From δu, δv, δs and δt, the new set of initial points are obtained as:

$$u_{i+1} = u_i + \delta u, \;\; v_{i+1} = v_i + \delta v, \;\; s_{i+1} = s_i + \delta s, \;\; t_{i+1} = t_i + \delta t.$$

The iterations above are repeated to determine the point on the intersecting curve of two homogeneous surfaces.

Lastly, we give a piece of advice. As is usual with Plücker coordinates and coefficients, there appear redundant common factors in the equations (see Section 16.4). Therefore it is strongly advisable to perform normalizations of coordinates and coefficients appropriately.

15.7 Type-D Homogeneous Method

The type-D homogeneous method is the one that deals with the doubly-homogenized curves or type-D homogeneous curves (see Section 10.3.2).

15.7.1 Outline

We consider determining an intersection point between a type-D2 homogeneous curve [1]:

$$\overline{\boldsymbol{HP}(\eta,\sigma)} = \overline{[w(\eta,\sigma)\;X(\eta,\sigma)\;Y(\eta,\sigma)]}$$

and a homogeneous line segment:

$$\overline{\boldsymbol{V}(t)} = \overline{(1-t)\boldsymbol{V}_a + t\boldsymbol{V}_b}.$$

If an intersection point exists between the homogeneous curve and homogeneous line segment, then the following is satisfied at that point:

$$\boldsymbol{HP}(\eta,\sigma) = \alpha \boldsymbol{V}(t), \quad \alpha \neq 0, \tag{15.56}$$

where α is a non-zero scalar.

Now, if $\overline{\boldsymbol{HP}(\eta_i,\sigma_i)}$ and $\overline{\boldsymbol{V}(t_i)}$ are sufficiently close to the intersection point, then there exist $\delta\eta, \delta\sigma$ and δt such that the following equation holds:

$$\boldsymbol{HP}(\eta_i + \delta\eta, \sigma_i + \delta\sigma) = \alpha \boldsymbol{V}(t_i + \delta t). \tag{15.57}$$

Applying the Taylor expansion to both sides and extracting up to the first-order term, we obtain:

$$\begin{aligned} \boldsymbol{HP}(\eta_i,\sigma_i) + \delta\eta \boldsymbol{HP}_\eta(\eta_i,\sigma_i) + \delta\sigma \boldsymbol{HP}_\sigma(\eta_i,\sigma_i) &\doteqdot \alpha\{\boldsymbol{V}(t_i) + \delta t \dot{\boldsymbol{V}}(t_i)\} \\ &= \alpha\{(1 - t_i - \delta t)\boldsymbol{V}_a + (t_i + \delta t)\boldsymbol{V}_b\}. \end{aligned} \tag{15.58}$$

[1] The relations for a type-D1 homogeneous curve can be derived in a similar way. See Section 25.2.1 for a comparison of the characteristics between the homogeneous Newton-Raphson methods for type-D1 and type-D2 curves.

This shows that vector $\boldsymbol{HP}(\eta_i,\sigma_i)+\delta\eta\boldsymbol{HP}_\eta(\eta_i,\sigma_i)+\delta\sigma\boldsymbol{HP}_\sigma(\eta_i,\sigma_i)$ is linearly dependent on $\boldsymbol{V}_a$ and $\boldsymbol{V}_b$, so we have:

$$\begin{vmatrix} \boldsymbol{HP}(\eta_i,\sigma_i)+\delta\eta\boldsymbol{HP}_\eta(\eta_i,\sigma_i)+\delta\sigma\boldsymbol{HP}_\sigma(\eta_i,\sigma_i) \\ \boldsymbol{V}_a \\ \boldsymbol{V}_b \end{vmatrix} = 0.$$

From the linearity property of a determinant, we have:

$$\begin{vmatrix} \boldsymbol{HP}(\eta_i,\sigma_i) \\ \boldsymbol{V}_a \\ \boldsymbol{V}_b \end{vmatrix} + \delta\eta \begin{vmatrix} \boldsymbol{HP}_\eta(\eta_i,\sigma_i) \\ \boldsymbol{V}_a \\ \boldsymbol{V}_b \end{vmatrix} + \delta\sigma \begin{vmatrix} \boldsymbol{HP}_\sigma(\eta_i,\sigma_i) \\ \boldsymbol{V}_a \\ \boldsymbol{V}_b \end{vmatrix} = 0. \tag{15.59}$$

We put as below:

$$HF(\eta,\sigma) = \begin{vmatrix} \boldsymbol{HP}(\eta,\sigma) \\ \boldsymbol{V}_a \\ \boldsymbol{V}_b \end{vmatrix} = \begin{vmatrix} w(\eta,\sigma) & X(\eta,\sigma) & Y(\eta,\sigma) \\ w_a & X_a & Y_a \\ w_b & X_b & Y_b \end{vmatrix}. \tag{15.60}$$

Then eq.(15.59) becomes:

$$HF(\eta_i,\sigma_i) + \delta\eta \cdot HF_\eta(\eta_i,\sigma_i) + \delta\sigma \cdot HF_\sigma(\eta_i,\sigma_i) = 0. \tag{15.61}$$

$HF(\eta,\sigma)$ is the equivalent function for type-D2 homogeneous curve. That is, determining an intersection point is equivalent to finding a root of $HF(\eta,\sigma) = 0$. Therefore, from eq.(15.61), $HF_\eta(\eta_i,\sigma_i)$ and $HF_\sigma(\eta_i,\sigma_i)$ can not be zeros simultaneously while an intersection point is not reached:

$$(HF_\eta(\eta_i,\sigma_i),\ HF_\sigma(\eta_i,\sigma_i)) \neq (0,\ 0). \tag{15.62}$$

Now, we note here that from eqs.(10.18) and (15.21)

$$\begin{vmatrix} \boldsymbol{HP}(\eta,\sigma) \\ \boldsymbol{V}_a \\ \boldsymbol{V}_b \end{vmatrix} = \begin{vmatrix} (\eta+\sigma)^m \boldsymbol{P}(t) \\ \boldsymbol{V}_a \\ \boldsymbol{V}_b \end{vmatrix} = (\eta+\sigma)^m F(t).$$

Thus,

$$HF(\eta,\sigma) = (\eta+\sigma)^m F(t). \tag{15.63}$$

Any $(\delta\eta,\delta\sigma)$ satisfying eq.(15.61) can give a corresponding ordinary parameter increment δt with one exceptional pair. That is,

$$\frac{\delta\sigma}{\delta\eta} \neq \frac{\sigma_i}{\eta_i}. \tag{15.64}$$

When the condition above is not observed, δt becomes zero and the algorithm does not proceed.

One satisfactory method of determining $(\delta\eta,\delta\sigma)$ is to compute an intersection between the line eq.(15.61) and the perpendicular line passing through the origin in $\delta\eta$-$\delta\sigma$ plane (Fig. 15.10):

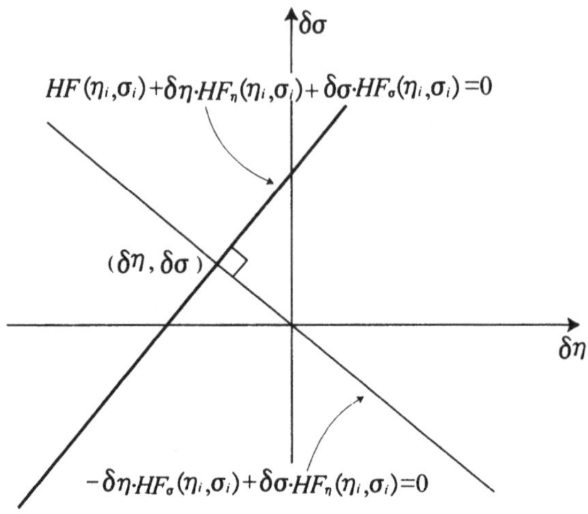

Figure 15.10: Control of homogeneous parameters.

$$-\delta\sigma \cdot HF_\eta(\eta_i, \sigma_i) + \delta\eta \cdot HF_\sigma(\eta_i, \sigma_i) = 0. \tag{15.65}$$

This method minimizes $(\delta\eta)^2 + (\delta\sigma)^2$.

$\delta\eta$ and $\delta\sigma$ are derived in this case as follows:

$$\begin{cases} \delta\eta = -\frac{HF(\eta_i,\sigma_i)\cdot HF_\eta(\eta_i,\sigma_i)}{\{HF_\eta(\eta_i,\sigma_i)\}^2+\{HF_\sigma(\eta_i,\sigma_i)\}^2}, \\ \delta\sigma = -\frac{HF(\eta_i,\sigma_i)\cdot HF_\sigma(\eta_i,\sigma_i)}{\{HF_\eta(\eta_i,\sigma_i)\}^2+\{HF_\sigma(\eta_i,\sigma_i)\}^2}. \end{cases} \tag{15.66}$$

Therefore, we can rewrite η_{i+1} and σ_{i+1} such that the new ones are multiplied by the common denominator of eq.(15.66):

$$\begin{cases} \eta_{i+1} = \eta_i\{\{HF_\eta(\eta_i, \sigma_i)\}^2 + \{HF_\sigma(\eta_i, \sigma_i)\}^2\} - HF(\eta_i, \sigma_i) \cdot HF_\eta(\eta_i, \sigma_i)\}, \\ \sigma_{i+1} = \sigma_i\{\{HF_\eta(\eta_i, \sigma_i)\}^2 + \{HF_\sigma(\eta_i, \sigma_i)\}^2\} - HF(\eta_i, \sigma_i) \cdot HF_\sigma(\eta_i, \sigma_i)\}. \end{cases} \tag{15.67}$$

Repeating the computations of eq.(15.67) determines an intersection point.

For the termination conditions of the convergent process of the type-D homogeneous geometric Newton-Raphson method, see Section 19.2.3.

15.7.2 Local Uniqueness

So far we have mainly discussed non-robustness of convergence often encountered in the conventional Euclidean geometric Newton-Raphson method when it is applied to a rational curve. There is another type of problems, i.e., non-local uniqueness of solutions in the conventional Newton-Raphson method. That is, initial parameter values corresponding to a solution are not in a unique continuous range, but scatter in different ranges. This could also be a serious problem.

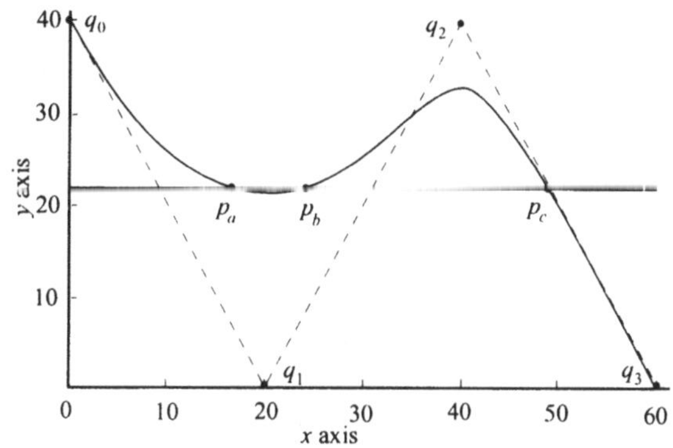

(1) Test data

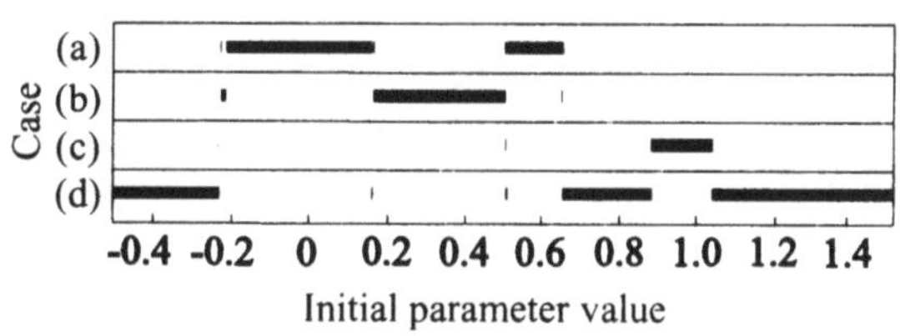

(2) Conventional Euclidean method

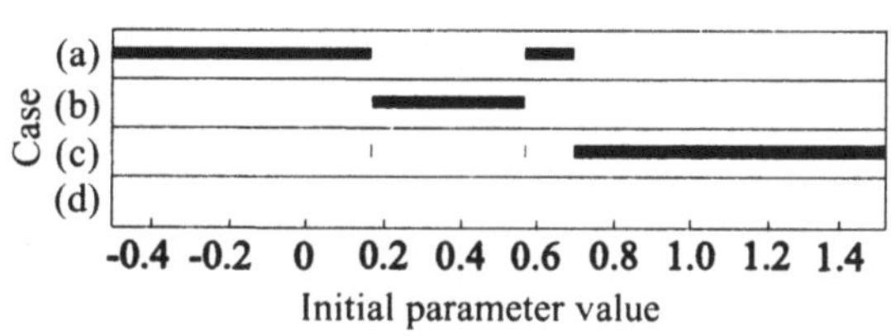

(3) Type-S homogeneous method

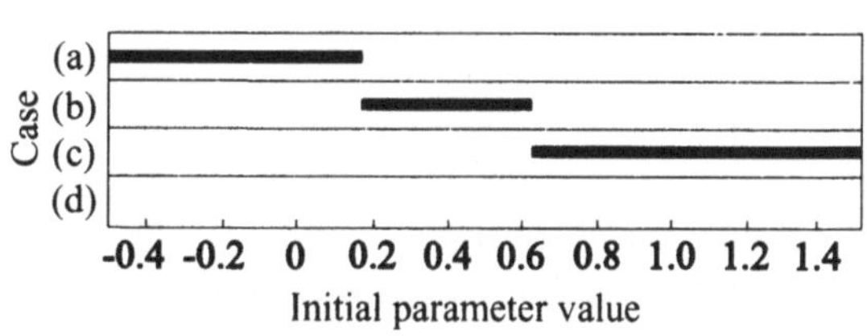

(4) Type-D2 homogeneous method

Figure 15.11: Typical test results.

Let us look at an experiment shown in Fig. 15.11. Fig. 15.11 (2) and (3) depict the results of the conventional Euclidean, and type-S homogeneous Newton-Raphson methods, respectively, applied to determining intersection points between a cubic rational Bézier curve and a line segment shown in Fig. 15.11 (1). In the figures, (a), (b), (c) and (d) correspond to the following cases:

(a) This represents the case where the parameter converges to point p_a,

(b) This represents the case where the parameter converges to point p_b,

(c) This represents the case where the parameter converges to point p_c,

(d) This represents the case where solutions can not be obtained because of the divergence of parameter values.

We have already discussed the detrimental effect of vertical asymptotes of an equivalent function to the local uniqueness property of solutions. From Fig. 15.11 (3), the type-S homogeneous Newton-Raphson method has better local uniqueness than that of the Euclidean method, but still depicts non-local uniqueness although there is no vertical asymptote in the equivalent function (Fig. 15.12). This implies that there is another factor except vertical asymptotes which affects the local uniqueness property.

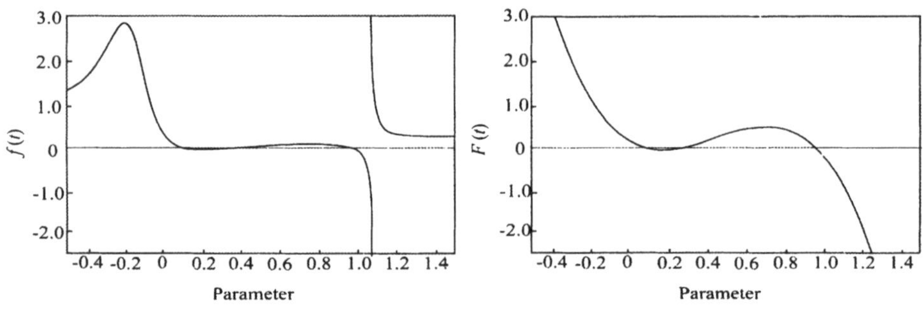

Euclidean method   Type-S homogeneous method

Figure 15.12: Equivalent functions for Euclidean and type-S homogeneous methods corresponding to (2) and (3) of Fig. 15.11, respectively.

Let us look at Fig. 15.11 (4) which shows the test result of type-D2 homogeneous geometric Newton-Raphson method. It exhibits that the type-D2 homogeneous parameter method has superior characteristics of local uniqueness of intersection points with respect to initial parameter value ranges in addition to outstanding characteristics of convergence robustness. Since the algorithm determines the parameter increments in a special way, this fact indicates that the parameter values are controlled appropriately to produce such a nice local uniqueness in the type-D2 homogeneous geometric Newton-Raphson method.

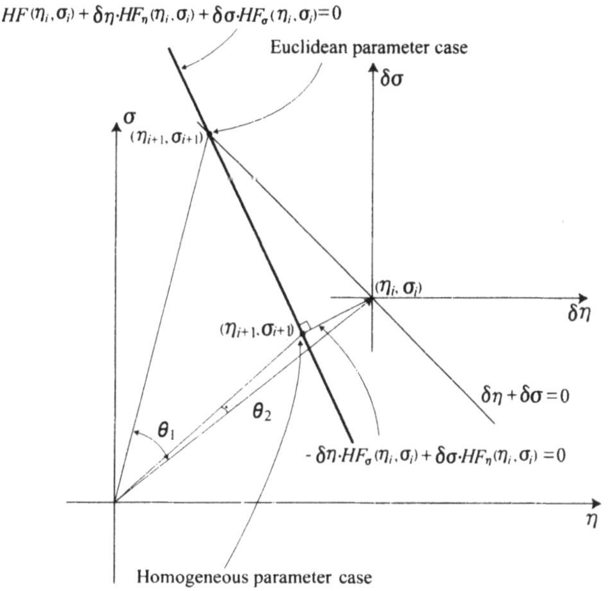

Figure 15.13: Control of homogeneous parameters (1).

Here, we shall analyse the local uniqueness properties of the type-S and type-D2 homogeneous cases, in η-σ space geometrically (Fig. 15.13). Suppose (η_i, σ_i) is already found and $(\eta_{i+1}, \sigma_{i+1})$ is going to be determined. In either case, the next constraint relation must be satisfied:

$$HF(\eta_i, \sigma_i) + \delta\eta \cdot HF_\eta(\eta_i, \sigma_i) + \delta\sigma \cdot HF_\sigma(\eta_i, \sigma_i) = 0. \tag{15.68}$$

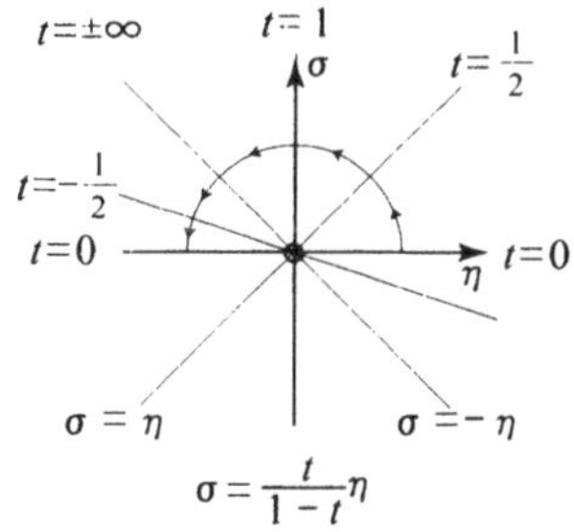

Figure 15.14: Relation of ordinary and homogeneous parameters.

1. **Type-S homogeneous case**

   The ordinary parameter case can be represented using homogeneous parameters as below (see eq.(8.29)):

$$\delta\eta + \delta\sigma = 0. \tag{15.69}$$

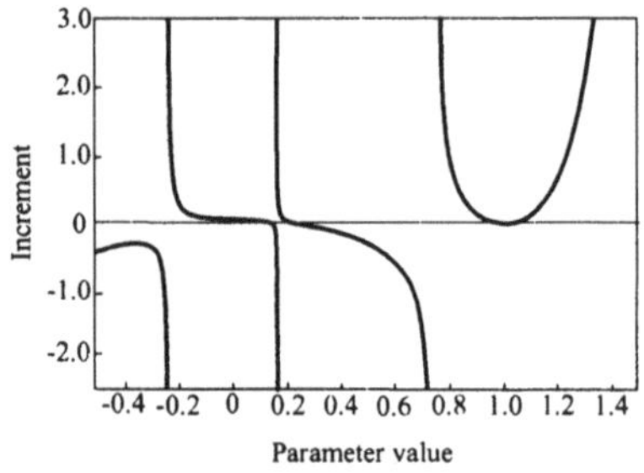

(1) Conventional Euclidean method

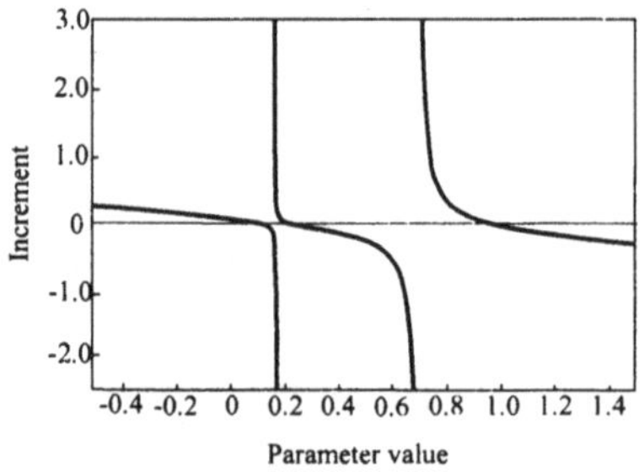

(2) Type-S homogeneous method

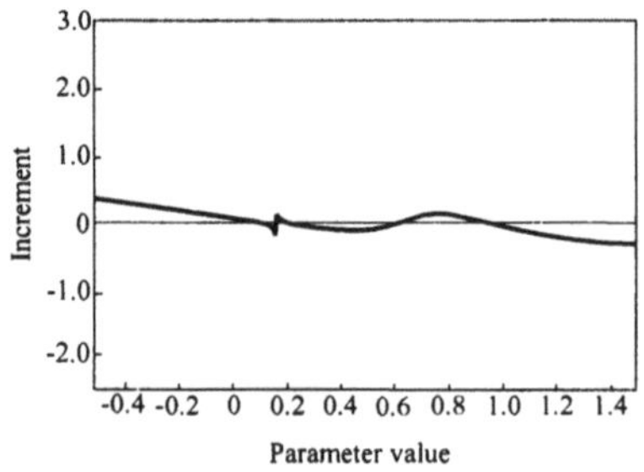

(3) Type-D2 homogeneous method

Figure 15.15: Ordinary parameter increments δt in three cases.

Therefore, the next point $(\eta_{i+1}, \sigma_{i+1})$ is automatically determined as the intersection of the line of the constraint equation, eq.(15.68) and the line of eq.(15.69), in η-σ space. There is no way of controlling the magnitude of δt. Note that the ordinary parameter increment δt becomes very large when the two lines are almost parallel (Fig. 15.14). This is the reason why type-S homogeneous method does not have good local uniqueness property. The ordinary parameter increment δt of Fig. 15.11 (1) case is shown in (2) of Fig. 15.15 (The results were derived experimentally from the Newton-Raphson algorithm).

2. **Type-D2 homogeneous case**

   The type-D2 homogeneous method has a freedom of determining the next parameters, and thus they are determined such that the corresponding ordinary parameter increment δt does not become too large over a wide range of parameter values. In order to attain this purpose, the next point $(\eta_{i+1}, \sigma_{i+1})$ is determined such that $(\delta\eta)^2 + (\delta\sigma)^2$ is minimized. Because the next point is ordinarily in the vicinity of the present point, δt is kept small in almost all cases over a wide range of t. The corresponding ordinary parameter increment δt of Fig. 15.11 (1) case is shown in (3) of Fig. 15.15, along with those of conventional Euclidean and type-S homogeneous methods.

In fact there are two types of local uniquenesses, i.e., one is projective and the other Euclidean. For these, see Example 4 in Section 25.2.1.

15.8 Type-C Homogeneous Method

As long as we deal with real roots, type-S and type-D geometric Newton-Raphson methods are sufficiently satisfactory. If there exists a complex root and the parameter happens to approach the area, however, it will oscillate around the solution and not converge. This raises another kind of non-robustness problem.

Let us consider adapting the homogeneous method to complex root cases as well. We shall consider two types. One is the application of type-S homogeneous method, and the other that of type-D.

15.8.1 Type-CS Homogeneous Method

Let us consider applying the type-S homogeneous method to complex root cases.

We express the parameter t in complex number:

$$t = t_r + t_i \cdot i,$$

where i represents imaginary unit.

In this case the equivalent function is also represented in a complex form:

$$\begin{aligned} F(t) &= F(t_r, t_i) \\ &= FR(t_r, t_i) + FI(t_r, t_i) \cdot i. \end{aligned} \tag{15.70}$$

Solving for the roots of the equivalent function $F(t) = 0$ is equivalent to determining the parameter values corresponding to the intersection points. At a solution point,

$$FR(t_r, t_i) = 0 \text{ and } FI(t_r, t_i) = 0, \tag{15.71}$$

since $F(t_r, t_i)=0$ there.

Applying the Taylor expansion to eq.(15.71) and extracting up to the first-order term, we obtain:

$$FR(t_r, t_i) + \delta t_r \cdot FR_{t_r}(t_r, t_i) + \delta t_i \cdot FR_{t_i}(t_r, t_i) = 0, \tag{15.72}$$

$$FI(t_r, t_i) + \delta t_r \cdot FI_{t_r}(t_r, t_i) + \delta t_i \cdot FI_{t_i}(t_r, t_i) = 0. \tag{15.73}$$

From the two equations above, we have:

$$\begin{aligned} \delta t_r &= \frac{FR_i \cdot FI - FR \cdot FI_i}{FR_r \cdot FI_i - FR_i \cdot FI_r}, \\ \delta t_i &= \frac{FR \cdot FI_r - FR_r \cdot FI}{FR_r \cdot FI_i - FR_i \cdot FI_r}, \end{aligned} \tag{15.74}$$

where

$$\begin{aligned} &FR \equiv FR(t_r, t_i), \quad FR_r \equiv FR_{t_r}(t_r, t_i), \quad FR_i \equiv FR_{t_i}(t_r, t_i), \\ &FI \equiv FI(t_r, t_i), \quad FI_r \equiv FI_{t_r}(t_r, t_i), \quad FI_i \equiv FI_{t_i}(t_r, t_i). \end{aligned}$$

From δt_r and δt_i, the new set of parameter values are obtained as:

$$t_{r,j+1} = t_{r,j} + \delta t_r, \quad t_{i,j+1} = t_{i,j} + \delta t_i \ (j = 0, 1, 2, \ldots).$$

The iterations above are repeated to determine the solution. We shall call this algorithm "type-CS homogeneous method."

It is possible to apply the type-D homogeneous method to complex root cases (see Section 8.6). We shall call this "type-CD homogeneous method."It is regrettable that the author can not discuss it here.

Chapter 16

Exact Arithmetic

16.1 Geometric Computations

In the Four-dimensional Processing, geometric elements defined in a projective space are treated consistently in its associated vector space $\mathbf{R}^4$. The computations in the space are usually done without the use of division operations. If required, exact computations might be carried out using long integer data. In this case the concept of vector space used in Section 3.1 must be generalized such that it is defined as module based on ring of integers (see Section 16.3).

Projective transformations are performed as linear transformations by the well-known 4×4 matrix method (see Chapter 6).

Geometric tests are carried out by making the most use of Plücker coordinates and coefficients (see Sections 9.1.2), i.e., by the homogeneous determinant method (see Chapter 14). In the method the orientations of the vectors defined by Plücker coordinates or coefficients are tested, where signs of 2×2, 3×3 or 4×4 determinants are checked.

16.2 Long Integer Representation

16.2.1 Various Errors

In the early days of computer graphics and geometric modeling, numerical data were expressed using fixed decimal point representation. With this method, however, it was necessary to carry out scaling frequently during computations in order to maintain accuracy. This was a tedious step for the programmer, as well as being a source of programming errors. Nowadays, floating-point representation has replaced fixed decimal point one as the standard of numerical data representation.

With floating-point representation, scaling is carried out automatically using the proper scaling index, and this has eased the programmer's burden considerably. Moreover, the introduction of a floating-point processing unit (FPU) that handles floating-point arithmetic has made high-speed processing possible.

Now, computational errors can cause serious problems in geometric modeling. For instance, when carrying out set operations in solid modeling, an erroneous geometric test result stemming from the slightest computational error may conflict with topological data descriptions pertaining to the solid in question, and thus create a serious hang-up situation in computer processing. In cases where the computational error merely results in lowering the representational accuracy of shapes, the problem is trivial. If, however, the error creates conflicting judgments against topological data representation, it cannot be ignored. A major issue in computer aided geometric design field nowadays, therefore, is to minimize or eliminate those errors that occur in the geometric modeling process.

Since computer carries out calculations based on finite data length, it is impossible, when dealing with real numbers, to represent all numbers exactly that lie between two given representable limits, regardless of whether floating-point or fixed decimal point representation is used. Consider to express the decimal 0.6, for example (see page 529). Thus the only choice we have left is to depend on approximation by employing the numbers that are representable. Division also is a source of error when its results are represented. Such minute errors will naturally accumulate in the computational process, and so a certain margin of error has always been considered unavoidable.

In the Four-dimensional Processing, on the other hand, all the geometric elements are represented in homogeneous coordinates or coefficients, which can thus be expressed in integers as long as rational numbers are dealt with. This means that the computations could be carried out exactly using only integers.

Below we compare the computations, by fixed-length integer and by floating-point representations for the case when computations involve integers only, and no division is carried out.

There are, in general, five types of errors that occur in numerical computations.

1. **Round-off error (rounding error)**

   When all computations are carried out using a finite, fixed number of digits, the lower-end digits are sometimes discarded. That is, when the result falls between two consecutive representable numbers on the real line, one of the two must be chosen to represent that result. The error in this case is the *round-off error.*

   With floating-point representation, one cannot always express all integers that lie between two given limits because the distance between two consecutive representable numbers widens with increasing exponent. Consequently, addition, subtraction and multiplication all produce round-off errors.

   Meanwhile, there are no round-off errors with fixed-length integer representation.

2. **Loss of information**

   When adding or subtracting between two numbers whose absolute values differ greatly, the lower-end digits of the smaller number are sometimes lost as a result of digit alignment. This is called *loss of information.*

   This error occurs with floating-point representation, which uses exponents to express numbers, but not with fixed-length integer representation.

3. **Cancellation**

   The addition of, or subtraction between two numbers, whose absolute values are almost the same can result in the disappearance of some significant digits. This is called *cancellation.*

   This type of error can occur with floating-point representation, which uses powers to represent numbers, but not with fixed-length integer representation.

4. **Overflow**

   Overflow occurs when the computational result becomes too large and can no longer be expressed within the representable range.

   While this type of error can occur with both floating-point and fixed-length integer representations, it occurs much less with the former, which has separate bits for expressing powers, although it can occur fairly often with fixed-length integer representation with its narrow expressible range.

5. **Underflow**

   Underflow occurs when the computational result is smaller than the smallest possible number that can be represented. This error does not occur when computations involve integers only and with no division, whether using floating-point or fixed-length integer representation.

As we have seen, neither fixed-length integer nor floating-point representation is completely free from errors when a finite, fixed data length is employed. While overflow occurs infrequently in floating-point representation, this method is subject to round-off errors, loss of information and cancellation even when only integers are dealt with.

Meanwhile, fixed-length integer arithmetic has neither round-off error, loss of information nor cancellation, but the extremely narrow range of representable numbers can often lead to overflow. To resolve the problem of overflow that accompanies fixed-length integer arithmetic and achieve error-free computation, we shall employ variable word-length integer data.

The Four-dimensional Processing, based on variable word-length integers, enables an error-free computation as long as the computations involve rational numbers only.

16.2.2 Variable Word-length Integer Data

Variable word-length integers adhere to a certain data arrangement. Figure 16.1 shows the memory image of a variable word-length integer representation. That is, the first 16 bits express the word-length of the data, and this is followed by the data proper beginning with the lower-end words. The word-length part expresses, in complements of two, the sign and word-length of the data in question. The number "zero" has a word-length of 0, and is expressed by one word (32 bits). Since there are many computational situations where a zero must be retained, this method serves to save memory. The data proper is expressed as an absolute value.

In computers, two's complements are generally employed to represent numbers for the following reasons:

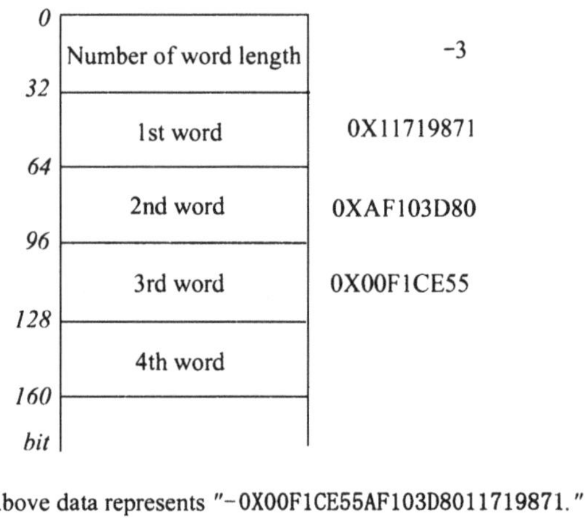

Figure 16.1: Memory image of variable word-length integer representation.

(1) If absolute values are used, two kinds of "zeros," +0 and −0, can occur. This situation does not arise with two's complements.

(2) With absolute values, one cannot simply add or subtract the bits representing two numbers if they are of different signs. With two's complements, however, this is possible.

Yet:

1. Bit-by-bit addition or subtraction (item (2) above) is not a straightforward operation when the word-length is variable;

2. For multiplication and division, numbers must in any case be converted to absolute values;

3. In the adaptive sign detection method, shifting is carried out to increase computational speed, but for this, we need to determine the maximum absolute value of the numbers involved (see Section 16.7);

4. The sign of a variable word-length integer can be easily ascertained if a word is assigned for the purpose.

For the reasons above, we shall employ absolute values rather than two's complements when using variable word-length integers.

With the variable word-length integer representation, any rational number can be expressed exactly by using the smallest relevant unit. Yet, if one uses the smallest unit pertaining to some object to describe its basic data, an unnecessary amount of digits must be kept, resulting in lower computational speed and wasted memory space. If, instead, we use the most frequently appearing unit (which we shall call the MFA unit) to describe the object's basic data, we can increase the computational speed and effectively utilize memory space.

Let us take an example of describing point coordinates of some geometric figure, for which the smallest unit is $1[\mu m]$ and the MFA unit $1[mm]$.

When the coordinates of points A and B are given as:

$$\begin{aligned} x_A &= 100[mm], & y_A &= 35[mm], & z_A &= 500[mm] \text{ (ordinary coordinates)},\\ x_B &= 100.35[mm], & y_B &= 35[mm], & z_B &= 500[mm] \text{ (ordinary coordinates)}, \end{aligned}$$

the numerical expressions for the cases when the smallest unit and the MFA unit are respectively used as the basic unit are as follows.

1. **Using the smallest unit as the standard unit (homogeneous coordinates)**

$$\begin{aligned} w_A &= 1, & x_A &= 100000[\mu m], & y_A &= 35000[\mu m], & z_A &= 500000[\mu m],\\ w_B &= 1, & x_B &= 100350[\mu m], & y_B &= 35000[\mu m], & z_B &= 500000[\mu m]. \end{aligned}$$

2. **Using the MFA unit as the standard unit (homogeneous coordinates)**

$$\begin{aligned} w_A &= 1, & x_A &= 100[mm], & y_A &= 35[mm], & z_A &= 500[mm],\\ w_B &= 100, & x_B &= 10035[mm], & y_B &= 3500[mm], & z_B &= 50000[mm]. \end{aligned}$$

A comparison of (1) and (2) above shows that the MFA unit is more convenient because it can describe the basic data (point coordinates) more concisely.

16.3 Generalization of Vector Space

The ordinary vector space is defined on a *field*. By the use of vectors in this vector space, projective spaces can be defined, where geometric elements of the Four-dimensional Processing are also defined.

Now, consider to use integer arithmetic in the Four-dimensional Processing for the purpose of carrying out exact computations. Since the set of integer does not make a field, the ordinary vector space can not be used for the definitions of projective spaces in this case.

For the purpose of performing exact computations by integer arithmetic, we must generalize the concept of vector space. Note that the set of integer makes a *commutative ring*. We define projective space by using a generalized vector space, i.e., a *module* on a commutative ring such that letting R a commutative ring and $\boldsymbol{S}$, $\boldsymbol{T}$ elements of modules on R, the equivalence relation for defining classical projective space is given as follows:

$$\boldsymbol{S} \sim \boldsymbol{T} \Leftrightarrow \exists\zeta \in R,\ \exists\eta \in R,\ \zeta \neq 0, \eta \neq 0 : \zeta\boldsymbol{S} = \eta\boldsymbol{T}. \tag{16.1}$$

The relation for defining two-sided space is obtained by replacing $\zeta\neq0, \eta\neq0$ by $\zeta>0, \eta>0$ in eq.(16.1).

Since the equivalence relations for defining projective spaces in the generalized vector space are different from those in the ordinary one, the definitions of geometric elements, and derivation processes of the formulas of the Four-dimensional Processing are somewhat different between these vector spaces, but many results turn out to be the same.

16.4 Data Length for Exact Computations

Exact computations generally require very long integer data, and the lengths of the data increase with repetition of computations. We shall discuss this problem, by taking as an example, the intersection point computation of two planar lines L_0 and L_1.

We assume L_0 goes through points $\overline{(h, -hx_0, -Y_0)}$ and $\overline{(h, hx_0, Y_0)}$, and L_1 through points $\overline{(h, -hx_0, Y_0)}$ and $\overline{(h, hx_0, -Y_0)}$ (see Fig. 16.2). When the value of h increases, then the intersecting angle of the two line segments decreases while the Euclidean x-value of each endpoint is kept fixed.

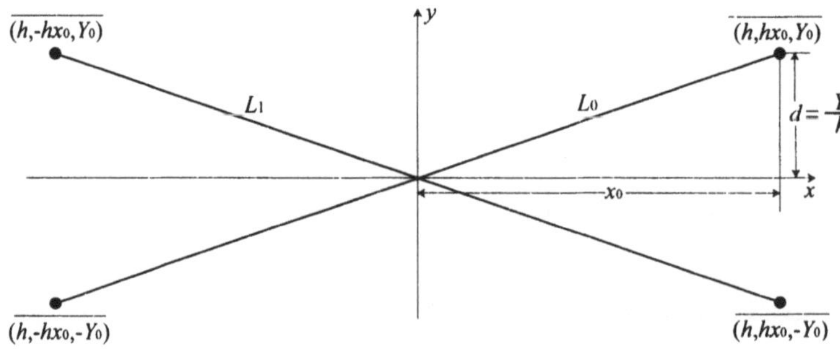

Figure 16.2: Data length increases as intersecting angle decreases.

Line Equations for L_0 and L_1

From the Plücker coordinate formula in Table C.1, we have line equations for L_0 and L_1 as follows:

Case 1

$$\begin{aligned} \text{Line } L_0 : &\quad 2hY_0 \cdot X - 2h^2 x_0 \cdot Y = 0, \\ \text{Line } L_1 : &\quad 2hY_0 \cdot X + 2h^2 x_0 \cdot Y = 0. \end{aligned} \tag{16.2}$$

Or in simplified forms, assuming $h \neq 0$:

Case 2

$$\begin{aligned} \text{Line } L_0 : &\quad Y_0 \cdot X - hx_0 \cdot Y = 0, \\ \text{Line } L_1 : &\quad Y_0 \cdot X + hx_0 \cdot Y = 0. \end{aligned} \tag{16.3}$$

Intersection Point of Lines L_0 and L_1

From eq.(16.2), we have homogeneous coordinates of the intersection point as follows:

Case 1

$$(w, X, Y) \equiv (8h^3 x_0 Y_0, 0, 0). \tag{16.4}$$

From eq.(16.3), we have another homogeneous representation of the same point as follows:

Case 2

$$(w, X, Y) \equiv (2hx_0 Y_0, 0, 0). \tag{16.5}$$

Increase of Data Length

The w-value above can be written in the form of the increase of data length in bits in terms of the ratio of h with respect to the original value h_0:

Case 1

$$\log_2 \left(\frac{h}{h_0}\right)^3 \quad \text{(bits)}, \tag{16.6}$$

Case 2

$$\log_2 \frac{h}{h_0} \quad \text{(bits)}. \tag{16.7}$$

Eq.(16.4) shows that w-value of the intersection point is proportional to h^3. This means that the data length of w increases by 10 bits when h is increased by a factor of 10, as is also shown in eq.(16.6). On the other hand, eq.(16.5) shows that w-value is linearly proportional to h. This means that the data length of w increases by 10 bits when h is increased by a factor of as many as 1000, as is also shown in eq.(16.7). The difference of the increases of data lengths between the two approaches is very big.

This analysis suggests that deleting common factors among homogeneous coordinates and coefficients prior to computations if possible, is very important and useful in terms of computing efficiency and memory space (see Section 25.1.1).

16.5 Computational Considerations in Practice

In the Totally Four-dimensional Processing we deal with data represented in homogeneous coordinates or coefficients (Plücker coordinates or coefficients). These data representations often have redundancies (common factors) in numerical formulas and numerical data. The redundancies could cause to deteriorate accuracy and efficiency. Therefore we had better remove these redundancies before performing computations if possible.

As for numerical data, the redundancy can be removed by the normalizations of homogeneous coordinates as discussed in Section 2.4.

The redundancy of a numerical formula, on the other hand, can be removed by the simplification of the formula as we saw in an example of homogeneous line coefficients of previous section.

Generally speaking, we should first simplify the formula and then normalize the numerical data of coordinates or coefficients, before we perform computations.

The details follow below:

1. **Integer format case**

   In the case of integer format, the normalization of integer homogeneous coordinates removes the redundancies of the numerical formula as well as numerical data. It would be more efficient, however, to remove the redundancy of the formula before doing that of numerical data.

2. **Floating-point format case**

   In the case of floating-point format, we must remove the redundancy of the numerical formula before we do that of numerical data (normalization of floating-point homogeneous coordinates), otherwise the truncation error of the floating-point representation of unsimplified, long digits could prevent from removing the redundancy of the numerical data.

16.6 Hybrid Approach to Exact Arithmetic

Although long integer arithmetic based on the Four-dimensional Processing makes it possible to realize exact arithmetic, it is generally very time-consuming.

Note that rational numbers of homogeneous representation can be transformed to integers, and therefore exact arithmetic is also possible with floating-point arithmetic coupled with the Four-dimensional Processing while the digits of the integer coordinates are within the expressible range of the mantissa of the floating-point representation (see Tables 25.1, 25.4 and 25.5). By the use of a floating-point processing unit obtainable commonly, the floating-point exact arithmetic can be accelerated (see Tables 25.2 and 25.10).

What is desired in the Four-dimensional Processing environment is a hybrid computation routine which switches between the long integer and floating-point exact arithmetic units, adaptively to the anticipated data lengths.

16.7 Adaptive Sign Detections

One of the major features of the Four-dimensional Processing as proposed in this book is that it is free from division operations and, combined with integer arithmetic, enables us to carry out computations without error. Yet, rigorously carrying out geometric operations without error might require the use of very long integer data and be very time consuming. Indeed, very long integer data are generally necessary to identify intersection points without error. On the other hand, over 90% of determinants appearing in most normal applications are used only to determine some geometric relationship. For such tests, we only need to know the sign, not the actual value, of the determinants, and this can be accurately established with short data lengths. Thus, one can simplify computations by employing only the necessary and sufficient bits of very long data and shorten computation time.

Since the computation of a determinant can be reduced to that of a scalar product, we discuss adaptive error-free sign tests of scalar products of two vectors, first involving word-based (see next section), then bit-based manipulations (see Section 16.7.2). Finally, we present an adaptive, error-free sign test by using an FPU in order to accelerate the computations.

16.7.1 Scalar Product of 4-D Vectors

A 4×4 determinant S is supposed to have components consisting of data of multi-words and to have been represented as (see eq.(13.99)):

$$\begin{aligned} S &= \boldsymbol{V}_a \cdot \boldsymbol{F}_{012} \\ &= [w_a \ X_a \ Y_a \ Z_a] \begin{bmatrix} A_{012} \\ B_{012} \\ C_{012} \\ D_{012} \end{bmatrix} . \end{aligned} \tag{16.8}$$

Let us consider determining the sign of a 4×4 determinant, S, by computing the scalar product above.

First, each component is transformed (i.e., shifted) into one-word data composed of the upper bits (we shall call this "shift operation"), then the scalar product (i.e., determinant) is computed. The absolute value of the computed result is then compared to the "maximum error limit" (discussed below); if the absolute value of the result is larger, it has the correct sign (i.e., same as that of the original 4×4 determinant).

The algorithm is shown below:

1. **Shift operations**

   The word-lengths of A_{012}, B_{012}, C_{012} and D_{012} are first checked.

   If one or more of these components have data lengths exceeding one word, the component with the greatest absolute value is shifted to make a one-word data consisting of the upper bits; the rest of the components are also shifted by the same number of bits. The shifted data are then returned along with the information "shifted."

   If none of the components exceeds one word in data length, no shifting takes place and the information "unshifted" is returned.

   The components w_a, X_a, Y_a and Z_a of vector $\boldsymbol{V}_a$ are also shifted in the same way.

2. **Computation of determinant**

   If all coordinates of $\boldsymbol{F}_{012}$ and $\boldsymbol{V}_a$ have data lengths of within one word, the determinant value, S, is directly computed.

   In all other cases, a determinant is computed by obtaining the scalar product using the shifted one-word data; we shall call the result S_{shift}. Clearly S_{shift} is different from the true determinant value, S.

3. **Comparison and recomputation**

   The absolute value of S_{shift} is compared to the maximum error limit E_{max} (discussed later); when it is found to be smaller than E_{max}, then S_{shift} may have a different sign from S . In this case, exact S must be computed (see discussion below).

4. **Sign test**

   The sign of S_{shift} or S is determined.

We now discuss the maximum error limit E_{max}. We want E_{max} to be as small as possible, for if it were needlessly large, S would have to be frequently re-computed, and the processing efficiency will suffer. E_{max} can be determined beforehand regardless of the data.

Below, we shall determine E_{max} when obtaining S as the scalar product of four-dimensional vectors.

Assume that the homogeneous plane coefficient vector $\boldsymbol{F}_{012} = [A_{012}\ B_{012}\ C_{012}\ D_{012}]^T$ has been obtained with no error. Denoting the components of $\boldsymbol{V}_a$ by w_a, X_a, Y_a and Z_a, the 4×4 determinant S is given by:

$$S = A_{012}w_a + B_{012}X_a + C_{012}Y_a + D_{012}Z_a. \tag{16.9}$$

w_a, X_a, Y_a, Z_a and A_{012}, B_{012}, C_{012}, D_{012} can be expressed as follows:

$$\begin{cases} w_a = w_{aH} \cdot 2^m + w_{aL}, & A_{012} = A_H \cdot 2^l + A_L, \\ X_a = X_{aH} \cdot 2^m + X_{aL}, & B_{012} = B_H \cdot 2^l + B_L, \\ Y_a = Y_{aH} \cdot 2^m + Y_{aL}, & C_{012} = C_H \cdot 2^l + C_L, \\ Z_a = Z_{aH} \cdot 2^m + Z_{aL}, & D_{012} = D_H \cdot 2^l + D_L, \end{cases} \tag{16.10}$$

where w_{aH}, X_{aH}, Y_{aH}, Z_{aH} and A_H, B_H, C_H, D_H represent values of the shifted upper one word, and w_{aL}, X_{aL}, Y_{aL}, Z_{aL} and A_L, B_L, C_L, D_L those of the discarded portions, consisting respectively of m and l bits.

Substituting eq.(16.10) into eq.(16.9) and rearranging, we obtain:

$$\begin{aligned} S = {} & (w_{aH}A_H + X_{aH}B_H + Y_{aH}C_H + Z_{aH}D_H) \cdot 2^{m+l} \\ & + (w_{aH}A_L + X_{aH}B_L + Y_{aH}C_L + Z_{aH}D_L) \cdot 2^m \\ & + (w_{aL}A_H + X_{aL}B_H + Y_{aL}C_H + Z_{aL}D_H) \cdot 2^l \\ & + w_{aL}A_L + X_{aL}B_L + Y_{aL}C_L + Z_{aL}D_L, \end{aligned} \tag{16.11}$$

where we know that

$$\begin{aligned} -2^m < w_{aL},\ X_{aL},\ Y_{aL},\ Z_{aL} < 2^m, \\ -2^l < A_L,\ B_L,\ C_L,\ D_L < 2^l. \end{aligned} \tag{16.12}$$

Denoting by S_{shift} the 4×4 determinant obtained from the shifted data, we have:

$$S_{shift} = w_{aH}A_H + X_{aH}B_H + Y_{aH}C_H + Z_{aH}D_H.$$

So eq.(16.11) can be written:

$$\begin{aligned} S = {} & S_{shift} \cdot 2^{m+l} \\ & + (w_{aH}A_L + X_{aH}B_L + Y_{aH}C_L + Z_{aH}D_L) \cdot 2^m \\ & + (w_{aL}A_H + X_{aL}B_H + Y_{aL}C_H + Z_{aL}D_H) \cdot 2^l \\ & + w_{aL}A_L + X_{aL}B_L + Y_{aL}C_L + Z_{aL}D_L. \end{aligned} \tag{16.13}$$

From eq.(16.12), we obtain the following relationships for the 2-nd, 3-rd and 4-th terms on the right-hand side of eq.(16.13):

$$\begin{aligned} & -(|w_{aH}| + |X_{aH}| + |Y_{aH}| + |Z_{aH}|) \cdot 2^{m+l} < \\ & (w_{aH}A_L + X_{aH}B_L + Y_{aH}C_L + Z_{aH}D_L) \cdot 2^m \\ & < (|w_{aH}| + |X_{aH}| + |Y_{aH}| + |Z_{aH}|) \cdot 2^{m+l}, \\ \\ & -(|A_H| + |B_H| + |C_H| + |D_H|) \cdot 2^{m+l} < \\ & (w_{aL}A_H + X_{aL}B_H + Y_{aL}C_H + Z_{aL}D_H) \cdot 2^l \\ & < (|A_H| + |B_H| + |C_H| + |D_H|) \cdot 2^{m+l}, \\ \\ & -4 \cdot 2^{m+l} < w_{aL}A_L + X_{aL}B_L + Y_{aL}C_L + Z_{aL}D_L < 4 \cdot 2^{m+l}. \end{aligned} \tag{16.14}$$

From eqs.(16.13) and (16.14), we obtain the following inequality:

$$(S_{shift} - E_{max})2^{m+l} < S < (S_{shift} + E_{max})2^{m+l}, \tag{16.15}$$

where

$$\begin{aligned} E_{max} &= (|w_{aH}| + |X_{aH}| + |Y_{aH}| + |Z_{aH}| \\ &\quad +|A_H| + |B_H| + |C_H| + |D_H|) + 4. \end{aligned} \tag{16.16}$$

When the absolute value of S_{shift} satisfies the relationship:

$$|S_{shift}| > E_{max}, \tag{16.17}$$

then S_{shift} and S have the same sign.

To determine an E_{max} value that does not depend on the given data, we write E_{max} as follows:

$$\begin{aligned} E_{max} &= (|w_{aH}| + |X_{aH}| + |Y_{aH}| + |Z_{aH}| \\ &\quad +|A_H| + |B_H| + |C_H| + |D_H|) + 4 \\ &\leq 8 \cdot max(|w_{aH}|, |X_{aH}|, |Y_{aH}|, |Z_{aH}|, |A_H|, |B_H|, |C_H|, |D_H|) + 4 \\ &\leq 8 \cdot (fffffff(H)) + 4 \\ &= 7ffffffc(H). \end{aligned} \tag{16.18}$$

Thus, E_{max}, when computing the scalar product of four-dimensional vectors, is given by:

$$E_{max} = 7ffffffc(H). \tag{16.19}$$

When S_{shift} obtained from shifted data has an absolute value greater than the maximum error limit, processing is fast. If this is smaller than the error limit, however, this method actually takes more processing time since S has to be computed anew. This inefficiency can be minimized by using the previously computed value for S_{shift} so that only the remainder needs computing. That is, we see from eq.(16.13) that S can be computed accurately if S_{shift} is shifted to the left by $(m+l)$ bits and the 2-nd, 3-rd and 4-th terms are added.

16.7.2 Scalar Product of n-D Vectors

In this section, our discussion on adaptive sign testing is further generalized to scalar products of n-dimensional vectors, and the sign is determined by adjusting data on a per-bit basis [68], [69].

Let $\boldsymbol{A} = [A_1\ A_2\ \dots\ A_n]$ and $\boldsymbol{B} = [B_1\ B_2\ \dots\ B_n]$ be n-dimensional vectors with integer components. Let ρ denote the number of bits needed to represent the component of $\boldsymbol{A}$ with the largest absolute value, $A_{iH,m}$ the upper m-bit portion of the components, and A_{iL} the remaining lower portion. For $\boldsymbol{B}$, the corresponding items are denoted by σ, $B_{iH,m}$ and B_{iL} (see Fig. 16.3).

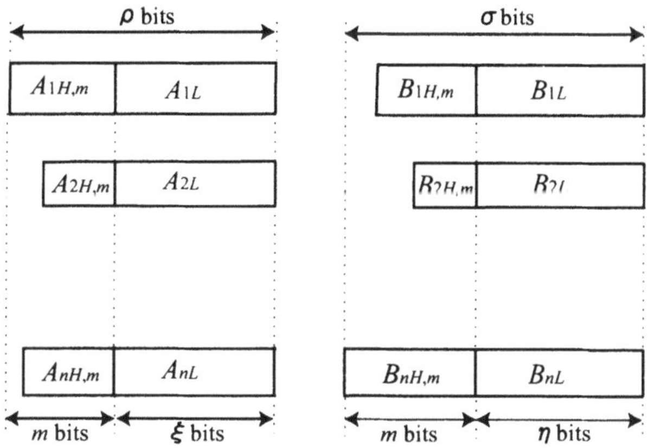

Figure 16.3: Upper and lower data of vectors $\boldsymbol{A}$ and $\boldsymbol{B}$.

Denoting by A_{max} and B_{max} the components of $\boldsymbol{A}$ and $\boldsymbol{B}$ with the largest absolute values, respectively, ρ and σ can be expressed as follows:

$$\rho = \lfloor \log_2 |A_{max}| \rfloor + 1, \quad \sigma = \lfloor \log_2 |B_{max}| \rfloor + 1, \tag{16.20}$$

where A_{max} and B_{max} are assumed to be nonzero.

By extracting the upper m bits of the vector components, starting at the position of the leading bit of the component with the largest absolute value, they can be written as follows:

$$A_i = A_{iH,m} \cdot 2^{\xi} + A_{iL}, \quad B_i = B_{iH,m} \cdot 2^{\eta} + B_{iL}, \quad (1 \le i \le n), \tag{16.21}$$

where

$$\xi = \rho - m, \quad \eta = \sigma - m, \tag{16.22}$$

$$A_{iL} < 2^{\xi}, \quad B_{iL} < 2^{\eta}. \tag{16.23}$$

Denoting the scalar product of only the upper-level data for the two vectors by $(\boldsymbol{A} \cdot \boldsymbol{B})_{H,m}$, we have:

$$(\boldsymbol{A} \cdot \boldsymbol{B})_{H,m} = \sum_{i=1}^{n} A_{iH,m} B_{iH,m}. \tag{16.24}$$

The scalar product of vectors $\boldsymbol{A}$ and $\boldsymbol{B}$ is given from eq.(16.21) as:

$$\begin{aligned} \boldsymbol{A} \cdot \boldsymbol{B} = & \sum_{i=1}^{n} A_{iH,m} B_{iH,m} \cdot 2^{\xi+\eta} + \sum_{i=1}^{n} A_{iH,m} B_{iL} \cdot 2^{\xi} \\ & + \sum_{i=1}^{n} A_{iL} B_{iH,m} \cdot 2^{\eta} + \sum_{i=1}^{n} A_{iL} B_{iL}. \end{aligned} \tag{16.25}$$

The 1-st term on the right-hand side of eq.(16.25) is the scalar product of upper-level data, multiplied by $2^{\xi+\eta}$. If the 1-st term has an absolute value greater than the sum of those of the 2-nd, 3-rd and 4-th terms, then it has the same sign as the accurately determined scalar product.

From eq.(16.23), the following inequalities exist for the 2-nd, 3-rd and 4-th terms on the right-hand side of eq.(16.25):

$$\begin{aligned} |\sum_{i=1}^{n} A_{iH,m} B_{iL} \cdot 2^{\xi}| &< (\sum_{i=1}^{n} |A_{iH,m}|) \cdot 2^{\xi+\eta}, \\ |\sum_{i=1}^{n} A_{iL} B_{iH,m} \cdot 2^{\eta}| &< (\sum_{i=1}^{n} |B_{iH,m}|) \cdot 2^{\xi+\eta}, \\ |\sum_{i=1}^{n} A_{iL} B_{iL}| &< n \cdot 2^{\xi+\eta}. \end{aligned} \tag{16.26}$$

Therefore, the sum of the absolute values of the 2-nd, 3-rd and 4-th terms is smaller than the product of $2^{\xi+\eta}$ and:

$$(\sum_{i=1}^{n} |A_{iH,m}| + \sum_{i=1}^{n} |B_{iH,m}|) + n.$$

Because $|A_{iH,m}|$ or $|B_{iH,m}|$ can be at most 2^m-1, the sum of the absolute values of the 2-nd, 3-rd and 4-th terms is smaller than the product of $2^{\xi+\eta}$ and:

$$E_{max,m} = 2n \cdot 2^m - n. \tag{16.27}$$

$E_{max,m}$ is the maximum error limit we seek. The following relationship then holds among the scalar product using upper-level data, the maximum error limit and the accurately determined scalar product:

$$((\boldsymbol{A} \cdot \boldsymbol{B})_{H,m} - E_{max,m})2^{\xi+\eta} < \boldsymbol{A} \cdot \boldsymbol{B} < ((\boldsymbol{A} \cdot \boldsymbol{B})_{H,m} + E_{max,m})2^{\xi+\eta}. \tag{16.28}$$

So if the absolute value of $(\boldsymbol{A} \cdot \boldsymbol{B})_{H,m}$ is compared to $E_{max,m}$ and is found to be larger, $(\boldsymbol{A} \cdot \boldsymbol{B})_{H,m}$ and $\boldsymbol{A} \cdot \boldsymbol{B}$ have the same sign.

If, however, the absolute value of $(\boldsymbol{A} \cdot \boldsymbol{B})_{H,m}$ is smaller than $E_{max,m}$, in which case the sign cannot be found from adaptive testing of the vectors' upper m bits, then processing efficiency can be maintained by retaining the value for $(\boldsymbol{A} \cdot \boldsymbol{B})_{H,m}$ and adding further data to determine the sign.

Below we discuss how to compute the scalar product and maximum error limit when another k bits of data are added.

Let $A_{iH,m}$ and $B_{iH,m}$ be the upper m-bit data of the vectors' components, and $A_{iM,k}$ and $B_{iM,k}$ the additional k-bit data (see Fig. 16.4). Components consisting of the upper $(m+k)$-bit data are then written as follows:

$$A_{iH,m+k} = A_{iH,m} \cdot 2^k + A_{iM,k}, \quad B_{iH,m+k} = B_{iH,m} \cdot 2^k + B_{iM,k}. \tag{16.29}$$

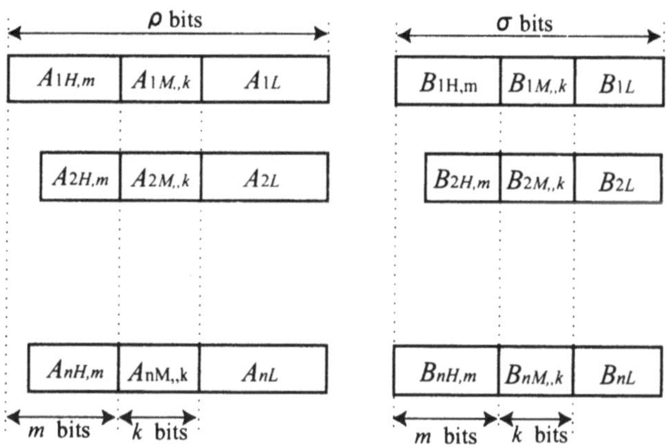

Figure 16.4: Upper, middle and lower data of vectors $\boldsymbol{A}$ and $\boldsymbol{B}$.

$(\boldsymbol{A}\cdot\boldsymbol{B})_{H,m+k}$ can then be written as:

$$\begin{aligned}(\boldsymbol{A}\cdot\boldsymbol{B})_{H,m+k} &= 2^{2k}\cdot\sum_{i=1}^{n} A_{iH,m}B_{iH,m}\\ &+ 2^{k}\sum_{i=1}^{n}(A_{iM,k}B_{iH,m}+A_{iH,m}B_{iM,k})+\sum_{i=1}^{n}A_{iM,k}B_{iM,k}\\ &= 2^{2k}\cdot(\boldsymbol{A}\cdot\boldsymbol{B})_{H,m}\\ &+ 2^{k}\sum_{i=1}^{n}(A_{iM,k}B_{iH,m}+A_{iH,m}B_{iM,k})+\sum_{i=1}^{n}A_{iM,k}B_{iM,k}.\end{aligned} \tag{16.30}$$

Furthermore, the maximum error limit for $(m+k)$-bit data can be obtained from that for m-bit data as a recurrence formula as follows:

$$\begin{aligned}E_{max,m+k} &= 2n\cdot 2^{m+k}-n\\ &= 2^{k}\cdot E_{max,m}+n(2^{k}-1),\end{aligned} \tag{16.31}$$

where $E_{max,1}=3n$.

Let us determine the maximum error limit for the case of 4×4 determinants, which are obtained:

1. **As the scalar product of four-dimensional vectors**

   Letting $n=4$ in eq.(16.27), we obtain:

   $$E_{max,m} = 8\cdot 2^{m}-4. \tag{16.32}$$

   If we let $m=32$, we have:

   $$E_{max,m} = 8\cdot 2^{32}-4$$

$$= 7ffffffc(H),$$

which agrees with eq.(16.19).

2. **As the scalar product of 6-dimensional vectors (see eq.(13.102))** Letting $n=6$ in eq.(16.27), we obtain:

$$E_{max,m} = 12 \cdot 2^m - 6. \tag{16.33}$$

We have seen that the adaptive sign testing method uses only the necessary data-length to establish the signs of scalar products of n-dimensional vectors, and thus serves to keep processing time at a minimum.

In this section, we first expressed the determinant as a scalar product of n-dimensional vectors, then extracted the upper m bits of the vector components to establish the determinant's sign.

Alternatively, one could directly extract m bits from each component of the determinant. In this case, the maximum error limit for a determinant of degree n is given by [69]:

$$E_{max,m} = n! \sum_{i=1}^{n} \binom{n}{i} (2^m - 1)^{n-i}. \tag{16.34}$$

For a 4×4 determinant, $n=4$ yields:

$$E_{max,m} = 96(2^m - 1)^3 + 144(2^m - 1)^2 + 96(2^m - 1) + 24. \tag{16.35}$$

16.8 Acceleration by FPU

As discussed in Chapter 14, we can deal with the interference problems between simplices by computing 2×2, 3×3 and 4×4 determinants. A difficulty, in this case, lies in how to accelerate the computation of a 4x4 determinant (see Section 16.8.2).

We shall deal with this problem with the aid of a floating point unit or FPU, along with an adaptive sign detection technique.

16.8.1 Adaptive Sign Detection of a 4×4 Determinant

We can write a 4x4 determinant:

$$\boldsymbol{M} = [m_{ij}], \quad (i,j = 0,1,2,3), \tag{16.36}$$

in terms of row vectors as follows:

$$\boldsymbol{M} = \begin{bmatrix} \boldsymbol{V}_0 \\ \boldsymbol{V}_1 \\ \boldsymbol{V}_2 \\ \boldsymbol{V}_3 \end{bmatrix}, \tag{16.37}$$

where

$$\boldsymbol{V}_i = [m_{i0}\ m_{i1}\ m_{i2}\ m_{i3}]. \tag{16.38}$$

The components of the vector $\boldsymbol{V}_i$ are expressed in variable word-length integers, which we now subdivide into 16-bit processing units (As for the length of a processing unit, we shall discuss it in Section 16.8.2).

We define l_i as the largest number of the processing units in the components of the row vector $\boldsymbol{V}_i$. Then, the processing units making up m_{ij} of the vector $\boldsymbol{V}_i$ are numbered from the lowest end beginning with "zero," so that $m_{ij,k}$ denotes the k-th unit $(0 \leq k \leq l_i)$ of m_{ij}. Thus, using the expression

$$\boldsymbol{V}_{i,k} = [m_{i0,k}\ m_{i1,k}\ m_{i2,k}\ m_{i3,k}], \tag{16.39}$$

the vector $\boldsymbol{V}_i$ can be written as

$$\boldsymbol{V}_i = \sum_{k=0}^{l_i} 2^{16k} \boldsymbol{V}_{i,k}. \tag{16.40}$$

So the determinant D is given by

$$D = \begin{vmatrix} \sum_{k=0}^{l_0} 2^{16k} \boldsymbol{V}_{0,k} \\ \sum_{k=0}^{l_1} 2^{16k} \boldsymbol{V}_{1,k} \\ \sum_{k=0}^{l_2} 2^{16k} \boldsymbol{V}_{2,k} \\ \sum_{k=0}^{l_3} 2^{16k} \boldsymbol{V}_{3,k} \end{vmatrix} = \sum_{r=0}^{l_s} 2^{16r} \left(\sum_{i=0}^{l_0} \sum_{j=0}^{l_1} \sum_{k=0}^{l_2} \begin{vmatrix} \boldsymbol{V}_{0,i} \\ \boldsymbol{V}_{1,j} \\ \boldsymbol{V}_{2,k} \\ \boldsymbol{V}_{3,r-(i+j+k)} \end{vmatrix} \right), \tag{16.41}$$

where $\boldsymbol{V}_{3,r-(i+j+k)} = \boldsymbol{0}$ if

$$r - (i + j + k) < 0 \quad \text{or} \quad r - (i + j + k) > l_3, \tag{16.42}$$

and where

$$l_s = l_0 + l_1 + l_2 + l_3. \tag{16.43}$$

Let $D(\alpha)$ now denote an approximation of the determinant obtained by reducing the range of r from $0 \leq r \leq l_s$ to $l_s - \alpha \leq r \leq l_s$, thus discarding the lower processing units of eq.(16.41), so that,

$$D(\alpha) = \sum_{r=l_s-\alpha}^{l_s} 2^{16r} \left(\sum_{i=0}^{l_0} \sum_{j=0}^{l_1} \sum_{k=0}^{l_2} \begin{vmatrix} \boldsymbol{V}_{0,i} \\ \boldsymbol{V}_{1,j} \\ \boldsymbol{V}_{2,k} \\ \boldsymbol{V}_{3,r-(i+j+k)} \end{vmatrix} \right), \tag{16.44}$$

where α $(0 \leq \alpha \leq l_s)$ represents the number of times of recomputation.

Let $D'(\alpha)$ denote the value obtained by dividing $D(\alpha)$ by $2^{16(l_s-\alpha)}$. This can be expressed by the recurrence formula:

$$D'(0) = \begin{vmatrix} \boldsymbol{V}_{0,l_0} \\ \boldsymbol{V}_{1,l_1} \\ \boldsymbol{V}_{2,l_2} \\ \boldsymbol{V}_{3,l_3} \end{vmatrix}, \tag{16.45}$$

$$D'(\alpha) = 2^{16}D'(\alpha - 1) + \sum_{i=0}^{l_0}\sum_{j=0}^{l_1}\sum_{k=0}^{l_2} \begin{vmatrix} \boldsymbol{V}_{0,i} \\ \boldsymbol{V}_{1,j} \\ \boldsymbol{V}_{2,k} \\ \boldsymbol{V}_{3,l_s-\alpha-(i+j+k)} \end{vmatrix}. \tag{16.46}$$

The error $E_r(\alpha)$ between the actual determinant D and the approximation $D(\alpha)$ is given from eqs.(16.41) and (16.44) as follows:

$$\begin{aligned} E_r(\alpha) &= D - D(\alpha) \\ &= \sum_{r=0}^{l_s-(\alpha+1)} 2^{16r} \left(\sum_{i=0}^{l_0}\sum_{j=0}^{l_1}\sum_{k=0}^{l_2} \begin{vmatrix} \boldsymbol{V}_{0,i} \\ \boldsymbol{V}_{1,j} \\ \boldsymbol{V}_{2,k} \\ \boldsymbol{V}_{3,r-(i+j+k)} \end{vmatrix} \right) \\ &\equiv \sum_{r=0}^{l_s-(\alpha+1)} 2^{16r} E_s(r), \end{aligned} \tag{16.47}$$

where

$$E_s(r) = \sum_{i=0}^{l_0}\sum_{j=0}^{l_1}\sum_{k=0}^{l_2} \begin{vmatrix} \boldsymbol{V}_{0,i} \\ \boldsymbol{V}_{1,j} \\ \boldsymbol{V}_{2,k} \\ \boldsymbol{V}_{3,r-(i+j+k)} \end{vmatrix}. \tag{16.48}$$

$E_s(r)$ expresses the sum of $(l_0+1)(l_1+1)(l_2+1)$ 4×4 determinants. Note that a determinant will vanish when its particular combination of (i,j,k) satisfies eq.(16.42). Thus, there is no need to compute all of the 4×4 determinants, of which there are $(l_0+1)(l_1+1)(l_2+1)$, but only those that satisfy:

$$0 \leq r - (i+j+k) \leq l_3. \tag{16.49}$$

$$\underbrace{0,\ldots,l_s-\alpha,\ldots,}_{r}\underbrace{r,\ldots,l_s}_{t}$$

Figure 16.5: Relation among parameters, r and t.

Let $P(t)$ be the number of these non-zero determinants expressed in parameter t $(= l_s - r)$ (see Fig. 16.5). Because the components of the determinants consist of 16-bit integers, the maximum value that a determinant can assume is $16(2^{16}-1)^4$ (see eq.(13.96)). Therefore, the minimum error boundary $EB(\alpha)$ for $D(\alpha)$ is given by:

$$EB(\alpha) = \sum_{r=0}^{l_s-(\alpha+1)} 2^{16r} \cdot 16(2^{16}-1)^4 P(t), \tag{16.50}$$

where

$$P(t) = \sum_{i=0}^{l_0} \sum_{j=0}^{l_1} \sum_{k=0}^{l_2} N(l_s - t - (i + j + k)), \tag{16.51}$$

$$N(x) = \begin{cases} 1 & (0 \leq x \leq l_3), \\ 0 & \text{(outside above range)}. \end{cases} \tag{16.52}$$

Dividing $EB(\alpha)$ by $2^{16(l_s-\alpha)}$, we obtain the error boundary $EB'(\alpha)$ that corresponds to $D'(\alpha)$ as:

$$EB'(\alpha) = \sum_{r=0}^{l_s-(\alpha+1)} 2^{16(r-l_s+\alpha)} \cdot 16(2^{16}-1)^4 P(t). \tag{16.53}$$

Computation of this, however, is quite cumbersome and requires considerable time. Instead, we can make use of the relation (see Appendix E):

$$EB'(\alpha) \leq 16 \times 2^{48} P'(\alpha + 1) \tag{16.54}$$

and use the expression on the right-hand side as the error boundary, where

$$P(t) \leq P'(t) = \frac{(t+1)(t+2)(t+3)}{6}. \tag{16.55}$$

Then, the error boundary $E'_r(\alpha)$ is given by:

$$E'_r(\alpha) = 16 \times 2^{48} P'(\alpha + 1). \tag{16.56}$$

Therefore, the result of the adaptive sign detection is final when

$$|D'(\alpha)| \geq E'_r(\alpha) \tag{16.57}$$

is satisfied, and $D'(\alpha)$ will have the same sign as the actual determinant. When, however, eq.(16.57) is not satisfied, α is increased by 1, and $D'(\alpha)$ and $E'_r(\alpha)$ are computed once again. The computation is repeated until either eq.(16.57) is met, or $\alpha = l_s$.

16.8.2 Length of Processing Units

In adaptive sign detection, fixed-length data are extracted and used to determine the sign of the determinant. When a long unit data length is used for this extraction, sign detection can be successfully completed with fewer processing cycles, thus improving efficiency. While the unit data length can be specified in bits, however, higher processing speed is possible when a byte-sized unit is used, as it does not require shifting or other extra processing.

The adaptive sign detection method discussed in this section adopts the extended double precision floating point system used in the Intel FPU's. This system has one sign bit, 15 bits for the exponent and 64 bits for the mantissa, so that unsigned integers of up to 64 bits can be exactly represented. Any integer within this range can be operated upon without introducing such numerical errors as round-off or digit cancellation.

For an $n \times n$ matrix Δ, all components of which have an absolute value of m or less, we have from Hadamard's inequality:

$$|\Delta| \leq n^{n/2} \cdot m^n. \tag{16.58}$$

Table 16.1: Bit length needed to calculate an $n \times n$ determinant.

Processing unit length	2×2 **det.**	3×3 **det.**	4×4 **det.**
8	17	27	36
16	33	51	68
32	65	99	132

unit: bits

From this, we can find the number of bits needed to exactly express the computed values of 2×2, 3×3 and 4×4 determinants when using processing unit lengths of 8, 16 and 32 bits (see Table 16.1). The numbers used in the extended double precision floating point system, whether during computation or to express the final result, must be an integer of 64 bits or less in length. Thus, Table 16.1 shows that 2×2 and 3×3 determinants can be computed using 16-bit data units, but that computation of 4×4 determinants may require more than 64 bits when 16-bit units are used. For this reason, the adaptive sign detection of 4×4 determinants cannot be done with 16-bit data in a straightforward manner.

With the method proposed in this section, however, it is possible to exactly express 96-bit integers, which enables the adaptive sign detection of 4×4 determinants based on 16-bit data units. Meanwhile, if we were to use 32-bit data units, 96 bits would still be insufficient and 132 bits are needed to exactly express a 4×4 determinant. We thus employ 16-bit data units.

16.8.3 Shortening the Processing Time

The 64-bit mantissa of the extended double precision floating point system is insufficient for expressing the 68-bit data length that may result when 16-bit units are employed for adaptive sign detection of 4×4 determinants.

Below, we discuss a method in which multiple registers of the FPU are used to accurately represent the results of 4×4 determinants, which allows the adaptive sign detection of 4×4 determinants based on 16-bit unit length. This method is faster than the one based on 8-bit unit length, as the use of a larger unit length speeds up processing time.

Representation of Data Lengths Exceeding 64 Bits

In the extended double precision floating point system, integer numbers with data lengths of 64 bits or less are exactly expressed. Those exceeding 64 bits, however, cannot be expressed exactly and thus contain numerical errors. Whenever a computational result exceeds 64 bits in data length, therefore, we shall assign to it two FPU registers. Using this method, it is possible to exactly express integer numbers with data lengths up to 96 bits.

Let a be an integer whose data length exceeds 64 bits. As a 96-bit integer, it can be expressed as the sum of two 64-bit integers a_0 and a_1, with a_1 being shifted to the left by 32 bits (see Fig. 16.6).

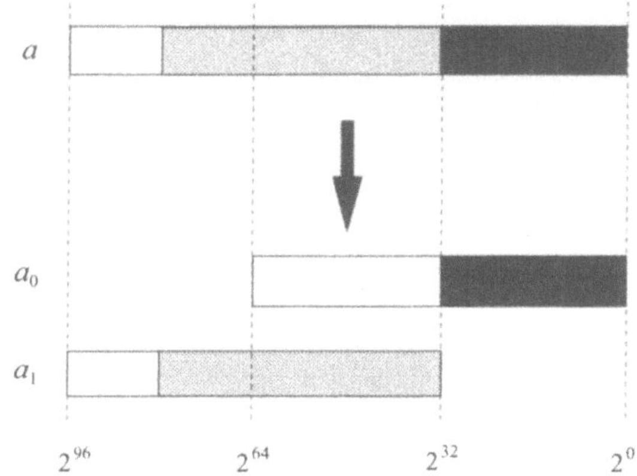

Figure 16.6: Representation of a 96-bit length integer.

$$a = a_0 + a_1 \times 2^{32}. \tag{16.59}$$

Multiplication of the 96-bit integer a by a 64-bit integer b is written as follows:

$$a \times b = a_0 \times b + a_1 \times b \times 2^{32}, \tag{16.60}$$

which amounts to multiplying two 64-bit integers, a_0 and a_1, each by b. Such a multiplication may produce overflowing, in which case some means are necessary to prevent numerical errors (this is discussed later).

The addition of two 96-bit integers, a and c, is written as follows:

$$a + c = a_0 + c_0 + (a_1 + c_1) \times 2^{32}, \tag{16.61}$$

which is processed as the addition of the respective 64-bit integers. Overflowing can occur here as well.

Thus, multiplications and additions in a 4×4 determinant must be carried out in a manner that will avoid overflowing.

Computation of a 4×4 Determinant

Here we describe the computation of a 4×4 determinant consisting of 16-bit unit length data components.

The 16-bit data, extracted from a variable word-length integer, expresses an integer without sign. To express it as a signed integer, therefore, 17 bits are needed. We thus transform the unsigned 16-bit integer to form a signed 32-bit integer.

We develop a 4×4 determinant S_{a012} with respect to the first row as follows (see Section 13.2.7):

$$\begin{aligned} S_{a012} &= w_a(+S_{01}X_2 + T_{01}Y_2 + U_{01}Z_2) \\ &+ X_a(-S_{01}w_2 + R_{01}Y_2 - Q_{01}Z_2) \\ &+ Y_a(-T_{01}w_2 - R_{01}X_2 + P_{01}Z_2) \\ &+ Z_a(-U_{01}w_2 + Q_{01}X_2 - P_{01}Y_2), \end{aligned} \qquad (16.62)$$

where P_{01}, Q_{01}, R_{01}, S_{01}, T_{01} and U_{01} are Plücker coordinates of line V_0V_1.

Using the FPU, we employ the following algorithm to evaluate a 4×4 determinant.

1. Compute the Plücker coordinates $P_{01}, Q_{01}, \ldots, U_{01}$. At most 33 bits are needed to store the results, so the 64-bit mantissa register of the FPU is sufficient.

2. Compute the expressions within the parentheses in eq.(16.62). The results are still expressible within the 64-bit mantissa of the FPU register.

3. Multiply the results above by $w_a, \ldots, Z_a$, in corresponding manner. As this multiplication may produce values exceeding 64 bits in length, first the results of step 2. above are expressed in the format of eq.(16.59), then the two 64-bit integers, a_0 and a_1, are each multiplied by $w_a, \ldots, Z_a$, whichever corresponds. Before multiplication the upper 32 bits of a_0 and a_1 of eq.(16.59) are empty, while $w_a, \ldots, Z_a$ are composed of 17 significant digits. Thus multiplication of these terms will produce no overflowing.

4. Add together the four terms obtained in step 3. Each term is expressed in the form $a = a_0 + a_1 \times 2^{32}$, where at least the upper 15 bits of a_0 and a_1 are empty, so the summation here will not produce overflowing.

The algorithm above describes the first cycle of computation needed for adaptive sign detection. In subsequent cycles, the results obtained in the previous cycle must first be shifted to the left by 16 bits, and then the term after the processing of step 4. is added to the shifted data.

Comparison with Error Boundary

The 4×4 determinant result is expressed in the form of eq.(16.59) as a 96-bit integer, while the error boundary is expressed as a 64-bit integer, so they cannot be compared directly. They must be converted into the same form for comparison.

From eq.(16.56), we know that only those bits occupying 2^{48} and above are relevant to the error boundary. Thus, we need only compare the portions of the determinant and error boundary lying at and above 2^{48}. This is a straightforward comparison between two 64-bit integers.

Upper Limit for the Recomputation Cycles

To carry out adaptive sign detection using the FPU, we compute the determinant's approximation, $D'(\alpha)$, expressing it as a 96-bit integer. If the determinant's sign cannot be established from the first approximation, the approximation is carried out again so as to approach the actual value, and this recomputation process is continued until the sign can be determined with certainty. When the recomputation cycle is carried out too many times, however, $D'(\alpha)$ may exceed 96 bits in length. When this occurs, the sign can no longer be exactly established because of numerical error. We thus need to know the maximum number of recomputations within which $D'(\alpha)$ will not exceed 96 bits.

For $D'(\alpha)$ to be 96 bits or less in length, the first and second terms of eq.(16.46) must each be 95 bits or less.

The first term, $D'(\alpha-1)$, is the determinant's approximate value obtained in the previous computational cycle. If $D'(\alpha-1)$ exceeds the error boundary, $E_r'(\alpha-1)$, which corresponds to that cycle, it means that sign detection has been successfully completed at this point. Thus, $E_r'(\alpha-1)$ is the greatest absolute value that $D'(\alpha-1)$ can assume, or

$$|D'(\alpha-1)| \leq E_r'(\alpha-1) = 16 \times 2^{48} P'(\alpha). \tag{16.63}$$

So we can state that the first term will have 95 bits or less when

$$2^{16}(16 \times 2^{48} P'(\alpha)) \leq 2^{95}. \tag{16.64}$$

Now, we also know that

$$P'(\alpha) = \frac{(\alpha+1)(\alpha+2)(\alpha+3)}{6}, \tag{16.65}$$

we obtain as the integer satisfying this condition $\alpha = 928$.

The second term of eq.(16.46) is the sum of $P(\alpha)$ 4×4 determinants. So we know that it will be 95 bits or less when:

$$16(2^{16}-1)^4 P(\alpha) \leq 2^{95}. \tag{16.66}$$

Using $P'(\alpha)$ instead of $P(\alpha)$, we obtain as the integer satisfying this condition $\alpha = 928$. Therefore, $D'(\alpha)$ will not exceed 96 bits in length as long as the cycle of recomputations remains at $\alpha = 928$ or below.

We now consider the error boundary. This is a 64-bit number with the value $16P'(\alpha+1)$, which was the portion lying at and above 2^{48}. Thus, it can be expressed without error as long as:

$$16P'(\alpha+1) \leq 2^{64}. \tag{16.67}$$

This yields $\alpha = 1905386$.

So $\alpha_{max} = 928$ is the maximum number of recomputations that can be made for exactly assessing the determinant's sign.

16.8.4 Experiment

An experiment was conducted to test the performance of the algorithm described above.

Experiment Environment

Used computer: Dell Dimension XPS Txxx
(Pentium III 500MHz, memory: 384MB)
OS: Microsoft Windows NT 4.00
Used software: Microsoft Visual C++ 6.0

Method of Experiment

The times needed to successfully establish the sign of a 4×4 determinant were measured and then compared among the next four methods:

(a) Computation of variable word-length integers using their total lengths,

(b) Adaptive sign detection without the use of the FPU,

(c) Adaptive sign detection based on 8-bit processing units using the FPU,

(d) Adaptive sign detection based on 16-bit processing units using the FPU.

Each method was tested against sets of randomly produced determinants, each set containing 100 determinants whose components were of fixed data length: 1, 2, 4, ..., 256, 512 and 1024 bytes. The mean value for that set was adopted as the time needed to establish the sign of a 4×4 determinant of a certain data length for the respective method. For (d), in particular, the data length needed for successful sign detection was also determined. For this experiment, the variable-length integers were expressed as integers employed in the GNU's C++ class library.

Results

The results are shown in Table 16.2 and Fig. 16.7. In (a), which employs the entire data length for computation, processing times increase exponentially with increasing data lengths. Meanwhile, in (b), (c) and (d), which all employ an adaptive strategy, the computation times needed for sign detection remain fairly level against changes in data lengths. We see further that the use of the FPU considerably improves the processing speed. Thus, compared to (b), the method of (c) is about 40 times faster, and that of (d) about 60 times faster. Comparing (c) and (d), we see that the use of 16-bit processing units is faster than the use of 8-bit units. With regard to (d), the success rate in establishing the determinant's sign was over 99 percent when processing was based on one word (16 bits), and 100 percent when using two words. From this also, we see that the time required for successful sign detection is nearly constant regardless of data length.

Table 16.2: Computation times of 4×4 determinants.

Data length (byte)	**(a)** (ms)	**(b)** (ms)	**(c)** (ms)	**(d)** (ms)
1	0.3285	0.4313	0.0096	0.0071
2	0.3238	0.4127	0.0098	0.0070
4	0.3484	0.4143	0.0096	0.0071
8	0.4378	0.4163	0.0096	0.0069
16	0.7319	0.4117	0.0099	0.0070
32	1.7476	0.4171	0.0106	0.0071
64	5.4443	0.4284	0.0107	0.0071
128	19.6178	0.4136	0.0111	0.0070
256	75.5340	0.4145	0.0103	0.0070
512	296.7711	0.4161	0.0107	0.0070
1024	1261.6750	0.4496	0.0108	0.0074

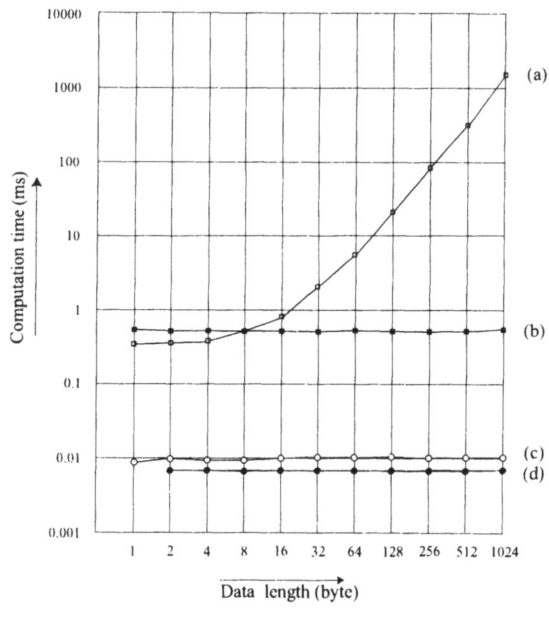

Figure 16.7: Computation time of a 4×4 determinant.

Chapter 17

Fundamentals of Topology

As discussed before, strict duality exists in the four-dimensional computations. Since the data for computations are stored in the data structure of a computer aided geometric design system, however, it is necessary to dualize the relevant topology relations and data structure in order to attain a total duality. This is the reason why Chapters 17 and 18 are included in this book.

17.1 Topology

Topology is a branch of mathematics that deals with connectivity among geometric elements. While Euclidean and affine geometries investigate whether two or more figures are congruent or similar, concepts like length and parallelism do not exist in topology. Instead, it deals with the connectivity relationships of constituent elements existing in various figures.

Topology derives from the concept of topological space, which is based on the theory of "neighborhoods."

In Fig.17.1, the figures shown in (a), (b), (c), (d) and (e) are, within each set, topologically equivalent, or *homeomorphic*, to one another. The respective sets representing (a), (b), (c), (d) and (e) are, however, topologically different from one another. One way to visualize this is to imagine the various figures as made from rubber strings; if one figure can be stretched to make another, then one can consider them to be homeomorphic. If not, then they are most likely not homeomorphic. Note that, during this process, two originally separate figures must stay separate, while those in contact must remain in contact. While Fig.17.1 shows homeomorphic line figures in one-dimensional space, homeomorphic spaces can be defined in two dimensions, three dimensions and so on just as well.

Fig. 17.2 shows examples of two-dimensional homeomorphic figures. As before, the figures in (a), (b), (c) and (d) are homeomorphic within each set, but not homeomorphic between sets. Here, one can visualize by thinking of the figures as being made from thin rubber sheets.

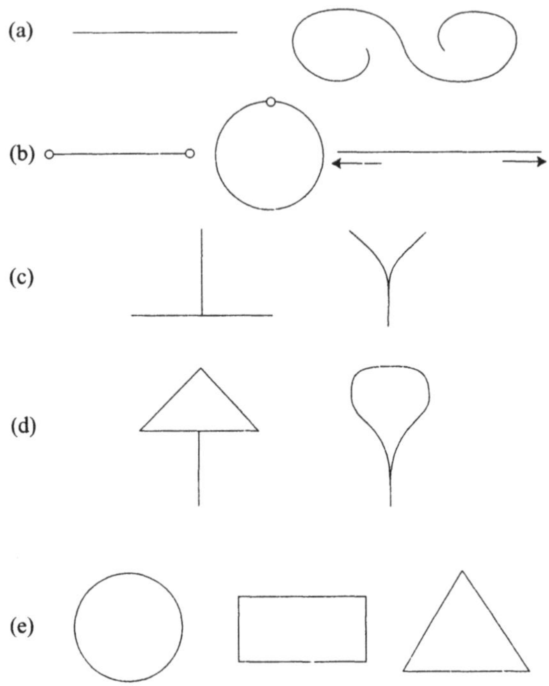

Figure 17.1: Homeomorphic figures (one dimension).

Below we define in a rigorous manner "homeomorphism" and its related terms. X and Y are assumed to be sets.

Definition 17.1 (Surjection)
Given the mapping $f : X \to Y$, if $f(X) = Y$ holds, that is, for an arbitrary point y in Y, there exists a point x in X such that $f(x) = y$, then f is called a surjection or onto-mapping.

Definition 17.2 (Injection)
Given the mapping $f : X \to Y$, if $x \neq x'$, it holds that $f(x) \neq f(x')$ (or, *if $f(x) \neq f(x')$, it holds that $x \neq x'$*), *then f is called an injection or one-to-one mapping.*

Definition 17.3 (Bijection)
If the mapping $f : X \to Y$ is, at the same time, a surjection and an injection, it is called a bijection. This is sometimes also called an onto and one-to-one mapping.

Definition 17.4 (Homeomorphism)
Let X and Y be subsets of Euclidean space $\mathbf{E}^n$. If mapping $f : X \to Y$ is a bijection, and if f and its inverse mapping $g : Y \to X$ are both continuous, then f is called a homeomorphism.

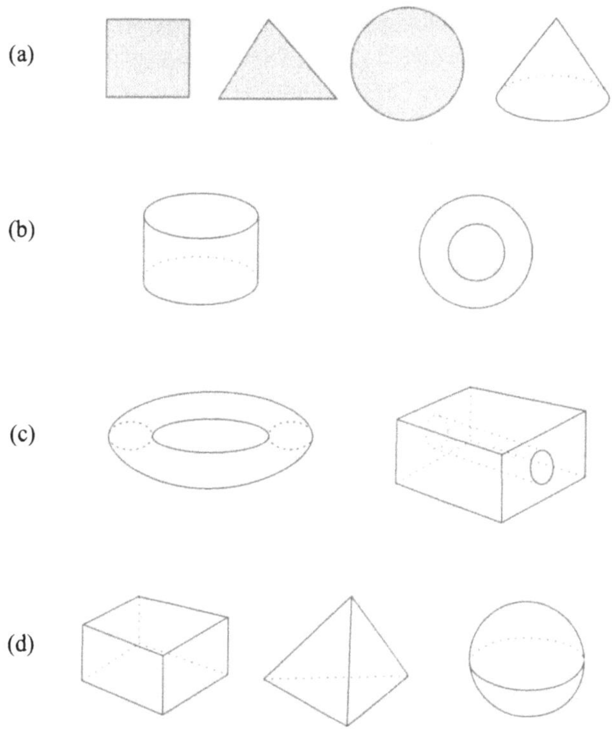

Figure 17.2: Homeomorphic figures (two dimension).

Definition 17.5 (Homeomorphic)
Let X and Y be subsets of Euclidean space $\mathbf{E}^n$. If there exists between X and Y a homeomorphism $f : X \to Y$, then X and Y are homeomorphic.

That is, two homeomorphic spaces are topologically equivalent.

17.2 Euler Formulas

An eighteenth-century mathematician, Leonhard Euler, discovered a formula showing the relationship among the numbers of vertices, edges (line segments) and faces of polyhedra [1]. This formula was later further generalized by H. Poincaré. In this section, we shall classify various geometric figures according to the concept of the Euler formula.

17.2.1 Figures of Points and Line Segments

A geometric figure consisting only of points and line segments is called a *graph*. The set of points one passes when setting out from some point on the graph

[1] The formula discovered by Euler is the equation for a particular polyhedron which is shown in eq.(17.9). In this book we call, however, various equations showing the relationships among the numbers of points, line segments and faces for various figures, Euler formulas.

and arriving at another point is called a *route*. A closed route is called a *cycle*.

Figures with No Cycle

A figure which has no cycle and consists of a connected series of points and line segments is called a *tree graph*. The conditions of a tree graph are that:

1. it must be connected; and
2. it must contain no cycle.

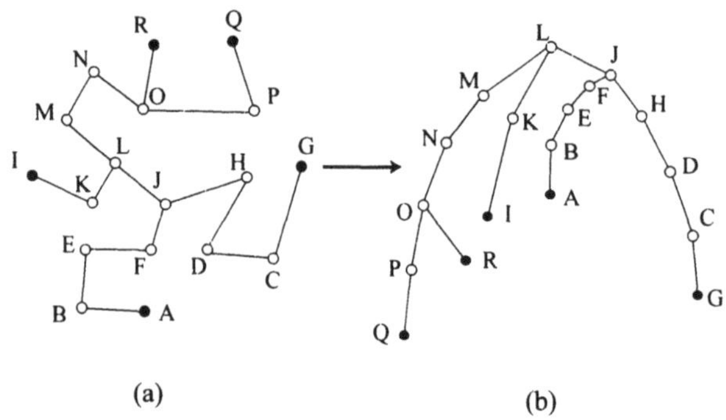

Figure 17.3: A tree graph.

Fig. 17.3 shows a tree graph. A point from which only a single line segment originates is called a *terminal point*, which in the figure is given by a solid dot. Fig. 17.3(a) can be changed into an upside-down tree, by taking for example point L as the root, as shown in (b). The tree graph has the following properties.

Theorem 17.1 (Tree graph)

1. *There always exists one and only one route connecting two arbitrary points in a tree graph.*
2. *If any line segment other than a lower end line segment is removed from the tree graph, the tree graph will be divided into two.*

Let us now construct a tree graph. One must initially set down a point. A tree graph can be produced by repeating the procedure of connecting a line segment to a pre-existing arbitrary point, then attaching to the other end of the line segment a point.

Conversely, to eliminate a tree graph, one repeats the procedure of removing a terminal point and its attached line segment, until a single point remains, which is then removed.

We can see from the discussion above that in a tree graph the number of points is larger than that of line segments by one. Denoting by v and e the number of points and line segments, respectively, this is expressed as

$$v - e = 1. \tag{17.1}$$

This is called the Euler formula for tree graphs, while $v-e$ is called the *Euler characteristic*. In other words, "the Euler characteristic of a tree graph is one."

A figure consisting of two or more tree graphs is called a *forest* (see Fig. 17.4). Thus, for a forest which consists of k tree graphs, the Euler formula is given by:

$$v - e = k. \tag{17.2}$$

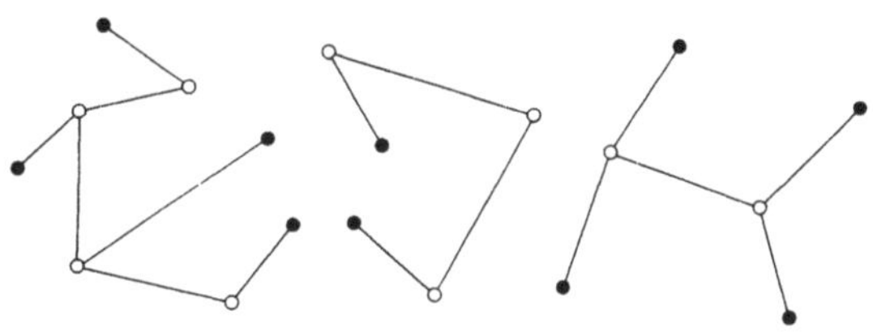

Figure 17.4: A forest.

An Italian mathematician E. Betti proposed a method of classifying geometric figures using what is now known as *Betti numbers*.

The *0-Betti number* is the number of parts into which a given figure is divided. In other words, it is the number of connected components. That is, if two points (which have zero dimension, hence 0-Betti number) can suitably be chosen in the figure, between which there is no connecting route, then the 0-Betti number is two. If three suitable points can be selected, among which there are no connecting routes, the 0-Betti number is three. We denote the 0-Betti number by β_0. The 0-Betti number for the forest shown in Fig. 17.4 is three. Thus, the 0-Betti number is equal to the Euler characteristic of a forest.

Figures with Cycles

We shall now determine the Euler characteristic for figures that contain cycles. We can begin by making a cycle in a tree graph. As Fig. 17.5 shows, this is done by connecting two points with a line segment. Thus, the Euler characteristic of a graph containing a single cycle is:

$$v - e = 0. \tag{17.3}$$

Because the Euler characteristic is reduced by one for each cycle formed, for a graph with c cycles, it is:

$$v - e = 1 - c. \tag{17.4}$$

This formula was that of a single graph with c cycles. The Euler formula for a forest which has the 0-Betti number β_0 and c cycles is given by:

$$v - e = \beta_0 - c. \tag{17.5}$$

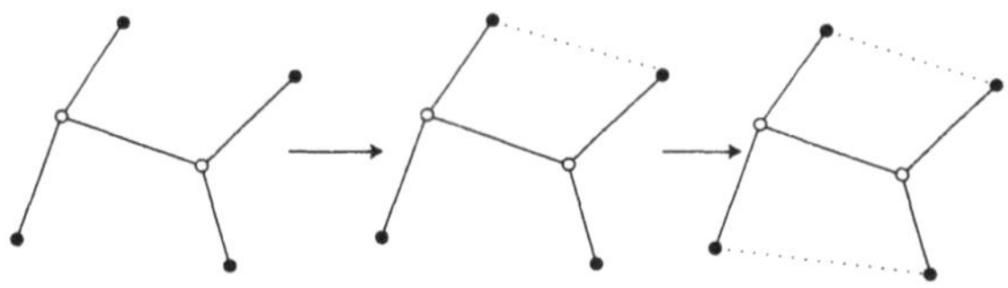

Figure 17.5: Making cycles from a tree graph.

We now introduce the *1-Betti number*, which we denote by β_1. This is the number of independent cycles. For instance, $\beta_1=1$ for the letter "A," and $\beta_1=2$ for the symbol "⋈ ." So c on the right-hand side of eq.(17.5) can be replaced by β_1, or:

$$v - e = \beta_0 - \beta_1. \tag{17.6}$$

This is the generalized Euler formula for graphs.

17.2.2 Figures of Points, Line Segments and Faces

Figures on an Open Surface

Let us take some graph containing a cycle and made of points and line segments, and assume that a surface has been stretched across that cycle, bordered by points and line segments. To distinguish it from the entire surface, we shall call this surface portion covering the cycle a face. Denoting by f the number of faces, we then have $f=c$. So eq.(17.5) can be written as:

$$v - e + f = \beta_0. \tag{17.7}$$

The left-hand side is called the Euler characteristic of a surface figure. Note that the face does not have to be planar and can be a curved surface as well.

Before we move on, we should discuss the types of figures to which the Euler formula can apply. The figures for e can include curves as well. The only requirement is that they must be homeomorphic to a line segment. Also, a figure counted under "f" must be homeomorphic to a triangular face. Fig. 17.6 presents a disc and an annulus, partitioned to be applied to the Euler formula. Note that a line segment here means an open one, i.e., one excluding the end points.

Let us now examine the Betti numbers of geometric figures consisting of points, line segments and faces on an open surface. Given two arbitrary, distinct points on the surface figure, it is always possible to draw a line or curve connecting those points, regardless of whether the surface figure contains a line figure or not. So we know that the 0-Betti number is 1.

Before we discuss *1-Betti number*, it is necessary to introduce the concept of homology.

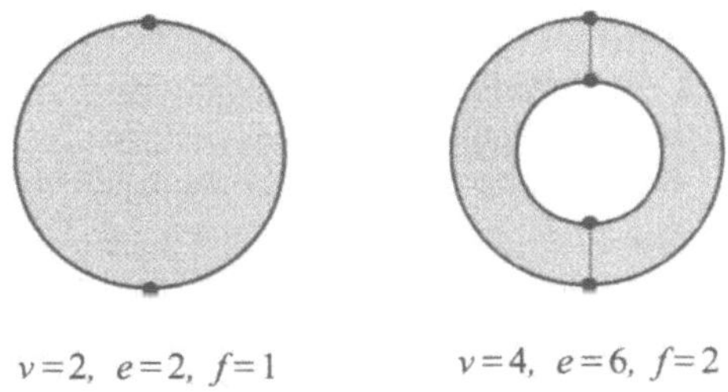

Figure 17.6: Partition of disc surface and annulus surface.

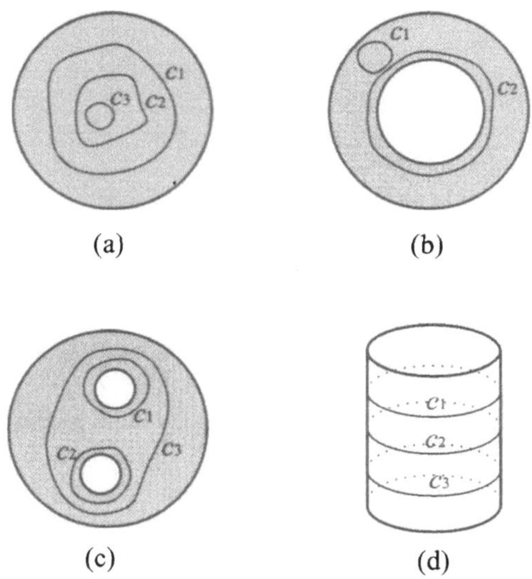

Figure 17.7: Circles homologous to 0 and 1-Betti number.

Let us first take a disc and draw on it a circle c_1 (see Fig. 17.7(a)). There is no need for the circle to be precise. Next, draw another smaller circle, c_2, inside c_1. Repeating this procedure an infinite number of times will eventually reduce the circle to a single point. The circle c_1, in this case, is said to be *homologous* to 0.

Next, Fig. 17.7(b) shows two circles drawn on an annulus. While circle c_1 is homologous to 0, circle c_2 is not.

Fig. 17.7(d) shows a group of circles, c_1, c_2 and c_3, on the side of a cylinder. Although none of these circles is homologous to 0, they are homologous to one another.

1-Betti number, then, is the number of independent circles that are not homologous to 0. Returning to Fig. 17.7(a), we see that any circle drawn on the disc is homologous to 0, hence $\beta_1 = 0$. In (b), $\beta_1 = 1$ since it is possible to draw only one circle that is not homologous to 0. In (c), it is possible to draw three circles that cannot be reduced to a point, i.e., that are not homologous to 0. However, setting down two circles automatically determines the third, so there are only two independent circles, hence $\beta_1 = 2$. We see that, with regard to discs with holes, 1-Betti number equals the number of holes.

2-Betti number is the number of space regions produced by connected surfaces. Triangular surfaces, discs and annuli are all open surfaces, so can not create any spatial region, hence $\beta_2 = 0$. Meanwhile, a closed surface like a spherical surface or torus creates a spatial region, so $\beta_2 = 1$, which is also the case for ordinary polyhedra.

Let us now return to our main discussion on the Euler formula. Writing the right-hand side of eq.(17.7) in the general form of eq.(17.6), we get:

$$v - e + f = \beta_0 - \beta_1 + \beta_2. \tag{17.8}$$

For a hole-less figure on an open surface, the right-hand side yields:

$$\begin{aligned} \beta_0 - \beta_1 + \beta_2 &= 1 - 0 + 0 \\ &= 1, \end{aligned}$$

which satisfies eq.(17.8). In fact, eq.(17.8) is the general formula applicable to any geometric figure consisting of points, line segments and faces, drawn on a surface.

We saw above that, for a geometric figure which consists of points, line segments and faces, drawn on a surface, and which is homeomorphic to a disc (or, for that matter, a triangular surface), the Euler characteristic equals 1. For the case of single-hole figures on a surface, i.e., those homeomorphic to an annulus, we have $\beta_0 = 1$, $\beta_1 = 1$ and $\beta_2 = 0$, which gives us an Euler characteristic of 0. If the figure has 2 holes, $\beta_1 = 2$. Then the Euler characteristic is -1. In other words, the Euler characteristic decreases by 1 for each additional hole.

Figures on Closed Surfaces

In the previous section, we started out with a point from which we constructed a tree graph, then closed the tree graph to create a cycle; we then "surfaced" the cycle to produce a figure on an open surface. After investigating such figures, we saw that the Euler characteristic of a hole-less figure on an open surface was 1.

Let us now consider stretching another face onto the back of this surface, thus creating a closed surface. It should be immediately clear that such a figure on a closed surface would possess an Euler characteristic of 2, or:

$$v - e + f = 2. \tag{17.9}$$

This is a well-known formula for *simple polyhedra* (also called *Eulerians*), that is, polyhedra that are homeomorphic to a spherical surface. In fact, formula eq.(17.8), which is a more general formula, applies to figures on a closed surface

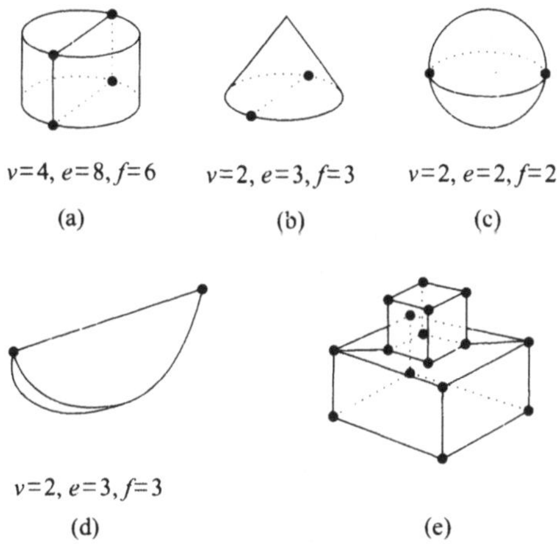

Figure 17.8: Partitioning of geometric figures.

as well. That is, for a simple polyhedron, the right-hand side of eq.(17.8) is:

$$\begin{aligned}\beta_0 - \beta_1 + \beta_2 &= 1 - 0 + 1 \\ &= 2,\end{aligned} \tag{17.10}$$

which agrees with eq.(17.9).

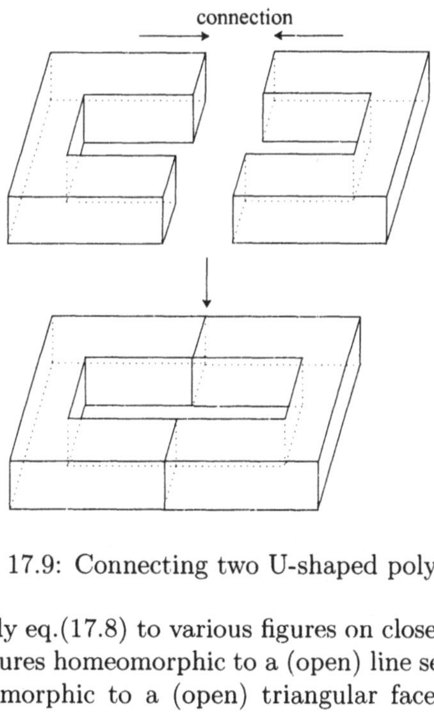

Figure 17.9: Connecting two U-shaped polyhedra.

As before, to apply eq.(17.8) to various figures on closed surfaces, the count for e must include figures homeomorphic to a (open) line segment, while f must include those homeomorphic to a (open) triangular face. The surfaces of a sphere, cylinder, cone, etc. can be partitioned as shown in Fig. 17.8, in which cases the Euler characteristic can be shown to be 2. In the case of (e), however, the upper surface of the lower rectangular parallelepiped is homeomorphic to an annulus, in which case the Euler formula cannot be directly applied, so it must be partitioned into two faces (see Section 17.6.1).

Let us now construct a polyhedron with a penetrating hole. This can be done, for example, by connecting two U-shaped simple polyhedra, as in Fig. 17.9. At the connections, 2×4 vertices, 2×4 edges and 4 faces disappear. Denoting by v, e and f the number of vertices, line segments and faces, respectively, of one of the original polyhedra, the Euler formula after connection is as follows:

$$\begin{aligned} & (2 \times v - 2 \times 4) - (2 \times e - 2 \times 4) + (2 \times f - 4) \\ = & \; 2 \times (v - e + f) - 4 \\ = & \; 2 \times 2 - 4 \\ = & \; 0. \end{aligned}$$

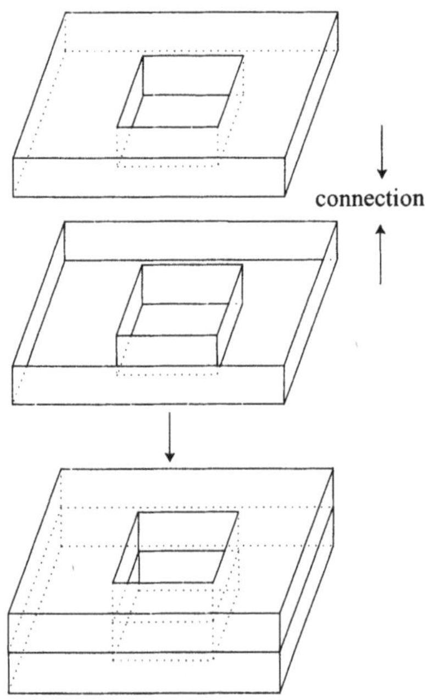

Figure 17.10: Connecting surfaces homeomorphic to an annulus.

Alternatively, a holed polyhedron can be made by connecting two open surfaces that are each homeomorphic to an annulus, as in Fig. 17.10. Denoting by v, e and f the vertices, line segments and faces, respectively, of the open surface, the Euler formula after connection is written:

$$(2 \times v - 2 \times 4) - (2 \times e - 2 \times 4) + 2 \times f$$

$$= 2 \times (v - e + f)$$
$$= 2 \times 0$$
$$= 0.$$

Thus the Euler formula for a polyhedron with a single penetrating hole is given by:

$$v - e + f = 0. \tag{17.11}$$

The number of penetrating holes a polyhedron has ordinarily equals its *genus*; one with no holes has a genus of 0, one with g penetrating holes has a genus of g. In other words, the genus of a closed surface is the maximum number of non-intersecting, independent closed curves that can be traced on the surface without dividing it into two (for example, c_1, c_2 and c_3 in Fig. 17.11). It is verified that the Euler characteristic for a polyhedron with genus g satisfies the general form, eq.(17.8).

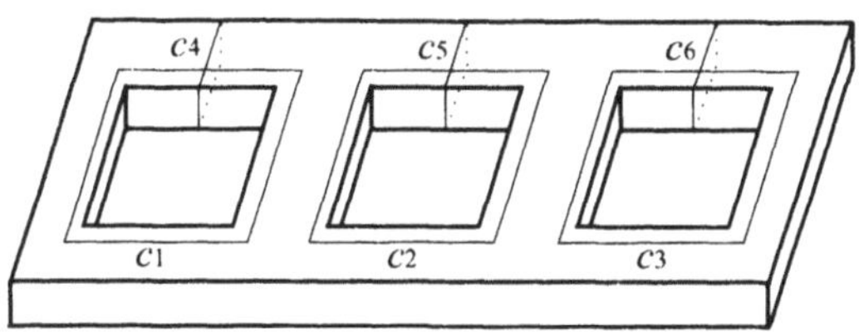

Figure 17.11: Determining 1-Betti number of a polyhedron with genus 3.

We saw that a polyhedron with genus 0 has an Euler characteristic of 2, while one with genus 1 has an Euler characteristic of 0. How about a polyhedron with genus g ? Let us approach this problem by considering the Betti numbers in eq.(17.8). Fig. 17.11 shows a polyhedron with genus 3. Now, 0-Betti number is 1 when a single polyhedron exists, whether it has holes or not. 2-Betti number is also 1. For 1-Betti number, we see that two independent closed curves, not homologous to 0, can be traced for each hole, making for a total of 6 curves. 1-Betti number thus is 6, or more generally, $2g$ when there are g holes. The Euler characteristic of a polyhedron with genus g is therefore $2-2g$, or

$$v - e + f = 2 - 2g. \tag{17.12}$$

A connected surface is called a *shell* (see Fig. 17.12 and Section 17.7.1).

If we denote by s the number of shells, we have:

$$v - e + f = 2(s - g). \tag{17.13}$$

Eq.(17.13) is widely used as a practical Euler formula.

The Euler formulas were later generalized by Henri Poincaré to the case of n dimensions.

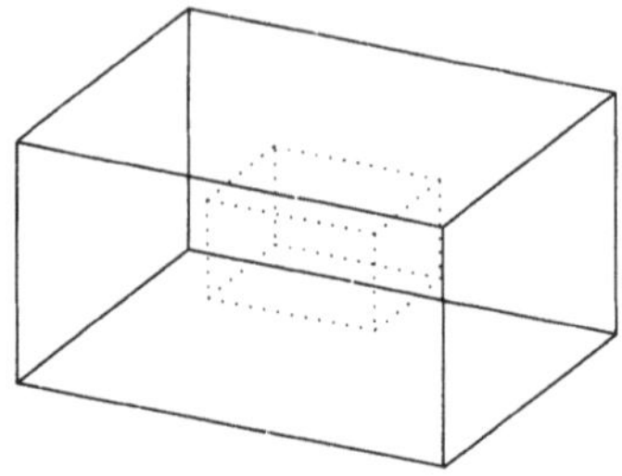

Figure 17.12: Solid with two shells.

Theorem 17.2 (Euler-Poincaré formula)
Given a polyhedron, divide it into simplices. Denoting its r-Betti numbers by $\beta_r(r = 0, 1, 2, ..., n)$ and the number of r-simplices by α_r $(r = 0, 1, 2, ...n)$, the following relation holds:

$$\sum_{r=0}^{n}(-1)^r\alpha_r = \sum_{r=0}^{n}(-1)^r\beta_r. \tag{17.14}$$

Eq. (17.14) is called the Euler-Poincaré formula.

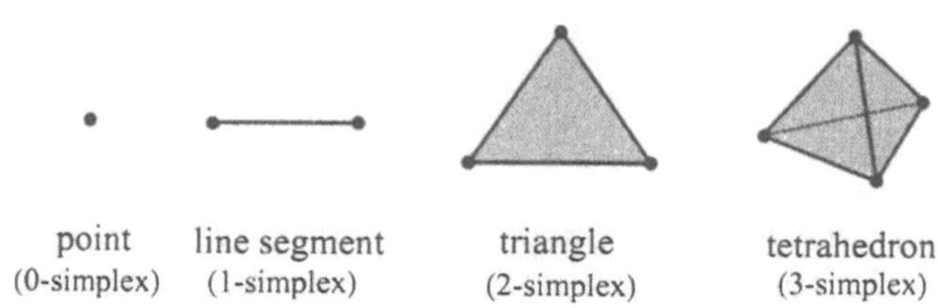

Figure 17.13: Simplices.

17.3 Simplices, Complexes and Cells

As stated in Section 9.2, a point, line segment (including the end points), triangle (including the three edges and three vertices) and solid tetrahedron (including the four faces, six edges and four vertices) are respectively called a *0-*, *1-*, *2-* and *3-simplices* (see Fig. 17.13).

The end points of a 1-simplex σ_1 are called the *0-faces* of σ_1; the three edges and three vertices of a 2-simplex σ_2 are called the *1-* and *0-faces* of σ_2, respectively. Similarly, the four faces, six edges and four vertices of a 3-simplex σ_3 are called the *2-*, *1-* and *0-faces* of σ_3, respectively.

Simplices can be thought of as the basic figures in their respective dimension. By combining simplices, various geometric figures can be constructed. For example, the polygon shown in Fig.17.14 can be thought of as a combination

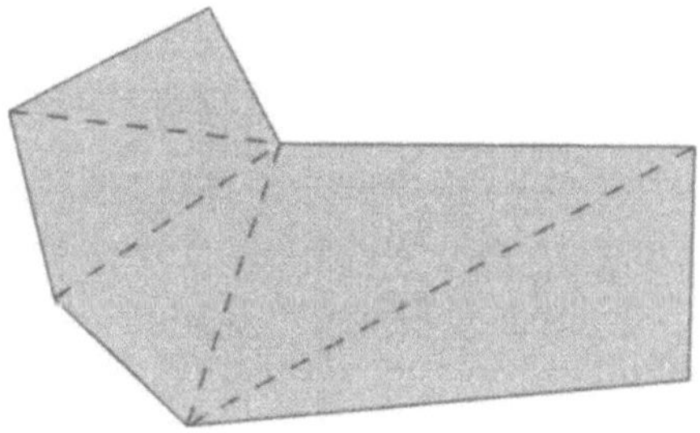

Figure 17.14: Combining simplices to construct a figure.

of five triangles. The reverse process, that is, dividing an arbitrary figure into simplices is called *simplicial decomposition.* In general, the simplicial decomposition of a figure is not unique.

A geometric figure which is produced by combining simplices, and for which the intersection of two arbitrary simplices forms a face simplex is called a *complex.*

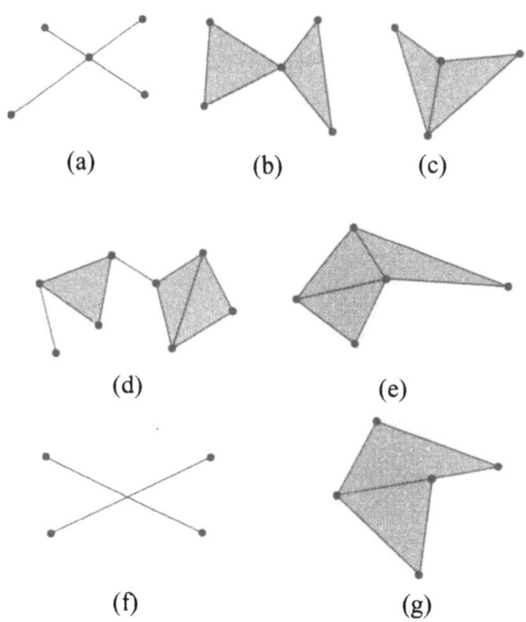

Figure 17.15: Complexes and non-complexes.

We now give the definition of a complex for the respective dimension [39].

Definition 17.6 (Complexes)

1. *A 0-complex is a set consisting of a finite number of points.*

2. *A 1-complex is a set which consists of a finite number of line segments and points and which satisfies the following conditions:*

   (a) *Given two arbitrary line segments, they either have no common point or have a common end point which is an element of the set.*

   (b) *Any given point either does not belong to any line segment, or is an end point of some line segment. The end points of line segments are elements of this set.*

3. *A 2-complex is a set which consists of a finite number of triangular faces, line segments and points and which satisfies the following conditions:*

   (a) *Given two elements of the set, they either have no common point or the set of common points is an element that belongs to both given elements.*

   (b) *Any element belonging to an element of the set is also an element of this set.*

In Fig.17.15, (a) is a 1-complex, while (b), (c), (d) and (e) are 2-complexes. (f) and (g) are not complexes, but upon simplicial decomposition become complexes that are identical to (a) and (e), respectively. When a complex is subdivided into smaller simplices, the resulting complex is called a *subdivision* of the original complex (see Fig.17.16).

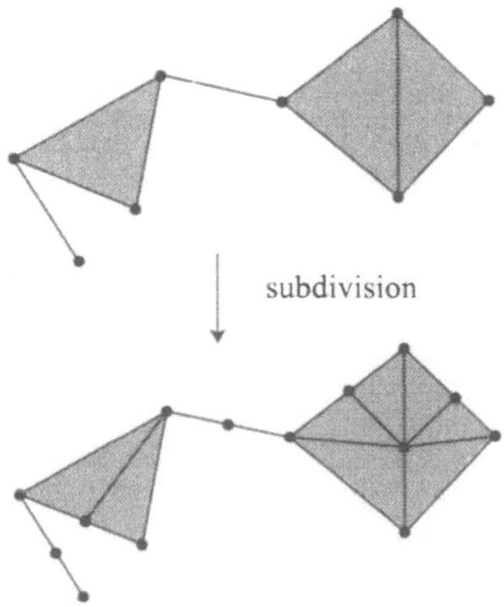

Figure 17.16: Subdivision of a complex.

By extending simplices, we obtain what is known as *cells*. An n-cell is a convex open set: that is, *0-*, *1-*, *2-* and *3-cells* are, respectively, points, open line segments, the interiors of convex polygons and the interiors of convex polyhedra (see Fig.17.17).

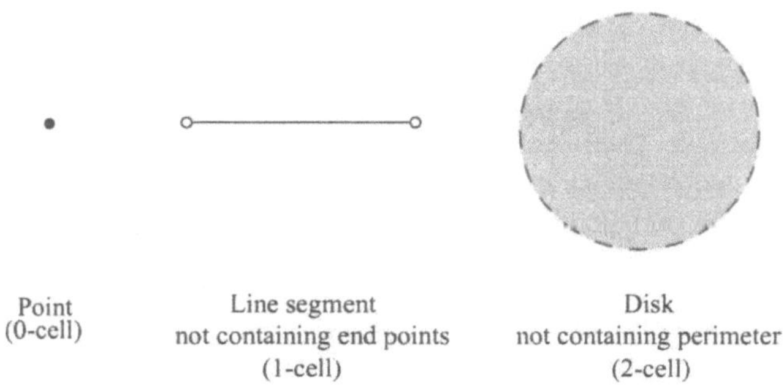

Figure 17.17: Cells.

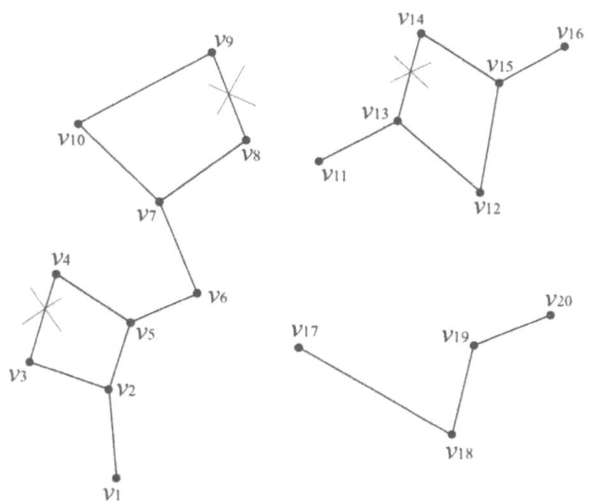

Figure 17.18: Connectivity number of 1-complex.

17.4 Connectivity Number of Complexes

We now discuss the connectivity number of 1-complexes.

Definition 17.7 (Connectivity number of 1-complex)
Given a 1-complex C, the maximum number of line segments that can be removed without changing the number of connected components (i.e., its 0-Betti number β_0) is called the connectivity number of C.

Let us illustrate using Fig.17.18. Here, the number of connected complexes, or connected components, is $\beta_0 = 3$. The line segments referred to in the definition above must be open, that is, they exclude the end points. For instance, removal of line segment v_1v_2 will isolate point v_1, thus increasing the number of connected components by one. One may, however, remove a line segment from a cycle without changing the number of connected components. There are three cycles in the figure shown, so as many as three line segments can be removed without affecting the number of components: for example, v_3v_4, v_8v_9 and $v_{13}v_{14}$. So the complex of Fig.17.18 has a connectivity number of three. Thus, the connectivity number of a 1-complex is equal to the number of cycles present, or its 1-Betti number.

We are now ready to examine the *connectivity number* of *2-complexes.*

Definition 17.8 (Connectivity number of 2-complex)
Given some curved surface F, we obtain by triangulation a connected 2-complex C. Suppose that the removal of a 1-complex of connectivity number q will leave C connected as one. The largest such q is called the connectivity number of the curved surface F.

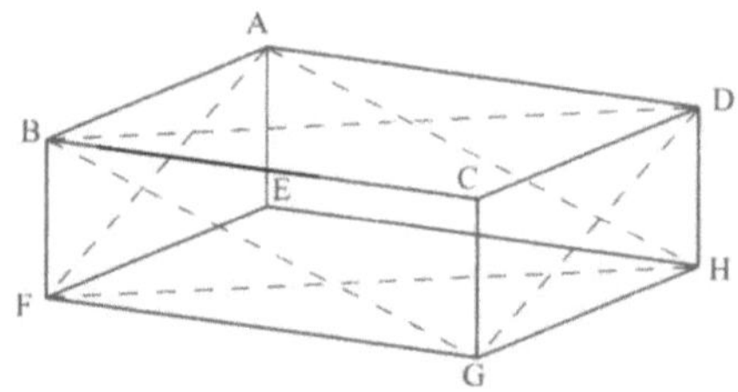

Figure 17.19: Determining the connectivity number of a 2-complex.

Let us first examine the connectivity number of a cube (see Fig.17.19). Here, removing any closed polygonal line will end up splitting the cube into two parts. For instance, if we remove the closed polygonal line $ABCDA$, the top surface will become separated. Because the cube surface will always be divided by removing a closed polygonal line, which is a 1-complex of connectivity number 1, we know that the cube surface has a connectivity number of 0.

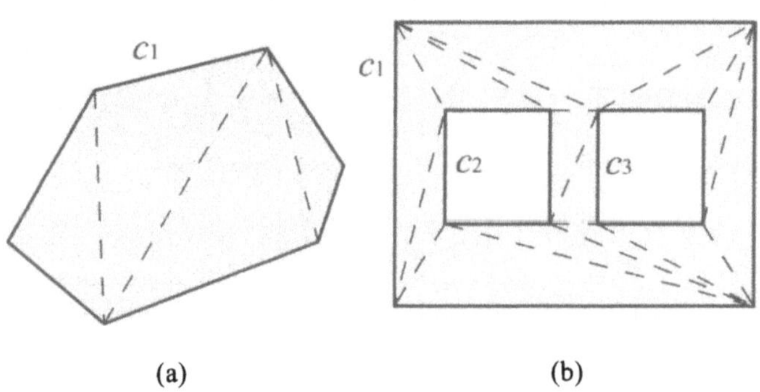

Figure 17.20: Determining the connectivity number of open surfaces.

For our next example, let us check the connectivity numbers of a plain face and that with two holes (see Fig.17.20). The face of (a) will remain as one part when its perimeter c_1 is removed, so has a connectivity number of 1. Meanwhile, the figure of (b) remains undivided by the removal of its three boundaries, c_1, c_2 and c_3, so has a connectivity number of 3.

We have the following theorem regarding the connectivity number of surfaces.

Theorem 17.3 (Connectivity number formula)
Given some curved surface F, we obtain by triangulation a connected 2-complex C, for which we denote the numbers of points, line segments and triangles by v, e and f, respectively. Denoting the connectivity number of surface F by q, the following formula holds:

$$v - e + f = 2 - q. \tag{17.15}$$

Let us check this formula against Figs.17.19 and 17.20.
For Fig.17.19, we have:

$$\begin{aligned} q &= 2 - v + e - f \\ &= 2 - 8 + 18 - 12 \\ &= 0. \end{aligned}$$

For Fig.17.20(a), we have:

$$\begin{aligned} q &= 2 - v + e - f \\ &= 2 - 6 + 9 - 4 \\ &= 1. \end{aligned}$$

For Fig.17.20(b), we have:

$$\begin{aligned} q &= 2 - v + e - f \\ &= 2 - 12 + 27 - 14 \\ &= 3. \end{aligned}$$

A face with connectivity number 1 is called a *simply-connected face*, while one with a connectivity number of 2 or more is called a *multiply-connected face.*

17.5 Manifolds

Lines, line segments and closed polygonal lines are one-dimensional figures. In general, an n-dimensional figure is one in which n independent variables are needed to specify the position of a point. A point in itself requires no variable to specify its given position, so is a zero-dimensional figure. Infinite planes and the closed surfaces of objects are two-dimensional figures. Cubes and spheres, including their interior spaces as well, are examples of three-dimensional figures.

By imposing a certain constraint onto these figures, we arrive at the concept of a *manifold.*

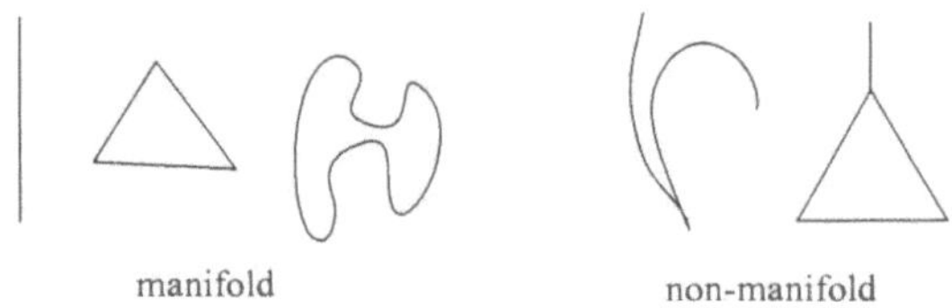

(a) One dimensional figure

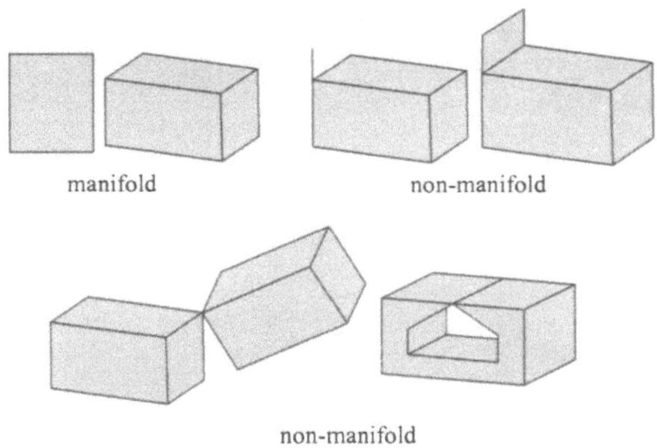

(b) Two dimensional figure

Figure 17.21: Manifolds and non-manifolds.

Definition 17.9 (Manifolds)
A 1-manifold is a figure which is homeomorphic to a line, line segment or closed polygonal line. A 2-manifold is a figure such that the neighborhood of any point is homeomorphic to a single plane or half-plane.

The two figures on the right in Fig.17.21(a) are not manifolds, since the junction points do not possess the properties of a line segment. In Fig.17.21(b), the cube, which is homeomorphic to a sphere, is a 2-manifold; a cube with a protruding line segment or surface, however, is no longer a 2-manifold. Neither is a manifold figure with parts that connect at a vertex or edge, since the neighborhood of that common vertex or edge forms more than two planes instead of one.

17.6 Generalizing Practical Euler Formula

In this section we shall generalize the practical Euler formula, eq.(17.13), such that it can be easily applied to non-manifold solids. Note that as will be explained in Section 20.5, use of non-manifold data structure allows to simplify the set operations of manifold solids, and at the same time allows dual topological processing.

17.6.1 Face-loop

As we saw, the original Euler formula for a simple polyhedron was later generalized as the Euler-Poincaré formula, eq.(17.14), which involved a count of simplex for each dimension. In applying this formula, however, it is not always necessary to triangulate the faces of a polyhedron. For instance, the diagonal in the face of Fig.17.22 can be removed without affecting the formula; this is because the numbers of line segments and faces both decrease by one. Therefore, such a face, i.e., one homeomorphic to a triangle, can be counted as one face for the f count in the Euler formula.

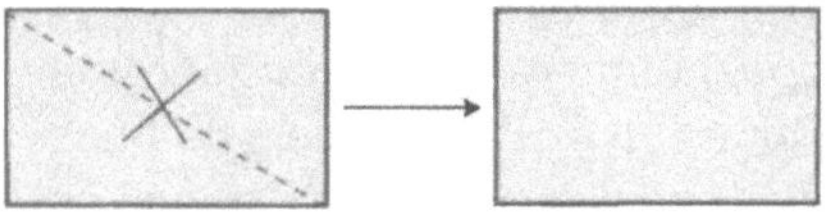

Figure 17.22: Face that does not require triangulation.

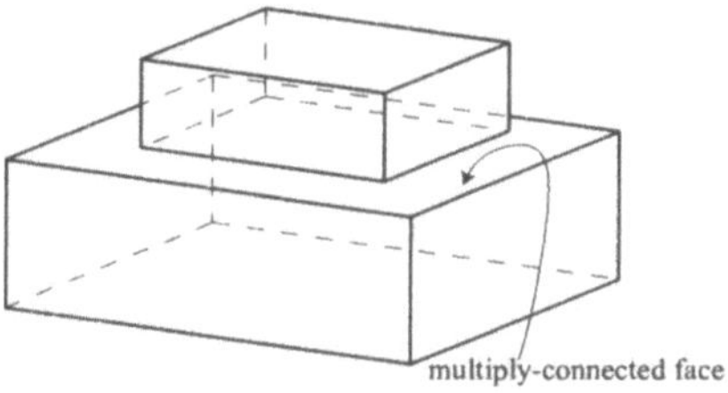

Figure 17.23: Polyhedron with a multiply-connected face.

This does not apply, however, for a face such as shown in Fig.17.23. That is, based on a simple count (i.e., without triangulating the faces), we obtain for the Euler characteristic:

$$v - e + f = 16 - 24 + 11 = 3,$$

which fails to satisfy the Euler formula.

The error here lies in dealing with the polygonal face with a hole (multiply-connected face) without distinction from an ordinary face (simply-connected face). It should be stressed that the count for f must only involve faces that are homeomorphic to a triangular face.

Let us therefore triangulate this face (see Fig.17.24(b)). We then have for the Euler characteristic:

$$v - e + f = 16 - 32 + 18 = 2,$$

which indeed satisfies the Euler formula.

Let us now remove from (b) a single line segment to arrive at the figure in (c). The Euler formula still stands because, along with the removed line segment,

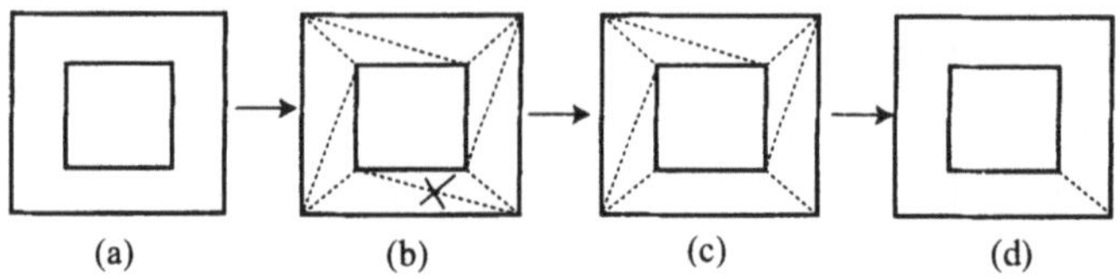

Figure 17.24: Removal of line segments from a triangulated multiply-connected face.

the number of faces also decreases by one. We see here that there is no need for all faces involved to be triangles, only that they must be homeomorphic to a triangle. With this in mind, we shall continue removing the line segments one by one. We soon arrive at (d), with a single line segment remaining. This one, however, cannot be removed since doing so will not accompany a reduction in the number of faces. Note here that the remaining line segment or edge is peculiar in that it has the same face on both sides, although it has different vertices at its ends.

From this, we can conclude that the Euler formula also applies to a polyhedron containing multiply-connected faces, with each face being counted as one, and with additional "virtual edges" being counted as many as the number of holes.

We now introduce an element called the *loop*. A loop is a cycle of vertices that form the boundary of a face. In this book, we shall call such a loop associated with a face a *face-loop*. Ordinarily, these vertices are connected by edges, and at least one face-loop is associated with a face. A simply-connected face has one face-loop, while a multiply-connected face has face-loops equal to the number of holes plus one. In a simply-connected face the multiplicity of the face-loop is said to be one.

Then if we denote by l_f the total number of face-loops of an arbitrary polyhedron, the total number of holes is given by $l_f - f$. We shall insert $l_f - f$ edges. Since this edge insertion does not affect the right hand side of Eq.(17.13), it can then be written as:

$$v - (e + l_f - f) + f = 2(s - g).$$

Or as:

$$v - e + f - (l_f - f) = 2(s - g). \tag{17.16}$$

In eq.(17.16), we do not have to take into account the "virtual edges" any more.

The process above can be considered to be composed of the following three steps:

1. **Insertion of edges**

   Because of the multiplicity of the face loop, eq.(17.13) can not directly be applied to a solid having such a face as (a) of Fig. 17.24. Thus we insert as many "virtual edges" as the total number of the face-loops minus the number of faces in order to turn the solid into one, where eq.(17.13) can directly be applied.

2. **Application of Euler formula**

   We apply eq.(17.13) to the modified shape, considering the count of the "virtual edges."

3. **Change of point of view**

   The result of the step 2. above, i.e., eq.(17.16), includes the total number of face loops, l_f, in place of that of the "virtual edges."

   Thus we consider the original solid to satisfy eq.(17.16) by taking the count of face-loops into account, without considering the insertion of the "virtual edges."

17.6.2 Vertex-loop

The author has been proposing the Four-dimensional Processing in this book. The concept of the Processing applies not only to geometric representations and computations, but to topological processing as well. This means that duality, a property of four-space, is also extended to and fully utilized in topological representations and operations, thus creating a consistent framework.

Let us then examine the practical Euler formula, eq.(17.16), from the standpoint of duality. We see that the equation does not have a symmetric form with respect to vertices and faces.

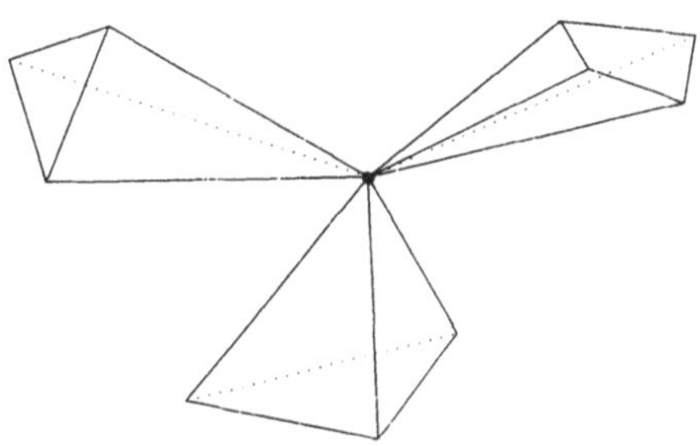

Figure 17.25: Multiple-loop vertex.

We have so far considered only manifold solids. In order to realize duality we shall deal with such a non-manifold shown in Fig.17.25. In a manifold, only single cycles of faces exist around each vertex, but for a non-manifold as in Fig.17.25, multiple cycles of faces can exist. We call the former a *single-loop vertex* and the latter a *multiple-loop vertex.* We shall call in this book such cycles associated with vertices as *vertex-loops.* A vertex-loop is dual to a face-loop. Ordinarily, these faces are connected by edges, and at least one vertex-loop is associated with a vertex. In a single-loop vertex the multiplicity is said to be one.

Just as in the case of face-loops, we can decrease the multiplicity of vertex-loops by inserting "virtual edges" [27]. The inserted edge this case must be dual to the one that we used to decrease the number of face-loops, i.e., edge that has

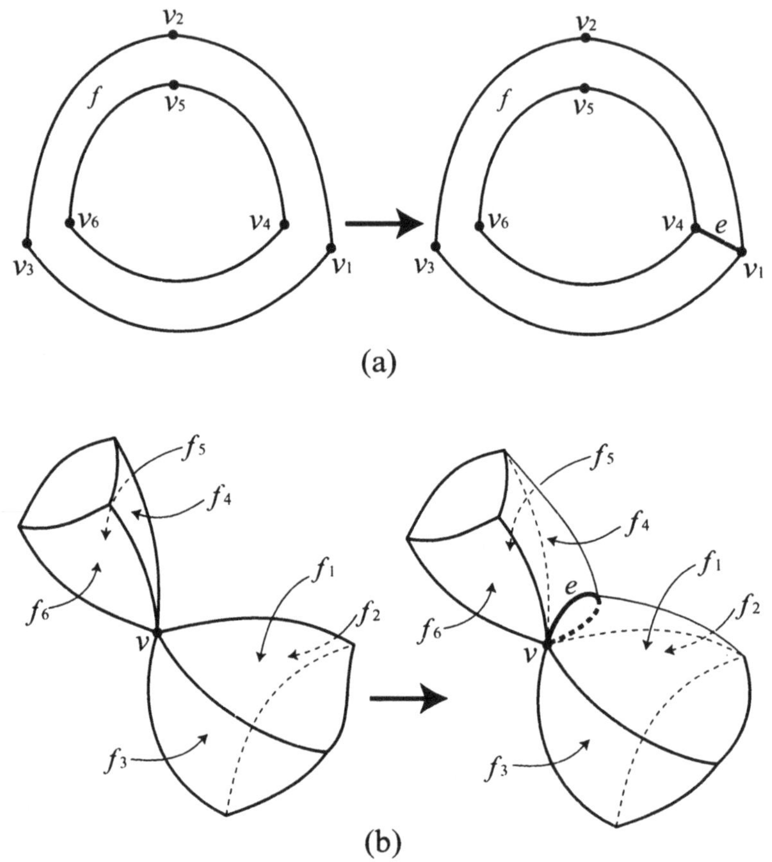

Figure 17.26: Inserting an edge to decrease the number of multiplicity of face- or vertex-loops by one.

an identical end vertex and has different adjacent faces. Fig. 17.26 illustrates contrastively how an inserted edge decreases the number of the multiplicity of face-loops or vertex-loops respectively. We shall take the three step approach that we have done in the face-loop.

1. **Insertion of edges**

   Insert as many "virtual edges" as the total number of vertex-loops minus the number of vertices in order to turn the solid into one, where all the vertices have single-loops and thus eq.(17.16) can directly be applied.

2. **Application of Euler formula**

   Apply eq.(17.16) to the modified shape. There are two special cases shown in Figs. 17.27 and 17.28 respectively. Take into account a penetrating hole or genus in Fig. 17.27 (see Section 17.7.1), but do not in Fig. 17.28.

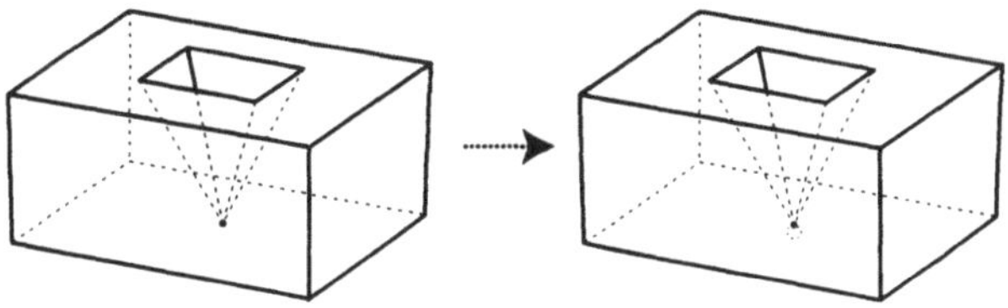

Figure 17.27: Special case of vertex-loop (1).

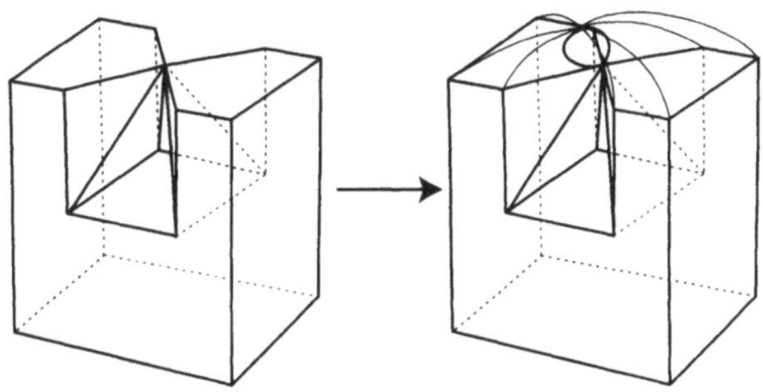

Figure 17.28: Special case of vertex-loop (2).

Thus, if we denote by l_v the total number of vertex-loops of an arbitrary polyhedron, the total number of edges to be inserted is given by $l_v - v$. Eq.(17.16) can then be written as:

$$v - (e + l_f - f + l_v - v) + f = 2(s - g).$$

Or as:

$$v - e + f - (l_v - v) - (l_f - f) = 2(s - g). \tag{17.17}$$

3. **Change of point of view**

   Eq.(17.17) includes the total number of vertex-loops, l_v, in place of the number of the "virtual edges." Thus consider the original solid to satisfy eq.(17.17) by taking the count of vertex-loops into account, without considering the insertion of the "virtual edges."

In eq.(17.17), we do not have to worry about edge insertion. The equation is really dual with respect to vertex and face.

17.6.3 Edge-loop

In addition to a face-loop and a vertex-loop, there is a loop associated with an edge, i.e., *edge-loop* (Fig. 17.29). An edge-loop is a cycle composed of exactly two incident faces and two incident vertices.

An ordinary edge is usually composed of one pair of two incident faces and two incident vertices. Such an edge is called a *single-loop edge*. An edge which

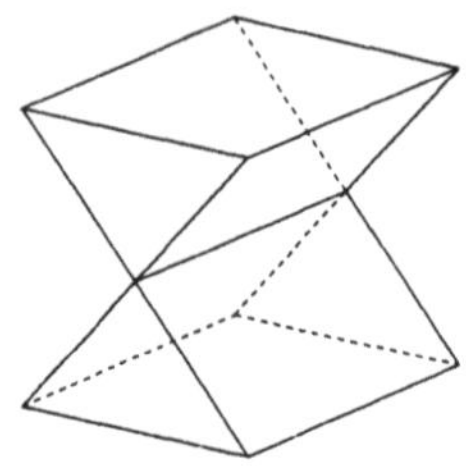

Figure 17.29: Multiple-loop edge.

is composed of more than two pairs of such faces and vertices is called *multiple-loop edge*. In a single-loop edge the multiplicity of the edge-loop is said to be one.

Just as in the case of face-loops or vertex-loops, we consider edge insertion to decrease the number of the multiplicity of edge-loops [27]. Fig. 17.30 illustrates how an inserting edge decreases the number of the multiplicity of edge-loops. Here we shall also take the same approach as before:

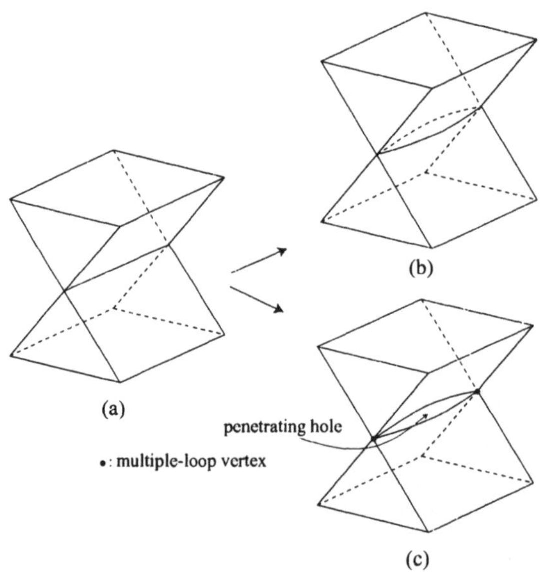

Figure 17.30: Inserting an edge to decrease the number of the multiplicity of edge-loop by one (1).

1. **Insertion of edges**

   Insert as many "virtual edges" as the total number of the edge-loops minus the number of edges in order to turn the solid into one, where all the edges have single-loops and thus eq.(17.17) can directly be applied.

   In the case of edge-loops, the situations, however, are not so simple as in face-loops or vertex-loops because there are always two ways of inserting an edge (Fig. 17.30). One is shown in (b), where the two inner spaces are united into one and the other is in (c), where a penetrating hole or a genus is created. Eq.(17.17) can directly be applied to (b) since it is a manifold. As for (c) it is a non-manifold since the two vertices have multiple-loops, but eq.(17.17) can be applied as discussed in Section 17.6.2.

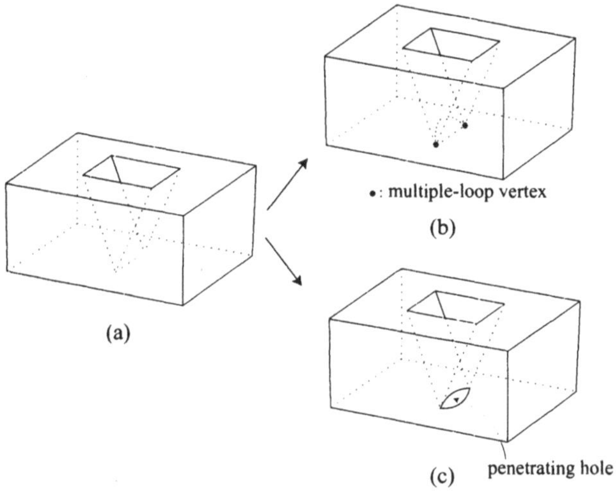

Figure 17.31: Inserting an edge to decrease the number of the multiplicity of edge-loop by one (2).

Next, let us look at Fig. 17.31. One modified shape is shown in (b), where two multiple-loop vertices are created, and the other is in (c), where a penetrating hole is created. Eq.(17.17) can be applied to either case as discussed in Section 17.6.2.

Lastly, look at Fig. 17.32. In (b) one multiple-loop vertex appears at the inner point, while in (c) a penetrating hole is created in addition to a multiple-loop vertex at the outer point. As discussed in Section 17.6.2, eq.(17.17) can be applied to these cases as well.

2. **Application of Euler formula**

Apply eq.(17.17) to the modified shape. If we denote by l_e the total number of edge-loops of an arbitrary polyhedron, the total number of edges to be inserted is given by $l_e - e$. Eq.(17.17) can then be written as:

$$v - (l_v - v) - (e + l_e - e) + f - (l_f - f) = 2(s - g).$$

Or as:

$$v - e + f - \{(l_v - v) + (l_e - e) + (l_f - f)\} = 2(s - g). \qquad (17.18)$$

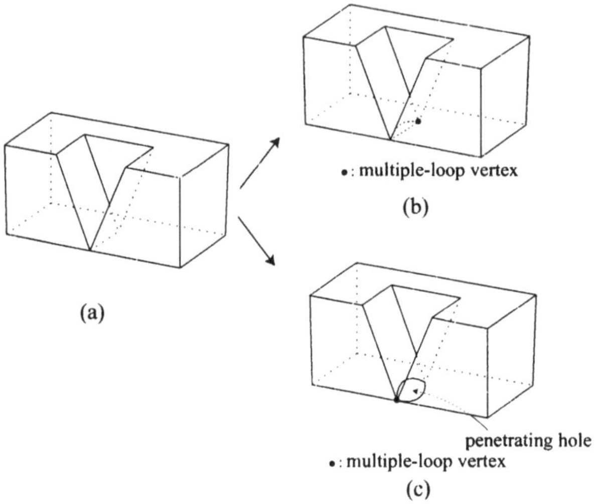

Figure 17.32: Inserting an edge to decrease the multiplicity of edge-loop by one (3).

3. **Change of point of view**

   Eq.(17.18) includes the total number of edge-loops, l_e, in place of that of the "virtual edges." Thus consider the original solid to satisfy eq.(17.18) by taking the count of edge-loops into account, without considering the insertion of the "virtual edges."

17.6.4 Revisit of Genus

Ordinarily genus g of a solid equals the number of penetrating holes. In the case of Fig 17.33, we can not determine the number of penetrating holes, however. Therefore we face a problem of how to evaluate the genus of a given solid.

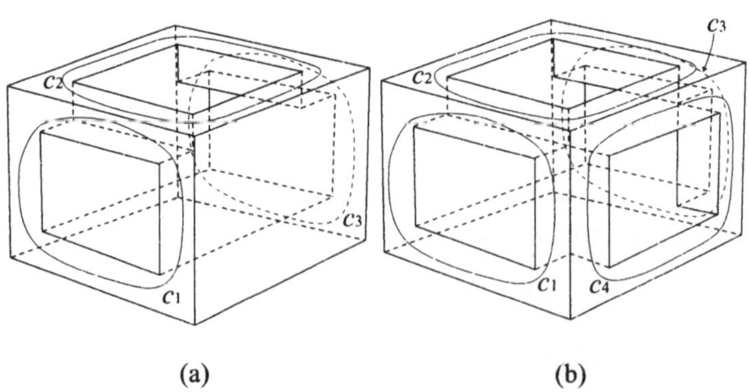

Figure 17.33: Solids having ambiguous numbers of penetrating holes.

Let us recall the definition of genus (see Section 17.2.2); the genus of a closed surface is the maximum number of non-intersecting, independent closed curves that can be traced on the surface without dividing it into two.

In Fig. 17.33 there is one connecting hole having three mouths in (a) and one connecting hole having four mouths in (b). With respect to each mouth we can draw a closed curve, but one of them is not independent of the others. For instance, c_3 is derived automatically in (a) if c_1 and c_2 are specified. Similarly, c_4 is determined automatically in (b) if c_1, c_2 and c_3 are specified.

Therefore if there are p connecting holes having m_i mouths in a solid, then the genus of the solid is:

$$g = \sum_i^p (m_i - 1). \tag{17.19}$$

Substituting the equation above into eq.(17.18) yields our final Euler formula:

$$v - e + f - \{(l_v - v) + (l_e - e) + (l_f - f)\} = 2(s - \sum_i^p (m_i - 1)), \tag{17.20}$$

v: number of vertices, e: number of edges, f: number of faces,
s: number of shells, m_i: number of mouths,
l_v: total number of vertex-loops,
l_e: total number of edge-loops,
l_f: total number of face-loops.

In this book, we shall use the generalized practical Euler formula, eq.(17.18) or eq.(17.20), for topological processing (see Section 18.2.3).

17.7 Application Examples

Here, we shall discuss some matters that we must be careful in applying the practical Euler formulas derived in the preceding section and give its various application examples to non-manifold solids.

17.7.1 Shells and Implicit Holes

In this section we discuss the right hand side of the Euler formula, eq.(17.18).

Shells

As described in Section 17.2.2, "s" in eq.(17.18) or (17.20) represents the number of shells, i.e., the number of connected surface (or the number of connected component).

There arises a question of how to count the number of shells s in the case of Fig. 17.34. Is it one or two ?

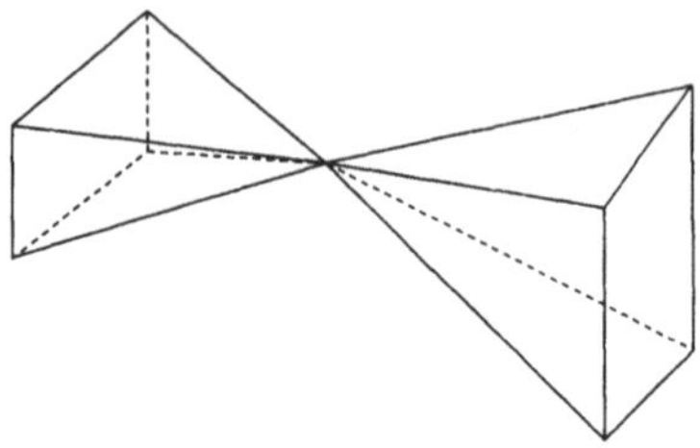

Figure 17.34: A solid having one shell.

Let us apply eq.(17.18) to this case. Except the number of shells s, other values are easily given as follows:

$$v = 9,\ e = 16,\ f = 10,\ g = 0,\ l_v - v = 1,\ l_e - e = 0,\ l_f - f = 0.$$

From eq.(17.18), we have $s = 1$. That is, these surfaces are connected, not separate. Thus the number of shells is one.

Implicit Holes

Consider the vertex-face contact case shown in Fig. 17.35. Then:

$$v = 13,\ e = 20,\ f = 10,\ l_v - v = 1,\ l_e - e = 0,\ l_f - f = 2,\ s = 1.$$

Thus we obtain $g = 1$. As discussed in Section 17.6.2, vertex-face contact case must be considered such that the contact face has an implicit hole (Fig. 17.35).

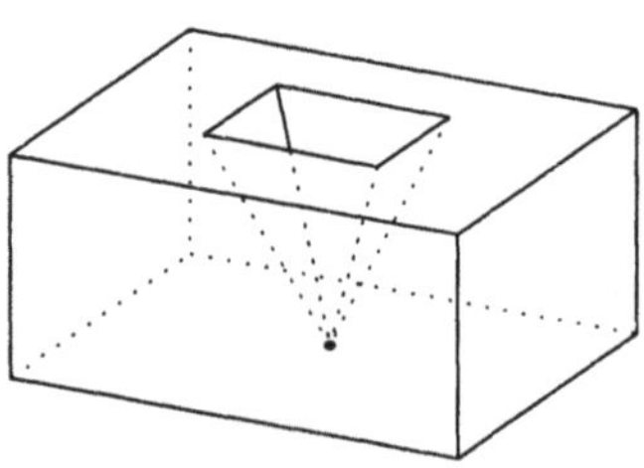

Figure 17.35: A solid having an implicit hole.

On the other hand, edge-face contact cases can be considered in either way, i.e., holed or not holed. See Example 5 in Section 17.7.2.

17.7.2 Application Examples

We shall apply the generalized practical Euler formula, eq.(17.18) or (17.20), to various cases. In applying the formula, we must take into account what we discussed in the preceding section. We do not consider the number of inserted edges, but instead consider the count of face-, vertex-, or edge-loops.

Example 1 (Fig. 17.25)

We give the following numbers to eq.(17.18):

$$v = 11,\ e = 20,\ f = 13,\ s = 1,\ g = 0,\ l_v - v = 2,\ l_e - e = 0,\ l_f - f = 0.$$

Example 2 (Fig. 17.35)

We consider there is a penetrating hole because of the existence of a vertex-face contact. Each of the top and bottom faces has multiplicity of two. We give the following numbers to eq.(17.18):

$$v = 13,\ e = 20,\ f = 10,\ s = 1,\ g = 1,\ l_v - v = 1,\ l_e - e = 0,\ l_f - f = 2.$$

Example 3 (Fig. 17.28)

We give the following numbers to eq.(17.18):

$$v = 17,\ e = 30,\ f = 14,\ s = 1,\ g = 1,\ l_v - v = 1,\ l_e - e = 0,\ l_f - f = 0.$$

Example 4 (Fig. 17.30(a))

We give the following numbers to eq.(17.18):

$$v = 10,\ e = 17,\ f = 10,\ s = 1,\ g = 0,\ l_v - v = 0,\ l_e - e = 1,\ l_f - f = 0.$$

For reference we also apply to (b) and (c). For (b) we give the following numbers to eq.(17.18):

$$v = 10,\ e = 18,\ f = 10,\ s = 1,\ g = 0,\ l_v - v = 0,\ l_e - e = 0,\ l_f - f = 0,$$

and for (c) we give:

$$v = 10,\ e = 18,\ f = 10,\ s = 1,\ g = 1,\ l_v - v = 2,\ l_e - e = 0,\ l_f - f = 0.$$

Example 5 (Fig. 17.31(a))

In the figure (a) we consider there is a penetrating hole having three mouths because of the existence of two vertex-face contacts. Each of the top and bottom faces has multiplicity of two. We give the following numbers to eq.(17.20):

$$v = 14,\ e = 21,\ f = 10,\ s = 1,\ g = 2,\ l_v - v = 2,\ l_e - e = 1,\ l_f - f = 2.$$

For reference we also apply to (b) and (c). For (b) we give the following numbers to eq.(17.20):

$$v = 14,\ e = 22,\ f = 10,\ s = 1,\ g = 2,\ l_v - v = 2,\ l_e - e = 0,\ l_f - f = 2,$$

and for (c) we give:

$$v = 14,\ e = 22,\ f = 10,\ s = 1,\ g = 1,\ l_v - v = 0,\ l_e - e = 0,\ l_f - f = 2.$$

Example 6 (Fig. 17.36(a))

We give the following numbers to eq.(17.18):

$$v = 14,\ e = 23,\ f = 10,\ s = 1,\ g = 1,\ l_v - v = 0,\ l_e - e = 1,\ l_f - f = 0.$$

For reference we also apply to (b) and (c). For (b) we give the following numbers to eq.(17.18):

$$v = 14,\ e = 24,\ f = 10,\ s = 1,\ g = 1,\ l_v - v = 0,\ l_e - e = 0,\ l_f - f = 0,$$

and for (c), where there is a penetrating hole having three mouths, we give the following numbers to eq.(17.20):

$$v = 14,\ e = 24,\ f = 10,\ s = 1,\ g = 2,\ l_v - v = 2,\ l_e - e = 0,\ l_f - f = 0.$$

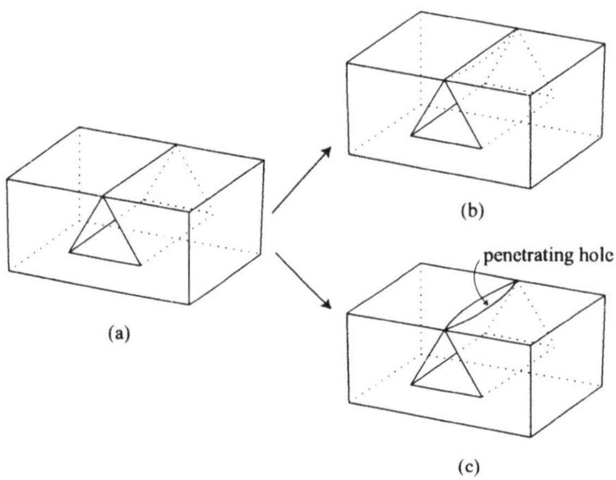

Figure 17.36: Example 6.

Example 7 (Fig. 17.32(a))

We apply to (a), where there is a penetrating hole because of the existence of a vertex-face contact. We give the following numbers to eq.(17.18):

$$v = 14,\ e = 22,\ f = 10,\ s = 1,\ g = 1,\ l_v - v = 1,\ l_e - e = 1,\ l_f - f = 0.$$

For reference we also apply to (b) and (c). For (b) we give the following numbers:

$$v = 14,\ e = 23,\ f = 10,\ s = 1,\ g = 1,\ l_v - v = 1,\ l_e - e = 0,\ l_f - f = 0,$$

For (c) the numbers we give are the same as in (b). That is,

$$v = 14,\ e = 23,\ f = 10,\ s = 1,\ g = 1,\ l_v - v = 1,\ l_e - e = 0,\ l_f - f = 0.$$

Chapter 18

Data Structures

18.1 Winged Edge Data Structure

18.1.1 Outline

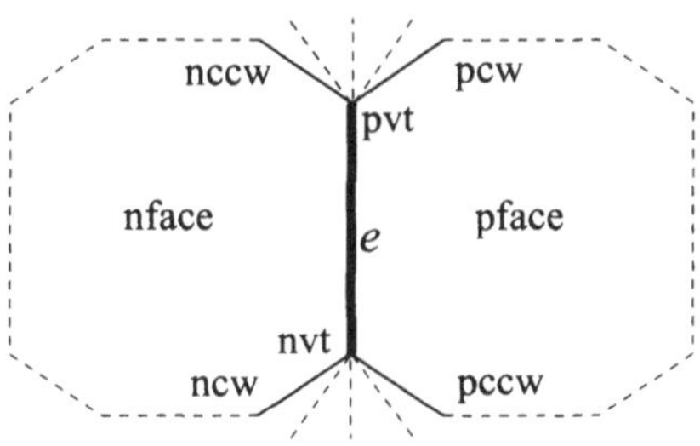

Figure 18.1: Winged edge data structure.

The basic concept for the data structure of solid modeling which is used in today's practical CAD systems was first proposed in 1974 by B. G. Baumgart [2]. This is known as the *winged edge data structure* (Fig. 18.1). This data structure deals with polyhedra consisting of only simply-connected faces, whose fronts and backs are distinguished, and explicitly describes the relations between an edge, and its incident vertices, edges and faces. The use of this data structure together with the Euler operators for creating solids (which will be discussed shortly) ensures that no solids will be produced with unrealistic topologies such as the Klein bottle. Moreover, the winged edge data structure expresses in a manner suited to computer processing, the property that solids have, that is, that its shape elements are continuously connected; this leads to efficient solid modeling.

The end points of some edge e of a polyhedron are given the symbols *pvt* and *nvt*. The letters p and n are used merely to distinguish between a pair of elements and have no special meaning. This also applies to other elements.

The polyhedron is viewed from the outside. Once *pvt* and *nvt* are established, the two faces adjacent to this edge are named *pface* and *nface* based on their positions relative to *pvt* and *nvt* as shown in the figure. Then, the edge which belongs to *pface* and which connects to e in the clockwise direction is named *pcw*, while that which connects in the counterclockwise direction is called *pccw*. Similarly, the edge belonging to *nface* and connecting to e clockwise is called *ncw*, and that counterclockwise *nccw*.

The winged edge data structure is characterized by its property that not only *pvt*, *nvt* and *pface*, *nface* are used to explicitly describe the data for an edge, but *pcw*, *pccw*, *ncw* and *nccw* as well. The edges, *pcw*, *pccw*, *ncw* and *nccw* form wings, hence the name "winged edge." The data on the winged edges make it possible to trace for shape elements efficiently. The fields of an edge block are shown in Fig.18.2(a).

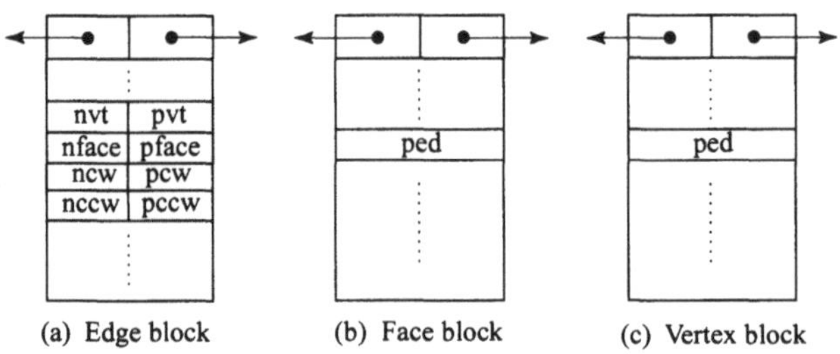

Figure 18.2: Edge block, face block and vertex block.

A vertex has several edges converging to it, while a face is surrounded by several edges. In a winged edge data structure, each vertex block and face block includes a pointer to one such edge (Figs.18.2 and 18.3). We shall denote such an edge by *ped*.

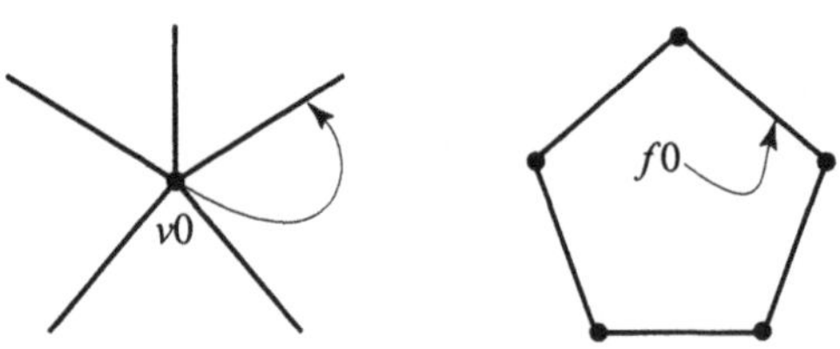

Figure 18.3: *ped*.

Baumgart proposed a group of nine functions used for tracing shape elements in a solid. These are:

$$\textbf{fcwv}\ (e0, v0),\quad \textbf{fccwv}\ (e0, v0),$$
$$\textbf{ecwv}\ (e0, v0),\quad \textbf{eccwv}\ (e0, v0),$$
$$\textbf{ecwf}\ (e0, f0),\quad \textbf{eccwf}\ (e0, f0),$$
$$\textbf{vcwf}\ (e0, f0),\quad \textbf{vccwf}\ (e0, f0),$$
$$\textbf{other}\ (e0, v0 \text{ or } f0).$$

The first letter of a function denotes the type of shape element to be outputted, the **cw** or **ccw** that follows indicates the rotation direction, and the final letter, **v** or **f**, is the type of shape element around which rotation takes place. The first argument in the parentheses specifies an edge from which rotation is to begin, and the second is the shape element around which rotation takes place (Fig.18.4).

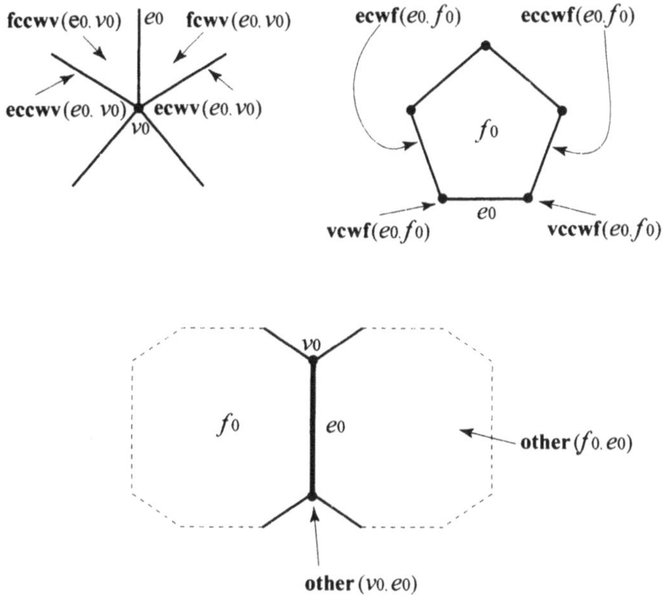

Figure 18.4: Trace functions for geometric elements.

Consider the example **ecwv** $(e0, v0)$. Having specified an edge $e0$ which converges to vertex $v0$, this function outputs the first edge encountered when rotating clockwise starting from $e0$.

We now show a sample program for **ecwv**$(e0, v0)$.

[**program** ①]

```
edge *ecwv(e0,v0), *e0;
vertex *v0;
{ if (e0 -> pvt == v0)
      return (e0 -> nccw);
   else if (e0 -> nvt == v0)
      return (e0 -> pccw);
   else { error(); return (null); }
}
```

The program for **ecwf**$(e0, f0)$ is as follows:

[**program** ②]

```
edge *ecwf(e0,f0), *e0;
face *f0;
{ if (e0 -> pface == f0)
      return (e0 -> pcw);
   else if (e0 -> nface == f0)
      return (e0 -> ncw);
   else { error(); return (null); }
}
```

Using these functions, we may write simple programs to carry out various operations.

As an example, a program that traces through all the edges e connecting to a vertex $v0$, and carries out some operation at each edge is given below:

[**program** ③]

```
{ e = v0 -> ped;
   do { func(e); e = ecwv(e,v0); }
   while (e != v0 -> ped);
}
```

Below is a program that traces through all the edges e surrounding a face $f0$, then carries out some operation function at each edge.

[**program** ④]

```
{ e = f0 -> ped;
   do { func(e); e = ecwf(e,f0); }
   while (e != f0 -> ped);
}
```

18.1.2 Euler Operators

The winged edge data structure was developed to deal with polyhedra which consist of simply-connected faces and which satisfy the following formula:

$$v - e + f = 2, \tag{18.1}$$

where v, e and f denote the number of vertices, edges and faces, respectively, that make up the polyhedron.

Baumgart has proposed a group of basic operators for topologically modifying a polyhedron. Being based on the Euler's formula, they are known as *Euler operators.* An Euler operator manipulates the shape by adding or removing either a vertex and an edge, or a face and an edge. Since the pair of elements in these combinations have opposite signs in eq.(18.1), the formula still holds for a polyhedron modified by an Euler operator. Thus, eq.(18.1) remains valid even when a polyhedron has been modified repeatedly by Euler operators, and it will remain an Eulerian polyhedron (Section 17.2.2). The Euler operators based on eq.(18.1) consist of the following four types (the inverse operators are given in the parentheses):

1. **mvfs** (**kvfs**)

   mvfs is read "make vertex, face, shell" and **kvfs** "kill vertex, face, shell." When **mvfs** is executed, it creates from an empty state in the data structure a block sn for a special "core" polyhedron with one vertex and one null face. That is:

   $$sn = \mathbf{mvfs};$$

   Note that the Euler's formula holds in this state.

   If **kvfs** is executed against a "core" polyhedron sn with one vertex and one null face, the data structure returns to an empty state. That is:

   $$\mathbf{kvfs}(sn);$$

2. **mev** (**kev**)

   mev is read "make edge, vertex" and **kev** "kill edge, vertex." After having specified a face f and one of its vertices v, **mev** creates a new edge en that connects to v and a new vertex vn at its end (Fig. 18.5);

   $$vn = \mathbf{mev}(f, v);$$

   Also, wing pointers are written between en and its connecting edges. Note that it is possible to have either $en{-}{>}\ nvt == vn$ or $en{-}{>}\ pvt == vn$, but processing can be simplified if this is determined beforehand. In our case, we shall choose $en{-}{>}\ nvt == vn$.

   If there is an edge and a vertex which could be created by an **mev** operator, the **kev** operator, upon specifying the vertex vn, will return the face back to its original state;

   $$v = \mathbf{kev}(vn);$$

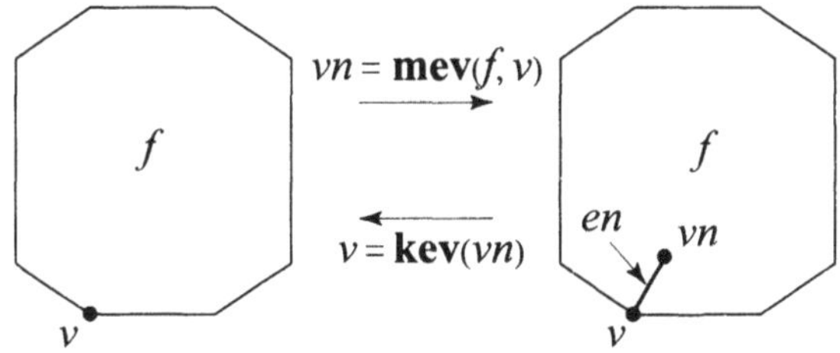

Figure 18.5: Euler operators **mev** and **kev**.

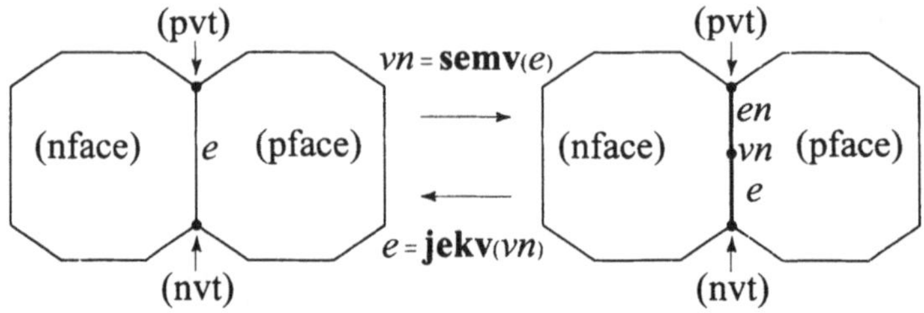

Figure 18.6: Euler operators **semv** and **jekv**.

3. **semv** (**jekv**)

   semv reads "split edge, make vertex" and **jekv** "join edge, kill vertex." With an edge e as its argument, **semv** creates vertex vn on e, thus splitting e into e and en (Fig. 18.6). That is,

$$vn = \mathbf{semv}(e);$$

   The wing pointers of the edges connected to the newly created edge en are changed appropriately. To simplify processing, we shall say that $en{-}{>}nvt == vn$ and $vn{-}{>}ped == en$.

   jekv carries out the inverse topological operation to **semv**. That is,

$$e = \mathbf{jekv}(vn);$$

4. **mef** (**kef**)

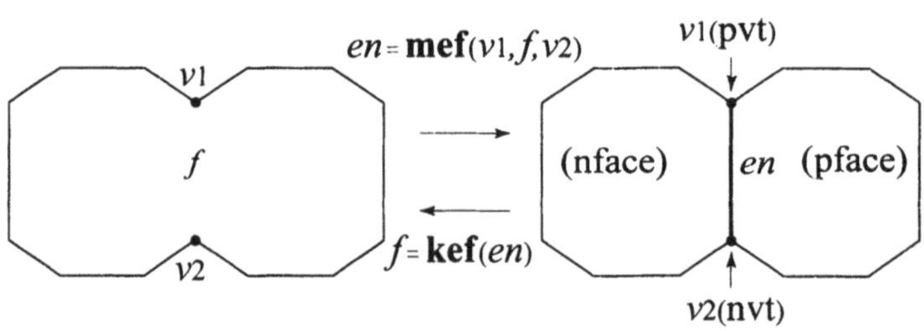

Figure 18.7: Euler operators **mef** and **kef**.

   mef reads "make edge, face" and **kef** "kill edge, face." With face f and two of its vertices $v1$ and $v2$ as its arguments, **mef** creates an edge en between $v1$ and $v2$ to split f into f and fn (Fig. 18.7). That is,

$$en = \mathbf{mef}(v1, f, v2);$$

   The wing pointers of the edges connected to the newly created edge en are changed appropriately. To simplify processing, we shall say that $en{-}{>}nface == fn$ and $fn{-}{>}ped == en$.

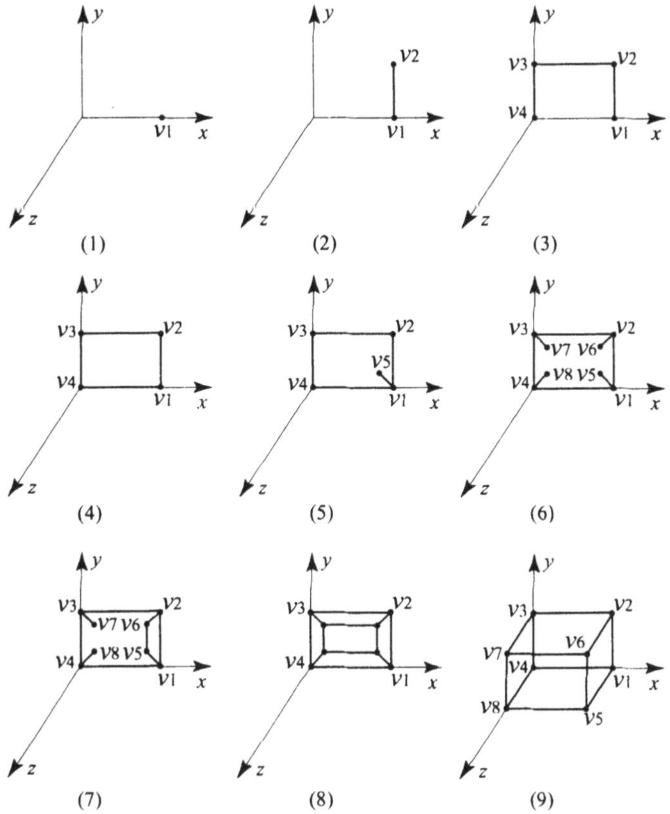

Figure 18.8: Creating a cuboid.

kef carries out the inverse topological operation to **mef**. That is,

$$f = \mathbf{kef}(en);$$

Creating a Cuboid Using Euler Operators

With Euler operators, the solid modeling of shapes can be done using relatively simple and reliable programs. Below we present a program in the style of C language for making a cuboid with the dimensions $w \times h \times d$ (Fig. 18.8).

```
makecuboid (w,h,d)   int w, h, d;
solid *s;
face *f;
edge *e;
vertex *v1,*v2,*v3,*v4,*v5,*v6,*v7,*v8;

s = mvfs;
```

/* Face f and vertex $v1$ are created in the face group ring and vertex group ring, respectively. These are reached by following pointers to the face group ring and vertex group ring of solid s. */

$v1$->xwc = w; $v1$->ywc = 0; $v1$->zwc = 0;

/* Specifying the coordinates of $v1$ (Fig. 18.8(1)). The coordinates of a vertex are stored in the "xwc," "ywc" and "zwc" fields of the vertex block. */

$v2$ = **mev**(f,$v1$); $v2$->ywc = h;
$v3$ = **mev**(f,$v2$); $v3$->xwc = 0;
$v4$ = **mev**(f,$v3$); $v4$->ywc = 0:

/* We suppose the output vertex of **mev** assumes the same coordinates as its argument vertex. The coordinates of $v2$, $v3$ and $v4$ are specified (Fig. 18.8(2),(3)). The line segments shown here are sometimes called *wires.* */

e = **mef**($v4$,f,$v1$); f = e->pface;   /* see Fig. 18.8(4). /*

/* A new edge e is created between vertices $v4$ and $v1$, so that f is split into two. The front face becomes f. We now have a rectangular sheet of thickness 0 with a distinct front and back. Such a thin sheet is often called a *lamina.* */

$v5$ = **mev**(f,$v1$); $v6$ = **mev**(f,$v2$);
$v7$ = **mev**(f,$v3$); $v8$ = **mev**(f,$v4$);

/* Four edges which serve as "struts" are created. Such an edge, where the same face exists on both sides, is sometimes called a *strut edge* (Fig. 18.8(5),(6)). */

e=**mef**($v5$,f,$v6$); e=**mef**($v6$,f,$v7$);
e=**mef**($v7$,f,$v8$); e=**mef**($v8$,f,$v5$);

/* Note here that the face f in the argument remains unchanged (Fig. 18.8(7),(8)). */

$v5$->zwc=d; $v6$->zwc=d; $v7$->zwc=d; $v8$->zwc=d;
/* See Fig. 18.8(9). */

makecuboid = s;

Euler operators were developed by extracting and systematizing commonly used, basic topological operations for solid modeling. Although processing can be done without the use of Euler operators, their use has several merits:

1. They apply universally when carrying out topological operations for various geometrical modeling situations;

2. Their use ensures that topological validity is maintained in the resulting configuration; and

3. Topological operations can be carried out for various types of data structures without much concern for their differences.

18.1.3 Remarks

We now examine the winged edge data structure from a critical standpoint. The data structure is shown again in Fig. 18.9.

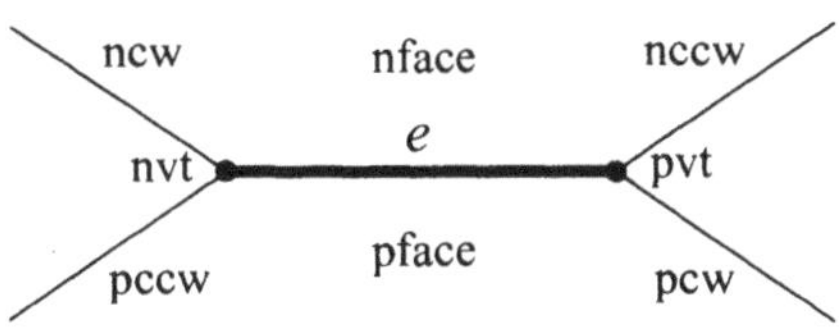

nvt	pvt
nface	pface
ncw	pcw
nccw	pccw

Figure 18.9: Winged edge data structure.

Problem ①

As discussed earlier, to make a tracing in the data structure, the edges or faces surrounding a vertex, or the edges or vertices surrounding a face are traced. This is done using the nine functions for tracing shape elements introduced earlier. Program ① on page 383 (Section 18.1.1) represented a function for tracing for edges around a vertex, while program ② traced for edges around a face. Let us now compare the central portions of these programs.

Central portion of program ①	**Central portion of program ②**
if ($e0$-> pvt == $v0$) **return** ($e0$-> nccw); **else if** ($e0$-> nvt == $v0$) **return** ($e0$-> pccw);	**if** ($e0$-> pface == $f0$) **return** ($e0$-> pcw); **else if** ($e0$-> nface == $f0$) **return** ($e0$-> ncw);

An edge can be considered to be shared by the two vertices at its ends, or alternatively by the two faces on both sides. Thus, programs ① and ② show that, when tracing around a vertex, we cannot establish the relationship existing among shape elements until we know whether the vertex, the central shape element, has been classified as a *pvt* or *nvt*; similarly, when tracing around a face, we need a test to determine whether the face, as the central shape element, is a *pface* or *nface*. If we could eliminate this testing procedure, tracing could be carried out more efficiently.

Problem ②

The winged edged data structure was proposed to deal with polyhedra consisting of simply-connected faces. Although Baumgart treated multiply-connected faces by dividing them into simply-connected ones, not only is this cumbersome but it would also be better if a face, whether simply- or multiply-connected, can be treated as a single unit.

Problem ③

Central portion of program ③	**Central portion of program ④**
e = $v0$-> ped; **do** { func(e); e= **ecwv**(e, $v0$); } **while** (e != $v0$-> ped)	e = $f0$-> ped; **do** { func(e); e= **ecwf**(e, $f0$); } **while** (e != $f0$-> ped)

Notice that programs ③ and ④ are very similar. Program ③ becomes program ④ if "v" is substituted by "f." Thus, these two programs appear to form a dual relationship with respect to vertices and faces. If they indeed form a true dual relation, a single program should suffice to execute the two operations. This kind of duality is one of the basic components of the paradigm of the Four-dimensional Processing which is set forth in this book. Yet if we compare programs ① and ②, we see that **ecwv** and **ecwf** do not form a dual. This shows that the winged edge data structure does not possess a dual structure with regard to vertices and faces.

18.2 Half Edge Data Structure

18.2.1 Half Edge

As we saw in problem ① above, frequent testing is needed when conducting a trace in the winged edge data structure. If there were another type of data structure that required no such testing, this should make processing more efficient.

One way to accomplish this is to add another type of edges called *half edge*, for efficient tracing purpose in addition to the ordinary edge type. The half edge could be considered to arise when an edge is divided into two parts; each half is then uniquely assigned to a set consisting of a face and a vertex. A data structure based on half edges is called a *half edge data structure*. This is the most commonly used data structure in CAD today. The half edge data structure can be divided into the following three types.

FE Type

Consider a face and assume each edge is oriented counterclockwise, viewed from the front. This oriented edge, i.e., half edge, h, is assumed to belong to the set consisting of the face and the beginning vertex (Fig. 18.10). Furthermore, the adjacent half edges, *Hccwf* and *Hcwf*, around the face are stored. *Hcwf* is not always necessary, but helps to improve processing efficiency. *Hpair* refers to the other half edge which forms a pair with the half edge under consideration.

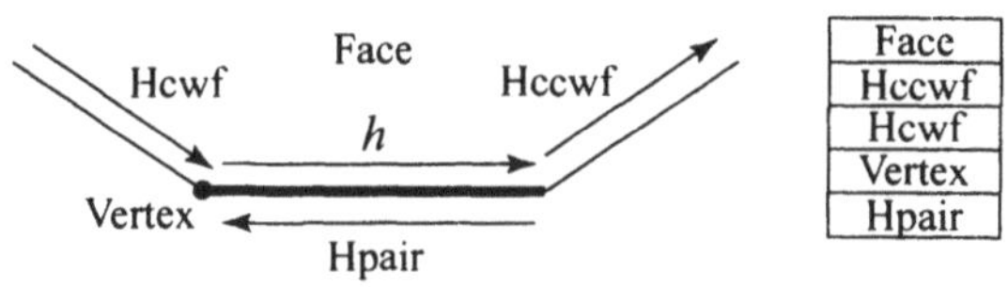

Figure 18.10: FE-type half edge data structure.

VE Type

Consider a vertex and assume each incident edge is oriented radiating outward from the vertex. The oriented edge, i.e., half edge, h, belongs to the set consisting of the vertex and the first face encountered when the half edge is turned counterclockwise (Fig. 18.11). The edges of *Hccwv* and *Hcwv*, originating from the vertex, are stored. VE and FE types form a dual relationship.

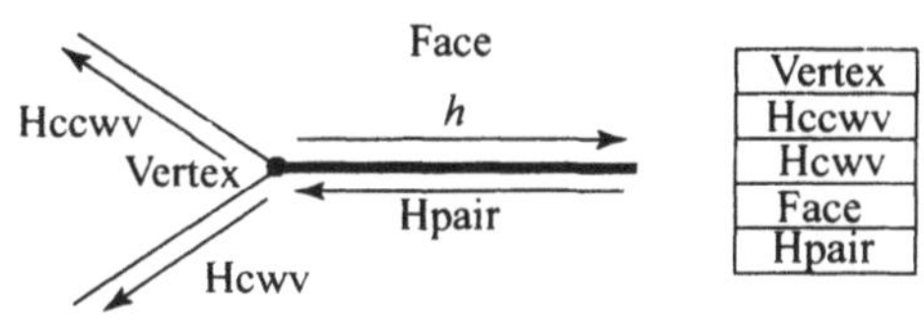

Figure 18.11: VE-type half edge data structure.

Combined Type

This type combines the FE- and VE-type data structures (Fig. 18.12), incorporating information on both FE- and VE-type adjacent edges. Although the amount of stored data is relatively large, this data structure allows one to take advantage of the features of both FE- and VE-types. *Hpair* is not absolutely necessary because it can be obtained from another field.

The definitions of a half edge and edge structure in the *combined half edge data structure* are presented as an example in Fig. 18.13. A single edge is divided

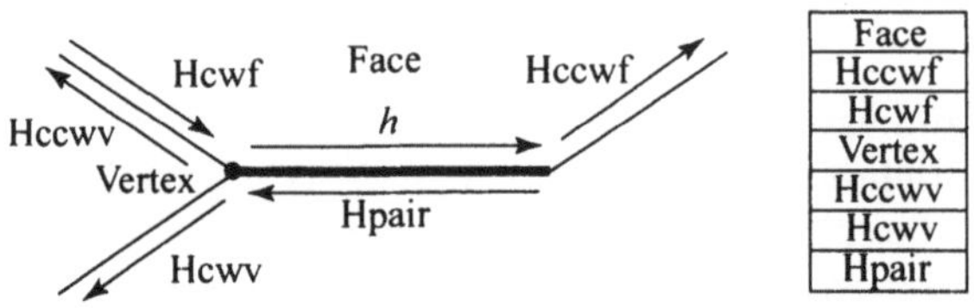

Figure 18.12: Combined-type half edge data structure.

```
typedef struct d_halfedge {
        index                    index;
        identifier               identifier;
        void                     *attr;
        struct d_halfedge *Hccwf;
        struct d_halfedge *Hcwv;
        struct d_halfedge *Hcwf;
        struct d_halfedge *Hccwv;
        struct d_halfedge *Hloop;
        struct d_halfedge *Hpair;
        struct d_halfedge *Hedge;
} Half;

typedef struct d_edge {
        index               index;
        identifier          identifier;
        void                *attr;
        struct d_edge *next;
        struct d_edge *prev;
        struct d_edge *Eshell;
        struct d_edge *Phalf;
        struct d_edge *Nhalf;
} Edge;
```

Figure 18.13: Definitions of half edge and edge structures.

into two half edges. An edge structure, therefore, has two pointers – *Phalf* and *Nhalf* - to identify the two half edges. Viewed from the half edge, *Hedge* specifies the edge to which the half edge belongs. Here, "index" refers to the overall serial number, "identifier" identifies the type, "*attr" is the pointer connecting to the node's attribute data, "*next" and "*prev" are pointers to the next and previous blocks on the ring-structured list, and "*Eshell" is the pointer to the shell to which the edge belongs. "*Hloop" will be discussed in Section 18.2.2 below. Pointers to faces and vertices are omitted in the structural definition statement of half edges.

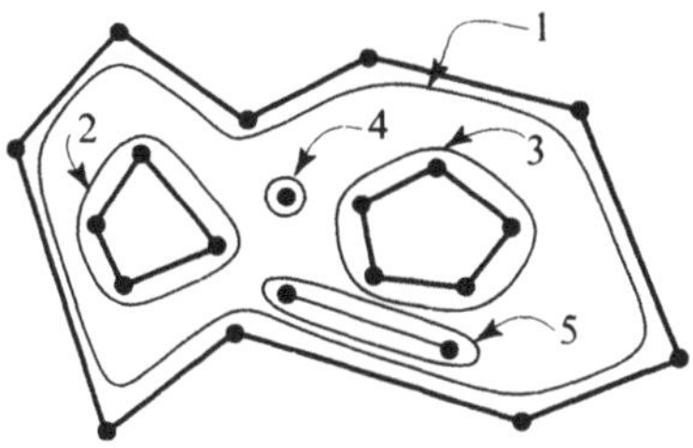

Figure 18.14: Face-loops.

18.2.2 Introducing Face-loops

As a solution to problem ②, face-loops are usually employed to describe multiply-connected faces. Here, we introduce a generalized form of face-loop into the half edge data structure. As shown in Fig. 18.14, a face is generally bordered by cycles consisting of one or more vertices (and edges). These cycles are called face-loops (see Section 17.6.1). The number of face-loops in Fig. 18.14 is five [1].

The relations among a vertex, edge, face and face-loop are expressed using the symbol { : } as follows [7]:

① $\{e : l(1 \text{ or } 2)\}$, ② $\{e : v(1 \text{ or } 2)\}$, ③ $\{v : e(\geq 0)\}$,
④ $\{l : e(\geq 0)\}$, ⑤ $\{f : l(\geq 1)\}$,

where the first letter denotes a geometric element type under consideration, and the second letter refers to the element type associated with the first element.

We now discuss these relations.

[1] In Fig. 18.14, loop 1 is the outer perimeter, while loops 2, 3, 4 and 5 are inner perimeter loops. Some methods distinguish inner loops from outer loop, calling inner loops "rings" and treating them as separate geometric elements in an associated Euler operator. Although this distinction holds for flat faces, it does not in general hold for curved surfaces (Fig. 18.15). Data structures deal with the topology of geometric figures, and Euler operators are used to carry out topological operations, yet rings are geometry-dependent elements. For this reason, in this book, we do not give special status to rings by setting up an Euler operator for them.

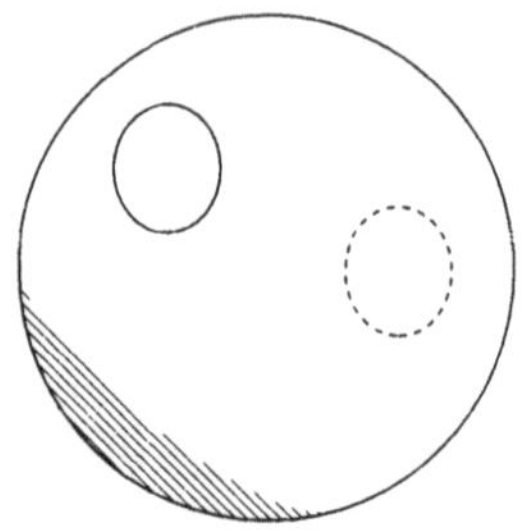

Figure 18.15: Sphere with holes.

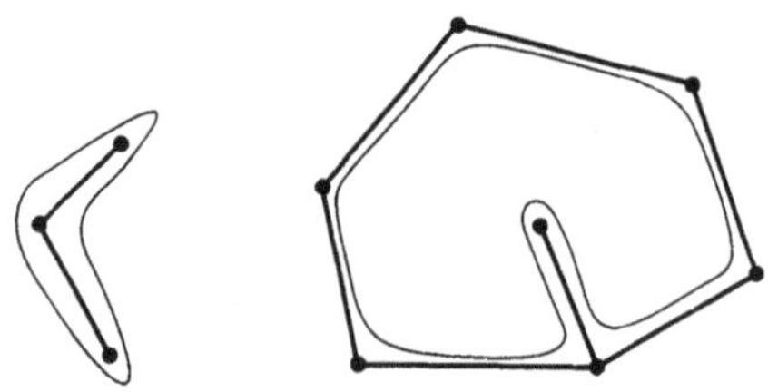

Figure 18.16: Case when an edge belongs to a single face-loop.

1. ① means that an edge normally is shared by two face-loops, but in special cases belongs only to a single face-loop. An edge belonging to a single (or same) face-loop occurs, for example, when a wire is first created when constructing a figure, or when a strut edge occurs temporarily in the middle of an operation (Fig. 18.16; see also Section 18.1.2).

2. ② indicates that an edge normally connects to two vertices, but in special cases, connects to a single vertex (Fig. 18.17). Such an edge, i.e., one that forms a *self loop* [2], can occur in association with a curve that forms the boundary of a curved face.

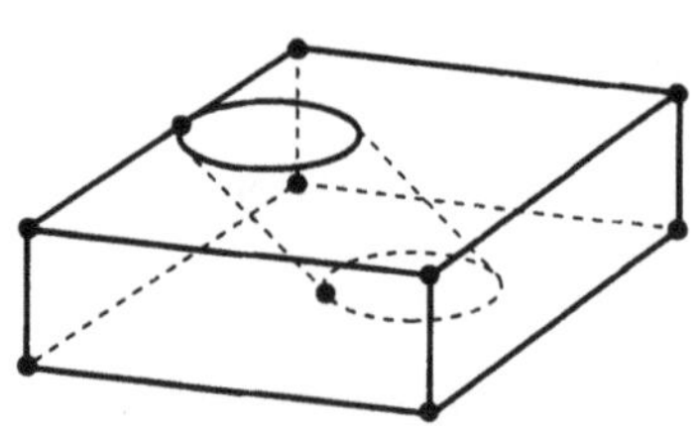

Figure 18.17: Edge forming a self-loop.

3. ③ means that several edges normally converge to a vertex, but in special cases, a vertex has no incoming edge, that is, it is an isolated point (Fig. 18.14).

[2] A self-looping edge is one in which the end vertices are identical. This forms a dual to the strut edge (see Section 18.1.2), for which the faces on both sides are identical.

4. ④ means that normally a face-loop will contain several edges, but in special cases, a vertex alone, with no edge, can be a face-loop (Fig. 18.14).

5. ⑤ means that a face has at least one face-loop.

The discussion above concerns face-loops, that is, loops that form boundaries to faces. These form a dual relation to vertex-loops, i.e., loops about vertices, which were discussed in Section 17.6.2.

18.2.3 Euler Operators

We now present a more generalized version of Euler operators which, by incorporating face-loops, applies to multiply-connected faces as well [3]. The elements treated by these Euler operators are vertices, edges, faces, loops (we are concerned here only with face-loops, so "loop" will hereafter be used to mean a face-loop), shells and genuses. For the Euler formula, we use the form:

$$v - e + f - (l_f - f) = 2(s - g). \tag{18.2}$$

Based on this formula, we employ five Euler operators which are now discussed. Below, the plane model is used to describe topological changes taking place in a solid [33]. For example, to represent the rectangular parallelepiped shown on the left of Fig. 18.18, the bottom face f_1 is removed and the parallelepiped is squashed flat onto a plane; face f_1 is reversed and presented as shown at right in the figure.

Of operator's arguments, the underlined ones are those elements that are outputted.

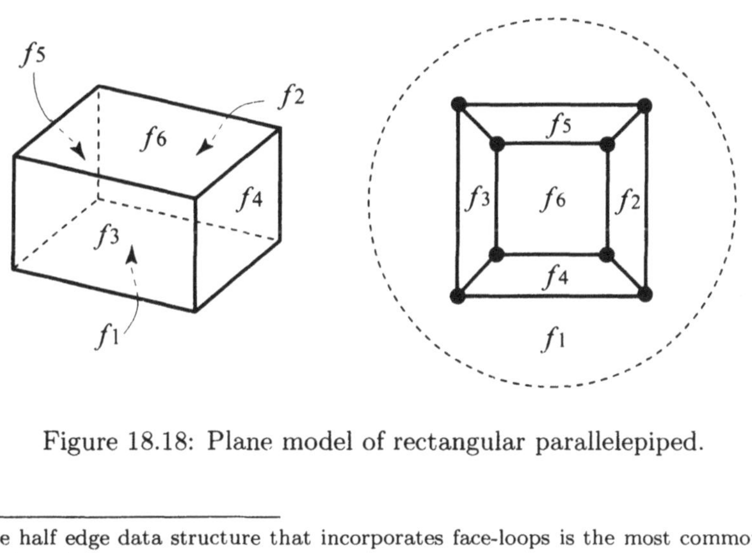

Figure 18.18: Plane model of rectangular parallelepiped.

[3] The half edge data structure that incorporates face-loops is the most commonly used data structure today.

1. **Operator for generating the core solid**

   mvfls ($\underline{v}, \underline{f}$) ... "make vertex, face, loop, shell"
   kvfls () .... "kill vertex, face, loop, shell"

   mvfls is the first operator to be executed when creating a solid; it produces a degenerate shell consisting of a vertex, null face and a loop (Fig. 18.19). Note that the Euler formula (18.2) already applies at this stage.

   kvfls is the inverse operation of **mvfls**: if a degenerate *shell* consisting of a vertex, a (null) face and a loop exists, this operation wipes out these elements and returns to an empty state.

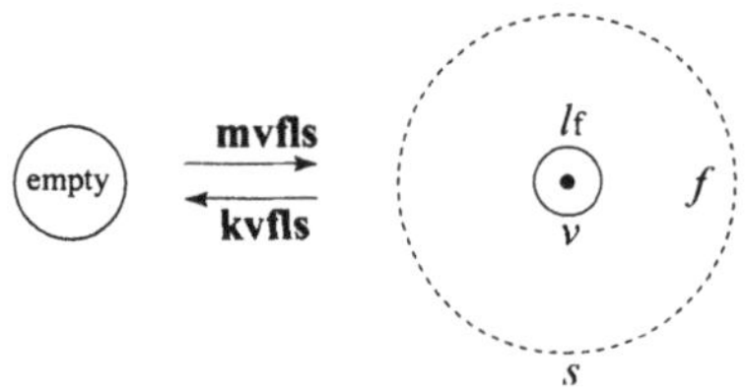

Figure 18.19: The operations of **mvfls** and **kvfls**.

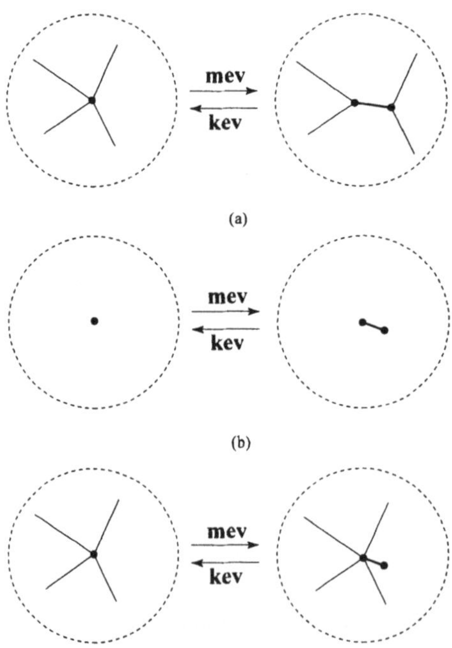

Figure 18.20: The operations of **mev** and **kev**.

Local topological operations are carried out by the following three operators.

2. **Local operators**

   mev $(v1, \underline{v2}, \underline{e})$ ... "make edge, vertex"
   kev $(v2, e, \underline{v1})$ ..... "kill edge, vertex"

   mev splits an existing vertex into two vertices and creates an edge connecting the two vertices; as a result, the number of vertices and edges each increases by one (Fig. 18.20(a)). **mev** can apply to an isolated point newly generated by **mvfls** (Fig. 18.20(b)), or it can also be used to create a strut edge as in Fig. 18.20(c).

   kev reverses the three operations of **mev** shown in Fig. 18.20. In other words, given an edge that connects two vertices, **kev** removes the edge and fuses the two vertices into a single vertex.

   mefl $(v1, v2, f1, \underline{f2}, \underline{e})$ ... "make edge, face, loop"
   kefl $(e, \underline{f1})$ .... "kill edge, face, loop"

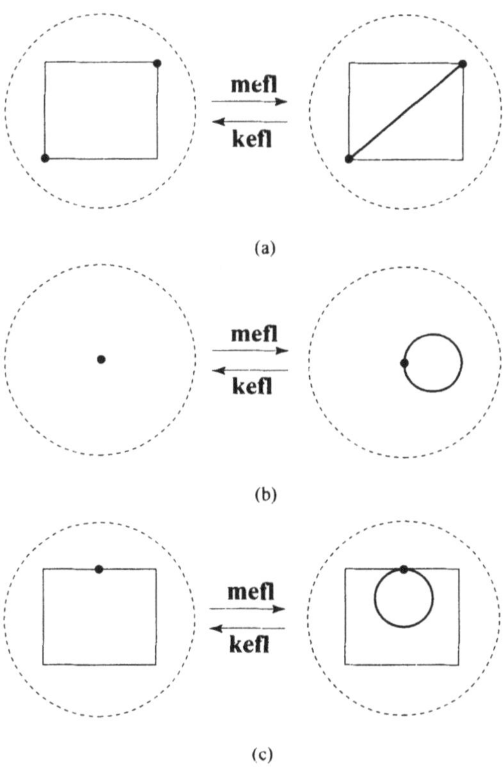

Figure 18.21: The operations of **mefl** and **kefl**.

mefl divides a face into two by connecting two of its vertices with an edge; as a result, the number of faces, edges as well as loops each increases by one (Fig. 18.21(a)). **mefl** can apply to an isolated vertex generated by **mvfls** (Fig. 18.21(b)), and to cases like Fig. 18.21(c) as well.

kefl reverses the three operations shown in Fig. 18.21, that is, given an edge shared by two faces, **kefl** removes the edge to create a single face.

keml (e) .... "kill edge, make loop"
mekl $(v1, v2, \underline{e})$ .... "make edge, kill loop"

keml removes an edge that appears twice when tracing a loop, thus splitting the loop into two loops (Fig. 18.22(a)). **keml** also applies to the special cases shown in Fig. 18.22 (b) and (c).

mekl, its inverse operator, connects the vertices of two loops with an edge to create a single loop.

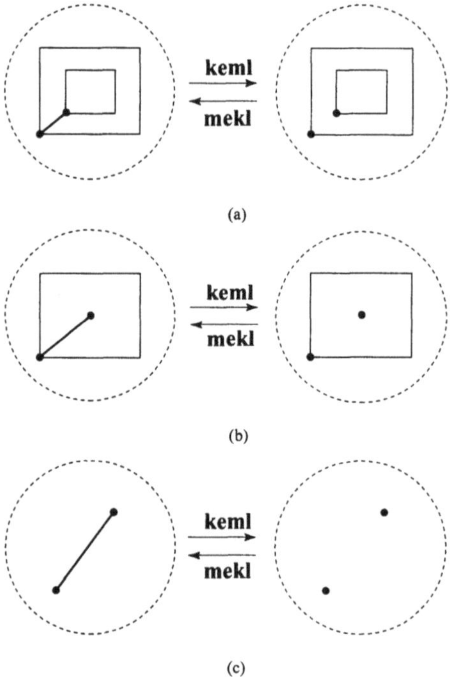

Figure 18.22: The operations of **keml** and **mekl**.

3. **Global operators**

While the operators above were limited to local topological operations, **kfmg** and **mfkg** discussed next execute global topological operations such as dividing a shell into two or opening a penetrating hole in a shell.

kfmg ($\underline{f1}, f2$) ... "kill face, make genus"
mfkg ($\overline{f1}, \underline{f2}$) ... "make face, kill genus"

Given two faces $f1$ and $f2$, **kfmg**($\underline{f1}, f2$) makes a hole by removing $f2$ and incorporating $f2$'s loop into $\overline{f1}$, which then becomes a multiply-connected holed face (Fig. 18.23(a)). Thus, the central portion of the right figure in Fig. 18.23(a) is now a hole. Usually, that is, when $f1$ and $f2$ belong to the same shell, this operation raises the genus by one. If $f1$ and $f2$ belong to different shells, **kfmg** fuses the two shells into a single shell (this is discussed later). Figure 18.23(b) shows when **kfmg** is used to produce a torus.

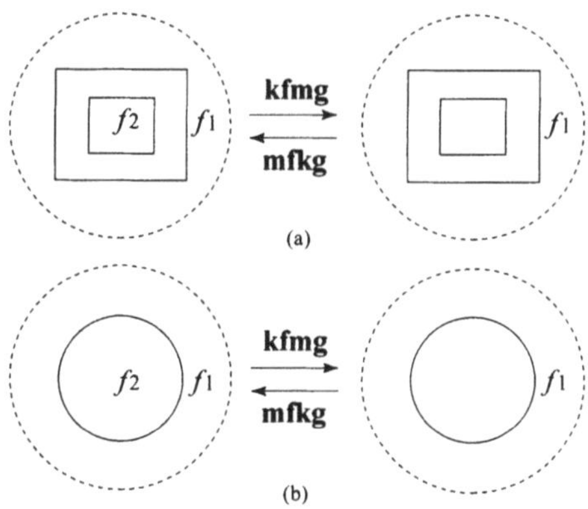

Figure 18.23: The operations of **kfmg** and **mfkg**.

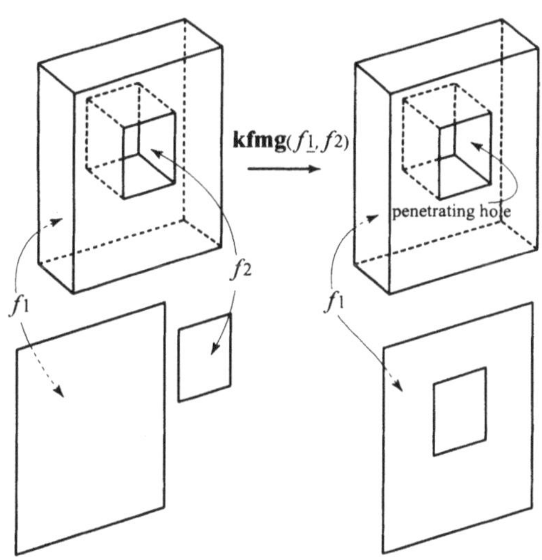

Figure 18.24: Application of **kfmg** (case 1).

In normal situations, **mfkg**, the inverse operator of **kfmg**, covers a penetrating hole and reduces the genus by one. With **kfmg** and **mfkg**, the total number of the loops remains constant.

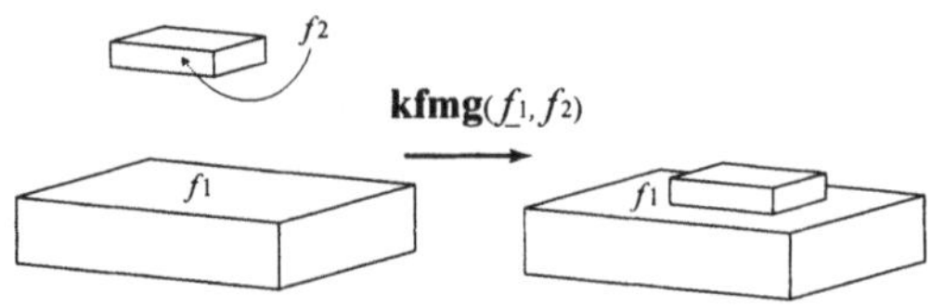

Figure 18.25: Application of **kfmg** (case 2).

Figs. 18.24 and 18.25 show how **kfmg** can be applied. In Fig. 18.25, it is used to fuse two contacting solids together.

While the other Euler operators (excepting **mvfls** and **kvfls**) keep the Euler characteristic constant, **kfmg** either eliminates a shell or opens a penetrating hole, thus reducing the Euler characteristic by two; meanwhile, **mfkg**, by doing the inverse, increases the Euler characteristic by two.

Although the following operators are not required, they are convenient to have.

4. **Supplementary operators**

   semv $(e1, \underline{v}, \underline{e2})$ ... "split edge, make vertex"
   jekv $(\underline{e1}, e2)$ .... "join edges, kill vertex"

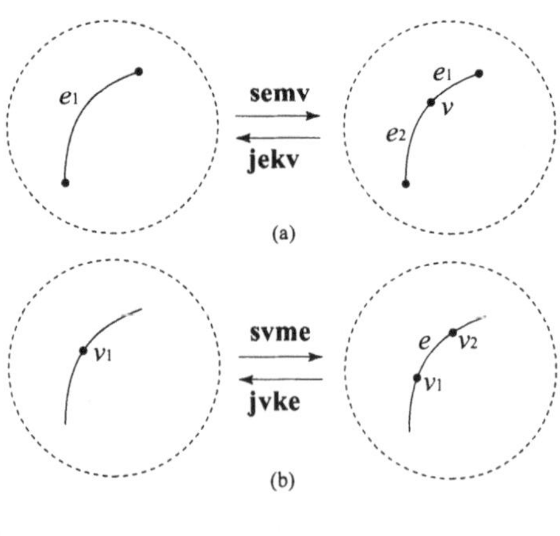

Figure 18.26: The operations of **semv**, **jekv**, **svme** and **jvke**.

The operator **semv** $(e1, \underline{v}, \underline{e2})$ splits a given edge $e1$ into e1 and $e2$ by creating a vertex v at the interior of the edge (Fig. 18.26(a)).

jekv ($\underline{e1}, e2$) does the inverse operation of **semv**. When a vertex has two and only two converging edges, having specified these two edges $e1$ and $e2$, this operator joins the edges and removes the vertex (Fig. 18.26(a)).

svme ($v1, \underline{v2}, \underline{e}$) ... "split vertex, make edge"
jvke ($\underline{v1}, v2$) .... "join vertices, kill edge"

When two edges meet at vertex $v1$, the operator **svme** ($v1, \underline{v2}, \underline{e}$) splits $v1$ into $v1$ and $v2$ and inserts an edge e in between (Fig. 18.26(b)).

jvke ($\underline{v1}, v2$) removes an edge e connecting two separate vertices and fuses them into a single vertex (Fig. 18.26(b)).

Table 18.1 shows how the Euler operators above affect the Euler characteristic.

Creating a Cuboid with a Hole Using Euler Operators

Fig. 18.27 shows the process for making a rectangular parallelepiped with a penetrating hole using the Euler operators.

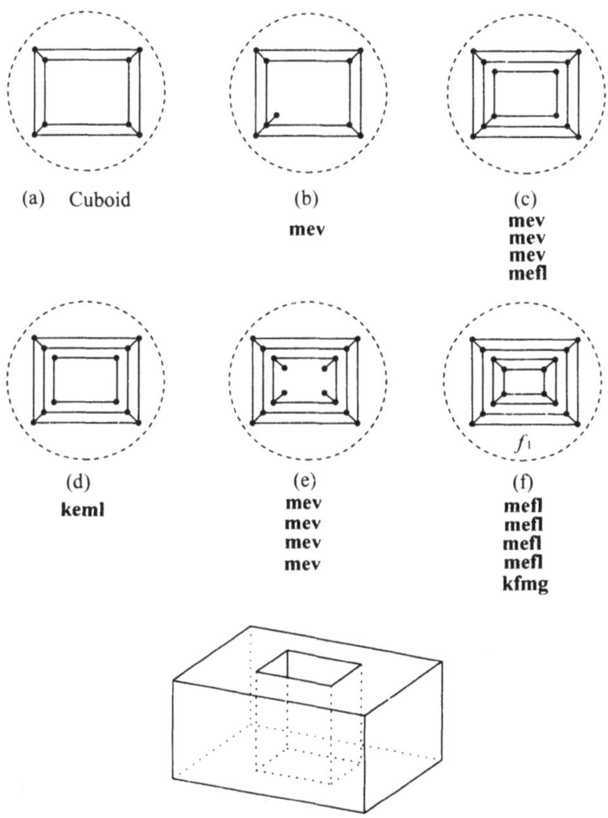

Figure 18.27: Constructing a cuboid with a hole using Euler operators.

Table 18.1: Euler operators and Euler characteristics.

No	Operator	v	e	f	$l_f - f$	s	g
(1)	**mvfls**	+1		+1		+1	
	kvfls	−1		−1		−1	
(2)	**mev**	+1	+1				
	kev	−1	−1				
(3)	**mefl**		+1	+1			
	kefl		−1	−1			
(4)	**keml**		−1		+1		
	mekl		+1		−1		
(5)	**kfmg**			−1(−1)	+1(+1)	0(−1)	+1(0)
	mfkg			+1(+1)	−1(−1)	0(+1)	−1(0)
(6)	**semv**	+1	+1				
	jekv	−1	−1				
(7)	**svme**	+1	+1				
	jvke	−1	−1				

In (b), **mev** produces a strut edge so that a loop can be created inside. In (c), a connected figure consisting of vertices and edges is constructed, although it is not yet a loop at this stage. In (d), the strut edge is removed so that the figure created in (c) forms a loop. In (e), four strut edges are created. In (f), five faces are created in the center. The four faces other than the very central one will become the sides of the penetrating hole. The final operation **kfmg** $(\underline{f1}, f2)$ opens the penetrating hole. When constructing an actual solid, the coordinates must be specified in addition to the topological operations by the Euler operators. This is done immediately after executing the operators **mvfls** and **mev**.

18.2.4 Algebraic Investigation of Euler Operators

In this section, we discuss the algebraic properties of the Euler operators based on the Euler formula:

$$v - e + f - (l_f - f) - 2(s - g) = 0. \tag{18.3}$$

Whenever the Euler operators are employed to create a solid, the first step always begins with executing **mvfls**, which produces a vertex, a face, a loop and a shell. At this stage, eq.(18.3) is already satisfied. The respective values of v, e, f, l_f, s and g of eq.(18.3) will vary with subsequent Euler operations, but the relationship of eq.(18.3) will always hold. This property allows us to carry out the following algebraic investigation [7].

Consider a six-dimensional numerical vector space with the coordinate axes v, e, f, l_f, s and g. Then eq.(18.3) represents a five-dimensional hyperplane in this vector space. Furthermore, it defines a lattice lying on this hyperplane because the variables can only assume non-negative integers. Thus, any three-dimensional solid created by the Euler operators above will correspond to some lattice point on the hyperplane. If we represent lattice points on the hyperplane by vectors, then a three-dimensional solid for which the number of vertices, edges, faces, loops, shells and genuses are respectively given by v, e, f, l_f, s and g, corresponds to the point (or vector)

$$\boldsymbol{S} = [v \; e \; f \; l_f \; s \; g]$$

in the 6-dimensional vector space.

Any lattice point on the five-dimensional hyperplane can be expressed as a linear combination of five linearly independent vectors on the hyperplane. Thus, from the viewpoint of solid construction, the Euler operators correspond to basis vectors as in Table 18.2.

If in order to construct the solid $\boldsymbol{S} = [v \; e \; f \; l_f \; s \; g]$ the Euler operators **mvfls**, **mev**, **mefl**, **keml** and **kfmg** must be carried out A, B, C, D and E times each, then we have the following equation:

$$[A \; B \; C \; D \; E] \begin{bmatrix} 1 & 0 & 1 & 1 & 1 & 0 \\ 1 & 1 & 0 & 0 & 0 & 0 \\ 0 & 1 & 1 & 1 & 0 & 0 \\ 0 & -1 & 0 & 1 & 0 & 0 \\ 0 & 0 & -1 & 0 & 0 & 1 \end{bmatrix} = [v \; e \; f \; l_f \; s \; g]. \tag{18.4}$$

Table 18.2: Euler operators as basis vectors.

	v	e	f	l_f	s	g		v	e	f	l_f	s	g
mvfls	1		1	1	1		**kvfls**	−1		−1	−1	−1	
mev	1	1					**kev**	−1	−1				
mefl		1	1	1			**kefl**		−1	−1	−1		
keml		−1		1			**mekl**		1		−1		
kfmg			−1			1	**mfkg**			1			−1

We add a sixth row, which is an identity relation, to the 5×6 matrix above to convert it into a square matrix so that its inverse matrix can be determined:

$$[A\ B\ C\ D\ E\ 1]\begin{bmatrix}1 & 0 & 1 & 1 & 1 & 0\\ 1 & 1 & 0 & 0 & 0 & 0\\ 0 & 1 & 1 & 1 & 0 & 0\\ 0 & -1 & 0 & 1 & 0 & 0\\ 0 & 0 & -1 & 0 & 0 & 1\\ 0 & 0 & 0 & 0 & 0 & 1\end{bmatrix} = [v\ e\ f\ l_f\ s\ g+1]. \tag{18.5}$$

So,

$$[A\ B\ C\ D\ E\ 1] = [v\ e\ f\ l_f\ s\ g+1]\begin{bmatrix}1 & 0 & 1 & 1 & 1 & 0\\ 1 & 1 & 0 & 0 & 0 & 0\\ 0 & 1 & 1 & 1 & 0 & 0\\ 0 & -1 & 0 & 1 & 0 & 0\\ 0 & 0 & -1 & 0 & 0 & 1\\ 0 & 0 & 0 & 0 & 0 & 1\end{bmatrix}^{-1}$$
$$= \frac{1}{2}[v\ e\ f\ l_f\ s\ g+1]\begin{bmatrix}0 & 2 & -1 & 1 & -1 & 1\\ 0 & 0 & 1 & -1 & 1 & -1\\ 0 & 0 & 0 & 0 & -2 & 2\\ 0 & 0 & 1 & 1 & 1 & -1\\ 2 & -2 & 0 & -2 & 2 & -2\\ 0 & 0 & 0 & 0 & 0 & 2\end{bmatrix}. \tag{18.6}$$

Given a solid $\boldsymbol{S} = [v\ e\ f\ l_f\ s\ g]$, eq.(18.6) calculates the minimum number of the Euler operators needed for its construction. Let us apply this to the rectangular parallelepiped with a penetrating hole discussed above (Figs. 18.8 and 18.27). We have $v = 16$, $e = 24$, $f = 10$, $l_f = 12$, $s = 1$ and $g = 1$, so

$$[A\ B\ C\ D\ E\ 1] = \frac{1}{2}[16\ \ 24\ \ 10\ \ 12\ \ 1\ \ 2]\begin{bmatrix}0 & 2 & -1 & 1 & -1 & 1\\ 0 & 0 & 1 & -1 & 1 & -1\\ 0 & 0 & 0 & 0 & -2 & 2\\ 0 & 0 & 1 & 1 & 1 & -1\\ 2 & -2 & 0 & -2 & 2 & -2\\ 0 & 0 & 0 & 0 & 0 & 2\end{bmatrix}$$
$$= [1\ \ 15\ \ 10\ \ 1\ \ 1\ \ 1].$$

Thus, we need to carry out at least **mvfls** once, **mev** 15 times, **mefl** ten times, **keml** once and **kfmg** once in order to create a rectangular parallelepiped with a penetrating hole. This indeed matches the number of operators used in Figs. 18.8 and 18.27, showing that the procedure used was optimal.

From eq.(18.6), we can determine the number of Euler operators needed to construct a solid $\boldsymbol{S}=[v\ c\ f\ l_f\ 1\ g]$ consisting of a single shell ($s=1$):

mvfls 1
mev ....$v-1$
mefl .... $f+g-1$
keml ... l_f-f-g
kfmg 1

If calculation yields a negative result for a particular Euler operator, this indicates that its inverse operator (for instance, **kev** for **mev**) must be carried out.

18.3 Quarter Edge Data Structure

18.3.1 Quarter Edges

Although the half edge data structure requires more data storage than the winged edge data structure, it allows for a more efficient processing. Yet, because it is not symmetric with respect to vertices and faces, the half edge data structure still retains the problem stated earlier in Problem ③ (Section 18.1.3) concerning the winged edge data structure, namely, that dual processing is not possible.

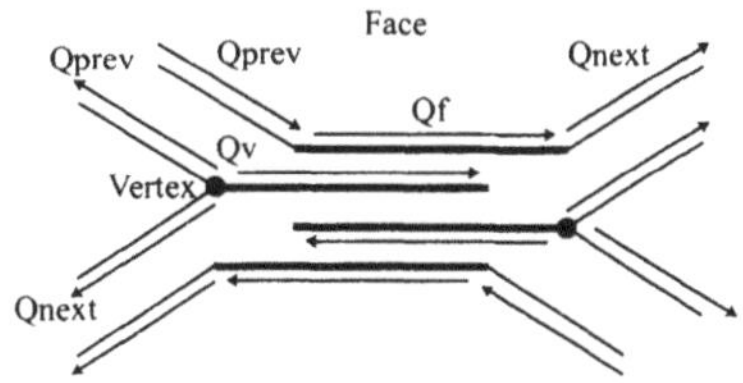

Figure 18.28: Quarter edge

As a solution to the two problems (① and ③) cited with respect to the winged edge data structure, one could divide the edge into four parts so that the "FE" and "VE" types are both represented separately. This is called the *quarter edge data structure* (Fig. 18.28) [41]. One type of quarter edge is defined around a face and the other around a vertex. To determine which processing to carry out – whether that around the face or that around the vertex – pointers are used. The two ways of processing form a dual relation. "Qpair" is a pointer used by the pair of *quarter edges*, one face-centered and the other vertex-centered, to point to each other; in Fig. 18.28, the upper two *quarter edges* and the lower two each form such a pair. When a pair of quarter edges are combined, it is equal in function to a half edge.

The biggest advantage of the quarter edge data structure is that, as the argument of functions, it is possible to specify face-centered and vertex-centered quarter edges separately. As we shall see later, this feature allows us to use Euler operators that possess complete duality.

The main advantage of a data structure possessing duality is that it allows duality to be introduced into Euler operators and other geometric operations; this cuts down on the types of programs needed and simplifies internal processing; in addition, the theory of dual processing leads to a more reliable and consistent programming. Dual processing can also lead to a greater functioning range in some cases, as when the use of dual operators results in an expanded modeling space.

A simplified structure of the quarter edge and edge are defined as an example in Fig. 18.29. To express the corresponding relationship, an edge structure has four pointers, each pointing to a respective quarter edge.

```
typedef struct d_quarteredge {
        index                   index;
        identifier              identifier;
        void                    *attr;
        struct d_quarteredge    *Qnext;
        struct d_quarteredge    *Qprev;
        struct d_loop           *Qloop;
        struct d_quarteredge    *Qpair;
        struct d_edge           *Qedge;
} Quarter;

typedef struct d_edge {
        index                   index;
        identifier              identifier;
        void                    *attr;
        struct d_edge           *next;
        struct d_edge           *prev;
        struct d_shell          *Eshell;
        struct d_quarteredge    *Epquarter[2];
        struct d_quarteredge    *Enquarter[2];
} Edge;
```

Figure 18.29: Definitions of quarter edge and edge structures.

Epquarter[0] and Enquarter[0] point to quarter edges belonging to two faces that connect via an edge, respectively; each quarter edge constitutes the "other" from its counterpart [4].

Epquarter[1] and Enquarter[1] point to quarter edges that belong to two vertices that connect via an edge; these form the "other" relation as well.

Epquarter[0] and Epquarter[1] are quarter edges that are pointed to by the pointer "Qpair" and so are Enquarter[0] and Enquarter[1].

From a quarter edge, "Qedge" points to the edge to which it belongs. "index" refers to the index number, "identifier" identifies the type, and "*next" and "*prev" are respective pointers to the next and previous blocks in the ring-structured list.

In order to maintain processing efficiency, the definition statement for the quarter edge structure does not include pointers to faces or vertices [5]. These elements must be accessed via "Qloop."

Data access

With the combined half edge data structure, edge data were accessed using "Hccwf," "Hcwf," "Hccwv" and "Hcwv." In the quarter edge data structure, these are accessed as follows (where "Qf" represents a face-centered quarter edge and "Qv" a vertex-centered quarter edge):

Hccwf...........Qf->Qnext,
Qv->Qpair->Qnext,

Hcwf.............Qf->Qprev,
Qv->Qpair->Qprev,

Hccwv..........Qf->Qpair->Qprev,
Qv->Qprev,

Hcwv............Qf->Qpair->Qnext,
Qv->Qnext.

We now describe how to access the "other" of a quarter edge. From a face-centered quarter edge this refers to the "other" face-centered quarter edge, and from a vertex-centered it is the other vertex-centered quarter edge.

"other"of Qf...........Qf->Qnext->Qpair->Qprev->Qpair,
or Qf->Qpair->Qnext->Qpair->Qprev.

"other" of Qv...........Qv->Qnext->Qpair->Qprev->Qpair,
or Qv->Qpair->Qnext->Qpair-->Qprev.

---

[4] See Section 18.1.1 for the meaning of "other."

[5] In processing with Euler operators, it occurs frequently that a loop switches the face to which it belongs. So if quarter edges had pointers to faces, they would have to be rewritten every time such change took place, thus considerably lowering the processing efficiency.

It is also possible to access the "other" through the edge. Thus "Qpair" is not an essential pointer.

To enable dual processing, the quarter edge data structure is structured so that face-centered processing can be carried out totally independently of vertex-centered processing. Consequently, if vertex-centered information is to be accessed from a face-centered quarter edge, or conversely face-centered information is to be accessed from a vertex-centered edge, frequent referrals to pointers must be made, and the processing efficiency suffers.

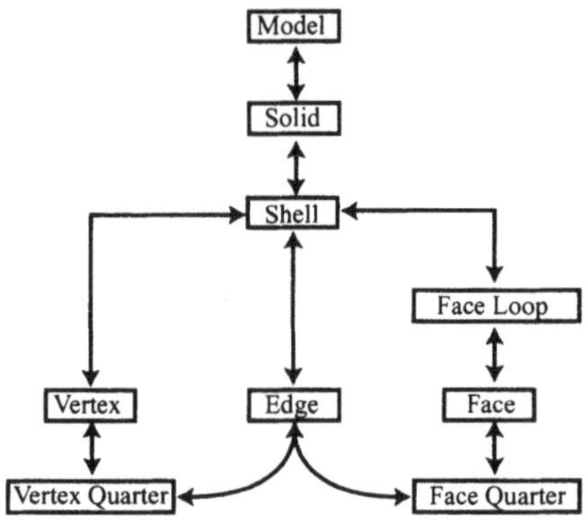

Figure 18.30: A hierarchical structure of solid model geometric elements.

18.3.2 Introducing Vertex- and Edge-loops

Let us now examine the hierarchical structure of shape elements of the solid model from the viewpoint of duality. Fig. 18.30 represents a hierarchical data structure of solid model geometric elements using quarter edges. Since clearly there is no element on the left side which forms a dual to the face-loop on the right, the structure is not symmetric with respect to vertices and faces.

We thus introduce the vertex-loop as a dual element to the face-loop (Fig. 17.25). From the standpoint of the quarter edge data structure, the vertex-loop is a cycle of faces centered on a vertex and consisting of quarter edges that belong to faces, while the face-loop is a cycle of vertices around a face, consisting of quarter edges belonging to vertices. By introducing vertex-loops, a face or a vertex can either have multiple cycles about it. We now have a dual hierarchical structure for solid model shape elements.

We further include the edge-loop to complete the generality of data structure (Fig. 17.29). The edge-loop helps to simplify the set operation algorithm (see Section 20.5.2). As already discussed, an edge-loop is a cycle composed of exactly two incident faces and two incident vertices.

Note that the conventional hierarchical structure for solid modeling of manifolds is wholly contained within the generalized non-manifold dual structure (Fig. 18.31).

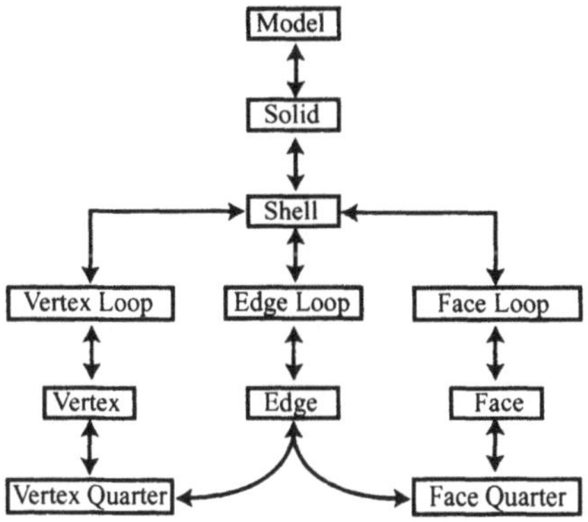

Figure 18.31: Dual hierarchical structure of solid model geometric elements.

18.3.3 Euler Operators

The Euler operators proposed in this book are based on the following generalized Euler formula:

$$v - e + f - \{(l_v - v) + (l_e - e) + (l_f - f)\} = 2(s - g), \tag{18.7}$$

where
v: number of vertices, e: number of edges, f: number of faces,
l_v: number of vertex-loops, l_e: number of edge-loops, l_f: number of face-loops,
s: number of shells, g: number of genuses.

Based on this equation, we can now construct Euler operators and their inverse operators. These operators form duals with either itself or another operator.

(1) mvfs (make vertex, face, shell)
(1') kvfs (kill vertex, face, shell)

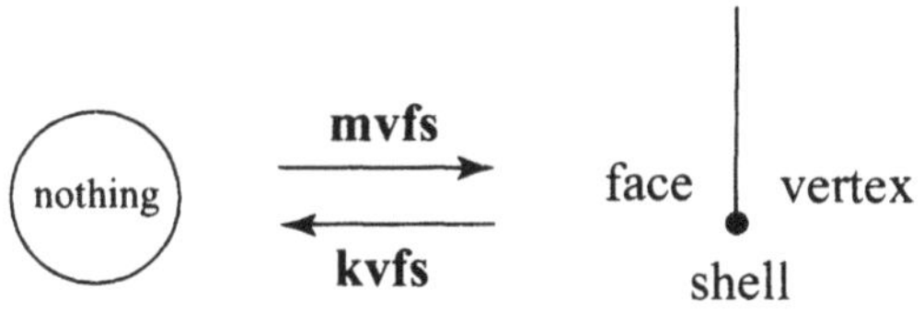

Figure 18.32: **mvfs** and **kvfs**.

The operation **mvfs** creates a vertex and a null face, as well as a quarter edge associated with each (Fig. 18.32).

kvfs is the inverse operator of **mvfs**.

Switching the vertex and face does not alter either operator **kvfs** or **mvfs**. So each of them is a self-dual operator (i.e., it is its own dual).

Below we present a pair of dual operators side by side.

(2) mev (make edge, vertex) ⇔ **(3) mef** (make edge, face)

mev splits a vertex into two and inserts an edge between them, while **mef** splits a face into two and inserts an edge between them (Fig. 18.33).

mev and **mef** are dual each other and are executed by a single program.

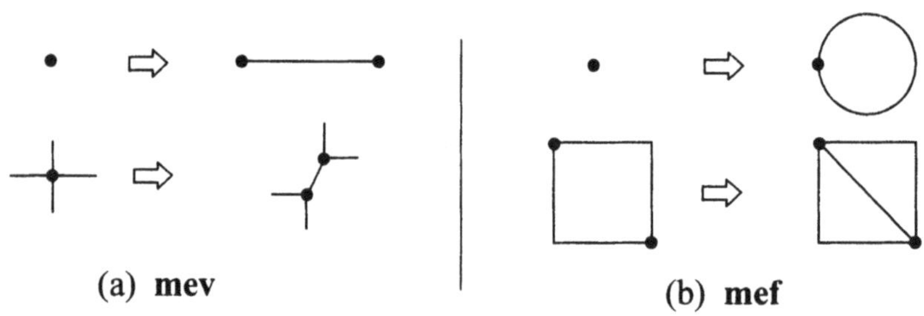

Figure 18.33: **mev** and **mef**.

(2') kev (kill edge, vertex) ⇔ **(3') kef** (kill edge, face)

kev performs the inverse operation of **mev**, that is, it deletes a vertex-connecting edge and unites the two incident vertices into one, while **kef** performs the inverse operation of **mef**, that is, it deletes a face-connecting edge and unites the two incident faces into one (Fig. 18.34).

kev and **kef** are dual each other and are executed by a single program.

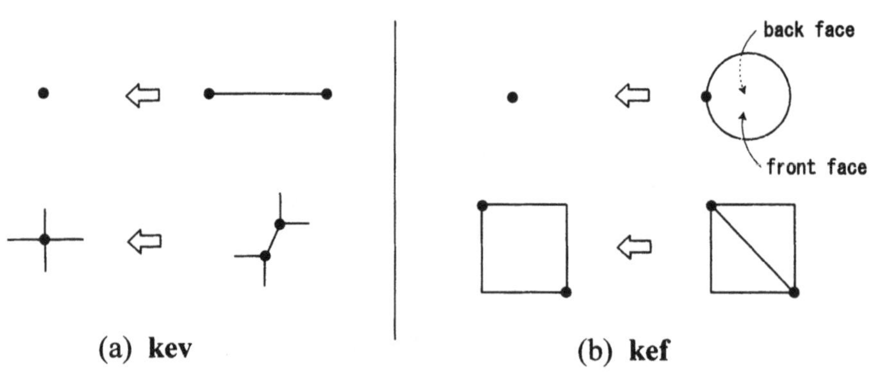

Figure 18.34: **kev** and **kef**.

(4) keml$_v$ (kill edge, make vertex-loop)⇔**(6) keml$_f$** (kill edge, make face-loop)

keml$_v$ specifies an edge whose incident vertices are identical. It increases the number of the loop-multiplicity of the vertex by one, by deleting the specified edge, while **keml$_f$** specifies an edge whose incident faces are identical. It increases the number of the loop-multiplicity of the face by one, by deleting the specified edge (Fig. 18.35).

keml$_v$ and **keml$_f$** are dual each other and are executed by a single program.

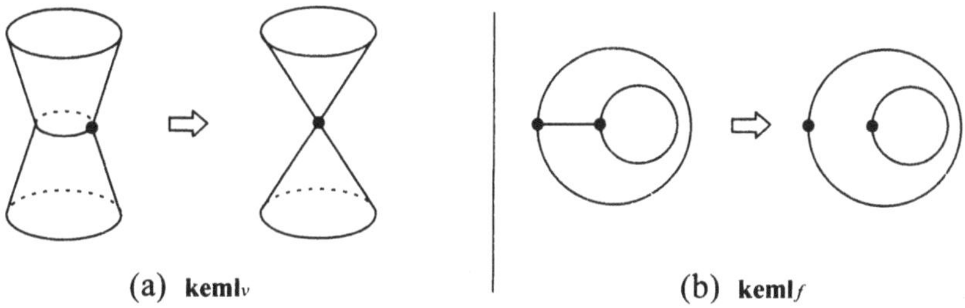

Figure 18.35: **keml$_v$** and **keml$_f$**.

(4') mekl$_v$ (make edge, kill vertex-loop)⇔**(6') mekl$_f$** (make edge, kill face-loop)

mekl$_v$ performs the inverse operation of **keml$_v$**, that is, it specifies a vertex whose loop-multiplicity is more than two. It decreases the number of the loop-multiplicity of the vertex by one by inserting an edge between two faces belonging to two distinct loops of the vertex, while **mekl$_f$** performs the inverse operation of **keml$_f$**, that is, it specifies a face whose loop-multiplicity is more than two. It decreases the number of the loop-multiplicity of the face by one by inserting an edge between two vertices belonging to two distinct loops of the face (Fig. 18.36).

mekl$_v$ and **mekl$_f$** are dual each other and are executed by a single program.

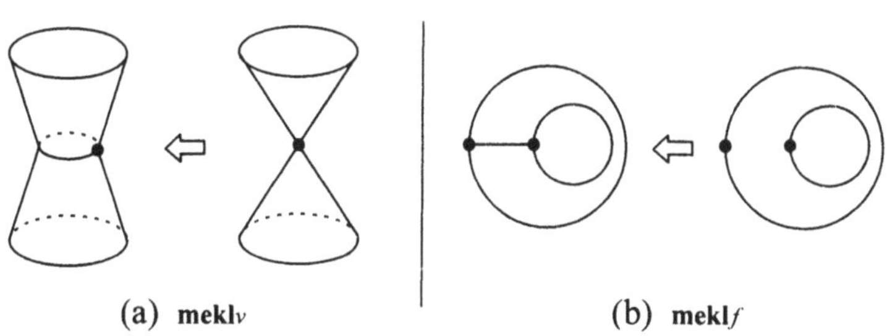

Figure 18.36: **mekl$_v$** and **mekl$_f$**.

(5) keml$_e$ (kill edge, make edge-loop)

keml$_e$ specifies two edges whose each end-vertex is identical respectively.

In one case it unites them into one edge by deleting the other and increases the number of the loop-multiplicity of the remaining edge by one (Fig. 18.37(a)).

In another case it not only unites them into one edge by deleting the other and increases the number of the loop-multiplicity of the remaining edge by one, but also decreases the genus and the number of the loop-multiplicity of each end-vertex by one, respectively (Fig. 18.37(b)).

This is a self dual operator.

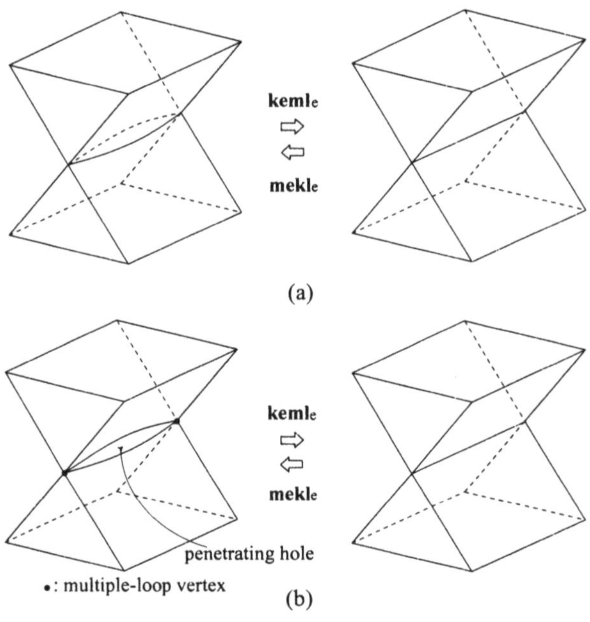

Figure 18.37: **keml$_e$** and **mekl$_e$**.

(5') mekl$_e$ (make edge, kill edge-loop)

mekl$_e$ performs the inverse operation of **keml$_e$**. It specifies an edge whose loop-multiplicity is more than two, and whose each end-vertex is identical respectively. **mekl$_e$** splits the edge into two.

In one case it decreases the number of the loop-multiplicity of the specified edge by one (Fig. 18.37(a)).

In another case it not only decreases the number of the loop-multiplicity of the specified edge by one, but also increases the genus and the number of the loop-multiplicity of each end-vertex by one, respectively (Fig. 18.37(b)).

This is a self dual operator.

(7) kvmg (kill vertex, make genus) ⇔ **(8) kfmg** (kill face, make genus)

In one case **kvmg** specifies two distinct vertices. It unites them into one vertex by deleting the other and increases the genus and the number of the loop-multiplicity of the remaining vertex by one respectively. On the other hand **kfmg** specifies two distinct faces. It unites them into one face by deleting the other and increases the genus and the number of the loop-multiplicity of the remaining face by one respectively (Fig. 18.38(1)).

In another case **kvmg** also specifies two distinct vertices. It unites them into one vertex by deleting the other and decreases the number of shells and increases the loop-multiplicity of the remaining vertex by one respectively. On the other hand **kfmg** also specifies two distinct faces. It unites them into one face by deleting the other and decreases the number of shells and increases the number of the loop-multiplicity of the remaining face by one respectively (Fig. 18.38(2)).

kvmg and **kfmg** are dual each other and are executed by a single program.

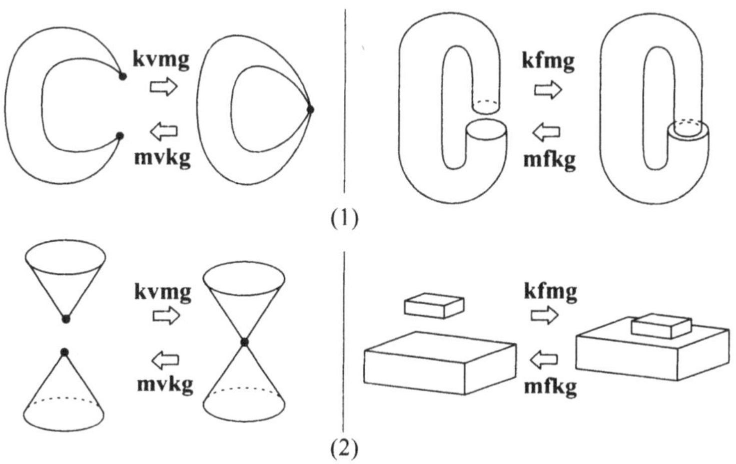

Figure 18.38: **kvmg**, **kfmg**, **mvkg** and **mfkg**.

(7') mvkg (make vertex, kill genus) ⇔ **(8') mfkg** (make face, kill genus)

In one case **mvkg** specifies a vertex whose loop-multiplicity is more than two, decreases the genus and the number of loop-multiplicity of the specified vertex by one respectively by splitting the vertex into two, while **mfkg** specifies a face whose loop-multiplicity is more than two, decreases the genus and the number of loop-multiplicity of the specified face by one respectively by splitting the face into two (Fig. 18.38(1)).

In another case **mvkg** specifies a vertex whose loop-multiplicity is more than two, increases the number of shells and decreases the number of the loop-multiplicity of the specified vertex by one respectively by splitting the vertex into two, while **mfkg** specifies a face whose loop-multiplicity is more than two, increases the number of shells and decreases the number of the loop-multiplicity of the specified face by one respectively by splitting the face into two (Fig. 18.38(2)).

mvkg and **mfkg** are dual each other and are executed by a single program.

These Euler operators are summarized in Table 18.3.

Using the Euler operators above, we can construct not only any solid possible with conventional Euler operators based on the half edge data structure, but a wider range of other solids as well. Furthermore, as we have seen, duality is established between the operators as follows:

(a) **mvfs** (self dual),	(a') **kvfs** (self dual),
(b) **mev** and **mef** (dual),	(b') **kev** and **kef** (dual),
(c) $\mathbf{keml}_e$ (self dual),	(c') $\mathbf{mekl}_e$ (self dual)
(d) $\mathbf{keml}_v$ and $\mathbf{keml}_f$ (dual),	(d') $\mathbf{mekl}_v$ and $\mathbf{mekl}_f$ (dual),
(e) **kvmg** and **kfmg** (dual),	(e') **mvkg** and **mfkg** (dual).

The Euler operators that form a dual relationship can be executed by a common program. If we use the letter "d" (for "dual") to express both "f" and "v," we can simplify as follows:

mvfs → **mvfs**	**kvfs** → **kvfs**
mev and **mef** → **med**	**kev** and **kef** → **ked**
$\mathbf{keml}_v$ and $\mathbf{keml}_f$ → $\mathbf{keml}_d$	$\mathbf{mekl}_v$ and $\mathbf{mekl}_f$ → $\mathbf{mekl}_d$
$\mathbf{keml}_e$ → $\mathbf{keml}_e$	$\mathbf{mekl}_e$ → $\mathbf{mekl}_e$
kvmg and **kfmg** → **kdmg**	**mvkg** and **mfkg** → **mdkg**

Therefore, we only need to prepare the ten functions, **mvfs**, **kvfs**, **med**, **ked**, $\mathbf{keml}_d$, $\mathbf{mekl}_d$, $\mathbf{keml}_e$, $\mathbf{mekl}_e$, **kdmg** and **mdkg**, for all operators including the inverse ones. We shall call these "dual Euler operators." When executing a dual operator, the argument determines which operations to take (i.e., for either "f" or "v"). For **med**, for instance, specifying a face-centered quarter edge executes **mef**, while a vertex-centered quarter edge will result in the operation **mev**.

Last of all, note that the Euler's formula, eq.(18.7), represents a seven-dimensional hyperplane in eight-dimensional vector space, and thus the minimum number of the operators required is seven (see Section 18.2.4).

Table 18.3: Euler operators based on generalized practical Euler formula.

No	Operators	v	e	f	$l_v - v$	$l_e - e$	$l_f - f$	s	g
(1)	**mvfs**	+1		+1				+1	
(1')	**kvfs**	−1		−1				−1	
(2)	**mev**	+1	+1						
(2')	**kev**	−1	−1						
(3)	**mef**		+1	+1					
(3')	**kef**		−1	−1					
(4)	**keml$_v$**		−1		+1				
(4')	**mekl$_v$**		+1		−1				
(5)	**keml$_e$**		−1			+1			
(5')	**mekl$_e$**		+1			−1			
			+1		+2	−1			+1
(6)	**keml$_f$**		−1				+1		
(6')	**mekl$_f$**		+1				−1		
(7)	**kvmg**	−1			+1				+1
(7')	**mvkg**	+1			−1				−1
		+1			−1			+1	
(8)	**kfmg**			−1			+1		+1
(8')	**mfkg**			+1			−1		−1
				+1			−1	+1	

Chapter 19

Euclidean and Affine

The Four-dimensional Processing proposed in this book is mainly based on the concepts of projective geometry. Therefore, it is quite natural to wonder how Euclidean metric quantities and affine concepts are treated in the Processing.

Recall that the main playground of the Four-dimensional Processing is the associated vector space, $\mathbf{R}^4$, of a projective space, not the projective space itself and that in dealing with Euclidean or affine concepts, the space $\mathbf{R}^4$ is considered a set of sections representing Euclidean spaces $\mathbf{E}^3$ of different scales (see Section 7.1).

There can be two approaches to Euclidean and affine problems in the Four-dimensional Processing:

One is to convert homogeneous coordinates, (w, X, Y, Z), of a point to $(1, x, y, z)$ such that each point has a unit scale [1]. This conversion involves division operations. The other is to convert homogeneous coordinates to (w', X', Y', Z') such that each point has a common scale value w'.

Since the first approach is straightforward, this chapter deals with the second one.

19.1 Basic Approach

As a simple example, let us consider the Euclidean distance between two points, $V_0 = \overline{(w_0, X_0, Y_0, Z_0)}$, $V_1 = \overline{(w_1, X_1, Y_1, Z_1)}$ (Fig. 19.1).

At this point, it is impossible to compute the distance because the scales, w_0, w_1, of the two points are different, where we assume w_0, w_1 are positive. Thus we adjust the scales such that the two points take on the same value, by multiplying V_0 and V_1 by k_0 and k_1 respectively:

$$\begin{aligned} k_0 V_0 &= \overline{(k_0 w_0, k_0 X_0, k_0 Y_0, k_0 Z_0)} \equiv V_0^* \equiv \overline{(M_{01}, X_0^*, Y_0^*, Z_0^*)} \equiv \overline{(M_{01}, v_0^*)}, \\ k_1 V_1 &= \overline{(k_1 w_1, k_1 X_1, k_1 Y_1, k_1 Z_1)} \equiv V_1^* \equiv \overline{(M_{01}, X_1^*, Y_1^*, Z_1^*)} \equiv \overline{(M_{01}, v_1^*)}, \end{aligned}$$

[1] In this chapter we call w "scale" instead of "weight."

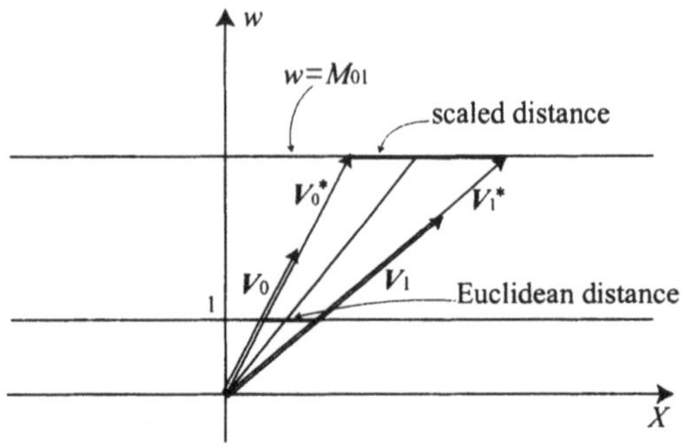

Figure 19.1: Scale adjustment of two vectors.

$$\begin{aligned} v_0^* &= (X_0^*, Y_0^*, Z_0^*), \\ v_1^* &= (X_1^*, Y_1^*, Z_1^*), \end{aligned} \tag{19.1}$$

$$k_0 w_0 = k_1 w_1 = M_{01} > 0, \tag{19.2}$$

where an asterisk mark * is attached on each scaled point or coordinate.

After the scale adjustments in eq.(19.2), the scales of the two points are equal and the distance computation becomes possible. Then we look upon points, v_0^* and v_1^*, as having ordinary coordinates (X_0^*, Y_0^*, Z_0^*) and (X_1^*, Y_1^*, Z_1^*) respectively and compute the distance as follows:

$$\begin{aligned} &\sqrt{(X_1^* - X_0^*)^2 + (Y_1^* - Y_0^*)^2 + (Z_1^* - Z_0^*)^2} \\ &= M_{01}\sqrt{(x_1 - x_0)^2 + (y_1 - y_0)^2 + (z_1 - z_0)^2} \\ &= M_{01} \times \text{Euclidean distance}. \end{aligned} \tag{19.3}$$

A simple way of choosing a scale value M_{01} is to take the product of all the scales of relevant points. In case of integer arithmetic however, taking the least common multiple of the scales of the relevant points would be a better choice.

Here, let us generally consider computing and dealing with Euclidean quantities in the Four-dimensional Processing. Euclidean quantities are computed by using homogeneous coordinates of points and/or homogeneous coefficients of planes, which are basic geometric elements. A difference of the Four-dimensional Processing from Euclidean one is that not only a plane but also a point has its scale in the Four-dimensional Processing. Thus a Euclidean quantity computed from scaled geometric elements has its scale in the Four-dimensional Processing. Therefore we must adjust the scales of the quantities in adding or subtracting them.

Now, let us consider the angle relation between planar line segments V_0V_1 and V_0V_2. We adjust the scales of the three points to M_{012} such that:

$$\overline{(w_i^*, X_i^*, Y_i^*)} = \overline{(k_i w_i, k_i X_i, k_i Y_i)} \equiv \overline{(M_{012}, v_i^*)}, \tag{19.4}$$

$$k_i w_i = M_{012} > 0, \tag{19.5}$$

$$i = 0, 1, 2.$$

Then the original line segment vectors $\overrightarrow{v_0v_1}$ and $\overrightarrow{v_0v_2}$ in Euclidean plane is scaled to $\overrightarrow{v_0^*v_1^*}$ and $\overrightarrow{v_0^*v_2^*}$ respectively:

$$\begin{aligned}
\overrightarrow{v_0v_1} &= [x_1 - x_0 \; y_1 - y_0] \\
\Rightarrow \overrightarrow{v_0^*v_1^*} &= [k_1X_1 - k_0X_0 \; k_1Y_1 - k_0Y_0] \\
&= M_{012} \cdot \overrightarrow{v_0v_1}, \\
\overrightarrow{v_0v_2} &= [x_2 - x_0 \; y_2 - y_0] \\
\Rightarrow \overrightarrow{v_0^*v_2^*} &= [k_2X_2 - k_0X_0 \; k_2Y_2 - k_0Y_0] \\
&= M_{012} \cdot \overrightarrow{v_0v_2}.
\end{aligned}$$

The angle between $\overrightarrow{v_0^*v_1^*}$ and $\overrightarrow{v_0^*v_2^*}$ on Euclidean plane $w = M_{012}$ is the same as that between vectors $\overrightarrow{v_0v_1}$ and $\overrightarrow{v_0v_2}$ on Euclidean plane $w = 1$. That is, we can deal with angles after the scaling in just the same way as in the ordinary Euclidean plane. This is also true in space geometry case because:

$$\frac{(\overrightarrow{v_0^*v_1^*} \cdot \overrightarrow{v_0^*v_2^*})}{|\overrightarrow{v_0^*v_1^*}||\overrightarrow{v_0^*v_2^*}|} = \frac{(M_{012})^2(\overrightarrow{v_0v_1} \cdot \overrightarrow{v_0v_2})}{M_{012}|\overrightarrow{v_0v_1}|M_{012}|\overrightarrow{v_0v_2}|} = \frac{(\overrightarrow{v_0v_1} \cdot \overrightarrow{v_0v_2})}{|\overrightarrow{v_0v_1}||\overrightarrow{v_0v_2}|} = \cos\theta.$$

The fact that the angle between two line segments is maintained after the scaling means also that perpendicularity and parallelism are maintained.

By this technique we can realize a three-dimensional Euclidean space in $\mathbf{R}^4$, where a line segment is scaled by a factor of its scale and angle relations are maintained. In the scaled Euclidean space we can play without performing a division operation.

In this method the space $\mathbf{R}^4$ is considered a set of three-dimensional Euclidean spaces having different scales (see Fig. 7.1).

19.2 Scaled Euclidean Metric Quantities

We assume all the scales w_i for relevant points V_i are positive.

19.2.1 Plane Geometry Case

Distance between Two Points

Given two points $V_0 = \overline{(w_0, X_0, Y_0)}$ and $V_1 = \overline{(w_1, X_1, Y_1)}$, the scaled distance $Dist^*_{01}$ between the two points is given by:

$$\begin{aligned}
Dist^*_{01} &= \sqrt{(X_1^* - X_0^*)^2 + (Y_1^* - Y_0^*)^2} \\
&= M_{01} \times \text{Euclidean distance},
\end{aligned} \tag{19.6}$$

where

$$\begin{aligned}
(w_i^*, X_i^*, Y_i^*) &= (k_iw_i, k_iX_i, k_iY_i), \quad i = 0, 1, \\
M_{01} &= k_0w_0 = k_1w_1 > 0.
\end{aligned}$$

Area of Triangle

Given three points $V_0=\overline{(w_0,X_0,Y_0)}$, $V_1=\overline{(w_1,X_1,Y_1)}$ and $V_2=\overline{(w_2,X_2,Y_2)}$, we define the scaled area, $Area^*_{012}$, of the triangle $V_0V_1V_2$ as follows:

$$\begin{aligned} Area^*_{012} &= \frac{1}{2}\begin{vmatrix} w_0 & X_0 & Y_0 \\ w_1 & X_1 & Y_1 \\ w_2 & X_2 & Y_2 \end{vmatrix} = w_0w_1w_2 \cdot \left(\frac{1}{2}\begin{vmatrix} 1 & x_0 & y_0 \\ 1 & x_1 & y_1 \\ 1 & x_2 & y_2 \end{vmatrix}\right) \\ &= M_{012} \times \text{Euclidean triangle area}, \end{aligned} \tag{19.7}$$

where $M_{012}=w_0w_1w_2$.

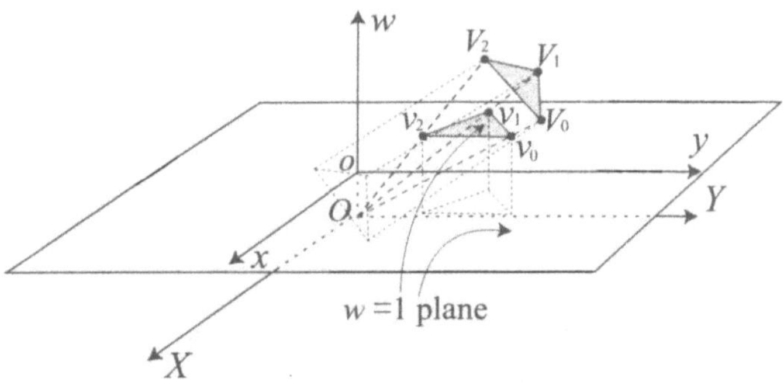

Figure 19.2: Scaled triangle.

Note that the scaled area of the triangle is defined as the volume of a triangular prism sweeped by the scaled triangle in parallel until its plane includes the origin $O(0,0,0)$ (Fig. 19.2).

If V_2 is the origin $o\overline{(1,0,0)}$, then:

$$\begin{aligned} Area^*_{012} &= \frac{1}{2}\begin{vmatrix} X_0 & Y_0 \\ X_1 & Y_1 \end{vmatrix} = w_0w_1 \cdot \left(\frac{1}{2}\begin{vmatrix} x_0 & y_0 \\ x_1 & y_1 \end{vmatrix}\right) \\ &= M_{01} \times \text{Euclidean triangle area}, \end{aligned} \tag{19.8}$$

where $M_{01} = w_0w_1$. In passing, note the following fact: if points V_0 and V_1 are identical, i.e., $V_0 = kV_1$, $k \neq 0$, then the three determinants or Plücker coordinates of planar line (see Table C.1):

$$\overline{\left(\begin{vmatrix} X_0 & Y_0 \\ X_1 & Y_1 \end{vmatrix}, -\begin{vmatrix} w_0 & Y_0 \\ w_1 & Y_1 \end{vmatrix}, \begin{vmatrix} w_0 & X_0 \\ w_1 & X_1 \end{vmatrix}\right)}$$

are all zeros. Conversely, if the Plücker coordinates are all zeros, then the two points V_0 and V_1 are identical.

19.2.2 Space Geometry Case

Distance between Two Points

Given two points $V_0 = \overline{(w_0, X_0, Y_0, Z_0)}$ and $V_1 = \overline{(w_1, X_1, Y_1, Z_1)}$, the scaled distance $Dist^*_{01}$ between the two points is given by:

$$\begin{aligned} Dist^*_{01} &= \sqrt{(X_1^* - X_0^*)^2 + (Y_1^* - Y_0^*)^2 + (Z_1^* - Z_0^*)^2} \\ &= M_{01} \times \text{Euclidean distance}, \end{aligned} \tag{19.9}$$

where

$$\begin{aligned} (w_i^*, X_i^*, Y_i^*, Z_i^*) &= (k_i w_i, k_i X_i, k_i Y_i, k_i Z_i), \quad i = 0, 1, \\ M_{01} &= k_0 w_0 = k_1 w_1 > 0. \end{aligned}$$

Area of Triangle

Given three points $V_0 = \overline{(w_0, X_0, Y_0, Z_0)}$, $V_1 = \overline{(w_1, X_1, Y_1, Z_1)}$ and $V_2 = \overline{(w_2, X_2, Y_2, Z_2)}$, we define the scaled area, $Area^*_{012}$, of the triangle $V_0V_1V_2$ as follows:

$$Area^*_{012} = \frac{1}{2}\sqrt{\begin{vmatrix} w_0 & Z_0 & Y_0 \\ w_1 & Z_1 & Y_1 \\ w_2 & Z_2 & Y_2 \end{vmatrix}^2 + \begin{vmatrix} w_0 & X_0 & Z_0 \\ w_1 & X_1 & Z_1 \\ w_2 & X_2 & Z_2 \end{vmatrix}^2 + \begin{vmatrix} w_0 & Y_0 & X_0 \\ w_1 & Y_1 & X_1 \\ w_2 & Y_2 & X_2 \end{vmatrix}^2} \tag{19.10}$$

$$\begin{aligned} &= w_0 w_1 w_2 \cdot \left(\frac{1}{2}\sqrt{\begin{vmatrix} 1 & z_0 & y_0 \\ 1 & z_1 & y_1 \\ 1 & z_2 & y_2 \end{vmatrix}^2 + \begin{vmatrix} 1 & x_0 & z_0 \\ 1 & x_1 & z_1 \\ 1 & x_2 & z_2 \end{vmatrix}^2 + \begin{vmatrix} 1 & y_0 & x_0 \\ 1 & y_1 & x_1 \\ 1 & y_2 & x_2 \end{vmatrix}^2} \right) \\ &= M_{012} \times \text{Euclidean triangle area}, \end{aligned} \tag{19.11}$$

where $M_{012} = w_0 w_1 w_2$.

Volume of Tetrahedron

Given V_a, V_0, V_1 and V_2, we define the scaled volume, Vol^*_{a012}, of the tetrahedron $V_aV_0V_1V_2$ as follows [2]:

$$Vol^*_{a012} = \frac{1}{6}\begin{vmatrix} w_a & X_a & Y_a & Z_a \\ w_0 & X_0 & Y_0 & Z_0 \\ w_1 & X_1 & Y_1 & Z_1 \\ w_2 & X_2 & Y_2 & Z_2 \end{vmatrix} = \frac{1}{6}S_{a012} \tag{19.12}$$

$$= w_a w_0 w_1 w_2 \cdot \left(\frac{1}{6}\begin{vmatrix} 1 & x_a & y_a & z_a \\ 1 & x_0 & y_0 & z_0 \\ 1 & x_1 & y_1 & z_1 \\ 1 & x_2 & y_2 & z_2 \end{vmatrix} \right) \tag{19.13}$$

$$= M_{a012} \times \text{Euclidean tetrahedron volume}, \tag{19.14}$$

[2] The author uses a point set V_a, V_0, V_1, V_2 in place of V_0, V_1, V_2, V_3 in consideration of S_{a012} in the determinant method (see Chapter 13).

where $M_{a012}=w_a w_0 w_1 w_2$.

$Vol\ ^*_{a012}$ is positive if V_0, V_1, V_2 are viewed clockwise from V_a and negative if viewed counter-clockwise.

If V_a is the origin $V_G=\overline{(1,0,0,0)}$, then

$$Vol\ ^*_{G012} = \frac{1}{6}\begin{vmatrix} X_0 & Y_0 & Z_0 \\ X_1 & Y_1 & Z_1 \\ X_2 & Y_2 & Z_2 \end{vmatrix} = \frac{1}{6}A_{012} \tag{19.15}$$

$$= w_0 w_1 w_2 \cdot \left(\frac{1}{6}\begin{vmatrix} x_0 & y_0 & z_0 \\ x_1 & y_1 & z_1 \\ x_2 & y_2 & z_2 \end{vmatrix}\right) \tag{19.16}$$

$$= M_{012} \times \text{Euclidean tetrahedron volume,} \tag{19.17}$$

where $M_{012}=w_0 w_1 w_2$.

$Vol\ ^*_{G012}$ is positive if V_0, V_1, V_2 are viewed clockwise from the origin and negative if viewed counter-clockwise.

In passing, note the following fact: from eq.(19.10), if points V_0, V_1 and V_2 are collinear, $Area\ ^*_{012}$ vanishes and

$$\begin{vmatrix} w_0 & Z_0 & Y_0 \\ w_1 & Z_1 & Y_1 \\ w_2 & Z_2 & Y_2 \end{vmatrix} = \begin{vmatrix} w_0 & X_0 & Z_0 \\ w_1 & X_1 & Z_1 \\ w_2 & X_2 & Z_2 \end{vmatrix} = \begin{vmatrix} w_0 & Y_0 & X_0 \\ w_1 & Y_1 & X_1 \\ w_2 & Y_2 & X_2 \end{vmatrix} = 0. \tag{19.18}$$

Therefore, if points V_0, V_1 and V_2 are collinear, then the four determinants or Plücker coordinates of plane (see eq.(19.16)):

$$\overline{\left(\begin{vmatrix} X_0 & Y_0 & Z_0 \\ X_1 & Y_1 & Z_1 \\ X_2 & Y_2 & Z_2 \end{vmatrix}, \begin{vmatrix} w_0 & Z_0 & Y_0 \\ w_1 & Z_1 & Y_1 \\ w_2 & Z_2 & Y_2 \end{vmatrix}, \begin{vmatrix} w_0 & X_0 & Z_0 \\ w_1 & X_1 & Z_1 \\ w_2 & X_2 & Z_2 \end{vmatrix}, \begin{vmatrix} w_0 & Y_0 & X_0 \\ w_1 & Y_1 & X_1 \\ w_2 & Y_2 & X_2 \end{vmatrix}\right)}$$

are all zeros. Conversely, if the Plücker coordinates are all zeros, then the three points V_0, V_1 and V_2 are collinear (see Section 14.3).

Normal Distance from a Point to a Planar Line

Denoting by h^* the scaled normal distance from a point $V_0=\overline{(w_0, X_0, Y_0)}$ to a line $aw+bX+cY=0$, then:

$$\begin{aligned} h^* &= aw_0 + bX_0 + cY_0 \\ &= w_0\sqrt{b^2+c^2} \times \text{Euclidean normal distance.} \end{aligned} \tag{19.19}$$

Normal Distance from a Point to a Plane

Denoting by h^* the scaled normal distance from a point $V_0=\overline{(w_0, X_0, Y_0, Z_0)}$ to a plane $aw+bX+cY+dZ=0$, then:

$$\begin{aligned} h^* &= aw_0 + bX_0 + cY_0 + dZ_0 \\ &= w_0\sqrt{b^2+c^2+d^2} \times \text{Euclidean normal distance.} \end{aligned} \tag{19.20}$$

Normal Distance from Origin to a Space Line

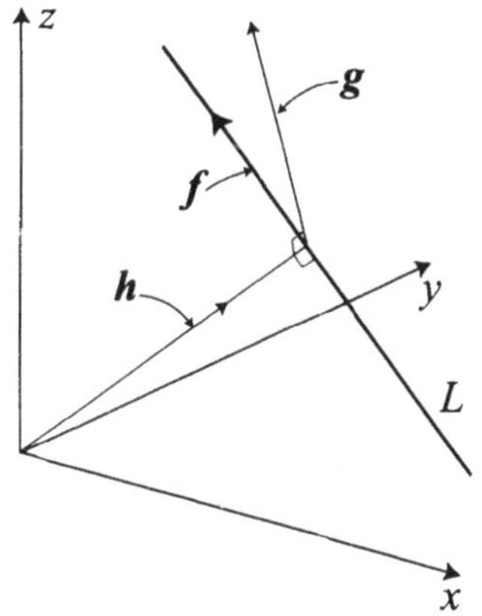

Figure 19.3: Distance from origin to space line L.

Space lines are discussed in detail in Section 9.1.1. Let the Plücker coordinates of a line L be $\overline{(P, Q, R, S, T, U)}$. The direction vector of the space line is given from Section 9.1.2 by $\boldsymbol{f} = [P\ Q\ R]$ (see Fig. 19.3). We also know from Section 9.1.2 that the origin and that line form a plane which has the normal vector $\boldsymbol{g} = [S\ T\ U]$.

To obtain the direction vector $\boldsymbol{h}$ of the normal line from the origin to the given space line, we take the vector product of $\boldsymbol{f}$ and $\boldsymbol{g}$:

$$\begin{aligned}\boldsymbol{h} &= \boldsymbol{f} \times \boldsymbol{g} \\ &= [UQ - TR\ \ SR - UP\ \ TP - SQ]. \end{aligned} \tag{19.21}$$

Using the identity of eq.(9.29), we find the vector $\boldsymbol{h}$ has the magnitude:

$$|\boldsymbol{h}| = \sqrt{(P^2 + Q^2 + R^2)(S^2 + T^2 + U^2)}. \tag{19.22}$$

Denoting by d_n the normal distance from the origin to the space line, the normal line meets the space line at a point with the homogeneous coordinates:

$$\overline{(1,\ d_n \frac{UQ - TR}{|\boldsymbol{h}|},\ d_n \frac{SR - UP}{|\boldsymbol{h}|},\ d_n \frac{TP - SQ}{|\boldsymbol{h}|})}.$$

So the following equation holds:

$$[1\ \ d_n \frac{UQ - TR}{|\boldsymbol{h}|}\ \ d_n \frac{SR - UP}{|\boldsymbol{h}|}\ \ d_n \frac{TP - SQ}{|\boldsymbol{h}|}]\boldsymbol{L} = [0\ \ 0\ \ 0\ \ 0]. \tag{19.23}$$

d_n can thus be determined as:

$$d_n = \sqrt{\frac{S^2 + T^2 + U^2}{P^2 + Q^2 + R^2}}. \tag{19.24}$$

Or, if we denote the scaled distance by d_n^*, then

$$\begin{aligned} d_n^* &= \sqrt{S^2+T^2+U^2} \\ &= \sqrt{P^2+Q^2+R^2} \times \text{Euclidean distance.} \end{aligned} \tag{19.25}$$

Length of Common Perpendicular

The length of the common perpendicular between two skew lines can be shown to be proportional to trace ($\boldsymbol{N}$) of eq.(12.12) as follows (see Fig. 19.4) [3].

Let the direction vectors of the two lines be $[P_1\ Q_1\ R_1]$ and $[P_2\ Q_2\ R_2]$ (see Section 9.1.2). Let $[P_0\ Q_0\ R_0]$ be the vector product of these two, that is:

$$[P_1\ \ Q_1\ \ R_1] \times [P_2\ \ Q_2\ \ R_2] = [P_0\ \ Q_0\ \ R_0].$$

Vector $[P_0\ Q_0\ R_0]$ is then perpendicular to the two lines.

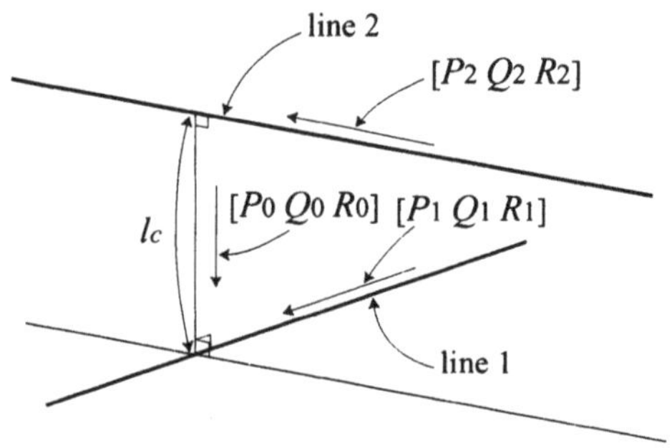

Figure 19.4: Length of common perpendicular between skew lines.

Now, suppose that one of the lines ("line 2") is translated in the direction of $[P_0\ Q_0\ R_0]$ until it intersects with the other line ("line 1"); the length of the common perpendicular of the two lines is the perpendicular distance between the two parallel lines, i.e., those before and after translation.

Any plane with the coefficients $b=P_0$, $c=Q_0$ and $d=R_0$ is parallel to both "line 1" and "line 2". Attaching the condition that one plane contains "line 1" and another contains "line 2", we can determine the first coefficient "a" for each case as follows (see eq.(9.32)):

$$\boldsymbol{K}_1 \begin{bmatrix} a_1 \\ P_0 \\ Q_0 \\ R_0 \end{bmatrix} = \begin{bmatrix} 0 \\ 0 \\ 0 \\ 0 \end{bmatrix}, \quad \boldsymbol{K}_2 \begin{bmatrix} a_2 \\ P_0 \\ Q_0 \\ R_0 \end{bmatrix} = \begin{bmatrix} 0 \\ 0 \\ 0 \\ 0 \end{bmatrix}. \tag{19.26}$$

Each matrix equation consists of four equations, which yield the same result in each case:

$$a_1 = -P_2S_1 - Q_2T_1 - R_2U_1, \tag{19.27}$$
$$a_2 = P_1S_2 + Q_1T_2 + R_1U_2. \tag{19.28}$$

The normal distances, A_1 and A_2, from the origin to the two planes are then given as:

$$A_1 = \frac{a_1}{\sqrt{{P_0}^2 + {Q_0}^2 + {R_0}^2}}, \quad A_2 = \frac{a_2}{\sqrt{{P_0}^2 + {Q_0}^2 + {R_0}^2}}. \tag{19.29}$$

So the distance between the two planes, that is, the length of the common perpendicular l_c between the two lines is given by:

$$l_c = A_2 - A_1 = \frac{a_2 - a_1}{\sqrt{{P_0}^2 + {Q_0}^2 + {R_0}^2}} = \frac{trace(\boldsymbol{N})}{2\sqrt{{P_0}^2 + {Q_0}^2 + {R_0}^2}}. \tag{19.30}$$

Or if we denote the scaled distance by l_c^*, then

$$\begin{aligned} l_c^* &= trace(\boldsymbol{N}) \\ &= 2\sqrt{{P_0}^2 + {Q_0}^2 + {R_0}^2} \times \text{Euclidean distance.} \end{aligned} \tag{19.31}$$

The two lines intersect when $trace(\boldsymbol{N})$ is zero, otherwise l_c expresses the length of the common perpendicular.

We already know the Plücker coordinates P_0, Q_0 and R_0 for the common perpendicular; the remaining coordinates, S_0, T_0 and U_0, can be determined from the following conditions:

1. S_0, T_0 and U_0 satisfy eq.(9.29), or

$$P_0 S_0 + Q_0 T_0 + R_0 U_0 = 0.$$

2. The common perpendicular intersects with "line 1", so

$$trace(\boldsymbol{K}_1 \boldsymbol{L}_0) = 0.$$

3. The common perpendicular intersects with "line 2", so

$$trace(\boldsymbol{K}_2 \boldsymbol{L}_0) = 0.$$

These three equations can be solved to yield S_0, T_0 and U_0.

Outward Normal Vector of Face

Any face of a polyhedron has two orientations: one in the direction away from the polyhedron's body (front), and the other toward the polyhedron (back). In computer aided geometric design, one often makes use of the outward (or inward) normal vector of a face in addition to its plane equation. This occurs for instance when removing hidden lines and faces or in the set operations of solid modeling. Below we present a rational method for determining outward normal vectors.

We assume that a face is expressed by the homogeneous coordinates of its vertices in sequence as $V_0, V_1, V_2, \ldots, V_{n-1}, V_n$, in the clockwise direction when viewed from front, and that all $w_i(>0)$ coordinates are scaled to a certain value $M_{0\ldots n}$ by multiplying the coordinates by k_i (see Fig. 19.5):

$$\begin{aligned}(w_i^*, X_i^*, Y_i^*, Z_i^*) &= (k_i w_i, k_i X_i, k_i Y_i, k_i Z_i), \quad i = 0, \ldots, n,\\ k_0 w_0 = \ldots &= k_n w_n = M_{0\ldots n},\\ v_i^* &= (X_i^*, Y_i^*, Z_i^*).\end{aligned} \tag{19.32}$$

We deal with scaled vertices v_i^* in eq.(19.32) and use $A_{k,0ij}^*$, $B_{k,0ij}^*$, $C_{k,0ij}^*$ and $D_{k,0ij}^*$ to denote those A_{0ij}^*, B_{0ij}^*, C_{0ij}^* and D_{0ij}^* (with respect to points v_0^*, v_i^* and v_j^* of a face) specifically pertaining to a face f_k of a polyhedron.

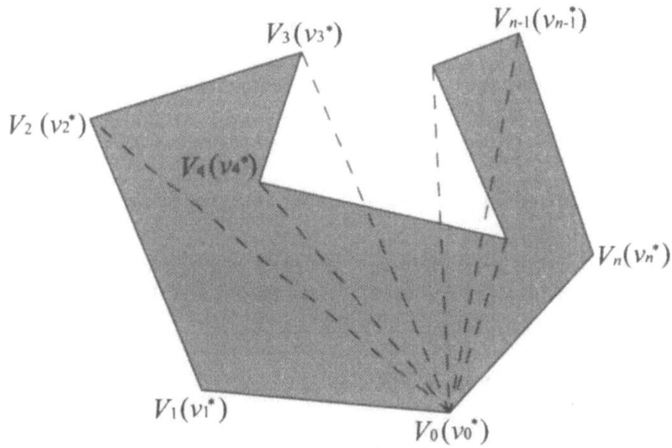

Figure 19.5: Calculating an outward normal vector of a face.

We now draw a line radiating from v_0^* to each of the vertices; lines to v_1^* and v_n^* are assumed to be present from the outset. These lines form $(n-1)$ triangles. From the vectors $\overrightarrow{v_0^* v_1^*}$ and $\overrightarrow{v_1^* v_2^*}$, we obtain the following vector product:

$$\overrightarrow{v_1^* v_2^*} \times \overrightarrow{v_0^* v_1^*}.$$

This is a face's normal vector, which has a magnitude twice the area of the triangle formed by the two specified vectors, and an outward direction in the present case. We move to the next radial line and take the vector product of the edge vector $\overrightarrow{v_2^* v_3^*}$ and $\overrightarrow{v_0^* v_2^*}$:

$$\overrightarrow{v_2^* v_3^*} \times \overrightarrow{v_0^* v_2^*}.$$

This also is a normal vector with a magnitude twice the area of the triangle formed by the vectors $\overrightarrow{v_2^* v_3^*}$ and $\overrightarrow{v_0^* v_2^*}$, and has an outward direction. This process of obtaining vector products is repeated for the entire polygonal face. Note that for the face shown in Fig. 19.5, the vector product of $\overrightarrow{v_3^* v_4^*}$ and $\overrightarrow{v_0^* v_3^*}$ produces a normal vector in the inward direction. The last normal vector is obtained as the vector product of the edge vector $\overrightarrow{v_{n-1}^* v_n^*}$ and $\overrightarrow{v_0^* v_{n-1}^*}$. When all of the normal vectors thus obtained are added, the result is an outward normal vector which has a magnitude twice the area of the scaled face. Denoting the outward normal vector of the face f_k by $\boldsymbol{n}_k$, we obtain:

$$\boldsymbol{n}_k = [n_{kx} \quad n_{ky} \quad n_{kz}], \tag{19.33}$$

$$\left.\begin{aligned} n_{kx} &= \sum_{i=0}^{n} (Y_i^* - Y_j^*)(Z_i^* + Z_j^*), \\ n_{ky} &= \sum_{i=0}^{n} (Z_i^* - Z_j^*)(X_i^* + X_j^*), \\ n_{kz} &= \sum_{i=0}^{n} (X_i^* - X_j^*)(Y_i^* + Y_j^*), \end{aligned}\right\} \tag{19.34}$$

where $j = i+1$ when $i \neq n$, and $j = 0$ when $i = n$.

So the scaled area $Area_k^*$ of f_k is given by:

$$\begin{aligned} Area_k^* &= \frac{1}{2}\sqrt{n_{kx}{}^2 + n_{ky}{}^2 + n_{kz}{}^2} \\ &= M_{0\ldots n}{}^2 \times \text{Euclidean area}. \end{aligned} \tag{19.35}$$

The outward unit normal vector is given by:

$$\frac{1}{2Area_k^*}[n_{kx} \quad n_{ky} \quad n_{kz}].$$

In the 4×4 determinant method, the outward normal vector $\boldsymbol{n}_k = [n_{kx}\ n_{ky}\ n_{kz}]$ of f_k is obtained, after the scaling mentioned above:

$$\begin{aligned} \boldsymbol{n}_k &= [n_{kx} \quad n_{ky} \quad n_{kz}] \\ &= [\sum_i B_{k,0ij}^* \quad \sum_i C_{k,0ij}^* \quad \sum_i D_{k,0ij}^*] \end{aligned} \tag{19.36}$$

The scaled area of f_k is:

$$\begin{aligned} Area_k^* &= \frac{1}{2}\sqrt{n_{kx}{}^2 + n_{ky}{}^2 + n_{kz}{}^2} \\ &= \frac{1}{2}\sqrt{(\sum_i B_{k,0ij}^*)^2 + (\sum_i C_{k,0ij}^*)^2 + (\sum_i D_{k,0ij}^*)^2} \\ &= M_{0\ldots n}{}^2 \times \text{Euclidean area}. \end{aligned} \tag{19.37}$$

Now, vector $[b\ c\ d]$, composed of three coefficients of plane equation $aw + bX + cY + dZ = 0$, expresses one of two normal vectors of that plane, the other being $[-b\ \ -c\ \ -d]$. Thus, if the outward normal vector (or the outward unit normal vector) of a face is known, we can determine the plane coefficients from the coordinates (w_f, X_f, Y_f, Z_f) of a point lying on that face. From n_{kx}, n_{ky} and n_{kz}, the coefficients of the plane are:

$$a = -(n_{kx}X_f + n_{ky}Y_f + n_{kz}Z_f), \quad b = w_f n_{kx}, \quad c = w_f n_{ky}, \quad d = w_f n_{kz}. \tag{19.38}$$

It is useful to have the outward normal vector in association with the plane equation.

Surface Area and Volume of Polyhedron

We assume that each face is expressed by the homogeneous coordinates of its vertices sequentially in the clockwise direction when viewed from front, and that all the scales w_i of the vertices are adjusted to a certain value $M_{0\ldots n}$ by multiplying the coordinates by k_i:

$$\begin{aligned}(w_i^*, X_i^*, Y_i^*, Z_i^*) &= (k_i w_i, k_i X_i, k_i Y_i, k_i Z_i), \quad i = 0, \ldots, n, \\ k_0 w_0 &= \ldots = k_n w_n = M_{0\ldots n}.\end{aligned} \tag{19.39}$$

The scaled surface area, $Area^*$, of a polyhedron is simply the sum of the scaled areas of each face, which is scaled equally, i.e. ${M_{0\ldots n}}^2$:

$$\begin{aligned} Area^* &= \sum_k Area_k^* \\ &= {M_{0\ldots n}}^2 \times \text{Euclidean polyhedron surface area.} \end{aligned} \tag{19.40}$$

We now determine the scaled volume V^* of a polyhedron using a method similar to the one that we used when we calculated the area of a face.

Assume that, for each face of the polyhedron, lines radiate from a reference vertex to other vertices as in Fig. 19.5, and also that lines radiate from the origin of the coordinate system to all the vertices (see Fig. 19.6).

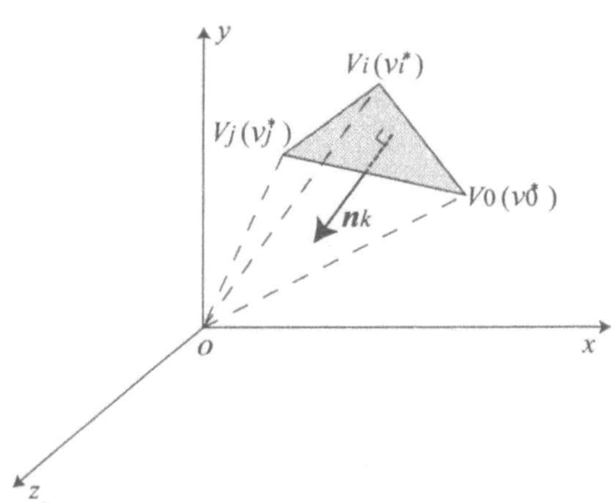

Figure 19.6: Tetrahedron $ov_0^*v_i^*v_j^*$ formed when dividing a face.

The signed, scaled volume Vol^*_{ki} of a tetrahedron formed by origin $o^*(0,0,0)$, the reference point $v^*_0(X^*_0, Y^*_0, Z^*_0)$ and two successive vertices, $v^*_i(X^*_i, Y^*_i, Z^*_i)$ and $v^*_j(X^*_j, Y^*_j, Z^*_j)$ of f_k, is obtained as follows (see eq.(19.15)):

$$Vol^*_{ki} = \frac{1}{6}\begin{vmatrix} X^*_0 & Y^*_0 & Z^*_0 \\ X^*_i & Y^*_i & Z^*_i \\ X^*_j & Y^*_j & X^*_j \end{vmatrix}. \tag{19.41}$$

This equation gives a positive result when the points v^*_0, v^*_i and v^*_j lie clockwise when viewed from the origin, and a negative result when they lie counterclockwise.

Denoting by Vol^*_k the signed, scaled volume of the pyramid formed by the origin and f_k, we then have:

$$Vol^*_k = \sum_i Vol^*_{ki}, \tag{19.42}$$

where each Vol^*_{ki} has an equal scale of ${M_{0\ldots n}}^3$.

In the 4×4 determinant method, the signed scaled volume Vol^*_{ki} of a tetrahedron formed by the origin and triangle $v^*_0 v^*_i v^*_j$ is given by (see eq.(19.15)):

$$Vol^*_{ki} = \frac{1}{6} A^*_{k,0ij}. \tag{19.43}$$

The scaled volume Vol^*_k of the pyramid formed by the origin and f_k is then given by:

$$Vol^*_k = \sum_i Vol^*_{ki} = \frac{1}{6} \sum_i A^*_{k,0ij}. \tag{19.44}$$

Therefore, the scaled volume Vol^* of the polyhedron is given by [3]:

$$\begin{aligned} Vol^* &= -\sum_k Vol^*_k \\ &= -\sum_k \sum_i Vol^*_{ki} \\ &= {M_{0\ldots n}}^3 \times \text{Euclidean polyhedron volume.} \end{aligned} \tag{19.45}$$

Center of Gravity of Face and Polyhedron

In Fig. 19.6, the scaled position vector $\boldsymbol{g}^*_{ki}$ for the center of gravity of the triangle formed by three points, v^*_0, v^*_i and v^*_j of f_k is given by:

$$\begin{aligned} \boldsymbol{g}^*_{ki} &= [\frac{X^*_0 + X^*_i + X^*_j}{3} \quad \frac{Y^*_0 + Y^*_i + Y^*_j}{3} \quad \frac{Z^*_0 + Z^*_i + Z^*_j}{3}] \\ &= M_{0\ldots n} \times [\frac{x_0 + x_i + x_j}{3} \quad \frac{y_0 + y_i + y_j}{3} \quad \frac{z_0 + z_i + z_j}{3}] \\ &= M_{0\ldots n} \times \text{Euclidean center of gravity position vector.} \end{aligned} \tag{19.46}$$

[3] "−" sign is appended such that the volume of a polyhedron becomes positive.

The scaled center of gravity position vector $\boldsymbol{g}_k^*$ of the face f_k is written, using the signed, scaled volume Vol_{ki}^* of a tetrahedron formed by the origin and triangle $v_0^* v_i^* v_j^*$, as follows:

$$\begin{aligned} \boldsymbol{g}_k^* &= \frac{1}{Vol_k^*} \sum_i Vol_{ki}^* \boldsymbol{g}_{ki}^* \\ &= M_{0\ldots n} \times \text{Euclidean center of gravity position vector.} \end{aligned} \tag{19.47}$$

Let us now determine the scaled center of gravity position vector $\boldsymbol{G}^*$ of a polyhedron in a similar manner.

In Fig. 19.6, the position vector $\boldsymbol{G}_{ki}^*$ for the center of gravity of the tetrahedron formed by three points v_0^*, v_i^* and v_j^* of f_k and the origin is given by:

$$\boldsymbol{G}_{ki}^* = [\frac{X_0^* + X_i^* + X_j^*}{4} \quad \frac{Y_0^* + Y_i^* + Y_j^*}{4} \quad \frac{Z_0^* + Z_i^* + Z_j^*}{4}]. \tag{19.48}$$

The scaled center of gravity position vector $\boldsymbol{G}^*$ of the polyhedron is thus obtained as:

$$\begin{aligned} \boldsymbol{G}^* &= \frac{1}{Vol^*} \sum_k Vol_k^* (\frac{1}{Vol_k^*} \sum_i Vol_{ki}^* \boldsymbol{G}_{ki}^*) \\ &= \frac{1}{Vol^*} \sum_k \sum_i Vol_{ki}^* \boldsymbol{G}_{ki}^* \\ &= M_{0\ldots n} \times \text{Euclidean center of gravity position vector.} \end{aligned} \tag{19.49}$$

Straightforward applications of the method presented in this chapter could cause data overflow error because the data lengths tend to increase. Perform homogeneous coordinate normalization, if appropriate, against the pair:

$$[\textit{scale} \quad \textit{scaled Euclidean quantity}]$$

as a homogeneous coordinate representation (see page 18).

19.2.3 Parameter Changes

We consider a tolerance value of the parameter change for terminating the algorithm of the type-D homogeneous geometric Newton-Raphson method (see Section 15.7). We consider two types of homogeneous parameters, i.e., "type-1" and "type-2" (see Section 8.6). t is used for denoting the ordinary parameter corresponding to the homogeneous parameters.

1. **Homogeneous parameters "type-1"** $(t = \frac{s}{h})$:

   Let point sequences in the geometric Newton-Raphson method be, ..., $V_i(\overline{h_i, s_i}), V_{i+1}(\overline{h_{i+1}, s_{i+1}}), \ldots,$. We adjust the scales such that:

$$\begin{aligned} V_i k_i = V_i^*, \quad V_{i+1} k_{i+1} = V_{i+1}^*, \\ \text{where} \quad h_i k_i = h_{i+1} k_{i+1} \equiv M_{i,i+1} > 0. \end{aligned} \tag{19.50}$$

In this case, scaled tolerance, $tol^*_{i,i+1}$ is:

$$\begin{aligned} tol^*_{i,i+1} &= s^*_{i+1} - s^*_i \\ &= s_{i+1}k_{i+1} - s_i k_i \\ &= M_{i,i+1}(t_{i+1} - t_i) \\ &= M_{i,i+1} \times \text{Euclidean tolerance.} \end{aligned} \tag{19.51}$$

2. **Homogeneous parameters "type-2"** $(t = \frac{\sigma}{\eta+\sigma})$:

Let point sequences in the geometric Newton-Raphson method be, ..., $\overline{V_i(\eta_i, \sigma_i)}, \overline{V_{i+1}(\eta_{i+1}, \sigma_{i+1})}, \ldots,$. We adjust the scales such that:

$$\begin{aligned} V_i k_i = V_i^*, \quad V_{i+1}k_{i+1} = V^*_{i+1}, \\ \text{where } (\eta_i + \sigma_i)k_i = (\eta_{i+1} + \sigma_{i+1})k_{i+1} \equiv M_{i,i+1} > 0. \end{aligned} \tag{19.52}$$

In this case, scaled tolerance, $tol^*_{i,i+1}$ is:

$$\begin{aligned} tol^*_{i,i+1} &= \sigma^*_{i+1} - \sigma^*_i \\ &= \sigma_{i+1}k_{i+1} - \sigma_i k_i \\ &= M_{i,i+1}(t_{i+1} - t_i) \\ &= M_{i,i+1} \times \text{Euclidean tolerance.} \end{aligned} \tag{19.53}$$

19.3 Affine Concepts

19.3.1 Ratio

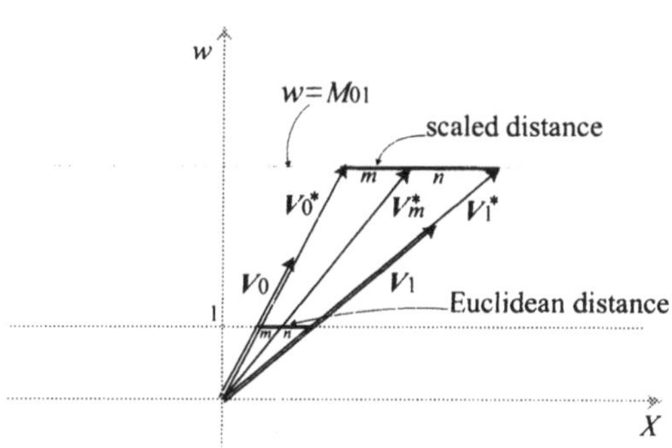

Figure 19.7: Scale adjustment of two vectors.

We consider determining a point V_m dividing two points V_0 and V_1 in the ratio of $m : n$ (Fig. 19.7). As described before, we adjust the scales of the points to a same value by multiplying V_0 and V_1 by k_0 and k_1 respectively such that:

$$\begin{aligned} k_0 V_0 &= \overline{(k_0 w_0, k_0 X_0, k_0 Y_0, k_0 Z_0)} \equiv V_0^* \equiv \overline{(M_{01}, X_0^*, Y_0^*, Z_0^*)} \equiv \overline{(M_{01}, v_0^*)}, \\ k_1 V_1 &= \overline{(k_1 w_1, k_1 X_1, k_1 Y_1, k_1 Z_1)} \equiv V_1^* \equiv \overline{(M_{01}, X_1^*, Y_1^*, Z_1^*)} \equiv \overline{(M_{01}, v_1^*)}, \end{aligned}$$

$$\begin{aligned} v_0^* &= (X_0^*, Y_0^*, Z_0^*), \\ v_1^* &= (X_1^*, Y_1^*, Z_1^*), \end{aligned} \tag{19.54}$$

$$k_0 w_0 = k_1 w_1 \equiv M_{01} > 0. \tag{19.55}$$

Then divide the scaled points v_0^* and v_1^* in the ratio of $m : n$ and determine the dividing point v_m^*:

$$\boldsymbol{v}_m^* = \frac{n\boldsymbol{v}_0^* + m\boldsymbol{v}_1^*}{m+n}. \tag{19.56}$$

Therefore the homogeneous coordinate representation of the dividing point is

$$\begin{aligned} V_m = V_m^* = \overline{(M_{01}, v_m^*)} &= \overline{(M_{01}, \frac{nX_0^* + mX_1^*}{m+n}, \frac{nY_0^* + mY_1^*}{m+n}, \frac{nZ_0^* + mZ_1^*}{m+n})} \\ &= \overline{((m+n)w_0w_1, nw_1X_0 + mw_0X_1, nw_1Y_0 + mw_0Y_1, nw_1Z_0 + mw_0Z_1)}. \end{aligned} \tag{19.57}$$

19.3.2 Parallelism

As can be estimated from the discussion so far in this chapter, we can deal with parallelism in the Four-dimensional Processing in just the same way as we do in Euclidean space, by adjusting the scales of all the relevant vertices to a common, same value. By this scale adjustment operation we are supposed to play in a three-dimensional Euclidean space having a different scale from unity.

Alternatively we can play by using the property of a projective space. It is true that the notion of parallelism is forfeit in projective geometry. This seems dreadful in the context of graphics and CAGD applications since the notion of parallelism is absolutely essential [12]. That the parallelism notion does not exist means any two distinct geometric elements have an intersection whether they are parallel or not. Parallel elements have an intersection in a hyperplane at infinity. The author considers this fact of projective geometry to be rather advantageous than dreadful because we ordinarily do not have to worry about special cases and we can easily detect the parallel cases if necessary.

We shall show some of parallel cases in the following.

Two Planar Lines

Given two distinct lines $\gamma_0 = \overline{(a_0, b_0, c_0)^T}$ and $\gamma_1 = \overline{(a_1, b_1, c_1)^T}$, the intersection point P_c is from eq.(12.2):

$$\begin{aligned} P_c &= \overline{(w_c, X_c, Y_c)} \\ &= \overline{\left(\begin{vmatrix} b_0 & b_1 \\ c_0 & c_1 \end{vmatrix}, - \begin{vmatrix} a_0 & a_1 \\ c_0 & c_1 \end{vmatrix}, \begin{vmatrix} a_0 & a_1 \\ b_0 & b_1 \end{vmatrix} \right)}. \end{aligned} \tag{19.58}$$

When

$$w_c = \begin{vmatrix} b_0 & b_1 \\ c_0 & c_1 \end{vmatrix} = b_0c_1 - c_0b_1 = 0, \tag{19.59}$$

or,

$$\frac{b_0}{c_0} = \frac{b_1}{c_1},$$

the two lines γ_0 and γ_1 are parallel.

Two Planes

Given two distinct planes $\gamma_0 = \overline{(a_0, b_0, c_0, d_0)^T}$ and $\gamma_1 = \overline{(a_1, b_1, c_1, d_1)^T}$, the intersection line $\boldsymbol{L}'$ is from eqs.(9.36) and (9.37):

$$[w\ X\ Y\ Z]\boldsymbol{L}' = [0\ 0\ 0\ 0]. \tag{19.60}$$

The condition that the line eq.(19.60) represents a line at infinity is that the plane made by an arbitrary point at infinity $(0, X, Y, Z)$ and the line is the plane at infinity ($w=0$). This condition yields:

$$u_{01} = t_{01} = 0, \quad u_{01} = s_{01} = 0, \quad t_{01} = s_{01} = 0. \tag{19.61}$$

Each of the equations above gives the same result:

$$\frac{b_0}{b_1} = \frac{c_0}{c_1} = \frac{d_0}{d_1}. \tag{19.62}$$

Line and Plane

Given a plane $\gamma = \overline{(a_0, b_0, c_0, d_0)^T}$ and a non-coplanar line of type-K representation, the intersection point $P_c = \overline{(w_c, X_c, Y_c, Z_c)}$ is given from eq.(12.16) as:

$$P_c = \overline{(w_c, X_c, Y_c, Z_c)} = \overline{\left(\boldsymbol{K}\begin{bmatrix} a_0 \\ b_0 \\ c_0 \\ d_0 \end{bmatrix}\right)^T}.$$

When

$$w_c = -b_0P - c_0Q - d_0R = 0,$$

or

$$b_0P + c_0Q + d_0R = 0, \tag{19.63}$$

the plane γ and space line K are parallel. Recall that $[P\ Q\ R]$ is a direction vector of the line K (see Section 9.1.2).

Two Space Lines

We suppose two distinct lines K_1 and L_2 are given:

$$\boldsymbol{K}_1 = \begin{bmatrix} 0 & -P_1 & -Q_1 & -R_1 \\ P_1 & 0 & -U_1 & T_1 \\ Q_1 & U_1 & 0 & -S_1 \\ R_1 & -T_1 & S_1 & 0 \end{bmatrix}, \quad \boldsymbol{L}_2 = \begin{bmatrix} 0 & S_2 & T_2 & U_2 \\ -S_2 & 0 & R_2 & -Q_2 \\ -T_2 & -R_2 & 0 & P_2 \\ -U_2 & Q_2 & -P_2 & 0 \end{bmatrix}.$$

The intersection point P_c is from eq.(12.14):

$$\begin{aligned}
P_c &= \overline{(w_c, X_c, Y_c, Z_c)} \\
&= \overline{(P_1S_2 + Q_1T_2 + R_1U_2,\ U_1T_2 - T_1U_2,\ S_1U_2 - U_1S_2,\ T_1S_2 - S_1T_2)} \\
&= \overline{(Q_1R_2 - R_1Q_2,\ P_1S_2 + U_1R_2 + T_1Q_2,\ Q_1S_2 - S_1Q_2,\ R_1S_2 - S_1R_2)} \\
&= \overline{(R_1P_2 - P_1R_2,\ P_1T_2 - T_1P_2,\ Q_1T_2 + U_1R_2 + S_1P_2,\ R_1T_2 - T_1R_2)} \\
&= \overline{(P_1Q_2 - Q_1P_2,\ P_1U_2 - U_1P_2,\ Q_1U_2 - U_1Q_2,\ R_1U_2 + T_1Q_2 + S_1P_2)}.
\end{aligned} \tag{19.64}$$

Requiring $w_c = 0$ yields:

$$[P_1\ Q_1\ R_1] = k[P_2\ Q_2\ R_2], \quad k \neq 0,$$

or

$$\frac{P_1}{P_2} = \frac{Q_1}{Q_2} = \frac{R_1}{R_2}. \tag{19.65}$$

Eq.(19.65) is evident since $[P_1\ Q_1\ R_1]$ and $[P_2\ Q_2\ R_2]$ are direction vectors of line 1 and line 2 respectively.

Chapter 20

Set Operations

Solid modeling is an important technique for achieving automation in geometric modeling, which forms the basis of CAD/CAM. The solid modeler employs set operations to compute sum-, difference- and product-sets between operand solids to generate a new solid, where a solid is expressed rigorously, that is, it has no representational ambiguity. In set operations, the state of interference between solids is numerically determined, and the result is used to modify their topological relation.

Floating-point arithmetic used in set operations, however, carries with it numerical errors, which can sometimes lead to conflicting information on the topological structure, and results in a breakdown in processing. This is a problem in current CAD technology for which a completely satisfactory general solution has yet to be found.

This chapter examines this issue of robustness and presents a completely robust solution for the set operations of polyhedra. One of the important features with this solid modeler is that the Four-dimensional Processing, coupled with integer arithmetic, makes it possible to completely separate the problems of topology from those of geometry.

For the reader who wishes to review the basics of set operations, refer to reference materials [24], [35], [38].

20.1 Difficulty of Robust Set Operation

The causes of non-robustness in set operations can broadly be divided into two types [35].

In the first type, the set operation algorithm encounters a geometric relation that it cannot handle, causing the program to crash. This rarely occurs nowadays, however, since most conceivable situations have been studied and documented in detail [35].

The second type derives from processing inaccuracy. Let us examine this in some detail. In a set operation, an assessment is made from geometric computation and the topological structure is modified accordingly. If there is a problem with the result of the geometric computation, however, the topological structure may be modified improperly, which may cause processing crash. It is therefore extremely important to ensure that set operations are robust. Yet, it is very difficult to develop an algorithm that will unfailingly perform a robust set operation under all circumstances. Let us see why this is so.

For a robust set operation, the geometric model must be described accurately in a topologically consistent manner. As we saw in Section 1.1, it is impossible, for instance, to represent with rigorous accuracy the polygonal faces of a polyhedron as a series of vertex coordinates as long as we insist on using Euclidean coordinates (see Fig. 20.1). That is, the following equations used for determining Euclidean coordinates,

$$x = \frac{\Delta_x}{\Delta}, \ y = \frac{\Delta_y}{\Delta}, \ z = \frac{\Delta_z}{\Delta}, \tag{20.1}$$

have divisions, and so contain round-off errors. Therefore, a point determined by this method does not really lie on the plane of the face, and there is no guarantee that geometric processing based on such imperfect data will be robust.

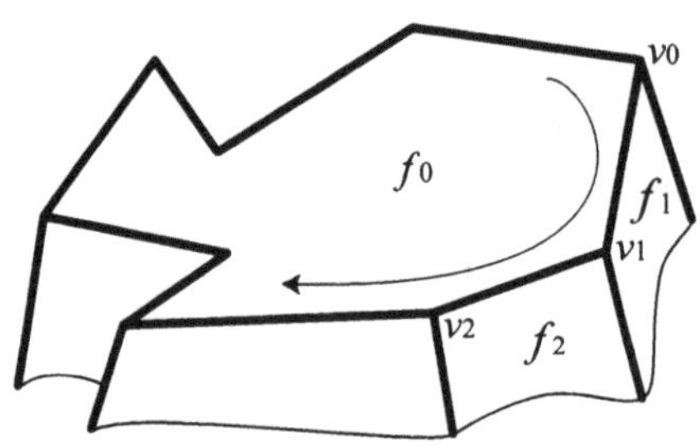

Figure 20.1: Defining a polygon in terms of vertices.

Let us now consider the geometric computations themselves. Clearly, geometric computations usually involve many divisions, the source of round-off errors, and with every division the error accumulates. In addition, there are errors such as loss of information or digit-cancellation that accompany floating-point arithmetic.

We have seen that set operations always accompany errors which arise from the representations of the geometric model, and from the geometric computations themselves, and that this could lead to an improper modification resulting in a contradictory topological structure and possible processing breakdown.

Studies are being conducted to develop floating-point arithmetic algorithms, allowing for their built-in errors, that would avoid such contradictions between geometry and topology. The outcome of this research, however, is likely to produce highly complex algorithms because of the complex processing needed to maintain consistency between geometry and topology. In only a few simple special cases has this research effort been successful so far.

In the following sections, we discuss the robustness issue with regard to set operations on polyhedra.

20.2 Error-free Processing

We saw above that as long as we follow conventional methods of geometric computations, error-free processing is not possible and a completely robust set operation is hard to achieve, where by error-free processing, we mean that rigorous accuracy is maintained in both the representation of solids and the execution of geometric computation. We saw also that there are two sources of errors when dealing with solids describable in rational numbers:

1. **Division operation**,
2. **Number representation**.

We shall discuss these in turn below as we explore the possibility of error-free processing.

1' **Issue of division operation**

Conventional methods of geometric computations deal with Euclidean figures, which are processed in Euclidean space. Let us take again the problem of defining a polygonal face in terms of vertex coordinates. We see that eq.(20.1) employs divisions to determine the Euclidean coordinates. If we use four dimensional coordinates $(\Delta, \Delta_x, \Delta_y, \Delta_z)$ consisting of predivision data, i.e., four-dimensional homogenous coordinates, instead of Euclidean coordinates (x, y, z), however, division operations would become unnecessary.

2' **Issue of number representation**

Nowadays, it is common to employ floating-point representation. Then we do not have to worry about tedious scaling operations required when we use fixed-point representation. Furthermore we can accelerate geometric computations by using a floating-point processing unit (FPU).

In solid modeling, however, computational accuracy is of prime importance as mentioned before. We saw how errors can cause a program to crash in the processing; so completely error-free processing is desirable. This is why, in our paradigm, we shall employ variable word-length integer representation instead of floating-point representation for applications like set operations where rigorous accuracy is needed.

We shall discuss the effects of using homogeneous coordinate system in set operations of solid modeling.

(1) **Range of representable numbers**

With the use of homogeneous coordinates in our paradigm, the representable number range expands considerably. Furthermore, we use variable word-length integers to be able to deal flexibly with a wide range of numbers (see Section 16.2). These two measures should provide a sufficiently broad range of numbers for most normal CAD applications.

(2) **Computational accuracy**

As long as we consider only geometric figures that can be expressed by rational numbers, any figure can be described exactly using four-dimensional integer homogeneous data.

Furthermore, the geometric computations involve no division, so there is no round-off error caused by division, and because integer arithmetic is used, there is neither round-off error, loss of information nor digit cancellation, associated with floating-point computations.

All these enable error-free processing.

(3) **Computational efficiency**

Because variable word-length data are used, there is a need to increase computational efficiency. The first approach is to employ the hybrid method to exact arithmetic mentioned in Section 16.6. The second one is to use the FPU to carry out error-free, adaptive sign tests for variable word-length integer data (see Section 16.7).

(4) **Programmer's burden**

Because of the use of an adaptive computational strategy based on variable word-length integers as well as four-dimensional processing, totally four-dimensional programming may be too troublesome and burdensome for programmers unfamiliar with it. To ease the programmer's burden, therefore, it is desirable to prepare a 4-D geometric computation library consisting of the basic geometric routines.

20.3 Achieving Robust Set Operations

With the use of variable word-length integers in the Four-dimensional Processing, it becomes possible to achieve rigorous accuracy both in the representation of polyhedral shapes that are describable in rational numbers, and in the execution of computations.

Let us then examine how error-free processing can actually achieve robustness in set operations.

20.3.1 Contradiction-free Solids

We first consider the conditions for achieving a completely robust set operation. The data structure of a boundary-representation solid model consists of geometric information like vertex coordinates or plane coefficients, and topological information, which describes how geometric elements connect to each other. When there is no contradiction between the results obtained from a solid's geometric information and those from its topological information, the solid is called *contradiction-free* [69]. The contradiction-free state of a solid is expressed as follows:

(C1) When four arbitrary vertices V_0, V_1, V_2 and V_3 in a data structure sharing a common face are chosen, $S_{0123} = 0$ always holds. This is the condition that the vertices are coplanar (see eq. (14.13)).

(C2) When four arbitrary faces f_0, f_1, f_2 and f_3 in a data structure sharing a common vertex are chosen, $T_{0123} = 0$ always holds. This is the condition that the faces are concurrent (see eq. (14.14)).

The condition (C1) concerns vertices, while (C2) concerns faces. Some solid modelers use vertex coordinates for basic data, while others use plane coefficients. Thus, the condition (C1) must be met in the former, and (C2) met in the latter case. If there is a solid modeler that uses both vertex coordinates and plane coefficients as its basic data, then the conditions (C1) and (C2) must both be satisfied.

20.3.2 An Overview of the Issues

Let us now look at the actual process of set operations and identify what types of problems we encounter. We saw above that a contradiction-free state must be kept at each stage of the set operation process to avoid processing crash.

① Solids in set operations

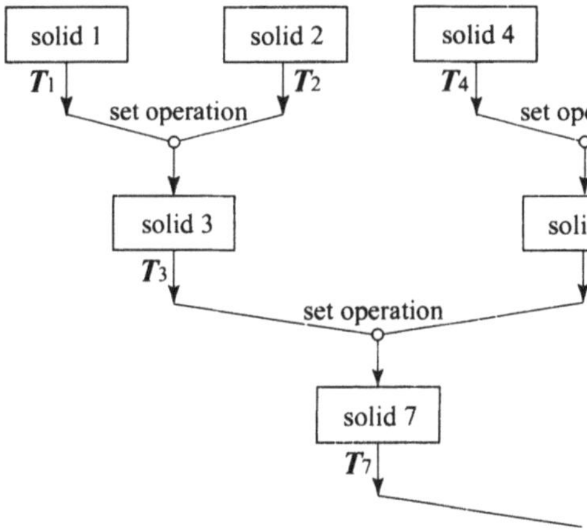

Figure 20.2: Set operation process.

A single set operation has as its operands two solids (which we shall call "solid-1" and "solid-2") (see Fig. 20.2). The operand solid may be a primitive element, or it can be a solid obtained as the result of a previous set operation. At this stage,

(1) the operand solid must be contradiction-free.

② Modeling transformation

"Solids 1" and "2" are subjected to transformations $\boldsymbol{T}_1$ and $\boldsymbol{T}_2$, respectively, to position them properly for the set operation. This is called *modeling transformation*. It consists of affine transformations such as translation, rotation and scaling. The operation involves multiplying a 4×4 matrix to the homogeneous coordinate vectors of the vertices. When transforming a plane equation, the adjoint of this matrix is used instead (see Section 6.1).

At this stage, the following problems arise:

(1) how do we represent a matrix containing trigonometric functions in terms of integers ?

(2) the solid after modeling transformation must be contradiction-free; and

(3) as a result of matrix multiplication, the data lengths of the vertice's homogeneous coordinates and the faces's plane coefficients will increase.

③ Set operation

Through the set operation, the intersections of the two solids are found; new vertices are created and intersecting faces are subdivided to form a new solid.

Here, the issues are that:

(1) the new vertices will have homogeneous coordinates that have longer data lengths than the other vertices; and

(2) the new solid formed by the set operation must be contradiction-free.

We must also keep in mind that such modeling transformations and set operations will occur repeatedly.

Let us then address each of these issues.

Issue ①-(1):

The basic units of solids in a set operation are primitives. So to begin with, the primitives must be contradiction-free. Section 20.3.3 discusses how to generate such a primitive.

Issue ②-(1):

When the modeling transformation matrix includes rotation, its elements will contain irrational numbers, and these cannot be expressed rigorously by integer-based homogeneous representations. This matter is discussed in Section 20.3.4.

Issue ②-(2):

The subject of maintaining the contradiction-free state of solids undergoing modeling transformations is discussed in Section 20.3.5.

Issues ②-(3), ③-(1) and ③-(2):

If solids are to be kept contradiction-free through a series of repeated modeling transformations and set operations, the homogeneous coordinates of their vertices (or the plane coefficients of their faces) will keep on increasing indefinitely in data length.

Consider vertices of a solid, for example. With the initial modeling transformation, their coordinate data increase. Then with a set operation, new vertices are generated. Their data lengths will be longer compared to the other vertices because their computation must be strictly accurate to keep a contradiction-free state. Most cases will involve repeated applications of these operations and, as a result, the vertices's homogeneous coordinates will grow increasingly longer in data length. We discuss this issue in Section 20.3.6.

20.3.3 Generating Contradiction-free Primitives

To realize a failure-free system based on exact integer arithmetic, we must be able to generate primitives containing no contradictions. However, the shape data of some primitives such as a cylinder or sphere are expressed in trigonometric functions and so cannot be represented exactly with rational numbers or integers. To generate a contradiction-free primitive, one must be able to recognize those parts for which errors are permitted, and others where errors cannot be allowed because they could create contradictions between topology and geometry, otherwise.

We shall now describe how to generate some primitives including the rectangular parallelepiped, cone, cylinder, sphere and torus. As our basic data, we shall employ the homogeneous coordinates of vertices.

1. **Rectangular parallelepiped**

   The six faces of the rectangular parallelepiped are generated so that each face is parallel to one of the coordinate planes. Therefore, the vertices belonging to a particular face all share the same value for one of the Euclidean coordinates x, y or z. Thus a rectangular parallelepiped satisfies the condition (C1).

2. **Cone**

   The base of the cone is assumed parallel to the xy-plane. Its vertices all have the same z-value and so satisfy the condition (C1). The cone's side surface can be approximated by a set of triangles, so it also meets the coplanar condition.

3. **Cylinder**

   Assume that the bases are parallel to the xy-plane. For reasons identical to the cone, the two bases satisfy the condition (C1). In a cylinder with bases parallel to the xy-plane, any arbitrary vertex can be represented by its radius r, two angles α_0 and α_1, and the two z-values of 0 and h

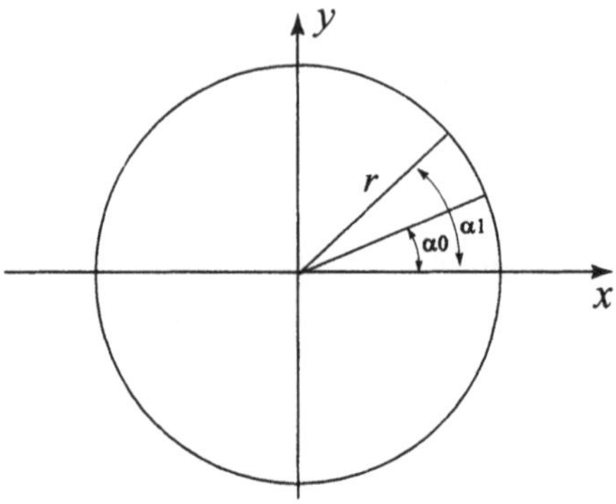

Figure 20.3: Base of cylinder.

(see Fig. 20.3). Thus, four points on the side surface can be expressed by homogeneous coordinates as follows:

$$\begin{aligned} V_0 &= (1, r\cos\alpha_0, r\sin\alpha_0, 0), \\ V_1 &= (1, r\cos\alpha_1, r\sin\alpha_1, 0), \\ V_2 &= (1, r\cos\alpha_1, r\sin\alpha_1, h), \\ V_3 &= (1, r\cos\alpha_0, r\sin\alpha_0, h). \end{aligned}$$

Allowing for some error in the computation process, we make the following approximations for the trigonometric functions:

$$\begin{aligned} x_1 &\leftarrow r\cos\alpha_0, \quad y_1 \leftarrow r\sin\alpha_0, \\ x_2 &\leftarrow r\cos\alpha_1, \quad y_2 \leftarrow r\sin\alpha_1. \end{aligned}$$

Then, the determinant S_{0123} formed by the four points V_0, V_1, V_2 and V_3 is given by:

$$S_{0123} = \begin{vmatrix} 1 & x_1 & y_1 & 0 \\ 1 & x_2 & y_2 & 0 \\ 1 & x_2 & y_2 & h \\ 1 & x_1 & y_1 & h \end{vmatrix}. \tag{20.2}$$

S_{0123} is identically zero. Thus, the side of the cylinder also satisfies the condition (C1).

4. **Sphere**

A sphere can be approximated by polygons using two angles α and β, as shown in Fig. 20.4. Thus, a point on the sphere is expressed as follows:

$$\begin{aligned} x &= r\cos\beta\cos\alpha, \\ y &= r\cos\beta\sin\alpha, \\ z &= r\sin\beta. \end{aligned}$$

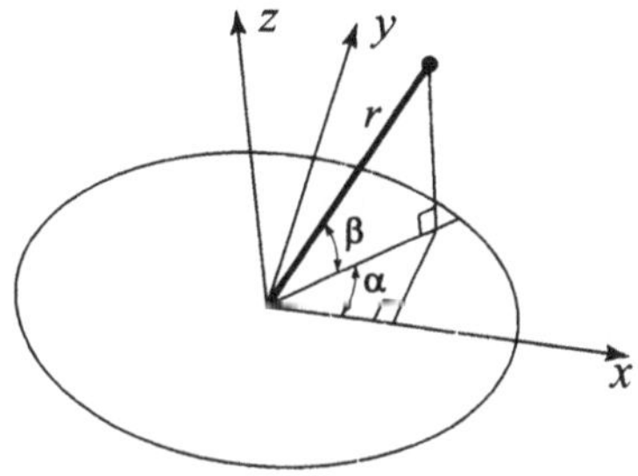

Figure 20.4: Point on sphere.

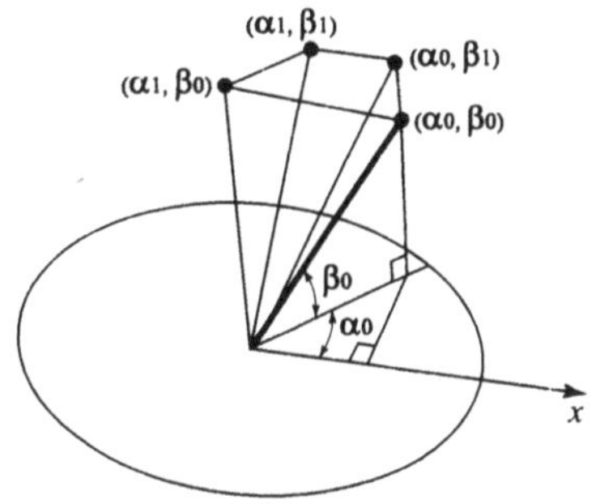

Figure 20.5: Four points on sphere.

We now denote four points approximating the sphere surface using the two angles as $V_0(\alpha_0, \beta_0)$, $V_1(\alpha_0, \beta_1)$, $V_2(\alpha_1, \beta_1)$ and $V_3(\alpha_1, \beta_0)$ (Fig. 20.5). In homogeneous coordinates, they are written:

$$\begin{aligned}
V_0 &= (1,\ r\cos\beta_0\cos\alpha_0,\ r\cos\beta_0\sin\alpha_0,\ r\sin\beta_0),\\
V_1 &= (1,\ r\cos\beta_1\cos\alpha_0,\ r\cos\beta_1\sin\alpha_0,\ r\sin\beta_1),\\
V_2 &= (1,\ r\cos\beta_1\cos\alpha_1,\ r\cos\beta_1\sin\alpha_1,\ r\sin\beta_1),\\
V_3 &= (1,\ r\cos\beta_0\cos\alpha_1,\ r\cos\beta_0\sin\alpha_1,\ r\sin\beta_0).
\end{aligned}$$

Allowing for some error in the computation process, we make the following approximations for the trigonometric functions:

$$\begin{aligned}
&ca_0 \leftarrow \cos\alpha_0,\quad rcb_0 \leftarrow r\cos\beta_0,\quad sa_0 \leftarrow \sin\alpha_0,\quad rsb_0 \leftarrow r\sin\beta_0,\\
&ca_1 \leftarrow \cos\alpha_1,\quad rcb_1 \leftarrow r\cos\beta_1,\quad sa_1 \leftarrow \sin\alpha_1,\quad rsb_1 \leftarrow r\sin\beta_1.
\end{aligned}$$

The homogeneous coordinates of the four points after approximations are then:

$$\begin{aligned}
V_0 &= (1,\ rcb_0 \cdot ca_0,\ rcb_0 \cdot sa_0,\ rsb_0),\\
V_1 &= (1,\ rcb_1 \cdot ca_0,\ rcb_1 \cdot sa_0,\ rsb_1),
\end{aligned}$$

$$V_2 = (1,\ rcb_1 \cdot ca_1,\ rcb_1 \cdot sa_1,\ rsb_1),$$
$$V_0 = (1,\ rcb_0 \cdot ca_1,\ rcb_0 \cdot sa_1,\ rsb_0).$$

In computing the coordinate components above, the product denoted by "·" is assumed to be error-free.

The homogeneous coordinates of the four points V_0, V_1, V_2 and V_3 after approximation are used to form the 4×4 determinant:

$$S_{0123} = \begin{vmatrix} 1 & rcb_0 \cdot ca_0 & rcb_0 \cdot sa_0 & rsb_0 \\ 1 & rcb_1 \cdot ca_0 & rcb_1 \cdot sa_0 & rsb_1 \\ 1 & rcb_1 \cdot ca_1 & rcb_1 \cdot sa_1 & rsb_1 \\ 1 & rcb_0 \cdot ca_1 & rcb_0 \cdot sa_1 & rsb_0 \end{vmatrix},$$

which is identical to zero. So the sphere surface also satisfies the condition (C1). Thus, the sphere can be expressed using only rational numbers, that is, homogeneous coordinates, so as to make it contradiction-free.

5. **Torus**

A torus can be approximated by polygons using the two radii R and r and two angles α and β, as in Fig. 20.6. A point V on the torus surface is expressed as follows:

$$x = (R + r\cos\beta)\cos\alpha,$$
$$y = (R + r\cos\beta)\sin\alpha,$$
$$z = r\sin\beta.$$

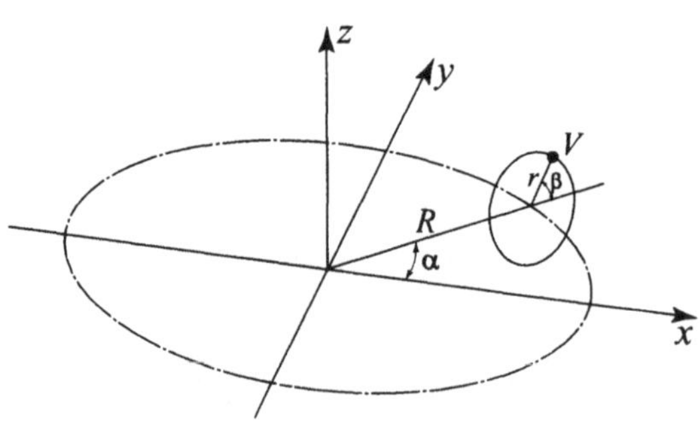

Figure 20.6: A point on torus.

Four points approximating the torus surface are denoted using the two angles as $V_0(\alpha_0, \beta_0)$, $V_1(\alpha_1, \beta_0)$, $V_2(\alpha_1, \beta_1)$ and $V_3(\alpha_0, \beta_1)$ (see Fig. 20.7). In homogeneous coordinates, they are written:

$$V_0 = (1,\ (R + r\cos\beta_0)\cos\alpha_0,\ (R + r\cos\beta_0)\sin\alpha_0,\ r\sin\beta_0),$$

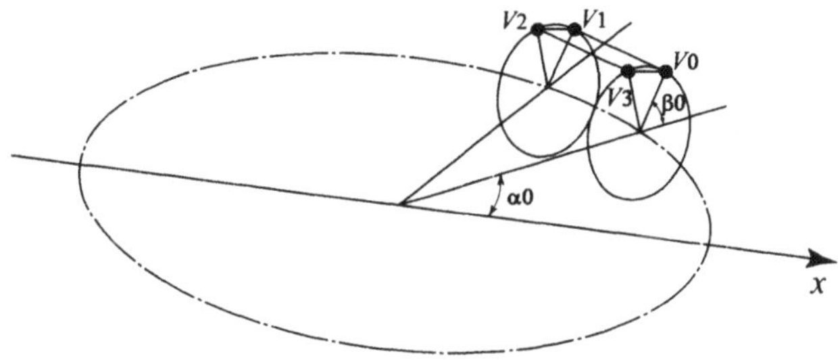

Figure 20.7: Four points on torus.

$$\begin{aligned}V_1 &= (1,\ (R + r\cos\beta_0)\cos\alpha_1,\ (R + r\cos\beta_0)\sin\alpha_1,\ r\sin\beta_0),\\ V_2 &= (1,\ (R + r\cos\beta_1)\cos\alpha_1,\ (R + r\cos\beta_1)\sin\alpha_1,\ r\sin\beta_1),\\ V_3 &= (1,\ (R + r\cos\beta_1)\cos\alpha_0,\ (R + r\cos\beta_1)\sin\alpha_0,\ r\sin\beta_1).\end{aligned}$$

Allowing for some error in the computation of trigonometric functions, we make the following approximations:

$$\begin{aligned}&rrcb0 \leftarrow R + r\cos\beta_0,\ ca0 \leftarrow \cos\alpha_0,\ rsb0 \leftarrow r\sin\beta_0,\ sa0 \leftarrow \sin\alpha_0,\\ &rrcb1 \leftarrow R + r\cos\beta_1,\ ca1 \leftarrow \cos\alpha_1,\ rsb1 \leftarrow r\sin\beta_1,\ sa1 \leftarrow \sin\alpha_1.\end{aligned}$$

The homogeneous coordinates of the four points after approximation are then:

$$\begin{aligned}V_0 &= (1,\ rrcb0\cdot ca0,\ rrcb0\cdot sa0,\ rsb0),\\ V_1 &= (1,\ rrcb0\cdot ca1,\ rrcb0\cdot sa1,\ rsb0),\\ V_2 &= (1,\ rrcb1\cdot ca1,\ rrcb1\cdot sa1,\ rsb1),\\ V_3 &= (1,\ rrcb1\cdot ca0,\ rrcb1\cdot sa0,\ rsb1).\end{aligned}$$

In computing the coordinate components above, the product denoted by "$\cdot$" is assumed to be error-free.

The homogeneous coordinates of the four points V_0, V_1, V_2 and V_3 after approximation are used to form the 4×4 determinant:

$$S_{0123} = \begin{vmatrix} 1 & rrcb0\cdot ca0 & rrcb0\cdot sa0 & rsb0\\ 1 & rrcb0\cdot ca1 & rrcb0\cdot sa1 & rsb0\\ 1 & rrcb1\cdot ca1 & rrcb1\cdot sa1 & rsb1\\ 1 & rrcb1\cdot ca0 & rrcb1\cdot sa0 & rsb1 \end{vmatrix},$$

which is identical to zero. So the torus surface also satisfies the condition (C1). Thus, the torus can be expressed using only rational numbers, that is, homogeneous coordinates, to make it contradiction-free.

Note that the vertices of the primitives above are expressed in homogeneous coordinates with rational numbers, and they can easily be expressed as integer-component coordinates by multiplying by the least common multiples of the denominators of the components.

6. **Other primitives**

   There are many other primitives conceivable except those described above. To produce a contradiction-free primitive, one only needs to ensure that, for all of its faces, the 4×4 determinant formed by four arbitrary vertices on that face always vanishes. If this is a difficult procedure, another possible method is to triangulate the faces.

   Let us now see how to determine the plane coefficients of the primitive's faces. In general, it is not easy to express homogeneous plane coefficients within a prescribed data length using the homogeneous coordinates of vertices. But in the solid modeling method discussed in this chapter, the vertices are always given exact coordinate values and lie on the same plane, and this coplanar condition is preserved through subsequent transformations (see Section 20.3.5). Therefore, we only need to choose three points V_0, V_1 and V_2, when forming a primitive, such that the normal vector they define points outward from the face. Then, the homogeneous plane coefficients a, b, c and d are given as follows:

$$a = \begin{vmatrix} X_0 & Y_0 & Z_0 \\ X_1 & Y_1 & Z_1 \\ X_2 & Y_2 & Z_2 \end{vmatrix}, \quad b = \begin{vmatrix} w_0 & Z_0 & Y_0 \\ w_1 & Z_1 & Y_1 \\ w_2 & Z_2 & Y_2 \end{vmatrix},$$

$$c = \begin{vmatrix} w_0 & X_0 & Z_0 \\ w_1 & X_1 & Z_1 \\ w_2 & X_2 & Z_2 \end{vmatrix}, \quad d = \begin{vmatrix} w_0 & Y_0 & X_0 \\ w_1 & Y_1 & X_1 \\ w_2 & Y_2 & X_2 \end{vmatrix}. \tag{20.3}$$

   The homogeneous plane coefficients will have data lengths within certain limits since they are computed from homogeneous vertex coordinates having limited data length.

20.3.4 Transformation Matrix in Integer

We now discuss how to express the components of the modeling transformation matrix in terms of integers.

First, we must find a way to deal with the trigonometric functions in the rotation matrix since, obviously, irrational numbers cannot be exactly represented by integers. Here, by using an angle θ' that differs slightly from the rotation angle θ, we can obtain $\cos\theta'$ and $\sin\theta'$ which consist of rational numbers. In other words, we employ the following parametric representation of the unit circle:

$$\cos\theta' = \frac{1-t^2}{1+t^2}, \qquad \sin\theta' = \frac{2t}{1+t^2}, \tag{20.4}$$

of which the geometric relationship is shown in Fig. 20.8. Here, $t = \tan(\theta/2)$. By approximating t by an appropriate rational number m/n, we have:

$$\cos\theta' = \frac{n^2-m^2}{n^2+m^2}, \qquad \sin\theta' = \frac{2nm}{n^2+m^2}. \tag{20.5}$$

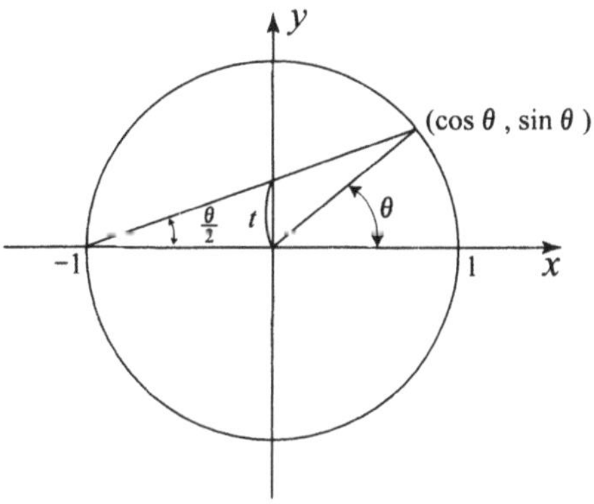

Figure 20.8: Geometric meaning of parameter t.

Recall now that a 4×4 transformation matrix is not changed by multiplication by an arbitrary scalar (or positive number in the case of signed homogeneous coordinates). Therefore, by multiplying by the least common multiples of the denominators of the matrix components, we can obtain without loss of generality a transformation matrix with integer components.

Normally, the inverse of the transformation matrix for points is used to transform homogeneous plane coefficients. However, the adjoint matrix can also be used for the same purpose. Thus, if we accurately compute the adjoint, it can be used to accurately transform the homogeneous plane coefficients by integer arithmetic (see Section 6.1).

20.3.5 Contradiction-free Modeling Transformation

We now discuss the issue of preserving the contradiction-free state of solids in modeling transformations.

Consider the following modeling transformation matrix consisting of real-number components:

$$\boldsymbol{T} = \begin{bmatrix} s & t_x & t_y & t_z \\ 0 & r_{00} & r_{01} & r_{02} \\ 0 & r_{10} & r_{11} & r_{12} \\ 0 & r_{20} & r_{21} & r_{22} \end{bmatrix}. \tag{20.6}$$

When $\boldsymbol{V} = [w\ X\ Y\ Z]$ becomes transformed to $\boldsymbol{V}^* = [w^*\ X^*\ Y^*\ Z^*]$, we have the following relation:

$$\boldsymbol{V}^* = \boldsymbol{V}\boldsymbol{T}. \tag{20.7}$$

Earlier in Section 20.3.1, we defined the contradiction-free state of a solid. Let us now examine how a solid's contradiction-free state is affected by modeling transformation. Denoting the homogeneous coordinate vectors of the four points by $\boldsymbol{V}_0$, $\boldsymbol{V}_1$, $\boldsymbol{V}_2$ and $\boldsymbol{V}_3$, and those after transformation $\boldsymbol{T}$ by $\boldsymbol{V}_0^*$, $\boldsymbol{V}_1^*$, $\boldsymbol{V}_2^*$ and $\boldsymbol{V}_3^*$, we have:

$$\begin{bmatrix} w_0^* & X_0^* & Y_0^* & Z_0^* \\ w_1^* & X_1^* & Y_1^* & Z_1^* \\ w_2^* & X_2^* & Y_2^* & Z_2^* \\ w_3^* & X_3^* & Y_3^* & Z_3^* \end{bmatrix} = \begin{bmatrix} w_0 & X_0 & Y_0 & Z_0 \\ w_1 & X_1 & Y_1 & Z_1 \\ w_2 & X_2 & Y_2 & Z_2 \\ w_3 & X_3 & Y_3 & Z_3 \end{bmatrix} \begin{bmatrix} s & t_x & t_y & t_z \\ 0 & r_{00} & r_{01} & r_{02} \\ 0 & r_{10} & r_{11} & r_{12} \\ 0 & r_{20} & r_{21} & r_{22} \end{bmatrix}. \tag{20.8}$$

It follows from linear algebra that:

$$\begin{vmatrix} w_0^* & X_0^* & Y_0^* & Z_0^* \\ w_1^* & X_1^* & Y_1^* & Z_1^* \\ w_2^* & X_2^* & Y_2^* & Z_2^* \\ w_3^* & X_3^* & Y_3^* & Z_3^* \end{vmatrix} = \begin{vmatrix} w_0 & X_0 & Y_0 & Z_0 \\ w_1 & X_1 & Y_1 & Z_1 \\ w_2 & X_2 & Y_2 & Z_2 \\ w_3 & X_3 & Y_3 & Z_3 \end{vmatrix} \begin{vmatrix} s & t_x & t_y & t_z \\ 0 & r_{00} & r_{01} & r_{02} \\ 0 & r_{10} & r_{11} & r_{12} \\ 0 & r_{20} & r_{21} & r_{22} \end{vmatrix}. \tag{20.9}$$

Therefore, for:

$$\begin{vmatrix} s & t_x & t_y & t_z \\ 0 & r_{00} & r_{01} & r_{02} \\ 0 & r_{10} & r_{11} & r_{12} \\ 0 & r_{20} & r_{21} & r_{22} \end{vmatrix} \neq 0,$$

$$\text{If } \begin{vmatrix} w_0 & X_0 & Y_0 & Z_0 \\ w_1 & X_1 & Y_1 & Z_1 \\ w_2 & X_2 & Y_2 & Z_2 \\ w_3 & X_3 & Y_3 & Z_3 \end{vmatrix} = 0, \text{ then } \begin{vmatrix} w_0^* & X_0^* & Y_0^* & Z_0^* \\ w_1^* & X_1^* & Y_1^* & Z_1^* \\ w_2^* & X_2^* & Y_2^* & Z_2^* \\ w_3^* & X_3^* & Y_3^* & Z_3^* \end{vmatrix} = 0.$$

In other words, a contradiction-free state is preserved by modeling transformation as long as multiplication by the transformation matrix $\boldsymbol{T}$ takes place without error [69]. In the usual case, however, the transformation of eq.(20.8) is carried out against floating point data and so a contradiction-free solid may not always produce a contradiction-free solid after transformation. Meanwhile, the method introduced here involves error-free processing based on integers and thus preserves the contradiction-free state of a solid.

From the discussion above, it is also clear that this method will preserve the contradiction-free state of solids not only for the transformation eq.(20.6) but also under any arbitrary projective transformation:

$$\boldsymbol{T} = \begin{bmatrix} s & t_x & t_y & t_z \\ p & r_{00} & r_{01} & r_{02} \\ q & r_{10} & r_{11} & r_{12} \\ r & r_{20} & r_{21} & r_{22} \end{bmatrix}.$$

20.3.6 Keeping Data Length under Control

As we saw in Section 20.2, repeatedly carrying out modeling transformations and set operations while preserving the contradiction-free state will produce ever-increasing data length for the homogeneous vertex coordinates and homogeneous plane coefficients. Modeling transformations (particularly rotation) contribute greatly to increasing data length.

As discussed in Section 20.2, the two operand solids were both subjected to modeling transformation. Note, however, that keeping one operand fixed while transforming the other operand relative to the fixed one will produce equivalent results. Thus, transformation is unnecessary for the fixed solid. Along with this method, we impose the following rule concerning set operations:

Of the two operands, use a primitive for the one which is not fixed.

By applying modeling transformation to one operand only and using the above rule, any primitive that makes up a solid formed by the set operations will undergo modeling transformation only once, regardless of how many modeling transformations and set operations are carried out to generate the final solid. This makes it possible to contain the increase of the data length of homogeneous vertex coordinates (or plane coefficients) within prescribed limits (see Fig. 20.9).

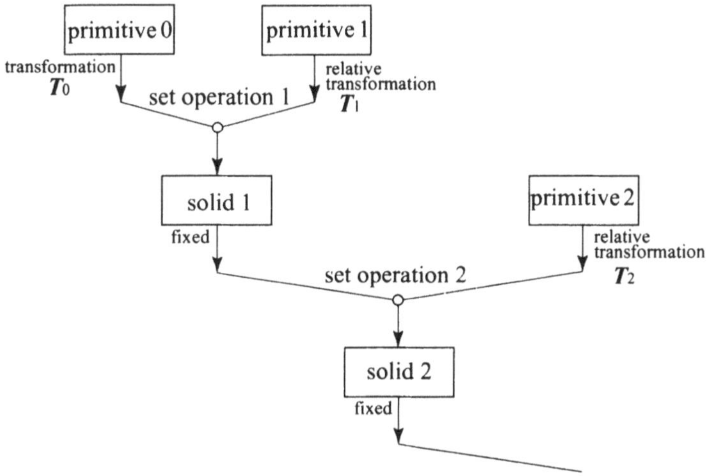

Figure 20.9: Set operation with a given rule.

Let us examine this process in some detail. For the initial set operation, both operands are primitives: primitive-0 and primitive-1. Primitive-0 undergoes modeling transformation $\boldsymbol{T}_0$, which places the primitive in the working area. Primitive-1 then undergoes modeling transformation $\boldsymbol{T}_1$ relative to primitive-0's coordinate system. Set operation 1 is carried out against these two operands to form solid-1. The next set operation takes place against solid-1 and primitive-2, where solid-1 remains fixed (i.e., no modeling transformation is carried out) but primitive-2 first undergoes a relative transformation $\boldsymbol{T}_2$. Set operation 2 thus yields solid-2. This procedure is then repeated, where the generated solid remains fixed; a primitive is first subjected to modeling transformation.

The faces that form the solid generated by the set operations are either complete or partial faces belonging to a primitive. As we have seen, such faces undergo modeling transformation only once. As a result, the homogeneous plane coefficients of all faces, and the homogeneous coordinates of all vertices that initially belonged to primitives, will have data lengths within prescribed limits.

Although a set operation does not create a new face that does not belong to a primitive, it ordinarily generates new vertices. If these new vertices are used in subsequent set operations to obtain further new vertices, the coordinates are likely to keep on growing in data length. This situation can be avoided if we compute a new vertex not from other vertices but as the intersection of three planes, as given by the following equations, which form a dual to eq.(20.3):

$$w = \begin{vmatrix} b_0 & b_1 & b_2 \\ c_0 & c_1 & c_2 \\ d_0 & d_1 & d_2 \end{vmatrix}, \quad X = \begin{vmatrix} a_0 & a_1 & a_2 \\ d_0 & d_1 & d_2 \\ c_0 & c_1 & c_2 \end{vmatrix},$$

$$Y = \begin{vmatrix} a_0 & a_1 & a_2 \\ b_0 & b_1 & b_2 \\ d_0 & d_1 & d_2 \end{vmatrix}, \quad Z = \begin{vmatrix} a_0 & a_1 & a_2 \\ c_0 & c_1 & c_2 \\ b_0 & b_1 & b_2 \end{vmatrix}. \tag{20.10}$$

Note that we are assuming exact computations. Therefore, if the normalization of integer homogeneous coordinates are supposed to be done every time a new point is generated, the coordinate lengths of the generated point do not depend on the type or process of intersecting point computations, but on the coordinates of a point to be represented because the representation of exact homogeneous coordinates of a point is unique when there is no common factor among the coordinates [1)].

We have seen that by observing the above-stated rule throughout the set operation process for polyhedra, we can keep data lengths within certain limits and thus achieve a failure-free, completely robust algorithm.

20.4 Investigation of Data Length

Let us now find the maximum data length required for the completely robust algorithm in the set operations on polyhedra we have discussed so far, assuming we do not normalize integer homogeneous coordinates.

Let the homogeneous coordinates of a primitive's vertex and the matrix components for modeling transformation be L and M bits in data length respectively.

Then, from eq.(20.3), the homogeneous coefficient of a primitive's plane is obtained by adding six terms of data length $3L$, so

Data length of homogeneous coefficient of a primitive's plane:

$$< 3L + 3 \text{ (bits)}. \tag{20.11}$$

For the adjoint matrix of the modeling transformation, we have from the footnote (page 78) in Chapter 6:

[1)] As for the normalization of integer homogeneous coordinates, see Section 2.4.

Data length of adjoint matrix component:

$$< \ 3M + 3 \text{ (bits).} \tag{20.12}$$

How then are data lengths affected by each computation relevant to a set operation ?

First, we consider modeling transformations by a 4×4 matrix. A vertex of data length L is multiplied by a matrix of data length M, so four terms of data length $L+M$ are added, and we have:

Data length of primitive vertex coordinate after transformation:

$$< \ L + M + 2 \text{ (bits).} \tag{20.13}$$

Meanwhile in the modeling transformation, a face of data length $3L+3$ is multiplied by an adjoint matrix of data length $3M+3$, so four terms of data length $(3L+3)+(3M+3)=3(L+M)+6$ are added, and:

Data length of primitive plane coefficient after transformation:

$$< \ 3(L + M) + 8 \text{ (bits).} \tag{20.14}$$

A set operation generates new vertices.

Computing a new vertex as the intersection of three planes, we have from eqs.(20.10) and (20.14):

Data length of new vertex coordinate in set operation:

$$< \ (3L + 3M + 8) \times 3 + 3 = 9(L + M) + 27 \text{ (bits).} \tag{20.15}$$

If we assume that $L=M=32$, the maximum data length is then 603 bits.

However, if such a very precise rotation angle is specified in the modeling transformation, or such a fine subdivision is made in the generation of a primitive solid, that can not be expressed in 32 bits (i.e., $L, M > 32$), the maximum data length will become more than 603 bits (see Sections 16.4 and 25.1.1).

Above is the theoretical maximum number of bits. In reality we perform the normalization of homogeneous coordinates while executing set operations. Therefore the maximum number of bits required for set operations is faily smaller than the values above.

20.5 Simplification of Set Operation Algorithm

Set operation algorithms are very complicate. Therefore it is important to have some techniques for making the algorithm as simple as possible. In this section we shall present a simplified and efficient set operation algorithm by capitalizing on the multiple-loop edge of non-manifold solid data structure (see Section 17.6.3).

Let us begin with reviewing the conventional set operation algorithm.

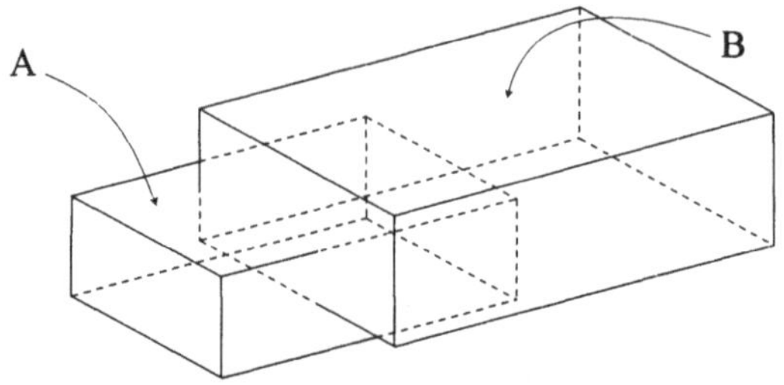

Figure 20.10: Operand solids "A" and "B" before set operation.

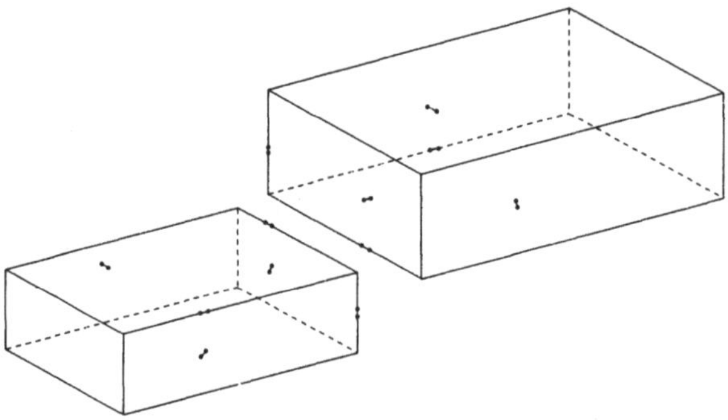

Figure 20.11: Null edge insertions at intersecting points.

20.5.1 Outline of Conventional Algorithm

The conventional set operation algorithm is performed in a sequence of "divide and then merge." It consists of the following steps [34] (Fig. 20.10): (note that used Euler operators are for the half edge data structure (see Section 18.2.3))

1. **Intersections between edges of one solid and faces of the other**

   Intersection points are computed between edges of one solid and faces of the other, and then null edges are inserted there by the use of Euler operators **mev**, **keml** and **mev** in this order when the intersection point is in the middle of a face (Fig. 20.11).

2. **Connections of null edges**

   These null edges are connected to produce null faces along the intersection lines by the use of operators **mekl** and **mefl** (Fig. 20.12). This connection process requires a very complicate and time-consuming algorithm.

3. **Connection of null faces**

   These null edges are deleted to connect the null faces by the use of operators **kefl** and **keml** (Fig. 20.13). As the result of these operations, there is only one bent shaped null face left in each solid.

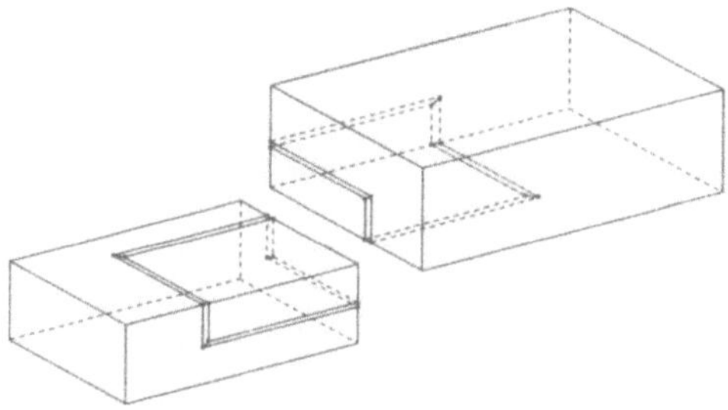

Figure 20.12: Null edge connections.

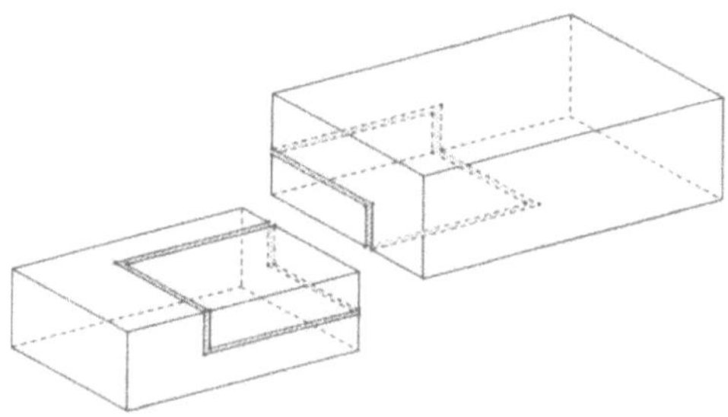

Figure 20.13: Null face connections by null edge deletions.

4. **Division of solids into four parts**

   The operand solids "A" and "B" are divided into four solid parts by the use of an operator **mfkg** (Fig. 20.14).

5. **Completion of final solid**

   A final solid is produced by merging two of the divided solids, corresponding to a specified operation (Fig. 20.15). The operation is done by the use of an operator **kfmg**.

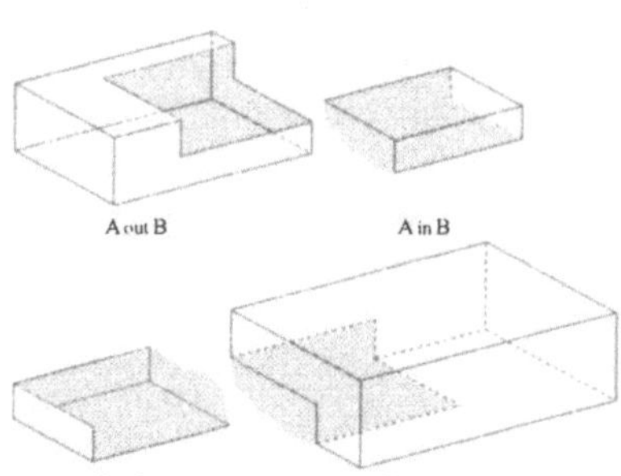

Figure 20.14: A out B, A in B, B out A and B in A.

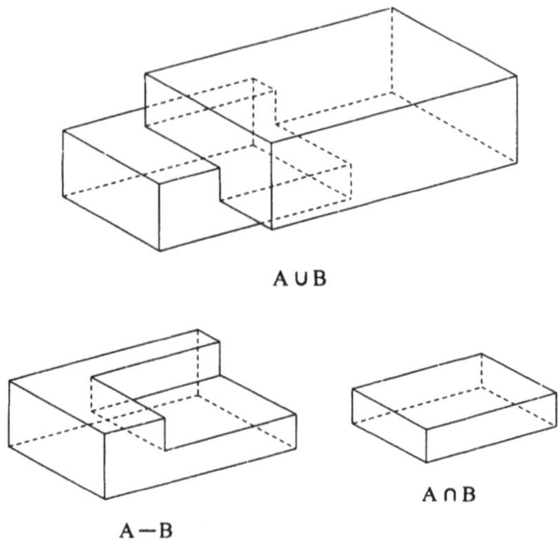

Figure 20.15: Results of set operations.

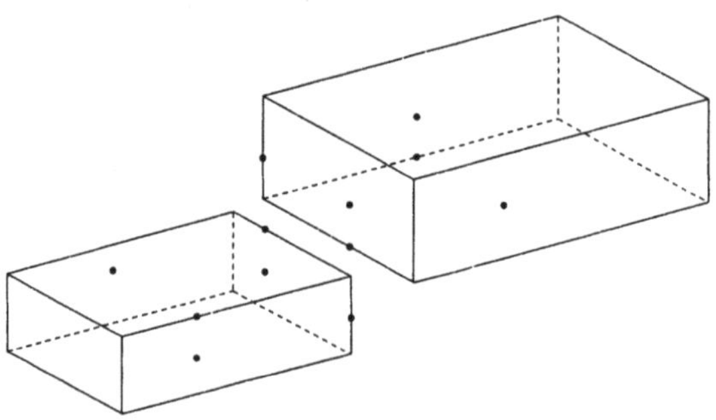

Figure 20.16: Vertex insertions at intersecting points.

20.5.2 Simplified Set Operation Algorithm

As discussed in the previous section, the conventional set operation algorithm is performed in a sequence of "divide and then merge." On the other hand the simplified algorithm to be presented here is done in a sequence of "merge and then divide."[23],[55] It capitalizes on the capability of the multiple-loop edge of non-manifold data structure (see Sections 17.6.3 and 18.3.2). It consists of the following steps: (note that used Euler operators are for the quarter edge data structure (see Section 18.3.3))

1. **Determining intersection points between two operand solids**

   Intersection line segment and face pairs are identified and vertices are inserted at intersecting points (Fig. 20.16). A vertex insertion is done by operators **mev** and **keml**$_f$ when the intersection point is in the middle of a face.

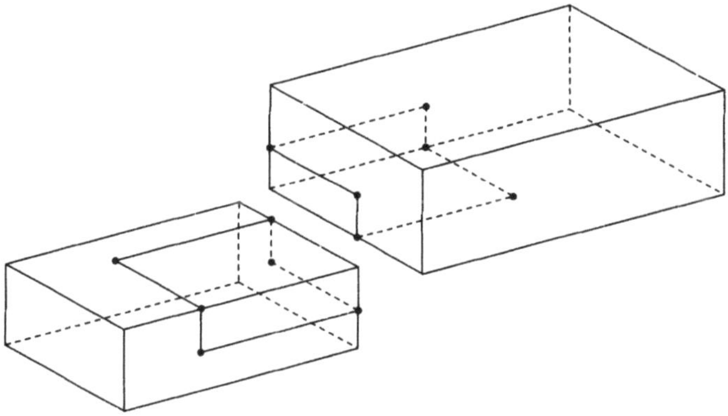

Figure 20.17: Edge insertions between vertices.

2. **Insertion of edges**

   Edges are inserted on the intersection lines of both solids (Fig. 20.17).

   Edge insertions are done by an operator **mekl**$_f$ or **mef**, depending on the intersection types.

3. **Merging corresponding vertices between two solids**

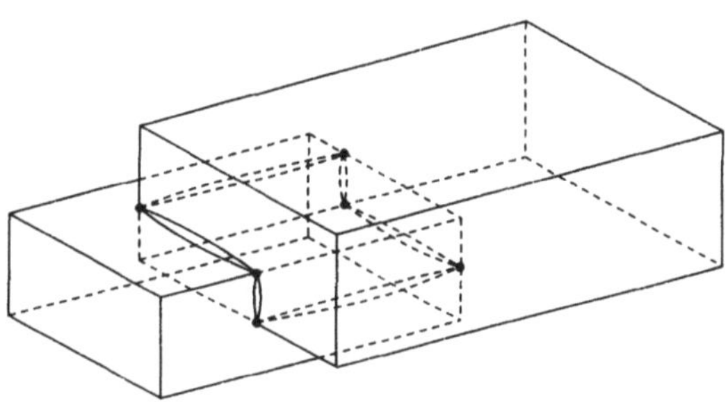

Figure 20.18: Merging vertices.

We first transform the two solids into one having two shells by using an operator **sld2shl** [2], and then merge corresponding vertices between the two solids into one respectively, using an operator **kvmg** (Fig. 20.18). Each operation of **kvmg** creates a hole except the first one. This step does not have to be performed in the order of the intersection line loop, but can be done at random.

At the end of this step the solid turns out to have one shell, and at each intersection point the vertex-loop multiplicity is two.

[2] **sld2shl** is a special operator used only for set operations. It takes out a shell in a solid and moves it to another solid, which turns out to increase the number of shells by one. The former solid is finally killed.

4. **Merging corresponding edges between two solids**

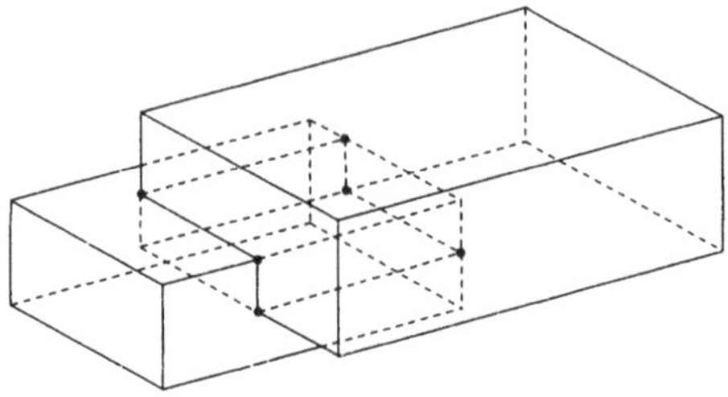

Figure 20.19: Merging edges.

We merge all the corresponding edges between the two solids into one respectively by using an operator $\mathbf{keml}_e$ (Fig. 20.19). By this operation two edges are transformed into one whose loop-multiplicity is two. This data structure representation was made possible owing to the capability of the multiple-loop edge.

The operation of this step can be performed randomly irrespectively of the order of edges of the intersection line loop.

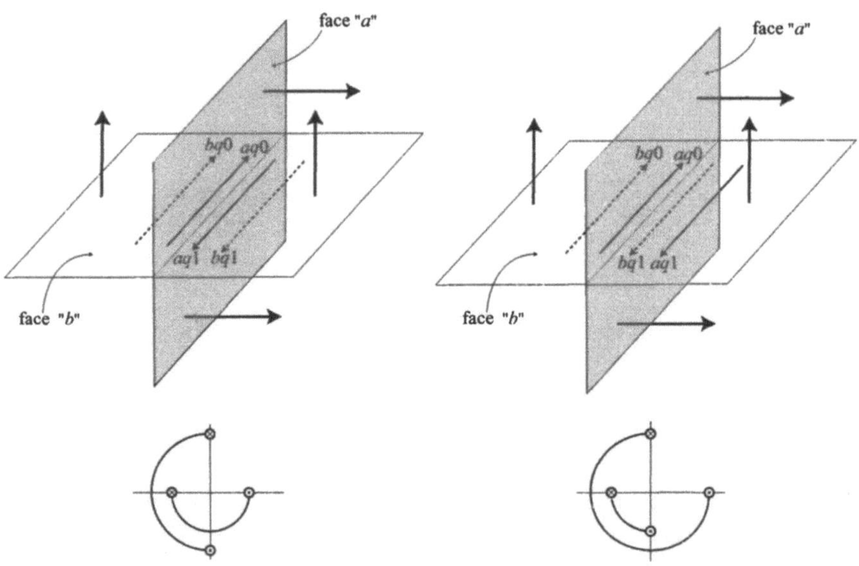

Figure 20.20: Interchange between quarter edges.

5. **Interchange between quarter edges**

In this algorithm *union* and *intersection* solids of input operands are generated simultaneously by interchange operations between quarter edges.

At this stage the quarter edges of face "a" in solid "A" and face "b" in solid "B" are recorded as shown in (a) of Fig. 20.20. In the figure (a), "aq0" and "aq1" represent quarter edges (solid directed lines) of face "a" (dark face), and "bq0" and "bq1" do those (dotted directed lines) of face "b" (white one).

In the bottom of each figure, these quarter edge relations are shown symbolically in a sectional view of an edge neighborhood: the symbol ⊙ represents the quarter edge directing frontside and ⊗ does the one directing backside, and an arrowed arc shows a solid.

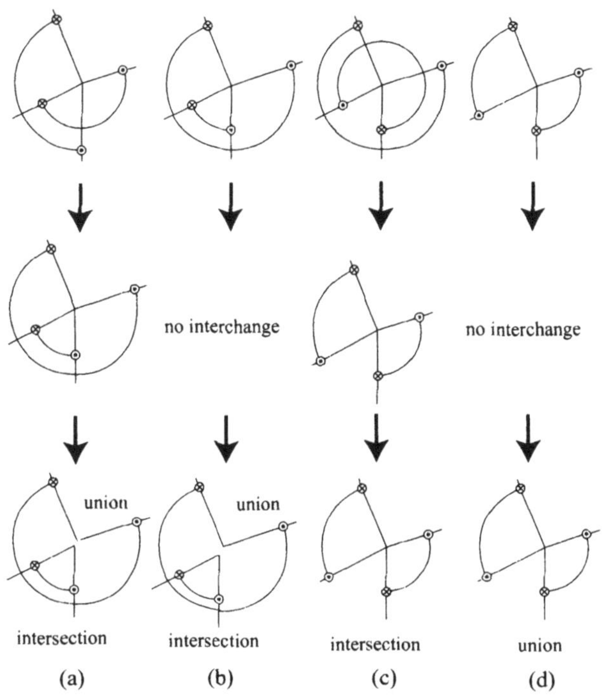

Figure 20.21: Various cases of quarter edge interchanges.

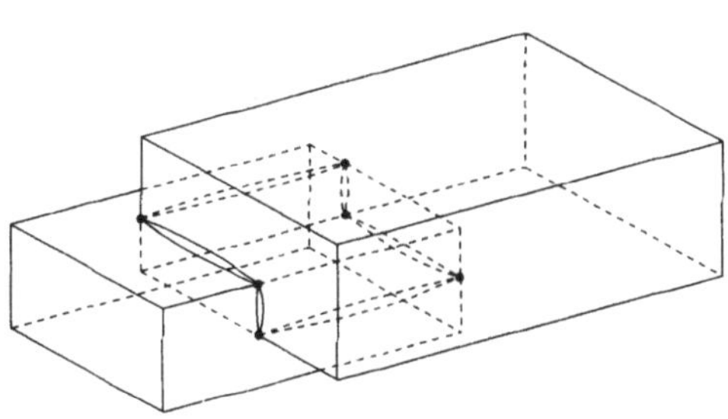

Figure 20.22: Dividing edge loops.

Here, we swap between the same directed quarter edges in a different edge-loop by using an operator **swapl**$_e$ [3]. In Fig. 20.20 we swap either between "aq1" and "bq1," or, between "aq0" and "bq0." Fig.20.20(b) shows a swap between "aq1" and "bq1."

This operation can be performed in a random fashion with respect to all the intersection line edges.

The quarter edge interchanges are done in accordance with intersection types (Fig. 20.21).

6. **Division of edge**

   With respect to all the intersection edges that have been interchanged between the quarter edges, we divide the multiple-loop edge (multiplicity=2) into two simple-loop edges by using an operator **mekl**$_e$(Fig. 20.22). This step can also be performed randomly, irrespectively of the order of edges of the intersection line loop.

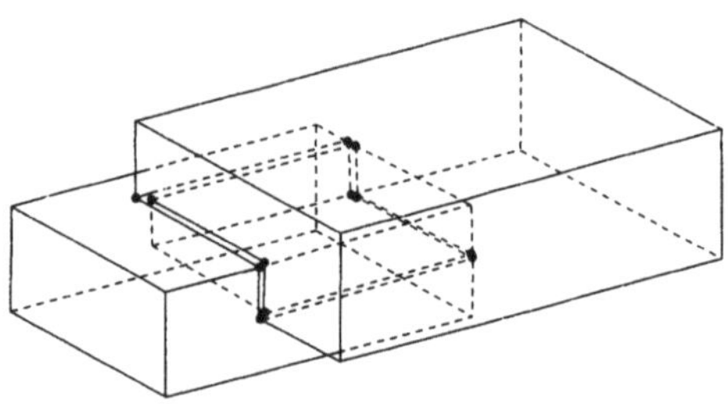

Figure 20.23: Dividing vertices.

7. **Division of vertices**

   At this point of processing, each vertex of intersection lines has the loop-multiplicity=2. Thus we divide each such vertex into two simple-loop ones by using an operator **mvkg**, and part the solid into two, i.e., *union* and *intersection* solids (Fig. 20.23).

8. **Division of solid**

   At the end of the preceding step we have two solids visually, but have in reality one solid having two shells in the data structure. All we have to do at the final step is to perform an operator **shl2sld** [4]. This assigns each shell to a solid. Then the solid divisioning is complete (Fig. 20.24).

---

[3] **swapl**$_e$ is a special operator used only for set operations. It swaps the combination of faces on an edge-loop.

[4] **shl2sld** is a special operator used only for set operations. The operator takes out one shell in a solid and makes a new solid including it.

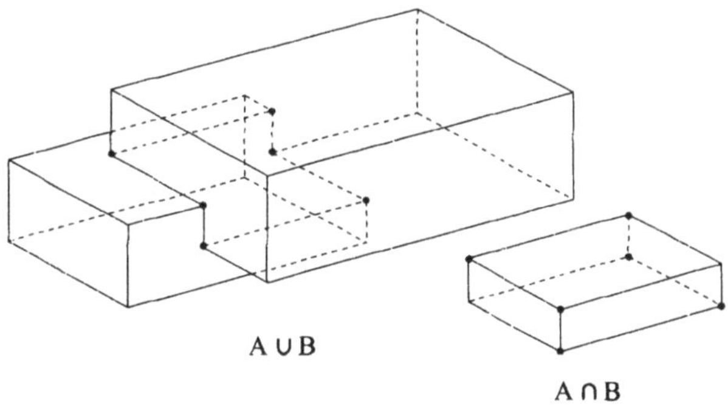

Figure 20.24: Dividing solid.

20.6 Set Operations on Curved Objects

In the preceding sections of this chapter we have presented a completely robust set operation algorithm on polyhedra. A question may arise; is it possible to attain the same complete robustness in the set operations between curved objects ? This is a very difficult problem.

When dealing with this problem algebraically, we must solve polynomials of very high degree. For instance the degree of the intersection curve between bi-cubic Bézier surfaces is 324. It is known that we cannot solve a polynomial equation algebraically having a higher degree than 5. It seems almost impossible to construct a completely robust set operation algorithm on curved objects.

Note, however, that what we need essentially in making a robust set operation algorithm is not to get exact coordinates of intersection points, but to find exactly if there exists an intersection point in a given surface region or not.

In this section we shall show a technique of attaining this purpose by using the Sturm's theorem and exact arithmetic of the Four-dimensional Processing [66],[37],[30](see Chapter 16).

20.6.1 Sturm's Theorem

The Sturm's theorem enables to exactly detect the number of real roots of a polynomial equation in a given interval.

We shall detect the number of the real roots of the following polynomial:

$$a_0x^n + a_1x^{n-1} + a_2x^{n-2} + \ldots + a_{n-1}x + a_n = 0. \tag{20.16}$$

We write the left side of the equation above as $S_1(x)$:

$$S_1(x) = a_0x^n + a_1x^{n-1} + a_2x^{n-2} + \ldots + a_{n-1}x + a_n \tag{20.17}$$

and write the derivative of $S_1(x)$ as $S_2(x)$:

$$S_2(x) = na_0x^{n-1} + (n-1)a_1x^{n-2} + (n-2)a_2x^{n-3} + \ldots + a_{n-1}. \tag{20.18}$$

From eqs.(20.17) and (20.18), we generate $S_k(x)$:

$$S_k(x) = \{\text{remainder of } (S_{k-2}(x)/S_{k-1}(x))\} \times (-1) \tag{20.19}$$

until $S_k(x)$ becomes a constant. Here, we denote the last polynomial by $S_m(x)$; that is, $S_{m-1}(x)$ is exactly divisible by $S_m(x)$ and

$$S_{m+1}(x) = 0. \tag{20.20}$$

Sequence of functions $S_k(x)$ $(1 \leq k \leq m)$ generated as above is called *Sturm sequence*. We denote the number of sign changes of $S_k(x)$ $(1 \leq k \leq m)$ at $x = x$ as $var(S(x))$, where we count the number by ignoring 0. We also denote the number of no sign-changes by $per(S(x))$:

$$per(S(x)) = m - 1 - var(S(x)). \tag{20.21}$$

Now, we introduce the Sturm's theorem.

Theorem 20.1 (Sturm's theorem)
The number of real solutions in interval $[a, b]$ *is equal to* $per(S(b)) - per(S(a))$, *where we suppose* a *and* b *are not the solutions, and count one for multiple root.*

20.6.2 Sturm's Theorem of Several Variables

Extending the Sturm sequence yields Sturm sequence of several variables. By using this, we can detect the number of common real roots contained in an n-dimensional parallelepiped with respect to n polynomial equations of n variables.

Computation of Volume Function

In order to generate the Sturm sequence of several variables, we must first compute a volume function.

We shall detect the number of common roots among n polynomial equations of n variables:

$$f_i(x_1, x_2, \ldots, x_n) \quad (1 \leq i \leq n)$$

and put

$$f_{n+1} = u + (x_1 - a_1)(x_2 - a_2)\ldots(x_n - a_n). \tag{20.22}$$

The volume function is computed by eliminating n new variables a_i $(1 \leq i \leq n)$ from the $n+1$ equations of $f_i(x_1, x_2, \ldots, x_n)$ $(1 \leq i \leq n)$ and eq.(20.22) [37].

When $n = 2$, the volume function is given as follows:

$$V(u, x_1, x_2) = \frac{Res_{a_2}(Res_{a_1}(f_1(a_1, a_2), f_3), Res_{a_1}(f_2(a_1, a_2), f_3))}{u^{deg(f_1(x_1,0))deg(f_2(x_2,0))}}, \tag{20.23}$$

where

$$f_3(u, x_1, x_2, a_1, a_2) = u + (x_1 - a_1)(x_2 - a_2). \tag{20.24}$$

In eq.(20.23), $Res_x(f_1(x), f_2(x))$ is a resultant for the elimination of variable x from $f_1(x)$ and $f_2(x)$, and $deg(f(x))$ represents the degree of $f(x)$. We use the Sylvester resultant for the elimination of one variable from two polynomial equations [30].

Generation of Sturm Sequence of Several Variables

We consider the volume function as a function of one variable u, and generate Sturm sequence:

$$V_k(u, x_1, \ldots, x_n) \ (1 \leq k \leq m).$$

We denote the sequence above when $u=0$ by $M_k(x_1, \ldots, x_n)$:

$$M_k(x_1, \ldots, x_n) \equiv V_k(0, x_1, \ldots, x_n) \ (1 \leq k \leq m), \tag{20.25}$$

which is the Sturm sequence of n variables.

Detection of the Number of Real Roots

The detection of the number of real roots is performed by counting the numbers of sign changes of the Sturm sequence at the ends of a given domain.

Let an n-dimensional parallelepiped, which is parallel to coordinate axes, be:

$$I_i = [a_1, b_1] \times \ldots \times [a_i, b_i] \ (1 \leq i \leq n), \tag{20.26}$$

where a_i and b_i are the minimum and maximum values of variable x_i within its range, respectively. The n-dimensional parallelepiped represents a line segment, a rectangle and a cuboid when $n=1, 2$ and 3, respectively.

If we denote the Sturm sequence of n variables by M, then an evaluation function $E(M, I)$ to detect the number of common real roots in I_i is given as follows:

$$E_0(M, I) = 2per(M), \tag{20.27}$$

$$E_i(M, I) = \frac{1}{2}(E_{i-1}(M(x_i \leftarrow b_i), I) - E_{i-1}(M(x_i \leftarrow a_i), I)), \tag{20.28}$$

where $f(x_i \leftarrow a_i)$ represents substitution of a_i into x_i.

From eqs.(20.27) and (20.28), we have the evaluation functions for $n=1$ and $n=2$ as follows:

$$E_1(M, I) = per(M(b)) - per(M(a)), \tag{20.29}$$

$$E_2(M, I) = \frac{1}{2}\{per(M(b_1, b_2)) + per(M(a_1, a_2)) - per(M(b_1, a_2)) - per(M(a_1, b_2))\}. \tag{20.30}$$

Eqs.(20.29) and (20.30) represent the numbers of real roots contained in a range $[a, b]$ and a rectangular interval $[a_1, b_1] \times [a_2, b_2]$, respectively.

20.6.3 Existence Detection of Intersection Points

We shall discuss the existence detection of the intersection point of three surfaces and determine the existence region in both parameter space and Euclidean coordinate space.

Existence Detection in Parameter Space

We write a parametric, homogeneous surface patch (surface patch 1) as:

$$(w_1(s,t), X_1(s,t), Y_1(s,t), Z_1(s,t)). \qquad (20.31)$$

Substitution of the surface representation above into two other surface patch representations, which are in implicit forms:

$$f_2(w, X, Y, Z) = 0, \qquad (20.32)$$
$$f_3(w, X, Y, Z) = 0, \qquad (20.33)$$

yields two representations in parameters s and t:

$$f_2(s,t) = 0, \qquad (20.34)$$
$$f_3(s,t) = 0. \qquad (20.35)$$

Eqs.(20.34) and (20.35) represent two intersection space curves between the surface patch 1 and patch 2, and between the surface patch 1 and patch 3, respectively. The intersection of these two curves is the intersection point of surface patches 1, 2 and 3 (see Fig. 20.25).

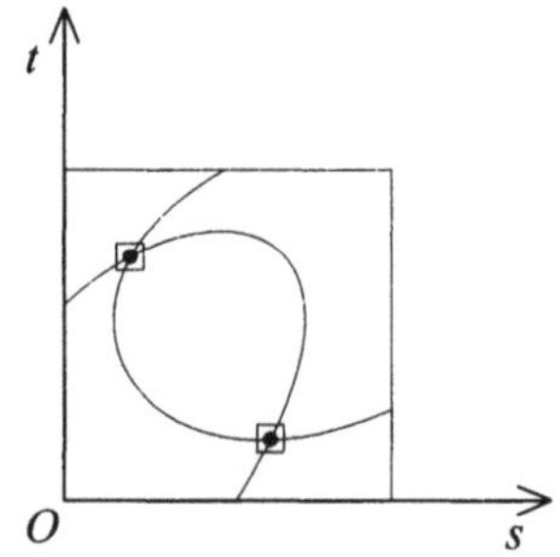

Figure 20.25: A parameter space of a surface.

We generate the Sturm sequence of two variables, s and t, from these equations. By using the evaluation function, eq.(20.30), we detect the number of real roots contained in the rectangular interval $[0,1] \times [0,1]$, that is, in the surface patch 1.

If an intersection point is found to exist, then its region of existence is determined. Rectangular interval $[0,1] \times [0,1]$ is subdivided into four and each sub-region is tested for existence of the intersection point. By repeating this

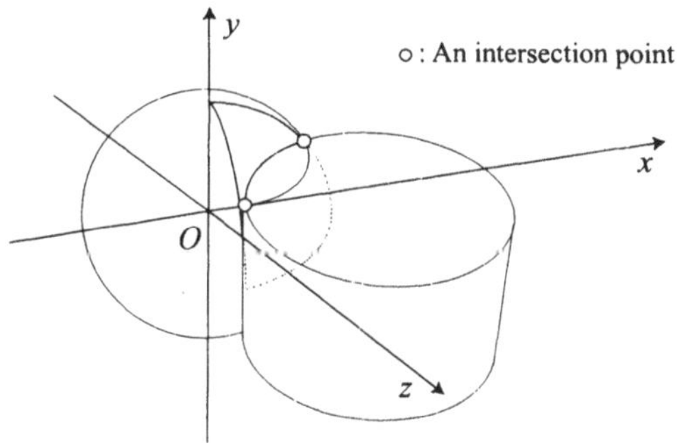

Figure 20.26: Intersection points of a sphere and a cylinder.

operation, an infinitesimal rectangular area containing the intersection point is obtained (see Fig. 20.25).

The four corner points of the rectangular area can also be used for the containment test of the intersection point in another surface area. If the test results for the four points are the same, we take the result for the intersection point. Otherwise, we subdivide the rectangle and perform the same test. Because the four corner points are obtained exactly, the containment test is exact.

As mentioned above, we can determine the existence region of an intersection point in the parameter space of the surface patch 1. Similarly we can determine the region with respect to the surface patches 2 and 3.

Existence Detection in Euclidean Coordinate Space

First, we generate the Sturm sequence of three variables from three implicit functions of surfaces. Next, we count the number of real roots in an appropriately given rectangular interval. The enclosing box for the surface patch may be a good choice for the interval. If an intersection point is found to exist, then the interval is made smaller and smaller. Finally we get an infinitesimal parallelepiped region containing the intersection point. The eight corner points of the parallelepiped region can also be used for the exact containment test of the intersection point in another surface area.

20.6.4 An Example

We shall demonstrate an example by detecting the number of intersection points among a spherical surface, a cylindrical surface and a plane (upper plane of the cylinder), using the methods discussed in the preceding sections (Fig. 20.26). For the computations of the example, MATHEMATICA was used.

We assume that the sphere is centered at $(0, 0, 0)$ and its radius is 4, and the cylinder is centered at the axis of $(x=0, z=4)$ and its radius is 4.

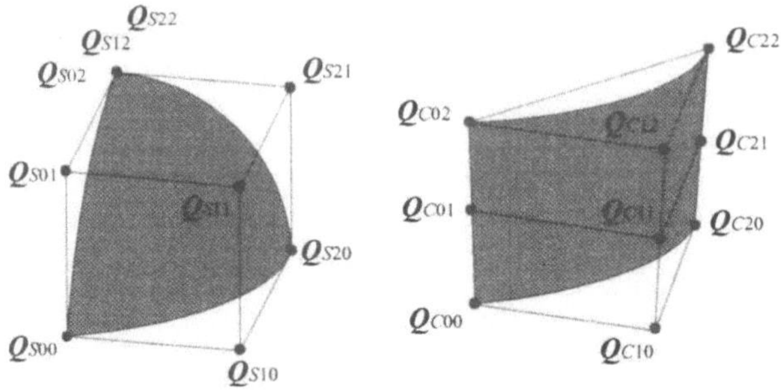

(a) (b)

Figure 20.27: Homogeneous Bézier rectangular surfaces.

Surface Patch for a Sphere

Control vectors are (see Fig. 20.27(a)):

$$\begin{aligned}
\boldsymbol{Q}_{s00} &= [1\ 0\ 0\ 4],\ \boldsymbol{Q}_{s01} = [1\ 0\ 4\ 4],\ \boldsymbol{Q}_{s02} = [2\ 0\ 8\ 0],\\
\boldsymbol{Q}_{s10} &= [1\ 4\ 0\ 4],\ \boldsymbol{Q}_{s11} = [1\ 4\ 4\ 4],\ \boldsymbol{Q}_{s12} = [2\ 0\ 8\ 0],\\
\boldsymbol{Q}_{s20} &= [2\ 8\ 0\ 0],\ \boldsymbol{Q}_{s21} = [2\ 8\ 8\ 0],\ \boldsymbol{Q}_{s22} = [4\ 0\ 16\ 0].
\end{aligned}$$

Parametric representation

$$w = (s^2+1)(t^2+1), \tag{20.36}$$
$$X = -8s(t^2-1), \tag{20.37}$$
$$Y = 8t(s^2+1), \tag{20.38}$$
$$Z = 4(s^2-1)(t^2-1). \tag{20.39}$$

Implicit representation

$$X^2+Y^2+Z^2-16w^2=0. \tag{20.40}$$

Surface patch for a cylinder

Control vectors are (see Fig. 20.27(b)):

$$\begin{aligned}
\boldsymbol{Q}_{c00} &= [1\ 4\ \ -3\ 0],\ \boldsymbol{Q}_{c01} = [1\ 4\ 0\ 0],\ \boldsymbol{Q}_{c02} = [1\ 4\ 3\ 0],\\
\boldsymbol{Q}_{c10} &= [1\ 0\ \ -3\ 0],\ \boldsymbol{Q}_{c11} = [1\ 0\ 0\ 0],\ \boldsymbol{Q}_{c12} = [1\ 0\ 3\ 0],\\
\boldsymbol{Q}_{c20} &= [2\ 0\ \ -6\ 8],\ \boldsymbol{Q}_{c21} = [2\ 0\ 0\ 8],\ \boldsymbol{Q}_{c22} = [2\ 0\ 6\ 8].
\end{aligned}$$

Parametric representation

$$w = s^2+1, \tag{20.41}$$

$$X = 4(s-1)^2, \tag{20.42}$$
$$Y = 3(s^2+1)(2t-1), \tag{20.43}$$
$$Z = 8s^2. \tag{20.44}$$

Implicit representation

$$X^2 + Z^2 - 8Xw - 8Zw + 16w^2 = 0. \tag{20.45}$$

Upper plane of cylinder

$$Y = 3w. \tag{20.46}$$

Detection in Parameter Space

Here we detect the number of intersection points in the parameter space of the spherical surface.

Substituting the parametric representations, eqs.(20.36)~(20.39), into eqs. (20.45) and (20.46) yields:

$$f_1(s,t) = 64(s^2+1)(st^4+t^4+s^2-s), \tag{20.47}$$
$$f_2(s,t) = -(s^2+1)(3t^2-8t+3). \tag{20.48}$$

From the equations above we generate the Sturm sequence of two variables M and determine the number of no sign-change in interval [0,1]×[0, 1], that is, the value of *per* operators. The results are shown below:

$$\begin{array}{l} per(M(0,0)) = 2,\ per(M(0,1)) = 0, \\ per(M(1,0)) = 0,\ per(M(1,1)) = 2. \end{array} \tag{20.49}$$

Therefore we obtain the number of intersection points contained in the surface patch by using the evaluation function:

$$E_2(M,I) = \frac{1}{2}(2+2-0-0) = 2, \tag{20.50}$$

which is correct.

Because there exist intersection points, the region containing the point is repeatedly subdivided into four, and the number of intersection points is tested for each subdivided region. Finally we get infinitesimal small regions containing intersection points as follows:

$$\begin{aligned}(s,t) = &\left(\left[\frac{745}{16384}, \frac{373}{8192}\right], \left[\frac{1849}{4096}, \frac{7397}{16384}\right]\right), \\ &\left(\left[\frac{7479}{8192}, \frac{14959}{16384}\right], \left[\frac{1849}{4096}, \frac{7397}{16384}\right]\right) \\ = &([0.04547119140625, 0.0455322265625], \\ &[0.451416015625, 0.45147705078125]), \\ &([0.9129638671875, 0.91302490234375], \\ &[0.451416015625, 0.45147705078125]). \end{aligned} \tag{20.51}$$

Approximated parameter values of the intersection point is shown below:

$$
\begin{aligned}
(s,t) = {} & (0.0454821797493118, 0.451416229645136), \\
& (0.912992912494754, 0.451416229645136).
\end{aligned}
\tag{20.52}
$$

Detection in Euclidean Space

We generate the Sturm sequence of three variables x, y and z from eqs.(20.40), (20.45) and (20.46), and count the number of intersection points contained in the enclosing box for the spherical patch, that is, interval $[0,4]\times[0,4]\times[0,4]$. The test result yields two intersection points. Then we repeatedly subdivide the parallelepiped region into eight and determine the number of intersection points in each region. The final result is as follows:

$$
\begin{aligned}
(x,y,z) = {} & \left(\left[\frac{1967}{8192}, \frac{3935}{16384}\right], 3, \left[\frac{43169}{16384}, \frac{21585}{8192}\right]\right), \\
& \left(\left[\frac{43169}{16384}, \frac{21582}{8192}\right], 3, \left[\frac{1967}{8192}, \frac{3935}{16384}\right]\right) \\
= {} & ([0.2401123046875, 0.24017333984375], 3, \\
& [2.63482666615625, 2.6348876953125]), \\
& ([2.63482666615625, 2.6348876953125], 3, \\
& [0.2401123046875, 0.24017333984375]).
\end{aligned}
\tag{20.53}
$$

An approximated coordinate representation of the intersection point is:

$$
\begin{aligned}
(x,y,z) = {} & (0.240172246208248, 3, 2.63482775379175), \\
& (2.63482775379175, 3, 0.240172246208248).
\end{aligned}
\tag{20.54}
$$

Chapter 21

Polyhedron Subdivisions

This chapter is included to show a simple application of the Four-dimensional Processing to surface generation by polyhedron subdivision, and to show an example of how generality of representational capability is increased by a simple homogenization.

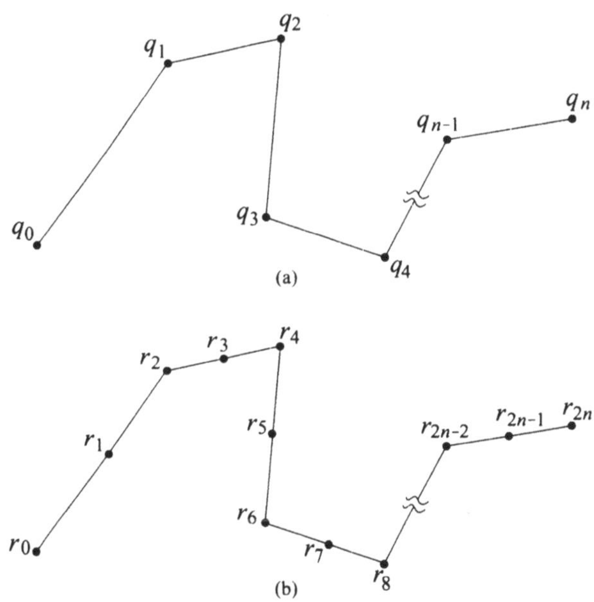

Figure 21.1: Chaikin's algorithm (1).

21.1 Chaikin's Algorithm

G.M. Chaikin proposed a method of generating curves procedurally, using a very simple geometrical algorithm, without depending on mathematical representations [9]. Suppose that a polygon $q_0 q_1 \ldots q_n$ is given, as in Fig. 21.1(a). Find the midpoints of all of the sides, and relabel the initially given vertices and these points as $r_0, r_1, \ldots, r_{2n}$ (Fig. 21.1(b)).

Fig. 21.2(a) shows just the vertex $b(r_i)$ of the initial polygon and the midpoints $a(r_{i-1})$ and $c(r_{i+1})$ of the two sides attached to it.

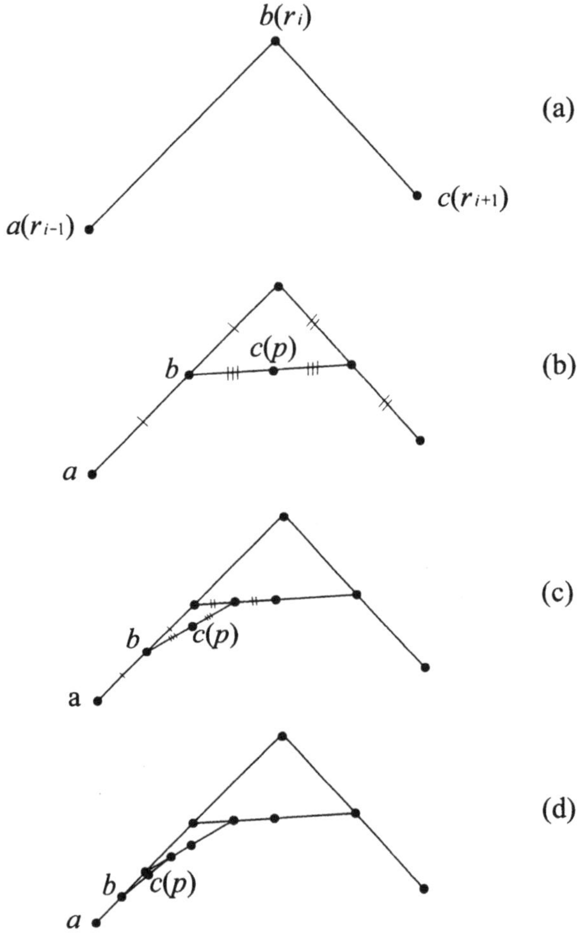

Figure 21.2: Chaikin's algorithm (2).

Letting p be the midpoint of the line segment formed by connecting the midpoints of sides ab and bc, we have:

$$p = \frac{\frac{a+b}{2} + \frac{b+c}{2}}{2} = \frac{a + 2b + c}{4}. \tag{21.1}$$

This point p becomes one point on the curve being generated. This division produces a set of 2 sides on either side of the point p. Eq.(21.1) can be applied to both of these sides. We push the set of 2 sides on the right side, for example, into stack and then apply eq.(21.1) again to the set of 2 sides on the left. This operation is repeated, pushing the set of 2 sides on the right into stack each time, until the length of the set of 2 sides on the left reaches a certain limit. At this point the contents of stack are poped up and similar operations are performed on them until stack is empty. This generates a sequence of points on the curve corresponding to $r_{i-1}r_ir_{i+1}$. If the processing above is performed for all groups of $r_{i-1}r_ir_{i+1}(i = 2, 4, \ldots, 2n-2)$, a curve corresponding to the given polygon $q_0q_1\ldots q_n$ is generated. An example of such a curve is shown in Fig. 21.3 .

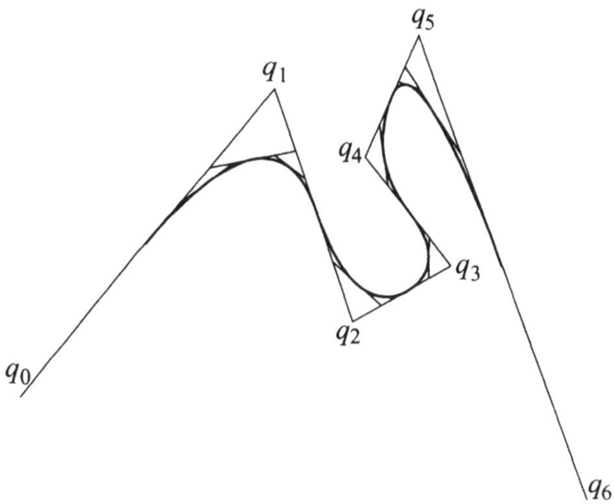

Figure 21.3: An example of a curve generated by Chaikin's method.

As can be understood from the generation process above, the curve segment is completely determined by only 3 points r_{i-1}, r_i, r_{i+1}. It has one end at r_{i-1} and the other at r_{i+1}. Its slope at r_{i-1} is in the direction of the line segment $\overrightarrow{r_{i-1}r_i}$, and its slope at r_{i+1} is in the direction of the line segment $\overrightarrow{r_ir_{i+1}}$. Since the curve passes through the point p calculated with eq.(21.1), it is evident that the curve is a parabola [1)].

Let us find the equation of this parabola [48]. Writing the curve function in the form

$$\boldsymbol{p}_i(t) = [t^2\ t\ 1]\begin{bmatrix}\boldsymbol{a}\\\boldsymbol{b}\\\boldsymbol{c}\end{bmatrix}, \tag{21.2}$$

we obtain:

$$\dot{\boldsymbol{p}}_i(t) = [2t\ 1\ 0]\begin{bmatrix}\boldsymbol{a}\\\boldsymbol{b}\\\boldsymbol{c}\end{bmatrix}. \tag{21.3}$$

[1)] See page 340 of [58].

Since we have the relations $\boldsymbol{p}_i(0)=\boldsymbol{r}_{i-1}$, $\boldsymbol{p}_i(1)=\boldsymbol{r}_{i+1}$, $\dot{\boldsymbol{p}}_i(0)=h(\boldsymbol{r}_i-\boldsymbol{r}_{i-1})$, $\dot{\boldsymbol{p}}_i(1)=k(\boldsymbol{r}_{i+1}-\boldsymbol{r}_i)$, the following equation is obtained:

$$\begin{bmatrix} \boldsymbol{r}_{i-1} \\ \boldsymbol{r}_{i+1} \\ h(\boldsymbol{r}_i - \boldsymbol{r}_{i-1}) \\ k(\boldsymbol{r}_{i+1} - \boldsymbol{r}_i) \end{bmatrix} = \begin{bmatrix} 0 & 0 & 1 \\ 1 & 1 & 1 \\ 0 & 1 & 0 \\ 2 & 1 & 0 \end{bmatrix} \begin{bmatrix} \boldsymbol{a} \\ \boldsymbol{b} \\ \boldsymbol{c} \end{bmatrix}. \tag{21.4}$$

Converting the first matrix on the right-hand side into a square matrix gives:

$$\begin{bmatrix} \boldsymbol{r}_{i-1} \\ \boldsymbol{r}_{i+1} \\ h(\boldsymbol{r}_i - \boldsymbol{r}_{i-1}) \\ k(\boldsymbol{r}_{i+1} - \boldsymbol{r}_i) \end{bmatrix} = \begin{bmatrix} 0 & 0 & 1 & 1 \\ 1 & 1 & 1 & 1 \\ 0 & 1 & 0 & 1 \\ 2 & 1 & 0 & 1 \end{bmatrix} \begin{bmatrix} \boldsymbol{a} \\ \boldsymbol{b} \\ \boldsymbol{c} \\ \boldsymbol{0} \end{bmatrix}. \tag{21.5}$$

This implies:

$$\begin{aligned} \begin{bmatrix} \boldsymbol{a} \\ \boldsymbol{b} \\ \boldsymbol{c} \\ \boldsymbol{0} \end{bmatrix} &= \begin{bmatrix} 0 & 0 & 1 & 1 \\ 1 & 1 & 1 & 1 \\ 0 & 1 & 0 & 1 \\ 2 & 1 & 0 & 1 \end{bmatrix}^{-1} \begin{bmatrix} \boldsymbol{r}_{i-1} \\ \boldsymbol{r}_{i+1} \\ h(\boldsymbol{r}_i - \boldsymbol{r}_{i-1}) \\ k(\boldsymbol{r}_{i+1} - \boldsymbol{r}_i) \end{bmatrix} \\ &= \begin{bmatrix} 0 & 0 & -1/2 & 1/2 \\ -1 & 1 & 1/2 & -1/2 \\ 0 & 1 & -1/2 & -1/2 \\ 1 & -1 & 1/2 & 1/2 \end{bmatrix} \begin{bmatrix} \boldsymbol{r}_{i-1} \\ \boldsymbol{r}_{i+1} \\ h(\boldsymbol{r}_i - \boldsymbol{r}_{i-1}) \\ k(\boldsymbol{r}_{i+1} - \boldsymbol{r}_i) \end{bmatrix} \\ &= \begin{bmatrix} \frac{h}{2}\boldsymbol{r}_{i-1} - \frac{1}{2}(h+k)\boldsymbol{r}_i + \frac{k}{2}\boldsymbol{r}_{i+1} \\ -(1+\frac{h}{2})\boldsymbol{r}_{i-1} + \frac{1}{2}(h+k)\boldsymbol{r}_i + (1-\frac{k}{2})\boldsymbol{r}_{i+1} \\ \frac{h}{2}\boldsymbol{r}_{i-1} + \frac{1}{2}(k-h)\boldsymbol{r}_i + (1-\frac{k}{2})\boldsymbol{r}_{i+1} \\ (1-\frac{h}{2})\boldsymbol{r}_{i-1} + \frac{1}{2}(h-k)\boldsymbol{r}_i - (1-\frac{k}{2})\boldsymbol{r}_{i+1} \end{bmatrix}. \end{aligned} \tag{21.6}$$

Equating the 4-th rows of the matrices on both sides gives:

$$(1-\frac{h}{2})\boldsymbol{r}_{i-1} + \frac{1}{2}(h-k)\boldsymbol{r}_i - (1-\frac{k}{2})\boldsymbol{r}_{i+1} = \boldsymbol{0}, \tag{21.7}$$

which yields:

$$h=k=2. \tag{21.8}$$

Therefore:

$$\begin{bmatrix} \boldsymbol{a} \\ \boldsymbol{b} \\ \boldsymbol{c} \end{bmatrix} = \begin{bmatrix} \boldsymbol{r}_{i-1} - 2\boldsymbol{r}_i + \boldsymbol{r}_{i+1} \\ 2\boldsymbol{r}_i - 2\boldsymbol{r}_{i-1} \\ \boldsymbol{r}_{i-1} \end{bmatrix}. \tag{21.9}$$

Thus, the parabola function $\boldsymbol{p}_i(t)$ becomes:

$$\boldsymbol{p}_i(t) = [t^2 \ t \ 1] \begin{bmatrix} \boldsymbol{a} \\ \boldsymbol{b} \\ \boldsymbol{c} \end{bmatrix}$$

$$
\begin{aligned}
&= [t^2\ t\ 1] \begin{bmatrix} \boldsymbol{r}_{i-1} - 2\boldsymbol{r}_i + \boldsymbol{r}_{i+1} \\ 2\boldsymbol{r}_i - 2\boldsymbol{r}_{i-1} \\ \boldsymbol{r}_{i-1} \end{bmatrix} \\
&= [t^2\ t\ 1] \begin{bmatrix} 1 & -2 & 1 \\ -2 & 2 & 0 \\ 1 & 0 & 0 \end{bmatrix} \begin{bmatrix} \boldsymbol{r}_{i-1} \\ \boldsymbol{r}_i \\ \boldsymbol{r}_{i+1} \end{bmatrix} \\
&= [(1-t)^2\ 2t(1-t)\ t^2] \begin{bmatrix} \boldsymbol{r}_{i-1} \\ \boldsymbol{r}_i \\ \boldsymbol{r}_{i+1} \end{bmatrix} \\
&\equiv [B_{0,2}(t)\ B_{1,2}(t)\ B_{2,2}(t)] \begin{bmatrix} \boldsymbol{r}_{i-1} \\ \boldsymbol{r}_i \\ \boldsymbol{r}_{i+1} \end{bmatrix}, (i=2,4,\ldots,2n-2),
\end{aligned} \tag{21.10}
$$

where $B_{0,2}(t), B_{1,2}(t), B_{2,2}(t)$ are Bernstein polynomials of degree 2. It is clear that $p_i(t)$ is a quadratic Bézier curve segment corresponding to the sequence of vertices r_{i-1}, r_i, r_{i+1}. It is easy to confirm that the following relations hold in this case (see Fig. 21.4):

$$
\boldsymbol{p}_i(1/2) = \frac{\boldsymbol{r}_{i-1} + 2\boldsymbol{r}_i + \boldsymbol{r}_{i+1}}{4}, \quad \dot{\boldsymbol{p}}_i(1/2) = \boldsymbol{r}_{i+1} - \boldsymbol{r}_{i-1}. \tag{21.11}
$$

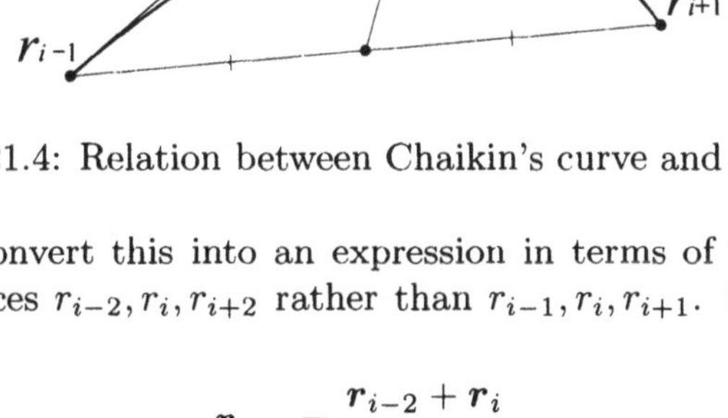

Figure 21.4: Relation between Chaikin's curve and polygon.

Let us now convert this into an expression in terms of the initially given sequence of vertices r_{i-2}, r_i, r_{i+2} rather than r_{i-1}, r_i, r_{i+1}. Since we have the relations:

$$
\begin{aligned}
\boldsymbol{r}_{i-1} &= \frac{\boldsymbol{r}_{i-2} + \boldsymbol{r}_i}{2}, \\
\boldsymbol{r}_{i+1} &= \frac{\boldsymbol{r}_i + \boldsymbol{r}_{i+2}}{2},
\end{aligned}
$$

the curve becomes:

$$
\boldsymbol{p}_i(t) = [(1-t)^2\ 2t(1-t)\ t^2] \begin{bmatrix} \boldsymbol{r}_{i-1} \\ \boldsymbol{r}_i \\ \boldsymbol{r}_{i+1} \end{bmatrix}
$$

$$= [(1-t)^2 \; 2t(1-t) \; t^2] \begin{bmatrix} 1/2 & 1/2 & 0 \\ 0 & 1 & 0 \\ 0 & 1/2 & 1/2 \end{bmatrix} \begin{bmatrix} \boldsymbol{r}_{i-2} \\ \boldsymbol{r}_i \\ \boldsymbol{r}_{i+2} \end{bmatrix}$$

$$= [\frac{1}{2}(1-t)^2 \quad -t^2+t+\frac{1}{2} \;\; \frac{1}{2}t^2] \begin{bmatrix} \boldsymbol{r}_{i-2} \\ \boldsymbol{r}_i \\ \boldsymbol{r}_{i+2} \end{bmatrix}$$

$$\equiv [N_{0,3}(t) \; N_{1,3}(t) \; N_{2,3}(t)] \begin{bmatrix} \boldsymbol{r}_{i-2} \\ \boldsymbol{r}_i \\ \boldsymbol{r}_{i+2} \end{bmatrix}, (i=2,4,\ldots,2n-2).$$

If we let $i/2$ be a new subscript and call this i instead, then

$$\boldsymbol{p}_i(t) = [N_{0,3}(t) \; N_{1,3}(t) \; N_{2,3}(t)] \begin{bmatrix} \boldsymbol{q}_{i-1} \\ \boldsymbol{q}_i \\ \boldsymbol{q}_{i+1} \end{bmatrix}, (i=1,2,\ldots,n-1). \tag{21.12}$$

This means that the function expresses a uniform B-spline curve of order 3 with respect to polygon $q_0q_1q_2 \ldots q_{n-1}q_n$.

21.2 Homogenization of Chaikin's Algorithm

We shall homogenize the Chaikin's algorithm. Suppose a sequence of vectors $\boldsymbol{Q}_0, \boldsymbol{Q}_1, \ldots, \boldsymbol{Q}_n$ is given in homogeneous coordinate vectors $[w_i \; X_i \; Y_i]$, and in vector space $\mathbf{R}^3$ we shall perform exactly the same operations as we did in the preceding section.

For $r_0, r_1, \ldots, r_{2n}$ in the preceding section we use capital bold letters $\boldsymbol{R}_0, \boldsymbol{R}_1, \ldots, \boldsymbol{R}_{2n}$ this time (see Fig. 21.5(a)). By using an operation corresponding to eq.(21.1) we get a new sequence of vectors.

This subdivision generates the following homogeneous Bézier curve of degree 2, which is equivalent to a rational quadratic Bézier curve:

$$\overline{\overline{\boldsymbol{P}_i(t)} = [B_{0,2}(t) \; B_{1,2}(t) \; B_{2,2}(t)] \begin{bmatrix} \boldsymbol{R}_{i-1} \\ \boldsymbol{R}_i \\ \boldsymbol{R}_{i+1} \end{bmatrix}}, \quad (i=2,4,\ldots,2n-2), \tag{21.13}$$

where $\boldsymbol{R}_i = [w_i \; X_i \; Y_i]$.

Or, the curve form is also represented as below (see Fig. 21.5(b)):

$$\overline{\overline{\boldsymbol{P}_i(t)} = [N_{0,3}(t) \; N_{1,3}(t) \; N_{2,3}(t)] \begin{bmatrix} \boldsymbol{Q}_{i-1} \\ \boldsymbol{Q}_i \\ \boldsymbol{Q}_{i+1} \end{bmatrix}}, \quad (i=1,2,\ldots,n-1). \tag{21.14}$$

Eq.(21.14) is the homogeneous representation of a rational B-spline curve of order 3 (degree 2).

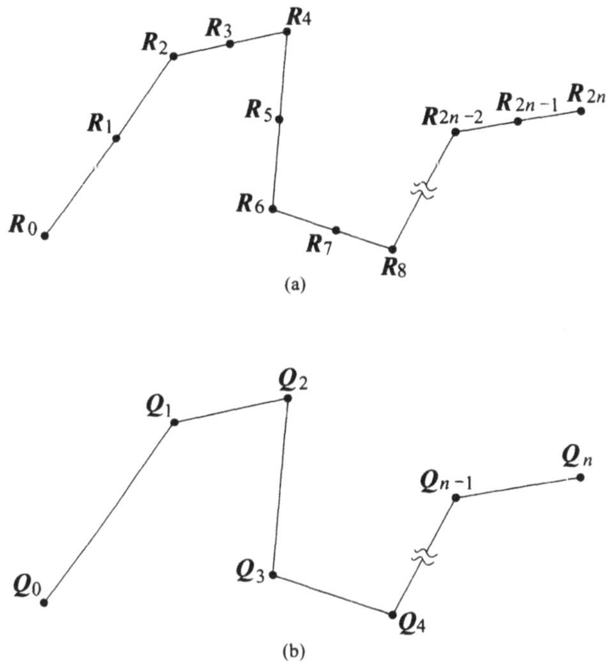

Figure 21.5: Homogenized Chaikin's algorithm.

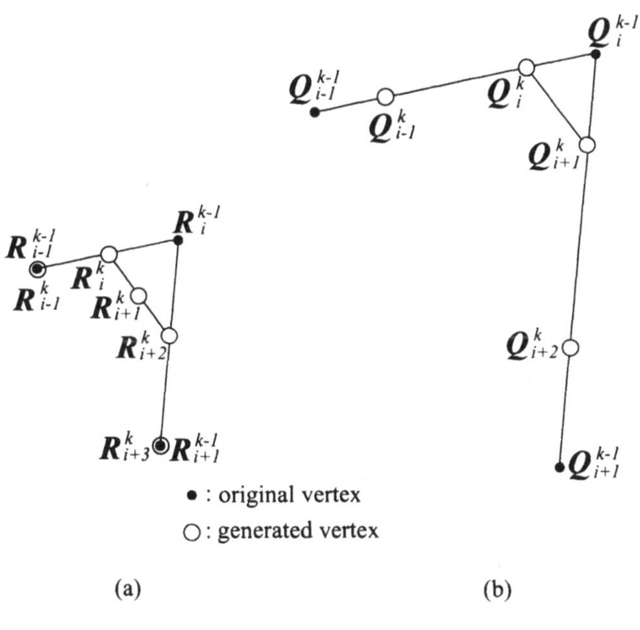

Figure 21.6: Homogenized subdivision.

At a subdivision level k, the generated vectors from points $\boldsymbol{R}_{i-1}^{k-1}\boldsymbol{R}_i^{k-1}\boldsymbol{R}_{i+1}^{k-1}$ are as follows (Fig. 21.6(a)):

$$\begin{aligned}
\boldsymbol{R}_{i-1}^k &= \boldsymbol{R}_{i-1}^{k-1}, \\
\boldsymbol{R}_i^k &= \frac{\boldsymbol{R}_{i-1}^{k-1} + \boldsymbol{R}_i^{k-1}}{2}, \\
\boldsymbol{R}_{i+1}^k &= \frac{\boldsymbol{R}_{i-1}^{k-1} + 2\boldsymbol{R}_i^{k-1} + \boldsymbol{R}_{i+1}^{k-1}}{4}, \\
\boldsymbol{R}_{i+2}^k &= \frac{\boldsymbol{R}_i^{k-1} + \boldsymbol{R}_{i+1}^{k-1}}{2}, \\
\boldsymbol{R}_{i+3}^k &= \boldsymbol{R}_{i+1}^{k-1}.
\end{aligned}$$

We can redefine all the vectors $\boldsymbol{R}_i$ generated at a subdivision level by multiplying them by 4 such that the subdivision does not include a division operation.

$$\begin{aligned}
\boldsymbol{R}_{i-1}^k &= 4\boldsymbol{R}_{i-1}^{k-1}, \\
\boldsymbol{R}_i^k &= 2\boldsymbol{R}_{i-1}^{k-1} + 2\boldsymbol{R}_i^{k-1}, \\
\boldsymbol{R}_{i+1}^k &= \boldsymbol{R}_{i-1}^{k-1} + 2\boldsymbol{R}_i^{k-1} + \boldsymbol{R}_{i+1}^{k-1}, \\
\boldsymbol{R}_{i+2}^k &= 2\boldsymbol{R}_i^{k-1} + 2\boldsymbol{R}_{i+1}^{k-1}, \\
\boldsymbol{R}_{i+3}^k &= 4\boldsymbol{R}_{i+1}^{k-1}.
\end{aligned} \tag{21.15}$$

Similarly, $\boldsymbol{Q}_i$ can be redefined as follows (Fig. 21.6(b)):

$$\begin{aligned}
\boldsymbol{Q}_{i-1}^k &= 3\boldsymbol{Q}_{i-1}^{k-1} + \boldsymbol{Q}_i^{k-1}, \\
\boldsymbol{Q}_i^k &= \boldsymbol{Q}_{i-1}^{k-1} + 3\boldsymbol{Q}_i^{k-1}, \\
\boldsymbol{Q}_{i+1}^k &= 3\boldsymbol{Q}_i^{k-1} + \boldsymbol{Q}_{i+1}^{k-1}, \\
\boldsymbol{Q}_{i+2}^k &= \boldsymbol{Q}_i^{k-1} + 3\boldsymbol{Q}_{i+1}^{k-1}.
\end{aligned} \tag{21.16}$$

21.3 Bi-quadratic Surface Generation

21.3.1 Polyhedron Subdivision Algorithm

Based on the Chaikin's subdivision algorithm to generate a quadratic curve as explained in Section 21.1, several authors applied it to surface generation [8], [13], [14], [31].

Suppose a part $v_{00}^0 \cdots v_{11}^0 \cdots v_{22}^0$ of a polyhedron is given as in Fig. 21.7(a).

A polyhedron subdivision algorithm to generate a surface is explained in the following [8], [31].

1. Find centroids $f_0^0, f_1^0, f_2^0, f_3^0$ of the vertex set of each face, and also find midpoints $e_0^0, e_1^0, e_2^0, e_3^0$ on each edge. We have made an inner polyhedron $f_0^0 e_0^0 f_1^0 e_3^0 v_{11}^0 e_1^0 f_3^0 e_2^0 f_2^0$ which corresponds to the inner polygon $r_{i-1}r_ir_{i+1}$ in the curve generation case (see Figs. 21.2(a) and 21.7(a)).

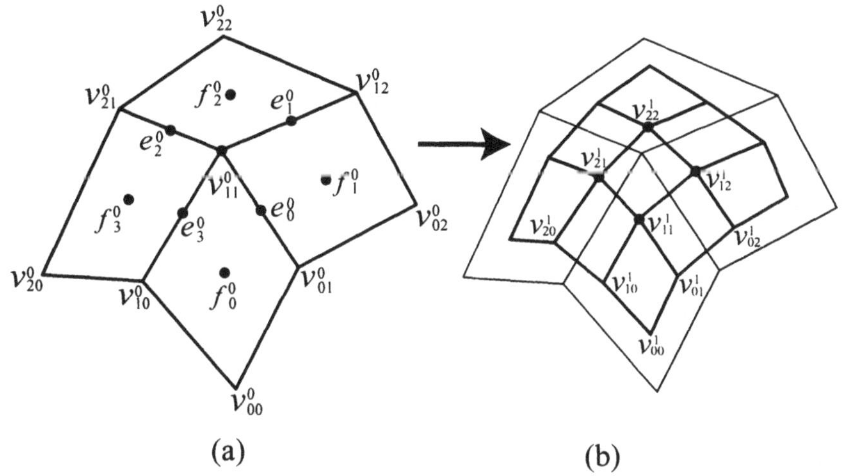

Figure 21.7: Polyhedron subdivision algorithm.

2. With respect to each inner polyhedron we apply a subdivision algorithm for surface generation. That is, find centroids $v^1_{11}, v^1_{12}, v^1_{22}, v^1_{21}$ among center vertex v^0_{11}, two midpoints e^0_j, e^0_k on each edge and centroid f^0_l of each face:

$$\left\{\begin{aligned} \boldsymbol{v}^1_{11} &= \frac{\boldsymbol{f}^0_0+\boldsymbol{e}^0_3+\boldsymbol{e}^0_0+\boldsymbol{v}^0_{11}}{4} = \frac{\boldsymbol{v}^0_{00}+3\boldsymbol{v}^0_{01}+3\boldsymbol{v}^0_{10}+9\boldsymbol{v}^0_{11}}{16}, \\ \boldsymbol{v}^1_{12} &= \frac{\boldsymbol{f}^0_1+\boldsymbol{e}^0_0+\boldsymbol{e}^0_1+\boldsymbol{v}^0_{11}}{4} = \frac{\boldsymbol{v}^0_{02}+3\boldsymbol{v}^0_{12}+3\boldsymbol{v}^0_{01}+9\boldsymbol{v}^0_{11}}{16}, \\ \boldsymbol{v}^1_{22} &= \frac{\boldsymbol{f}^0_2+\boldsymbol{e}^0_1+\boldsymbol{e}^0_2+\boldsymbol{v}^0_{11}}{4} = \frac{\boldsymbol{v}^0_{22}+3\boldsymbol{v}^0_{21}+3\boldsymbol{v}^0_{12}+9\boldsymbol{v}^0_{11}}{16}, \\ \boldsymbol{v}^1_{21} &= \frac{\boldsymbol{f}^0_3+\boldsymbol{e}^0_2+\boldsymbol{e}^0_3+\boldsymbol{v}^0_{11}}{4} = \frac{\boldsymbol{v}^0_{20}+3\boldsymbol{v}^0_{10}+3\boldsymbol{v}^0_{21}+9\boldsymbol{v}^0_{11}}{16}, \end{aligned}\right. \tag{21.17}$$

and make edges by connecting these centroids across edges. These edges are shown in bold lines in Fig. 21.7(b) which constitute a polyhedron after subdivision. Nine of these generated vertices are labeled as $v^1_{00}, \cdots, v^1_{22}$ in the figure (b).

By repeating the algorithm above, the generated polyhedron converges to a limit surface (see Section 21.3.3).

21.3.2 Transformation of a Polyhedron

Now, we shall study how a polyhedron is transformed by the subdivision algorithm [31].

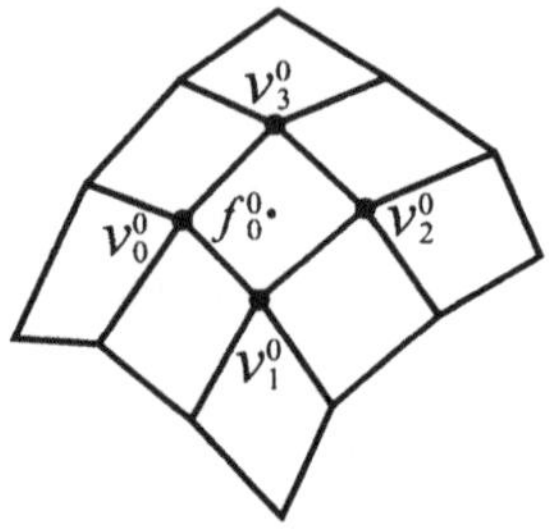

Figure 21.8: A polyhedron made up of four-sided faces.

Face Centroid

First, we suppose a polyhedron is made up of four-sided faces (see Fig. 21.8). We apply the subdivision algorithm to the polyhedron. The transformation of the central face is shown on the right in Fig. 21.9.

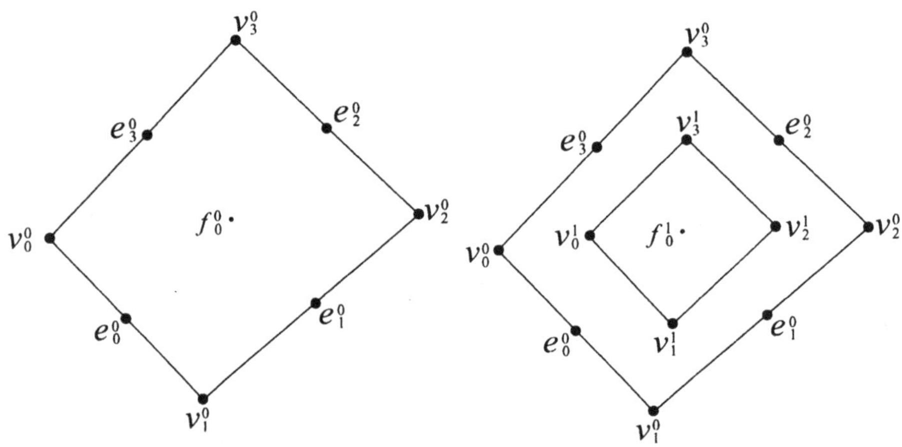

Figure 21.9: Transformation of a face.

The centroid f_0^1 of the central face after subdivision is:

$$\begin{aligned} \boldsymbol{f}_0^1 &= \frac{\boldsymbol{v}_0^1 + \boldsymbol{v}_1^1 + \boldsymbol{v}_2^1 + \boldsymbol{v}_3^1}{4} \\ &= \frac{\boldsymbol{v}_0^0 + \boldsymbol{v}_1^0 + \boldsymbol{v}_2^0 + \boldsymbol{v}_3^0 + 2\boldsymbol{e}_0^0 + 2\boldsymbol{e}_1^0 + 2\boldsymbol{e}_2^0 + 2\boldsymbol{e}_3^0 + 4\boldsymbol{f}_0^0}{16} \\ &= \frac{\boldsymbol{v}_0^0 + \boldsymbol{v}_1^0 + \boldsymbol{v}_2^0 + \boldsymbol{v}_3^0}{16} + \frac{\boldsymbol{e}_0^0 + \boldsymbol{e}_1^0 + \boldsymbol{e}_2^0 + \boldsymbol{e}_3^0}{8} + \frac{\boldsymbol{f}_0^0}{4} \\ &= \frac{\boldsymbol{f}_0^0}{4} + \frac{\boldsymbol{f}_0^0}{2} + \frac{\boldsymbol{f}_0^0}{4} = \boldsymbol{f}_0^0. \end{aligned} \tag{21.18}$$

Eq.(21.18) means that the centroid of a face after subdivision is the same as that of the face before subdivision.

In the case of n-sided face the centroid f_0^1 after subdivision is:

$$\begin{aligned} \boldsymbol{f}_0^1 &= \frac{\boldsymbol{v}_0^0 + \ldots + \boldsymbol{v}_{n-1}^0 + 2\boldsymbol{e}_0^0 + \ldots + 2\boldsymbol{e}_{n-1}^0 + n\boldsymbol{f}_0^0}{4n} \\ &= \frac{\boldsymbol{v}_0^0 + \ldots + \boldsymbol{v}_{n-1}^0}{4n} + \frac{\boldsymbol{e}_0^0 + \ldots + \boldsymbol{e}_{n-1}^0}{2n} + \frac{\boldsymbol{f}_0^0}{4} = \boldsymbol{f}_0^0. \end{aligned} \tag{21.19}$$

From eq.(21.19), we understand that the centroid of a face is stationary under subdivision, irrespective of the number of its sides.

Face, Vertex and Edge

Face

After subdivision, a face is contracted into a smaller one. Although these shapes are not similar, the numbers of vertices and edges are maintained. As mentioned before, the centroids of the faces before and after subdivision are in the same position.

Vertex

After subdivision a face is created around a vertex position whose number of sides coincides with that of edges incident to the vertex (see Fig. 21.10).

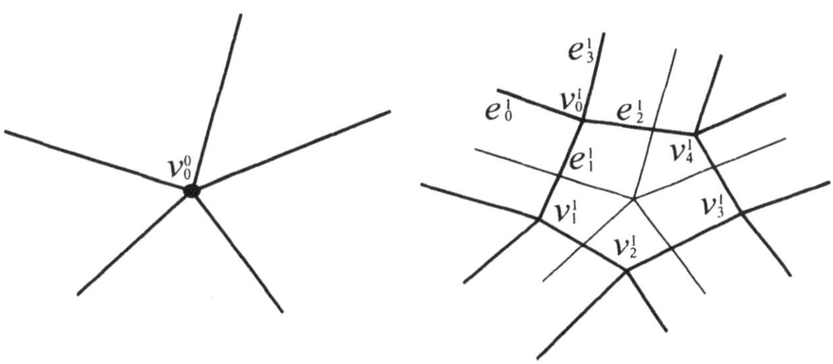

Figure 21.10: Transformation of a vertex.

Edge

After subdivision a four-sided face is created in the edge position (Fig. 21.7).

From the description above we understand that a face is always created in each face, vertex or edge position. We should note that a newly created vertex has always four incident edges (see Fig. 21.10).

In Fig. 21.11, the polyhedron transformation process is shown. From the figure, we understand the first subdivision is particular in that it turns all the generated vertices to have four incident edges, and then there is no vertex left

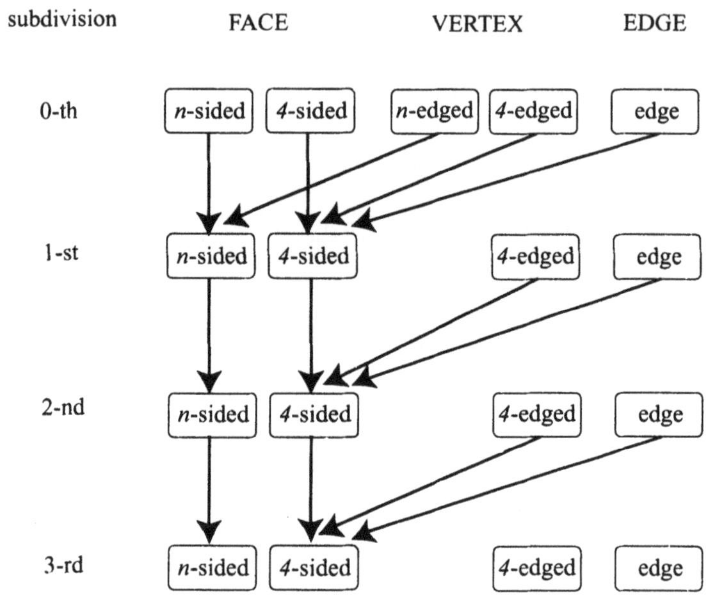

Figure 21.11: Polyhedron transformation process.

in the polygon whose number of incident edges is not four. That is, the first subdivision has an important role that it unifies the number of incident edges of every vertex to four.

21.3.3 Limit Surface

Let us consider applying the subdivision algorithm to a polyhedron whose number of edges of its constituent faces is not limited to four. With the repetition of subdivision, more and more, smaller faces are generated and almost all the faces are four-sided, arranged in a regular lattice. There are, however, a finite number of extraodinary points at which the regularity of the lattice is disturbed and non-four-sided faces are generated.

We shall consider the mathematical representation of the limit surface of the area in a regular lattice which occupies the majority part of the generated polyhedron.

Suppose an inner polyhedron $f_0^0 e_0^0 f_1^0 e_3^0 v_{11}^0 e_1^0 f_3^0 e_2^0 f_2^0$ is given as in Fig.21.12.

Let us consider three polygons $f_0^0 e_0^0 f_1^0$, $e_3^0 v_{11}^0 e_1^0$ and $f_3^0 e_2^0 f_2^0$ in u-direction, and subdivide each according to the Chaikin's algorithm (Fig. 21.13(a),(b)). Then subdivide, in v-direction, the 4 polygons including the newly generated ones ((b),(c)). This operation generates a newly subdivided polyhedron as shown in Figs. 21.13(d) and 21.14(b).

The newly generated vertices $v_{11}^1, v_{12}^1, v_{22}^1, v_{21}^1$ in the center of the polyhedron are expressed in terms of the old data:

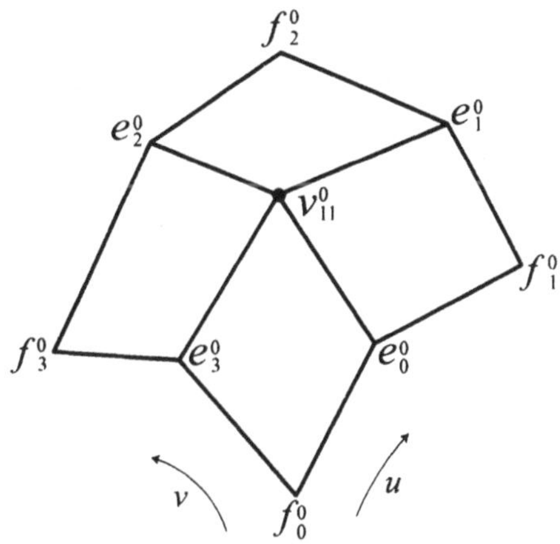

Figure 21.12: An inner polyhedron with only 4-sided faces.

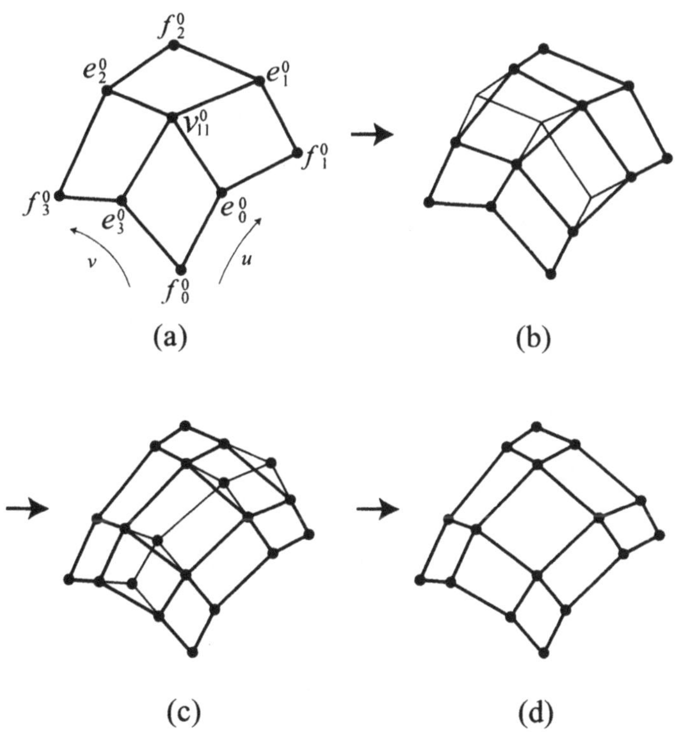

Figure 21.13: Alternate subdivisions of a polyhedron.

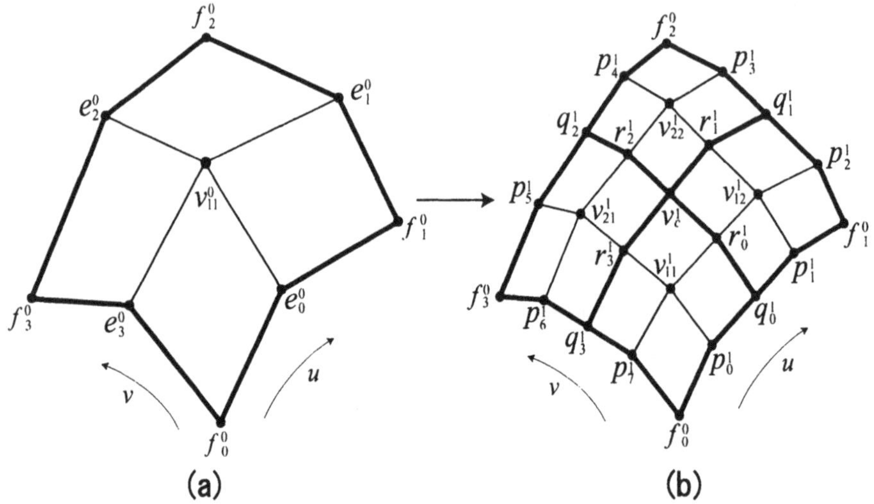

Figure 21.14: A subdivided polyhedron.

$$\begin{cases} \boldsymbol{v}_{11}^1 = \dfrac{\boldsymbol{f}_0^0+\boldsymbol{e}_3^0+\boldsymbol{e}_0^0+\boldsymbol{v}_{11}^0}{4}, & \boldsymbol{v}_{12}^1 = \dfrac{\boldsymbol{f}_1^0+\boldsymbol{e}_0^0+\boldsymbol{e}_1^0+\boldsymbol{v}_{11}^0}{4}, \\ \boldsymbol{v}_{22}^1 = \dfrac{\boldsymbol{f}_2^0+\boldsymbol{e}_1^0+\boldsymbol{e}_2^0+\boldsymbol{v}_{11}^0}{4}, & \boldsymbol{v}_{21}^1 = \dfrac{\boldsymbol{f}_3^0+\boldsymbol{e}_2^0+\boldsymbol{e}_3^0+\boldsymbol{v}_{11}^0}{4}. \end{cases} \tag{21.20}$$

Eq.(21.20) is the same as the relation in eq.(21.17). This shows that the polyhedron subdivision algorithm presented in Section 21.3.1 means the polyhedron transformation shown in Fig. 21.13.

Now, in addition to the generated vertices $v_{11}^1, v_{12}^1, v_{22}^1, v_{21}^1$, consider other points also (Fig. 21.14).

points $p_0^1, p_1^1, p_2^1, p_3^1, p_4^1, p_5^1, p_6^1, p_7^1$:

$$\begin{cases} \boldsymbol{p}_0^1 = \dfrac{\boldsymbol{f}_0^0+\boldsymbol{e}_0^0}{2}, \ \boldsymbol{p}_1^1 = \dfrac{\boldsymbol{e}_0^0+\boldsymbol{f}_1^0}{2}, \ \boldsymbol{p}_2^1 = \dfrac{\boldsymbol{f}_1^0+\boldsymbol{e}_1^0}{2}, \ \boldsymbol{p}_3^1 = \dfrac{\boldsymbol{e}_1^0+\boldsymbol{f}_2^0}{2}, \\ \boldsymbol{p}_4^1 = \dfrac{\boldsymbol{f}_2^0+\boldsymbol{e}_2^0}{2}, \ \boldsymbol{p}_5^1 = \dfrac{\boldsymbol{e}_2^0+\boldsymbol{f}_3^0}{2}, \ \boldsymbol{p}_6^1 = \dfrac{\boldsymbol{f}_3^0+\boldsymbol{e}_3^0}{2}, \ \boldsymbol{p}_7^1 = \dfrac{\boldsymbol{e}_3^0+\boldsymbol{f}_0^0}{2}, \end{cases} \tag{21.21}$$

points $q_0^1, q_1^1, q_2^1, q_3^1$:

$$\boldsymbol{q}_0^1 = \frac{\boldsymbol{p}_0^1+\boldsymbol{p}_1^1}{2}, \ \boldsymbol{q}_1^1 = \frac{\boldsymbol{p}_2^1+\boldsymbol{p}_3^1}{2}, \ \boldsymbol{q}_2^1 = \frac{\boldsymbol{p}_4^1+\boldsymbol{p}_5^1}{2}, \ \boldsymbol{q}_3^1 = \frac{\boldsymbol{p}_6^1+\boldsymbol{p}_7^1}{2}, \tag{21.22}$$

points $r_0^1, r_1^1, r_2^1, r_3^1$:

$$\boldsymbol{r}_0^1 = \frac{\boldsymbol{v}_{11}^1+\boldsymbol{v}_{12}^1}{2}, \ \boldsymbol{r}_1^1 = \frac{\boldsymbol{v}_{12}^1+\boldsymbol{v}_{22}^1}{2}, \ \boldsymbol{r}_2^1 = \frac{\boldsymbol{v}_{22}^1+\boldsymbol{v}_{21}^1}{2}, \ \boldsymbol{r}_3^1 = \frac{\boldsymbol{v}_{21}^1+\boldsymbol{v}_{11}^1}{2}, \tag{21.23}$$

and v_c^1:

$$\boldsymbol{v}_c^1 = \frac{\boldsymbol{v}_{11}^1 + \boldsymbol{v}_{12}^1 + \boldsymbol{v}_{22}^1 + \boldsymbol{v}_{21}^1}{4}. \tag{21.24}$$

The polyhedron subdivision algorithm generates four nine-vertex polyhedra from one nine-vertex polyhedron. Considering the relations of the equations from (21.20) to (21.24), the limit surface always passes the corner points of the nine-vertex polyhedron and that the tangents of the limit surface at the corner points are in the directions of the sides of the original polyhedra, for example $\overrightarrow{f_0^0 e_0^0}, \overrightarrow{f_0^0 e_3^0}$ at f_0^0. Therefore the four boundary curves are represented in a quadratic Bézier forms. It is verified that the limit surface is a Bézier surface patch of degree 2:

$$\boldsymbol{p}(u,v) = [B_{0,2}(u)\ B_{1,2}(u)\ B_{2,2}(u)] \begin{bmatrix} \boldsymbol{f}_0^0 & \boldsymbol{e}_0^0 & \boldsymbol{f}_1^0 \\ \boldsymbol{e}_3^0 & \boldsymbol{v}_{11}^0 & \boldsymbol{e}_1^0 \\ \boldsymbol{f}_3^0 & \boldsymbol{e}_2^0 & \boldsymbol{f}_2^0 \end{bmatrix} \begin{bmatrix} B_{0,2}(v) \\ B_{1,2}(v) \\ B_{2,2}(v) \end{bmatrix}, \tag{21.25}$$
$$0 \le u \le 1,\ 0 \le v \le 1.$$

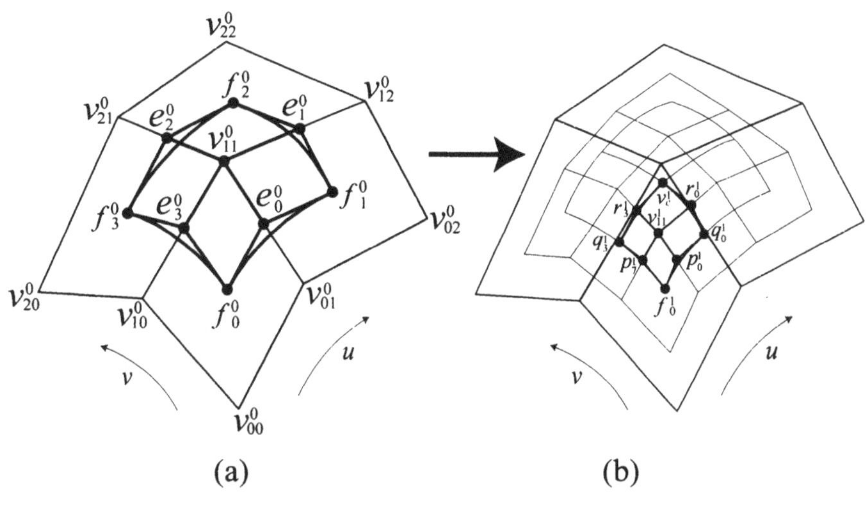

Figure 21.15: Relation between given polyhedron and Bézier surface patch.

A polyhedron subdivision generates four Bézier sub-patches. One of the four patches is expressed as (Fig. 21.15):

$$\boldsymbol{p}(u,v) = [B_{0,2}(u)\ B_{1,2}(u)\ B_{2,2}(u)] \begin{bmatrix} \boldsymbol{f}_0^1 & \boldsymbol{p}_0^1 & \boldsymbol{q}_0^1 \\ \boldsymbol{p}_7^1 & \boldsymbol{v}_{11}^1 & \boldsymbol{r}_0^1 \\ \boldsymbol{q}_3^1 & \boldsymbol{r}_3^1 & \boldsymbol{v}_c^1 \end{bmatrix} \begin{bmatrix} B_{0,2}(v) \\ B_{1,2}(v) \\ B_{2,2}(v) \end{bmatrix}, \tag{21.26}$$
$$0 \le u \le 1,\ 0 \le v \le 1.$$

Now, we shall express the quadratic Bézier patch eq.(21.25) in a form of

B-spline patch. For this purpose we rewrite eq.(21.25) as follows:

$$\begin{aligned} \boldsymbol{p}(u,v) &= [B_{0,2}(u)\ B_{1,2}(u)\ B_{2,2}(u)] \begin{bmatrix} \boldsymbol{f}_0^0 & \boldsymbol{e}_0^0 & \boldsymbol{f}_1^0 \\ \boldsymbol{e}_3^0 & \boldsymbol{v}_{11}^0 & \boldsymbol{e}_1^0 \\ \boldsymbol{f}_3^0 & \boldsymbol{e}_2^0 & \boldsymbol{f}_2^0 \end{bmatrix} \begin{bmatrix} B_{0,2}(v) \\ B_{1,2}(v) \\ B_{2,2}(v) \end{bmatrix} \\ &= [u^2\ u\ 1] \boldsymbol{M}_B \begin{bmatrix} \boldsymbol{f}_0^0 & \boldsymbol{e}_0^0 & \boldsymbol{f}_1^0 \\ \boldsymbol{e}_3^0 & \boldsymbol{v}_{11}^0 & \boldsymbol{e}_1^0 \\ \boldsymbol{f}_3^0 & \boldsymbol{e}_2^0 & \boldsymbol{f}_2^0 \end{bmatrix} \boldsymbol{M}_B{}^T \begin{bmatrix} v^2 \\ v \\ 1 \end{bmatrix}, \end{aligned} \tag{21.27}$$

where

$$\boldsymbol{M}_B = \begin{bmatrix} 1 & -2 & 1 \\ -2 & 2 & 0 \\ 1 & 0 & 0 \end{bmatrix}. \tag{21.28}$$

We assume eq.(21.25) can also be expressed in a B-spline form as:

$$\begin{aligned} \boldsymbol{p}(u,v) &= [N_{0,3}(u)\ N_{1,3}(u)\ N_{2,3}(u)] \begin{bmatrix} \boldsymbol{A} & \boldsymbol{B} & \boldsymbol{C} \\ \boldsymbol{D} & \boldsymbol{E} & \boldsymbol{F} \\ \boldsymbol{G} & \boldsymbol{H} & \boldsymbol{I} \end{bmatrix} \begin{bmatrix} N_{0,3}(v) \\ N_{1,3}(v) \\ N_{2,3}(v) \end{bmatrix} \\ &= [u^2\ u\ 1] \boldsymbol{M}_N \begin{bmatrix} \boldsymbol{A} & \boldsymbol{B} & \boldsymbol{C} \\ \boldsymbol{D} & \boldsymbol{E} & \boldsymbol{F} \\ \boldsymbol{G} & \boldsymbol{H} & \boldsymbol{I} \end{bmatrix} \boldsymbol{M}_N{}^T \begin{bmatrix} v^2 \\ v \\ 1 \end{bmatrix}, \end{aligned} \tag{21.29}$$

where

$$\boldsymbol{M}_N = \begin{bmatrix} \frac{1}{2} & -1 & \frac{1}{2} \\ -1 & 1 & 0 \\ \frac{1}{2} & \frac{1}{2} & 0 \end{bmatrix}. \tag{21.30}$$

Equating eqs.(21.27) and (21.29) yields:

$$\boldsymbol{M}_N \begin{bmatrix} \boldsymbol{A} & \boldsymbol{B} & \boldsymbol{C} \\ \boldsymbol{D} & \boldsymbol{E} & \boldsymbol{F} \\ \boldsymbol{G} & \boldsymbol{H} & \boldsymbol{I} \end{bmatrix} \boldsymbol{M}_N{}^T = \boldsymbol{M}_B \begin{bmatrix} \boldsymbol{f}_0^0 & \boldsymbol{e}_0^0 & \boldsymbol{f}_1^0 \\ \boldsymbol{e}_3^0 & \boldsymbol{v}_{11}^0 & \boldsymbol{e}_1^0 \\ \boldsymbol{f}_3^0 & \boldsymbol{e}_2^0 & \boldsymbol{f}_2^0 \end{bmatrix} \boldsymbol{M}_B{}^T.$$

From the equation above we have:

$$\begin{aligned} \begin{bmatrix} \boldsymbol{A} & \boldsymbol{B} & \boldsymbol{C} \\ \boldsymbol{D} & \boldsymbol{E} & \boldsymbol{F} \\ \boldsymbol{G} & \boldsymbol{H} & \boldsymbol{I} \end{bmatrix} &= \boldsymbol{M}_N{}^{-1} \boldsymbol{M}_B \begin{bmatrix} \boldsymbol{f}_0^0 & \boldsymbol{e}_0^0 & \boldsymbol{f}_1^0 \\ \boldsymbol{e}_3^0 & \boldsymbol{v}_{11}^0 & \boldsymbol{e}_1^0 \\ \boldsymbol{f}_3^0 & \boldsymbol{e}_2^0 & \boldsymbol{f}_2^0 \end{bmatrix} \boldsymbol{M}_B{}^T (\boldsymbol{M}_N{}^T)^{-1} \\ &= \begin{bmatrix} 4\boldsymbol{f}_0^0 - 2\boldsymbol{e}_0^0 - 2\boldsymbol{e}_3^0 + \boldsymbol{v}_{11}^0 & 2\boldsymbol{e}_0^0 - \boldsymbol{v}_{11}^0 & 4\boldsymbol{f}_1^0 - 2\boldsymbol{e}_0^0 - 2\boldsymbol{e}_1^0 + \boldsymbol{v}_{11}^0 \\ 2\boldsymbol{e}_3^0 - \boldsymbol{v}_{11}^0 & \boldsymbol{v}_{11}^0 & 2\boldsymbol{e}_1^0 - \boldsymbol{v}_{11}^0 \\ 4\boldsymbol{f}_3^0 - 2\boldsymbol{e}_2^0 - 2\boldsymbol{e}_3^0 + \boldsymbol{v}_{11}^0 & 2\boldsymbol{e}_2^0 - \boldsymbol{v}_{11}^0 & 4\boldsymbol{f}_2^0 - 2\boldsymbol{e}_2^0 - 2\boldsymbol{e}_1^0 + \boldsymbol{v}_{11}^0 \end{bmatrix}. \end{aligned}$$

Because

$$\begin{cases} \boldsymbol{f}_0^0 = \frac{\boldsymbol{v}_{00}^0 + \boldsymbol{v}_{01}^0 + \boldsymbol{v}_{10}^0 + \boldsymbol{v}_{11}^0}{4}, \quad \boldsymbol{f}_1^0 = \frac{\boldsymbol{v}_{01}^0 + \boldsymbol{v}_{02}^0 + \boldsymbol{v}_{12}^0 + \boldsymbol{v}_{11}^0}{4}, \\ \boldsymbol{f}_2^0 = \frac{\boldsymbol{v}_{12}^0 + \boldsymbol{v}_{21}^0 + \boldsymbol{v}_{22}^0 + \boldsymbol{v}_{11}^0}{4}, \quad \boldsymbol{f}_3^0 = \frac{\boldsymbol{v}_{10}^0 + \boldsymbol{v}_{20}^0 + \boldsymbol{v}_{21}^0 + \boldsymbol{v}_{11}^0}{4}, \\ \boldsymbol{e}_0^0 = \frac{\boldsymbol{v}_{01}^0 + \boldsymbol{v}_{11}^0}{2}, \ \boldsymbol{e}_1^0 = \frac{\boldsymbol{v}_{12}^0 + \boldsymbol{v}_{11}^0}{2}, \ \boldsymbol{e}_2^0 = \frac{\boldsymbol{v}_{21}^0 + \boldsymbol{v}_{11}^0}{2}, \ \boldsymbol{e}_3^0 = \frac{\boldsymbol{v}_{10}^0 + \boldsymbol{v}_{11}^0}{2}, \end{cases} \tag{21.31}$$

we have:

$$\begin{bmatrix} A & B & C \\ D & E & F \\ G & H & I \end{bmatrix} = \begin{bmatrix} \boldsymbol{v}_{00}^0 & \boldsymbol{v}_{01}^0 & \boldsymbol{v}_{02}^0 \\ \boldsymbol{v}_{10}^0 & \boldsymbol{v}_{11}^0 & \boldsymbol{v}_{12}^0 \\ \boldsymbol{v}_{20}^0 & \boldsymbol{v}_{21}^0 & \boldsymbol{v}_{22}^0 \end{bmatrix}. \tag{21.32}$$

Therefore, eq.(21.25) can be rewritten in a uniform B-spline form of order 3 (degree 2) (Fig. 21.16):

$$\boldsymbol{p}(u,v) = [N_{0,3}(u)\ N_{1,3}(u)\ N_{2,3}(u)] \begin{bmatrix} \boldsymbol{v}_{00}^0 & \boldsymbol{v}_{01}^0 & \boldsymbol{v}_{02}^0 \\ \boldsymbol{v}_{10}^0 & \boldsymbol{v}_{11}^0 & \boldsymbol{v}_{12}^0 \\ \boldsymbol{v}_{20}^0 & \boldsymbol{v}_{21}^0 & \boldsymbol{v}_{22}^0 \end{bmatrix} \begin{bmatrix} N_{0,3}(v) \\ N_{1,3}(v) \\ N_{2,3}(v) \end{bmatrix}, \tag{21.33}$$
$$0 \le u \le 1,\ 0 \le v \le 1.$$

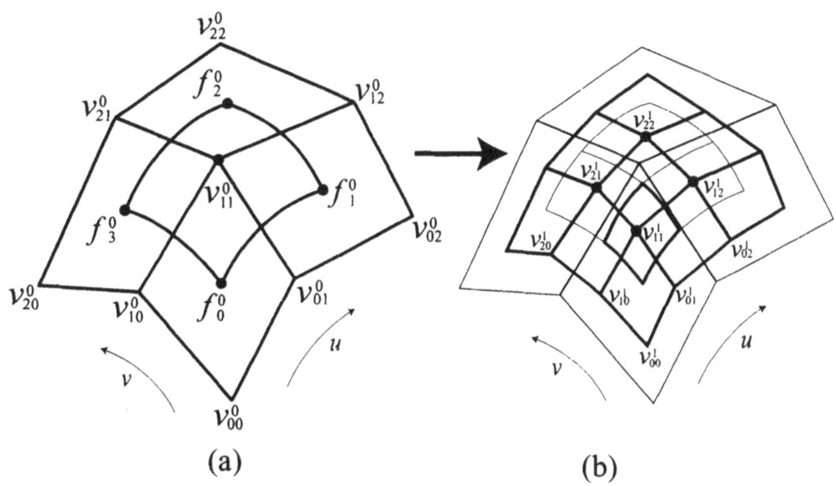

Figure 21.16: Relation between given polyhedron and B-spline surface patch.

The polyhedron subdivision can be considered to generate four B-spline sub-patches which define the original patch eq.(21.33) (Fig. 21.16). One of the four patches is expressed as:

$$\boldsymbol{p}(u,v) = [N_{0,3}(u)\ N_{1,3}(u)\ N_{2,3}(u)] \begin{bmatrix} \boldsymbol{v}_{00}^1 & \boldsymbol{v}_{01}^1 & \boldsymbol{v}_{02}^1 \\ \boldsymbol{v}_{10}^1 & \boldsymbol{v}_{11}^1 & \boldsymbol{v}_{12}^1 \\ \boldsymbol{v}_{20}^1 & \boldsymbol{v}_{21}^1 & \boldsymbol{v}_{22}^1 \end{bmatrix} \begin{bmatrix} N_{0,3}(v) \\ N_{1,3}(v) \\ N_{2,3}(v) \end{bmatrix}, \tag{21.34}$$
$$0 \le u \le 1,\ 0 \le v \le 1.$$

21.4 Homogenization of Surface Generation

We shall homogenize the subdivision algorithm for surface generation. Suppose a sequence of vectors $\boldsymbol{V}_{00}^0, \boldsymbol{V}_{01}^0, \ldots, \boldsymbol{V}_{22}^0$ is given in homogeneous coordinate vectors $[w_i\ X_i\ Y_i\ Z_i] \equiv [w_i\ w_i x_i\ w_i y_i\ w_i z_i]$, and we shall perform exactly the same operations in vector space $\mathbf{R}^4$ as we did in the preceding section (see eq.(21.17)):

$$\begin{cases} \boldsymbol{V}^1_{11} = \dfrac{\boldsymbol{V}^0_{00}+3\boldsymbol{V}^0_{01}+3\boldsymbol{V}^0_{10}+9\boldsymbol{V}^0_{11}}{16}, \\ \boldsymbol{V}^1_{12} = \dfrac{\boldsymbol{V}^0_{02}+3\boldsymbol{V}^0_{12}+3\boldsymbol{V}^0_{01}+9\boldsymbol{V}^0_{11}}{16}, \\ \boldsymbol{V}^1_{22} = \dfrac{\boldsymbol{V}^0_{22}+3\boldsymbol{V}^0_{21}+3\boldsymbol{V}^0_{12}+9\boldsymbol{V}^0_{11}}{16}, \\ \boldsymbol{V}^1_{21} = \dfrac{\boldsymbol{V}^0_{20}+3\boldsymbol{V}^0_{10}+3\boldsymbol{V}^0_{21}+9\boldsymbol{V}^0_{11}}{16}. \end{cases} \tag{21.35}$$

We can redefine all the vectors $\boldsymbol{V}_{ij}$ generated at a subdivision level by multiplying them by 16 such that the subdivision does not include a division operation:

$$\begin{cases} \boldsymbol{V}^1_{11} = \boldsymbol{V}^0_{00} + 3\boldsymbol{V}^0_{01} + 3\boldsymbol{V}^0_{10} + 9\boldsymbol{V}^0_{11}, \\ \boldsymbol{V}^1_{12} = \boldsymbol{V}^0_{02} + 3\boldsymbol{V}^0_{12} + 3\boldsymbol{V}^0_{01} + 9\boldsymbol{V}^0_{11}, \\ \boldsymbol{V}^1_{22} = \boldsymbol{V}^0_{22} + 3\boldsymbol{V}^0_{21} + 3\boldsymbol{V}^0_{12} + 9\boldsymbol{V}^0_{11}, \\ \boldsymbol{V}^1_{21} = \boldsymbol{V}^0_{20} + 3\boldsymbol{V}^0_{10} + 3\boldsymbol{V}^0_{21} + 9\boldsymbol{V}^0_{11}. \end{cases} \tag{21.36}$$

We call this "homogeneous polyhedron subdivision algorithm."

We obtain the following homogeneous B-spline limit surface [2]:

$$\overline{\boldsymbol{P}(u,v)} = \overline{[w(u,v)\ X(u,v)\ Y(u,v)\ Z(u,v)]}$$

$$= \overline{[N_{0,3}(u)\ N_{1,3}(u)\ N_{2,3}(u)] \begin{bmatrix} \boldsymbol{V}^0_{00} & \boldsymbol{V}^0_{01} & \boldsymbol{V}^0_{02} \\ \boldsymbol{V}^0_{10} & \boldsymbol{V}^0_{11} & \boldsymbol{V}^0_{12} \\ \boldsymbol{V}^0_{20} & \boldsymbol{V}^0_{21} & \boldsymbol{V}^0_{22} \end{bmatrix} \begin{bmatrix} N_{0,3}(v) \\ N_{1,3}(v) \\ N_{2,3}(v) \end{bmatrix}}, \tag{21.37}$$

$$0 \le u \le 1,\ 0 \le v \le 1.$$

The equation above is a homogeneous representation of a rational uniform B-spline surface of order 3.

The homogeneous polyhedron subdivision can be considered to generate four homogeneous B-spline sub-patches which define the initial patch (Fig. 21.17). One of the four patches is expressed as:

$$\overline{\boldsymbol{P}(u,v)} = \overline{[N_{0,3}(u)\ N_{1,3}(u)\ N_{2,3}(u)] \begin{bmatrix} \boldsymbol{V}^1_{00} & \boldsymbol{V}^1_{01} & \boldsymbol{V}^1_{02} \\ \boldsymbol{V}^1_{10} & \boldsymbol{V}^1_{11} & \boldsymbol{V}^1_{12} \\ \boldsymbol{V}^1_{20} & \boldsymbol{V}^1_{21} & \boldsymbol{V}^1_{22} \end{bmatrix} \begin{bmatrix} N_{0,3}(v) \\ N_{1,3}(v) \\ N_{2,3}(v) \end{bmatrix}}, \tag{21.38}$$

$$0 \le u \le 1,\ 0 \le v \le 1.$$

By homogenizing the polyhedron subdivision algorithm, we can obtain more general surface representation than the conventional one, i.e., rational surface. As for the comparison between the conventional and homogeneous subdivisions, see Section 25.4.1.

[2] For simplicity we shall show only B-spline representation in this and next sections.

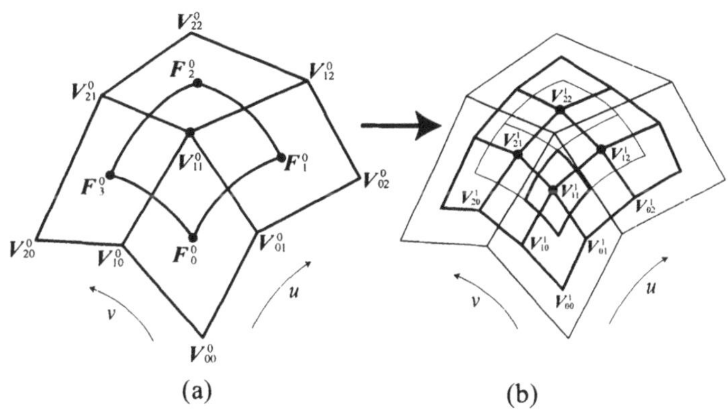

Figure 21.17: Relation between given homogeneous polyhedron and generated homogeneous B-spline surface patch.

21.5 Homogenized Bi-cubic Surface Generation

We shall deal with the homogenization of the polyhedron subdivision for bi-cubic surface generation [8] (Fig. 21.18).

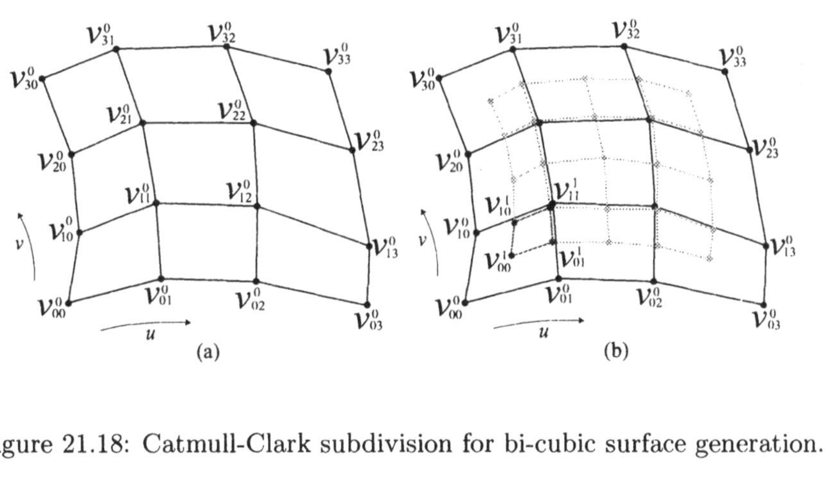

Figure 21.18: Catmull-Clark subdivision for bi-cubic surface generation.

Suppose a part $v_{00}^0 v_{01}^0 \cdots v_{11}^0 v_{12}^0 \cdots v_{32}^0 v_{33}^0$ of a polyhedron is given as shown in Fig. 21.18(a). These vertices define a bi-cubic B-spline surface patch:

$$\boldsymbol{p}(u,v) = [N_{0,4}(u)\ N_{1,4}(u)\ N_{2,4}(u)\ N_{3,4}(u)] \begin{bmatrix} \boldsymbol{v}_{00}^0 & \boldsymbol{v}_{01}^0 & \boldsymbol{v}_{02}^0 & \boldsymbol{v}_{03}^0 \\ \boldsymbol{v}_{10}^0 & \boldsymbol{v}_{11}^0 & \boldsymbol{v}_{12}^0 & \boldsymbol{v}_{13}^0 \\ \boldsymbol{v}_{20}^0 & \boldsymbol{v}_{21}^0 & \boldsymbol{v}_{22}^0 & \boldsymbol{v}_{23}^0 \\ \boldsymbol{v}_{30}^0 & \boldsymbol{v}_{31}^0 & \boldsymbol{v}_{32}^0 & \boldsymbol{v}_{33}^0 \end{bmatrix} \begin{bmatrix} N_{0,4}(v) \\ N_{1,4}(v) \\ N_{2,4}(v) \\ N_{3,4}(v) \end{bmatrix},$$

$$0 \le u \le 1,\ 0 \le v \le 1. \tag{21.39}$$

The Catmull-Clark algorithm of the polyhedron subdivision for a bi-cubic surface generates the following new vertices:

New face-point

$$\boldsymbol{v}_{00}^1 = \frac{\boldsymbol{v}_{00}^0 + \boldsymbol{v}_{01}^0 + \boldsymbol{v}_{10}^0 + \boldsymbol{v}_{11}^0}{4}, \tag{21.40}$$

New edge-point

$$\boldsymbol{v}_{01}^1 = \frac{\frac{\boldsymbol{c}+\boldsymbol{d}}{2} + \frac{\boldsymbol{v}_{01}^0+\boldsymbol{v}_{11}^0}{2}}{2}, \tag{21.41}$$

where

$$\boldsymbol{c} = \frac{\boldsymbol{v}_{00}^0 + \boldsymbol{v}_{01}^0 + \boldsymbol{v}_{10}^0 + \boldsymbol{v}_{11}^0}{4} \equiv \boldsymbol{v}_{00}^1,$$

$$\boldsymbol{d} = \frac{\boldsymbol{v}_{01}^0 + \boldsymbol{v}_{02}^0 + \boldsymbol{v}_{11}^0 + \boldsymbol{v}_{12}^0}{4} \equiv \boldsymbol{v}_{02}^1,$$

New vertex-point

$$\boldsymbol{v}_{11}^1 = \frac{\boldsymbol{q}}{4} + \frac{\boldsymbol{r}}{2} + \frac{\boldsymbol{v}_{11}^0}{4}, \tag{21.42}$$

where

$$\boldsymbol{q} = \frac{\boldsymbol{v}_{00}^1 + \boldsymbol{v}_{02}^1 + \boldsymbol{v}_{20}^1 + \boldsymbol{v}_{22}^1}{4},$$

$$\boldsymbol{r} = \frac{1}{4}\left(\frac{\boldsymbol{v}_{11}^0 + \boldsymbol{v}_{01}^0}{2} + \frac{\boldsymbol{v}_{11}^0 + \boldsymbol{v}_{12}^0}{2} + \frac{\boldsymbol{v}_{11}^0 + \boldsymbol{v}_{21}^0}{2} + \frac{\boldsymbol{v}_{11}^0 + \boldsymbol{v}_{10}^0}{2}\right).$$

These operations can be considered to subdivide the original patch eq.(21.39) into four B-spline subpatches (Fig. 21.18(b)). One of the four patches is expressed as:

$$\boldsymbol{p}(u,v) = [N_{0,4}(u)\ N_{1,4}(u)\ N_{2,4}(u)\ N_{3,4}(u)] \begin{bmatrix} \boldsymbol{v}_{00}^1 & \boldsymbol{v}_{01}^1 & \boldsymbol{v}_{02}^1 & \boldsymbol{v}_{03}^1 \\ \boldsymbol{v}_{10}^1 & \boldsymbol{v}_{11}^1 & \boldsymbol{v}_{12}^1 & \boldsymbol{v}_{13}^1 \\ \boldsymbol{v}_{20}^1 & \boldsymbol{v}_{21}^1 & \boldsymbol{v}_{22}^1 & \boldsymbol{v}_{23}^1 \\ \boldsymbol{v}_{30}^1 & \boldsymbol{v}_{31}^1 & \boldsymbol{v}_{32}^1 & \boldsymbol{v}_{33}^1 \end{bmatrix} \begin{bmatrix} N_{0,4}(v) \\ N_{1,4}(v) \\ N_{2,4}(v) \\ N_{3,4}(v) \end{bmatrix},$$
$$0 \le u \le 1,\ 0 \le v \le 1. \tag{21.43}$$

Suppose a sequence of vectors $\boldsymbol{V}_{00}^0 \boldsymbol{V}_{01}^0 \cdots \boldsymbol{V}_{11}^0 \boldsymbol{V}_{12}^0 \cdots \boldsymbol{V}_{32}^0 \boldsymbol{V}_{33}^0$ is given in homogeneous coordinate vectors $[w_i\ X_i\ Y_i\ Z_i] \equiv [w_i\ w_i x_i\ w_i y_i\ w_i z_i]$(Fig. 21.19(a)). These vectors define a bi-cubic homogeneous B-spline surface patch:

$$\overline{\boldsymbol{P}(u,v)} = [N_{0,4}(u)\ N_{1,4}(u)\ N_{2,4}(u)\ N_{3,4}(u)] \begin{bmatrix} \boldsymbol{V}_{00}^0 & \boldsymbol{V}_{01}^0 & \boldsymbol{V}_{02}^0 & \boldsymbol{V}_{03}^0 \\ \boldsymbol{V}_{10}^0 & \boldsymbol{V}_{11}^0 & \boldsymbol{V}_{12}^0 & \boldsymbol{V}_{13}^0 \\ \boldsymbol{V}_{20}^0 & \boldsymbol{V}_{21}^0 & \boldsymbol{V}_{22}^0 & \boldsymbol{V}_{23}^0 \\ \boldsymbol{V}_{30}^0 & \boldsymbol{V}_{31}^0 & \boldsymbol{V}_{32}^0 & \boldsymbol{V}_{33}^0 \end{bmatrix} \begin{bmatrix} N_{0,4}(v) \\ N_{1,4}(v) \\ N_{2,4}(v) \\ N_{3,4}(v) \end{bmatrix},$$
$$0 \le u \le 1,\ 0 \le v \le 1. \tag{21.44}$$

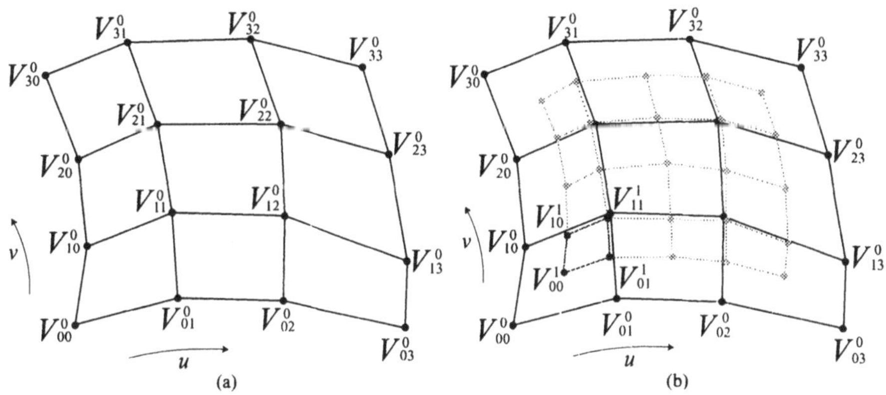

Figure 21.19: Homogenized subdivision for bi-cubic homogeneous surface generation.

We can redefine all the vectors $\boldsymbol{V}_{ij}$ generated at a subdivision level by multiplying them by 64 such that the subdivision does not include a division operation:

$$\boldsymbol{V}^1_{00} = 16\boldsymbol{V}^0_{00} + 16\boldsymbol{V}^0_{01} + 16\boldsymbol{V}^0_{10} + 16\boldsymbol{V}^0_{11}, \tag{21.45}$$

$$\boldsymbol{V}^1_{01} = 4\boldsymbol{C} + 4\boldsymbol{D} + 16\boldsymbol{V}^0_{01} + 16\boldsymbol{V}^0_{11}, \tag{21.46}$$

$$\boldsymbol{V}^1_{11} = \boldsymbol{C} + \boldsymbol{D} + \boldsymbol{E} + \boldsymbol{F} + 4(\boldsymbol{V}^0_{01} + \boldsymbol{V}^0_{12} + \boldsymbol{V}^0_{21} + \boldsymbol{V}^0_{10}) + 32\boldsymbol{V}^0_{11}, \tag{21.47}$$

where

$$\begin{aligned}
\boldsymbol{C} &= 4\boldsymbol{c} = \boldsymbol{V}^0_{00} + \boldsymbol{V}^0_{01} + \boldsymbol{V}^0_{10} + \boldsymbol{V}^0_{11},\\
\boldsymbol{D} &= 4\boldsymbol{d} = \boldsymbol{V}^0_{01} + \boldsymbol{V}^0_{02} + \boldsymbol{V}^0_{11} + \boldsymbol{V}^0_{12},\\
\boldsymbol{E} &= \boldsymbol{V}^0_{10} + \boldsymbol{V}^0_{11} + \boldsymbol{V}^0_{21} + \boldsymbol{V}^0_{20},\\
\boldsymbol{F} &= \boldsymbol{V}^0_{11} + \boldsymbol{V}^0_{12} + \boldsymbol{V}^0_{22} + \boldsymbol{V}^0_{21}.
\end{aligned}$$

The operations above can be considered to generate four homogeneous B-spline sub-patches which define the original patch eq.(21.44) (Fig. 21.19(b)). One of the four patches is expressed as:

$$\overline{\boldsymbol{P}(u,v)} = [N_{0,4}(u)\ N_{1,4}(u)\ N_{2,4}(u)\ N_{3,4}(u)] \begin{bmatrix} \boldsymbol{V}^1_{00} & \boldsymbol{V}^1_{01} & \boldsymbol{V}^1_{02} & \boldsymbol{V}^1_{03} \\ \boldsymbol{V}^1_{10} & \boldsymbol{V}^1_{11} & \boldsymbol{V}^1_{12} & \boldsymbol{V}^1_{13} \\ \boldsymbol{V}^1_{20} & \boldsymbol{V}^1_{21} & \boldsymbol{V}^1_{22} & \boldsymbol{V}^1_{23} \\ \boldsymbol{V}^1_{30} & \boldsymbol{V}^1_{31} & \boldsymbol{V}^1_{32} & \boldsymbol{V}^1_{33} \end{bmatrix} \begin{bmatrix} N_{0,4}(v) \\ N_{1,4}(v) \\ N_{2,4}(v) \\ N_{3,4}(v) \end{bmatrix},$$
$$0 \le u \le 1,\ 0 \le v \le 1. \tag{21.48}$$

According to the Four-dimensional Geometric Processing, the same operations as those of the Euclidean Processing enable to generate a more general surface (equivalent to a rational surface) in a more suitable form for geometric processing (see Chapter 11).

Chapter 22

Reconstruction of 3-D Points

In this chapter we shall deal with the reconstruction of three-dimensional points from a pair of projected images on two spherical surfaces. We discuss the application of the Four-dimensional Processing to this problem.

Similarly to the previous application (Chapter 21), this chapter also shows another example of how the application of the Four-dimensional Processing simplifies the processing and increases the generality.

22.1 Reconstruction of Surrounding Scene

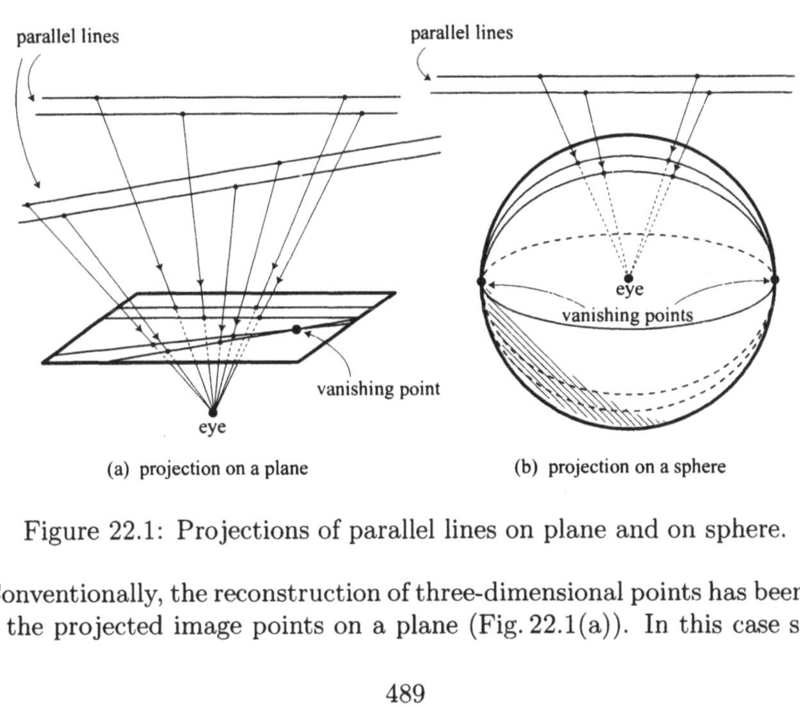

Figure 22.1: Projections of parallel lines on plane and on sphere.

Conventionally, the reconstruction of three-dimensional points has been tried from the projected image points on a plane (Fig. 22.1(a)). In this case special care must be paid when two parallel lines happen to be parallel to the projection plane since these lines do not create a vanishing point. Furthermore the view field for the reconstruction is limitted only to the front region of the projection plane.

Instead we shall assume a spherical projection surface, where any parallel lines always create vanishing points and thus we do not have to worry about special cases (Fig. 22.1(b)). Furthermore theoretically speaking we can take all objects surrounding us into consideration for the reconstruction purpose.

22.2 The Hough Transformations

We shall deal with the reconstruction problem by using a pair of projected images on two spherical surfaces (Fig. 22.2).

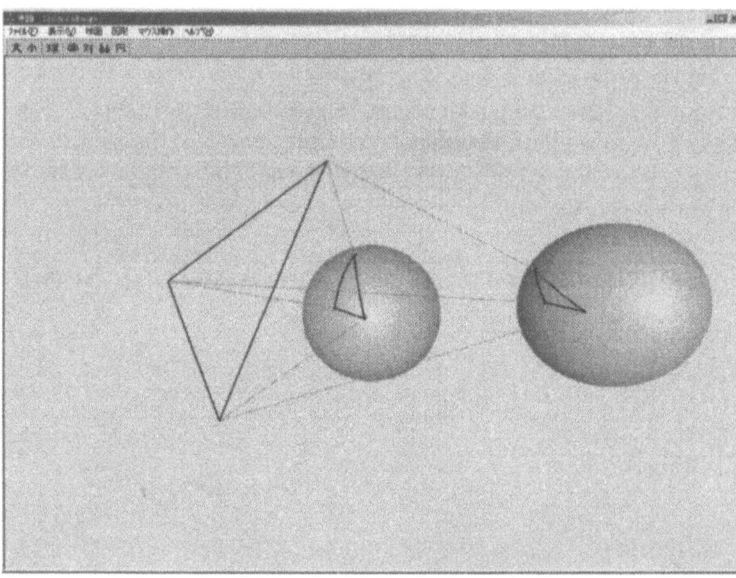

Figure 22.2: Projected images of a triangle on spherical surfaces.

We assume that the projected points are the images of points on edges of a polyhedron (Fig. 22.3).

Generally, the image points have some amount of noise and error. The Hough transformation is a powerful method to reject noises appropriately and to extract a line from such erroneous data in the case of planar projection surface [26],[15].

We represent the line equation in the form:

$$y = ax + b. \tag{22.1}$$

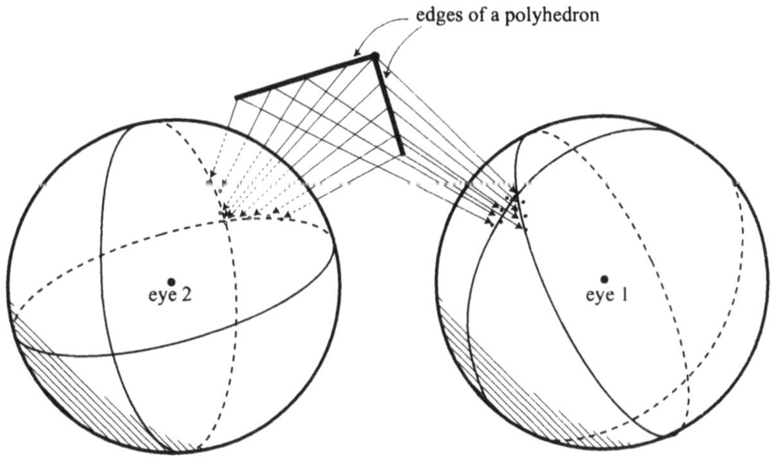

Figure 22.3: Projected images of line segments on spherical surfaces.

We substitute into eq.(22.1) the coordinates (x_0, y_0) of a point p_0 which is supposed to be on a line. Then

$$y_0 = ax_0 + b. \tag{22.2}$$

On a-b plane, eq.(22.2) represents a line. Repeat the line drawing operations with respect to all projected points which are considered to be on the line, then we have a set of lines (Fig. 22.4(b)). All the lines pass through a particular point if the projected points p_i are collinear. This can be shown as follows:

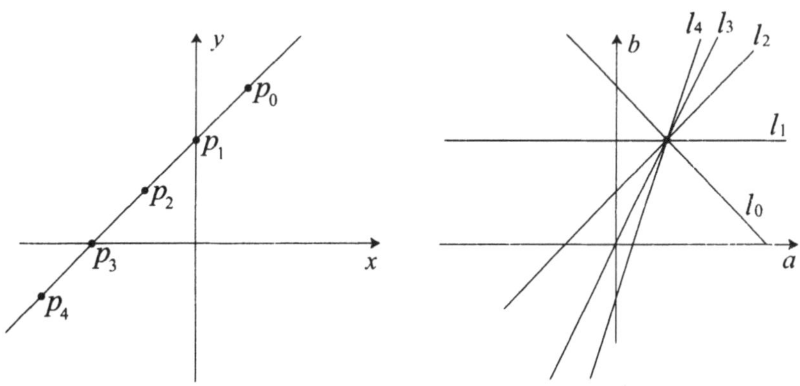

Figure 22.4: Basic Hough transformation.

The condition that point $p(x, y)$ is collinear to $p_0(x_0, y_0)$ and $p_1(x_1, y_1)$ is:

$$\begin{vmatrix} 1 & x & y \\ 1 & x_0 & y_0 \\ 1 & x_1 & y_1 \end{vmatrix} = 0, \tag{22.3}$$

or

$$y = \frac{y_0 - y_1}{x_0 - x_1}x + \frac{x_0 y_1 - x_1 y_0}{x_0 - x_1}. \tag{22.4}$$

Eq.(22.4) expresses that the point $p(x, y)$ is transformed into a line, in a-b plane, going through a point $(a, b) = (\frac{y_0-y_1}{x_0-x_1}, \frac{x_0y_1-x_1y_0}{x_0-x_1})$, which is also the intersection point of lines $y_0 = ax_0+b$ and $y_1 = ax_1+b$ in a-b plane.

In a real environment the intersection points of the set of lines are considered to center around the particular point or *accumulation point* (a_A, b_A). By determining the accumulation point with some means we get the approximating line equation $y = a_Ax+b_A$. This process is called *basic Hough transformation.*

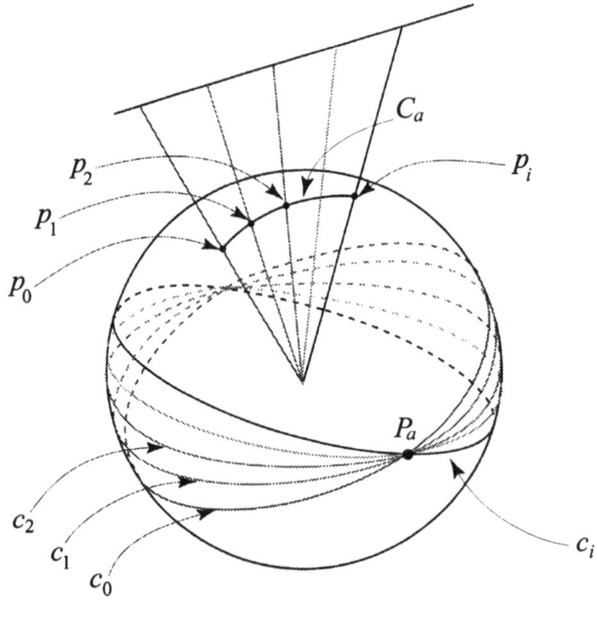

Figure 22.5: Polar complements as duomorphisms.

To the reconstruction problem from spherical surface images of the total solid angle, the Hough transformation mentioned above can not be applied straightforwardly, however. Instead we shall apply the polar complement transformations repeatedly, i.e., from points p_i to lines (great circles) c_i, then from an accumulation point P_a to an approximated line (great circle) C_a (see Section 4.11) (Fig. 22.5). We shall call this operations generalized Hough transformation or total solid angle Hough transformation.

22.3 Generation of Reconstructed Points

Through the repetition of polar complement transformations, we can get a plane equation γ' passing through the eye point, for each point set. This plane is represented in the eye coordinate system, and thus must be transformed into the expression γ in the world coordinate system.

Suppose we have two intersecting planes γ_0 and γ_1 represented in the world coordinate system (Fig. 22.6):

$$\gamma_0 = \overline{(a_0, b_0, c_0, d_0)^T}, \gamma_1 = \overline{(a_1, b_1, c_1, d_1)^T}.$$

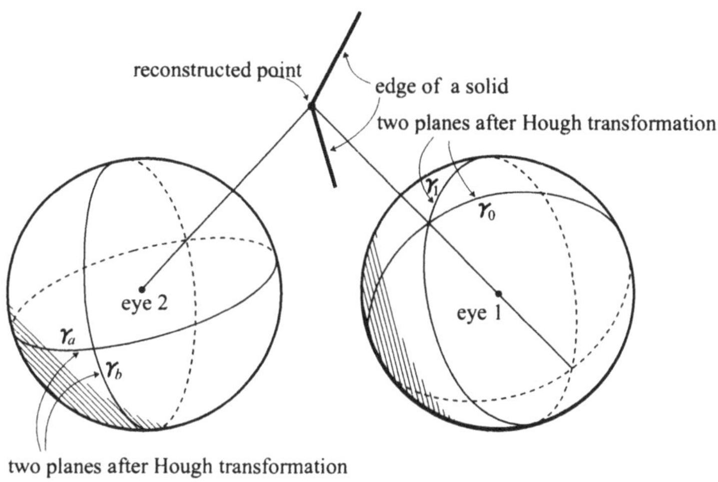

Figure 22.6: Intersection of two space lines.

As shown in Table 9.1, there are two types of space line representations defined by two planes, i.e., type-K' and type-L':

Type-K' space line representation

$$\begin{bmatrix} 0 & -s_{01} & -t_{01} & -u_{01} \\ s_{01} & 0 & -r_{01} & q_{01} \\ t_{01} & r_{01} & 0 & -p_{01} \\ u_{01} & -q_{01} & p_{01} & 0 \end{bmatrix} \begin{bmatrix} a \\ b \\ c \\ d \end{bmatrix} = \begin{bmatrix} 0 \\ 0 \\ 0 \\ 0 \end{bmatrix}.$$

Type-K' space line matrix is composed of four homogeneous coordinate row vectors of points collinear to the line.

Type-L' space line representation

$$[w\ X\ Y\ Z] \begin{bmatrix} 0 & p_{01} & q_{01} & r_{01} \\ -p_{01} & 0 & u_{01} & -t_{01} \\ -q_{01} & -u_{01} & 0 & s_{01} \\ -r_{01} & t_{01} & -s_{01} & 0 \end{bmatrix} = [0\ 0\ 0\ 0].$$

Type-L' space line matrix is composed of four homogeneous coefficient column vectors of planes collinear to the line.

Suppose we have two almost intersecting space lines emanating from two eye points (Fig. 22.6). One is the line made by planes γ_0 and γ_1, and the other the one by planes γ_a and γ_b.

We shall make a matrix product $\boldsymbol{K_1}'\boldsymbol{L_2}'$. Since the matrix $\boldsymbol{L_2}'$ is composed of four homogeneous coefficient column vectors of planes collinear to the line 2, the product generates four homogeneous coordinate column vectors of points between the line 1 and the four planes (see eq.(9.27)). That is,

$$\boldsymbol{N} = \boldsymbol{K_1}'\boldsymbol{L_2}' = \begin{bmatrix} w_0 & w_1 & w_2 & w_3 \\ X_0 & X_1 & X_2 & X_3 \\ Y_0 & Y_1 & Y_2 & Y_3 \\ Z_0 & Z_1 & Z_2 & Z_3 \end{bmatrix}. \tag{22.5}$$

These four points are considered to be very close to each other since they represent an identical point if the lines intersect exactly.

Similarly we make another matrix product $\boldsymbol{K_2}'\boldsymbol{L_1}'$. Since the matrix $\boldsymbol{L_1}'$ is composed of four homogeneous coefficient column vectors of planes collinear to the line 1, the product generates another set of four homogeneous coordinate column vectors of points between the line 2 and the four planes. These four points are also considered to be very close to each other.

Averaging these almost identical eight points would yield an appropriately approximated reconstruction of the point made by the intersection of edges of a solid.

The four-dimensional approach presented here has few special cases and can be looked upon as a more general one.

The final objective of the reconstruction problem would be to reconstruct surrounding solids (Fig. 22.7).

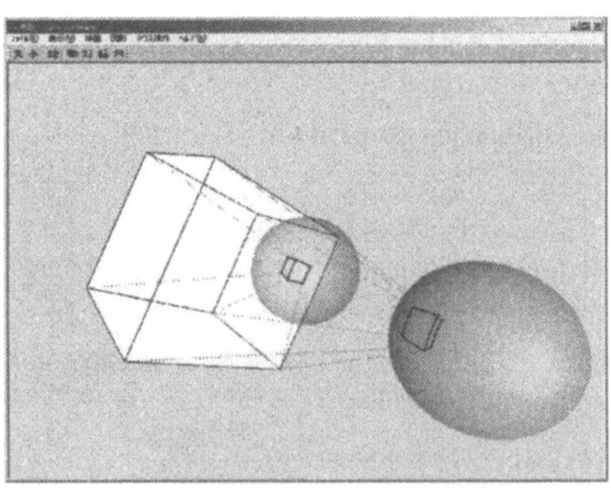

Figure 22.7: Reconstruction of a solid.

Chapter 23

Display Process

In this chapter, we present some important matrices used when generating perspective drawings. There are mainly four coordinate systems in this process, namely, the world-, eye-, normalized perspective- and 3-D screen-coordinate systems. In conventional practice, these coordinate systems, except for the world-coordinate system, have usually employed the left-hand system. One of the purposes of this book is to provide a consistent four-dimensional geometric computation system. For consistency, we shall use the standard right-hand coordinate approach for all coordinate systems related to the display process.

23.1 View Field Transformation Matrix

The coordinate system which defines the scene to be displayed is called the *world-coordinate system.* We assume that this is a right-hand system.

To create a perspective drawing, we first specify the "look-from" point or *eye point,* $p_f(x_f, y_f, z_f)$, and the "look-at" point, $p_a(x_a, y_a, z_a)$, in the world-coordinate system. We then define a second coordinate system, namely, the *eye-coordinate system,* $x_e y_e z_e$, of which the origin lies at the eye, and where the z_e-axis is in the direction from the look-at point to the eye point (we thus assume that the scene lies in the negative z_e-region). An additional condition that the x_e-axis is parallel to the $x_w z_w$-plane establishes the eye-coordinate system (see Fig. 23.1). The plane which contains the eye and which is normal to the line connecting the eye and look-at point is called the *eye plane.*

Now, let $\boldsymbol{T}_v$ denote a 4×4 matrix that transforms data described in the world-coordinate system into those of the eye-coordinate system, or:

$$\overline{[1\ x_w\ y_w\ z_w]}\boldsymbol{T}_v = \overline{[1\ x_e\ y_e\ z_e]}. \tag{23.1}$$

$\boldsymbol{T}_v$ is called the *view-field transformation* matrix.

Let us now derive $\boldsymbol{T}_v$. We first translate the world-coordinate system in the x_w-, y_w- and z_w-directions by $+x_f$, $+y_f$ and $+z_f$, respectively; the new coor-

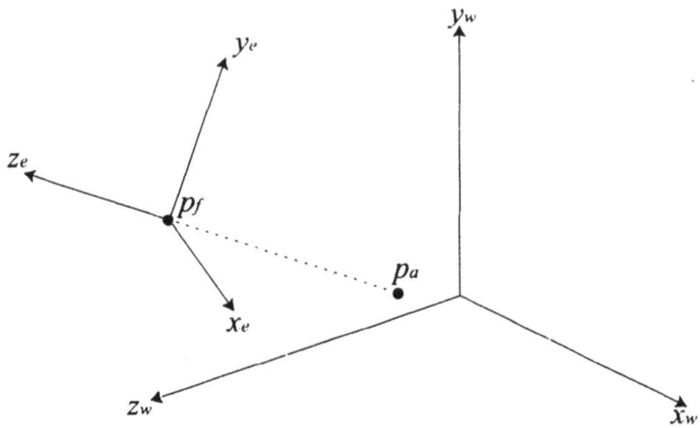

Figure 23.1: World- and eye-coordinate systems.

dinate system obtained from this operation is defined as the $x_1y_1z_1$-coordinate system (see Fig. 23.2).

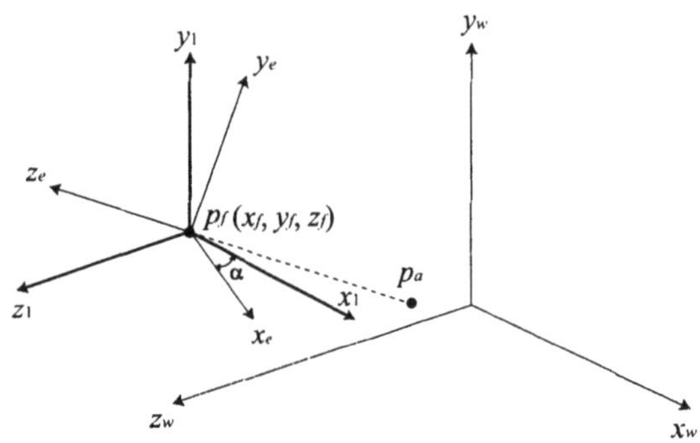

Figure 23.2: $x_1y_1z_1$-coordinate system.

Then, the following equation holds:

$$\overline{[1\ x_w\ y_w\ z_w]\boldsymbol{T}_1} = \overline{[1\ x_1\ y_1\ z_1]}, \tag{23.2}$$

where

$$\boldsymbol{T}_1 = \begin{bmatrix} 1 & -x_f & -y_f & -z_f \\ 0 & 1 & 0 & 0 \\ 0 & 0 & 1 & 0 \\ 0 & 0 & 0 & 1 \end{bmatrix}. \tag{23.3}$$

Now, the x_1- and x_e-axes both lie on a plane parallel to the x_wz_w-plane; let us denote by α the angle formed by these axes.

We then rotate the $x_1y_1z_1$-coordinate system around the y_1-axis by $-\alpha$ and call this the $x_2y_2z_2$-coordinate system. Then, the following equation holds (see Fig. 23.3):

$$\overline{[1\ x_1\ y_1\ z_1]\boldsymbol{T}_2} = \overline{[1\ x_2\ y_2\ z_2]}, \tag{23.4}$$

where

$$T_2 = \begin{bmatrix} 1 & 0 & 0 & 0 \\ 0 & \cos\alpha & 0 & -\sin\alpha \\ 0 & 0 & 1 & 0 \\ 0 & \sin\alpha & 0 & \cos\alpha \end{bmatrix}. \tag{23.5}$$

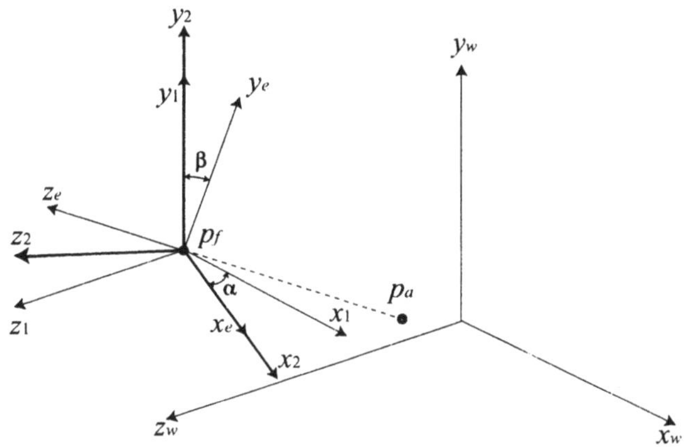

Figure 23.3: $x_2y_2z_2$-coordinate system.

Now, the y_2-axis lies on the y_ez_e-plane; let β denote the angle formed by the y_2- and y_e-axes. If we rotate $x_2y_2z_2$-coordinate system about the x_2-axis by $-\beta$, it will coincide with the $x_ey_ez_e$-coordinate system. The following equation then holds:

$$\overline{[1\ x_2\ y_2\ z_2]T_3} = \overline{[1\ x_e\ y_e\ z_e]}, \tag{23.6}$$

where

$$T_3 = \begin{bmatrix} 1 & 0 & 0 & 0 \\ 0 & 1 & 0 & 0 \\ 0 & 0 & \cos\beta & \sin\beta \\ 0 & 0 & -\sin\beta & \cos\beta \end{bmatrix}. \tag{23.7}$$

By combining eqs.(23.2), (23.4) and (23.6), we have:

$$\overline{[1\ x_w\ y_w\ z_w]T_1T_2T_3} = \overline{[1\ x_e\ y_e\ z_e]}, \tag{23.8}$$

and,

$$\begin{aligned} T_v &= T_1T_2T_3 \\ &= \begin{bmatrix} 1 & -x_f\cos\alpha - z_f\sin\alpha & -x_f\sin\alpha\sin\beta - y_f\cos\beta + z_f\cos\alpha\sin\beta \\ 0 & \cos\alpha & \sin\alpha\sin\beta \\ 0 & 0 & \cos\beta \\ 0 & \sin\alpha & -\cos\alpha\sin\beta \end{bmatrix.} \\ &\qquad \begin{matrix} x_f\sin\alpha\cos\beta - y_f\sin\beta - z_f\cos\alpha\cos\beta \\ -\sin\alpha\cos\beta \\ \sin\beta \\ \cos\alpha\cos\beta \end{matrix}\Bigg]. \end{aligned} \tag{23.9}$$

The inverse matrix of $\boldsymbol{T}_v$ is given by:

$$
\begin{aligned}
\boldsymbol{T}_v^{-1} &= (\boldsymbol{T}_1\boldsymbol{T}_2\boldsymbol{T}_3)^{-1} \\
&= \boldsymbol{T}_3^{-1}\boldsymbol{T}_2^{-1}\boldsymbol{T}_1^{-1} \\
&= \begin{bmatrix} 1 & 0 & 0 & 0 \\ 0 & 1 & 0 & 0 \\ 0 & 0 & \cos\beta & -\sin\beta \\ 0 & 0 & \sin\beta & \cos\beta \end{bmatrix}
\begin{bmatrix} 1 & 0 & 0 & 0 \\ 0 & \cos\alpha & 0 & \sin\alpha \\ 0 & 0 & 1 & 0 \\ 0 & -\sin\alpha & 0 & \cos\alpha \end{bmatrix}
\begin{bmatrix} 1 & x_f & y_f & z_f \\ 0 & 1 & 0 & 0 \\ 0 & 0 & 1 & 0 \\ 0 & 0 & 0 & 1 \end{bmatrix} \\
&= \begin{bmatrix} 1 & x_f & y_f & z_f \\ 0 & \cos\alpha & 0 & \sin\alpha \\ 0 & \sin\alpha\sin\beta & \cos\beta & -\cos\alpha\sin\beta \\ 0 & -\sin\alpha\cos\beta & \sin\beta & \cos\alpha\cos\beta \end{bmatrix}.
\end{aligned} \tag{23.10}
$$

From Fig. 23.4, we obtain the following relations:

$$
\begin{aligned}
\cos\alpha &= \frac{z_f - z_a}{\sqrt{(x_f-x_a)^2+(z_f-z_a)^2}}, \\
\sin\alpha &= \frac{x_a - x_f}{\sqrt{(x_f-x_a)^2+(z_f-z_a)^2}},
\end{aligned} \tag{23.11}
$$

$$
\begin{aligned}
\cos\beta &= \frac{\sqrt{(x_f-x_a)^2+(z_f-z_a)^2}}{\sqrt{(x_f-x_a)^2+(y_f-y_a)^2+(z_f-z_a)^2}}, \\
\sin\beta &= \frac{y_f - y_a}{\sqrt{(x_f-x_a)^2+(y_f-y_a)^2+(z_f-z_a)^2}}.
\end{aligned} \tag{23.12}
$$

Meanwhile, for a left-hand eye coordinate system (see Fig. 23.5), we have

$$
\boldsymbol{T}_v = \boldsymbol{T}_1\boldsymbol{T}_2\boldsymbol{T}_3\boldsymbol{T}_4, \tag{23.13}
$$

where

$$
\boldsymbol{T}_4 = \begin{bmatrix} 1 & 0 & 0 & 0 \\ 0 & 1 & 0 & 0 \\ 0 & 0 & 1 & 0 \\ 0 & 0 & 0 & -1 \end{bmatrix}, \tag{23.14}
$$

$$
\boldsymbol{T}_v = \begin{bmatrix} 1 & -x_f\cos\alpha - z_f\sin\alpha & -x_f\sin\alpha\sin\beta - y_f\cos\beta + z_f\cos\alpha\sin\beta & -x_f\sin\alpha\cos\beta + y_f\sin\beta + z_f\cos\alpha\cos\beta \\ 0 & \cos\alpha & \sin\alpha\sin\beta & \sin\alpha\cos\beta \\ 0 & 0 & \cos\beta & -\sin\beta \\ 0 & \sin\alpha & -\cos\alpha\sin\beta & -\cos\alpha\cos\beta \end{bmatrix}. \tag{23.15}
$$

$\boldsymbol{T}_v^{-1}$ for the left-hand system is given by:

$$
\boldsymbol{T}_v^{-1} = (\boldsymbol{T}_1\boldsymbol{T}_2\boldsymbol{T}_3\boldsymbol{T}_4)^{-1}
$$

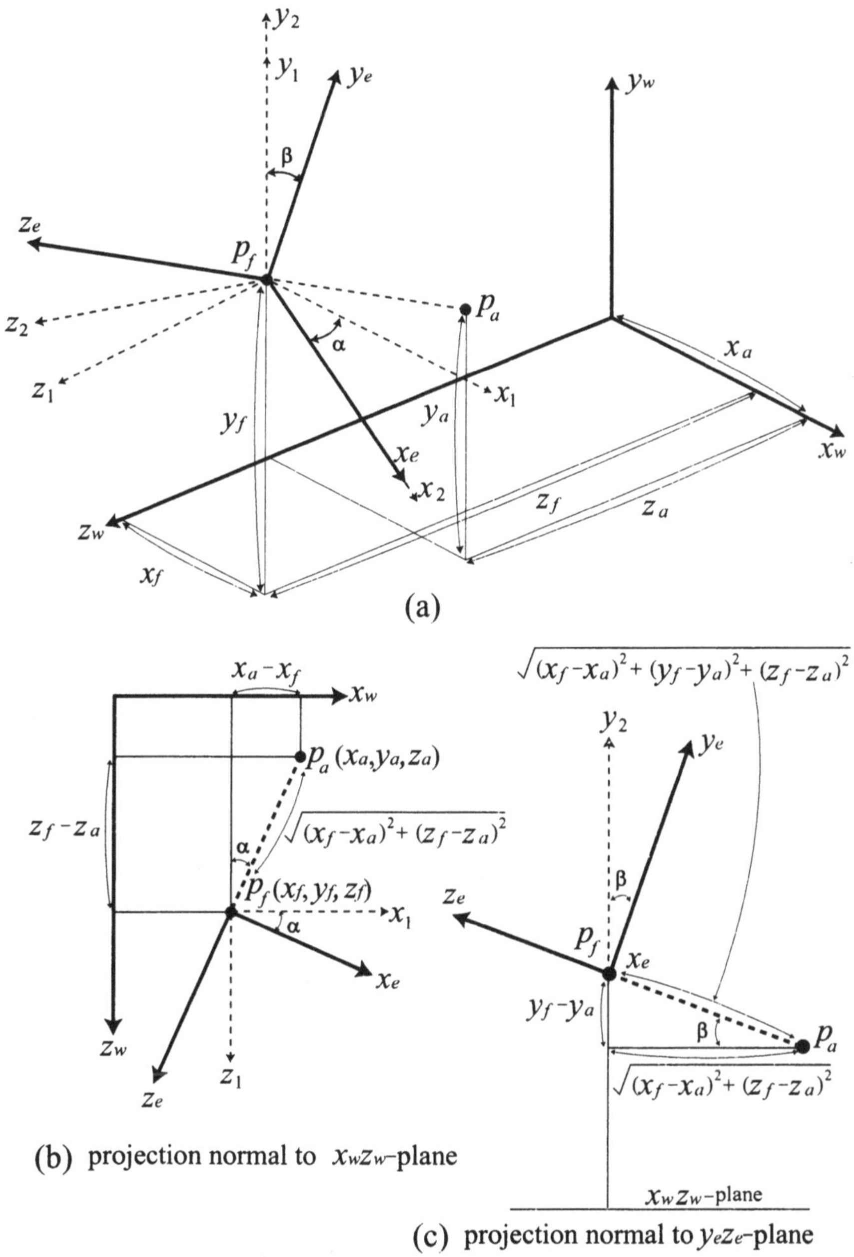

Figure 23.4: Relation between world- and eye-coordinate systems.

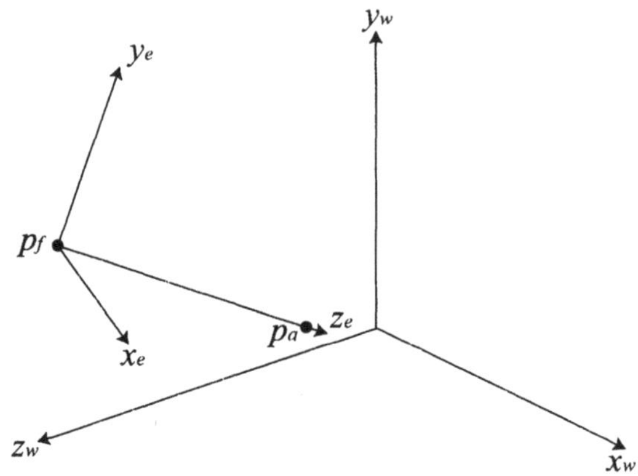

Figure 23.5: Left-hand eye-coordinate system.

$$= \boldsymbol{T}_4^{-1}\boldsymbol{T}_3^{-1}\boldsymbol{T}_2^{-1}\boldsymbol{T}_1^{-1}$$

$$= \begin{bmatrix} 1 & x_f & y_f & z_f \\ 0 & \cos\alpha & 0 & \sin\alpha \\ 0 & \sin\alpha\sin\beta & \cos\beta & -\cos\alpha\sin\beta \\ 0 & \sin\alpha\cos\beta & -\sin\beta & -\cos\alpha\cos\beta \end{bmatrix}. \tag{23.16}$$

23.2 Perspective Transformation Matrix

Let us assume that the plane on which the perspective drawing is to be drawn, i.e., the *projection plane*, has a dimension of $2k \times 2k$ and is located at a distance h from the eye (see Fig. 23.6). The pyramid having as its apex the eye and formed by the four corners of the projection plane is called the *viewing pyramid.* A perspective drawing can be obtained on the projection plane only for those figures located within the viewing pyramid (Fig. 23.7).

Let us determine the perspective transformation matrix for this case. We have already obtained in eq.(6.22) of Chapter 6 the perspective transformation relation in the xyz-coordinate system when the eye is located at h on the z-axis and the projection plane is the xy-plane, or:

$$\overline{[1\ x\ y\ z] \begin{bmatrix} 1 & 0 & 0 & 0 \\ 0 & 1 & 0 & 0 \\ 0 & 0 & 1 & 0 \\ -1/h & 0 & 0 & 1 \end{bmatrix}} = \overline{[w^*\ X^*\ Y^*\ Z^*]}. \tag{23.17}$$

We can consider the shape data of the scene as being originally defined in the world-coordinate system, then expressed in the eye-coordinate system after undergoing a view-field transformation. The right-hand xyz- and right-hand eye-coordinate systems have the following relations (see Fig. 23.6):

$$\begin{aligned} x = x_e, \quad y = y_e, \quad z = z_e + h, \\ x^* = x_e^*, \quad y^* = y_e^*, \quad z^* = z_e^* + h. \end{aligned} \tag{23.18}$$

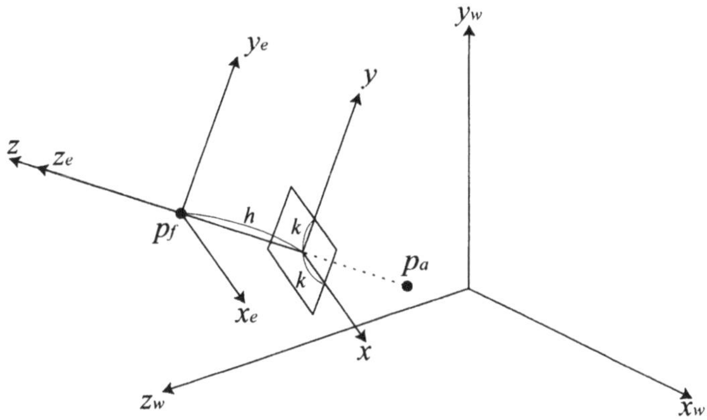

Figure 23.6: Relation between xyz- and eye-coordinate $x_e y_e z_e$-systems.

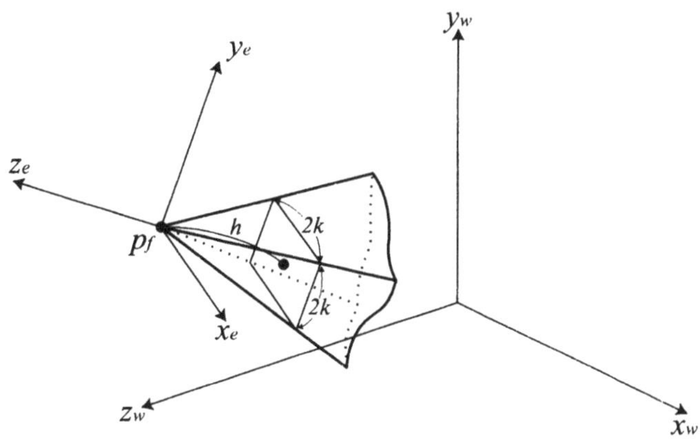

Figure 23.7: Viewing pyramid.

Substituting this into eq.(23.17) and rearranging, we obtain:

$$\overline{[1\ x_e\ y_e\ z_e]\begin{bmatrix} 0 & 0 & 0 & h \\ 0 & 1 & 0 & 0 \\ 0 & 0 & 1 & 0 \\ -1/h & 0 & 0 & 2 \end{bmatrix}} = \overline{[w_e^*\ X_e^*\ Y_e^*\ Z_e^*]}. \tag{23.19}$$

Thus, the transformed coordinates are given by:

$$x_e^* = -hx_e/z_e, \quad y_e^* = -hy_e/z_e, \quad z_e^* = -2h - h^2/z_e. \tag{23.20}$$

We now normalize the perspectively transformed coordinates. First, we normalize the x- and y-coordinates for points that are transformed onto the projection plane so that they satisfy $-1 \leq x, y \leq 1$, and the z coordinate so that $0 \leq z \leq 1$

corresponding to $-\infty \le z_e^* \le -h$. For points in the viewing pyramid, we have $-k \le x_e^*, y_e^* \le k$, and from eq.(23.20), we know that $-2h \le z_e^* \le -h$. Hence, x_e^* and y_e^* can be normalized by multiplying by $1/k$, while z_e^* is normalized by adding $2h$ then multiplying by $1/h$. The matrix for these operations is given by:

$$\begin{bmatrix} 0 & 0 & 0 & h \\ 0 & 1 & 0 & 0 \\ 0 & 0 & 1 & 0 \\ -1/h & 0 & 0 & 2 \end{bmatrix} \begin{bmatrix} 1 & 0 & 0 & 2h \\ 0 & 1/k & 0 & 0 \\ 0 & 0 & 1/k & 0 \\ 0 & 0 & 0 & 1 \end{bmatrix} \begin{bmatrix} 1 & 0 & 0 & 0 \\ 0 & 1 & 0 & 0 \\ 0 & 0 & 1 & 0 \\ 0 & 0 & 0 & 1/h \end{bmatrix}$$
$$= \frac{1}{k} \begin{bmatrix} 0 & 0 & 0 & k \\ 0 & 1 & 0 & 0 \\ 0 & 0 & 1 & 0 \\ -k/h & 0 & 0 & 0 \end{bmatrix}.$$

Since we are dealing with homogeneous coordinates, a transformation matrix can be scalar-multiplied without affecting the ordinary coordinates of the result. Thus, we multiply by k above to obtain:

$$\begin{bmatrix} 0 & 0 & 0 & k \\ 0 & 1 & 0 & 0 \\ 0 & 0 & 1 & 0 \\ -k/h & 0 & 0 & 0 \end{bmatrix}.$$

Therefore, the normalized perspective transformation relation is given by:

$$\overline{[w_e\ X_e\ Y_e\ Z_e]}\boldsymbol{T}_p = \overline{[w_p\ X_p\ Y_p\ Z_p]}, \tag{23.21}$$

$$\boldsymbol{T}_p = \begin{bmatrix} 0 & 0 & 0 & k \\ 0 & 1 & 0 & 0 \\ 0 & 0 & 1 & 0 \\ -k/h & 0 & 0 & 0 \end{bmatrix}. \tag{23.22}$$

Alternatively, we can use the following form, which does not include division:

$$\boldsymbol{T}_p{}' = \begin{bmatrix} 0 & 0 & 0 & hk \\ 0 & h & 0 & 0 \\ 0 & 0 & h & 0 \\ -k & 0 & 0 & 0 \end{bmatrix}. \tag{23.23}$$

From either eq.(23.22) or (23.23), we obtain the transformed coordinates:

$$x_p = \frac{X_p}{w_p} = -\frac{hx_e}{kz_e}, \quad y_p = \frac{Y_p}{w_p} = -\frac{hy_e}{kz_e}, \quad z_p = \frac{Z_p}{w_p} = -\frac{h}{z_e}, \tag{23.24}$$

which confirm that indeed the following relation is satisfied:

$$-1 \le x_p \le 1, \quad -1 \le y_p \le 1, \quad 0 \le z_p \le 1. \tag{23.25}$$

Eq.(23.21) transforms the space inside the viewing pyramid (formed by the eye and projection plane) to a rectangular parallelepiped space (see Fig. 23.8).

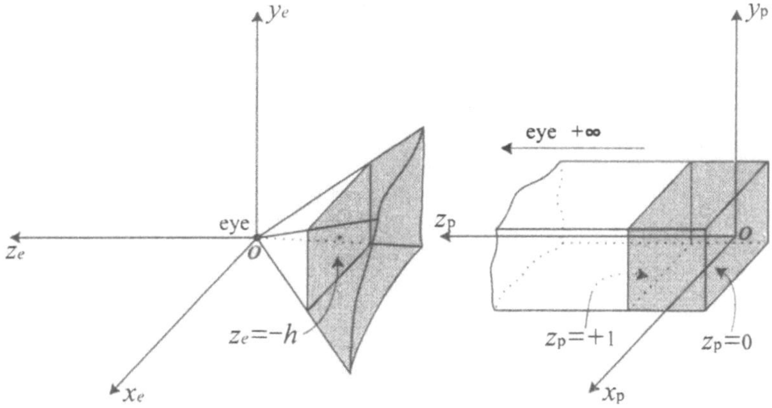

(a) before perspective transformation (b) after perspective transformation

Figure 23.8: Viewing pyramid before and after perspective transformation.

Thus, points lying on $z_e = -h$ are unaffected, while figures in the range $z_e < -h$ are reduced and those for $-h < z_e < 0$ magnified. The space expressed by the $x_p y_p z_p$-coordinate system is called the *normalized perspective space.*

Although the transformed z_p-coordinate is not needed to create the perspective drawing, it can be used for removing hidden lines and surfaces, and displaying depth effects. This is because perspective transformation has the important property that the z-coordinates are transformed so as to preserve lines as lines (this will be discussed later).

In some cases, a *near* (or *hither*) *plane* and *far* (or *yon*) *plane* are given to specify the display range (see Fig. 23.9).

In this case, we normalize so that $0 \le z \le 1$ for the z_e range of $-f$ to $-h$. The perspective transformation matrix is then obtained as follows:

$$\begin{bmatrix} 0 & 0 & 0 & h \\ 0 & 1 & 0 & 0 \\ 0 & 0 & 1 & 0 \\ -1/h & 0 & 0 & 2 \end{bmatrix} \begin{bmatrix} 1 & 0 & 0 & 2h - h^2/f \\ 0 & 1/k & 0 & 0 \\ 0 & 0 & 1/k & 0 \\ 0 & 0 & 0 & 1 \end{bmatrix} \begin{bmatrix} 1 & 0 & 0 & 0 \\ 0 & 1 & 0 & 0 \\ 0 & 0 & 1 & 0 \\ 0 & 0 & 0 & f/(fh - h^2) \end{bmatrix}$$
$$= \frac{1}{k} \begin{bmatrix} 0 & 0 & 0 & fk/(f-h) \\ 0 & 1 & 0 & 0 \\ 0 & 0 & 1 & 0 \\ -k/h & 0 & 0 & k/(f-h) \end{bmatrix}.$$

so the transformation matrix is given by:

$$\begin{bmatrix} 0 & 0 & 0 & fk/(f-h) \\ 0 & 1 & 0 & 0 \\ 0 & 0 & 1 & 0 \\ -k/h & 0 & 0 & k/(f-h) \end{bmatrix}. \tag{23.26}$$

Thus a normalized perspective transformation when the near and far planes are

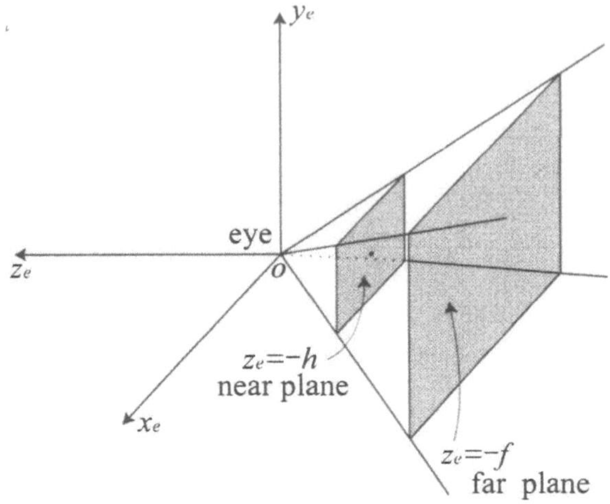

Figure 23.9: Near and far planes.

specified is expressed as:

$$\overline{[1\ x_e\ y_e\ z_e]\boldsymbol{T}_p{}'} = \overline{[w_p{}'\ X_p{}'\ Y_p{}'\ Z_p{}']}, \tag{23.27}$$

$$\boldsymbol{T}_p{}' = \begin{bmatrix} 0 & 0 & 0 & fk/(f-h) \\ 0 & 1 & 0 & 0 \\ 0 & 0 & 1 & 0 \\ -k/h & 0 & 0 & k/(f-h) \end{bmatrix}. \tag{23.28}$$

The transformed coordinates are given by:

$$\begin{aligned} x_p{}' &= \frac{X_p{}'}{w_p{}'} = -\frac{hx_e}{kz_e}, \\ y_p{}' &= \frac{Y_p{}'}{w_p{}'} = -\frac{hy_e}{kz_e}, \\ z_p{}' &= \frac{Z_p{}'}{w_p{}'} = -\frac{h}{f-h} - \frac{fh}{(f-h)z_e}. \end{aligned} \tag{23.29}$$

In this book, we shall mainly use eqs.(23.21) and (23.22) to carry out perspective transformations.

The inverse matrix of $\boldsymbol{T}_p$ is given by:

$$\boldsymbol{T}_p{}^{-1} = \begin{bmatrix} 0 & 0 & 0 & -h/k \\ 0 & 1 & 0 & 0 \\ 0 & 0 & 1 & 0 \\ 1/k & 0 & 0 & 0 \end{bmatrix}. \tag{23.30}$$

Meanwhile, in the left-hand coordinate system, we have:

$$\boldsymbol{T}_p = \begin{bmatrix} 0 & 0 & 0 & -k \\ 0 & 1 & 0 & 0 \\ 0 & 0 & 1 & 0 \\ k/h & 0 & 0 & k/h \end{bmatrix}, \tag{23.31}$$

$$\boldsymbol{T}_p{}^{-1} = \begin{bmatrix} 1/k & 0 & 0 & h/k \\ 0 & 1 & 0 & 0 \\ 0 & 0 & 1 & 0 \\ -1/k & 0 & 0 & 0 \end{bmatrix}. \tag{23.32}$$

23.3 Viewport Transformation Matrix

We define a three-dimensional rectangular parallelepiped viewport as follows (see Fig. 23.10):

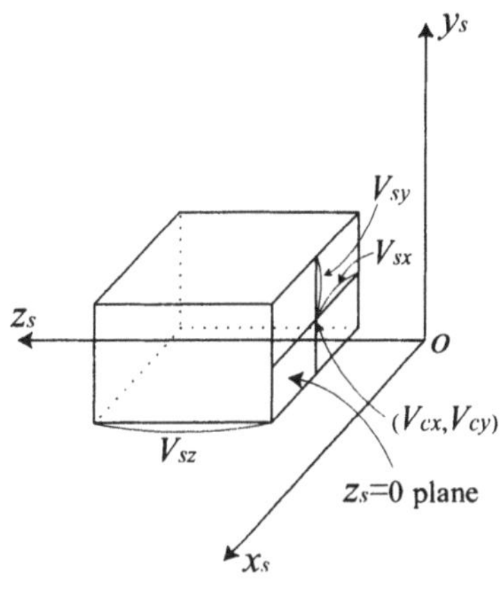

Figure 23.10: Rectangular parallelepiped viewport.

$$\begin{gathered} V_{cx} - V_{sx} \leq x_s \leq V_{cx} + V_{sx}, \\ V_{cy} - V_{sy} \leq y_s \leq V_{cy} + V_{sy}, \\ 0 \leq z_s \leq V_{sz}, \end{gathered} \tag{23.33}$$

where V_{cx} and V_{cy} are the coordinates of the viewport's center in the x- and y-directions, respectively, while V_{sx} and V_{sy} are 1/2 of the viewport's size (or length) in these directions. V_{sz} is the viewport's size in the z-direction.

The transformation from a normalized perspective space to a rectangular parallelepiped viewport is given by:

$$\overline{[w_p \; X_p \; Y_p \; Z_p]}\boldsymbol{T}_s = \overline{[w_s \; X_s \; Y_s \; Z_s]}, \tag{23.34}$$

$$\boldsymbol{T}_s = \begin{bmatrix} 1 & V_{cx} & V_{cy} & 0 \\ 0 & V_{sx} & 0 & 0 \\ 0 & 0 & V_{sy} & 0 \\ 0 & 0 & 0 & V_{sz} \end{bmatrix}. \tag{23.35}$$

To avoid distortion of the perspective drawing, we need the condition:

$$V_{sx} = V_{sy}. \tag{23.36}$$

The inverse matrix of $\boldsymbol{T}_s$ is given by:

$$\boldsymbol{T}_s{}^{-1} = \begin{bmatrix} 1 & -V_{cx}/V_{sx} & -V_{cy}/V_{sy} & 0 \\ 0 & 1/V_{sx} & 0 & 0 \\ 0 & 0 & 1/V_{sy} & 0 \\ 0 & 0 & 0 & 1/V_{sz} \end{bmatrix}, \tag{23.37}$$

or

$$\boldsymbol{T}_s{}^{-1} = \begin{bmatrix} V_{sx}V_{sy}V_{sz} & -V_{cx}V_{sy}V_{sz} & -V_{cy}V_{sx}V_{sz} & 0 \\ 0 & V_{sy}V_{sz} & 0 & 0 \\ 0 & 0 & V_{sx}V_{sz} & 0 \\ 0 & 0 & 0 & V_{sx}V_{sy} \end{bmatrix}. \tag{23.38}$$

23.4 Display Transformation Process

The equation transforming data (x_w, y_w, z_w) expressed in the world coordinate system to data (x_s, y_s, z_s) in the three-dimensional screen coordinate system is obtained by combining eqs.(23.1), (23.21) and (23.34), or:

$$\overline{[1\ x_w\ y_w\ z_w]}\boldsymbol{T}_a = \overline{[w_s\ X_s\ Y_s\ Z_s]}, \tag{23.39}$$

where

$$\boldsymbol{T}_a = \boldsymbol{T}_v\boldsymbol{T}_p\boldsymbol{T}_s. \tag{23.40}$$

The screen coordinates (x_s, y_s, z_s) are obtained as:

$$x_s = \frac{X_s}{w_s}, \quad y_s = \frac{Y_s}{w_s}, \quad z_s = \frac{Z_s}{w_s}. \tag{23.41}$$

The inverse matrix of $\boldsymbol{T}_a$ is given by:

$$\begin{aligned} \boldsymbol{T}_a{}^{-1} &= (\boldsymbol{T}_v\boldsymbol{T}_p\boldsymbol{T}_s)^{-1} \\ &= \boldsymbol{T}_s{}^{-1}\boldsymbol{T}_p{}^{-1}\boldsymbol{T}_v{}^{-1}. \end{aligned} \tag{23.42}$$

$\boldsymbol{T}_a^{-1}$ is sometimes used for removing hidden lines and surfaces.

23.5 Revisit of Perspective Transformations

Let us now take a closer look at the normalized perspective transformation equation (for clarity of notation, we write $X, Y, \ldots$ for $X_e, Y_e, \ldots$), which was earlier given as:

$$[w\ X\ Y\ Z] \begin{bmatrix} 0 & 0 & 0 & k \\ 0 & 1 & 0 & 0 \\ 0 & 0 & 1 & 0 \\ -k/h & 0 & 0 & 0 \end{bmatrix} = [w^*\ X^*\ Y^*\ Z^*]. \tag{23.43}$$

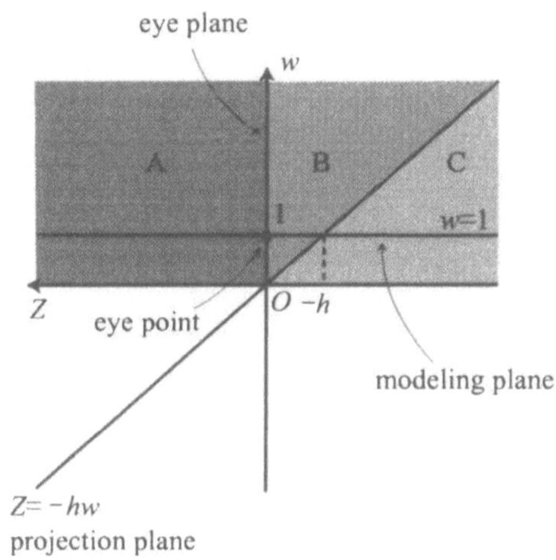

Figure 23.11: Vector space before perspective transformation.

Fig. 23.11 shows the $X = Y = 0$ section of $wXYZ$-space before perspective transformation. The geometric model is normally defined within the range $-\infty < Z/w < -h$ on the $w = 1$ plane, while the eye is at point $X = Y = Z = 0$ on the same plane. The projection plane is given by:

$$z = \frac{Z}{w} = -h,$$

or

$$Z = -hw.$$

We now divide the $w > 0$ region into three zones, A, B and C, and see how they are affected by perspective transformation.

1. **Zone behind the eye plane**

   We shall call the region behind the eye plane "zone A." A geometric model defined in this zone cannot be seen from the eye.

$$\text{Zone } A \ldots 0 < Z/w < +\infty.$$

2. **Zone between the eye plane and projection plane**

   We will designate as "zone B" the region between the eye plane and the projection plane.

$$\text{Zone } B \ldots -h < Z/w < 0.$$

3. **Zone forward of the projection plane**

   The region forward of the projection plane is where a geometric model is usually defined. This shall be designated as "zone C."

$$\text{Zone } C \ldots -\infty < Z/w < -h.$$

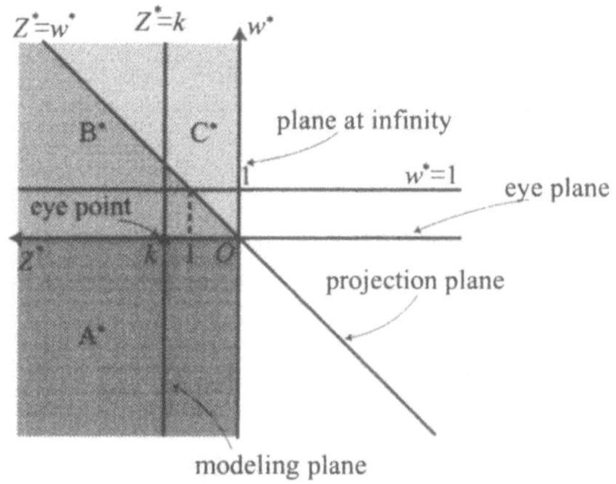

Figure 23.12: Vector space after perspective transformation.

Let us examine how certain planes and points are affected by the perspective transformation (Fig. 23.12).

a. $w=1$ **plane (modeling plane)**

   Substituting $w=1$ into eq.(23.43), we obtain $Z^*=k$. To obtain a perspective image, a point on this plane must be further projected onto the $w^*=1$ plane.

b. $w=0$ **plane (plane at infinity)**

   Substituting $w=0$ into eq.(23.43), we obtain $Z^*=0$, hence $z^*=0$. Thus, a point at infinity will have a z^*-value of 0 after transformation (this is because eq.(23.43) is a normalized transformation).

c. $Z=-hw$ **plane (projection plane)**

   Substituting $Z=-hw$ into eq.(23.43), we obtain $Z^*=w^*$, which represents the transformed projection plane. Here, we have $z^*=Z^*/w^*=1$ (again, this is because eq.(23.43) is a normalized transformation).

d. $Z = 0$ **(eye plane)**

Substituting $Z = 0$ into eq.(23.43), we obtain $w^* = 0$; this is the transformed eye plane.

e. **Eye**

Letting $X = Y = Z = 0$ and $w = 1$ in eq.(23.43), we obtain $(0, 0, 0, k)$. The eye is thus transformed to a point at $Z^* = k$ on the Z^*-axis.

As shown in Fig. 23.12, zones A, B and C are respectively transformed to A^*, B^* and C^*, that is:

$$\begin{aligned}&\text{Zone } A^* \ldots w^* < 0,\ Z^* > 0,\\ &\text{Zone } B^* \ldots 0 < w^* < Z^*,\\ &\text{Zone } C^* \ldots 0 < Z^* < w^*.\end{aligned}$$

Consider now the sign of w^* after the four-dimensional linear transformation eq.(23.43). We see that $w^* = 0$ for points on the eye plane, $w^* > 0$ for those in zones forward of the eye plane (i.e., B^* and C^*), and $w^* < 0$ for those behind (i.e., A^*). Note in particular the last case (for points behind the eye plane) where the sign of w^* becomes reversed (see Fig. 23.12).

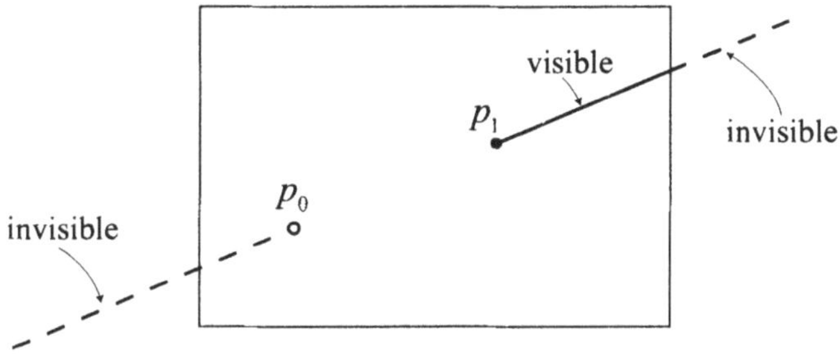

Figure 23.13: External line segment after perspective transformation.

How then is a line segment affected by perspective transformation?

When the entire line segment lies forward of the eye plane, the transformation is straightforward and nothing special occurs.

Special attention is needed, however, when a line segment crosses the eye plane. In this case, with end points having opposite w^* signs, perspective transformation produces an external line segment. When the end points are perspectively transformed and projected onto the $w^* = 1$ plane, both points may appear in the visible xy-region (see Fig. 23.13). It could be a laborious task to establish, after projection, the visibility for such an anomalous line segment.

This problem can be handled with relative ease if we clip all line segments while still in vector space, before being projected onto the $w^* = 1$ plane, i.e., before division operations (see page 358 of [40]) (this is discussed in Section 23.6.2). That is, only one kind of simple line segment, i.e., internal line segment, has to be dealt with if we perform the operations in vector space.

23.6 Homogeneous Clipping

We begin our discussion on homogeneous clipping by looking at the two-dimensional case.

23.6.1 2-D Homogeneous Clipping

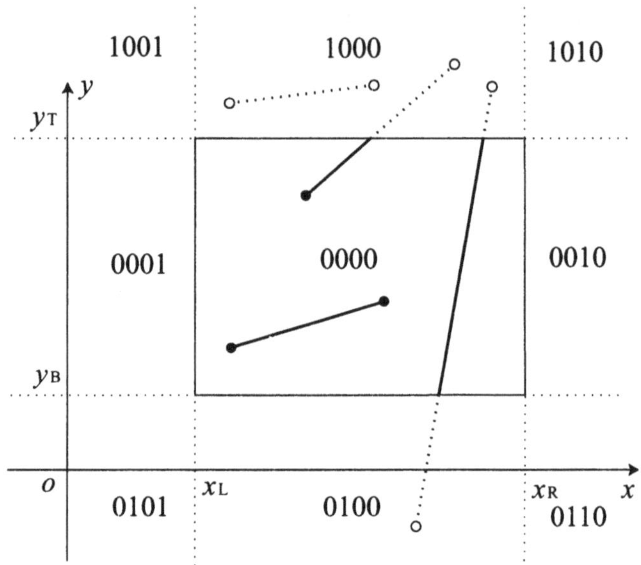

Figure 23.14: 2-D clipping using ordinary coordinates.

When the visible region is represented by a rectangle with boundaries parallel to x- and y-coordinate axes, two-dimensional clipping in ordinary coordinates is the process of determining prior to display those line segments and their parts that lie within the rectangular visible region (see Fig. 23.14). Two-dimensional clipping using ordinary coordinates means determining line segments satisfying the following conditions:

$$x_L \le x \le x_R, \quad y_B \le y \le y_T.$$

Clipping of a line segment expressed in ordinary coordinates is usually carried out by the following algorithm [52]:

(1) Determine the four-bit codes C_0 and C_1 for the end points of a given line segment p_0p_1. The four-bit codes represent the nine zones defined by the extensions of the rectangle's boundaries as shown in Fig. 23.14.

(2) Carry out the following simple tests:

(2.1) If $C_0 = C_1 = 0000$, the line segment lies entirely within the rectangle; no further processing is needed and we proceed to next line segment. If $C_0 = C_1 = 0000$ is not satisfied, proceed to (2.2).

(2.2) If the bit-by-bit logical product (AND) of C_0 and C_1 is not 0000, then the line segment lies entirely outside of the rectangle. This line segment is discarded and we proceed to next line segment.

If the bit-by-bit logical product is 0000, proceed to (3).

(3) At this stage, we know that at least one of the end points lies outside of the rectangle. We shall designate this point as p_0.

(3.1) When the bit-by-bit logical products between C_0 and each of 0001, 0010, 0100 and 1000 are obtained, one or more of the results will not be 0000. This information can be used to identify the zone where p_0 lies. This will in turn decide which boundary intersects with the line segment.

(3.2) The intersection point p_i with the boundary is determined.

(3.3) The line segment p_0p_i lies outside of the rectangle, so is discarded. Turning our attention now to the line segment p_ip_1, we return to step (1) and repeat the above process.

Consisting of repetitions of very simple steps, this algorithm allows us to carry out clipping in an efficient manner. But since it applies only to internal line segments, it cannot be used for treating external line segments or half-lines, which sometimes occur when displaying line segment approximations of rational curves or perspectively transformed line segments.

To deal with such situations, J. F. Blinn proposed the use of homogeneous coordinates for clipping [4] [1]. This is now discussed. The following is somewhat modified from his publication.

For convenience, we can simplify the conditions for two-dimensional clipping as follows:

$$-1 \leq x \leq +1, \quad -1 \leq y \leq +1. \tag{23.44}$$

This is expressed in homogeneous coordinates as:

$$-1 \leq \frac{X}{w} \leq +1, \quad -1 \leq \frac{Y}{w} \leq +1, \tag{23.45}$$

or,

$$\begin{cases} -w \leq X \leq w, & -w \leq Y \leq w, \quad (w > 0), \\ w \leq X \leq -w, & w \leq Y \leq -w, \quad (w < 0). \end{cases} \tag{23.46}$$

This is graphically shown in Fig. 23.15, where we see that there are two visible regions, i.e., one for $w>0$ and the other for $w<0$.

A line segment is usually represented in homogeneous coordinates using $w = 1$ as the first coordinate, i.e., as a line segment on the $w = 1$ plane. A

[1] Here, a two-dimensional line segment expressed in ordinary coordinates is processed in three-dimensional space. We shall call this "two-dimensional homogeneous clipping" in this book to distinguish it from conventional clipping processed in two-dimensional space. Thus, two-dimension refers here to the line segment's dimension when expressed in ordinary coordinates.

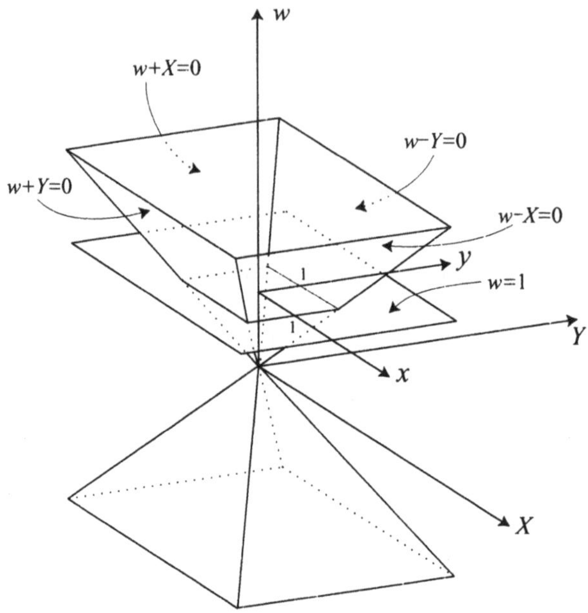

Figure 23.15: Visible regions in 2-D clipping using homogeneous coordinates.

rational curve, however, is expressed where the w-coordinate is not always equal to unity.

For instance, a circular arc expressed as:

$$[w\ X\ Y] = [1+t^2\ \ 2t\ \ 1-t^2]$$

has as its w-coordinate a positive number equal to or greater than unity.

Meanwhile, the hyperbola expressed by:

$$[w\ X\ Y] = [1-t^2\ \ \frac{1+t^2}{2}\ \ \sqrt{2}t] \tag{23.47}$$

is shown in wXY-space as in Fig. 23.16(a), while its projection onto the $w=1$ plane is given in Fig. (b). Note that, in wXY-space, the curve extends to the visible regions for both $w>0$ and $w<0$. Thus, the approximating line segments appearing on the $w=1$ plane can take either of the three forms: internal line segment, external line segment or half-line. An external line segment will appear as two segments.

To obtain the two line segments, we need only one clipping routine, i.e., that for the $w \geq 0$ clipping region. That is, the basic algorithm is as follows: if $w>0$ for both end points, or $w>0$ for one end point and $w=0$ for the other, the processing is straightforward. If $w<0$ for both end points, or $w<0$ for one end point and $w=0$ for the other, the signs of all coordinates are first reversed (i.e., end point coordinates are multiplied by -1), then processed. If

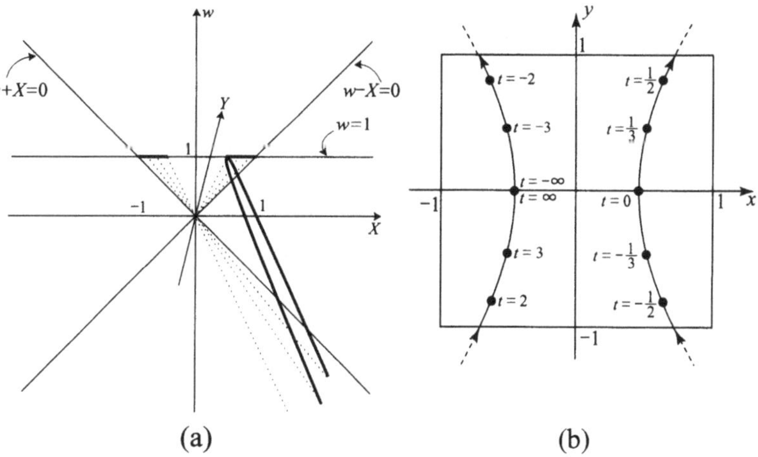

Figure 23.16: Projection of hyperbola onto $w = 1$ plane.

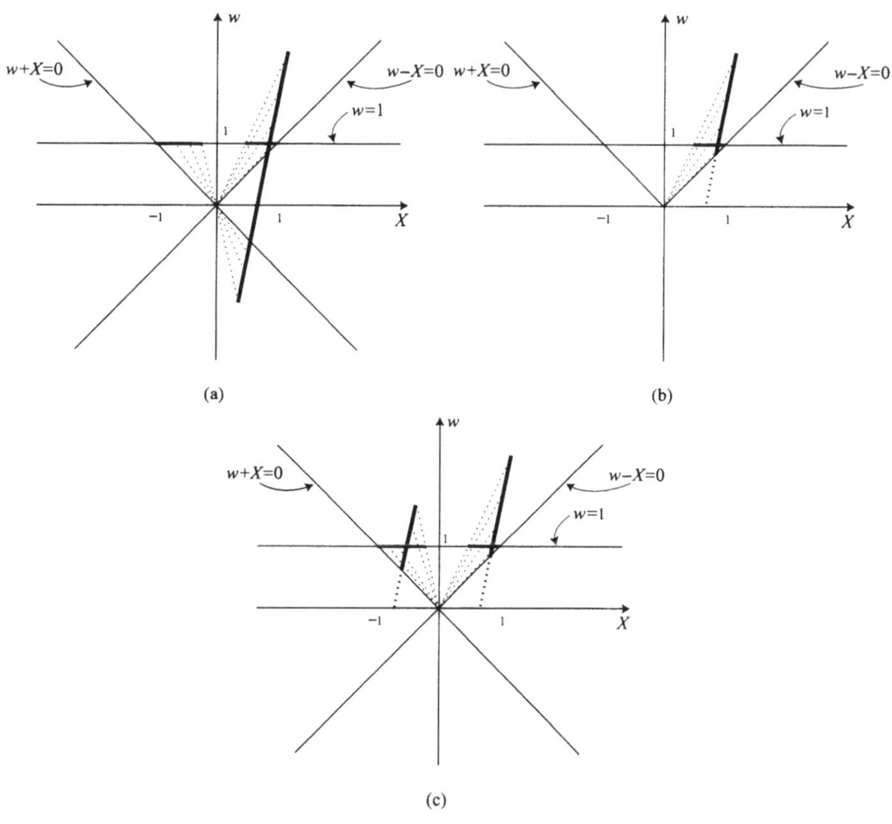

Figure 23.17: Clipping of external line segment.

the two w-coordinates have reverse signs (Fig. 23.17(a)), then the line segment is split into two pieces by $w = 0$ plane. Clipping is first carried out for the positive-w piece (Fig. (b)), and then again for the negative-w piece with the signs reversed (Fig. (c)); this will produce the two line segments we seek. This method is possible because multiplication of homogeneous coordinates by an arbitrary non-zero scalar leaves its ordinary coordinates unaffected.

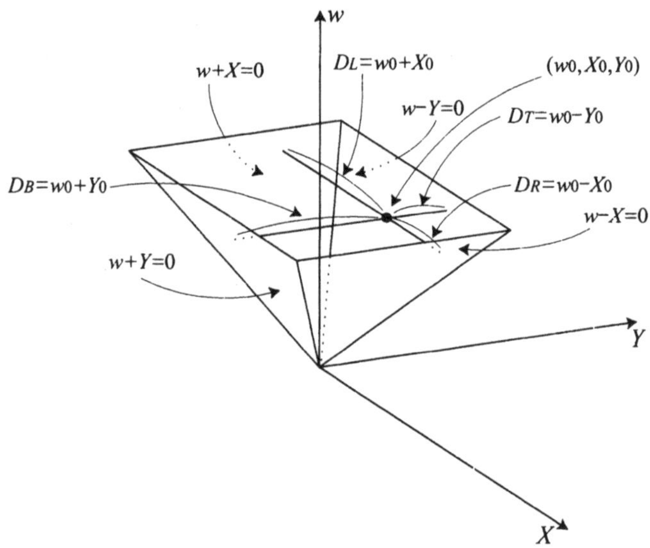

Figure 23.18: Distance coordinates.

As long as the following differences are noted, clipping in the $w \geq 0$ region can be carried out using an algorithm which is essentially the same as the one for ordinary coordinates. The signed distances from the point (w_0, X_0, Y_0) to the clipping plane along X- and Y-axes are given as follows (see Fig. 23.18):

$$\begin{aligned}
\text{Distance to } w - Y = 0 \text{ plane:} \quad & D_{T0} = w_0 - Y_0, \\
\text{Distance to } w + Y = 0 \text{ plane:} \quad & D_{B0} = w_0 + Y_0, \\
\text{Distance to } w - X = 0 \text{ plane:} \quad & D_{R0} = w_0 - X_0, \\
\text{Distance to } w + X = 0 \text{ plane:} \quad & D_{L0} = w_0 + X_0.
\end{aligned}$$

These four planes divide $w \geq 0$ space into nine zones. If the point lies in the visible region, all four distances are positive. However, if the point lies outside of the visible region, then at least one of the distances will be negative. The signed distances thus constitute a set of distance coordinates (D_T, D_B, D_R, D_L) indicating the zone in which the point exists. In other words, the four-bit codes in this case are given by the signs of distance coordinates, where zero distance is considered positive.

The intersecting point between a line segment and clipping plane can be determined as follows:

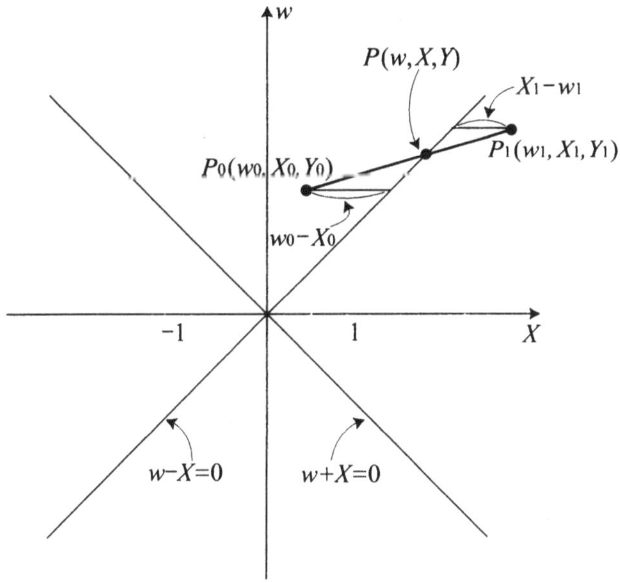

Figure 23.19: Calculation of intersection point with boundary plane.

Consider now the intersection point for a line segment P_0P_1 and the w–$X=0$ plane (see Fig. 23.19), where the coordinates are given by $P_0=(w_0,X_0,Y_0)$ and $P_1=(w_1,X_1,Y_1)$. The signed distances from P_0 and P_1 to the $w-X=0$ plane along X-axis are respectively given by w_0-X_0 and w_1-X_1, so the intersection point $P=(w,X,Y)$ is obtained as:

$$\overline{\boldsymbol{P}} = \overline{\boldsymbol{P}_0 + \frac{D_{R0}}{D_{R0}-D_{R1}}(\boldsymbol{P}_1 - \boldsymbol{P}_0)}$$
$$= \begin{cases} \overline{D_{R0}\boldsymbol{P}_1 - D_{R1}\boldsymbol{P}_0} & (D_{R0} \geq 0 \wedge D_{R1} \leq 0), \\ \overline{D_{R1}\boldsymbol{P}_0 - D_{R0}\boldsymbol{P}_1} & (D_{R0} \leq 0 \wedge D_{R1} \geq 0). \end{cases} \tag{23.48}$$

If the intersection point lies on some other boundary plane, it can be obtained in the same way.

It should be clear that the algorithms for two-dimensional homogeneous clipping and for clipping using ordinary coordinates are quite similar as long as the differences above are noted.

23.6.2 3-D Homogeneous Clipping

Three-dimensional clipping means identifying those line segments that lie in the three-dimensional display region prior to display. The three-dimensional display region is that space within the viewing pyramid which is generally sandwiched between the front and back planes (see Section 23.2). This space is transformed by the normalized perspective transformation to the region:

$$-1 \leq x_p \leq +1, \quad -1 \leq y_p \leq +1, \quad 0 \leq z_p \leq +1. \tag{23.49}$$

Here, we consider three-dimensional clipping using homogeneous coordinates [4] [2]. The relations above are expressed in homogeneous coordinates as:

$$\begin{cases} -w_p \leq X_p \leq w_p, & -w_p \leq Y_p \leq w_p, \quad 0 \leq Z_p \leq w_p, \quad (w_p > 0), \\ w_p \leq X_p \leq -w_p, & w_p \leq Y_p \leq -w_p, \quad w_p \leq Z_p \leq 0, \quad (w_p < 0). \end{cases} \tag{23.50}$$

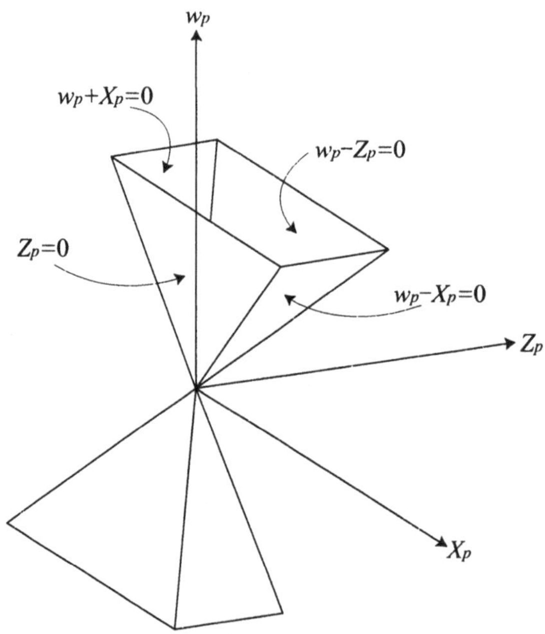

Figure 23.20: 3-D homogeneous clipping ($Y_p = 0$ section).

By comparing these conditions with those for two-dimensional homogeneous clipping, we see that the only difference is the addition of the third expressions, which are the conditions for the line segment to lie between the front and back planes. The clipping zone of eq.(23.50) is shown in Fig. 23.20, where the $w_p < 0$ clipping zone is relevant when dealing with rational curves and surfaces.

[2] Here, a three-dimensional line segment expressed in ordinary coordinates is processed in four-dimensional space. We shall call this "three-dimensional homogeneous clipping" in this book to distinguish it from conventional clipping processed in three-dimensional space. Thus, three-dimension refers here to the line segment's dimension when expressed in ordinary coordinates.

Three-dimensional homogeneous clipping is essentially the same as two-dimensional homogeneous clipping. That is, we prepare a clipping routine for the $w_p \geq 0$ clipping region. If $w_p > 0$ for both end points of the given line segment, or $w_p > 0$ for one end point and $w_p = 0$ for the other, process in a straightforward manner; if $w_p < 0$ for both end points, or $w_p < 0$ for one end point and $w_p = 0$ for the other, reverse the signs of all coordinates before processing; and if the two w_p-coordinates have reverse signs, split the segment into two pieces by $w_p = 0$ plane. Then carry out clipping of the positive-w_p piece, and then the negative-w_p piece. This process allows treating external line segments.

Whereas two-dimensional homogeneous clipping employed four distance coordinates to indicate an end point's position, three-dimensional homogeneous clipping involves six distance coordinates $(D_T, D_B, D_R, D_L, D_F, D_N)$, which represent the distances to the six planes referred to in eq.(23.50). Thus, If a pair of corresponding distance coordinates are of opposite signs, the intersection point P of a line segment P_0P_1 and the corresponding plane is given in the same form as in eq.(23.48):

$$\overline{\boldsymbol{P}} = \overline{\boldsymbol{P}_0 + \frac{D_{R0}}{D_{R0} - D_{R1}}(\boldsymbol{P}_1 - \boldsymbol{P}_0)}$$

$$= \begin{cases} \overline{D_{R0}\boldsymbol{P}_1 - D_{R1}\boldsymbol{P}_0} & (D_{R0} \geq 0 \wedge D_{R1} \leq 0), \\ \overline{D_{R1}\boldsymbol{P}_0 - D_{R0}\boldsymbol{P}_1} & (D_{R0} \leq 0 \wedge D_{R1} \geq 0). \end{cases} \tag{23.51}$$

$$\boldsymbol{P} = [w\ X\ Y\ Z], \quad \boldsymbol{P}_0 = [w_0\ X_0\ Y_0\ Z_0], \quad \boldsymbol{P}_1 = [w_1\ X_1\ Y_1\ Z_1],$$
$$D_{T0} = w_0 - Y_0, \quad D_{B0} = w_0 + Y_0, \quad D_{R0} = w_0 - X_0,$$
$$D_{L0} = w_0 + X_0, \quad D_{Y0} = w_0 - Z_0, \quad D_{H0} = Z_0.$$

Chapter 24

Classical or Two-Sided ?

In the Four-dimensional Processing we can deal with geometric elements defined either in classical projective space or in two-sided space. These geometric elements are processed in the associated vector space.

The geometric elements in two-sided space can be defined algebraically by specifying $\lambda > 0$ instead of $\lambda \neq 0$ in the equivalence relation of the classical projective space:

$$\boldsymbol{S} \sim \boldsymbol{T} \Leftrightarrow \exists \lambda \in \mathbf{R}^1, \lambda \neq 0 : \lambda \boldsymbol{S} = \boldsymbol{T}, \tag{24.1}$$

where $\boldsymbol{S}$ and $\boldsymbol{T}$ are vectors.

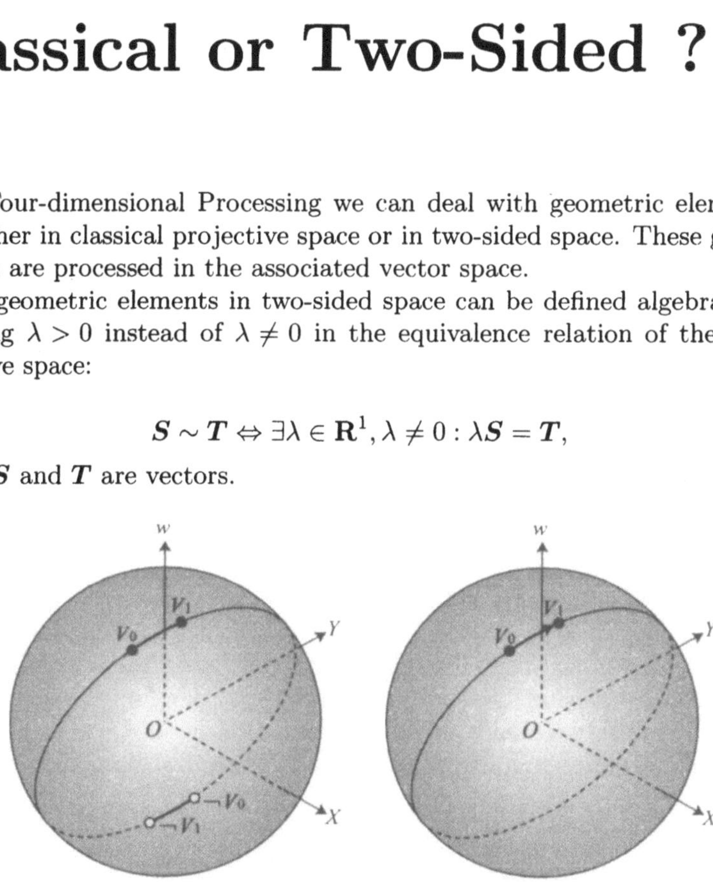

(a) Classical projective space (b) Two-sided space

Figure 24.1: Line segments defined in classical and two-sided projective spaces.

The geometrical differences between the classical projective space and the two-sided space are that the antipodal geometric element is identified in the classical projective space and not in the two-sided space (Figs.24.1, 24.2) and that the geometric elements are oriented in the two-sided space while they are not in the classical projective space.

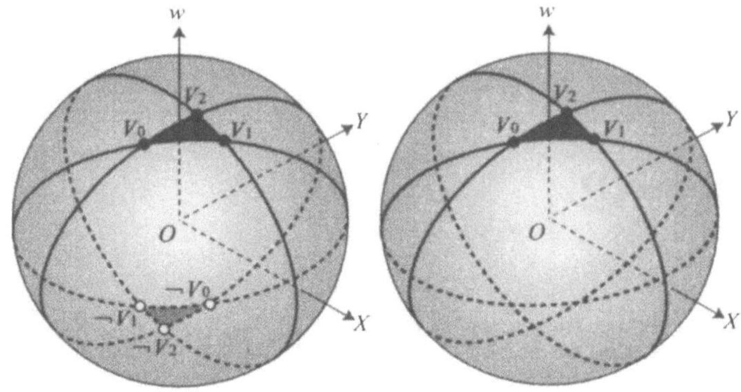

(a) Classical Projective Space (b) Two-sided Space

Figure 24.2: Triangles defined in classical and two-sided projective spaces.

Now, whether we deal with geometric elements defined in classical projective space or two-sided space, we can play without the use of a division operation which is considered to be "the root cause of all evil." Then how do we choose to use these two projective spaces appropriately ? A general rule is that we use geometric elements defined in two-sided space if we need to deal with directions or orientations, and otherwise those in classical projective space. In the following we shall explain two cases.

24.1 A Problem of Classical Projective Space

When we deal with rational curves or surfaces, we need them to be defined in classical projective space. We shall explain this by taking up an example of the intersection test of two planar rational curves.

In the Four-dimensional Processing approach a rational curve:

$$\boldsymbol{p}(t) = [\frac{X(t)}{w(t)} \; \frac{Y(t)}{w(t)}] \tag{24.2}$$

is treated as an ordinary polynomial form of dimension higher by one, that is, a homogeneous curve:

$$\overline{\boldsymbol{P}(t)} = \overline{[w(t) \; X(t) \; Y(t)]}. \tag{24.3}$$

Now, assume two planar rational curves expressed in the form eq.(24.2) are approximated by small line segments and two line segments derived from each curve are shown in Fig.24.3, where the weights w_0, w_1 of the endpoints of the line segment p_0p_1 are both positive and the weights w_a, w_b of the line segment p_ap_b are both negative. This case must be considered to be intersecting.

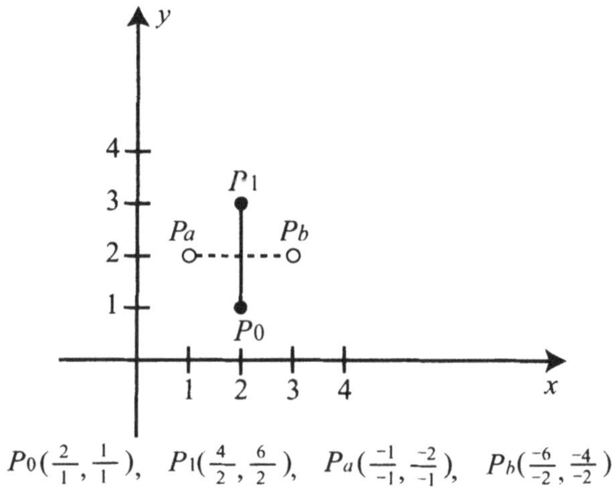

Figure 24.3: Intersection test of two line segments derived from planar rational polynomial curves.

Let us consider this case as the problem of two homogeneous curves expressed in eq.(24.3).

Assume, first, the curves are defined in classical projective space. In this case the two line segments are considered to be intersecting since the antipodal element is identified in the space.

Next, assume the curves are defined in two-sided space. Then the two line segments are considered to lie in different ranges, i.e., front range and back range, and considered not to be intersecting.

As discussed above, rational curves and surfaces need to be treated as defined in classical projective space in the Four-dimensional Processing. The reason for this lies in the convention of a division operation, where we do not distinguish the results of the operation by the signs of the denominator. For example we do not distinguish $\frac{1}{4}$ from $\frac{-1}{-4}$, but consider $\frac{1}{4} = \frac{-1}{-4}$. This convention is the same as that of classical projective space. On the other hand the convention of the two-sided space does distinguish these two results. Since we are supposed to compute and evaluate the coordinates of rational curves and surfaces according to the traditional evaluation convention of a division operation, we need to treat them to be defined in classical projective space.

24.2 A Problem of Two-sided Space

Let us consider performing a perspective transformation. The transformation which projects a point of negative z with an eye located at the origin of a right hand coordinate system is expressed as follows (see eq.(23.21)):

$$[w\ X\ Y\ Z]\begin{bmatrix} 0 & 0 & 0 & k \\ 0 & 1 & 0 & 0 \\ 0 & 0 & 1 & 0 \\ -k/h & 0 & 0 & 0 \end{bmatrix} = [w^*\ X^*\ Y^*\ Z^*], \tag{24.4}$$

where a $2k\times 2k$ projection plane is placed at $z=-h$, and the projected image is normalized such that $-1\leq x^*, y^*\leq +1$ corresponding to the projection plane square, and $0\leq z^*\leq +1$ corresponding to the region in front of the projection plane (Fig. 24.4).

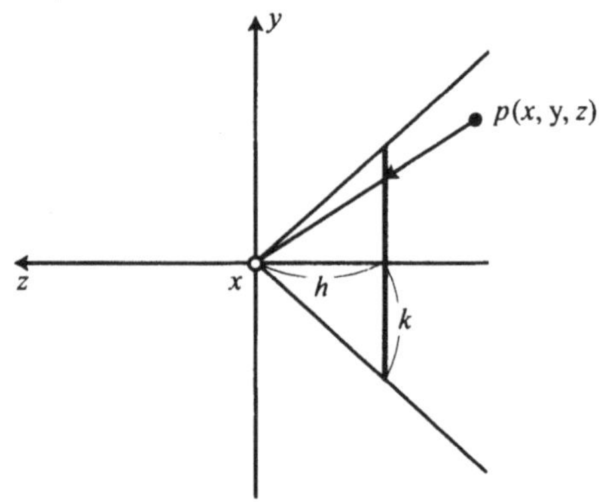

Figure 24.4: A perspective projection.

The relationships of four dimensional vector spaces before and after the perspective transformation are shown in Figs. 24.5 and 24.6.

We assume an object is defined in front of the projection plane with $w>0$. In Fig. 24.5, this region is shown as “A.” We ordinarily define an object on hyperplane $w=1$. In the figure we also show two other regions, one between the projection plane and the eye plane, and the other behind the eye plane, as “B” and “C” respectively, where we define the eye plane as the one that passes through the eye point and is perpendicular to z-axis.

In Fig. 24.6, each region after the transformation is shown as “A*”,“B*”and “C*.” The object definition plane $w=1$ is transformed into $Z^*=k$ after the transformation. Then finally the points on $Z^*=k$ are projected onto $w^*=1$. The $w^*>0$ points on $Z^*=k$ correspond to the space in front of the eye plane, and the $w^*<0$ points on the plane to the space behind the eye plane, before the perspective transformation.

It is the two-sided space approach to distinguish between $w^*>0$ and $w^*<0$ regions, where the former corresponds to “front range” and the latter to “back range” in the two-sided space. If some application requires us to distinguish between the spaces in front of and behind the eye plane, then it will be necessary to employ the two-sided space approach.

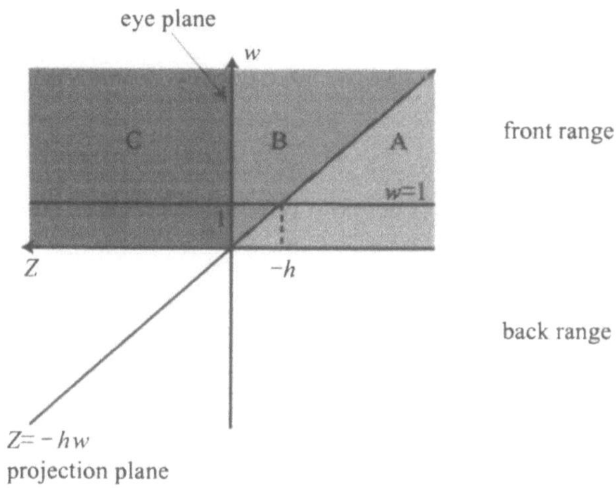

Figure 24.5: Before perspective transformation ($X = Y = 0$ section).

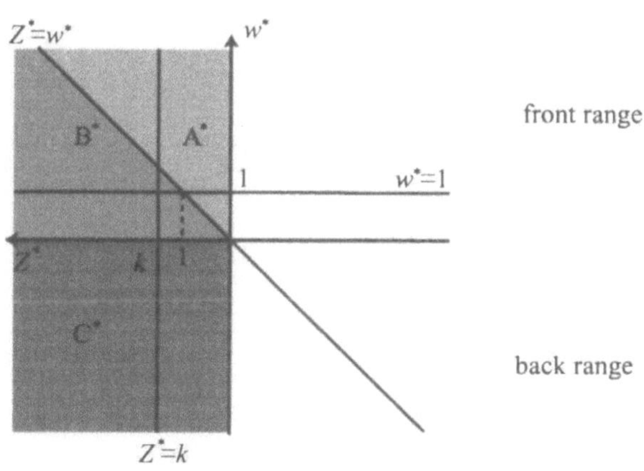

Figure 24.6: After perspective transformation ($X = Y = 0$ section).

Part III

Test Results

Chapter 25

Various Tests

25.1 Exactness

Theoretically speaking, the homogeneous processing, combined with integer arithmetic, is supposed to make it possible to attain exact computations as long as it deals with rational numbers.

This section demonstrates various, basic experimental results of the homogeneous processing in contrast to those of Euclidean processing on exactness.

For exact arithmetic, see Chapter 16.

25.1.1 Intersections of Two Planar Lines

The intersection computation of two planar lines or line segments would be one of the most fundamental geometric computations in a computer aided geometric design system.

This computation has, however, numerical error problems in ordinary floating-point computational environment. It is well known from numerical analysis that the most accurate results will be obtained if the two lines are perpendicular and that there will be severe numerical problems when the lines are almost parallel [20]. For such a small intersection angle, $\theta = 1/2^m$, between the lines as can be approximated as $\sin\theta \doteqdot \theta$, about $m+2$ binary digits are expected to be lost [24].

Experiments

We perform simple computations of the intersection point between two line segments by decreasing the intersection angle with respect to the three cases shown below (Fig. 25.1):

A. **Double-precision floating-point, real arithmetic**

   This case uses the double precision floating-point, real arithmetic (IEEE standard), where real coordinate data are directly expressed in floating-point format.

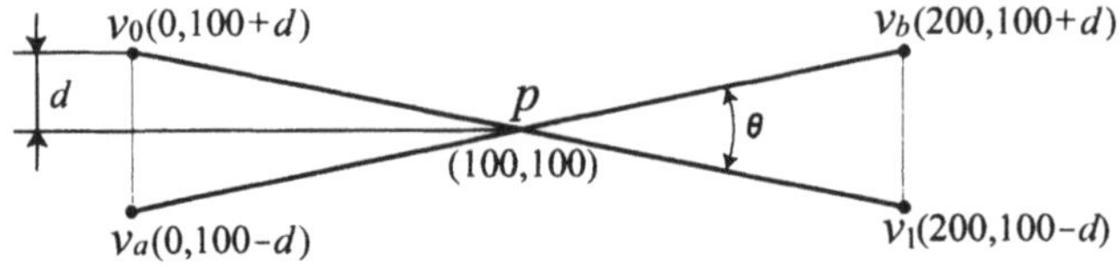

Figure 25.1: Intersection between two 2-D line segments.

From two end points, $v_0(x_0, y_0)$ and $v_1(x_1, y_1)$, line equation, $a+bx+cy=0$, is determined such that:

$$a = x_0y_1 - x_1y_0, \quad b = y_0 - y_1, \quad c = -(x_0 - x_1). \tag{25.1}$$

From two such lines, $a_0 + b_0x + c_0y = 0$ and $a_1 + b_1x + c_1y = 0$, the intersection point p is computed as follows:

Putting

$$\Delta = \begin{vmatrix} b_0 & b_1 \\ c_0 & c_1 \end{vmatrix}, \quad \Delta_x = -\begin{vmatrix} a_0 & a_1 \\ c_0 & c_1 \end{vmatrix}, \quad \Delta_y = \begin{vmatrix} a_0 & a_1 \\ b_0 & b_1 \end{vmatrix}, \tag{25.2}$$

we have

$$p = (x,\ y) = (\frac{\Delta_x}{\Delta}, \frac{\Delta_y}{\Delta}).$$

This type of computation is considered to be used commonly.

B. **Double-precision floating-point, integer arithmetic**

This case uses the double precision floating-point, integer arithmetic (IEEE standard).

In eq.(25.1), rational numbers a, b, c are transformed into integers by multiplying them the least common multiple, and then normalized. These integer coefficients are expressed in floating-point format.

C. **Variable word-length integer arithmetic**

In eq.(25.1), rational numbers a, b, c are transformed into integers by multiplying them the least common multiple, and then normalized. These integer coefficients are expressed in the variable word-length integer format presented in Section 16.2.

Test results are shown in Table 25.1, which shows the absolute errors of x-coordinates of the intersection points.

The test was done using a self-made computer with Ashlon 800MHz processor, 256MB memory.

Table 25.1: Absolute errors of intersection computations in three cases.

d	**Case A**	**Case B**	**Case C**
1×10^{0}	0	0	0
1×10^{-1}	5.68×10^{-12}	0	0
1×10^{-2}	-5.12×10^{-11}	0	0
1×10^{-3}	-4.77×10^{-10}	0	0
1×10^{-4}	-3.32×10^{-9}	0	0
1×10^{-5}	-5.50×10^{-8}	0	0
1×10^{-6}	-8.19×10^{-7}	0	0
1×10^{-7}	-9.55×10^{-7}	$+6.14 \times 10^{-6}$	0
1×10^{-8}	-1.07×10^{-4}	-3.32×10^{-5}	0
1×10^{-9}	$+3.98 \times 10^{-4}$	$+2.60 \times 10^{-4}$	0
1×10^{-10}	$+1.06 \times 10^{-2}$	-4.57×10^{-3}	0
1×10^{-11}	-4.36×10^{-2}	$+5.56 \times 10^{-2}$	0
1×10^{-12}	$+6.45 \times 10^{-1}$	-7.64×10^{-2}	0
1×10^{-13}	-6.38×10^{0}	-9.21×10^{-1}	0
1×10^{-14}	$6.38 \times 10^{+1}$	$-1.00 \times 10^{+2}$	0

Discussions

1. As expected, errors increase with the decrease of the intersection angle in the cases of floating-point arithmetic (due to digit-cancellation error). The errors become maximum when the intersection angle is minimum.

   On the other hand there is no such error involved in the case of variable word-length integer arithmetic.

2. Even in the floating-point computations, there is a clear difference in the error occurrences between the real and integer cases; the integer case shows no error while the intersection angle θ is not extremely small (while $d \geq 1 \times 10^{-6}$ or $\frac{\theta}{2} > 10^{-8}$). The reason is as follows:

   In expressing decimal fractions with floating-point representation, some amount of error must be involved in the real case (case A)(due to conversion error). For example, the decimal fraction 0.6 is equal to the periodic binary fraction 0.1001 1001... because $3/5 = \sum_{i=1}^{\infty} 9/16^{i}$ [24].

   In the integer case (case B), on the other hand, any scalar multiplication does not affect the coefficients. Thus we can express rational numbers exactly in floating-point format as long as the number of digits does not exceed the representable limit of mantissa. When a number exceeds the representable limit of mantissa, it has to be rounded. This incurs a round-off error.

3. From the results of cases A and B, we can conclude that the integerization

and normalization are effective in performing exact arithmetic while the numbers of digits involved are not extremely large (see Section 16.6).

4. In the variable word-length integer case or case C, there are no such errors as round-off, conversion or cancellation errors. Thus the results of computations are truly exact.

5. Table 25.2 shows the results of computing times in the three cases above. In cases B and C, homogeneous coefficient normalizations are done.

Table 25.2: Comparison of computing times in three cases.

d	**Case A**	**Case B**	**Case C**
1×10^{0}	0.0329	0.0811	0.3933
1×10^{-1}	0.0318	0.0833	0.3958
1×10^{-2}	0.0360	0.0867	0.4131
1×10^{-3}	0.0305	0.1048	0.4095
1×10^{-4}	0.0311	0.1096	0.4268
1×10^{-5}	0.0306	0.1244	0.4558
1×10^{-6}	0.0305	0.1243	0.4402
1×10^{-7}	0.0306	0.1523	0.4390
1×10^{-8}	0.0442	0.1655	0.4572
1×10^{-9}	0.0313	0.1858	0.4641
1×10^{-10}	0.0317	0.1972	0.4640
1×10^{-11}	0.0315	0.1960	0.4623
1×10^{-12}	0.0312	0.2099	0.4613
1×10^{-13}	0.0318	0.2257	0.4602
1×10^{-14}	0.0345	0.1629	0.4530

unit: milli-second

Data Length for Exact Computations

The characteristics of data length increases for the exact intersection point computations between two line segments were analysed in Section 16.4. This analysis was tested with respect to cases 1 and 2 against the data shown in Fig 25.2:

Case 1

This is the case where line equations are derived from Plücker coordinates and no common factors are deleted among the coefficients of the line equations (see eq.(16.2)). According to the analysis, the data length of w in this case increases by 10 bits when h is increased by a factor of 10.

Case 2

This is the case where line equations are derived from Plücker coordinates and common factors are deleted among the coefficients of the line equations (see eq.(16.3)). According to the analysis, the data length of w in this case increases by 10 bits when h is increased by a factor of as many as 1000.

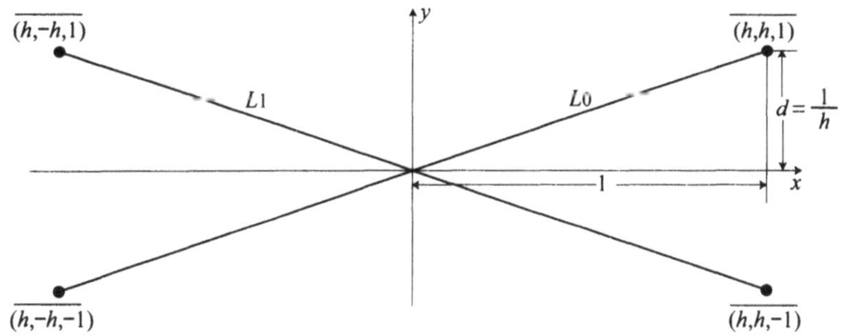

Figure 25.2: Test of data length increase.

Table 25.3: Increase of data length for exact computation.

h	**Lengths of w values of intersection point** (bits)	
	Case 1	Case 2
10^1	13	8
10^2	23	11
10^3	33	15
10^4	43	18
10^5	53	21
10^6	63	25
10^7	73	28
10^8	83	31
10^9	93	35
10^{10}	103	38
10^{11}	113	41
10^{12}	123	45
10^{13}	133	48
10^{14}	143	51

The test results are exactly the same as the results of the analysis (see Table 25.3).

The test results above indicate that in exact arithmetic it is very important to simplify and normalize integer homogeneous data prior to computations, in terms of computing efficiency and memory space saving (see Section 16.5).

25.1.2 Pentagon Problem

Next, we test the pentagon problem, where the output of one intersection computation becomes the input of the next. In this situation, precision losses in one computation may accumulate, and may be magnified by subsequent computations.

Experiments

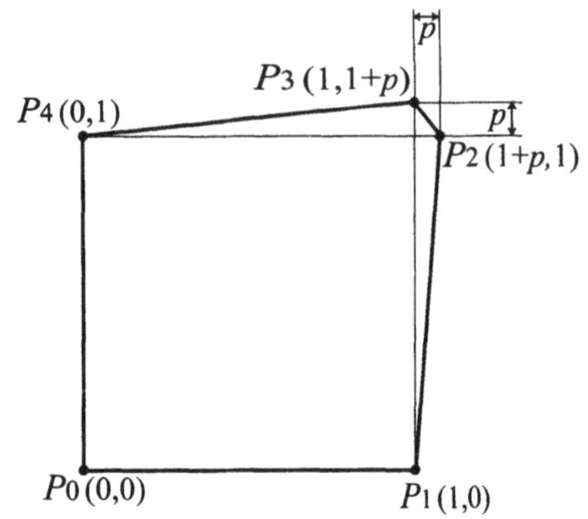

Figure 25.3: Pentagon to be tested.

We test the pentagon shown in Fig. 25.3 by decreasing the distance p (0.1, 0.01, 0.001) with respect to the three cases shown below. $In^N(out^N())$ cases are not tested because $out^N(in^N())$ cases produce much more errors than the former because the first going-in operations tend to make generating points closer each other.

The tests were done using a self-made computer with Ashlon 800MHz processor, 256MB memory.

A. **Double-precision floating-point arithmetic (Euclidean)**

This case uses the double precision floating-point, real arithmetic (IEEE standard), where real coordinate data are directly expressed in floating-point format. This type of computation is considered to be used commonly.

The results are shown on the left sides of Tables 25.4, 25.5 and 25.6.

B. **Double-precision floating-point arithmetic (homogeneous)**

This case employs the homogeneous processing and uses the double precision floating-point, integer arithmetic (IEEE standard).

By using the property of homogeneous coordinates and coefficients, coordinate and coefficient data are transformed into integer and expressed in double-precision floating-point format.

At each going-in or -out operation, homogeneous coordinate and coefficient data are exactly normalized, that is, the greatest common divisors are removed although the data are expressed in floating-point format (see Section 2.4.2).

The results are shown on the right sides of Tables 25.4, 25.5 and 25.6.

Table 25.4: x-, y-errors after $out^N(in^N())$(Floating-point) (p=0.1).

	N	**Errors** x (Euclid)	**Errors** y (Euclid)	**Errors** x (Homo.)	**Errors** y (Homo.)
p_0	1	-1.28×10^{-15}	-1.28×10^{-15}	0	0
	3	-2.60×10^{-13}	-2.60×10^{-13}	0	0
	5	3.64×10^{-12}	3.64×10^{-12}	0	0
p_1	1	0	-6.01×10^{-16}	0	0
	3	-1.48×10^{-13}	1.19×10^{-13}	0	0
	5	7.22×10^{-12}	-4.96×10^{-12}	0	0
p_2	1	0	0	0	0
	3	-1.22×10^{-14}	2.15×10^{-14}	0	0
	5	-1.84×10^{-12}	-2.27×10^{-12}	0	0
p_3	1	0	0	0	0
	3	2.15×10^{-14}	-1.22×10^{-14}	0	0
	5	-2.27×10^{-12}	-1.84×10^{-12}	0	0
p_4	1	-6.01×10^{-16}	0	0	0
	3	1.19×10^{-13}	-1.48×10^{-13}	0	0
	5	-4.96×10^{-12}	7.22×10^{-12}	0	0

Table 25.5: x-, y-errors after $out^N(in^N())$(Floating-point) (p=0.01).

	N	**Errors** x (Euclid)	**Errors** y (Euclid)	**Errors** x (Homo.)	**Errors** y (Homo.)
p_0	1	0	0	0	0
	3	-3.18×10^{-11}	-3.18×10^{-11}	0	0
	5	-2.40×10^{-7}	-2.40×10^{-7}	7.06×10^{-8}	7.06×10^{-8}
p_1	1	0	-5.50×10^{-15}	0	0
	3	8.64×10^{-13}	-7.07×10^{-12}	0	0
	5	-4.67×10^{-8}	-4.43×10^{-8}	-7.73×10^{-8}	1.05×10^{-7}
p_2	1	0	0	0	0
	3	-7.45×10^{-13}	-5.52×10^{-13}	0	0
	5	-1.06×10^{-9}	9.64×10^{-12}	8.27×10^{-10}	1.44×10^{-9}
p_3	1	0	0	0	0
	3	-5.52×10^{-13}	-7.45×10^{-13}	0	0
	5	9.64×10^{-12}	-1.06×10^{-9}	1.44×10^{-9}	8.27×10^{-10}
p_4	1	-5.50×10^{-15}	0	0	0
	3	-7.07×10^{-12}	8.64×10^{-13}	0	0
	5	-4.43×10^{-8}	-4.67×10^{-8}	1.05×10^{-7}	-7.73×10^{-8}

Table 25.6: x-, y-errors after $out^N(in^N())$(Floating-point) (p=0.001).

	N	**Errors x** (Euclid)	**Errors y** (Euclid)	**Errors x** (Homo.)	**Errors y** (Homo.)
	1	-1.11×10^{-13}	-1.11×10^{-13}	0	0
p_0	3	-5.16×10^{-9}	-5.16×10^{-9}	2.43×10^{-8}	2.43×10^{-8}
	5	6.43×10^{-5}	$+6.43 \times 10^{-5}$	-1.82×10^{-5}	-1.82×10^{-5}
	1	0	0	0	0
p_1	3	-3.37×10^{-8}	3.20×10^{-8}	9.14×10^{-8}	-8.46×10^{-8}
	5	-2.01×10^{-4}	2.27×10^{-4}	2.52×10^{-4}	-2.61×10^{-4}
	1	0	0	0	0
p_2	3	1.48×10^{-10}	1.49×10^{-10}	1.30×10^{-10}	-1.18×10^{-10}
	5	2.29×10^{-7}	4.17×10^{-7}	4.15×10^{-8}	-2.12×10^{-7}
	1	0	0	0	0
p_3	3	1.49×10^{-10}	1.48×10^{-10}	1.18×10^{-10}	1.30×10^{-10}
	5	4.17×10^{-7}	2.29×10^{-7}	-2.12×10^{-7}	4.15×10^{-8}
	1	0	0	0	0
p_4	3	3.20×10^{-8}	-3.37×10^{-8}	-8.46×10^{-8}	9.14×10^{-8}
	5	2.27×10^{-4}	-2.01×10^{-4}	-2.61×10^{-4}	2.52×10^{-4}

C. **Variable word-length integer arithmetic (homogeneous)**

By using the property of homogeneous coordinates and coefficients, coordinate and coefficient data are transformed into integer and represented in variable word-length integer format.

At each going-in or, -out operation, homogeneous coordinate and coefficient data were exactly normalized. The results are shown in Tables 25.7, 25.8 and 25.9.

The effects of the normalizations of variable word-length integer data are shown in Table 25.10 in terms of data lengths and processing times. In the table, the processing times are also compared with those of case B, where simple normalization, i.e., only exponent subtraction is done in this case. This test was done using DELL Dimension XPS T computer with Intel Pentium III/500MHz processor, 383MB memory.

Discussions

1. Cases A (Euclidean floating-point case) shows some amount of errors (Tables 25.4, 25.5 and 25.6). These errors increase when p becomes smaller. The more the going-in or going-out operations are repeated, the more the errors are accumulated.

2. Case B (Homogeneous floating-point case), on the other hand, does not show any error while the computations are not severe and do not require

Table 25.7: x-, y-errors after $out^N(in^N())$ (Homogeneous Integer) (p=0.1).

	N	**Errors** x	**Errors** y
p_0	1	0	0
	3	0	0
	5	0	0
p_1	1	0	0
	3	0	0
	5	0	0
p_2	1	0	0
	3	0	0
	5	0	0
p_3	1	0	0
	3	0	0
	5	0	0
p_4	1	0	0
	3	0	0
	5	0	0

Table 25.8: x-, y-errors after $out^N(in^N())$ (Homogeneous Integer) (p=0.01).

	N	**Errors** x	**Errors** y
p_0	1	0	0
	3	0	0
	5	0	0
p_1	1	0	0
	3	0	0
	5	0	0
p_2	1	0	0
	3	0	0
	5	0	0
p_3	1	0	0
	3	0	0
	5	0	0
p_4	1	0	0
	3	0	0
	5	0	0

Table 25.9: x-, y-errors after $out^N(in^N())$ (Homogeneous Integer) (p=0.001).

	N	**Errors** x	**Errors** y
p_0	1	0	0
	3	0	0
	5	0	0
p_1	1	0	0
	3	0	0
	5	0	0
p_2	1	0	0
	3	0	0
	5	0	0
p_3	1	0	0
	3	0	0
	5	0	0
p_4	1	0	0
	3	0	0
	5	0	0

Table 25.10: Computation times and decimal digits of data after $out^4(in^4())$.

p	**Unnormalized variable integer**		**Normalized variable integer**		**Homogeneous floating-point**
	data [digits]	times [ms]	data [digits]	times [ms]	times [ms]
0.1	21,924	13,377.608	2	13.037	0.482
0.01	41,712	48,637.537	2	15.061	0.484
0.001	62,033	111,831.305	2	17.367	0.484
0.0001	82,409	196,794.464	2	19.898	0.483
0.00001	102,792	305,751.916	2	21.941	0.482
0.000001	123,175	438,598.700	2	25.708	0.483

• In the table, "digits" mean decimal ones.

long digit data.

3. Case B shows some errors when the computations are severe and require long digit data. The error characteristics do not show much difference from those of case A.

4. In cases A and B, the errors appear symmetrically because the shape of the original pentagon is symmetrical with respect to line $y=x$.

5. As expected, case C (Homogeneous variable word-length integer case) does not show any error at all irrespective of p values and restores the original pentagon data perfectly (Tables 25.7, 25.8 and 25.9).

6. It is confirmed in case C that the original pentagon data are perfectly restored even if some lines happen to be parallel during going-in and -out operations.

7. Table 25.10 shows that the homogeneous coordinate normalizations are very effective and indispensable in case C.

8. Table 25.10 shows that even if the normalizations are done in the exact computations (case C), the processing speed is much slower compared with that of case A or case B.

25.1.3 Point Computations on a Rational Curve

We generate successive points on both the conventional NURBS curve and the type-I homogenized NURBS curve by applying the difference calculus method (see Section 10.7), and compare the errors between the two types of curves. In principle the difference calculus method can not be applied to the conventional NURBS curve because it is in a rational, not an ordinary polynomial form. Thus we apply the four-dimensional approach to the conventional NURBS curve. That is, we compute it as the type-S homogenized NURBS curve.

We measured coordinate values after computing 200, 600 and 1000 points of the homogenized NURBS curves of orders 3 and 4, where data are represented in floating-point format. Note that integer data are expressed in floating-point format even in the type-I homogenized NURBS curve.

The control vectors of these curves are shown below:

Order $M = 3$

$$[1\ 50\ 400\ 100],\quad [1\ 100\ 100\ 100],\quad [1\ 300\ 300\ 100].$$

Order $M = 4$

$$[1\ 50\ 400\ 100],\quad [1\ 100\ 100\ 100],\quad [1\ 300\ 300\ 100],\quad [1\ 500\ 50\ 100].$$

Used Computer

The experiment was done under the following environment:
computer: EPSON486 Note As

CPU: intel486DX2 50Mz (floating-point processing unit included)
OS: MS-DOS 5.00

The test results are shown in Tables 25.11 and 25.12.

Table 25.11: Accumulated relative errors (NURBS: order M=3).

Number of points	200	600	1000
Conventional NURBS	2.5×10^{-12}	1.24×10^{-11}	4.29×10^{-11}
Type-I homogenized NURBS	0	0	0

Table 25.12: Accumulated relative errors (NURBS: order M=4).

Number of points	200	600	1000
Conventional NURBS	7.88×10^{-10}	1.39×10^{-8}	2.27×10^{-7}
Type-I homogenized NURBS	0	0	0

Discussions

1. While the conventional NURBS curve exhibits error increase with the increase of the numbers of generation points, the type-I homogenized NURBS curve does not show any error in the experiment.
2. The errors in the conventional NURBS curve are caused by decimals of the coefficients in the normalized B-spline functions. If we multiply the numerator and denominator of the rational curve respectively, by the least common multiple, the errors would be eliminated.
3. The reason why the type-I homogenized NURBS curve does not show any error although the integer data are expressed in floating-point format is that the numbers of digits of the data do not exceed the representable limit of mantissa.
4. The normalization of homogeneous coordinate data (see Section 2.2) is effective in expanding the limit of exact integer computation in floating-point format although no normalization was done in the experiment.

25.2 Robustness

25.2.1 Geometric Newton-Raphson Method

Example 1....Convergence Robustness

Convergence robustness of geometric Newton-Raphson method is compared between the conventional Euclidean and the type-S homogeneous methods about

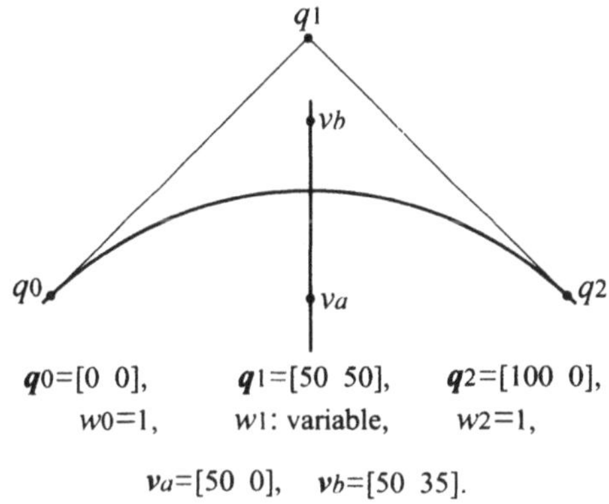

w_1: **weight for q_1**	**Conventional method**	**Type-S homogeneous method**
100.0	$-0.005 \sim 1.005$	$-\infty \sim \infty$
10.0	$-0.052 \sim 1.052$	$-\infty \sim \infty$
5.0	$-0.112 \sim 1.112$	$-\infty \sim \infty$
1.0	$-\infty \sim +\infty$	$-\infty \sim \infty$
0.5	$0.001 \sim 0.999$	$-\infty \sim \infty$
0.1	$0.181 \sim 0.819$	$-\infty \sim \infty$
0.0	$0.212 \sim 0.788$	$-\infty \sim \infty$
−0.1	$0.239 \sim 0.762$	$-\infty \sim \infty$
−0.5	$0.334 \sim 0.669$	$-\infty \sim \infty$
−1.0	—	$-\infty \sim \infty$
−5.0	$0.092 \sim 0.908$	$-\infty \sim \infty$
−10.0	$0.048 \sim 0.952$	$-\infty \sim \infty$
−100.0	$0.005 \sim 0.995$	$-\infty \sim \infty$

Figure 25.4: Intersection of a curve and a line.

the intersection point determination of a rational Bézier curve and a line. Robust ranges of initial parameter values are measured and shown in Fig. 25.4.

We see that the initial value must be chosen within a very narrow range for the parameter to successfully converge to a root in the conventional method. This is true whether w_1 is positive or negative. One must therefore choose the initial value very carefully when dealing with rational polynomial curves.

Note that the conventional method does not show any convergence problem only when $w = 1$, and that the curve in this case turns out to be an ordinary polynomial one, not a rational one !

Example 2....Effects of Weights of Control Points

The rational curve segment and line segment for the test is shown in Fig. 25.5. We shall examine in detail the effects of weights of control points.

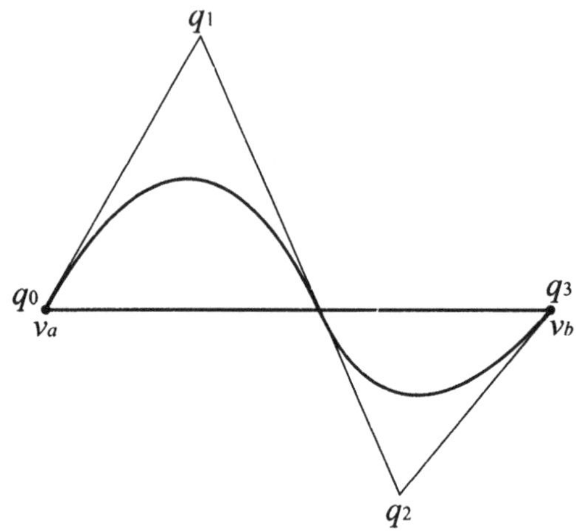

$\boldsymbol{q}_0$=[0 0], $\boldsymbol{q}_1$=[30 100], $\boldsymbol{q}_2$=[70 −60], $\boldsymbol{q}_3$=[100 0],

$\boldsymbol{v}_a$=[0 0], $\boldsymbol{v}_b$=[100 0].

Figure 25.5: Intersection of curve segment and line segment (Example 2).

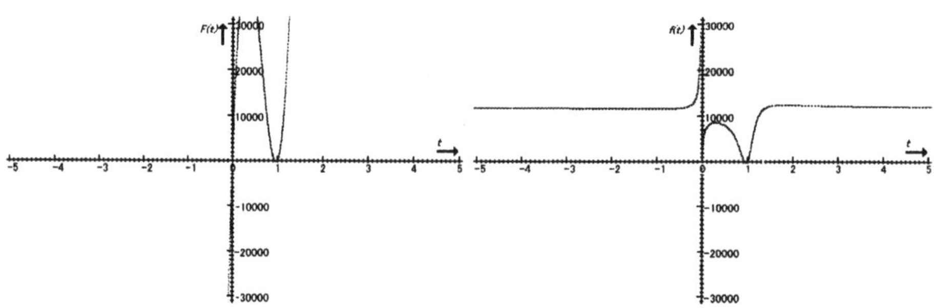

(a) $w_1 = 10$

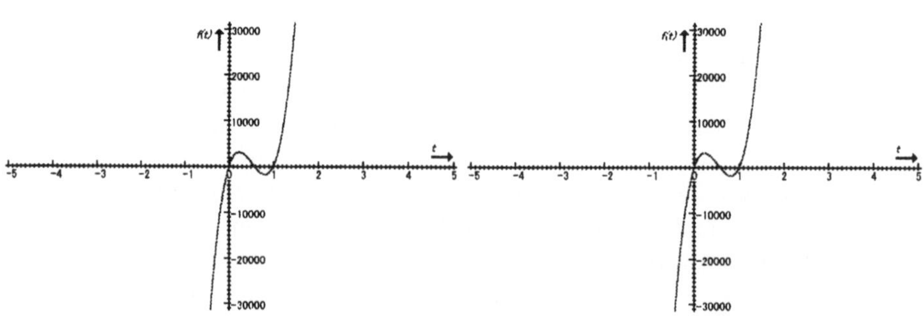

(b) $w_1 = 1$

Figure 25.6: Comparison of $f(t)$ (right) and $F(t)$ (left) for various w_1 values.

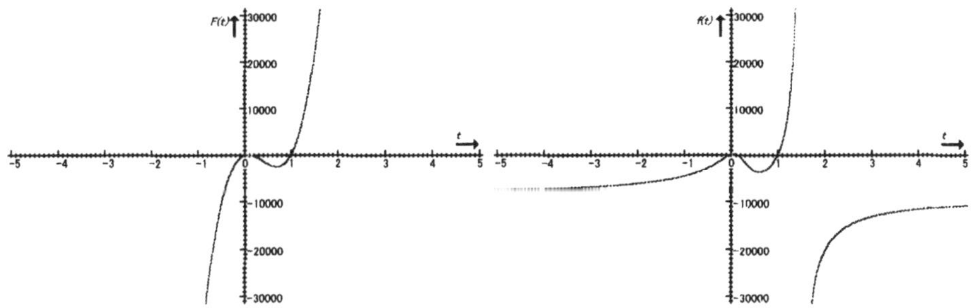

(c) $w_1 = 0.1$

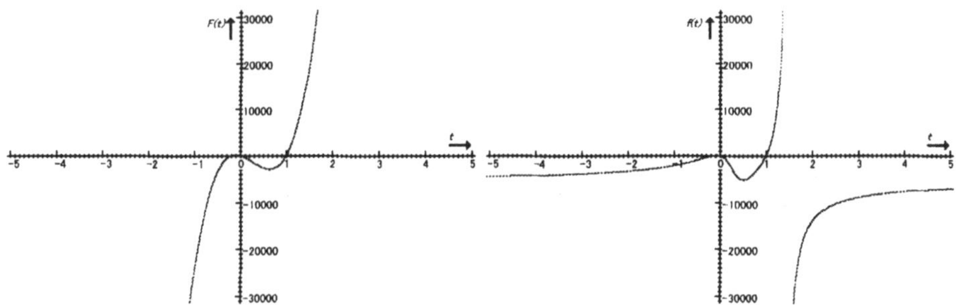

(d) $w_1 = -0.1$

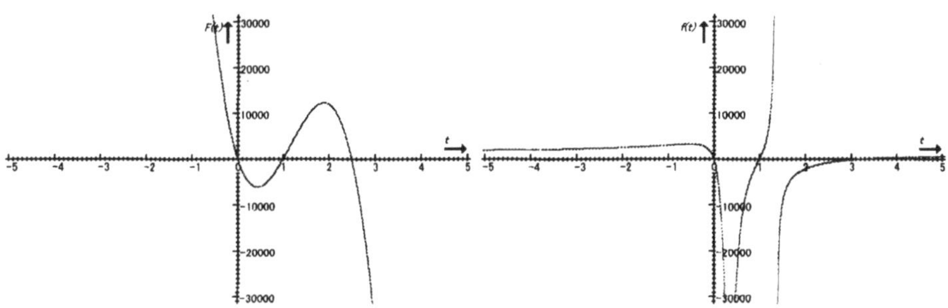

(e) $w_1 = -1$

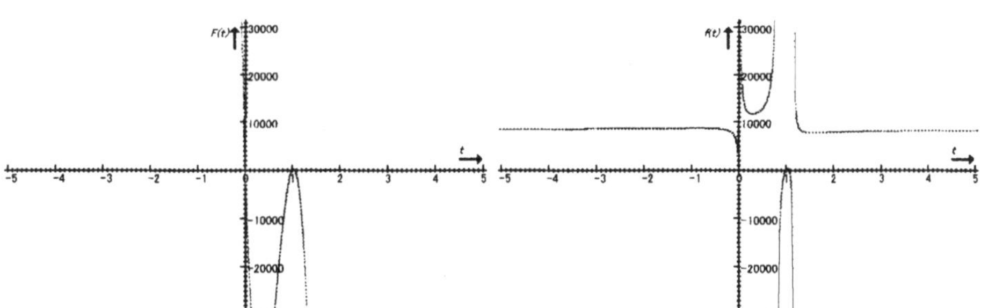

(f) $w_1 = -10$

Figure 25.6: *Continued.*

Fig. 25.2.1 shows plots for $f(t)$ (right) alongside those for $F(t)$ (left) for various w_1 values, for the intersection problem between the curve segment and the line segment. The plots of $f(t)$ have complex shapes, having asymptotes in both horizontal and vertical directions, and it is plain to see that processing by the geometric Newton-Raphson method can become quite unstable. In contrast, those for $F(t)$ are simple, ensuring that processing will be stable. Also, the plots for $f(t)$ are greatly affected by the weight, while those for $F(t)$ show very little variation. Fig. 25.2.1 shows how an equivalent function for a rational polynomial curve can assume a variety of shapes depending on the w_1 values.

Example 3....Convergence Robustness and Local Uniqueness

In this example we test local uniqueness of intersection points as well as convergence robustness with respect to a cubic rational Bézier curve segment and a line segment (Fig. 25.7):

Data for the rational Bézier curve
The data for the control points are

$$\begin{array}{llll} \boldsymbol{q}_0 = [0 \;\; 40], & \boldsymbol{q}_1 = [20 \;\; 0], & \boldsymbol{q}_2 = [40 \;\; 40], & \boldsymbol{q}_3 = [60 \;\; 0], \\ w_0 = 1, & w_1 = 3, & w_2 = 9, & w_3 = 1. \end{array}$$

Data for the line segment

$$\boldsymbol{v}_a = [0 \;\; 22], \qquad \boldsymbol{v}_b = [100 \;\; 22].$$

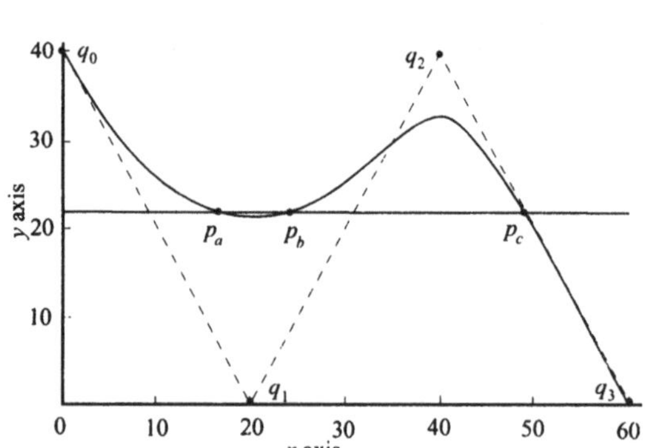

Figure 25.7: A cubic rational Beźier curve and a line segment.

This test was performed and compared among the next three methods:

(1) Conventional Euclidean method,

(2) Type-S homogeneous method,

(3) Type-D2 homogeneous method.

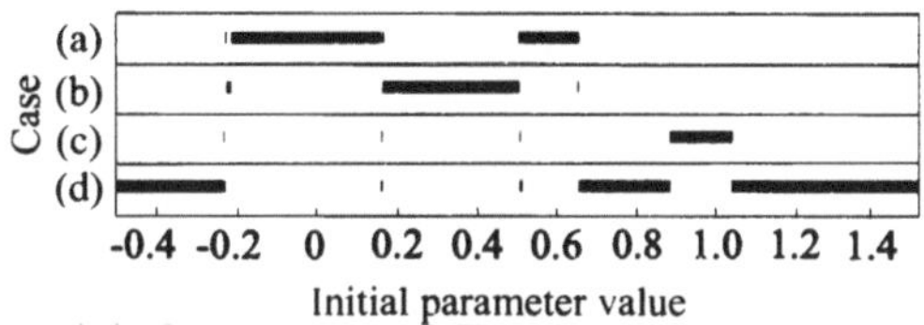

(1) Conventional Euclidean method

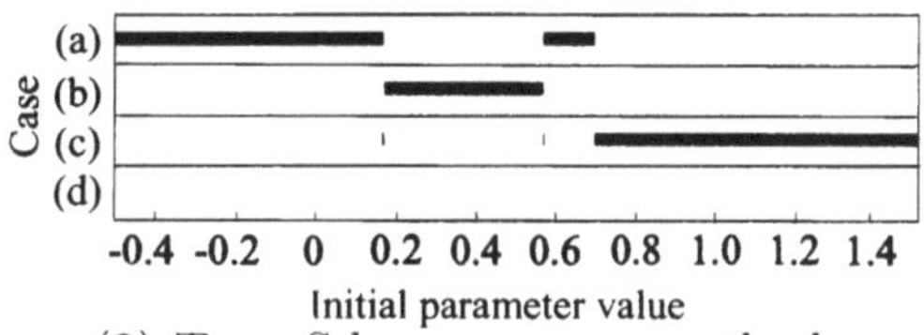

(2) Type-S homogeneous method

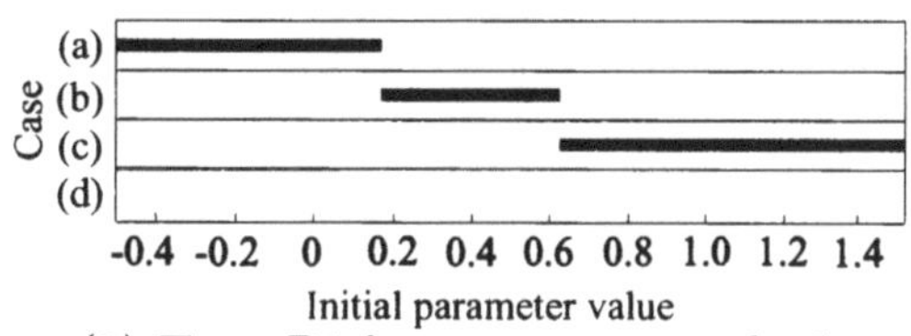

(3) Type-D2 homogeneous method

Figure 25.8: Test results for the data in Fig. 25.7.

The test results are shown in Fig. 25.8. We denote the three intersection points between the curve and the line segment by p_a, p_b and p_c (see Fig. 25.7). In Fig. 25.8, (a), (b) and (c) correspond to the convergences to points p_a, p_b and p_c respectively, and (d) corresponds to the case where a solution can not be obtained because of divergence of parameter value.

Each test was done with initial parameter values given every 0.001 unit from $t=-0.5$ to $t=1.5$.

From Fig. 25.8 (1), (2) and (3), we observe the followings:

1. In the conventional Euclidean method (Fig. 25.8 (1)), there are some initial parameter value ranges where the parameter value diverges and thus an intersection point can not be obtained.

   Furthermore the local uniqueness of solution with respect to initial parameter ranges is no good.

2. Fig. 25.8 (2) shows that in contrast to the Euclidean method the type-S homogeneous method improves very much in terms of convergence robustness. This could be understood by observing the equivalent functions of both methods (Fig. 25.9). While the equivalent function $f(t)$ of the Euclidean method has a horizontal asymptote, that of the type-S homogeneous method is very simple and does not have any asymptote.

This method still has the problem of local uniqueness of solutions, however.

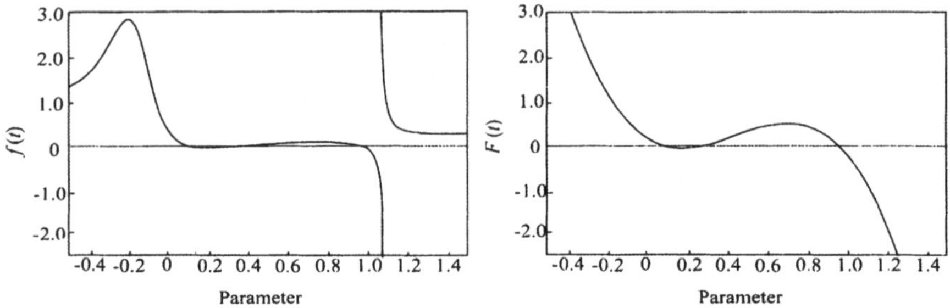

Euclidean method Type-S homogeneous method

Figure 25.9: Equiv. functions for Euclidean and type-S homogeneous methods.

3. Fig. 25.8 (3) shows that the type-D2 homogeneous method is satisfactory in terms of both convergence robustness and local uniqueness. This means that the control of homogeneous parameters is done appropriately.

   See Fig. 25.10 for the ordinary parameter increments δt's of the three methods.

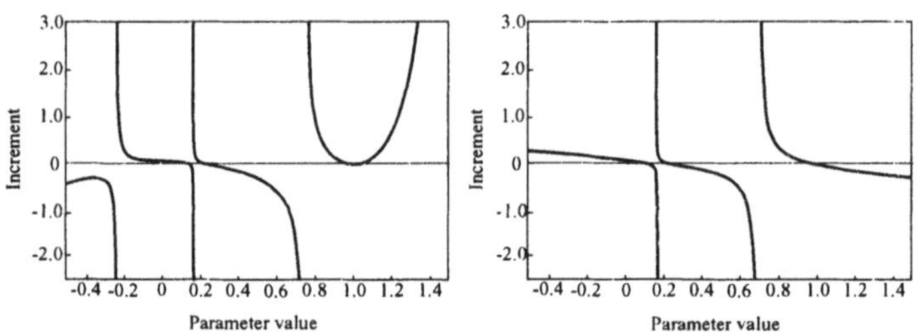

Euclidean Type-S homogeneous

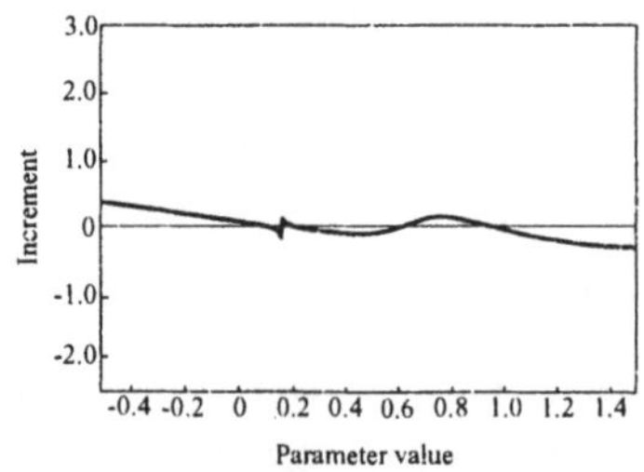

Type-D2 homogeneous

Figure 25.10: Ordinary parameter increments of three methods.

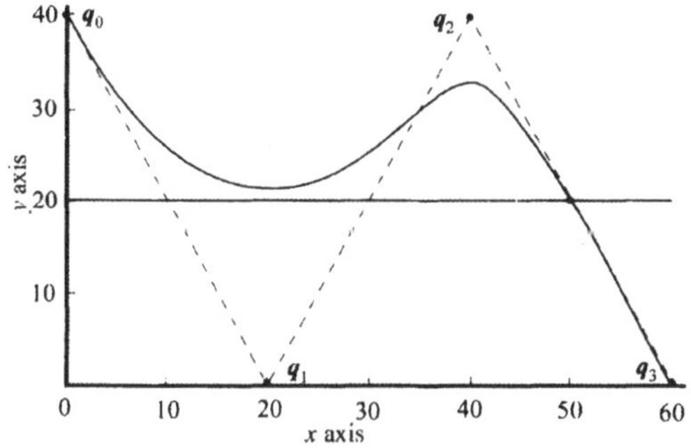

Figure 25.11: A cubic rational Beźier curve and a line segment.

Example 4....Comparison between Type-D1 and Type-D2 Methods

We shall examine the differences of characteristics between the homogeneous Newton-Raphson methods for type-D1 and type-D2 curves (Fig. 25.11). The test data in this case are shown as follows:

Data for the rational Bézier curve
The data for the control points are

$$\begin{array}{llll} \boldsymbol{q}_0 = [0 \;\; 40], & \boldsymbol{q}_1 = [20 \;\; 0], & \boldsymbol{q}_2 = [40 \;\; 40], & \boldsymbol{q}_3 = [60 \;\; 0], \\ w_0 = 1, & w_1 = 3, & w_2 = 9, & w_3 = 1. \end{array}$$

Data for the line segment

$$\boldsymbol{v}_a = [0 \;\; 20], \qquad \boldsymbol{v}_b = [100 \;\; 20].$$

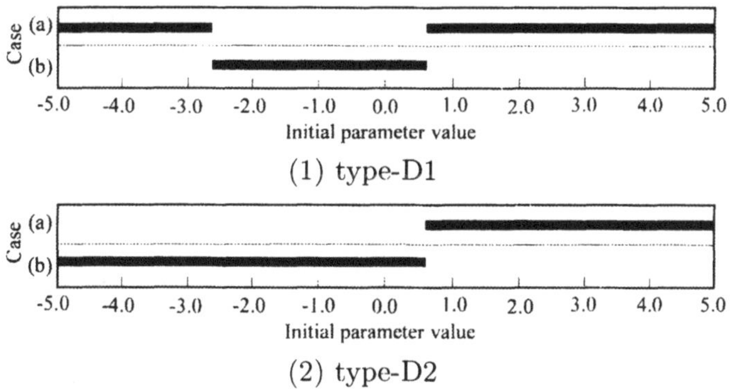

Figure 25.12: A convergence test between type-D1 and -D2 methods (1).

The example above has only one real solution. The results are shown in Fig. 25.12, where (a) corresponds to the convergence of the real solution and

(b) is supposed to correspond to a complex solution. In the latter case the algorithm does not terminate since it can not handle a complex solution.

While the solution ranges are clearly separated in Fig. 25.12(2), these ranges are not in (1). This result of the type-D1 demonstrates some problem on local uniqueness property. If we look upon the parameter space as $\mathbf{P}^1$, however, the local uniqueness of (1) is still maintained. Thus we shall call this type "projective local uniqueness" and the type of (2) "Euclidean local uniqueness." What we really desire is to acquire the Euclidean local uniqueness. See Fig. 25.13 for another example.

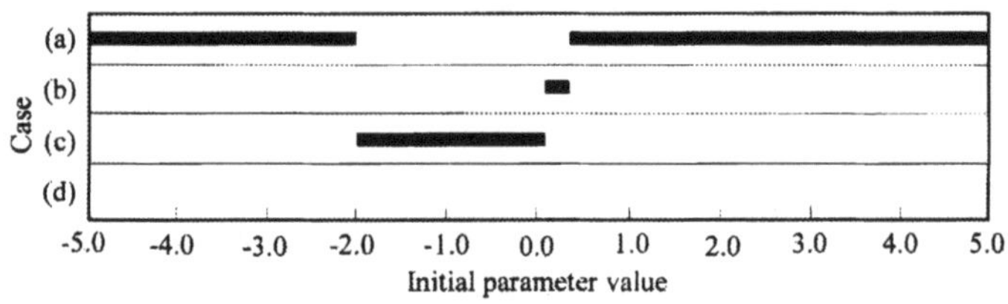

(a) type-D1

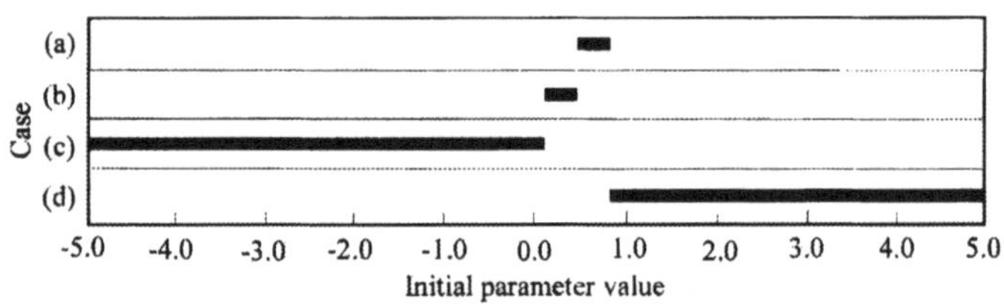

(b) type-D2

Figure 25.13: A convergence test between type-D1 and -D2 methods (2).

Example 5....Convergence Robustness and Local Uniqueness

A more striking test result on convergence robustness and local uniqueness was gained in determining intersection points between a high degree (seven-degree) rational Bézier curve segment and a line segment. The test data in this case are shown as follows:

Data for the seven-degree rational Bézier curve segment

The data for the control points are

$$\boldsymbol{q}_0 = [0 \;\; 10], \quad \boldsymbol{q}_1 = [30 \;\; 400], \quad \boldsymbol{q}_2 = [50 \;\; 30],$$
$$\boldsymbol{q}_3 = [70 \;\; 600], \quad \boldsymbol{q}_4 = [90 \;\; 20], \quad \boldsymbol{q}_5 = [120 \;\; 400],$$
$$\boldsymbol{q}_6 = [150 \;\; 10], \quad \boldsymbol{q}_7 = [170 \;\; 300],$$
$$w_0 = 1, \qquad w_1 = 6, \qquad w_2 = 6, \qquad w_3 = 1,$$
$$w_4 = 6, \qquad w_5 = 6, \qquad w_6 = 1, \qquad w_7 = 1.$$

Data for the line segment

$$\boldsymbol{v}_a = [0 \;\; 250], \qquad \boldsymbol{v}_b = [300 \;\; 250].$$

The equivalent function $F(t)$ in this case is shown in Fig. 25.14. There are three real roots in this case. On the right of the graph the value of the local minimum is positive, and thus there is no real root here. We denote these three real roots by p_a, p_b and p_c from left to right.

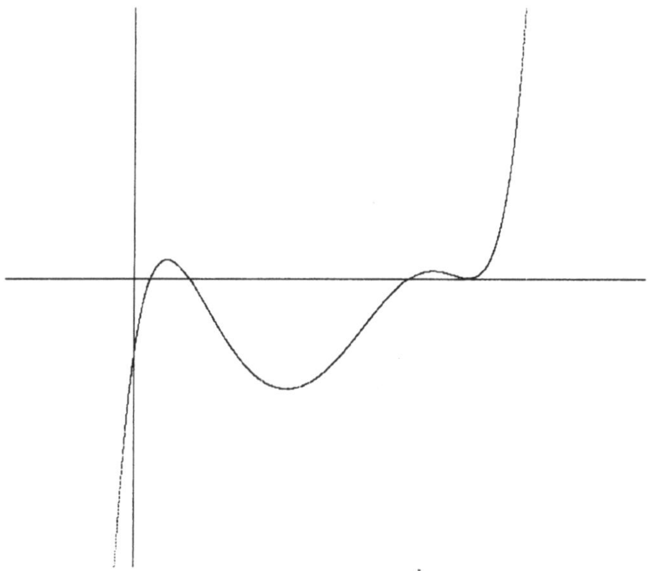

Figure 25.14: Equivalent function $F(t)$.

The results are shown in Fig. 25.15. In Fig. 25.15, (a), (b) and (c) correspond to the convergences to points p_a, p_b and p_c respectively, and (d) corresponds to the case where a solution can not be obtained because of non-stability.

1. In the conventional Euclidean method, there are many non-robust parameter ranges, and furthermore the local uniqueness is lost more severely than in Example 3 (Fig. 25.15(1)).

2. In the type-S homogeneous method, robustness is also maintained just as it is in Example 3 (Fig. 25.15(2)). The local uniqueness, however, is lost more severely than in Example 3.

3. The type-D2 homogeneous method shows satisfactory characteristics both on convergence robustness and local uniqueness even in a high degree curve (25.15(3)).

   Note that there is shown a non-robust parameter range when an initial parameter is larger than approximately 0.8. This is considered to be the range of initial parameters which should have converged to a complex root. It is expected that if homogenization is extended to the determination of complex roots, then this non-stability would disappear.

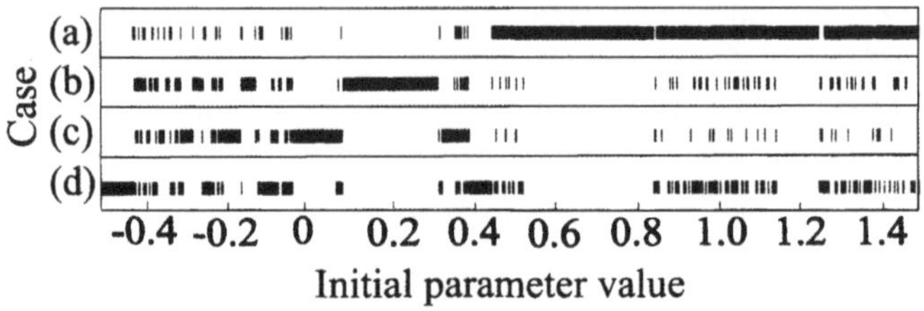

(1) Conventional Euclidean method

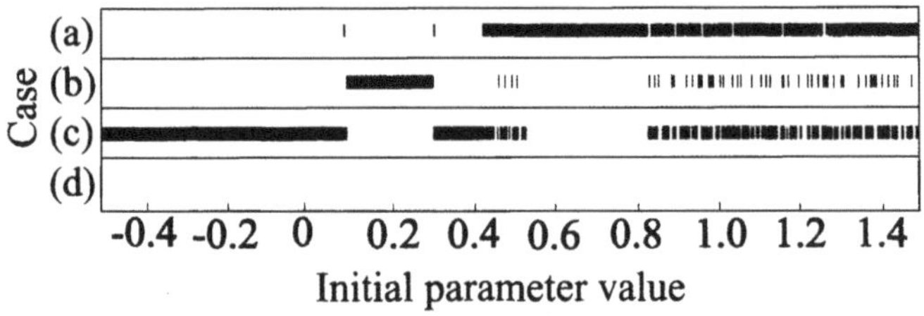

(2) Type-S homogeneous method

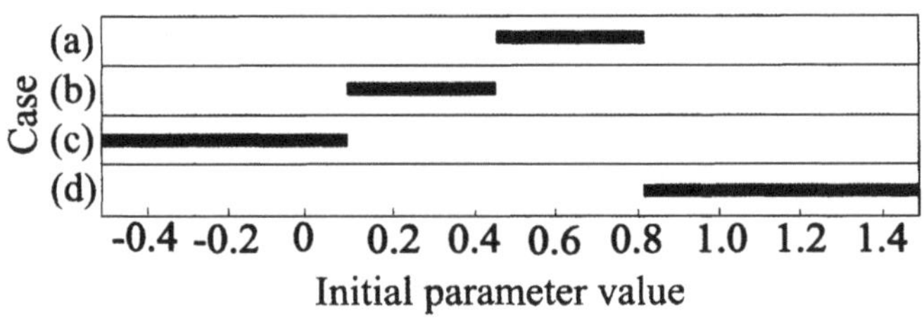

(3) Type-D2 homogeneous method

Figure 25.15: Intersection of a seven-degree rational Bézier curve and a line.

Example 6....Convergence Robustness and Local Uniqueness

Lastly, we shall show one more example, which shows the results of the intersection between an eight degree rational Bézier curve and a line, where there is a multiple root (p_d). This case has seven real roots (Fig. 25.16).

Data for the rational Bézier curve
The data for the control points are:

$$\boldsymbol{q}_0 = [0 \;\; 0], \;\; \boldsymbol{q}_1 = [20 \;\; 100], \;\; \boldsymbol{q}_2 = [40 \;\; 0], \;\; \boldsymbol{q}_3 = [60 \;\; 100], \;\; \boldsymbol{q}_4 = [80 \;\; 0],$$
$$\boldsymbol{q}_5 = [100 \;\; 100], \;\; \boldsymbol{q}_6 = [120 \;\; 0], \;\; \boldsymbol{q}_7 = [140 \;\; 100], \;\; \boldsymbol{q}_8 = [160 \;\; 0],$$
$$w_0 = 1, \quad w_1 = 5, \quad w_2 = 13, \quad w_3 = 20, \quad w_4 = 24,$$
$$w_5 = 20, \quad w_6 = 13, \quad w_7 = 5, \quad w_8 = 1.$$

Data for the line segment

$$\boldsymbol{v}_a = [0 \;\; 49.05], \qquad \boldsymbol{v}_b = [200 \;\; 49.05].$$

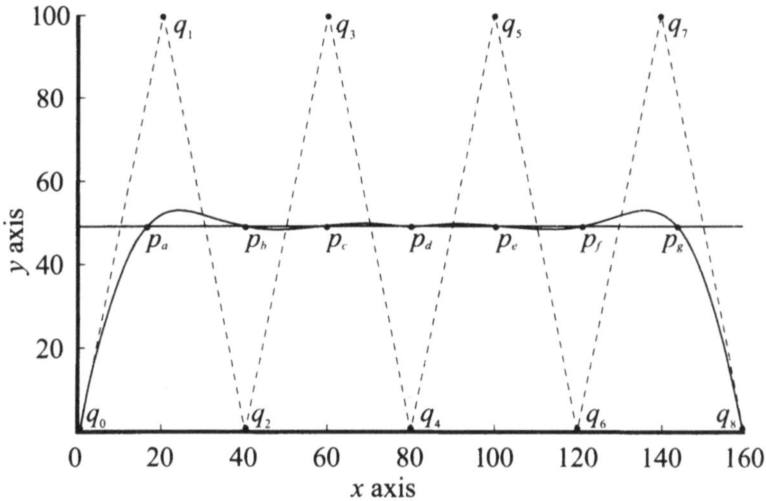

Figure 25.16: Eight degree rational Beźier curve and line (multiple root p_d).

The results are shown in Fig. 25.17.

In Fig. 25.17, (a), (b), (c), (d), (e), (f), (g) and (h) correspond to the following cases:

(a) This represents the case where the parameter converges to point $p_a(t_a = 0.03129892286)$,

(b) This represents the case where the parameter converges to point $p_b(t_b = 0.14631360702)$,

(c) This represents the case where the parameter converges to point $p_c(t_c = 0.32431412236)$,

(d) This represents the case where the parameter converges to multiple root point $p_d(t_d = 0.50)$,

(e) This represents the case where the parameter converges to point $p_e(t_e = 0.67568587763)$,

(f) This represents the case where the parameter converges to point $p_f(t_f = 0.85368639297)$,

(g) This represents the case where the parameter converges to point $p_g(t_g = 0.96870107713)$,

(h) This represents the case where a solution can not be obtained because of divergence or loop-entering of algorithm.

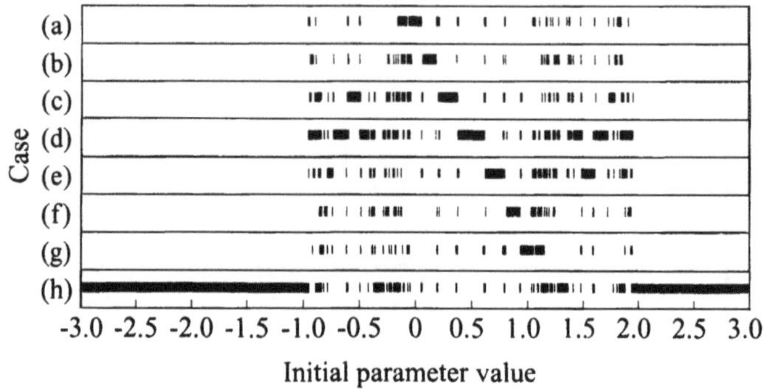

(1) Conventional Euclidean method

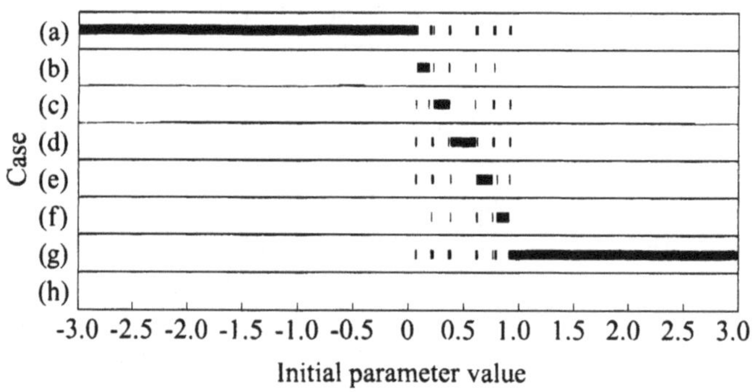

(2) Type-S homogeneous method

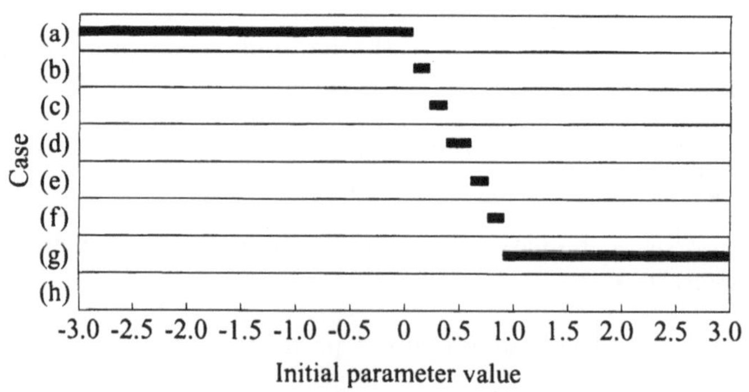

(3) Type-D2 homogeneous method

Figure 25.17: Eight-degree rational Bézier curve and a line ((d): multiple root).

In Fig. 25.17 (1), the conventional method exhibits many non-robust initial parameter ranges and at the same time poor local uniqueness property. On the other hand, the type-S homogeneous method does not show any non-robust parameter range, but still shows some problem in its local uniqueness property, as shown in Fig. 25.17 (2).

Note in Fig. 25.17 (3) that the type-D2 homogeneous method shows superior local uniqueness property as well as robust convergence property.

25.3 Efficiency

25.3.1 Computation Times of Points on a Rational Curve

The difference calculus method discussed in Section 10.7 can be applied to the generation of points on the homogeneous curves because they are represented in ordinary polynomials, while it can not in the case of rational curves without using four-dimensional approach. We shall test the efficiency of the difference calculus method, comparing with those of other approaches:

1. **de Boor's recurrence relation**

   We compute type-S B-spline functions by using the de-Boor recurrence relation eq.(10.44), compute each term of the curve representation by performing multiplications with control vectors, and add these terms.

2. **Simple polynomial computation**

   We arrange the curve in a power series and evaluate it straightforwardly.

3. **Hohner's method**

   We arrange the curve in a power series and evaluate it by using the Hohner's method.

4. **Difference calculus method**

   We use the type-I homogenized NURBS curve and apply the difference calculus method.

The control vectors of the curve (order 4) for the tests above are as follows:

$$[2\ 200\ 200\ 200],\quad [1\ 150\ 300\ 50],\quad [1\ 200\ 100\ 0],\quad [1\ 250\ 250\ 0].$$

Used Computer
The experiment was done under the following environment:
computer: EPSON486 Note As
CPU: intel486DX2 50Mz (floating-point processing unit included)
OS: MS-DOS 5.00

The test results are shown in Fig. 25.18 and Table 25.13. The times of preparatory arrangement of the curve forms for the tests are excluded from the table.

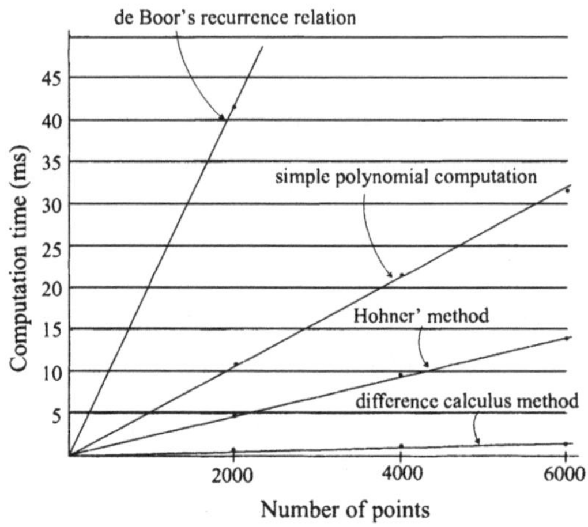

Figure 25.18: Computation times of points on a rational curve.

Table 25.13: Computation times of points on a rational curve.

Number of points	0	2,000	4,000	6,000
de Boor's recurrence relation	0	41.930	84.357	127.833
Simple polynomial computation	0	10.623	21.176	31.812
Hohner's method	0	4.741	9.460	14.160
Difference calculus method	0	0.494	0.977	1.474

unit: milli-second

Table 25.14: Number of times of arithmetic operations.

	Addition & subtraction	Multiplication & division
Simple polynomial comp.	$M-1$	$M(M-1)/2$
Horner's method	$M-1$	$M-1$
Difference operation	M	0

M: order of polynomial

In this experiment the normalization of homogeneous coordinates is not performed.

The numbers of arithmetic operations per coordinate are shown in Table 25.14.

25.4 Generality

25.4.1 Surfaces by Polyhedron Subdivision

As discussed in Chapter 21, the proposed homogeneous polyhedron subdivision generates a rational bi-quadratic, or bi-cubic B-spline surface while the conventional subdivision does an ordinary bi-quadratic or bi-cubic B-spline surface. Therefore the homogeneous subdivision is considered to provide more general surface than the conventional one although the former is based on the same simple algorithm as the latter. That is, the roundness of the generated surface part near an edge of the given polyhedron can be controlled by changing the weights of the vertices corresponding to the edge while it is fixed and thus can not be controlled in the conventional subdivision. Furthermore if the weights are controlled appropriately, the homogeneous subdivision allows us to generate a conic surface exactly.

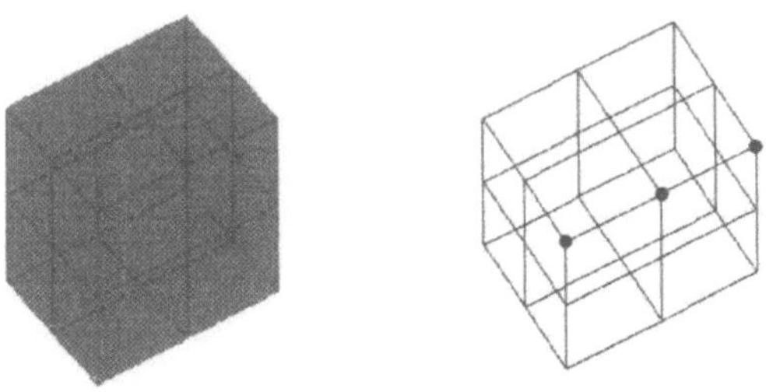

Figure 25.19: A sample solid.

From the sample solid of Fig. 25.19, the conventional polyhedron subdivision (quadratic case) generates the shape "weight=1" shown in Fig. 25.20. On the other hand the homogeneous polyhedron subdivision (quadratic case) generates the same shape as the conventional subdivision does when all the weights of the vertices are unity, but can generate the various shapes shown in Fig. 25.20 when the weights of the three dotted vertices in Fig. 25.19 are 0.1, 0.5, 1, 2, 10 and 100 respectively. The roundness of the edge corresponding to the dotted vertices is controlled.

Figs. 25.21 $\sim$ 25.30 are some of the designed shapes under the homogeneous polyhedron subdivision (quadratic case). Original polyhedra and the generated shapes are shown on the left and right respectively. In the figures of original polyhedra, a bigger solid dot vertex represents a bigger weight value and a vertex with no dot represents a unity weight.

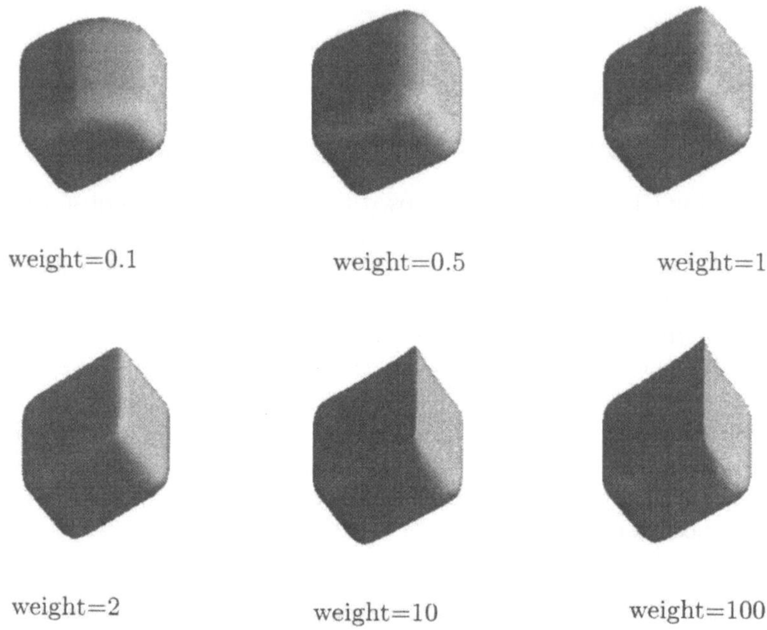

Figure 25.20: Generated shapes.

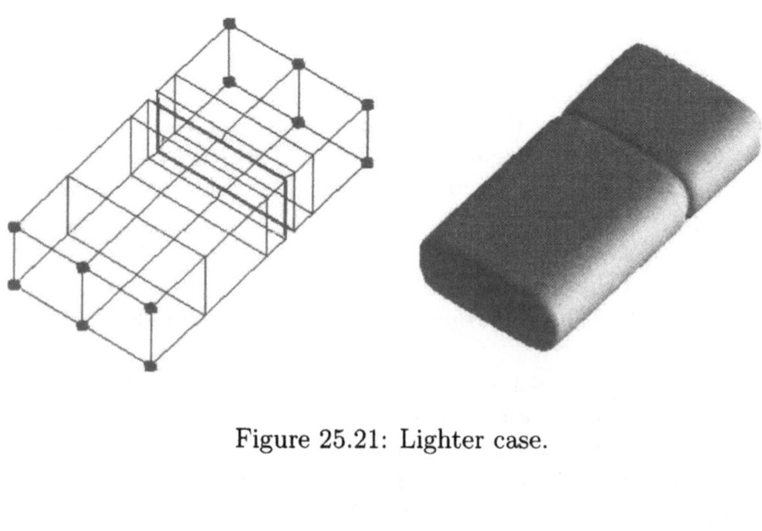

Figure 25.21: Lighter case.

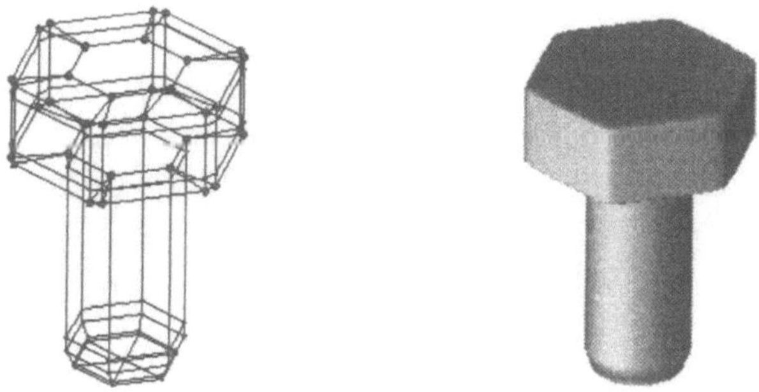

Figure 25.22: Bolt.

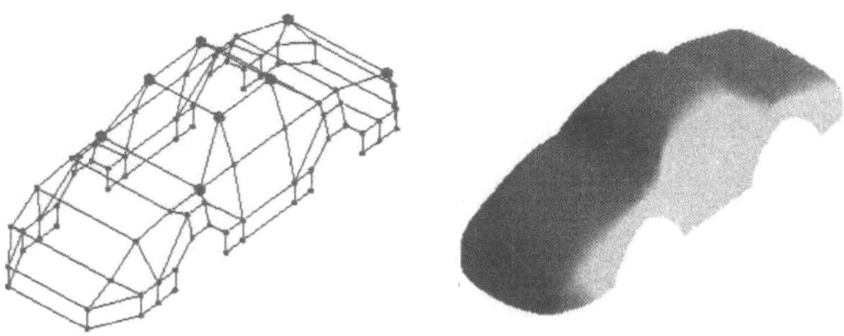

Figure 25.23: Model car body.

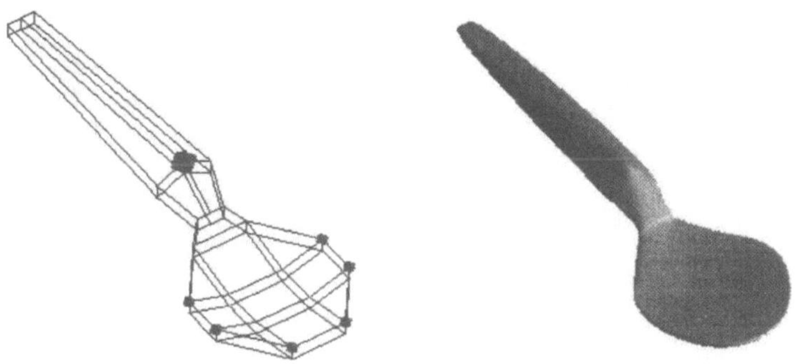

Figure 25.24: Spoon.

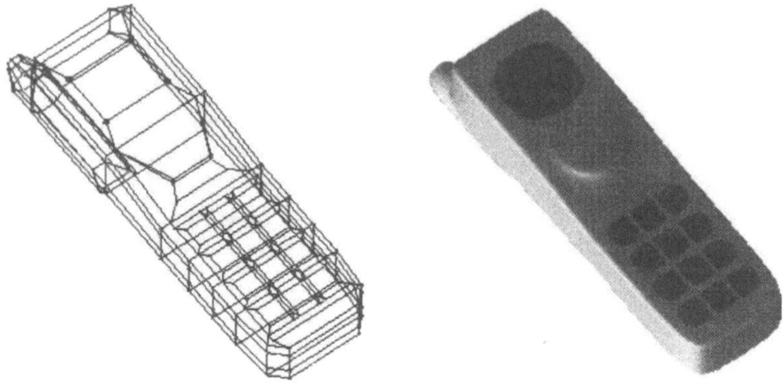

Figure 25.25: Portable telephone.

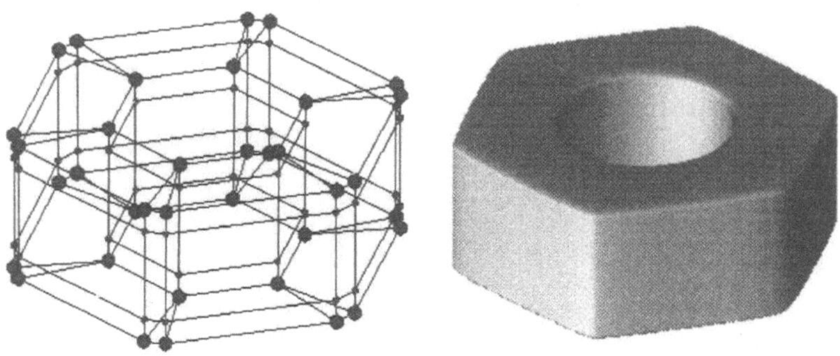

Figure 25.26: Nut.

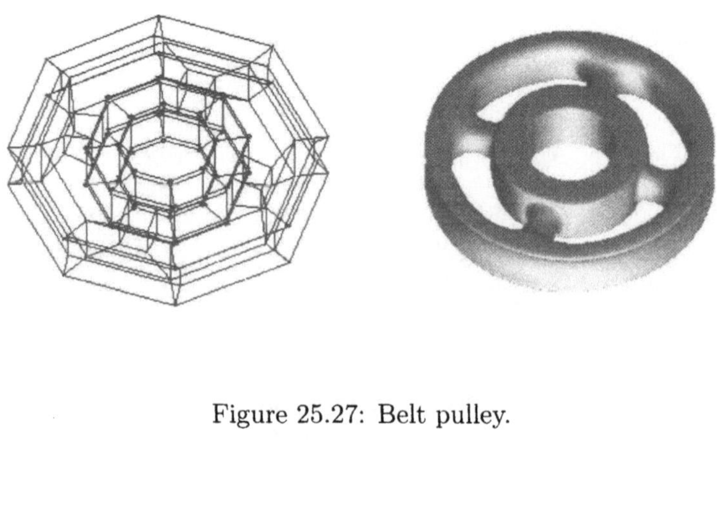

Figure 25.27: Belt pulley.

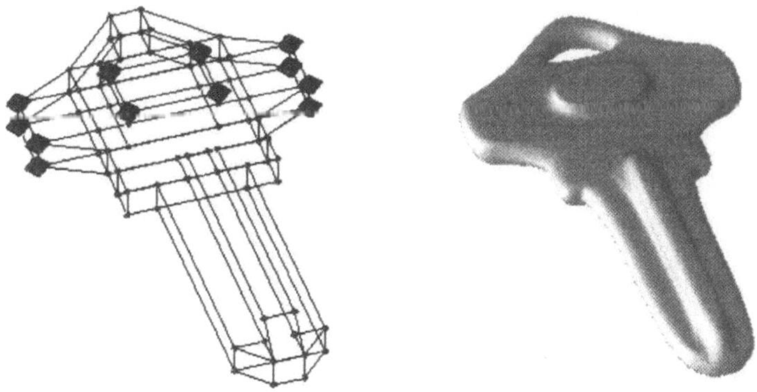

Figure 25.28: Key.

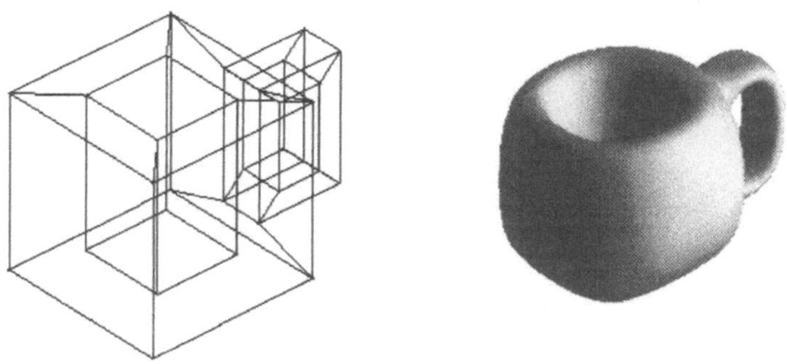

Figure 25.29: Mug.

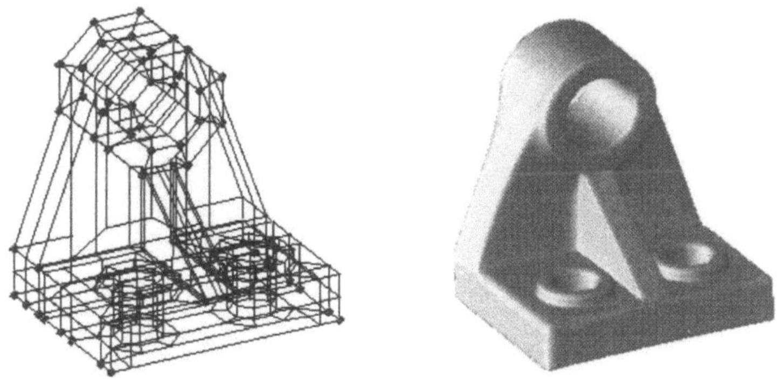

Figure 25.30: Bearing Bracket.

Part IV

Conclusions

Chapter 26

Evaluations

In this chapter the characteristics of the Four-dimensional Processing are discussed and evaluated in comparison to those of the conventional Euclidean Processing, taking into consideration, various discussions throughout this book and the test results presented in Chapter 25. Evaluation items are "exactness," "robustness," "compactness," "generality," "unifiability," "duality," "computational quantities" and "momory requirements."

Let us note here the difference between the Four-dimensional Processing and the Euclidean one that the former employs pre-division coordinates while the latter does post-division coordinates.

At the end of the discussion of each item, a conclusion will be derived.

1. **Exactness**

   According to the test results of the pentagon problem in Section 25.1.2, the conventional Euclidean Processing exhibited a large error after the iterations of the same number of times of going-in and going-out operations, even when the number is small.

   On the other hand, our experiments of using long integers in the homogeneous approach demonstrated complete restoration of the homogeneous coordinates of the original input vertices. The original pentagon data are perfectly restored even if some lines happen to be parallel during going-in and -out operations. In this experiment we performed normalizations [1)] of integer homogeneous coordinates after each going-in or -out operation.

   Note that the data lengths of the homogeneous coordinates or coefficients do not necessarily increase with the repetition of computations. They depend only on the point or plane to be represented, assuming the normalizations are done after each computation.

   Since the normalization eliminates redundant common factors among homogeneous coordinates and coefficients and makes it possible to represent

[1)] As for normalizations, see Section 2.2.

these with necessary and sufficient data lengths, we can attain and accelerate exact arithmetic even with floating-point representation in some types of computations not requiring extremely long data lengths (see Sections 25.1.1 and 25.1.2).

It can be said that the Four-dimensional Processing can perform exact computations as long as it deals with rational numbers.

The Euclidean Processing, on the other hand, is obliged to deal with approximated data which are the results of division operations inherent in this processing.

By the way, rational number arithmetic can be considered to be in between the Four-dimensional Processing and the Euclidean one. In principle it would be as exact as the Four-dimensional Processing since it does not perform division operations. At present the author thinks, however, that it could not easily treat parallel line intersections in the pentagon problem because the denominator of a rational number could not take on zero in an ordinary sense.

In conclusion, the Four-dimensional Processing is considered to be superior to the conventional, ordinary Euclidean Processing (which requires division operations) in terms of exactness. The Four-dimensional Processing seems to be a little superior to rational arithmetic in that the former can treat parallel intersection cases easily. The problem with the Four-dimensional Processing, however, is that it is time-consuming if exactness is required because a hardware accelerator, such as a floating-point unit in floating-point arithmetic, is not available at present in long integer arithmetic. The Euclidean Processing can not, in general, perform exact computation, though.

2. **Robustness**

   In the Four-dimensional Processing, there is no such instability as division by zero, because a division operation is not ordinarily performed except at the very end of whole process.

   In Chapter 15, three types of homogeneous geometric Newton-Raphson methods are presented. One is the type-S homogeneous geometric Newton-Raphson method, where point coordinates on the curve are homogenized. Another is the type-D homogeneous method, where the parameter is also homogenized in addition to point coordinates. The third is the type-C's, which are the applications of the type-S and -D to determinations of complex solutions.

   While the conventional geometric Newton-Raphson method occasionally fails when it is applied to <u>rational</u> polynomial curves, i.e., the parameter value diverges and finally halts the algorithm, the type-S homogeneous geometric Newton-Raphson method does not show such non-robustness inherent in rational polynomial curve processing because it treats a homogeneous curve which is expressed as an ordinary curve of dimension higher by one. This superiority is borne out by many experimental data (see Sections 15.5 and 25.2.1).

Although the type-S homogeneous geometric Newton-Raphson method is as robust as the case when the conventional algorithm is applied to an ordinary polynomial curve, it is not satisfactory on the local uniqueness property of the intersection point with respect to an initial value range just as the conventional Newton-Raphson method is not.

As shown in Section 25.2.1, the type-D2 homogeneous geometric Newton-Raphson method shows excellent characteristics on this local uniqueness as well as on the robust convergence.

The third problem of instability arises when the parameter happens to approach a complex solution. It oscillates around it and can not converge. This case can be overcome by the type-C homogeneous method. The author has remarkable results with the method, although they cannot be included in the book regrettably.

In solid modeling it is well known that the robustness of set operations is sometimes lost because of representational and computational errors. As discussed in **Exactness**, the Four-dimensional Processing is more favorable than conventional Euclidean Processing in performing accurate computations.

It could be concluded that the Four-dimensional Processing is much superior to conventional one in terms of robustness.

3. **Compactness**

   In the first place we notice that the Four-dimensional Processing is simpler because it completes the processing before performing division operations and dispenses with the operations. This is not necessary true, however, because the author recommends the normalization of homogeneous coordinates instead.

   In the second place we notice that a Euclidean geometry tends to be more complicated because it is considered to be a cut of homogeneous one (i.e., linear subspace) of which the dimension is higher by one than that of its counterpart.

   Take a line segment for example. Three types of Euclidean line segments are created by a cut of a homogeneous line segment which is in reality a wedge-shaped plane (see Fig. 7.3). As for triangle and tetrahedron, there are created five and eight Euclidean ones from a homogeneous triangle and tetrahedron, respectively (see Figs. 9.5 and 9.7).

   Consider the clipping operations of geometric elements before displaying them on the screen. As for the difficulty of clipping line segments after division operations, it was discussed in Section 23.5. In the case of polygon clipping, the operation after divisions would be prohibitively complex.

Another familiar example is a conic section. Euclidean curves such as a parabola, ellipse and hyperbola are section curves of a cone. In Euclidean geometry these curves are considered different geometric types and treated as such.

The increase of geometric types in the Euclidean Processing makes it much more complex. Each type must be mathematically represented individually, and the increased numbers of the combinations must be processed.

Take the intersection condition of two line segments V_aV_b and V_0V_1 for example. One routine expressed as one line of description is enough in the Four-dimensional Processing while six routines must be prepared in the Euclidean Processing (see Sections 14.4.1 and 14.4.3). That is, because the homogeneous line segment expression:

$$\overline{\boldsymbol{V}} = \overline{\xi_0 \boldsymbol{V}_0 + \xi_1 \boldsymbol{V}_1},$$
$$\xi_0, \xi_1 \geq 0 \ \text{ or } \ \xi_0, \xi_1 \leq 0, \ (\xi_0, \xi_1) \neq (0,0),$$

is projectively invariant, the intersection condition for the classical projective space is derived as follows:

$$(S_{01ab} = 0) \wedge (\boldsymbol{F}_{01a} \cdot \boldsymbol{F}_{01b} \leq 0) \wedge (\boldsymbol{F}_{ab0} \cdot \boldsymbol{F}_{ab1} \leq 0), \tag{26.1}$$

where S is a Plücker coordinate of three-space defined by the subscript points, and $\boldsymbol{F}$ is a four dimensional vector represented by Plücker coordinates of the plane defined by the subscript points.

In the third place, mathematical representations or formulas and algorithms of the Euclidean Processing tends to be more complex than those of the Four-dimensional Processing.

As for transformations, a projective transformation can be simply performed as a linear transformation in the Four-dimensional Processing while it is done in a more complicated fashion in the Euclidean Processing (see Chapter 6).

The mathematical representations or formulas of rational curves are more complex than those of homogeneous curves:

- Compare δt_i in eq.(15.16) with the one in eq.(15.20).
- Compare the de Casteljau's algorithm for a rational curve [2] with the one for a homogeneous curve which is of the same form as the one for an ordinary polynomial curve.

In conclusion the Four-dimensional Processing can be considered to be much better than the Euclidean Processing in terms of compactness.

[2] See Farin's book [16].

As discussed above, the Four-dimensional Processing is free from the root cause of all evil, i.e., division operations, inherent in the Euclidean Processing which may lead to decrease the reliability of a computer aided geometric design system. We notice that the Four-dimensional Processing is overwhelmingly superior to the Euclidean Processing in terms of "exactness," "robustness" and "compactness."

The Four-dimensional Processing also gains the properties of " generality," "unifiability" and "duality" which could be made the best use of in constructing a systematically organized CAGD system:

4. **Generality**

   The Four-dimensional Processing deals with geometric elements defined in classical projective space or two-sided space. It allows to represent points and lines at infinity in a natural way and accordingly, to reduce the number of special cases which we often encounter in the Euclidean Processing.

   Take the intersection of two planar lines as an example. The programmer does not have to worry about whether they are parallel or not. From the computed homogeneous coordinates, he can classify the intersection cases if he wants: ordinary intersection, parallel intersection or same line cases (see Section 12.1).

   A point at infinity, which is the intersection of two parallel lines, can be processed as if it were an ordinary finite point. See Section 6.2 and 6. of Section 25.1.2.

   The generality of the Four-dimensional Processing is pronounced in curves and surfaces. In rational curves and surfaces there is a severe restriction on the signs of weights of control points, i.e., they must not be mixed. In the Four-dimensional Processing on the other hand there is no such restrictions. The potential representational capability of rational curves and surfaces could be fully exploited in the Four-dimensional Processing (see Section 10.4).

   Furthermore the representation and processing of geometric elements including rational curves and surfaces are projectively invariant in the Four-dimensional Processing while it is affinely invariant with some condition imposed in the Euclidean Processing (see Sections 10.2 and 10.4).

   The homogeneous polyhedron subdivision presented in Chapter 21 is the result of a simple application of the homogeneous coordinate technique. Owing to the homogenization the generality is increased such that the roundness of each edge can be specified while it is fixed in the conventional polyhedron subdivision technique (see Section 25.4.1).

   The reconstruction of three-dimensional points discussed in Chapter 22 shows another example of how the Four-dimensional Processing provides a general approach requiring fewer special cases.

Therefore the Four-dimensional Processing is much more general than the Euclidean Processing.

5. **Unifiability**

   As for unifiability, the Four-dimensional Processing is particularly fine.

   Consider projective transformation. It is represented as a 4×4 matrix multiplication in a unified way. In the Euclidean Processing it can not be represented as a matrix multiplication form except linear transformation.

   In the Four-dimensional Processing geometric representations are projectively invariant (see Sections 9.3.2, 10.4 and also Geometric Interpretations 2. in Chapter 28). Thus many geometric computations are automatically unifiable. Take, as an example, the intersection condition of two line segments shown in eq.(26.1). It is applicable to six cases in Fig.1.7. The superiority of the Four-dimensional Processing, in this respect, seems self-evident.

   As for curves and surfaces, they are unifiable in a simpler form, i.e., ordinary polynomial form of dimension higher by one in the Four-dimensional Processing while they could be in a more complex form, i.e., rational form in the Euclidean Processing.

   In conclusion the Four-dimensional Processing is much better than the Euclidean one in terms of unifiability.

6. **Duality**

   The principle of duality holds strictly in the Four-dimensional Processing while it does not in the Euclidean Processing (see Section 7.4). As stated before, it can be capitalized on both in geometry definitions and computations (see Chapters 8, 9, 13, 12 and 14) and also in topology definitions and operations (see Chapters 17 and 18). Note that true duality is realized in the Four-dimensional Processing because the data structure is also dualized.

   In conclusion, the superiority of the Four-dimensional Processing on this item is self-evident because the principle of duality does not hold strictly in the Euclidean Processing.

The first three evaluation items, exactness, robustness and compactness, concern the reliability of a computer aided geometric design system and the next three items, generality, unifiability and duality, do the capability of systematic construction of a computer-aided design system.

The last items on which we evaluate the two processing methods are computational quantity and memory requirement.

7. **Computational Quantity**

   First, the Four-dimensional Processing terminates computations just before performing division operations. Therefore it dispenses with division operations. In place of division operations, however, the Four-dimensional Processing preferably requires the normalizations of homogeneous coordinates, coefficients, Plücker coordinates and coefficients occasionally.

Second, the Euclidean Processing deals with the cut shapes of four-dimensional figures. The cut produces a variety of shapes. Furthermore, the algorithms and formulas for rational forms are quite complex. Therefore, the Euclidean Processing tends to be more complex and accordingly is considered to need higher computational cost.

Third, rational polynomial curves and surfaces do not enjoy projective invariance while the homogeneous ones do. In perspectively transforming a rational polynomial curve, tranforming the control points and then computing the curve does not give its correct projected image. One must perspectively transform each generated point on the curve. This would be computationally much more expensive in the case of rational curves while one can transform the control points and then compute the curves in the case of the homogeneous curves.

It is hard to say conclusively that one method is superior to the other in terms of computational quantity.

8. **Memory Requirement**

As for the memory requirement for storing geometry data, it is true that the Four-dimensional Processing requires 33 percent more storage than the Euclidean Processing.

As for the memory for storing programs, on the other hand, the Four-dimensional Processing is better because the theories and algorithms are more compact, more general and more unified as discussed in 3., 4. and 5.

Overall Summary of Evaluations

On most evaluation items above the Four-dimensional Processing acquired better evaluations than the Euclidean Processing (see Table 26.1). The Four-dimensional Processing, however, is considered to have the following problems:

(a) It seems a little more difficult for ordinary programmers to understand.

(b) Although the Totally Four-dimensional Processing does not require performing a division operation, it preferably requires the normalizations of homogeneous coordinates, coefficients, Plücker coordinates and coefficients. This is troublesome and costly in the present-day computing environments.

(c) Manipulating Euclidean quantities and affine concepts is cumbersome since the weights of all the relevant vertices must be equalized.

(d) It uses arithmetic of very long data in the case of exact computations. This is inefficient in the present-day computing environments, although the Euclidean Processing can not generally attain exact arithmetic.

The discussions of the merits and demerits of the Totally Four-dimensional Processing above might lead to the appearance of a new type of computer for geometric use which reinforces the abilities of (b), (c) and (d) [65].

Table 26.1: Comparison between Euclidean and Four-dimensional Processing.

Items	**Euclidean processing**	**Four-dimensional processing**
Exactness	•not exact	•can be exact with respect to rational numbers
	4	5
Robustness	•possible zero division •possible unrobust cases with respect to rational curves in Newton-Raphson method	•no zero division operation •robust in Newton-Raphson method
	3	5
Compactness	•many special cases (parallel cases) •complex formula and algorithm	•few special cases •simpler formula and algorithms
	4	5
Generality	•restriction on weight sign in rational curves and surfaces	•no restriction on weight sign in rational curves and surfaces
	4	5
Unifiability	unifiable in rational form	unifiable in ordinary form
	4	5
Duality	not strict	strict
	4	5
Computational quantities	division operations complex routines	no division operations simpler routines normalization
	5	4.5
Memory requirements	less memory for data more memory for programs	more memory for data less memory for programs
	5	5
Transformation invariance	affine (conditional)	projective (no condition)
	4	5
Total points	37/45	44.5/45

Chapter 27

Role of Division Operations

27.1 A Paradox

In chapter 26, we compared the characteristics of the Four-dimensional Processing with those of the Euclidean one in terms of many evaluation items and found that the results turned out to be surprisingly favorable for the Four-dimensional Processing in almost all items. From our common sense this sounds strange. The results of the comparison seem to claim a paradox:

> "The Four-dimensional Processing, which gives a simpler system of techniques, provides, in reality, more general, more accurate, more robust and more systematic processing environment."

Then why does such a paradox hold in the Four-dimensional Processing ? The rationale of the paradox would have to be explained clearly.

27.2 Why Does the Paradox Hold ?

We shall again consider the pentagon problem. In the example, the output of the intersection computation of two line segments becomes the input to the next.

As stated in Section 1.1, a small amount of error is unavoidable in the division operations of eq.(1.2). There the (x, y) is derived, which includes the error and is input to the next process. Therefore the error is accumulated with the repetition of the computations.

Here we must note that the three dimensional homogeneous coordinates $(\Delta, \Delta_x, \Delta_y)$ of the intersection point have already been derived ! This example is the case of plane geometry. In the case of space geometry we can say the four dimensional homogeneous coordinates of the intersection point have already been derived before performing division operations ! Furthermore we must note that the homogeneous coordinates $(\Delta, \Delta_x, \Delta_y)$ can be represented exactly in integers, assuming the original input data are representable in rational numbers. Why do we need the division operations ? There is no need of deriving Euclidean coordinates (x, y) by performing detrimental division operations.

As mentioned before, our experiment demonstrated perfect restoration of the homogeneous coordinates of the original input vertex data after the iterations of the same number of times of going-in and going-out operations in the homogeneous approach (see Section 25.1.2).

As we see in this example, the Euclidean Processing can, in general, be considered to generate four-dimensional homogeneous coordinates in the beginning (space geometry case). Nevertheless it converts the homogeneous coordinates to Euclidean ones by performing detrimental division operations. Here there is no essential reason for doing such division operations. This is really unnatural processing ! It would not be difficult to justify the paradox mentioned above if we understand that the Euclidean Processing does such redundant and detrimental division operations.

From the observation above, we conclude that space geometry problems are preferably treated consistently as four-dimensional processing. Otherwise, the redundant division operations may cause "non-exactness," "non-robustness" or "non-compactness" problems in geometric modeling.

27.3 The Role of a Division Operation

As understood from the discussion of the previous section, there is no need of carrying out any division operation as long as next processing continues further. What is really needed in this stage is the ratios between the numerators and the denominator, but not the values of the ratios derived as the result of division operations. The homogeneous coordinate (or coefficient) data (i. e. ratios) are sufficient for subsequent processing. Division operations during each geometric processing do not produce any benefit but detrimental effects.

Then what is the real role of a division operation in a geometric processing system ?

It lies in the very end of the whole process, when the result of the process is to be interfaced to a human being for the confirmation of his intention. In this case the homogeneous data must be converted to Euclidean data by division operations in order that he can easily understand the result of computer. In some cases, division operations are carried out for performing perspective projections, or, in other cases, for deriving a Euclidean quantity with unit scale factor.

27.4 Problems in Geometric Systems

27.4.1 CAGD System

Present computer aided geometric design systems are considered to be mostly based on the Euclidean Processing, and therefore to contain the problems inherent in the processing, as discussed in Chapter 1 (Fig. 27.1(a)).

We expect that future systems will be based on the Four-dimensional Processing and organized as shown in Fig. 27.1(b). By dispensing with division operations, we can expect the two main advantages.

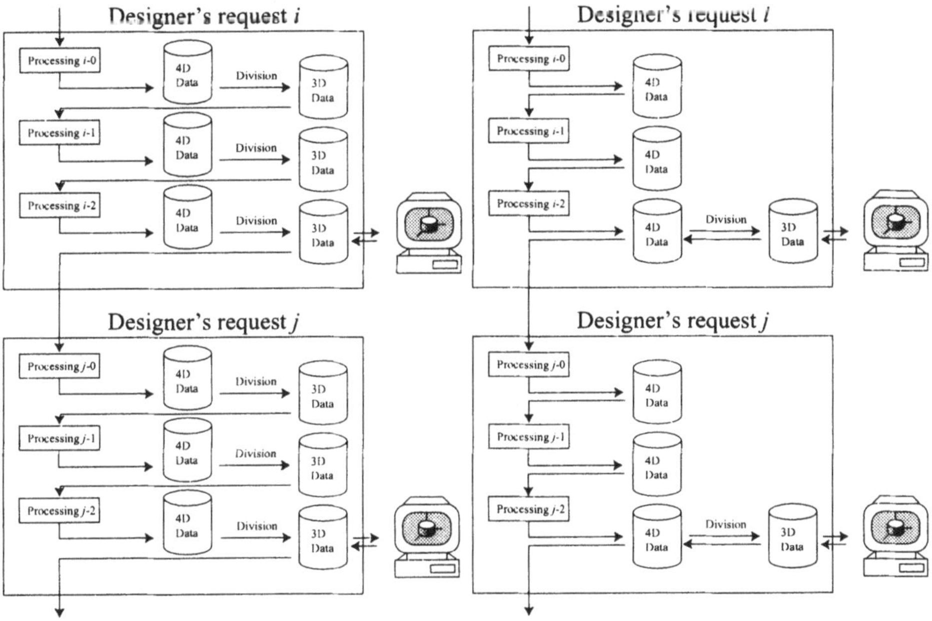

(a) Present CAGD system (b) Desirable CAGD system

Figure 27.1: Present and desirable CAGD systems.

1. The systems are expected to be free from the fundamental problems, i.e., "non-exactness," "non-robustness" and "non-compactness" existing in the Euclidean playground, and thus to be more reliable.

2. The systems are expected to be organized more simply and more systematically, based on the properties of "generality," "unifiability" and "duality," which are unique to the Four-dimensional Processing.

27.4.2 Other Geometric Systems

We have so far discussed the detrimental influences of division operations to CAGD systems. However, the discussions could be applicable to many other geometric processing systems as well. Such systems include geometric data communication systems on internet, data translators between different CAGD systems, numerical control machining systems and so on. Division operations are also considered to give detrimental effects upon the characteristics of these systems.

Take a data translator as an example. The purpose of a translator is to translate and convert the data formats of a sender CAGD system into those of the receiver CAGD system. A translator has its own intermediate data formats for the geometric elements in the system and therefore the conversions are performed in two stages, i.e., from the data formats of the sender to those of the intermediate descriptions, and then from those of the intermediate to those of the receiver.

First, the intermediate data descriptions must be as general as possible, otherwise some capabilities of the sender CAGD system may be lost. Here, the property of "generality" of the geometry descriptions in the Four-dimensional Processing could be capitalized on in the intermediate data descriptions.

Second, the data conversions must be as accurate as possible. Here, the property of "exactness" of the Four-dimensional Processing could be made the most of for this purpose. Four-dimensional coordinates should be used in place of Euclidean coordinates which are considered to be "deteriorated" by division operations.

Chapter 28

Various Interpretations

The Four-dimensional Processing might not be easy for an ordinary programmer to comprehend its true meaning. Therefore, it would be helpful to give some interpretations of the Four-dimensional Processing from various viewpoints for its further understanding. Followings are some of them.

Algebraic Interpretations

1. The Four-dimensional Processing can be considered to be such a geometric computation approach that the quadruple of a denominator w and three numerators X, Y, Z in division operations is looked upon as a coordinate representation of a point, and the division operations are omitted.

2. The Four-dimensional Processing can be considered to be a geometric computation approach to perform such computations systematically that a series of arithmetic operations in the Euclidean Processing are arranged into a single division form for each coordinate, computations of the numerators and the denominator are carried out separately, and division operations are performed only at the very end of the whole computational process.

3. The Four-dimensional Processing determines homogeneous coordinates while the Euclidean Processing does Euclidean coordinates. The homogeneous coordinate representation expresses "a ratio," not "a value" while the Euclidean coordinate one expresses "a value." Therefore the Four-dimensional Processing "processes relations" while the Euclidean Processing "computes values."

4. The three-dimensional Euclidean Processing generates, in reality, four-dimensional homogeneous coordinates, and then calculates Euclidean coordinates by division operations. The Four-dimensional Processing is such a method that eliminates the redundant and detrimental division opera-

tions from the Euclidean Processing and that generalizes [1] the generation of the four-dimensional data.

Geometric Interpretations

1. The Four-dimensional Processing is performed in the associated vector space of a projective space. A point in a projective space is represented as a line through the origin in the vector space.

   Therefore the Four-dimensional Processing deals with the set of lines through the origin in a space of dimension higher by one than that of the corresponding Euclidean space, while the Euclidean Processing deals with the set of points.

   This observation can be looked upon as a geometric view of the Algebraic Interpretation 3.

2. The Four-dimensional Processing deals with homogeneous geometric elements which are linear subspaces of dimension higher by one than that of the Euclidean counterparts while the Euclidean Processing can be considered to deal with the geometric elements produced by the cuts of the homogeneous elements by $w=1$ plane (Fig. 28.1).

   The shape of a Euclidean geometric element changes, depending on the relative position of the corresponding homogeneous element with respect to $w=0$ plane while that of the homogeneous element does not.

   That is, the homogeneous geometric elements are projectively invariant while the Euclidean elements are not.

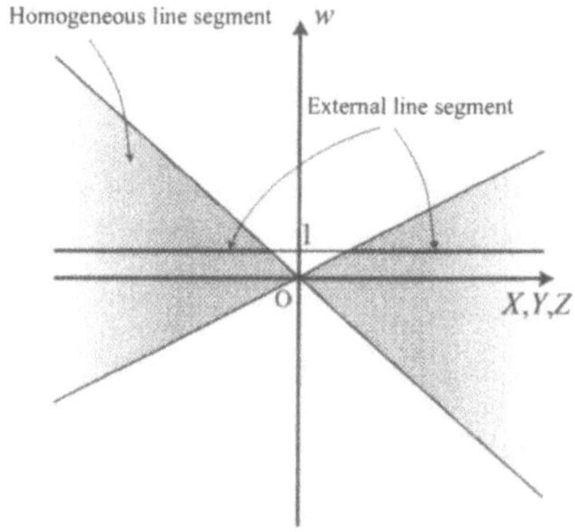

Figure 28.1: An external line segment as a cut of a homogeneous line segment by $w=1$ plane.

---

[1] In the Four-dimensional Processing, input point data are given in homogeneous coordinates while they are in ordinary coordinates in the Euclidean Processing.

Afterword

The author propounded the followings in this book:

1. In the past we had to be involved in the minutes of each numerical calculation, where we had to do division operations to confirm each computational result. Nowadays, however, since almost all the calculations are done in computer, we should consider the role of division operations once.

2. If you want to enhance the quality of the present computer aided geometric design system further, you had better shift the playground for the system from the three-dimensional to the four-dimensional one, because a limit of enhancement would be inevitable in the three-dimensional playground which is caused by division operations.

3. If you want to acquire the principles, properties and techniques by which you can construct a systematically structured CAD system, you had better shift the playground from the three-dimensional to the four-dimensional one, because the Four-dimensional Processing provides us with nice characteristics for the purpose such as generality, unifiability and duality.

The author expects further researches of the Four-dimensional Processing will be conducted. He does not dare to say that the Four-dimensional Processing is a panacea.

Bibliography

[1] Barr, S. Experiments in Topology. *Thomas Y. Crowell Co,* Newyork, 1964.

[2] Baumgart, B. G. Geometric Modeling for Computer Vision. *Stanford University, Computer Science Department* AIM-249,, STAN-CS-74-463, Oct., 1974.

[3] Blinn, J.F. A Homogeneous Formulation for Lines in 3-Space. *Computer Graphics*, Vol.11, No.2, 1977.

[4] Blinn, J. F. and M. E. Newell. Clipping Using Homogeneous Coordinates. *SIGGRAPH'78 proceedings*, August 1978.

[5] Bloomenthal, J. and J. Rokne. Homogeneous coordinates. *The Visual Computer*, Vol. 11, No.1, 1994.

[6] Böhm, W. Inserting new knots into B-spline curves. *Computer-Aided Design*, Vol.12, No.4, 1980.

[7] Braid, I.C., R.C. Hillyard and I. A. Stroud. Stepwise Construction of Polyhedra in Geometric Modelling in Mathematical Methods in Computer Graphics and Design (K. W. Brodlie, ed.). *Academic Press*, 1980.

[8] Catmull, E. and James Clark. Recursively generated B-spline Surfaces on Arbitrary Topological Meshes *Computer Aided Design* Vol.10, No.6, 1978.

[9] Chaikin, G. M. An Algorithm for High-Speed Curve Generation. *Computer Graphics and Image Processing*, Vol.14, No.3, 346-349,1974.

[10] Coons, S.A. Surfaces for Computer Aided Design of Space Forms. *MIT project MAC*, TR-41, June 1967.

[11] Coons, S.A. Transformations and Matrices. unpublished notes. *Univ. Michigan Short Course in Computer Aided Design*, 1971.

[12] DeRose, T. A Coordinate-Free Approach to Geometric Programming. *Theory and Practice of Geometric Modeling* Springer-Verlag, 1989.

[13] Doo, D.W.H. A Method of Smoothing highly Irregular Polyhedrons. *Interactive Techniques in Computer Aided Design Conference* Bologna, September, 1978.

[14] Doo, D.W.H. and M. Sabin. Behaviour of Recursive Division Surfaces near Extraodinary Points. *Computer Aided Design*, Vol.10, No.6,November 1978.

[15] Duda, R.O. and Hart, P.E. Use of Hough Transformation to Detect Lines and Curves in Pictures, Commun. ACM, Vol.15, No.1, pp.11-15, 1972.

[16] Farin, G. Curves and Surfaces for Computer Aided Geometric Design-A Practical Guide (Third Edition). *Academic Press*, 1993.

[17] Farin, G. NURB Curves and Surfaces from Projective Geometry to Practical Use. *A K Peters*, Massachusetts, 1995.

[18] Foley, J.D., Van Dam, A.,Feiner, S.K. and Hughes, J.F. Computer Graphics:Principles and Practice(Second Edition). *Addison-Wesley Publishing Company*, 1990.

[19] Forrest, A.R. Curves and Surfaces for Computer-Aided Design. *Doctorate Dissertation*, University of Cambridge, July 1968.

[20] Forrest, A.R. Computational Geometry in Practice. *Fundamental Algorithms for Computer Graphics, NATO ASI Series*, Vol.F17, Edited by R.A. Earnshaw, Springer-Verlag Berlin Heidelberg 1985.

[21] Goldman, R.N. Illicit expressions in vector algebra. *ACM Transactions on Graphics*,4(3):223-243, 1985.

[22] Hacker, R. Certification of algorithm 112: Position of a point relative to polygon. *Communication of the ACM*, Vol.5, 1962.

[23] Higashi, M., H. Yatomi, Y. Mizutani and S. Murabata. Unified Geometric Modeling by Non-Manifold Shell Operation. *2nd ACM Solid Modeling*, 1993.

[24] Hoffmann, C. M. Geometric and Solid Modeling —-An Introduction. *Morgan Kaufmann Publishers,Inc.*, California, 1989.

[25] Hoffmann, C. M. Advanced Aspects of Curves and Surfaces. *Tutorial Note, Eurographics'93*, Sept. 1993.

[26] Hough, P.V.C. Meathod and Means for Recognizing Complex Patterns, U.S Patent No.3069654(1962).

[27] Ikeno, Y., T. Minami and S. Enatsu. A Practical Equation for Euler-Poincaré's. Graduation Thesis, Yamaguchi Laboratory, Mechanical Engineering Dept., Waseda University, 2000.

[28] Iwahori, N. Linear Algebra(in Japanese). *Shoukabou book publishing Co.*, Oct. 1982.

[29] Kawada, Takayoshi. Affine Geometry and Projective Geometry (Fundamental Mathematics Series). *Iwanami Book Publishing Company*,1976.

[30] Keyser, J., S. Krishnan and D. Manocha. Efficient B-rep Generation of Low Degree Sculptured Solids using Exact Arithmetic, *4th ACM Symp. Solid Modeling, Atlanta*, 1997.

[31] Kurokawa, Hideki. A Proposal of a Free-form Surface Design Tool by Using a Polyhedron Subdivision Algorithm. *Master's Thesis, Mechanical Engineering Department*, Waseda University, Japan, March 1996.

[32] Lou, Lin, Norimasa Yoshida, Hiroaki Hanamitsu and Fujio Yamaguchi. The Homogeneous Representation of Rational Quadratic Bézier Curve and NURBS. *Journal of the Society of Precision Engineering (in Japanese)*, Vol. 63, No. 4, 1997.

[33] Mäntylä, M. and M. Sulonen. GWB-A Solid Modeller with Euler Operators. *IEEE Computer Graphics and Applications*, 2, 17-31,Sept. 1982.

[34] Mäntylä, M. Boolean set operations of 2-manifolds through vertex neighborhood classification. Transactions on Graphics, 5(1):1-29, Jan. 1986.

[35] Mäntylä, Martti. An Introduction to Solid Modeling. *Computer Science Press*, 1988.

[36] Matsumura, K., A. Yamada, F. Yamaguchi. A Geometric Newton Method for Interference Processing of Rational Curves and Surfaces in Homogeneous Space, *Proc. of Mathematics of Surfaces Sixth Conference, Oxford University Press*, 1996.

[37] Milne, P. S. On the Solution of a Set of Polyhedral Equation, *Symbolic and Numerical Computation for Artificial Intelligence, Academic Press*, 1992.

[38] Mortenson, M. Geometric Modeling, *Wiley*, New York, 1985.

[39] Nakamura, Katuhiko. Topology, *Kyouritu Shuppan Publishing Co.*, 1966.

[40] Newman, W.M. and R.F. Sproull. Principles of Interactive Computer Graphics, 2nd edition,*McGraw-Hill*, 1979.

[41] Niizeki, M.,F.Konishi,M.Yoshida and F. Yamaguchi. The Quarter-edge Data Structure. *Journal of Advanced Automation Technology*, Vol.6, No.4, 1994.

[42] Niizeki, M. and F. Yamaguchi. Projectively Invariant Intersection Detections for Solid Modeling. *ACM Transaction on Graphics*, Vol. 13, No.3, 279-299, 1994.

[43] Patterson, Richard R. Projective Transformations of the Parameter of a Bernstein-Bézier Curve. *ACM Transaction on Graphics*, Vol. 4, No.4, Oct. 1985.

[44] Penna, M.A. and R.R. Patterson. Projective Geometry and its Applications to Computer Graphics. *Prentice Hall*, 1986.

[45] Pottmann, Helmut. Studying NURBS Curves and Surfaces with Classical Geometry. *Mathematical Methods for Curves and Surfaces*, M. Daehlen, T. Lyche, and L.L. Schumaker (eds.), Vanderbilt University Press, pp. 413-438, 1995.

[46] Pottmann, Helmut, M. Peternell and B. Ravani. An introduction to line geometry with applications. *Computer-Aided Design*, 31(1999)3-16.

[47] Pottmann, Helmut and J. Wallner. Computational Line Geometry. *Springer-Verlag*, Berlin Heidelberg, 2001.

[48] Riesenfeld, R.F. On Chaikin's Algorithm. *Computer Graphics and Image Processing*, Vol.15, No.4, 304-310,1975.

[49] Riesenfeld, R.F. Homogeneous Coordinates and Projective Planes in Computer Graphics. *IEEE CG and A*, January 1981.

[50] Roberts, L.G. Homogeneous Matrix Representations and Manipulation of N-Dimensional Constructs. *Document MS 1405*, Lincoln Laboratory, Massachusetts, 1965.

[51] Sabin, Malcolm. Recursive subdivision. *The Mathematics of Surfaces*, edited by J. Gregory, pp.269-281, Claredon Press, 1986.

[52] Sproull, R. F. and I. E. Sutherland. A Clipping Divider. *FJCC 1968*, Thompson Books, Washington, D.C., 1968.

[53] Stolfi, J. Oriented Projective Geometry(A Framework for Geometric Computations). *Academic Press*, California, 1991.

[54] Sutherland, I.E. and G.W. Hodgman. Reentrant Polygon Clipping. *CACM*, Vol.17,No.1,Jan. 1974.

[55] Tsugane, H., N. Yoshida, H. Iguchi, M. Kitahara, J. Doi, R. Rou and F. Yamaguchi. Introduction of Edge Loop in the Quarter Edge Data Structure (in Japanese). *Proc. of the Society of Precision Engineering*, March 1997.

[56] Yamada, A. Interference problems of rational curves and surfaces based on the concept of homogeneous processing. *Doctorate dissertation*, Graduate school of science and engineering, Waseda University, Tokyo, June, 1995.

[57] Yamaguchi, F. A Unified Approach to Interference Problems Using a Triangle Processor. *Proc. of SIGGRAPH'85*. July 1985.

[58] Yamaguchi, F. Curves and Surfaces in Computer Aided Geometric Design. *Springer-Verlag.* 1988.

[59] Yamaguchi, F. and M. Niizeki. A New Paradigm for Geometric Processing. *Computer Graphics Forum.* Vol.12, No. 3(Proceeding of Eurographics '93),177-188,1993.

[60] Yamaguchi, F. and M. Niizeki. A Proposal of Geometric Processing of Rational Polynomial Curves and Surfaces. *Design and Application of Curves and Surfaces(Proc. of Mathematics of Surfaces conference).* Oxford University Press, 295-323, 1994.

[61] Yamaguchi, F., M. Niizeki, A. Yamada,N. Yoshida and K. Matsumura. Totally Homogeneous Paradigm for Geometric Processing Based on the Principle of Duality. *Proc. of Indian Mathematical Society,* December 1994.

[62] Yamaguchi, F. Computer Graphics and Geometric Modelling based on Four-Dimensional Theories (in Japanese). *Nikkan Kogyou Book Publishing Co.,* September 1996.

[63] Yamaguchi, F. and M. Niizeki. Some Basic Geometric Test Conditions in Terms of Plücker Coordinates and Plücker Coefficients, *The Visual Computer,* Vol.13, No.1, 1997.

[64] Yamaguchi, F. A Shift of Playground for Geometric Processing from Euclidean to Homogeneous One, *The Visual Computer,* 14(7):315–327, 1998.

[65] Yamaguchi, F. and N. Yoshida. A Homogeneous Computer, *in preparation.*

[66] Yamauchi, T. and F. Yamaguchi. The Existence Evaluation of Intersection Points in Curve/Surface Intersection using Multivariate Sturm Sequences (in Japanese), *Journal of Precision Engineering Society of Japan,* 67(3):498–503, 2001.

[67] Yap, C. Towards exact geometric computation. *Proc. 5th Canadian Conf. Computational Geometry,* Waterloo, 405, 1993.

[68] Yoshida, N., M. Shiokawa and F. Yamaguchi. Adaptive Sign Detection in 4×4 Determinant Method. *Journal of Advanced Automation Technology,* Vol.6, No.4, 1994.

[69] Yoshida, N, M. Shiokawa and F. Yamaguchi. Solid Modeling Based on a New Paradigm. *Computer Graphics Forum,* Vol. 13, No. 3, 1994.

Appendix A

Fundamentals on Euclidean Processing

A.1 Euclidean Space

Determining a coordinate origin o in space, an arbitrary point p has one-to-one correspondence to a vector $\overrightarrow{op}$ originating from the origin. The vector $\overrightarrow{op}$ is called a *position vector* with respect to the point p.

A position vector $\boldsymbol{p}$ is expressed as follows:

$$\boldsymbol{p} = \overrightarrow{op} = x\boldsymbol{i} + y\boldsymbol{j} + z\boldsymbol{k},$$

where $\boldsymbol{i}$, $\boldsymbol{j}$ and $\boldsymbol{k}$ are the fundamental vectors of three-dimensional vector space. In representing points and vectors, three orthogonal coordinate values are used.

The same relation exists in n-dimensional vector space. That is, an n-tuple $(x_1, x_2, \ldots, x_n)$ is considered to represent a point as well as a vector. In this case a position vector $\boldsymbol{p}$ is expressed as:

$$\boldsymbol{p} = \overrightarrow{op} = x_1\boldsymbol{e}_1 + x_2\boldsymbol{e}_2 + \ldots + x_n\boldsymbol{e}_n,$$

where $\boldsymbol{e}_1, \boldsymbol{e}_2, \ldots, \boldsymbol{e}_n$ are fundamental vectors of n-dimensional vector space.

The set of all points $p = (x_1, x_2, \ldots, x_n)$ is called n-dimensional *affine space*. An affine space is such that it represents a set of points associated with vectors. We say an n-dimensional affine space is associated with an n-dimensional vector space.

An affine space is often called a *Euclidean space* when the concept of distance is added to. Accordingly we can also say Euclidean space is associated with vector space. An n-dimensional Euclidean space is denoted by $\mathbf{E}^n$ and an n-dimensional vector space by $\mathbf{R}^n$.

In a vector space, two operations, i.e., addition and scalar multiplication are allowed and the space is closed under these two operations.

In an affine space, on the other hand, subtraction of two points and addition of a point and a vector are allowed (see A.2). The former produces a vector, and the latter another point.

A.2 Vector Operations of Position Vectors

As stated above, a point and vector are both represented in three-dimensional Euclidean space by a group of three real numbers. Yet it is highly important that points and vectors are strictly distinguished [21]. Simply stated, a point has a position but no direction or magnitude. In contrast, a vector has direction and magnitude but no position. The operations of vector algebra, that is, addition, subtraction, scalar multiplication, scalar product and vector product, are defined for vectors and should not be used when dealing with points. Yet, improper expressions such as $\boldsymbol{p}+\boldsymbol{q}$, $c\boldsymbol{p}$, $\boldsymbol{p}\cdot\boldsymbol{u}$ and $\boldsymbol{p}\times\boldsymbol{q}$ are sometimes found in graphics-related programs (where $\boldsymbol{p}$ and $\boldsymbol{q}$ are position vectors in $\mathbf{E}^3$, $\boldsymbol{u}$ a vector in $\mathbf{R}^3$, and c is a scalar). Thus, we must be careful not to use vector operations to treat points.

Let us consider a few examples. Let $\boldsymbol{p}$ and $\boldsymbol{q}$ denote position vectors, and $\boldsymbol{u}$ a vector defined as follows:

$$\boldsymbol{u}=\boldsymbol{q}-\boldsymbol{p}.$$

We now translate $\boldsymbol{p}$ and $\boldsymbol{q}$ by $\boldsymbol{v}$, so that they become $\boldsymbol{p}^*$ and $\boldsymbol{q}^*$ (see Fig. A.1), or:

$$\boldsymbol{p}^*=\boldsymbol{p}+\boldsymbol{v}, \quad \boldsymbol{q}^*=\boldsymbol{q}+\boldsymbol{v}.$$

Meanwhile, we have:

$$\boldsymbol{u}^*=\boldsymbol{q}^*-\boldsymbol{p}^*=(\boldsymbol{q}+\boldsymbol{v})-(\boldsymbol{p}+\boldsymbol{v})=\boldsymbol{u}.$$

Thus, translations affect points but leave vectors unchanged.

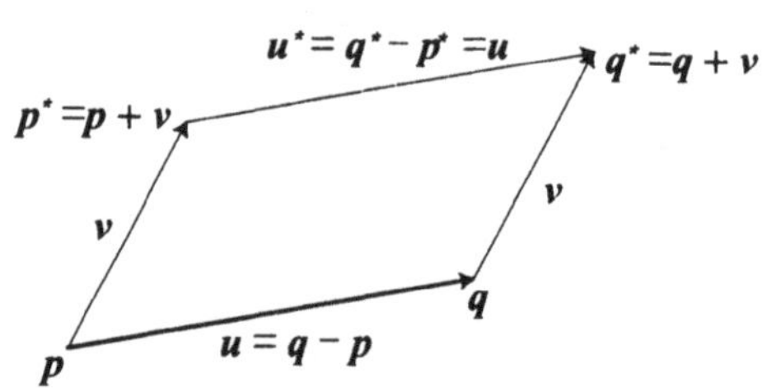

Figure A.1: Points are changed by translation but vectors unaffected.

Consider next the addition of two points $\boldsymbol{p}$ and $\boldsymbol{q}$ (see Fig. A.2). In the figure, $\boldsymbol{p}$ and $\boldsymbol{q}$ are shown in relation to two coordinate systems. The point $\boldsymbol{p}$+$\boldsymbol{q}$ can be considered that at $\overrightarrow{\mathrm{op}}+\overrightarrow{\mathrm{oq}}$, or at $\overrightarrow{\mathrm{o'p}}+\overrightarrow{\mathrm{o'q}}$. Or if $\boldsymbol{p}$+$\boldsymbol{q}$ is considered to be a vector, what then are its direction and magnitude ? As Fig. A.2 clearly shows, the point $\boldsymbol{p}$+$\boldsymbol{q}$ not only is determined from $\boldsymbol{p}$ and $\boldsymbol{q}$, but also depends on the coordinate system. Meanwhile, the operations of vector algebra are defined independently of coordinate systems. Therefore, $\boldsymbol{p}$+$\boldsymbol{q}$ is not a proper expression. Table A.1 presents vector operations that are proper and those that are not.

The value of an expression containing position vectors like $\boldsymbol{p},\boldsymbol{q},\boldsymbol{r},\ldots$, can be a scalar (e.g., $(\boldsymbol{p}-\boldsymbol{q})\cdot(\boldsymbol{q}-\boldsymbol{r})$), vector (e.g., $(\boldsymbol{q}-\boldsymbol{p})+(\boldsymbol{r}-\boldsymbol{p})$), or a point

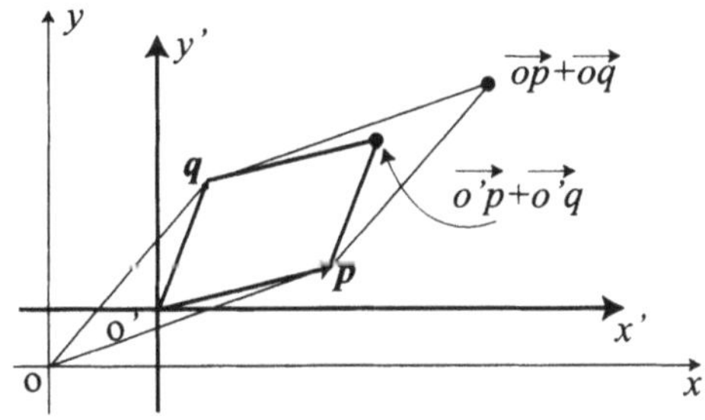

Figure A.2: Coordinate-dependent operation.

Table A.1: Proper and improper operations.

Operations	Proper operations	Improper operations
Addition	$\boldsymbol{u}+\boldsymbol{v}$(vector), $\boldsymbol{p}+\boldsymbol{u}$(point)	$\boldsymbol{p}+\boldsymbol{q}$
Subtraction	$\boldsymbol{u}-\boldsymbol{v}$(vector), $\boldsymbol{p}-\boldsymbol{u}$(point) $\boldsymbol{p}-\boldsymbol{q}$(vector)	$\boldsymbol{u}-\boldsymbol{p}$
Scalar multiplication	$c\cdot\boldsymbol{v}$(vector)	$c\cdot\boldsymbol{p}$
Scalar product	$\boldsymbol{u}\cdot\boldsymbol{v}$(scalar)	$\boldsymbol{p}\cdot\boldsymbol{u},\quad \boldsymbol{p}\cdot\boldsymbol{q}$
Vector product	$\boldsymbol{u}\times\boldsymbol{v}$(vector)	$\boldsymbol{p}\times\boldsymbol{u},\quad \boldsymbol{p}\times\boldsymbol{q}$

Note above that:
c: scalar,
$\boldsymbol{u},\boldsymbol{v}$: vectors in three-dimensional vector space $\mathbf{R}^3$,
$\boldsymbol{p},\boldsymbol{q}$: position vectors in three-dimensional Euclidean space $\mathbf{E}^3$.

(e.g., $\boldsymbol{p}+(\boldsymbol{q}-\boldsymbol{r})$). When the expression represents a scalar or vector, it must be invariant under translation. In other words, by their very definition, the scalar or vector value of the expression must not be affected when all points in the expression are translated by the same distance.

Below we present some examples of proper algebraic expressions $E(\boldsymbol{p}_0,\boldsymbol{p}_1,\ldots,\boldsymbol{p}_n)$ for position vectors.

Example 1

Midpoint of line segment pq

$$\frac{\boldsymbol{p}+\boldsymbol{q}}{2}.$$

Whereas $\boldsymbol{p}+\boldsymbol{q}$ is undefined, $(\boldsymbol{p}+\boldsymbol{q})/2$ represents the midpoint of line segment pq, which is properly and uniquely defined. A line segment's midpoint is unaffected by the coordinate system chosen.

Center of gravity of triangle pqr

$$\frac{\boldsymbol{p}+\boldsymbol{q}+\boldsymbol{r}}{3}.$$

The center of gravity of a triangle is unaffected by the coordinate system chosen.

Example 2

$$E(\boldsymbol{p},\boldsymbol{q},\boldsymbol{r}) = \boldsymbol{p}\times\boldsymbol{q}+\boldsymbol{q}\times\boldsymbol{r}+\boldsymbol{r}\times\boldsymbol{p}. \tag{A.1}$$

$E(\boldsymbol{p},\boldsymbol{q},\boldsymbol{r})$ is the normal vector of $\triangle pqr$. It has a magnitude twice the area of $\triangle pqr$.

Similarly,

$$E(\boldsymbol{v}_0,\boldsymbol{v}_1,\cdots,\boldsymbol{v}_n) = \boldsymbol{v}_0\times\boldsymbol{v}_1+\boldsymbol{v}_1\times\boldsymbol{v}_2+\cdots+\boldsymbol{v}_{n-1}\times\boldsymbol{v}_n+\boldsymbol{v}_n\times\boldsymbol{v}_0 \tag{A.2}$$

represents the normal vector of polygon $v_0v_1\ldots v_n$, and has a magnitude twice the area of the polygon.

Example 3

$$E(\boldsymbol{q}_0,\boldsymbol{q}_1,\cdots,\boldsymbol{q}_n) = \sum_i c_i\boldsymbol{q}_i. \tag{A.3}$$

Let us assume here that

$$\sum_i c_i = 0, \tag{A.4}$$

in which case, we can write:

$$\sum_i c_i\boldsymbol{q}_i = c_1(\boldsymbol{q}_1-\boldsymbol{q}_0)+c_2(\boldsymbol{q}_2-\boldsymbol{q}_0)+\cdots+c_n(\boldsymbol{q}_n-\boldsymbol{q}_0). \tag{A.5}$$

So $\sum c_i\boldsymbol{q}_i$ represents a vector when $\sum c_i=0$. It can also be shown that if $\sum c_i\boldsymbol{q}_i$ is a vector, then $\sum c_i=0$. Thus, $\sum c_i\boldsymbol{q}_i$ is a vector if and only if $\sum c_i=0$.

Next, let us assume that:

$$\sum_i c_i = 1, \tag{A.6}$$

in which case, we have:

$$\sum_i c_i\boldsymbol{q}_i = \boldsymbol{q}_0+c_1(\boldsymbol{q}_1-\boldsymbol{q}_0)+c_2(\boldsymbol{q}_2-\boldsymbol{q}_0)+\cdots+c_n(\boldsymbol{q}_n-\boldsymbol{q}_0). \tag{A.7}$$

So $\sum c_i\boldsymbol{q}_i$ represents a point when $\sum c_i=1$. It can also be shown that if $\sum c_i\boldsymbol{q}_i$ is a point, then $\sum c_i=1$. Thus, $\sum c_i\boldsymbol{q}_i$ is a point if and only if $\sum c_i=1$.

From these, we can say that $\sum c_i\boldsymbol{q}_i$ is undefined if $\sum c_i$ is neither 0 nor 1.

We present some examples below.

Examples of proper expressions:
Vector: $\boldsymbol{p}-\boldsymbol{q}$, $n\boldsymbol{p}-n\boldsymbol{q}$, $n\boldsymbol{p}+m\boldsymbol{q}-(n+m)\boldsymbol{r}$.
Point: $(\boldsymbol{p}+\boldsymbol{q})/2$, $(\boldsymbol{q}_1+\ldots+\boldsymbol{q}_m)/m$, $\boldsymbol{p}+\boldsymbol{q}-\boldsymbol{r}$.

Examples of improper expressions:
$2\boldsymbol{p}-3\boldsymbol{q}$, $(\boldsymbol{p}+\boldsymbol{q}+\boldsymbol{r})/2$.

Example 4

$$\boldsymbol{p}(t) = \sum_i f_i(t)\boldsymbol{q}_i. \tag{A.8}$$

As we can guess from **example 3**, only when:

$$\sum_i f_i(t) = 1, \tag{A.9}$$

will $\boldsymbol{p}(t) = \sum f_i(t)\boldsymbol{q}_i$ be a proper expression for a point. Since a curve is a set of points, condition (A.9) must always be satisfied in the definition of a curve. This is known as the *condition of affine invariance.*

Differentiating eqs.(A.8) and (A.9), we obtain:

$$\dot{\boldsymbol{p}}(t) = \sum_i \dot{f}_i(t)\boldsymbol{q}_i, \tag{A.10}$$

$$\sum_i \dot{f}_i(t) = 0. \tag{A.11}$$

Thus, $\dot{\boldsymbol{p}}(t)$ is a proper vector expression.

A.3 Barycentric Coordinates

We denote position vectors representing $(\nu+1)$ points, $p_0, p_1, \ldots, p_\nu$ in affine space, by $\boldsymbol{p}_0, \boldsymbol{p}_1, \ldots, \boldsymbol{p}_\nu$. If $\boldsymbol{p}_1 - \boldsymbol{p}_0, \boldsymbol{p}_2 - \boldsymbol{p}_0, \ldots, \boldsymbol{p}_\nu - \boldsymbol{p}_0$ are linearly independent, then points $p_0, p_1, \ldots, p_\nu$ are said to be linearly independent.

Linearly independent $(\nu+1)$ points define ν-dimensional affine subspace, and its parametric representation is shown below:

$$\boldsymbol{p} = t_0\boldsymbol{p}_0 + \ldots + t_\nu\boldsymbol{p}_\nu, \quad t_0 + \ldots + t_\nu = 1. \tag{A.12}$$

Since $p_0, \ldots, p_\nu$ are linearly independent, this representation is unique. Hence a point in ν-dimensional affine subspace has one-to-one correspondence with a $(\nu+1)$-tuple:

$$(t_0, \ldots, t_\nu), \quad t_0 + \ldots + t_\nu = 1.$$

This $(\nu+1)$-tuple is called *barycentric coordinate representation* with respect to the corresponding point p. A point with its barycentric coordinates (t_0, t_1, t_2, t_3) in three-dimensional Euclidean space is a barycenter of a system of point mass where each point p_0, p_1, p_2, p_3 has a positive or negative mass proportional to t_0, t_1, t_2, t_3 respectively.

A.4 Affine Invariance

We put a parametric curve as:

$$\boldsymbol{p}(t) = \sum a_j(t)\boldsymbol{q}_j, \tag{A.13}$$

where

$$\boldsymbol{p}(t) = [x(t)\ y(t)\ z(t)],\ \boldsymbol{q}_j = [x_j\ y_j\ z_j]. \tag{A.14}$$

Let us derive the condition that an affine transformation ϕ can be applied to eq.(A.13) (see eq.(A.9)). The condition is expressed as follows:

$$\phi(\boldsymbol{p}(t)) = \sum a_j(t)\phi(\boldsymbol{q}_j). \tag{A.15}$$

Now, we will treat an affine transformation as the sum of a linear transformation $\boldsymbol{M}$(3×3 matrix) and a translation $\boldsymbol{m} = [t_x\ t_y\ t_z]$. We first apply the linear transformation $\boldsymbol{M}$. Then

$$\begin{aligned}\sum a_j(t)\phi(\boldsymbol{q}_j) &= \sum a_j(t)(\boldsymbol{q}_j\boldsymbol{M}) \\ &= (\sum a_j(t)\boldsymbol{q}_j)\boldsymbol{M} \\ &= \phi(\boldsymbol{p}(t)).\end{aligned}$$

From the relation above, we say eq.(A.13) is invariant under linear transformation without any condition.

As for the invariant condition for translation,

$$\begin{aligned}\sum a_j(t)\phi(\boldsymbol{q}_j) &= \sum a_j(t)(\boldsymbol{q}_j + \boldsymbol{m}) \\ &= \sum a_j(t)\boldsymbol{q}_j + \boldsymbol{m}\sum a_j(t) \\ &= \boldsymbol{p}(t) + \boldsymbol{m}\sum a_j(t).\end{aligned}$$

Therefore we need

$$\sum a_j(t) \equiv 1. \tag{A.16}$$

Then we have

$$\begin{aligned}\sum a_j(t)\phi(\boldsymbol{q}_j) &= \boldsymbol{p}(t) + \boldsymbol{m} \\ &= \phi(\boldsymbol{p}(t)).\end{aligned}$$

Appendix B

Various Geometries

In 1872, a mathematician F. Klein presented in his Erlangen program [1] the concept of using various transformations to express the characteristics of different geometries.

Euclidean geometry is the study of invariant properties of geometric figures under rigid body motion. The transformation involved is congruence transformation (see Section 6.1), which comprises translation, rotation and reflection. A line is congruently transformed into a line, with line-segment lengths and angles remaining invariant. Inner products stay invariant through congruence transformations since the magnitude and angle of vectors are expressed by inner products. Concepts and properties that remain invariant under congruence transformations are called *Euclidean concepts* and *Euclidean properties*, respectively.

Affine geometry is the study of properties that remain invariant under affine transformations (see Section 6.1). Line segment lengths and angles are changed upon affine transformation. Meanwhile, invariant properties in affine transformations include the intersection point of lines, the line defined by two points, the parallelism of lines, the ratio of the division of a line segment by points, etc. As a set of points, the affine plane is identical to the Euclidean plane. Starting out with the plane in Euclidean geometry, affine geometry focuses on linear structures such as intersections while ignoring metrical structures such as length, angle, area and volume, etc. Affine transformation in fact re-examines, from a geometric standpoint, vector operations like addition, subtraction and translation, and also vector representation using components. When the concept of vector inner products is added to affine geometry, we have Euclidean geometry. Parallelism, meet, join and line segment ratios are all affine concepts.

[1] A paper submitted by Klein upon his appointment as Professor at Erlangen University. In this paper, Klein advocated a unified approach to various geometries, asserting that, given a transformation group for a manifold, the invariants associated with that group should be studied. Klein classified various geometries according to their transformation groups, each of which has corresponding invariant equations and quantities which are viewed as the geometric properties.

Projective geometry (classical and oriented) is the study of *projective notions* and *projective properties*, that is, notions and properties that remain invariant when a geometric figure is projectively transformed (see Section 6.1). In projective space, points at infinity are treated in the same manner as ordinary points, and lines and planes at infinity as ordinary lines and planes, respectively. A line and a plane are projectively transformed into a line and a plane, respectively.

A notable feature of projective space is that, through this transformation, the cross ratio of four points on a line remains invariant.

Projective space is also notable in that strict duality holds. Furthermore, incidence relations are maintained. Thus, if three points lie on the same line (i.e., are collinear), or if three lines intersect at a common point (i.e., are concurrent), this relation is retained through projective transformations.

A line segment has no meaning in classical projective geometry just as an angle has no meaning in affine geometry. Thus, specifying two points in projective space does not define a line segment (in our Four-dimensional Processing paradigm, line segments are defined in projective space by making use of the associated vector space; see Section 9.2). Furthermore, there is no notion for half-space, convex figures, parallelism or orientation in classical projective space. Notions related to orientation include front, back, right, left, clockwise, counterclockwise, etc.

In oriented projective space, on the other hand, the notions of line segment, half-space, convex figures and orientation exist. Table B.1 summarizes the concepts of the various geometries.

Table B.1: Concepts of various geometries.

Geometry	Transformations	Geometric concepts
Euclidean geometry	Congruence	line segment length angle magnitude scalar product
Affine geometry	Affine	parallelism, ratio mid point, barycenter join, meet
Classical projective geometry	Projective	duality, cross ratio point, line, plane at infinity
Oriented projective geometry	Projective	duality, cross ratio point, line, plane at infinity line segment, half space convex figure, orientation

Appendix C

Plane Determinant Method

C.1 Plücker Coordinates and Coefficients

Plücker coordinates and Plücker coefficients in plane geometry are shown in Table C.1.

Table C.1: Plücker coordinates and Plücker coefficients in plane geometry.

	Plücker coordinates		**Plücker coefficients**
Point	$V_0 = \overline{(w_0, X_0, Y_0)}$	Line	$\gamma_0 = \overline{(a_0, b_0, c_0)^T}$
Line	$L_{01} = \overline{(U_{01}, -Q_{01}, P_{01})^T}$ $P_{01} = \begin{vmatrix} w_0 & X_0 \\ w_1 & X_1 \end{vmatrix}$ $Q_{01} = \begin{vmatrix} w_0 & Y_0 \\ w_1 & Y_1 \end{vmatrix}$ $U_{01} = \begin{vmatrix} X_0 & Y_0 \\ X_1 & Y_1 \end{vmatrix}$	Point	$\pi_{01} = \overline{(u_{01}, -q_{01}, p_{01})}$ $p_{01} = \begin{vmatrix} a_0 & a_1 \\ b_0 & b_1 \end{vmatrix}$ $q_{01} = \begin{vmatrix} a_0 & a_1 \\ c_0 & c_1 \end{vmatrix}$ $u_{01} = \begin{vmatrix} b_0 & b_1 \\ c_0 & c_1 \end{vmatrix}$
Space	$F_{012} = \overline{(S_{012})}$ $S_{012} = \begin{vmatrix} w_0 & X_0 & Y_0 \\ w_1 & X_1 & Y_1 \\ w_2 & X_2 & Y_2 \end{vmatrix}$	Vacuum	$\tau_{012} = \overline{(T_{012})}$ $T_{012} = \begin{vmatrix} a_0 & a_1 & a_2 \\ b_0 & b_1 & b_2 \\ c_0 & c_1 & c_2 \end{vmatrix}$

In plane geometry, l_{01} and m_{01} represent the following:

$$l_{01} \in \{U_{01}, -Q_{01}, P_{01}\}, \ m_{01} \in \{u_{01}, -q_{01}, p_{01}\}, \tag{C.1}$$

respectively, which are different from what they do in space geometry (see "Notation used in this book").

C.2 Line L_{01} in Plücker Coordinates

From Table C.1,

$$L_{01} \equiv \overline{(U_{01}, -Q_{01}, P_{01})^T} \equiv \overline{\left(\begin{vmatrix} X_0 & Y_0 \\ X_1 & Y_1 \end{vmatrix}, - \begin{vmatrix} w_0 & Y_0 \\ w_1 & Y_1 \end{vmatrix}, \begin{vmatrix} w_0 & X_0 \\ w_1 & X_1 \end{vmatrix} \right)^T}. \quad \text{(C.2)}$$

In vector space $\mathbf{R}^3$, L_{01} represents an oriented plane which contains vectors $\boldsymbol{V}_0$ and $\boldsymbol{V}_1$ and, of which the normal vector is $\boldsymbol{L}_{01} = [U_{01}, -Q_{01}\ P_{01}]^T$ (see eq.(9.2) and Fig. C.1). The orientation of the normal vector agrees with that of the vector product of $\boldsymbol{V}_0$ and $\boldsymbol{V}_1$.

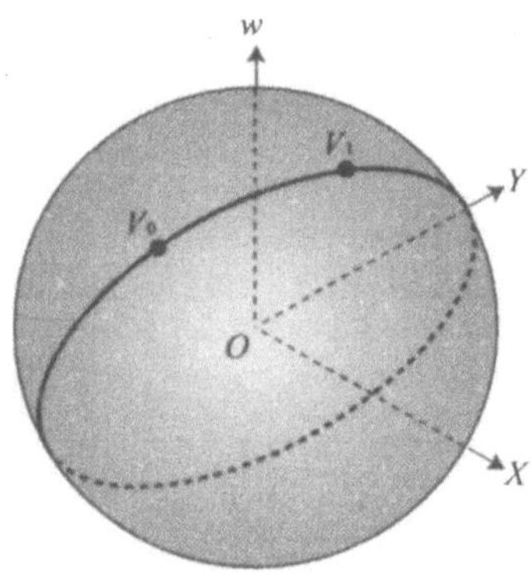

Figure C.1: Homogeneous line in wXY space.

In Euclidean space, L_{01} represents a line, where

$$[-Q_{01}\ P_{01}] = w_0 w_1[-(y_1 - y_0)\ \ (x_1 - x_0)] \quad \text{(C.3)}$$

is a normal vector to the line, and

$$U_{01} = \begin{vmatrix} X_0 & Y_0 \\ X_1 & Y_1 \end{vmatrix} = w_0 w_1 (x_0 y_1 - x_1 y_0) = w_0 w_1 \times (\text{parallelogram } o, v_0, v_1) \quad \text{(C.4)}$$

is a signed area of parallelogram $o(0,0)$, $v_0(x_0, y_0)$, $v_1(x_1, y_1)$, scaled by $w_0 w_1$ (see Fig. C.2). Unlike in $\mathbf{R}^3$, the roles of the coefficients of a line equation are different in two-dimensional Euclidean space case (see 6. of Section 2.2).

C.3 Space S_{012} in Plücker Coordinates

From Table C.1,

$$S_{012} = \begin{vmatrix} w_0 & X_0 & Y_0 \\ w_1 & X_1 & Y_1 \\ w_2 & X_2 & Y_2 \end{vmatrix}. \quad \text{(C.5)}$$

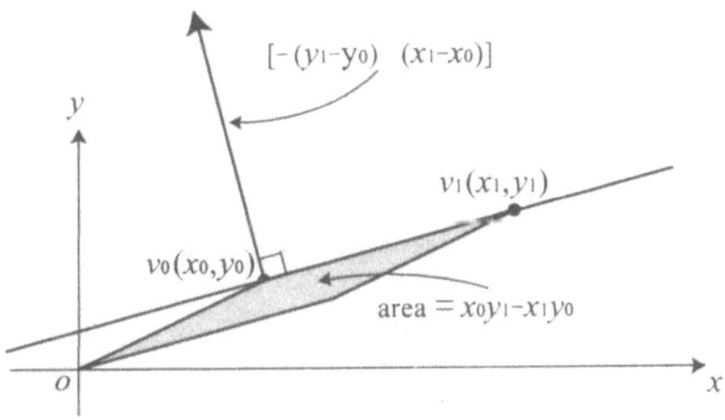

Figure C.2: Line in xy-plane.

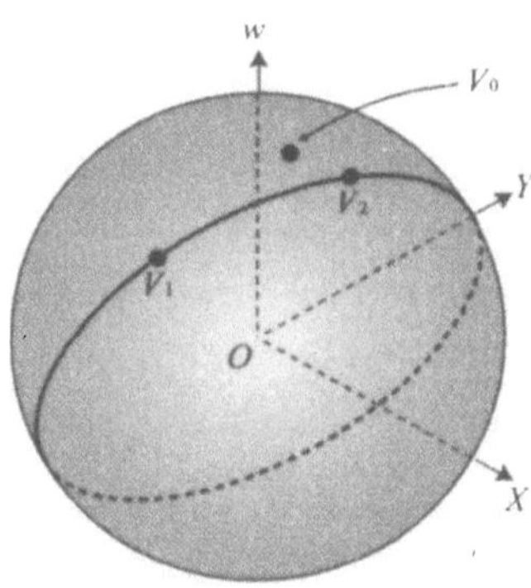

Figure C.3: Half space test in wXY-space.

In vector space $\mathbf{R}^3$, S_{012} represents the signed volume of a parallelepiped made by points V_0, V_1, V_2 and origin O (Fig. C.3):

$$S_{012} \begin{cases} > 0 & \cdots V_0 \text{ is in the positive (left) half-space of oriented line } V_1V_2, \\ = 0 & \cdots V_0 \text{ is on oriented line } V_1V_2, \\ < 0 & \cdots V_0 \text{ is in the negative (right) half-space of oriented line } V_1V_2. \end{cases} \quad \text{(C.6)}$$

As for S_{012}, see also Section 4.9.1.

We now modify eq.(C.5) assuming $w_0, w_1, w_2 \neq 0$:

$$S_{012} = \begin{vmatrix} w_0 & X_0 & Y_0 \\ w_1 & X_1 & Y_1 \\ w_2 & X_2 & Y_2 \end{vmatrix}$$

$$= w_0 w_1 w_2 \begin{vmatrix} 1 & x_0 & y_0 \\ 1 & x_1 & y_1 \\ 1 & x_2 & y_2 \end{vmatrix}$$

$$= 2w_0w_1w_2 \times (\text{signed area of triangle } v_0v_1v_2). \tag{C.7}$$

In Euclidean space, S_{012} represents a signed area of the triangle $v_0(x_0, y_0)$,$v_1(x_1, y_1)$, $v_2(x_2, y_2)$, scaled by $2w_0w_1w_2$.

C.4 Basic Geometric Relations

1. **Condition for coincident points**

   The Plücker coordinates of the line that passes through two points $\overline{V_0 = (w_0, X_0, Y_0)}$ and $V_1 = \overline{(w_1, X_1, Y_1)}$ are given by (see Table C.1):

$$\overline{(U_{01}, -Q_{01}, P_{01})^T}. \tag{C.8}$$

   When the two points V_0 and V_1 are either identical or antipodal, that is, $V_0 = kV_1$ $(k \neq 0)$, then:

$$\boldsymbol{L}_{01} \equiv [U_{01} \ -Q_{01} \ P_{01}]^T = [0 \ 0 \ 0]^T. \tag{C.9}$$

   Conversely, if eq.(C.9) holds, then eq.(C.8) does not represent a line, that is, the two points V_0 and V_1 are either identical or antipodal to each other.

   Thus, eq.(C.9) expresses the condition for two points V_0 and V_1 to be either identical or antipodal.

   When V_0 and V_1 satisfy eq.(C.9):

   - they are identical points if V_0 and V_1 are points in projective space;
   - the following test is needed if they are points in two-sided space:
     - $\boldsymbol{V}_0 \cdot \boldsymbol{V}_1 > 0 \cdots$ V_0 and V_1 are identical points,
     - $\boldsymbol{V}_0 \cdot \boldsymbol{V}_1 < 0 \cdots$ V_0 and V_1 are antipodal, and thus distinct.

2. **Condition for coincident lines**

   The condition for two lines $\gamma_0 = \overline{(a_0, b_0, c_0)^T}$ and $\gamma_1 = \overline{(a_1, b_1, c_1)^T}$ to be coincident is derived in the exactly same manner as, but forming a dual relationship to, the condition for two coincident points. That is, the necessary and sufficient condition for the two lines to be identical or to have reverse orientations can be expressed by the dual equation to eq.(C.9), or:

$$\boldsymbol{\pi}_{01} \equiv [u_{01} \ -q_{01} \ p_{01}] = [0 \ 0 \ 0]. \tag{C.10}$$

   When γ_0 and γ_1 satisfy eq.(C.10):

   - they are identical lines if γ_0 and γ_1 are lines in projective space;
   - the following test is needed if they are lines in two-sided space:
     - $\gamma_0 \cdot \gamma_1 > 0 \cdots$ γ_0 and γ_1 are identical lines,
     - $\gamma_0 \cdot \gamma_1 < 0 \cdots$ γ_0 and γ_1 are reversely oriented, and thus distinct.

Table C.2: Conditions for geometric elements to be coincident, concurrent and collinear in plane geometry.

Coincidence conditions for homogeneous elements	**Coincidence conditions for dual homogeneous elements**
Two points The condition for two points V_0 and V_1 to be either identical or antipodal is given by: $P_{01} = Q_{01} = U_{01} = 0$ or $\boldsymbol{L}_{01} = \boldsymbol{0}.$	**Two lines** The condition for two lines γ_0 and γ_1 to be identical or to have reverse orientations is given by: $p_{01} = q_{01} = u_{01} = 0$ or $\boldsymbol{\pi}_{01} = \boldsymbol{0}.$

Collinearity conditions	**Concurrent conditions**
Three points The condition for three points V_0, V_1 and V_2 to be collinear is given by: $S_{012} = 0.$	**Three lines** The condition for three lines γ_0, γ_1 and γ_2 to be concurrent is given by: $T_{012} = 0.$

3. **Condition for collinear points**

   The condition for three points V_0, V_1 and V_2 to be collinear is that they are linearly dependent:

$$S_{012} = \begin{vmatrix} w_0 & X_0 & Y_0 \\ w_1 & X_1 & Y_1 \\ w_2 & X_2 & Y_2 \end{vmatrix} = 0. \tag{C.11}$$

4. **Condition for concurrent lines**

   The condition for three lines γ_0, γ_1 and γ_2 to be concurrent is given by the dual to eq.(C.11), that is:

$$T_{012} = \begin{vmatrix} a_0 & a_1 & a_2 \\ b_0 & b_1 & b_2 \\ c_0 & c_1 & c_2 \end{vmatrix} = 0. \tag{C.12}$$

The above results are summarized in Table C.2.

C.5 Interference Tests between Simplices

We assume here that line segments and triangles are all defined by linearly independent homogeneous coordinate vectors.

C.5.1 Simplices in Classical Projective Space

1. **Containment of a point in a line segment**

   We derive the condition in classical projective space for a homogeneous point V_a to lie on a homogeneous line segment V_0V_1.

   First, we put the condition such that the point V_a and line segment V_0V_1 are collinear, which is given by eq.(C.11):

   $$S_{a01} = 0.$$

   Geometric Derivation

   The condition for the point V_a to be contained in the collinear line segment V_0V_1 is expressed in the spherical model as the condition for V_a to be contained in V_0V_1 or its antipode $\neg V_0 \neg V_1$ [1)](see Fig. C.4).

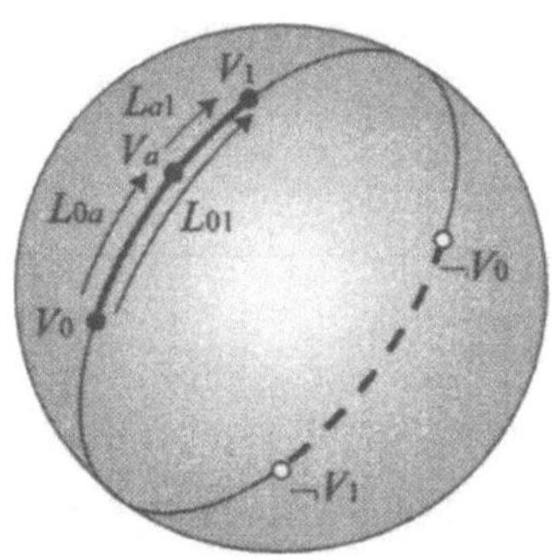

Figure C.4: Containment test of a point in a line segment (projective space).

   Referring to Section 4.6, this condition can be expressed, using vectors defined by Plücker coordinates of line in plane geometry, as follows:

   $$\begin{aligned} &(\boldsymbol{L}_{01} \cdot \boldsymbol{L}_{0a},\ \boldsymbol{L}_{01} \cdot \boldsymbol{L}_{a1} \geq 0) \\ \vee\ &(\boldsymbol{L}_{01} \cdot \boldsymbol{L}_{0a},\ \boldsymbol{L}_{01} \cdot \boldsymbol{L}_{a1} \leq 0). \end{aligned} \tag{C.13}$$

   This is further simplified as follows:

   $$\boldsymbol{L}_{a0} \cdot \boldsymbol{L}_{a1} \leq 0.$$

[1)] The "condition that $\neg V_a$ is contained in V_0V_1" is the same as the "condition that V_a is contained in $\neg V_0 \neg V_1$," while the "condition that $\neg V_a$ is contained in $\neg V_0 \neg V_1$" is the same as the "condition that V_a is contained in V_0V_1"(see Fig. C.4).

Together with the collinearity condition above, the final result is written as follows:

$$(S_{a01} = 0) \wedge (\boldsymbol{L}_{a0} \cdot \boldsymbol{L}_{a1} \leq 0). \tag{C.14}$$

Note that the order of vertices defining the line segment does not affect the containment condition eq.(C.14).

Algebraic Derivation

The condition for V_a to be contained in the line segment V_0V_1 is expressed as follows (see Section 9.2) [2]:

$$\xi_0 \boldsymbol{V}_0 + \xi_1 \boldsymbol{V}_1 = \boldsymbol{V}_a, \tag{C.16}$$

$$(\xi_0, \xi_1 \geq 0) \vee (\xi_0, \xi_1 \leq 0). \tag{C.17}$$

Note here that when the homogeneous equation (C.16), consisting of three simultaneous equations, is solved for the two variables, ξ_0 and ξ_1, three solution sets are possible depending on which equations are chosen.

We shall let l_{01} represent one of the three Plücker coordinates of line defined by two points (see eq.(C.1)):

$$L_{01} = \overline{(U_{01}, -Q_{01}, P_{01})},$$

that is,

$$l_{01} \in \{U_{01}, -Q_{01}, P_{01}\}. \tag{C.18}$$

Since the line segment is assumed to be linearly independent:

$$(U_{01}, -Q_{01}, P_{01}) \neq (0,0,0),$$

we can obtain ξ_0 and ξ_1 using the notation above. We assume $l_{01} \neq 0$. Then

$$(\xi_0, \xi_1) = (\frac{l_{a1}}{l_{01}}, \frac{l_{0a}}{l_{01}}). \tag{C.19}$$

From eq.(C.17), we have:

$$(l_{0a} \geq 0 \wedge l_{1a} \leq 0) \ \vee \ (l_{0a} \leq 0 \wedge l_{1a} \geq 0). \tag{C.20}$$

Combining the condition (C.20) with the collinearity one above gives the final result:

$$\begin{gathered} \text{With respect to } l_{01} \neq 0 \ (\in \{U_{01}, -Q_{01}, P_{01}\}), \\ (S_{a01} = 0) \\ \wedge \ ((l_{a0} \geq 0 \wedge l_{a1} \leq 0) \ \vee \ (l_{a0} \leq 0 \wedge l_{a1} \geq 0)). \end{gathered} \tag{C.21}$$

[2] Eq.(C.16) must be written as follows:

$$\xi_0 \boldsymbol{V}_0 + \xi_1 \boldsymbol{V}_1 = k\boldsymbol{V}_a, \quad k \neq 0. \tag{C.15}$$

Since the homogeneous parameters play the role of k, it is omitted for simplicity. The same simplification is taken throughout.

This expression represents eq.(C.14) in terms of its vector components.

Partition

Now, let us consider partitioning the line segment V_0V_1 using the point V_a, when it is found to lie in the line segment.

The first condition of eq.(C.17) is for the point to be contained in the line segment V_0V_1 and the second one for it to be in the antipodal line segment, in the spherical model.

Now, in $\mathbf{R}^3$, the orientations of geometric elements are distinguished although they are finally defined in projective space, where they are not. That is, we have a line segment ($l_{01}>0$) and a line segment ($l_{01}<0$).

Thus, from eqs.(C.17) and (C.19), the condition for V_a to be in V_0V_1 is:

$$\begin{aligned}&(l_{01} > 0 \wedge l_{a0} \leq 0 \wedge l_{a1} \geq 0)\\ \vee\ &(l_{01} < 0 \wedge l_{a0} \geq 0 \wedge l_{a1} \leq 0),\end{aligned} \tag{C.22}$$

and the condition for V_a to be in $\neg V_0 \neg V_1$ is:,

$$\begin{aligned}&(l_{01} > 0 \wedge l_{a0} \geq 0 \wedge l_{a1} \leq 0)\\ \vee\ &(l_{01} < 0 \wedge l_{a0} \leq 0 \wedge l_{a1} \geq 0).\end{aligned} \tag{C.23}$$

Therefore it is advisable to use the following vector $\boldsymbol{V}$ to maintain consistency in the vector signs between the line segment vertices and a partitioning point:

$$\left\{\begin{array}{l}\text{With respect to } l_{01} \neq 0\ (\in \{U_{01}, -Q_{01}, P_{01}\}),\\ \quad \textbf{If } (l_{01} > 0 \wedge l_{a0} \leq 0 \wedge l_{a1} \geq 0)\\ \quad \vee\ (l_{01} < 0 \wedge l_{a0} \geq 0 \wedge l_{a1} \leq 0)\\ \qquad \textbf{then } \boldsymbol{V} = \boldsymbol{V}_a\\ \qquad \textbf{else}\\ \quad \textbf{if } (l_{01} > 0 \wedge l_{a0} \geq 0 \wedge l_{a1} \leq 0)\\ \quad \vee\ (l_{01} < 0 \wedge l_{a0} \leq 0 \wedge l_{a1} \geq 0)\\ \qquad \textbf{then } \boldsymbol{V} = -\boldsymbol{V}_a.\end{array}\right. \tag{C.24}$$

2. **Containment of a point in a triangle**

   We now derive the condition in classical projective space for a homogeneous point V_a to lie inside a homogeneous triangle $V_0V_1V_2$.

   Geometric Derivation

   The condition for the point V_a to be contained in the triangle $V_0V_1V_2$ is expressed in the spherical model as the condition for V_a to be contained in $V_0V_1V_2$ or its antipode $\neg V_0 \neg V_1 \neg V_2$ [3](see Fig. C.5).

---

[3] The "condition that $\neg V_a$ is contained in $V_0V_1V_2$" is the same as the "condition that V_a is contained in $\neg V_0 \neg V_1 \neg V_2$," while the "condition that $\neg V_a$ is contained in $\neg V_0 \neg V_1 \neg V_2$" is the same as the "condition that V_a is contained in $V_0V_1V_2$"(see Fig. C.5).

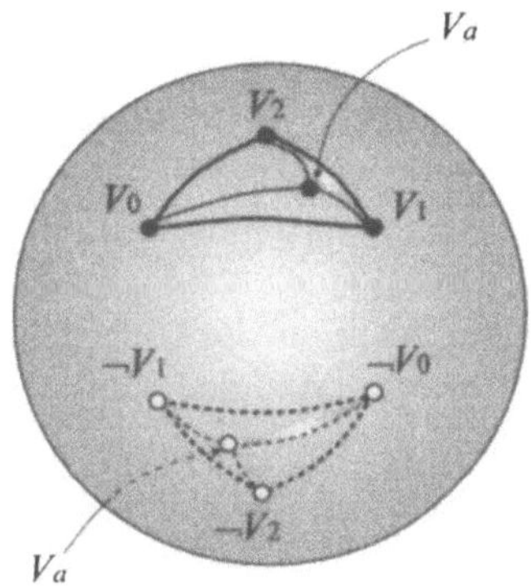

Figure C.5: Containment test of a point in a triangle (projective space).

Referring to Section 4.6, this condition can be expressed, using the Plücker coordinate of space in plane geometry, as follows:

$$\begin{aligned} &(S_{012} \cdot S_{a12},\ S_{012} \cdot S_{0a2},\ S_{012} \cdot S_{01a} \geq 0)) \\ \vee\ &(S_{012} \cdot S_{a12},\ S_{012} \cdot S_{0a2},\ S_{012} \cdot S_{01a} \leq 0)). \end{aligned} \tag{C.25}$$

This is further simplified as follows:

$$(S_{a12}, S_{a20}, S_{a01} \geq 0) \vee (S_{a12}, S_{a20}, S_{a01} \leq 0). \tag{C.26}$$

Note that the order of vertices defining the triangle does not affect the containment condition eq.(C.26).

Algebraic Derivation

The condition for the homogeneous point V_a to lie inside the homogeneous triangle $V_0V_1V_2$ is given by (see Section 9.2):

$$\xi_0 \boldsymbol{V}_0 + \xi_1 \boldsymbol{V}_1 + \xi_2 \boldsymbol{V}_2 = \boldsymbol{V}_a, \tag{C.27}$$

$$(\xi_0, \xi_1, \xi_2 \geq 0) \vee (\xi_0, \xi_1, \xi_2 \leq 0). \tag{C.28}$$

Eq.(C.27) expresses a set of three simultaneous linear equations with variables, ξ_0, ξ_1 and ξ_2.

Since V_0, V_1 and V_2 are assumed to be linearly independent, we have:

$$S_{012} \neq 0.$$

Thus, eq.(C.27) has a unique solution for ξ_0, ξ_1 and ξ_2, as given by:

$$\begin{aligned} (\xi_0, \xi_1, \xi_2) &= \left(\frac{S_{a12}}{S_{012}}, \frac{S_{0a2}}{S_{012}}, \frac{S_{01a}}{S_{012}} \right) \\ &= \frac{1}{S_{012}} (S_{a12}, S_{a20}, S_{a01}). \end{aligned} \tag{C.29}$$

From eq.(C.28), therefore, we have:

$$(S_{a12}, S_{a20}, S_{a01} \geq 0) \vee (S_{a12}, S_{a20}, S_{a01} \leq 0). \tag{C.30}$$

Partition

Now, let us consider partitioning the triangle $V_0V_1V_2$ using the point V_a, when it is found to lie in the triangle.

The first condition of eq.(C.28) is for the point to be contained in the triangle $V_0V_1V_2$ and the second one for it to be in the antipodal triangle, in the spherical model.

Now, in $\mathbf{R}^3$, the orientations of geometric elements are distinguished although they are finally defined in projective space. That is, we have a positive triangle ($S_{012}>0$) and a negative one ($S_{012}<0$).

Thus, from eqs.(C.28) and (C.29), the condition for V_a to be in $V_0V_1V_2$ is:

$$\begin{aligned}&(S_{012} > 0 \wedge S_{a12}, S_{a20}, S_{a01} \geq 0)\\ \vee\ &(S_{012} < 0 \wedge S_{a12}, S_{a20}, S_{a01} \leq 0),\end{aligned} \tag{C.31}$$

and the condition for V_a to be in $\neg V_0 \neg V_1 \neg V_2$ is:

$$\begin{aligned}&(S_{012} > 0 \wedge S_{a12}, S_{a20}, S_{a01} \leq 0)\\ \vee\ &(S_{012} < 0 \wedge S_{a12}, S_{a20}, S_{a01} \geq 0).\end{aligned} \tag{C.32}$$

These cases are shown in (a), (b) (corresponding to eq.(C.31)) and (c), (d) (corresponding to eq.(C.32)) in Fig. C.6.

Therefore it is advisable to use the following vector $\boldsymbol{V}$ to maintain consistency in the vector signs between the triangle vertices and a partitioning point:

$$\begin{cases} \textbf{If } (S_{012} > 0 \wedge S_{a12}, S_{a20}, S_{a01} \geq 0)\\ \ \vee (S_{012} < 0 \wedge S_{a12}, S_{a20}, S_{a01} \leq 0)\\ \qquad \textbf{then } \boldsymbol{V} = \boldsymbol{V}_a\\ \qquad\quad \textbf{else}\\ \textbf{if } (S_{012} > 0 \wedge S_{a12}, S_{a20}, S_{a01} \leq 0)\\ \ \vee (S_{012} < 0 \wedge S_{a12}, S_{a20}, S_{a01} \geq 0)\\ \qquad \textbf{then } \boldsymbol{V} = -\boldsymbol{V}_a. \end{cases} \tag{C.33}$$

3. **Intersection of two line segments**

We now derive the condition in classical projective space for two homogeneous line segments, V_0V_1 and V_aV_b, to intersect.

We assume the two line segments are not collinear. That is, at least one set of three points in the four endpoints V_0, V_1, V_a, V_b are not collinear:

$$(S_{01a}, S_{01b}, S_{ab0}, S_{ab1}) \neq (0,0,0,0). \tag{C.34}$$

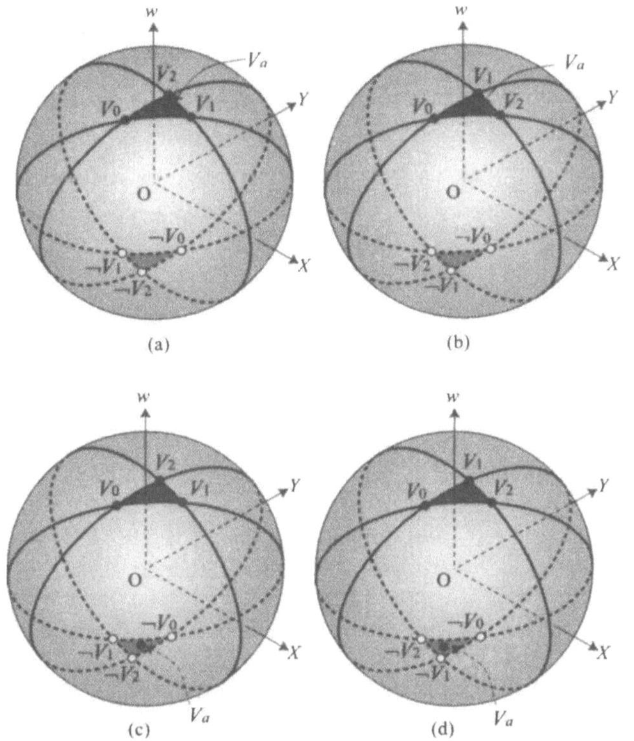

Figure C.6: Partitioning triangle $V_0V_1V_2$ using point V_a.

Geometric Derivation

To determine whether the two line segments intersect, we employ the sign zones relative to a triangle discussed in Section 4.6 (see Fig. C.7), using here the triangle $V_0V_1V_a$.

We see that the line segment V_aV_b intersects with V_0V_1 when V_b lies in the $++-$ zone (see Fig.C.7(a)), while it intersects with $\neg V_0 \neg V_1$ when V_b lies in the $---$ zone (see Fig. C.7(b)).

Using the Plücker coordinates of space in plane geometry, this is expressed as follows:

$$\begin{aligned}&(S_{01a} \cdot S_{b1a} \geq 0 \wedge S_{01a} \cdot S_{0ba} \geq 0 \wedge S_{01a} \cdot S_{01b} \leq 0)\\ \vee\ &(S_{01a} \cdot S_{b1a} \leq 0 \wedge S_{01a} \cdot S_{0ba} \leq 0 \wedge S_{01a} \cdot S_{01b} \leq 0),\end{aligned}$$

which can be simplified as:

$$S_{01a} \cdot S_{01b},\ S_{ab0} \cdot S_{ab1} \leq 0. \tag{C.35}$$

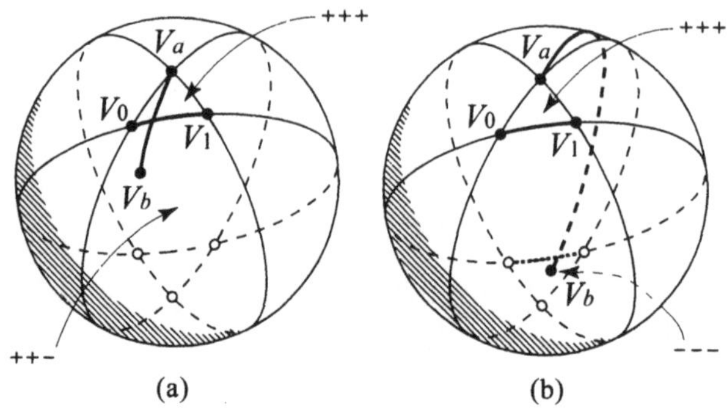

Figure C.7: Two cases of two line segment intersections (projective space).

Combining the relation above with eq.(C.34) yields:

$$\begin{array}{c}((S_{01a}, S_{01b}, S_{ab0}, S_{ab1}) \neq (0,0,0,0)) \\ \wedge(S_{01a} \cdot S_{01b},\ S_{ab0} \cdot S_{ab1} \leq 0).\end{array} \tag{C.36}$$

Algebraic Derivation

When the two line segments intersect, the following equations hold (see Table 9.2):

$$\boldsymbol{V} = \xi_0 \boldsymbol{V}_0 + \xi_1 \boldsymbol{V}_1 = \xi_a \boldsymbol{V}_a + \xi_b \boldsymbol{V}_b, \tag{C.37}$$

$$(\xi_0, \xi_1 \geq 0 \vee \xi_0, \xi_1 \leq 0) \ \wedge \ (\xi_a, \xi_b \geq 0 \vee \xi_a, \xi_b \leq 0). \tag{C.38}$$

Since the condition (C.34) exists, eq.(C.37) can be solved. For example, let us assume $S_{01a} \neq 0$. It is solved for ξ_0, ξ_1 and ξ_a in terms of ξ_b since it includes three equations:

$$(\xi_0, \xi_1, \xi_a, \xi_b) = \left(\xi_b \frac{S_{b1a}}{S_{01a}}, \xi_b \frac{S_{0ba}}{S_{01a}}, \xi_b \frac{S_{0b1}}{S_{01a}}, \xi_b \right). \tag{C.39}$$

Eqs.(C.38) and (C.39) yields:

$$\begin{array}{c}((S_{01a} \geq 0 \wedge S_{01b} \leq 0) \vee (S_{01a} \leq 0 \wedge S_{01b} \geq 0)) \\ \wedge\ ((S_{ab0} \geq 0 \wedge S_{ab1} \leq 0) \vee (S_{ab0} \leq 0 \wedge S_{ab1} \geq 0)).\end{array} \tag{C.40}$$

Combining eqs.(C.34) and (C.40) gives the final result:

$$\begin{array}{c}((S_{01a}, S_{01b}, S_{ab0}, S_{ab1}) \neq (0,0,0,0)) \\ \wedge\ ((S_{01a} \geq 0 \wedge S_{01b} \leq 0) \vee (S_{01a} \leq 0 \wedge S_{01b} \geq 0)) \\ \wedge\ ((S_{ab0} \geq 0 \wedge S_{ab1} \leq 0) \vee (S_{ab0} \leq 0 \wedge S_{ab1} \geq 0)).\end{array} \tag{C.41}$$

The condition above can also be expressed as:

$$\begin{array}{c}((S_{01a}, S_{01b}, S_{ab0}, S_{ab1}) \neq (0,0,0,0)) \\ \wedge\ (S_{01a} \cdot S_{01b},\ S_{ab0} \cdot S_{ab1} \leq 0).\end{array} \tag{C.42}$$

Intersection Point

By using eq.(C.39), we have the intersection point of the two line segments from eq.(C.37):

$$\begin{aligned}
\boldsymbol{V} &= \overline{\xi_0 \boldsymbol{V}_0 + \xi_1 \boldsymbol{V}_1} \\
&= \overline{\frac{\xi_b}{S_{01a}}(S_{ab1}\boldsymbol{V}_0 - S_{ab0}\boldsymbol{V}_1)} \\
&= \overline{S_{ab1}\boldsymbol{V}_0 - S_{ab0}\boldsymbol{V}_1} \qquad (C.43) \\
&= \overline{\xi_a \boldsymbol{V}_a + \xi_b \boldsymbol{V}_b} \\
&= \overline{\frac{\xi_b}{S_{01a}}(-S_{01b}\boldsymbol{V}_a + S_{01a}\boldsymbol{V}_b)} \\
&= \overline{S_{01b}\boldsymbol{V}_a - S_{01a}\boldsymbol{V}_b}. \qquad (C.44)
\end{aligned}$$

As stated in the discussion for Section 13.2.4, it is advisable to maintain the consistency of the signs to facilitate subsequent processing in $\mathbf{R}^3$, and so we present below only the intersection point that corresponds to the positive conditions of eqs.(C.43) and (C.44).

Expression in terms of points V_0 and V_1

$$\boldsymbol{V} = \begin{cases} \overline{S_{ab1}\boldsymbol{V}_0 - S_{ab0}\boldsymbol{V}_1}, & (S_{ab0} \le 0 \wedge S_{ab1} \ge 0), \\ \overline{-S_{ab1}\boldsymbol{V}_0 + S_{ab0}\boldsymbol{V}_1}, & (S_{ab0} \ge 0 \wedge S_{ab1} \le 0). \end{cases} \qquad (C.45)$$

Expression in terms of points V_a and V_b

$$\boldsymbol{V} = \begin{cases} \overline{S_{01b}\boldsymbol{V}_a - S_{01a}\boldsymbol{V}_b}, & (S_{01a} \le 0 \wedge S_{01b} \ge 0), \\ \overline{-S_{01b}\boldsymbol{V}_a + S_{01a}\boldsymbol{V}_b}, & (S_{01a} \ge 0 \wedge S_{01b} \le 0). \end{cases} \qquad (C.46)$$

C.5.2 Simplices in Two-sided Space

1. **Containment of a point in a line segment**

   We derive the condition in two-sided space for a homogeneous point V_a to lie on a homogeneous line segment V_0V_1.

   First, we add the condition that V_a and V_0V_1 are collinear, which is given by eq.(C.11):

$$S_{a01} = 0.$$

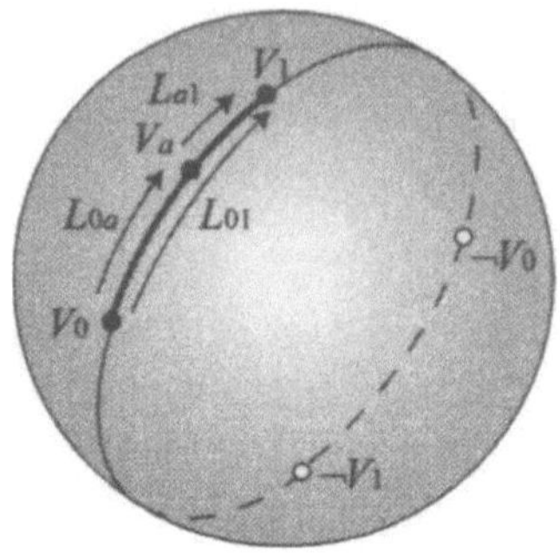

Figure C.8: Containment test of a point in a line segment (two-sided space).

Geometric Derivation

Referring to Section 4.6, the condition for V_a to be contained in collinear line segment V_0V_1 can be expressed, using vectors defined by Plücker coordinates of line in plane geometry, as follows (see Fig. C.8):

$$(\boldsymbol{L}_{01} \cdot \boldsymbol{L}_{0a} \geq 0) \wedge (\boldsymbol{L}_{01} \cdot \boldsymbol{L}_{a1} \geq 0). \tag{C.47}$$

Together with the collinearity condition above, the final result is written as follows:

$$(S_{a01} = 0) \ \wedge \ (\boldsymbol{L}_{01} \cdot \boldsymbol{L}_{a0} \leq 0 \wedge \boldsymbol{L}_{01} \cdot \boldsymbol{L}_{a1} \geq 0). \tag{C.48}$$

Algebraic Derivation

The condition for V_a to be contained in V_0V_1 is expressed as follows [4](see Section 9.2):

$$\xi_0 \boldsymbol{V}_0 + \xi_1 \boldsymbol{V}_1 = \boldsymbol{V}_a, \tag{C.50}$$

$$\xi_0, \xi_1 \geq 0. \tag{C.51}$$

Note here that when the homogeneous equation (C.50), consisting of three simultaneous equations, is solved for two variables, ξ_0 and ξ_1, three solution sets are possible depending on which equations are chosen.

We shall let l_{01} represent one of the three Plücker coordinates of line defined by two points (see eq.(C.1)):

$$L_{01} = \overline{(U_{01}, -Q_{01}, P_{01})},$$

[4] Eq.(C.50) must be written as follows:

$$\xi_0 \boldsymbol{V}_0 + \xi_1 \boldsymbol{V}_1 = k\boldsymbol{V}_a, \quad k > 0. \tag{C.49}$$

Since the homogeneous parameters play the role of k, it is omitted for simplicity. The same simplification is taken throughout.

that is,

$$l_{01} \in \{U_{01}, -Q_{01}, P_{01}\}. \tag{C.52}$$

Since the line segment is assumed to be linearly independent:

$$(U_{01}, -Q_{01}, P_{01}) \neq (0, 0, 0),$$

we can obtain ξ_0 and ξ_1 using the notation above. We assume $l_{01} \neq 0$. Then

$$(\xi_0, \xi_1) = (\frac{l_{a1}}{l_{01}}, \frac{l_{0a}}{l_{01}}). \tag{C.53}$$

From eq.(C.51), we have:

$$\begin{aligned} &(l_{01} > 0 \wedge l_{0a} \geq 0 \wedge l_{1a} \leq 0) \\ \vee\ &(l_{01} < 0 \wedge l_{0a} \leq 0 \wedge l_{1a} \geq 0). \end{aligned} \tag{C.54}$$

Combining eqs.(C.54) with the collinearity condition above gives the final result:

$$\begin{aligned} &\text{With respect to } l_{01} \neq 0 \ (\in \{U_{01}, -Q_{01}, P_{01}\}), \\ &(S_{a01} = 0) \\ \wedge\ &((l_{01} > 0 \wedge l_{a0} \leq 0 \wedge l_{a1} \geq 0) \\ \vee\ &\ (l_{01} < 0 \wedge l_{a0} \geq 0 \wedge l_{a1} \leq 0)). \end{aligned} \tag{C.55}$$

This expression represents eq.(C.48) in terms of its vector components.

Partition

In the case of two-sided space, we can partition the line segment by simply using V_a as a partitioning point.

2. **Containment of a point in a triangle**

We now derive the condition in two-sided space for a homogeneous point V_a to lie inside a homogeneous triangle $V_0V_1V_2$.

Geometric Derivation

The condition for the point V_a to be contained in the triangle $V_0V_1V_2$ is expressed in the spherical model simply as the condition for V_a to be contained in $V_0V_1V_2$ (see Fig. C.9).

Referring to Section 4.6, this condition can be expressed, using the Plücker coordinate of space in plane geometry, as follows:

$$(S_{012} \cdot S_{a12} \geq 0 \wedge S_{012} \cdot S_{0a2} \geq 0 \wedge S_{012} \cdot S_{01a} \geq 0). \tag{C.56}$$

This can be represented as below:

$$\begin{aligned} &(S_{012} > 0 \wedge S_{a12}, S_{a20}, S_{a01} \geq 0) \\ \vee\ &(S_{012} < 0 \wedge S_{a12}, S_{a20}, S_{a01} \leq 0). \end{aligned} \tag{C.57}$$

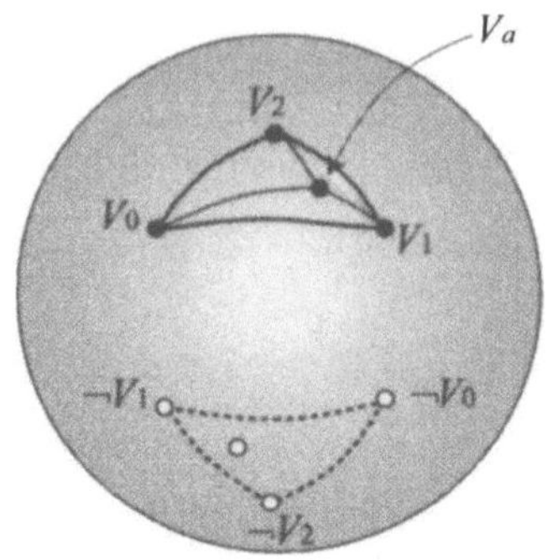

Figure C.9: Containment test of a point in a triangle (two-sided space).

Algebraic Derivation

The condition for the homogeneous point V_a to lie inside the homogeneous triangle $V_0V_1V_2$ is given by (see Section 9.2):

$$\xi_0 \boldsymbol{V}_0 + \xi_1 \boldsymbol{V}_1 + \xi_2 \boldsymbol{V}_2 = \boldsymbol{V}_a, \tag{C.58}$$

$$\xi_0, \xi_1, \xi_2 \geq 0. \tag{C.59}$$

Eq.(C.58) expresses a set of three simultaneous linear equations with variables, ξ_0, ξ_1 and ξ_2.

Since V_0, V_1 and V_2 are assumed to be linearly independent, we have:

$$S_{012} \neq 0.$$

Thus, eq.(C.58) has a unique solution for ξ_0, ξ_1 and ξ_2, as given by:

$$\begin{aligned}(\xi_0, \xi_1, \xi_2) &= \left(\frac{S_{a12}}{S_{012}}, \frac{S_{0a2}}{S_{012}}, \frac{S_{01a}}{S_{012}}\right) \\ &= \frac{1}{S_{012}}(S_{a12}, S_{a20}, S_{a01}).\end{aligned} \tag{C.60}$$

By incorporating eq.(C.60) into the condition (C.59), we have:

$$\frac{1}{S_{012}}(S_{a12}, S_{a20}, S_{a01}) \geq 0. \tag{C.61}$$

Thus, the final result is given by:

$$\begin{aligned}&(S_{012} > 0 \wedge S_{a12}, S_{a20}, S_{a01} \geq 0) \\ \vee\ &(S_{012} < 0 \wedge S_{a12}, S_{a20}, S_{a01} \leq 0).\end{aligned} \tag{C.62}$$

Partition

In the case of two-sided space, we can partition the triangle by simply using V_a as a partitioning point.

3. **Intersection of two line segments**

We now derive the condition in two-sided space for two homogeneous line segments, V_0V_1 and V_aV_b, to intersect.

We assume the two line segments are not collinear:

$$(S_{01a}, S_{01b}, S_{ab0}, S_{ab1}) \neq (0,0,0,0). \qquad \text{(C.63)}$$

Geometric Derivation

To determine whether the two line segments intersect, we employ the sign zones relative to a triangle in the spherical model, discussed in Section 4.6 (see Fig. C.10).

We see that the line segment V_aV_b intersects V_0V_1 when V_b lies in the $++-$ zone. Using the Plücker coordinates of space, this is expressed as follows:

$$(S_{01a} \cdot S_{b1a} \geq 0 \wedge S_{01a} \cdot S_{0ba} \geq 0 \wedge S_{01a} \cdot S_{01b} \leq 0). \qquad \text{(C.64)}$$

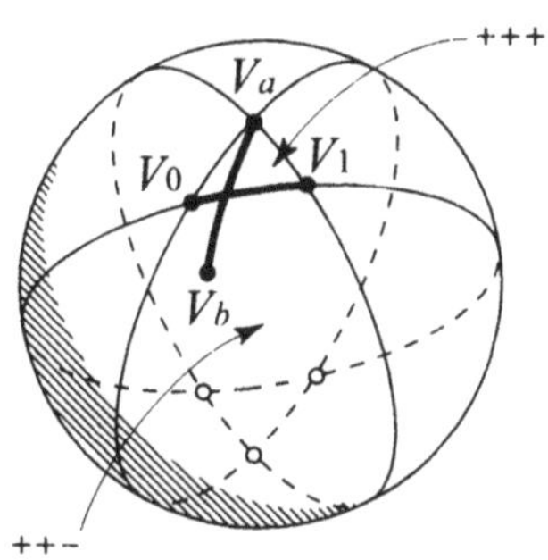

Figure C.10: Intersection test of two line segments (two-sided space).

From the first term, we can substitute S_{b1a} for S_{01a} in the second term to obtain:

$$(S_{01a} \cdot S_{b1a} \geq 0 \wedge S_{b1a} \cdot S_{0ba} \geq 0 \wedge S_{01a} \cdot S_{01b} \leq 0).$$

From the second term above, we can substitute S_{0ba} for S_{b1a} in the first term, then rearrange in a symmetrical manner to obtain:

$$(S_{01a} \cdot S_{01b},\ S_{ab0} \cdot S_{ab1},\ S_{01a} \cdot S_{ab0} \leq 0). \qquad \text{(C.65)}$$

The first and second terms express the condition for two line segments in classical projective space to intersect (see eq.(C.35)).

Note that the condition up to this point does not exclude the case where the antipodal element to a line segment intersects with the other line

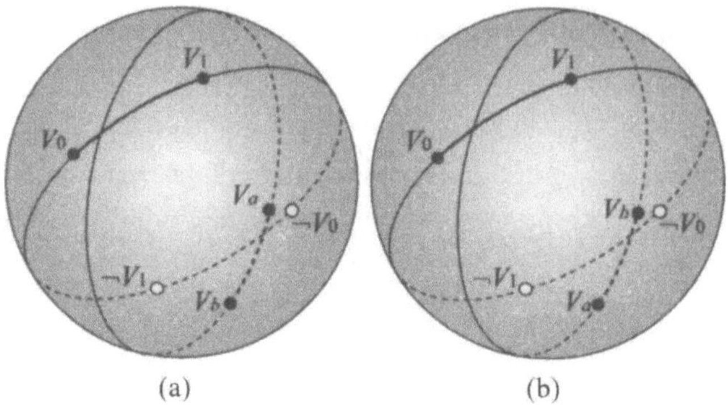

Figure C.11: Excluding intersection of antipodal line segment.

segment (see Fig. C.11). We need the third term to exclude this possibility.

Combining eq.(C.65) with eq.(C.63) yields:

$$\begin{aligned}&((S_{01a}, S_{01b}, S_{ab0}, S_{ab1}) \neq (0,0,0,0)) \wedge \\ &(S_{01a} \cdot S_{01b},\ S_{ab0} \cdot S_{ab1},\ S_{01a} \cdot S_{ab0} \leq 0).\end{aligned} \tag{C.66}$$

Algebraic Derivation

When the two line segments intersect, the following equations hold (see Table 9.2):

$$\boldsymbol{V} = \xi_0 \boldsymbol{V}_0 + \xi_1 \boldsymbol{V}_1 = \xi_a \boldsymbol{V}_a + \xi_b \boldsymbol{V}_b, \tag{C.67}$$

$$(\xi_0, \xi_1 \geq 0) \wedge (\xi_a, \xi_b \geq 0). \tag{C.68}$$

Since the condition (C.63) exists, eq.(C.67) can be solved. For example, let us assume $S_{01a} \neq 0$. It is solved for ξ_0, ξ_1 and ξ_a in terms of ξ_b since it includes three equations:

$$(\xi_0, \xi_1, \xi_a, \xi_b) = \left(\xi_b \frac{S_{b1a}}{S_{01a}}, \xi_b \frac{S_{0ba}}{S_{01a}}, \xi_b \frac{S_{0b1}}{S_{01a}}, \xi_b\right). \tag{C.69}$$

Eqs.(C.68) and (C.69) yields:

$$\begin{aligned}&(S_{01a} \geq 0 \wedge S_{01b} \leq 0 \wedge S_{ab0} \leq 0 \wedge S_{ab1} \geq 0) \\ \vee\ &(S_{01a} \leq 0 \wedge S_{01b} \geq 0 \wedge S_{ab0} \geq 0 \wedge S_{ab1} \leq 0).\end{aligned} \tag{C.70}$$

Combining eqs.(C.63) and (C.70) gives the final result:

$$\begin{aligned}&((S_{01a}, S_{01b}, S_{ab0}, S_{ab1}) \neq (0,0,0,0)) \\ \wedge\ &((S_{01a} \geq 0 \wedge S_{01b} \leq 0 \wedge S_{ab0} \leq 0 \wedge S_{ab1} \geq 0) \\ \vee\ &(S_{01a} \leq 0 \wedge S_{01b} \geq 0 \wedge S_{ab0} \geq 0 \wedge S_{ab1} \leq 0)).\end{aligned} \tag{C.71}$$

Eq.(C.71) is another expression of eq.(C.66). The intersection formulas in this case are the same as eqs.(C.45) and (C.46).

Appendix D

Analytical Geometry in Vector Space

D.1 Curves

We write a homogeneous curve as shown below:

$$\begin{aligned}\overline{\boldsymbol{P}(t)} &= \overline{[w(t)\ \ X(t)\ \ Y(t)]} \\ &= \overline{w(t)\boldsymbol{p}(t)},\quad (w(t)\neq 0), \qquad \text{(D.1)}\\ \text{where}\quad \boldsymbol{p}(t) &= [1\ \ x(t)\ \ y(t)] \qquad \text{(D.2)}\end{aligned}$$

or

$$\begin{aligned}\overline{\boldsymbol{P}(t)} &= \overline{[w(t)\ \ X(t)\ \ Y(t)\ \ Z(t)]} \\ &= \overline{w(t)\boldsymbol{p}(t)},\quad (w(t)\neq 0), \qquad \text{(D.3)}\\ \text{where}\quad \boldsymbol{p}(t) &= [1\ \ x(t)\ \ y(t)\ \ z(t)]. \qquad \text{(D.4)}\end{aligned}$$

A type-D2 homogeneous curve in plane is shown below as an example (see Section 8.6):

$$\begin{aligned}\overline{\boldsymbol{P}(\eta,\sigma)} &= \overline{[w(\eta,\sigma)\ \ X(\eta,\sigma)\ \ Y(\eta,\sigma)]} \\ &= \overline{w(\eta,\sigma)\boldsymbol{p}(\eta,\sigma)},\quad (w(\eta,\sigma)\neq 0), \qquad \text{(D.5)}\\ \text{where}\quad \boldsymbol{p}(\eta,\sigma) &= [1\ \ x(\eta,\sigma)\ \ y(\eta,\sigma)]. \qquad \text{(D.6)}\end{aligned}$$

In the discussion that follows, we introduce the following notation for simplicity whenever appropriate: $X(t_0)\equiv X_0$, $\dot{Y}(t_0)\equiv \dot{Y}_0$, $X_\sigma(\eta_0,\sigma_0)\equiv X_{\sigma 0}$, ..., etc.

D.1.1 First Derivative Vector

A homogeneous curve $\overline{\boldsymbol{P}(t)}$ is shown in the associated vector space as a conical surface of which the apex is at the origin and which passes through the simple curve $\boldsymbol{P}(t)$ [1)] (see Fig. D.1). One parameter of the surface is t and the other u (see Section 9.5). Thus the first derivative vector $\dot{\boldsymbol{P}}(t)$ is a tangent vector in the direction of t of the surface.

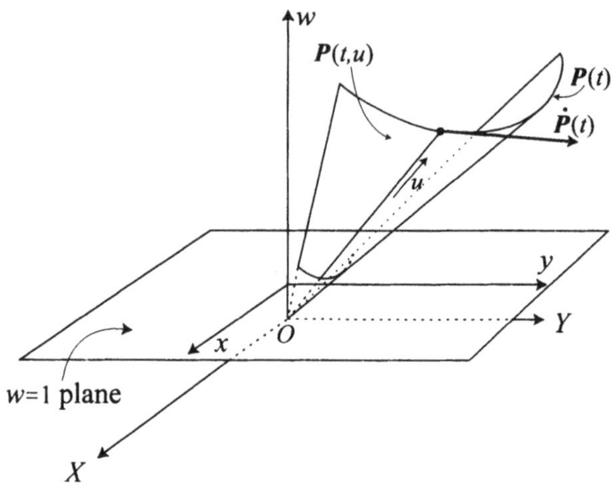

Figure D.1: Homogeneous tangent vector (ordinary parameter).

Next, let us consider two type-D homogeneous curve cases.

Type-D1 Homogeneous Curve

From eq.(10.15), we have:

$$\boldsymbol{HP}_h(h,s) = mh^{m-1}\boldsymbol{P}(t) - sh^{m-2}\dot{\boldsymbol{P}}(t), \tag{D.7}$$
$$\boldsymbol{HP}_s(h,s) = h^{m-1}\dot{\boldsymbol{P}}(t), \tag{D.8}$$

where m is the degree of the polynomial curve. These relations are illustrated in Fig. D.2.

Type-D2 Homogeneous Curve

From eq.(10.18), we have:

$$\boldsymbol{HP}_\eta(\eta,\sigma) = m(\eta+\sigma)^{m-1}\boldsymbol{P}(t) - \sigma(\eta+\sigma)^{m-2}\dot{\boldsymbol{P}}(t), \tag{D.9}$$
$$\boldsymbol{HP}_\sigma(\eta,\sigma) = m(\eta+\sigma)^{m-1}\boldsymbol{P}(t) + \eta(\eta+\sigma)^{m-2}\dot{\boldsymbol{P}}(t). \tag{D.10}$$

From these equations above, we also have:

$$\dot{\boldsymbol{P}}(t) = \frac{1}{(\eta+\sigma)^{m-1}}\{\boldsymbol{HP}_\sigma(\eta,\sigma) - \boldsymbol{HP}_\eta(\eta,\sigma)\}. \tag{D.11}$$

These relations are illustrated in Fig. D.3.

[1)] As for simple curve, see Section 9.5.

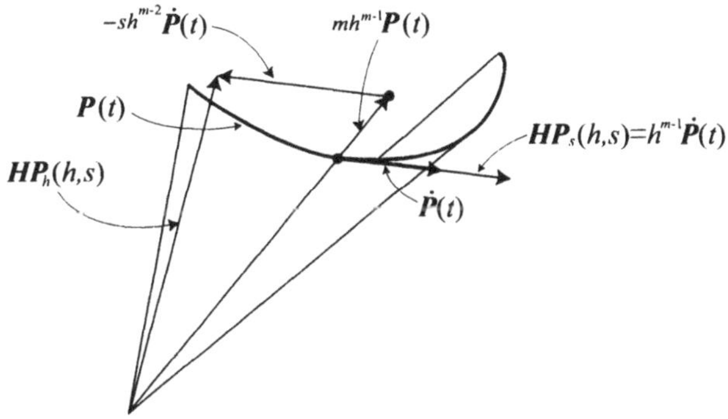

Figure D.2: Relation of homogeneous tangent vectors (type-1).

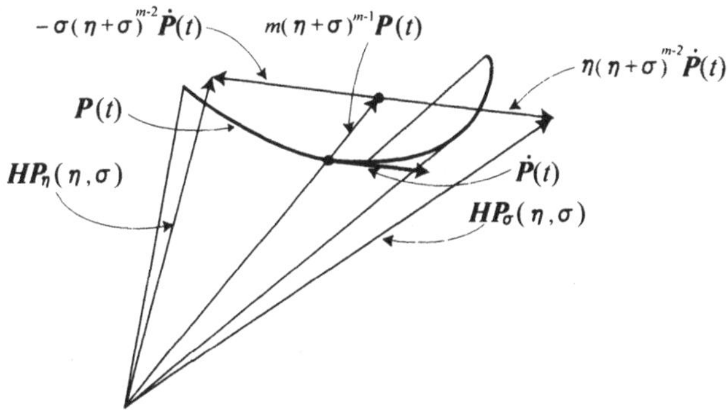

Figure D.3: Relation of homogeneous tangent vectors (type-2).

D.1.2 Tangent Line

We determine the tangent line of a planar curve at point $t=t_0$ (see Fig. D.4).

The tangent line of a curve is a line passing through point $P(t_0)$ and a point at infinity $\overline{(0, \dot{x}(t_0), \dot{y}(t_0))}$ in the direction of the tangent line. So from eq.(9.1), we have:

$$\begin{vmatrix} w & X & Y \\ w(t_0) & X(t_0) & Y(t_0) \\ 0 & \dot{x}(t_0) & \dot{y}(t_0) \end{vmatrix} = 0. \tag{D.12}$$

Now, from eq.(D.1) or (D.3), we obtain:

$$\dot{\boldsymbol{P}}(t_0) = \dot{w}(t_0)\boldsymbol{p}(t_0) + w(t_0)\dot{\boldsymbol{p}}(t_0) \tag{D.13}$$

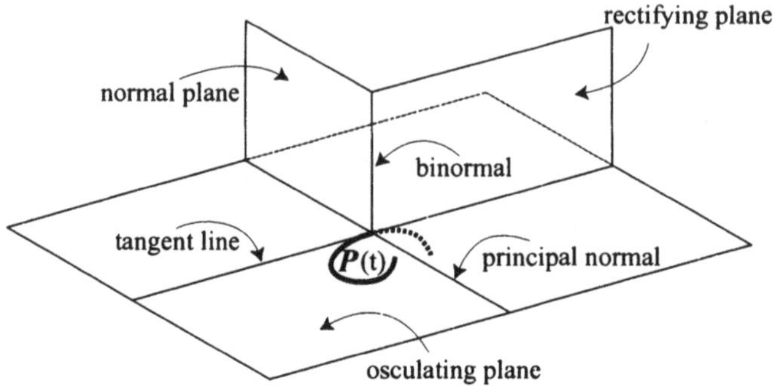

Figure D.4: Various lines and planes associated with a point on a curve.

and so:

$$\begin{cases} \dot{X}(t_0) = \dot{w}(t_0)x(t_0) + w(t_0)\dot{x}(t_0), \\ \dot{Y}(t_0) = \dot{w}(t_0)y(t_0) + w(t_0)\dot{y}(t_0). \end{cases} \tag{D.14}$$

We obtain from these $\dot{x}(t_0)$ and $\dot{y}(t_0)$ and substitute into eq.(D.12), which after rearranging yields:

$$\begin{vmatrix} w & X & Y \\ w(t_0) & X(t_0) & Y(t_0) \\ \dot{w}(t_0) & \dot{X}(t_0) & \dot{Y}(t_0) \end{vmatrix} = 0. \tag{D.15}$$

Let us consider the case where the homogeneous curve is represented, for example in type-2 homogeneous parameters (see Section 8.6). In this case,

$$\boldsymbol{P}(t) = \frac{1}{(\eta+\sigma)^m}\boldsymbol{HP}(\eta,\sigma) = \frac{1}{m(\eta+\sigma)^m}\{\eta\boldsymbol{HP}_\eta(\eta,\sigma) + \sigma\boldsymbol{HP}_\sigma(\eta,\sigma)\},$$

(from eqs.(10.18) and (10.22))

$$\dot{\boldsymbol{P}}(t) = \frac{1}{(\eta+\sigma)^{m-1}}\{\boldsymbol{HP}_\sigma(\eta,\sigma) - \boldsymbol{HP}_\eta(\eta,\sigma)\}.$$

(from eq.(D.11))

We obtain from eq.(D.15), using relations above and letting $\boldsymbol{R}$ represent a point vector $[w\ X\ Y]$ on the tangent line:

$$\begin{aligned} \begin{vmatrix} \boldsymbol{R} \\ \boldsymbol{P}(t) \\ \dot{\boldsymbol{P}}(t) \end{vmatrix} &= \frac{1}{m(\eta+\sigma)^{2m-1}} \begin{vmatrix} \boldsymbol{R} \\ \eta\boldsymbol{HP}_\eta(\eta,\sigma) + \sigma\boldsymbol{HP}_\sigma(\eta,\sigma) \\ \boldsymbol{HP}_\sigma(\eta,\sigma) - \boldsymbol{HP}_\eta(\eta,\sigma) \end{vmatrix} \\ &= \frac{1}{m(\eta+\sigma)^{2m-2}} \begin{vmatrix} \boldsymbol{R} \\ \boldsymbol{HP}_\eta(\eta,\sigma) \\ \boldsymbol{HP}_\sigma(\eta,\sigma) \end{vmatrix}. \end{aligned}$$

Therefore we have:

$$\begin{vmatrix} w & X & Y \\ w_\eta(\eta_0,\sigma_0) & X_\eta(\eta_0,\sigma_0) & Y_\eta(\eta_0,\sigma_0) \\ w_\sigma(\eta_0,\sigma_0) & X_\sigma(\eta_0,\sigma_0) & Y_\sigma(\eta_0,\sigma_0) \end{vmatrix} = 0. \tag{D.16}$$

Similarly, for type-1 homogeneous-parameter, homogeneous curve, we have:

$$\begin{vmatrix} w & X & Y \\ w_h(h_0,s_0) & X_h(h_0,s_0) & Y_h(h_0,s_0) \\ w_s(h_0,s_0) & X_s(h_0,s_0) & Y_s(h_0,s_0) \end{vmatrix} = 0. \tag{D.17}$$

Next, we consider determining Plücker coordinate representation of a tangent line of a space curve $\overline{\boldsymbol{P}(t)}$ [56]. Plücker coordinate representation of a space line passing through two points $P(t_0)$ and $P(t_1)$ on the curve is:

$$\begin{aligned} L_{01} &= \overline{(P_{01}, Q_{01}, R_{01}, S_{01}, T_{01}, U_{01})} \\ &= \overline{\left(\begin{vmatrix} w_0 & X_0 \\ w_1 & X_1 \end{vmatrix}, \begin{vmatrix} w_0 & Y_0 \\ w_1 & Y_1 \end{vmatrix}, \begin{vmatrix} w_0 & Z_0 \\ w_1 & Z_1 \end{vmatrix}, \begin{vmatrix} Y_0 & Z_0 \\ Y_1 & Z_1 \end{vmatrix}, \begin{vmatrix} Z_0 & X_0 \\ Z_1 & X_1 \end{vmatrix}, \begin{vmatrix} X_0 & Y_0 \\ X_1 & Y_1 \end{vmatrix}\right)}. \end{aligned}$$

P_{01} can be arranged for example as:

$$\begin{aligned} P_{01} &= \begin{vmatrix} w_0 & X_0 \\ w_1 & X_1 \end{vmatrix} \\ &= \begin{vmatrix} w_0 & X_0 \\ w_1 - w_0 & X_1 - X_0 \end{vmatrix} \\ &= (t_1 - t_0) \begin{vmatrix} w_0 & X_0 \\ \frac{w_1 - w_0}{t_1 - t_0} & \frac{X_1 - X_0}{t_1 - t_0} \end{vmatrix}. \end{aligned}$$

As t_1 approaches to t_0, line L_{01} becomes the tangent line at $t = t_0$, when the Plücker coordinates turn out to be:

$$\overline{\left(\begin{vmatrix} w_0 & X_0 \\ \dot{w}_0 & \dot{X}_0 \end{vmatrix}, \begin{vmatrix} w_0 & Y_0 \\ \dot{w}_0 & \dot{Y}_0 \end{vmatrix}, \begin{vmatrix} w_0 & Z_0 \\ \dot{w}_0 & \dot{Z}_0 \end{vmatrix}, \begin{vmatrix} Y_0 & Z_0 \\ \dot{Y}_0 & \dot{Z}_0 \end{vmatrix}, \begin{vmatrix} Z_0 & X_0 \\ \dot{Z}_0 & \dot{X}_0 \end{vmatrix}, \begin{vmatrix} X_0 & Y_0 \\ \dot{X}_0 & \dot{Y}_0 \end{vmatrix}\right)}. \tag{D.18}$$

If the homogeneous space curve is represented in using homogeneous parameters, we can easily obtain the following line representations in Plücker coordinates:

$$\overline{\left(\begin{vmatrix} w_{h0} & X_{h0} \\ w_{s0} & X_{s0} \end{vmatrix}, \begin{vmatrix} w_{h0} & Y_{h0} \\ w_{s0} & Y_{s0} \end{vmatrix}, \begin{vmatrix} w_{h0} & Z_{h0} \\ w_{s0} & Z_{s0} \end{vmatrix}, \begin{vmatrix} Y_{h0} & Z_{h0} \\ Y_{s0} & Z_{s0} \end{vmatrix}, \begin{vmatrix} Z_{h0} & X_{h0} \\ Z_{s0} & X_{s0} \end{vmatrix}, \begin{vmatrix} X_{h0} & Y_{h0} \\ X_{s0} & Y_{s0} \end{vmatrix}\right)}, \tag{D.19}$$

$$\overline{\left(\begin{vmatrix} w_{\eta 0} & X_{\eta 0} \\ w_{\sigma 0} & X_{\sigma 0} \end{vmatrix}, \begin{vmatrix} w_{\eta 0} & Y_{\eta 0} \\ w_{\sigma 0} & Y_{\sigma 0} \end{vmatrix}, \begin{vmatrix} w_{\eta 0} & Z_{\eta 0} \\ w_{\sigma 0} & Z_{\sigma 0} \end{vmatrix}, \begin{vmatrix} Y_{\eta 0} & Z_{\eta 0} \\ Y_{\sigma 0} & Z_{\sigma 0} \end{vmatrix}, \begin{vmatrix} Z_{\eta 0} & X_{\eta 0} \\ Z_{\sigma 0} & X_{\sigma 0} \end{vmatrix}, \begin{vmatrix} X_{\eta 0} & Y_{\eta 0} \\ X_{\sigma 0} & Y_{\sigma 0} \end{vmatrix}\right)}. \tag{D.20}$$

D.1.3 Osculating Plane

Letting $\boldsymbol{r} = [x\ y\ z]$ represent a point on the osculating plane of curve $p(t)$ at $t=t_0$, the equation for the osculating plane is given by [58]:

$$[\boldsymbol{r} - \boldsymbol{p}(t_0), \dot{\boldsymbol{p}}(t_0), \ddot{\boldsymbol{p}}(t_0)] = 0. \tag{D.21}$$

We modify this to obtain an expression for the osculating plane in homogeneous coordinates.

$$\begin{aligned}
[\boldsymbol{r} - \boldsymbol{p}(t_0), \dot{\boldsymbol{p}}(t_0), \ddot{\boldsymbol{p}}(t_0)] &= \begin{vmatrix} x - x(t_0) & y - y(t_0) & z - z(t_0) \\ \dot{x}(t_0) & \dot{y}(t_0) & \dot{z}(t_0) \\ \ddot{x}(t_0) & \ddot{y}(t_0) & \ddot{z}(t_0) \end{vmatrix} \\
&= \begin{vmatrix} 1 & 0 & 0 & 0 \\ 1 & x - x(t_0) & y - y(t_0) & z - z(t_0) \\ 0 & \dot{x}(t_0) & \dot{y}(t_0) & \dot{z}(t_0) \\ 0 & \ddot{x}(t_0) & \ddot{y}(t_0) & \ddot{z}(t_0) \end{vmatrix} \\
&= - \begin{vmatrix} 1 & x & y & z \\ 1 & x(t_0) & y(t_0) & z(t_0) \\ 0 & \dot{x}(t_0) & \dot{y}(t_0) & \dot{z}(t_0) \\ 0 & \ddot{x}(t_0) & \ddot{y}(t_0) & \ddot{z}(t_0) \end{vmatrix}.
\end{aligned} \tag{D.22}$$

The following relations exist between ordinary and homogeneous coordinates:

$$\begin{aligned}
(x, y, z) &= (X/w, Y/w, Z/w), \\
(\dot{x}, \dot{y}, \dot{z}) &= ((\dot{X}w - X\dot{w})/w^2, (\dot{Y}w - Y\dot{w})/w^2, (\dot{Z}w - Z\dot{w})/w^2), \\
(\ddot{x}, \ddot{y}, \ddot{z}) &= ((\ddot{X}w^2 - Xw\ddot{w} - 2\dot{X}w\dot{w} + 2X\dot{w}^2)/w^3 \\
&\quad , (\ddot{Y}w^2 - Yw\ddot{w} - 2\dot{Y}w\dot{w} + 2Y\dot{w}^2)/w^3 \\
&\quad , (\ddot{Z}w^2 - Zw\ddot{w} - 2\dot{Z}w\dot{w} + 2Z\dot{w}^2)/w^3).
\end{aligned} \tag{D.23}$$

Substituting these into eq.(D.22), we obtain the homogeneous osculating plane equation:

$$\begin{vmatrix} w & X & Y & Z \\ w(t_0) & X(t_0) & Y(t_0) & Z(t_0) \\ \dot{w}(t_0) & \dot{X}(t_0) & \dot{Y}(t_0) & \dot{Z}(t_0) \\ \ddot{w}(t_0) & \ddot{X}(t_0) & \ddot{Y}(t_0) & \ddot{Z}(t_0) \end{vmatrix} = 0. \tag{D.24}$$

D.2 Surfaces

We write a homogeneous surface patch as shown below:

$$\begin{aligned}
\overline{\boldsymbol{P}(u, v)} &= \overline{[w(u, v)\ \ X(u, v)\ \ Y(u, v)\ \ Z(u, v)]} \\
&= \overline{w(u, v)\boldsymbol{p}(u, v)}, \quad (w(u, v) \neq 0),
\end{aligned} \tag{D.25}$$

$$\text{where} \quad \boldsymbol{p}(u, v) = [1\ \ x(u, v)\ \ y(u, v)\ \ z(u, v)], \tag{D.26}$$

or in homogeneous-parameter form,

$$\overline{\boldsymbol{P}(h,r,s)} = \overline{[w(h,r,s)\ \ X(h,r,s)\ \ Y(h,r,s)\ \ Z(h,r,s)]}$$
$$= \overline{w(h,r,s)\boldsymbol{p}(h,r,s)}, \quad (w(h,r,s) \neq 0), \tag{D.27}$$
$$\text{where} \quad \boldsymbol{p}(h,r,s) = [1\ \ x(h,r,s)\ \ y(h,r,s)\ \ z(h,r,s)]. \tag{D.28}$$

We introduce the following notation for simplicity whenever appropriate:

$$X(u_0, v_0) \equiv X_0,\ \ X_u(u_0, v_0) \equiv X_{u0}, ..., \text{etc.}$$

D.2.1 Tangent Plane

A plane that contains tangent vectors for two directions at some point on a surface is called *tangent plane* at that point (see Fig. D.5).

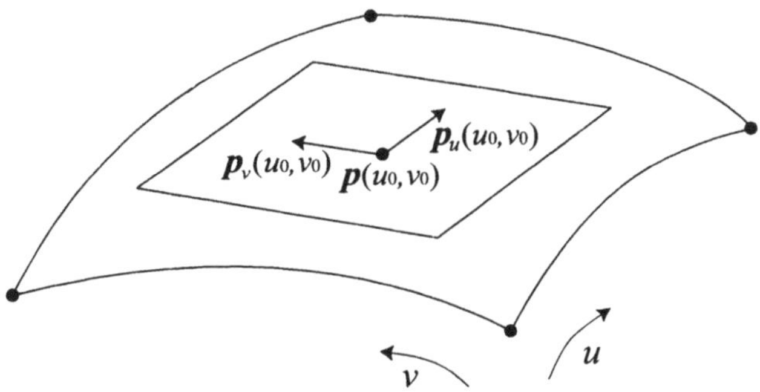

Figure D.5: Tangent plane.

Letting $\boldsymbol{r} = [x\ y\ z]$ represent a point on a tangent plane, the equation for the tangent plane in Euclidean space is given from its definition by:

$$\begin{vmatrix} x - x_0 & y - y_0 & z - z_0 \\ x_{u0} & y_{u0} & z_{u0} \\ x_{v0} & y_{v0} & z_{v0} \end{vmatrix} = 0. \tag{D.29}$$

Replacing the ordinary coordinates by homogeneous ones and rearranging, we obtain the homogeneous tangent plane equation:

$$\begin{vmatrix} w & X & Y & Z \\ w_0 & X_0 & Y_0 & Z_0 \\ w_{u0} & X_{u0} & Y_{u0} & Z_{u0} \\ w_{v0} & X_{v0} & Y_{v0} & Z_{v0} \end{vmatrix} = 0. \tag{D.30}$$

If the homogeneous surface is represented in using homogeneous parameters, we can obtain the following representation:

$$\begin{vmatrix} w & X & Y & Z \\ w_{h0} & X_{h0} & Y_{h0} & Z_{h0} \\ w_{r0} & X_{r0} & Y_{r0} & Z_{r0} \\ w_{s0} & X_{s0} & Y_{s0} & Z_{s0} \end{vmatrix} = 0. \tag{D.31}$$

Appendix E

Proofs for Chapter 16

E.1 Function $P(t)$

We shall prove the inequality (16.55):

$$P(t) \leq \frac{(t+1)(t+2)(t+3)}{6}, \tag{E.1}$$

which will be used in Section E.2.

Proof.

We define b_0, b_1, b_2 and b_3 corresponding to i, j, k and $r-(i+j+k)$ such that

$$b_0 = l_0 - i, \quad b_1 = l_1 - j, \quad b_2 = l_2 - k, \quad b_3 = l_3 - (r - (i+j+k)). \tag{E.2}$$

Since $r = l_s - t$, we have:

$$b_0 + b_1 + b_2 + b_3 = t, \quad 0 \leq b_i \leq l_i. \tag{E.3}$$

Thus we know that determining $P(t)$ is equivalent to finding the number of integer solutions satisfying eq.(E.3). Furthermore we understand that solving eq.(E.3) reduces to finding the coefficient of the term of x^t of $f(x)$ from the theory of combinatorial analysis:

$$f(x) = \prod_{j=0}^{3} \left(\sum_{i=0}^{l_j} x^i \right). \tag{E.4}$$

It is impossible to obtain $P(t)$ as an algebraical function, however. Therefore we instead consider a function $f_\infty(x)$ where l_j is put to infinity:

$$f_\infty(x) = \prod_{j=0}^{3} \left(\sum_{i=0}^{\infty} x^i \right). \tag{E.5}$$

We let $P'(t)$ be the coefficient of the term x^t of $f_\infty(x)$. Since $P'(t)$ is the number of solutions of the equation:

$$b_0 + b_1 + b_2 + b_3 = t, \quad 0 \le b_i, \tag{E.6}$$

then

$$P(t) \le P'(t). \tag{E.7}$$

Consider eq.(E.5). Because

$$\sum_{i=0}^{\infty} x^i = \frac{1}{1-x}, \tag{E.8}$$

then

$$f_\infty(x) = (1-x)^{-4}. \tag{E.9}$$

According to Newton's binomial theorem,

$$(1-x)^{-n} = \sum_{r=0}^{\infty} \binom{n+r-1}{r} x^r. \tag{E.10}$$

Thus the coefficient $P'(t)$ of the term x^t is:

$$P'(t) = \binom{3+t}{t} = \frac{(t+1)(t+2)(t+3)}{6}. \tag{E.11}$$

This proves eq.(E.1).

E.2 Error Boundary

We shall prove eq.(16.54), that is,

$$EB'(\alpha) \le 16 \times 2^{48} P'(\alpha+1).$$

Proof.

With respect to the summation of $EB'(\alpha)$, we change from r to t:

$$\begin{aligned} EB'(\alpha) &= \sum_{r=0}^{l_s-(\alpha+1)} 2^{16(r-l_s+\alpha)} \cdot 16(2^{16}-1)^4 P(t) \\ &= 16\left(\sum_{t=\alpha+1}^{l_s} 2^{16(\alpha-t)}(2^{16}-1)^4 P(t)\right). \end{aligned}$$

From eq.(E.7), we have:

$$EB'(\alpha) = 16\left(\sum_{t=\alpha+1}^{l_s} 2^{16(\alpha-t)}(2^{16}-1)^4 P(t)\right)$$

$$
\begin{aligned}
&\leq 16\left(\sum_{t=\alpha+1}^{l_s} 2^{16(\alpha-t)}(2^{16}-1)^4 P'(t)\right)\\
&= 16\left(\sum_{t=\alpha+1}^{l_s} 2^{16(\alpha-t)}(2^{64}-4\cdot 2^{48}+6\cdot 2^{32}-4\cdot 2^{16}+1)P'(t)\right)\\
&= 16\left(P'(\alpha+1)\cdot 2^{48}-(4P'(\alpha+1)-P'(\alpha+2))\cdot 2^{32}\right.\\
&\quad \left.+(6P'(\alpha+1)-4P'(\alpha+2)+P'(\alpha+3))\cdot 2^{16}+\ldots\right).
\end{aligned}
$$

Making use of eq.(E.11) yields:

$$
\begin{aligned}
&= 16\left(\frac{1}{6}(\alpha+2)(\alpha+3)(\alpha+4)\cdot 2^{48}-\frac{1}{2}(\alpha+1)(\alpha+3)(\alpha+4)\cdot 2^{32}\right.\\
&\quad \left.+\frac{1}{2}(\alpha+1)(\alpha+2)(\alpha+4)\cdot 2^{16}+\ldots\right)\\
&\leq 16\cdot\frac{1}{6}(\alpha+2)(\alpha+3)(\alpha+4)\cdot 2^{48}\\
&= 16\times 2^{48}P'(\alpha+1).
\end{aligned}
\tag{E.12}
$$

This proves eq.(16.54).

Index

MIX
Papier aus verantwortungsvollen Quellen
Paper from responsible sources
FSC® C105338

If you have any concerns about our products,
you can contact us on
ProductSafety@springernature.com

In case Publisher is established outside the EU,
the EU authorized representative is:
Springer Nature Customer Service Center GmbH
Europaplatz 3, 69115 Heidelberg, Germany

Printed by Libri Plureos GmbH
in Hamburg, Germany